Praise for *Coven*

'Its journalistic boldness, scope and energy make for stimulating reading . . . Lebrecht is also often brilliantly acute on the personalities stalking the corridor of power from dressing room to boardroom . . . [he] states the case with all the invigorating conviction that is his hallmark' *Daily Telegraph*

'Norman Lebrecht's history of Covent Garden, in which I figure, is rich in the qualities we expect from his *Daily Telegraph* column; it is vigorous, sometimes slapdash, opinionated . . . roistering and rumbustious' Sir Jeremy Isaacs, *Jewish Chronicle*

'A grandly stylish rant . . . Lebrecht is one of a small band of arts experts who can pontificate on just about anything' *Independent on Sunday*

'He is the critic the classical music industry dreads most' *The Scotsman*

'Its cultural doom-mongering makes a bracing read' *Financial Times*

'This book is as magnificent as it is irritating, as perceptive in its social analysis as it is cavalier in its artistic judgements. However, the combination of perspective, research and discussion is deep enough to mean that the conclusions have to be taken seriously' *BBC Music Magazine*

'The country's residual aversion to the arts gets another airing in Norman Lebrecht's compulsive page-turner' *The Times*

'Punchily provocative and good if not especially clean fun' *Gramophone*

'Sparklingly and economically written, *Covent Garden* tells it as it is . . . a superbly gripping and eye-catching "libretto"' *What's On In London*

Also by Norman Lebrecht

The Maestro Myth
When the Music Stops
The Complete Companion to 20th Century Music

Covent Garden
The Untold Story

Dispatches from the English Culture War, 1945–2001

NORMAN LEBRECHT

POCKET
BOOKS

LONDON · SYDNEY · NEW YORK · TOKYO · SINGAPORE · TORONTO

First published in Great Britain by Simon & Schuster UK Ltd, 2000
This edition first published by Pocket Books, 2001
An imprint of Simon & Schuster UK Ltd
A Viacom Company

1 3 5 7 9 10 8 6 4 2

Simon & Schuster UK Ltd
Africa House
64-78 Kingsway
London WC2B 6AH

www.simonsays.co.uk

Simon & Schuster Australia
Sydney

A CIP catalogue record for this book is available from the British Library

ISBN 0-671-01817-5

Typeset by SX Composing DTP, Rayleigh, Essex
Printed and bound in Great Britain by Cox and Wyman Ltd, Berkshire

For

Elbie, Naama, Abigail and Gabriella

Acknowledgements

I have received tremendous assistance in researching this book from dozens of people in all walks of life, some of whom do not wish to be named. I am particularly grateful to the 12th Earl of Drogheda for letting me look after and quote from his father's papers; to Ken Davison (Lord Brochaine) for his friendship and memories; to the Board of the Royal Opera House for allowing me partial access to their archives; to the ROH archivists Francesca Franchi and Jane Jackson; to the many artists, staff and directors who gave liberally of their time and memorabilia; to my assistants, Joanna Collins and Catherine Best; and to my nearest and dearest who put up with two years of mental absenteeism.

I have been helped in various ways, above and beyond the demands of friendship and collegiality, and sometimes more than they knew, by:

Mary Allen, Peter Alward, Helen Anderson, Peter Andry, Tim Ashley, Dave Ashton, Ewen Balfour, Lady Barbirolli, Richard Bebb, Eduardo Benarroche, Catherine Best, Sir Harrison Birtwistle, Gillian Brierley, Ismene Brown, Teresa Cahill, Patrick Carnegy, Alexander Chancellor, Joanna Collins, Keith Cooper, Jilly Cooper, Sarah Crompton, John Denison, Peter Diamand, Geoffrey Douch, Sir Anthony Dowell, Sir Edward Downes, David Drew, Paul and Francoise Findlay, Eva Foley-Comer, Massimo Freccia, Betty Freeman, Daniele Gatti, Peter Gellhorn, Paul Gent, Valery Gergiev, Lord Gibson, Lord Gilmour, Berthold Goldschmidt, Lord Gowrie, Judy Grahame, Rita Grudzien, Michael Haas, Dame Heather Harper, Seppo Heikinheimo, Gavin Henderson, Lillian and Victor Hochhauser, Manuela Hoelterhoff, Sir Jeremy Isaacs, Alan

Jefferson, Amanda Jones, Gilbert E. Kaplan, Ernest Keeling, Ron Kitaj, Lotte Klemperer, Elizabeth Latham, Alison Latham, Vera Langdon, Adele Leigh, Ruth Leon, Tamsin Lewis, Janine Limberg, Kathryn McDowell, John McLaren, John McMurray, Ginny Macbeth, Fiona Maddocks, Monica Mason, Jack Mastroianni, David Mellor, Margaret Mendel, Yehudi Menuhin, Elsie Morison, Antonio Pappano, Sir Hayden Phillips, Stephen Phillips, Andrew Porter, Christine Rankl, Andrew Renton, Ann Richards, Janet Ritterman, Zsuzsi Roboz, Henry Roche, Lord Rothschild, Steve Rubin, Naresh Samani, Maggie Sedwards, Sir Nicholas Serota, Constance Shacklock, Moira Shearer, Dame Antoinette Sibley, Prudence Skene, Sytze Smit, The Rt. Hon. Chris Smith MP, Daniel Snowman, Sir Georg Solti, Lady Solti, Lady Tooley, Robert Trory, Dame Ninette de Valois, Christel Wallbaum, Lilian Watson, Nick Webb, Sally and George Whyte, Gillian Widdicombe, Katharine Wilkinson, John Willan, Francesca Zambello.

Contents

I sometimes think that more has changed since 1945 than in all the years of history there have ever been. I don't know what to make of the end of so many things.

Lou Levov, in Philip Roth's *American Pastoral*

Introduction

The last of the founders died at 8.45 on the morning of 8 March, 2001. Ninette de Valois was three months short of 103 years old and had seen the light of three centuries. Racked by arthritis and irritably deaf, she had long told visitors to her sheltered apartment in Barnes, beside the River Thames, that she had no wish to stay alive. But the iron will that had implanted an alien art in stubborn British soil refused to yield until the prospect of survival seemed assured.

Without Ninette de Valois, the obituarists noted, there would have been no Royal Ballet, no school, no choreography, no tradition. Her fierce involvement may have lasted too long – to the point where any reform would be shot down on the grounds that 'Madam wouldn't like it' – but her legacy was intact. The Royal Ballet was resident at last in the Royal Opera House and the Royal Ballet School was moving into former ROH premises across the street. Her vision of making Covent Garden the hub of balletic art had been physically fulfilled. All that was lacking was spiritual impetus, moral leadership and singularity of purpose.

The cause upon which Covent Garden opera and ballet had been founded after the War was the regeneration of Britain through its language and culture, the cultivation of resources never previously esteemed to be properly British. The Royal Opera House was to be the stage on which the nation displayed the best of its legs and larynxes, its dexterity and imagination. It was on such ideals that the company shot to prominence, conquering America in the early 1950s and Europe soon after with an *esprit de corps* that was every bit as vital as its home-reared stars. The careers of Margot Fonteyn and Joan Sutherland, Kenneth MacMillan and Geraint Evans, Lynn Seymour and Jon Vickers, were triumphs as much of a collective ethos as of their innate talents.

That ethos, however, had ceased to function years before Madam expired. On the day of her death, there was only one British dancer, Jonathan Cope, among six principal males in the Royal Ballet and three British ballerinas among seven females. In the next rank of soloists, there were eight foreigners to four locals. The incoming director, Ross Stretton, was an Australian who had never danced with the company and could be expected to have no particular regard for its heritage. The head of the Royal Ballet School was another antipodean, Gailene Stock, who bewailed the couch-potato unfitness of native British stock and looked abroad for scholarship pupils. The Royal Ballet danced on, but not in any national interest.

The Royal Opera, for its part, trotted out casts that were indistinguishable from the ones that sang in Paris and Berlin. The repertoire was stale, the productions humdrum. Bernard Haitink, the Dutch music director, was drawing tetchily to the end of his term; Antonio Pappano, his American successor, was unable to break into rigid schedules and stamp his mark on the house. The company, such as it was, consisted of a work-to-rule orchestra and chorus. Casting precedence was given to 'international' singers, even in secondary roles.

Jane Eaglen, a Lincoln-born soprano, daughter of a steelworker, related that she had once been engaged to understudy Margaret Price as Norma. When Price called in sick one morning, the ROH flew in an unrehearsed substitute from Germany, sending the British girl home with a consolatory bottle of champagne. Eaglen, who achieved stardom at the Met, returned to London as Turandot in February 2001, a princess without honour in her own land. Snootier than the ballet, the Royal Opera actively snubbed native artists, depressing morale and destroying its own seedbed.

The low-light of its second season in the reopened house was Hans Werner Henze's *Boulevard Solitude*, a retrograde German opera almost fifty years old. A week before the premiere, with barely 20 per cent of the seats sold, a desperate administration tried giving away tickets to minor television celebrities in the hope that their tinselly allure would attract paparazzi and press headlines. Free oysters and champagne were offered as the ultimate inducement. A sour joke wafted up from the box-office.

Caller: 'What time does *Boulevard* begin?'

Sales clerk: 'What time can you get here?'

The episode exemplified how dismally the institution had lost its bearings. A worthy desire to celebrate the seventy-fifth birthday of an important composer faltered at the prospect of presenting one of his more challenging recent works. Nicholas Payne, the director who booked *Boulevard*, left soon after. His successors were unable to summon enough enthusiasm to convince sales staff and the public that it was worth seeing. In dire straits, the marketing department resorted to the kind of gimmicks employed to open supermarkets and second-hand car-lots – and the European press exploded in mirth. The Royal Opera had become a house without passion or shame.

Delusions of world rank had gone to its head. Cut off from the bulk of the nation it was supposed to serve by prohibitive seat prices and a no-touring policy, shunned by British singers and scorned by the upper echelons of the performing arts industry, the ROH had failed to redefine its mission for a post-national era.

The depth of its confusion was evoked by a revival of *Billy Budd*, in which surtitles were used to display the English text. Here was a rare occasion when the ROH presented a native work in the raw vernacular, yet the administration did not trust the singers to articulate or the public to understand their own mother-tongue.

'What's the story?' was the opening question posed by the new executive director, Tony Hall, the BBC's ex-Head of News. 'What is the ROH there for?' he demanded. No clear answer was forthcoming.

Hall, the sixth chief in as many years, had been selected from an embarrassingly short list. None of the obvious suspects had agreed to let their names go forward. Sarah Billinghurst of the Met issued a terse refusal. Brian McMaster renewed his contract with the Edinburgh Festival. Nicholas Payne stayed put at English National Opera. John Tusa of the Barbican made public his contempt in a newspaper article. The only eager beaver was Raymond Gubbay, the commercial impresario, who reckoned his company could run the ROH on the cheap and cheerful. His application was dismissed as 'inappropriate', amid a slew of free publicity.

Among the long-shots interviewed for the job were Pierre Bergé, the French fashion mogul who had run the Opéra Bastille into deep waters, and Richard Lyttleton, son of an earl and head of EMI Classics, who was wheeled in by the ROH chairman Sir Colin Southgate, his former boss. In a weak field, a cool-headed BBC careerist with an operagoing habit looked a reasonable choice. He had no artistic experience, and would devolve all artistic decisions to Stretton and Pappano.

There was a three-month delay before Hall could take office, a dangerous hiatus eerily reminiscent of Mary Allen's foredoomed arrival. Hall stipulated that he could not leave the BBC until he turned fifty in March 2001, when he was entitled to draw a generous corporate pension. There was much haggling and hedging over his remuneration. Southgate told a radio interviewer that Hall would receive 'nothing like' his BBC salary of £247,000, plus annual bonus and chauffeur-driven limo. In fact, Board sources revealed that Hall was to be paid precisely £247,000 – double the wages of his predecessor, Michael Kaiser – but without bonus and car.

Few were prepared to wager on his longevity, though Hall, like Kaiser, expressed keen interest in seeking a private solution to the company's future. It was, by now, generally accepted that the ROH could not continue unreformed. Chris Smith, the Culture Secretary, had told Southgate to weld together its various trusts and funds before making way for fresh blood on a sclerotic and deeply riven board. Smith had previously backed Southgate in getting rid of the deputy chair, Vivien Duffield, who had raised a hundred million pounds and was the ROH's key to private wealth. Duffield did not leave without a fight. 'I have immensely enjoyed my years on the Board,' she told staff, 'except for the last twelve months which have been largely unpleasant; and I am very unhappy to be leaving the Board when there is so much to be done and when the future of the House is once again unsure.' Smith himself was soon replaced in Tony Blair's post-re-election reshuffle.

Insecurity, boardroom turbulence, political machinations, public disaffection – the English culture war over Covent Garden rumbled on towards a seventh decade with no resolution in sight and the next financial crisis just around the corner. Any redeeming light would have to come from within, since politicians of both parties were disinclined to waste any more time or personal credit on a cause of diminishing importance. The centrality of the Royal Opera House was subsiding year by year.

The appearance of this book in September 2000 had the effect of concentrating many minds on the place of the performing arts in British society. The book was received with near-unanimous rancour by lobbyists and luvvies of the opera and ballet worlds. One over-zealous Covent Garden official sought to ban our launch party from the Crush Bar. One of the many defeated chief executives of the ROH denounced the book as 'unnecessary'.

All this was to be expected. Less predictable was the torrent of responses from performers, past and present, along with opera and ballet patrons of all ages, who concurred with the historical account and appeared grateful for the context it provided. More gratifying still were the reactions of an international readership and the appearance of an American edition – two indicators that the evolution of Covent Garden has served as a paradigm for theatrical progress in many parts of the civilized world.

The story is not over yet; there are bound to be further twists. But only the most myopic of operamanes would share Sir Jeremy Isaacs's contention that the history of Covent Garden has no wider significance – no bearing on the changing character and demographics of the British nation. Whether it will continue to manifest any national relevance in a new millennium cannot be foretold. Much will depend, as ever, on individual inspiration.

Ninette de Valois, the last of the titans, was laid to rest in a private ceremony, a gathering of great-nieces and -nephews untouched by media intrusion. The nation at large had barely noticed her passing, beyond a sheaf of broadsheet tributes. The BBC coughed up a small item at the end of its nightly news; ITN ignored her death altogether. A week beforehand, when the Australian cricketer Sir Donald Bradman died at ninety-two, the news media had wallowed in a veritable swamp of nostalgia.

The comparison, drawn by the *Daily Telegraph's* arts editor, amounted to a striking indication of the shifting values of sport and art: one up, the other down. Sport was now a mass pursuit, art an 'elite' activity. When Madam had set up stall, sport was ruled by class demarcations and art was generally democratic, open to all regardless of means. What would it take to restore core values?

Apart from Margaret Thatcher, no British woman had left a greater mark on the twentieth century. De Valois had performed what few mortals ever achieve, an act of *creatio ab nihilo*, making something out of nothing. She was responsible not just for founding British ballet, but for rocket-boosting the skills and prospects of British film, television, music, stage design and costumery.

Nor had she acted alone. It had required a Keynes and Lopokova, a Webster and Drogheda, a Lambert and Nureyev, to bring her vision to fruition and drag a wallflower nation to the dance. It would take personalities of comparable magnitude to galvanize it again, decoying the public imagination away from its passive fixation with soap operas and televised sport and up into the limitless realms of newborn art and magnificent self-reinvention.

Norman Lebrecht
St John's Wood
July 2001

CHAPTER 1

Come into the Garden, Awed

IN THE MIDDLE of most great cities there stands an opera house: part monument, part amenity. In teeming, congested New York, the Metropolitan Opera proclaims its importance with an extravagance of space and wealth. In Paris, the gilded, primping Opéra Garnier has been joined by the towering Opéra Bastille on a site soaked in revolutionary sentiment. In Berlin and Vienna, the opera houses represent the presumptions of an imperial past. In Helsinki, the opera house is dappled, like the country, by a forest lake. The symbolism of an opera house is often so powerful that one can easily forget the place is supposed to be dedicated to pleasure.

London's main opera house has occupied the same site at Covent Garden since 1732. The building burned down twice, in 1808 and 1856, and until the Second World War it was privately owned and operated, presenting seasons of international opera and ballet to coincide with 'the Season' when landed families came to town and presented their marriageable daughters at Court.

The Royal Opera House was a reflection of the country it served. The rich and noble entered by the front doors, were greeted by flunkeys and enjoyed light refreshments at the Crush Bar. The rest of the world entered by side-doors, scrambled up badly-lit stairs and enjoyed the show from on high with few interval luxuries. In a country which had five different classes of rail travel, the stratification was almost democratic.

It became problematic after 1945, when the Royal Opera House was reborn as a public company, in receipt of state subsidy. From this point on, the voting public felt it had a vested interest in the opera house, a right to share in triumphs and apportion blame for failure. The ROH, for its part, purported to conduct a national

mission while attaching itself to a social élite. In these tensions and
contradictions lay potential for high drama, which exploded at the
end of the century when the opera house awoke to discover that it
had lost the country upon which it had been moored.

There have been several histories of Covent Garden, some written
by former executives, others by dewy-eyed supporters. This writer is
neither. As a professional attender over twenty years, I have been
unstirred by the majesty of the ROH and unconvinced of the singular
importance attached to it by editors and politicians. My fault, no
doubt.

Whether watching a rehearsal, being hectored at a press
conference or wooed at lunch, embraced by artists or abused by
officials, it took no great effort to maintain a position of amused
neutrality towards a self-centred enterprise that demanded a diet of
undiluted praise. It was made clear in oh-so-many ways that the
press were given free tickets to Covent Garden in the interests of
public accountability but that this institution was so celestially
superior, so unutterably Royal, that criticism was not just
superfluous – it would be almost disloyal. Critics and journalists
were tolerated so long as we sang from an approved score. One press
officer of the Royal Opera House would sit purposefully behind the
row of press seats to make sure we all behaved like gentlemen,
stayed awake and stayed to the end.

My earliest transgression set in motion a whizzing *pas de deux*
that, I later discovered, was danced only in the most exalted circles.
In May 1983 I reported that Covent Garden had cancelled an
important Verdi production, supposedly for lack of funds but in
reality (I learned) because regular telephone contact could not be
established with its eccentric German producer. A Puccini production had already been replaced that season because its equally
uncontactable Italian designer had built a set that was too large for
the ROH stage. They could get it up, but they could not get it down
in time for the next production. The Italian conductor, threatening to
quit over an ill-prepared diva, was taken aside and firmly told that if
he walked out, with the Queen Mother due to attend, he would never
work again in Britain.

When a toned down version of this story appeared in early
editions of the *Sunday Times*, an irate Covent Garden chairman, Sir
Claus Moser, rang the editor, Frank Giles, late on Saturday night

demanding that the item be removed. Was it inaccurate? asked Giles. No, said Moser, but it was damaging to the opera house. When Giles refused to withdraw the piece, Moser hinted that the paper might be stripped of its free tickets.

Saturday night head-to-heads between editors and public figures were as common, and mostly as bloodless, as punch-ups outside East End pubs. The only noteworthy aspect of this particular spat was that the ROH was employing a weapon normally reserved for Downing Street, the Bank of England and Buckingham Palace. It was no more than coincidence, surely, that the Secretary to the Board of the ROH at this time was also Secretary to the Cabinet. No other place of entertainment was so conversant with power. No other theatre, museum, sports club or orchestra acted as if its selfish interests were, in fact, the national interest.

Preposterous as this might sound to millions who never set foot in the ROH and switched channels if ever it appeared on television, there was some validity in the confluence of interests. For Covent Garden was always more than a pleasure house. If the Church of England was the Conservative Party at prayer and the Savoy Grill displayed half the Cabinet at trough, Covent Garden epitomized certain aspects and aspirations of the national condition that were all the more interesting for being unrecognized. During half a century of social change, Covent Garden was solid and immovable in its narrow sense of purpose: to produce opera and ballet at the highest standard. Unlike the House of Commons, the BBC, the National Health Service, the Labour Party and other manifestations of the *vox populi*, the ROH stood so far above transient whims of public taste and demands for 'modernization' that it encapsulated a set of freeze-dried English values in a disinterested archival form – like the (supposedly) apocryphal shelf at Oxford University Press where unsold books were taken off and dusted once a century. And come the millennium, when England anguished over its eroding identity, Covent Garden stood out briefly as a template of fading Englishness.

Its human influx was a social cross-section, always more catholic than was caricatured. It ran, in ascending flights of stairs, from the lobby carousel of peers, tycoons, media stars and the odiously rich, up to the closed circle of predatory queens and nightingale fanciers, and beyond to the top gallery of donkey-jackets and student couples with full scores in their laps and coffee flasks in their backpack. Mingled at all levels were little girls all agasp at their first *Swan*

Lake, truck-drivers who would go 'anywhere' to hear Gwyneth Jones, old-age pensioners who 'never missed a *Figaro*', pop singers who freaked out at real voices and couples of every conceivable gender pairing who were there for a birthday, an anniversary, a corporate night out or because their eleven-year-old nephew was playing an urchin in *Peter Grimes*.

The mix varied from night to night. A première or gala audience differed markedly from a Saturday-afternoon ballet house. Verdi pulled a different public from Wagner. In every row there were divergent levels of commitment and privilege. Seats 10 and 11 might belong to Friends who attended pre-curtain talks and Sunday teas, and gave ten pounds to incessant appeals. Their neighbour on either side might be a first-time corporate guest and a fanatical music-buff who had queued all day for returns. That these patrons co-existed without rancour was itself a comment on the English compromise in the three centuries since the last civil war. A comparable conjunction would not have sat peacefully in the Vienna State Opera or the Palais Garnier, especially when the corporates started snoring and the queuers unlaced their pungent footwear.

Over half a century, the social code was rewritten. In 1946, the stalls wore black-tie and the gallery dress uniforms. In 1996, jeans were not uncommon and an ex-POW would greet Japanese moguls at the door. In 1946, the Lord Chamberlain exercised powers of censorship that eliminated acts of nudity, treason or blasphemy. By 1996, the Royal Ballet star Sylvie Guillem danced habitually topless and François Le Roux had his privates on parade in *Gawain*. A new production of the *Ring* ridiculed Wagner to a point where Bernard Haitink could hardly bring himself to conduct it, and homo-erotic images were pasted on street posters to attract a sexually-active audience.

In manners and morals, habits and hobbies, attitudes and ambitions, England changed fundamentally in the second half of the twentieth century. The upheavals were most visible in demographics and wealth distribution. In 1946, any non-white face at Covent Garden would certainly have belonged to a North American soldier or a Latin American diplomat. By 1996, opera appealed to Londoners of Asian and Caribbean descent. When Covent Garden reopened after the war, England was a manufacturing nation with a northern industrial base. When it closed in 1997, England was a post-industrial society that relied on 'invisible earnings' and

London-based service industries. Millennial England with its cluttered domes and multi-cultural correctnesses bore scant resemblance to the late-imperial world of 1946. The past, wrote L. P. Hartley, is a foreign country[1] – and many who chose to live in the past felt like foreigners in their own land. Covent Garden was one of the few points of constancy.

I became aware of its frozenness in time when, in May 1995, I took my eldest sister to watch *La Bohème* with Roberto Alagna and Cynthia Haymon. Beatrice, living on a windswept hilltop in Galilee, had not entered the ROH for forty-five years. While I toddled my first steps she, in her first job as a school secretary, used to visit the opera two or three times a month. It cost her two-and-sixpence (twelve and a half pence in decimal conversion; around two pounds in millennial values) and she developed a teenaged crush on the Irish tenor, James Johnston, before leaving to build a new country.

As we ate ices between acts of *Bohème* and surveyed the human promenade, Beatrice suddenly remarked how familiar it felt, how little had changed. London no longer belonged to her, but Covent Garden was a rock upon which her memories and values could safely be measured. This was the England she had left behind. Her observation sparked a train of thought in my mind. Could it be that an archaic institution like the Royal Opera House represented something more than the sum of its vanities? Was it, perhaps, a repository of unretouched reality, a laboratory specimen of an England we had lost in a wave of Europeanism and heteroethnicity?

Personally, I welcomed the new cosmopolitanism that turned greasy-spoon caffs into spic trattorias and Brylcreemed hair into beaded dreadlocks. I shuttled happily through the Channel Tunnel and rejoiced at the death of little-Englishness and mediocre English art. Every historian, however, feels a responsibility to conserve. In the remote, myopic and often comic self-absorption of Covent Garden there existed, I suspected, a classic model for examining what had happened to my country in my lifetime.

For an opera house to flourish, it must secure and sustain popular approval, fingering the pulse of the majority who never attend opera or ballet yet pay for them through taxes in Europe and tax-breaks in the United States. This is rather like asking a butcher to canvass the views of passing vegetarians, but it has become a prerequisite of modern opera management. Failure to attune to changing rhythms of public mood is a recipe for disaster. Covent Garden, in the second half of its public existence, recklessly courted disaster.

By aspiring to world class, it forsook the common touch. In chasing stars, it alienated earthlings. The higher it rose, the odder it seemed to that kind of Englishman who likes a dash of amateurism in his sport and prefers an honest English trier to a world-slaying foreign genius. Covent Garden, once it joined the Met, La Scala and Vienna as a cornerstone of world opera, lost its local footholds.

A ghetto mentality prevailed. In the minds of directors, staff and performers, the ROH represented an irresistible force of destiny. 'To work at Covent Garden with its wealth of history – let us be bold and say Tradition – would make anyone humble that he or she occupies the room where Melba or Caruso dressed for performances, or where Augustus Harris planned his seasons; it can make the same people proud that, a generation after his death, they are sharing in an attempt to give reality to Richter's dream of a national opera company for England, based on Covent Garden,'[2] marvelled the Queen's cousin, a senior Royal Opera House executive. His sentiments were meaningful, but only to a minority within a cultured minority who adored opera. To the man on the Clapham omnibus, the names of Melba and Caruso might ring a bell, but Harris and Hans Richter struck no chords. What was their dream, and who cared? Opera, the most inverted of arts, was forever invoking ancient gods, whose names usefully separated the true devotee from the cultural tourist. To the buff, going to the opera entailed a day's advance preparation: reading the libretto, studying the score or sampling a recording and, if time permitted, trawling a periphery of composer letters and philosophical essays. In a country where fanaticism is dismissed as bad manners, a schism opened between the committed and the occasional.

Every place where opera and ballet is performed is riddled with cliques and intrigues. Covent Graden was unusual in its unifying sense of purpose. 'People worked here for next to nothing,' said the house manager, Trevor Jones. 'We tried to give the public a sense of coming into something special. Our rewards, and theirs, were those nights when everything came off.'[3] 'The pay was atrocious,' said a 1960s secretary, 'fifteen pounds a week was half what I could have got outside. But you got swept up in the life of the house, the magic.

Everyone hung out in the canteen, stars and plebs and stagehands. It was wonderful.'[4]

Many of those who worked in the offices made opera and ballet as amateurs in their own spare time. They sang in choruses, directed village-hall productions, researched impossibly detailed programme notes and hung out in bars with fellow-devotees. They spent holidays in the crush of Bayreuth, Verona or an English summer school where the art would be mounted by night and studied by day. 'At Covent Garden, everybody loves the opera, from the porter to (the general director) Jeremy Isaacs,' said the international soprano, Angela Gheorghiu. 'I know all the people, the usherettes, the stage hands. If they like a performer, they collect money to buy her flowers. Only at Covent Garden does this happen, nowhere else in the world.'[5]

Only at Covent Garden would you find dancers rehearsing on stage at four in the morning, no other slot being available. Nowhere else did wage clerks stay on past midnight to proofread a report from another department that had to reach the Arts Council by morning. Here alone did stagehands knowingly risk and, on tragic occasion, sacrifice their lives on machinery that was defunct before the First World War and still in use decades later. Only at Covent Garden would the doorman look after the dogs of two dancers who were going on holiday, while the nonagenarian ballet founder, Dame Ninette de Valois, stood in a queue for a cup of canteen tea, shunning special treatment. In no other opera house would a music director, a knight of the realm, take a broom and sweep the pit floor before rehearsal, taking care not to knock down the table on which Puccini had stood during rehearsals for the first *Bohème*.

Such attitudes amounted to a vanishing ethos, preserved by the collective will of an ever-changing group of people who, in some ways, represented the English character at its finest – robust, optimistic, reserved, dry-witted, industrious and uncomplaining. People who, in former times, would have been called 'the salt of the earth'. People who lived for an ideal, but made no big deal of it. People who said 'you don't want to hear about *me*,' as they scuttled off to complete a twenty-hour day. People – artists, stagehands, make-up men, secretaries, programme editors, wig-makers, second violinists – who were the life's blood of the place, and would blush or snarl if you told them so. Singly, they were men and women of little consequence; collectively, they gave devoted service to something larger than themselves, their phlegmaticism calling to mind romanticized accounts of the yeomen of old England and the spirit of the Blitz.

The underside of such dedication was a tunnel vision that led company members to mistrust outsiders and feel threatened by change. True insiders were known as 'Gardeners'. They formed a secretive society, pledged to protect one another and preserve the sacred opera house from external encroachments. The corollary of their English staunchness was a poisonously English parochialism of the kind excoriated by Benjamin Britten in *Peter Grimes* and parodied in *Albert Herring*. As managers came and went, ancillary staff dug themselves into defensive positions, marrying self-interest with the survival of a company that was fast becoming unmanageable. Private papers were ransacked and computers hacked. News of a senior dismissal was leaked to the press before the victim could be told. Factions within the Floral Street offices were at war with one another, and the chairman spoke out at board meetings of 'a nest of vipers'. In the face of danger, the opera house turned inwards like a scorpion and stung itself almost to death in a series of misadventures that enthralled the nation. The full truth of those mortal passions can be revealed in this book for the first time.

There have been several books on Englishness, written either by wrily admiring foreigners or by acidly self-lacerating Brits. This author is neither. Born and raised in post-war London, I lived and worked in other lands and picked up several languages before returning home, convinced that this was still the best place to live and write. Mine was, I realized, an unfashionable choice. England was in decline, its populace unhappy, its world role abandoned. There was more money to be had in America, more fun in Europe and more excitement in the Middle East. The decisive lure of England was its Englishness, that amalgam of the qualities that enables fifty-five million people to live at peace and in comfort on a crowded island. It is a temperate cocktail composed of mild tolerance, good manners, bad food, fair play, mixed weather, anti-intellectualism and a refusal to take life and death too seriously.

That was the top of the coin. The obverse revealed a puzzling attachment to mediocrity and an exclusion of alien ideas. The composer Michael Finnissy viewed the adjective 'English' as 'a tactful euphemism for second-rate or, worse, a limited and limiting culture'.[6] The artist Ron Kitaj re-emigrated to America in 1997, blaming anti-Semitic reviews for the death of his wife. A Lancashire-born Jewish scholar said tellingly, 'Englishness is not available to me.'[7] 'Damn you, England!' said the playwright John Osborne in a famous rejection of Queen and country.

All of these perceptions viewed Englishness as a tangible unity, which it decidedly is not. Even after the devolution of Scotland, Wales and Northern Ireland, this remains a peaceably fissipated island: city knows nothing of country, town never meets gown, them are not us, and 'U' is the opposite of 'non-U'. There are many Englands and varied forms of Englishness. When the New Labour Government backed a measure to abolish fox-hunting, it thought it was attacking the landed gentry. Peaceful mass demonstrations brought threadbare crofters marching on to the streets beside estate-owners' wives in jodhpurs and pearls. They represented the English countryside, united against the spread of urban values. When the rights of hereditary peers were abolished in the House of Lords, it was the life peers who were seen to weep, mourning the passing of eight centuries of tradition.

'The Prime Minister has asked us to help create a new Britain, a new country,' declared one Labour MP,[8] but there will always be an England, and there will always be what the writer Michael Bracewell called 'a need within the psyche of Englishness to look back to an idealized past'.[9] The Royal Opera House catered primarily to that need, which may help explain the passions it aroused. But the ideals were never defined, and the murkier they grew the shakier was the ground on which the ROH stood. This history attempts to trace the parabola, from gleaming post-war ideals to complacent millennial posterity.

The sources of modern history are oral and documentary. At Covent Garden, the paper trail is tantalizingly thin. There is an official archive, which has been officially shut for two years. It has also been stripped of anything remotely contentious. There is no file of correspondence, for example, between the ballet director and the general administrator. There is a file for Lord Goodman, the Arts Council chairman and later a member of the ROH board, but it turned out to be completely empty.

Before I could enter the archives, the board demanded that I obtain the approval of all past chairmen, one of whom refused access to files pertaining to his period. I would later discover that he had little to hide. His response was typically that of an ROH grandee who saw no reason for the public to know what had been going on while he was in charge of a public-funded institution.

Other papers had to be treated with care. Maynard Keynes, by the time of his involvement with Covent Garden, was aware of his frailty and wrote with an eye to posterity. David Webster, the first administrator, never committed himself to paper if he could avoid it, and what he wrote often differed from what he meant.

In the most glaring of lacunae, Ninette de Valois, founder of English ballet, sent her papers for safe-keeping to her mother in Ireland. When she came to visit, she found they had been thrown on the fire. 'I didn't realize you wanted that stuff kept,' said Mum.

Happily, I stumbled across the papers of the 11th Earl of Drogheda, secretary to the ROH Board for six years and chairman for sixteen, conserved in a cardboard suitcase beneath an old gentleman's bed in Chelsea. With the permission of the 12th earl, his son, I have been able to unravel some of the more stubborn mysteries of the formative period. The widows of two music directors, Karl Rankl and Georg Solti, allowed me to examine items from their archives. During the upheavals of the late 1990s, several executives kept diaries and conversation notes, sometimes at the demand of their lawyers. Several of these eye-opening documents passed beneath my incredulous eyes.

Almost every artist and executive whom I approached for information responded positively and generously. There was a collective desire, it seemed, almost an urgency, to discover the past, dispel the clouds and start again on fresh foundations to bring art to an undemanding nation. Impartial as I remain, they have earned my gratitude, admiration and every good wish.

Norman Lebrecht
St John's Wood
July 2000

CHAPTER 2

Drinks at the Bar, 6.45

(1945 European time)

THE WAR ENDED in Europe on 7 May 1945, news of the German surrender being relayed over the BBC as England sat down to lunch. There was no public eruption, but the next morning, VE-Day, thousands converged on Whitehall where Winston Churchill, having addressed Parliament and offered thanks to God at St Margaret's, Westminster, went onto the balcony of the Ministry of Health to tell the milling crowds, 'My dear friends, this is *your* victory . . .'

That night, London was floodlit for the first time in five and a half years, its gutted and gapped glories exposed like a grand dowager's mouth in the dentist's chair. St Paul's stood miraculously intact on a mound of devastation; the National Gallery gleamed once more in Georgian splendour, though its west side was wrecked. On Trafalgar Square, Nelson on his leonine column surveyed a tide of deferred and fairly decorous revelry. The police had been ordered to treat excessive jubilation 'in a fatherly manner',[1] but there was not much to exercise the arm of the law apart from one bright spark who led community singing from on top of the gates of Buckingham Palace and another who set a tree ablaze in Green Park. Pubs began to run dry by eight in the evening and restricted beer-drinkers to half-pints. Two young women hopped into the Trafalgar Square fountains to pose in clinging-wet sweaters with a pair of pop-eyed sailors. But there was no repeat of the unbridled relief and pavement copulations that, in the same streets, greeted the end of the First World War.

Men and women of all ranks and nations donned paper hats, embraced one another and danced into the night but most drew back from acts they might regret in grey daylight. Something in the national mood suggested that this was not the moment for letting go. The war with Japan was still to be won, the full horrors of Hitler's crimes had yet to be absorbed and the immediate future portended as much of a life-and-death struggle as the recent past. Although British losses in battle were barely half the 750,000 toll of the 1914–1918 War, the home front this time was torn to shreds. More than 780,000 buildings had been destroyed or heavily damaged by German bombing. Some 147,000 civilians had been killed or severely injured and many more were in urgent need of rehousing. One-third of the City of London had been laid waste. The merchant fleet was reduced to two-thirds of its pre-war size, eliminating any early resumption of overseas trading.

To pay for the war, the United Kingdom had sold £1,118 million of assets and incurred foreign debts of three billion pounds. The world's richest nation had become its biggest debtor. All it had earned in return was a stubborn independence and a swelling of self-pride. 'When shall the reputation and faith of this generation of English men and women fail?' exulted Churchill on VE-Day. 'I say that in the long years to come, not only the people of this island, but from all over the world, wherever the bird of freedom chirps in human hearts, they will look back to what we have done and they will say, "Don't despair, don't yield to violence and tyranny. March straight forward and die, if need be, unconquered."' Churchill, however, was about to be swept away in an electoral landslide, and the bill for victory was due for payment.

No sooner had the results been declared than the incoming Labour Government faced a stark warning from the Treasury adviser, Lord Keynes, that Britain had 'not a hope of escaping what might be described, without exaggeration, and without implying that we might not eventually recover from it, a financial Dunkirk'. Industry had been turned over to military production and could not quickly be domesticated; export markets had been lost, perhaps for ever; and the United States was about to end its expensive line of credit known as Lend-Lease. Resorting to darkest-hour Churchillian rhetoric, Keynes, the foremost living economist, said the situation could only be saved 'by a combination of the greatest enterprise, ruthlessness and tact'.[2]

Britain was, in a word, broke. Its cities lay in ruins, its citizens were shabbily dressed and its daily food and fuel would be strictly rationed for the next ten years. It had won the war and lost the peace, before the peace had even begun. The country was entering an era of austerity so bleak that unborn historians of a future generation could grasp it only by experiencing conditions in shard republics of the dismantled Soviet empire. Fear of national bankruptcy, added to exceptionally harsh winters, industrial unrest and the threat of nuclear confrontation with the Russians, would give rise to a siege mentality more pervasive and morale-sapping than the fearsome Blitz – an atmosphere captured with only slight exaggeration in George Orwell's apocalyptic novel, *1984*.

The early summer of 1945 was a critical moment that did not permit English people the luxury of relief and rejoicing. It was a time to tighten belts and think of bare necessities. There were neither the resources nor the urge for frivolity. Yet – and this decision would appear all the more striking in light of political attitudes in a later, wealthier age – within weeks of the end of war and with creditors baying at the door, an almost indigent nation resolved without controversy to set up three cost-intensive new cultural institutions: the Arts Council, the BBC's third programme of music, drama and serious talks, and the Royal Opera House, Covent Garden.

In a society that had always left the organization of art in the hands of enthusiastic amateurs and refused to allocate tax revenue to support mere 'entertainments', this triple conception amounted to nothing less than a Damascene conversion, a blinding act of faith. The endowment of three publicly-funded promoters of culture amounted to a penitent admission by the authorities of their moral responsibility for the state of the arts. Setting aside the BBC's initiative, which was the kind of public-spirited gesture the BBC tends to make when its Charter is up for renewal, the founding of the Arts Council and the Royal Opera House at a time when there was not enough gold in Threadneedle Street to pay the nation's energy bills marked a substantial shift in the core values and priorities of the island's inhabitants, the unarticulated quintessentials of Englishness.

'The English will never develop into a nation of philosophers,' wrote Orwell around this time. 'They will always prefer instinct to logic and character to intelligence. But they must get rid of their downright contempt for "cleverness". They cannot afford it any longer. They must grow less tolerant of ugliness and mentally more adventurous. And they must stop despising foreigners.'[3] To survive in a post-war landscape, Orwell believed the English had to shed their chauvinism and philistinism and show more respect for intelligence and ideas, wherever they originated. 'The intellectual atmosphere of England is already very much livelier than it was,' he noted. 'The War scotched if it did not kill certain kinds of folly. But there is still a need for a conscious effort at national re-education.'[4]

Orwell's words were, as so often, reflective and prophetic of the national mood. No serious objection was raised to the introduction of state funding for the arts. A revolution achieved almost by stealth, but with tacit public support, was regarded as one of a series of necessary measures that would modernize the country without altering its character. 'They remained a peaceful and civilized people, tolerant, patient and generous,' was A. J. P. Taylor's assessment of the English at the end of war. 'Traditional values lost much of their force. Other values took their place. Imperial greatness was on the way out; the welfare state was on the way in. The British empire declined; the condition of the people improved.'[5] Times changed, England endured. Amid the irritating privations, most people shared the view that they were building a better country, a New Britain (to borrow a future slogan), and the arts had a vital role to play in improving the national condition.

Ever since the tide of war began to turn, the British had been led, by a sheaf of multi-party Government reports, to look forward to a better, fairer way of life. They were promised free education, the eradication of poverty and, by Labour, a welfare state that would care for everyone from cradle to grave. When the war ended, Britain awoke to Blakeian visions of a New Jerusalem. When Labour was elected, that utopia seemed at hand.

Welfare, however, is a cumbersome behemoth, slow to rise and costly to run. It was 1946 before the National Insurance Act offered decent benefits to the sick and unemployed and November 1948 before the National Health Service provided free health care, dentures and spectacles. These tangible blessings and shibboleths of a caring society took years to organize, against bitter resistance from the medical profession and others. When the war ended, there was need for an immediate sign that *laissez-faire* had been abolished and the caring state had been born. Nothing expensive could be undertaken before a general election, but all parties were united in wanting to give the country a taste of times to come. That appetizer was placed before the House of Commons on 12 June 1945 by the Chancellor of the Exchequer, Sir John Anderson, who announced the introduction of public subsidy for culture by setting up an Arts Council of Great Britain to foster a 'knowledge, understanding and practice of the fine arts'.[6]

If the Welfare State had a defining moment, it was not in the delivery of the first benefit cheque or the cutting of a free tonsillectomy but in this momentous, consensual decree that the arts – the creative voice of the nation – were from now on to be a paternal concern of central government. The new Arts Council was granted £235,000, worth around six million pounds by end-of-century values. Its remit was as modest as its resources – a friendly tweak here, a helping hand there. In the outlay of the first four years, there was nothing for orchestras in London, a hundred pounds for opera in Wales and three thousand for converting a barracks cinema in Salisbury into a fully-fledged arts theatre. By far the largest Arts Council grant, £25,000 and double the next year, was set aside for the Royal Opera House, a symbolic act of favouritism that would join the two bodies in a macabre alliance for the next half-century and almost destroy them both. This shady union was not the fault of any individual or either organization. It was by the expressed will of Government and Parliament that the Arts Council and the Royal Opera House were created inseparably in a single act and with a parallel mission – to revive the nation.

To endow two new agencies at a moment of extreme fiscal stringency and on the eve of a general election required political courage and cross-party consensus. To formulate the legislation alone demanded time that had to be stolen from more pressing matters, yet there is little sign of dissent in the surviving documentation. Covent Garden and the Arts Council were created with as much unity, or sufferance, as the nation had shown in waging war against Hitler. More remarkable still, this double extravagance was impelled and inaugurated not by some impractical dreamer but by the rigorist prophet and architect of national austerity, the high-domed and walrus-eyed Treasury adviser, John Maynard Keynes.

On the day of his Chancellor's statement in the House of Commons, the free-spirited Baron Keynes called a press conference at an address in Bloomsbury, the central London district that had lent its name to a libertarian artists' group in which the eminent economist was a pivotal and beloved figure. Keynes, who planned to become chairman of both the Arts Council and the Royal Opera House, cheerily gave the press his own gloss to the Chancellor's speech. The Arts Council, he said, had many objectives but reopening Covent Garden was absolutely its top priority – 'thereby restoring to this country something it should never have lost'.[7]

Four weeks later, in a prime-time radio address Keynes added: 'We look forward to a time when the theatre and the concert hall and the gallery will be a living element in everyone's upbringing, and regular attendance at the theatre and at concerts a part of organized education.'[8] Culture and creativity were the key to national revival. If England was to rise again, it would rise enlightened from its economic Dunkirk.

'I do not believe it is yet realized what an important thing has happened,' Keynes continued. 'State patronage of the arts has crept in. It has happened in a very *English*, informal, unostentatious way – half-baked, if you like. A semi-independent body is provided with modest funds to stimulate, comfort and support any societies and bodies . . . which are striving with serious purpose and a reasonable prospect of success to present for public enjoyment the arts of drama, music and painting.' He went on to extol the artist 'who walks where the breath of the spirit blows him. He cannot be told his direction; he does not know it himself. But he leads the rest of us into fresh pastures and teaches us to love and enjoy what we often begin by rejecting, enlarging our sensibility and purifying our instincts.'

This was no mere blueprint for a new bureacracy. The dialectics of Keynes's speech left no room for doubt that he was talking about a resurrection of a national spirit in which his infant Arts Council and Royal Opera House would nurture the necessary growth. He talked of preserving not just an English way of art, but Englishness in all its regional and social variants. In the one passage of his talk that sparked controversy Keynes declared: 'Let every part of Merrie England make merry in its own way. Death to Hollywood!'

This rallying cry drew a yelp of protest from the dream factories. Mr J. Pole, publicity director of United Artists, wrote to *The Times* complaining of Keynes's ingratitude for Hollywood's part in winning the war. Keynes, visiting America with a begging bowl ('there is no source from which we can raise sufficient funds except the United States,'[9] he told the Government) hurriedly ate his words. 'What I ought to have said,' he recanted, 'was Hollywood for Hollywood.' His meaning, though, was unmitigated by half-apology. Unless England preserved its Englishness through the arts and the Royal Opera House, the country would be reduced to dependence not just on American material aid but on the crassness of its commercial culture. The British economy might some day recover,

Keynes told his Government, but no country could ever restore a culture that had been allowed to become extinct.

The notion that culture could define nationhood was not a novel proposition. Nationalism had raged through the arts in the nineteenth century as embryonic nation-states applied great art to inflame revolution and justify independence. Verdi was, in no small measure, the catalyst of unified Italy as Beethoven and Wagner were of Bismarck's Germany. Such confluences had no place in English culture, grounded as it was in fine painting and dramatic poetry. Britain had conquered half the world without recourse to its arts and when Victorian romantics painted or poetized a 'spirit of Empire' their effusions were richly embarrassing.

Music, the most inflammatory of arts, played little part in English culture until the ascent of Edward Elgar, whose success was founded more on continental than on national strands. Elgar developed a synthesis of Franco-German orchestral textures, bowing to Berlioz, Gounod and Saint-Saëns in one bar, Brahms and Wagner in the next, albeit in a robustly English manner. Composers who set out to trace native sonorities found themselves half a century behind European researches; Ralph Vaughan Williams and Gustav von Holst, the first to be perceived as nationally 'English', were identifiably so only insofar as their music conscientiously refused to score points and make propaganda for a national agenda. English culture as a whole was individualist, self-contained, phlegmatic, witty and overwhelmingly static, fixed to the page, the canvas and the dramatic stage.

The performing arts, while well-attended, were imported wholesale. No city apart from New York paid higher fees to foreign singers, actors and musicians than imperial London. No metropolis had less by way of year-round entertainment. Opera and ballet were confined to 'the Season' when the landed gentry decamped on the capital to go shopping and display their marriageable daughters. No symphony orchestra existed in London until 1904. A national theatre, first mooted in 1848, did not come into being until 1962. The German rhetorician who defamed England as 'the land without music'[10] was not altogether wide of the mark. It took one world war to persuade English theatres and concert halls to accept indigenous artists and a second to convince the public of their merits.

The catalyst was a woman called Lilian Baylis who, inheriting her Aunt Emma's temperance hall on the wrong side of Waterloo

Bridge, made it her mission at the Old Vic to provide drama and opera at prices that were affordable to all classes. Baylis set her sights high, announcing an annual Shakespeare season in 1914 when no classics were to be seen in the West End. Sybil Thorndike played most of the female leads and the first cycle reached completion with *Troilus and Cressida* in the tercentenary year of 1923, a stark alternative to the prevailing Twenties frivolity.

Lilian Baylis's contribution to English arts and culture cannot be overstated. Over quarter of a century and on cruelly pinched means, she laid the foundations of three great ensembles: the Royal National Theatre, English National Opera and the Royal Ballet. Stout, bespectacled, thick-lipped and almost execrably ugly, her mouth twisted in midlife by a stroke, Baylis spoke in a Cockney accent that provoked middle-class derision and disparagement even from firm supporters. 'Poor dear, she has no imagination of what any opera might be, if only it was put on properly,'[11] exclaimed the music scholar Edward J. Dent, a member of her board. Whatever she lacked in artistic discernment, she made up for with an uncanny knack for recognizing good artists and persuading them to work for pennies – 'doing our bit for the Vic,' they called it. Actors who asked Baylis for a ten-shilling raise were told, 'Sorry, dear, God says No.' She was often to be found by the side of her rolltop desk, 'down on her knees, praying for a tenor'.

The operas Baylis espoused were sung resolutely in English for the greater public edification. 'My people must have The Best,' she declared. 'God tells me The Best in music is grand opera. Therefore my people must have grand opera.'[12] Stagings were unspectacular and the sets were constantly recycled. Opera played three times a week at the Vic, but the appetite for plays grew faster, especially once John Gielgud, Peggy Ashcroft and Ralph Richardson emerged at the head of a thrilling new generation. So 'the Lady', as Baylis was ironically known, decided to keep the Old Vic for drama and to find a new home for opera.

In 1928 she bought and started rebuilding the derelict Sadler's Wells theatre in seedy, run-down Islington. It was a daring move, an act of faith. To fill the bill, she knew, would require more than grand opera. Just as she was surveying her options, the God of her prayers sent along Ninette de Valois, a 'slightly fanatical young woman'[13] in her late twenties who had danced as a *soliste* for Serge Diaghilev and was now determined to create a distinctively British ballet company.

Irish-born and baptized Edris Stannis, de Valois had retired from the stage with arthritis and founded a ballet school. She needed more outlets for her talented pupils. Baylis engaged her to choreograph dance scenes for Shakespeare plays and furnish a *corps de ballet* for the opera. De Valois seized the opening and formed a full-time ballet company. The missionary zeal of 'the Lady' was met by the visionary force of a natural leader who became known to her subordinates as 'Madam'.

Baylis, who died in 1937, clung to the belief that working people could be lured from dreary pubs into the higher temples of art with a promise of entertainment and self-betterment. Some deemed her approach archaic, arguing that more modern works would attract a loyal and enthusiastic following among teachers, young secretaries, shipping clerks and the rest of the educated underclass. But the Lady was set in her ways and unsusceptible to intellectual argument. Others could raise the tone if they liked, and they did. While Gay Young Things bopped and bed-hopped the night away, England was experiencing a high-cultural revolution. Its performing landscape suddenly burst into flower. The number of symphony orchestras doubled as Birmingham, the BBC and Sir Thomas Beecham tapped a surgent demand for good music. Repertory theatres sprang up in several towns. An opera festival was started at Glyndebourne, in the Sussex Downs, by a bullish landowner, John Christie, who had married an English soprano, Audrey Mildmay.

The combined impact of these uncoordinated and often mutually hostile initiatives on English artists was electrifying. Composers and librettists found a market for their works. Home-trained English singers and ballerinas made débuts before a supportive public. A country that had neither opera nor ballet before the war was finding its voice and feet and advancing on the world stage. The legacy of Lilian Baylis and her contemporaries amounted to nothing less than a spontaneous expression of a national will to excel in the unEnglish realm of the lyric arts. The ultimate goal was to present outstanding English performers in immortal English works before a discerning English public.

Covent Garden, meanwhile, continued to serve the nobility with international seasons of opera and ballet, a parade of celebrated singers and dancers under Sir Thomas Beecham's stylish if capricious leadership. An inveterate intriguer and omnivorous wit, Beecham had been the centrifugal force in British opera since the early years of the century, spending most of his father's money and some of his mistress's on seasons and schemes that foundered as much on the shimmer of his brilliant inconstancy as on the rock of English indifference. He fluttered from the dazzle of Diaghilev, whose troupe he imported in 1913 and 1914, to the dreariness of an all-British Opera Company; from the shock value of Strauss, conducting the premières of *Elektra* and a censored *Salome*, to the soporific worthiness of Frederick Delius. A butterfly personality that illuminated all it touched, Beecham lacked the patience to dig foundations and the application to fulfil bureaucratic and legal requirements. Puffed up with vanity and frustrated by mundane obstacles, he directed a withering hail of barbed aphorisms at any would-be national revivers who did not follow his wavery beat.

'The English may not like music,' he opined, 'but they absolutely love the noise it makes.'[14] British music, he snorted, 'is in a state of perpetual promise. It might almost be said to be one long promissory note.' Modern art, he drawled, 'is a gigantic racket, run by unscrupulous men for unhealthy women.'[15] Spying the growing audience at Sadler's Wells he sent Lady Cunard, his moneybags and mistress, on a bid to take financial control of the Vic-Wells Company and send it on provincial tours. Baylis, however, was not prepared to be bought out and bridled in ripe Cockney language at her ladyship's deprecations of the company's musical standards.

Between Beecham's all-stars and the jolly-good-triers there was an unbridgeable gulf in quality, both artistic and social. No English-sung Carmen could match Conchita Supervia's. No one who was anyone in the Covent Garden audience would be seen dead watching opera in English. Nevertheless, despite the disparities, or perhaps because of them, Covent Garden was losing ground. Facing top-note competition from Glyndebourne's Continentals and rising standards at Sadler's Wells, the Royal Opera House was becoming an oddity rather than the apex of artistic life. Beside the constructive, year-round work of home-based companies, its ephemeral seasons seemed extravagant, antediluvian, even ridiculous.

What does England do when war breaks out? runs the joke. It calls up the army and shuts the theatres.[16] While *ganz* Berlin and *tout* Paris flocked to opera and music-halls, London was masked in darkness from September 1939 until Neville Chamberlain's nervous government realized that lack of entertainment was sapping morale and putting artists on the dole. Night-life resumed by official decree in November 1939. Soon after, on 14 December, a meeting took place that would transform the casual status of English arts for all time to come.

It was convened in a private room at the University of London and brought together two Cabinet ministers with little personally in common. Herbrand Sackville, ninth Earl De La Warr, was President of the Board of Education, a lover of bright lights and loose women.* Lord Macmillan, an austere Scottish jurist of great intellect and discretion, was the inept Minister of Information. Both had served in the 1924 Labour administration before drifting into National Governments with the Conservatives; both would soon be sacked.

What tore these two public figures from their duties on a working Thursday in the middle of a war was the guile of a Welsh charmer called Thomas Jones. A former Deputy Secretary to the Cabinet, Jones had been unable to accept retirement when he reached the statutory age in 1930. Having served four Prime Ministers through war, peace, Irish troubles, a General Strike and a financial crash, he had come to consider his counsel indispensable to the nation. For the next decade until Churchill shut him out, this white-haired ex-preacher and sometime economics professor was in and out of Downing Street hustling for many causes, chiefly for easing poverty in Wales and making friends with Germany. Jones had been received by Hitler in his Munich apartment and was over-friendly with his crass ambassador in London, Joachim von Ribbentrop. Using unique access to men in power, he took the former Prime Minister David Lloyd George to see the Führer and almost persuaded the incumbent Stanley Baldwin to follow suit. Known in Whitehall as 'T.J.', Jones wheedled tirelessly for an alliance between Germany and Britain. He voiced some sympathy for Hitler's Jewish victims, but was committed at all costs to achieving an understanding with the master-race.

In or out of office, Tom Jones assiduously blurred the lines between public service and personal favours, between duty and booty. Friends considered him 'incorruptible', but as Lloyd George's closest confidant from 1916 onwards, 'he had not merely touched pitch; he had been up to his neck in it, and not been

---

* his sister, Lady Idina, was at the centre of a colonial scandal when her husband, Lord Erroll, was murdered in Kenya in 1941, conceivably by her lover

defiled.'[17] Through his friendship with Baldwin, Jones became Secretary of the Pilgrim Trust, endorsed by the New York financier and philanthropist, Edward S. Harkness' Pilgrim Trust, to improve the quality of British life.

T.J. was in clover, sitting on a fortune to spend as he alone saw fit. Baldwin, the trust chairman, trusted him unreservedly and Macmillan, who succeeded as chairman in 1934, was equally friendly if more frugal. Jones sailed to America to survey its many charities. On his return he lavished large amounts on the repair of Lincoln Cathedral, Durham Castle and St David's Cathedral in Wales. Next came gifts to an experimental nursery school in the deprived London borough of Deptford and to Lilian Baylis's ever-needy Old Vic. There were grants to preserve the natural beauty of the Malvern Hills and the grandeur of Parliament Square. Sir Isaac Newton's birthplace was bought for the nation and Jones even passed a proposal, remarkably given his Nazi friendships, to offer relief to Jewish refugees.

But what most concerned the busy Secretary was the blight of mass unemployment. He began looking for 'pivotal people',[18] Gauleiters perhaps, who could lead communities out of the vale of despair by running clubs and recreation centres at which the workless might learn crafts and arts. The idea caught on in depressed Wales where, by 1933, there were one hundred and fifty such centres attended by thirty thousand men. Paying a penny a week, many labourers acquired new skills that enabled them to find or create work; others applied their idle time to reinforcing the principality's enviable choral traditions. T. J. became a hero in his homeland. In the rest of the kingdom, he sought to stem graduate emigration by giving Pilgrim Trust bursaries to impecunious students.

All of his schemes and wheezes came to a halt, however, with the outbreak of a war he had worked so shadily to prevent. The Pilgrim Trust suspended its grants for the duration of hostilities and T.J., now 69, was left casting around for a role. Back home in Wales, he wondered whether his grass-roots arts and crafts movement might not raise spirits across the nation during the Phoney War, perhaps with Government aid. Just then, he took a phone call from 'Buck' De La Warr at the Board of Education, who was thinking along similar lines. Jones proposed a chat with the Pilgrims' chairman, Lord Macmillan.

The oleaginous Jones has left a much-quoted minute of this

historic meeting, a document compromised only by its author's manipulative disingenuousness. 'Lord De La Warr,' wrote Jones, 'was enthusiastic. He had Venetian visions of a post-war Lord Mayor's Show in which the Board of Education led the Arts in triumph from Whitehall to Greenwich in magnificent barges and gorgeous gondolas; orchestras, madrigal singers, Shakespeare from the Old Vic, ballet from Sadler's Wells, shining canvases from the Royal Academy, folk dancers from village greens – in fact, Merrie England. Lord Macmillan's grave judicial calm collapsed suddenly and completely. At the moment he was responsible for the national morale, and in the President's dream he saw employment for actors, singers and painters, and refreshment for the multitude of war workers for the duration. Supply and Demand kissed. Would £25,000 be any use?'[19]

'It is characteristic of our national way of doing things,' wrote Macmillan in his memoirs, 'that the beginnings of what was to become the first State-subsidized organization for the provision and promotion of music, drama and painting for the people were entirely informal and unofficial ... The Pilgrim Trust made a first grant of £25,000 and Lord De La Warr persuaded the Treasury to contribute pound for pound with us, up to £50,000.'[20]

Four days later, with uncommon haste for Whitehall even in wartime, Macmillan and Jones called on De La Warr at his office. With them were Sir Kenneth Clark, director of the National Gallery, and two of Jones's Welsh cronies, the composer and popular broadcaster Sir Walford Davies and the adult education propagator William Emrys Williams. Having made sure that any decision was stacked in his favour, Jones proposed the formation of a Committee for the Encouragement of Music and the Arts, known as CEMA, to be funded jointly by the Pilgrim Trust and the state.

There was just one hitch. Jones's plan for milking the Treasury was designed, in part, to procure himself a last niche in public life. Unhappily for the little wizard, politics intervened. A fortnight before CEMA's inaugural meeting on 19 January 1940, Lord Macmillan was dismissed by Neville Chamberlain. With time on his hands and a noble desire to serve, Macmillan volunteered to become chairman of CEMA, depriving Jones of one post he wanted. Whitehall then claimed the job of CEMA Secretary for one of its own, a former schools inspector and French linguist called Mary Glasgow. That left T.J. out in the cold, with only a deputy chairmanship for comfort and a seat on the board for his two Welsh chums.

So long as CEMA ran on Pilgrim benefice, Jones continued to be its driving force. But Macmillan, late in 1941, ruled that the Trust might be exceeding its legal remit and would have to withdraw, leaving sole responsibility for funding the arts with the Treasury. Thus, the unintended outcome of Jones's plot, before he trickled off into oblivion, was to make the arts an affair of state – administered at 'arm's length' from political interference but accepted by all parties as a natural concern of central Government.

This was, by any measure, an historic achievement. It was also, in terms of war aims, a victory on the home front as Pilgrim and Treasury money revived the spirits in every corner of the land. CEMA sent six 'Music Travellers' up and down the country; in six months they organized 254 concerts and founded 37 orchestras and 244 choirs. William Emrys Williams circulated 'Art for the People' exhibitions, complete with easy-to-understand lecturers and guides. Sir Walford Davies organized symphony concerts in factory canteens.

When the Blitz began, CEMA put on 'emergency' concerts in air-raid shelters. The demand for distraction swelled. Men in desert fatigues faced Panzer tanks in North Africa with Penguin tracts and Mozart scores in their pockets. The Old Vic gave *The Merchant of Venice* in mining towns and moved office to Burnley. Divisions between serious and popular art narrowed. Every show, high or low, sold out and newspapers remarked on the growth of a mass audience for culture. Covent Garden, meanwhile, served as a Mecca ballroom.

Sadler's Wells Ballet and the London Philharmonic Orchestra – forsaken by its founder, Beecham, who fled the country on the outbreak of war – were sustained by an independent charity, the Carnegie Trust. Other professional ensembles stayed alive by entertaining troops, for which they were paid by ENSA out of army budgets. CEMA saw itself more as 'an extension of the social service',[21] designed to ease unemployment and foster self-help. The priority, for Jones, was to serve the public, not the arts.

CEMA was, nonetheless, the centrifugal force in a cultural upsurge that contributed materially to a myth of mass resistance – 'we can take it' – during the worst of the Blitz. 'The Treasury thought that CEMA would end with the war,' noted Kenneth Clark, who was privy to Whitehall thinking and despised Jones's lowly aims.

The Director of the National Gallery believed in great art, loved grand opera and loathed provincialism. An arrogant young man of inherited wealth who became the nation's chief curator in 1934 at the age of thirty, Clark packed off his canvases to caves in North Wales and engaged the redoubtable Myra Hess to give daily piano recitals in the bare-walled National Gallery. No event of CEMA's so captured the spirit of the times as Dame Myra playing to a thousand men and women in an evacuated, dome-shattered gallery. 'This was what we had been waiting for,' extolled Clark, 'an assertion of eternal values.'[22]

Jones, for his part, sent musicians to 'dreary Dagenhams' and kept them out of the capital, 'where amenities are abundant'.[23] Clark's dissatisfaction increased when Jones's blinkered cronies refused the brilliant actor-manager Donald Wolfit funding for a national tour in May 1940, on the grounds that Wolfit was a 'commercial' London-based enterprise. That Wolfit's lunchtime Shakespeare performances were addressing the same urgent need as Myra Hess's recitals somehow failed to register with the Joneses, locked as they were in their petty rules and pathetic resentments. This fatal misjudgement earned CEMA an unnecessary enemy.

Wolfit had lately performed a sold-out season at the Arts Theatre in Cambridge, enthralling its founder, the economist Maynard Keynes. Puzzled by the denial of subsidy, Keynes consulted Kenneth Clark, who told him that CEMA was frittering away public money on mediocrity. In July 1940, *The Times* ran a leading article attacking CEMA for spending too much on amateur art and too little on professional companies. Keynes, a Treasury advisor, duly summoned the CEMA Secretary, Mary Glasgow and, in her words, 'made mincemeat of me when I tried (as I had to) to justify my masters on the Council. I reeled out into the night, bloody but I hope unbowed, feeling I had been in the presence of a very great man.'[24]

She was not alone in that impression. Clark found Keynes 'every bit as clever and charming as he is reported to have been'.[25] Bertrand Russell, the Cambridge philosopher, wrote: 'Keynes's intellect was the sharpest and clearest that I have ever known. When I argued with him, I felt that I took my life in my hands.'[26] Keynes's brain, said the novelist H. G. Wells, was 'the best in the country'.[27] Even Tom Jones recognized his 'prismatic genius'.[28] Keynes was both an intellectual

giant and a bully who used his superior mind like a bulging muscle
to daunt would-be rivals and opponents. 'I did not enjoy his company,' said Russell, 'he made me feel a fool.'[29]

To put Wolfit on the road, Keynes personally underwrote a quarter
of his losses and advised CEMA to guarantee the rest. The incident
brought CEMA into his sights. When offered its chairmanship by
'Rab' Butler, President of the Board of Education and 'the best
Prime Minister Britain never had', Keynes hesitated at first, protesting that he suffered from heart disease, was overworked at the
Treasury and had no sympathy for CEMA's aims. But Butler was a
persuasive man and his father-in-law, the philanthropist Samuel
Courtauld, was a friend of Keynes. Butler knew the great economist
was 'not impervious to flattery';[30] a peerage clinched it and Keynes
became chairman. Upon the tittle of titles does English history turn.

In April 1942 Keynes took charge of CEMA, moved it to
Bloomsbury and transferred departmental responsibility from
Education to the Treasury, shifting brick walls of authority like so
many breeze-blocks. Over the next three years, amid frail health and
fiscal crisis, he overcame all obstacles to establish an Arts Council
and Royal Opera House. Without Keynes, neither would exist. His
appointment might seem fortuitous, a clever improvisation by a
rising politician, but the foregoing events indicate that it was part of
an organic process – the kind of evolutionary adjustment for which
the English system is widely envied and profoundly misunderstood.
Whitehall was working in mysterious ways, its wonders to perform.

Officialdom had acted unofficially, creating precedents that
foreshadowed all future relations between Government and the arts.
CEMA, conceived at an informal meeting of two ministers and run
by Whitehall nominees, was funded by the Treasury without formal
legislation and, when its directors proved inadequate, they were
replaced without a ripple appearing on the public record. This was a
manner of administration that had functioned since the reign of
Henry the Eighth. Self-selecting from a narrow social and
educational base, the senior levels of the civil service clung to
unreformed privileges by being acutely sensitive to failure. Their
rules were designed to deter hotheads, avert corruption and put the
right man in the right job most of the time. They did not always
succeed at first, but setting Keynes at the head of arts funding was a
mark of the system at its best. Here was a man with all the necessary
qualities and a passionate commitment who could also be trusted by

the Establishment not to traduce its authority.

Keynes was at once an insider – Eton, Cambridge, Whitehall – and a lion of bohemia; a public official and a self-made millionaire; a servant of the Crown with an independent mind. The arts, he once said, 'owe no vow of obedience'.[31] Without Keynes as arts commissar, England would probably have reverted to its usual state of artlessness and the Royal Opera House would never have risen from the disgrace of a dance-hall floor.

Few men of ideas have exerted such influence on their century as John Maynard Keynes, designer of the modern economy. From the early 1930s when he formulated the *General Theory of Employment, Interest and Money* to the 1970s when it was held responsible for renewed economic crisis, Keynes held sway in the study of economics to the point where anyone questioning his formula was dismissed as stupid or heartless. While never quite a household name, Keynes was widely held to be the 'saviour'* of capitalism as Karl Marx was of communism and Jesus Christ of sinful humanity – an immaculate conceptualizer. His teachings possessed poetic simplicity and empirical apparatus, glorious turns of phrase and just enough historical evidence to convince the doubters.

Before Keynes, economics was taught in England as a minor branch of moral philosophy. After Keynes, economics became a political formula of immense practical value. Until Keynes published his *General Theory* in February 1936, governments were led to believe that economies were intractable and could not be manipulated. Ministers who asked awkward questions were fed a pre-industrial aphorism from eighteenth-century France. Known as Say's Law, this theorem held that 'supply creates its own demand'. Production resulted in income which, in turn, got spent on other products. Unemployment and stagflation were temporary aberrations, adjusting themselves like the weather after a record heatwave. That was the way of the world, said the classical economists, and had been ever since fiscal trade replaced the bartering of goods. *Quod erat demonstrandum*.

What Keynes proposed, in the depths of world Depression, was that Government could, and should, make a difference. By lowering and raising interest rates it could stimulate spending or saving, as

* the title of the second volume of Skidelsky's important biography

desired. By borrowing money and spending it on industrial pur-
chases and investments, it could increase levels of employment. The
state, Keynes argued, needed to spend more than it earned in order
to secure jobs for most working men and boost their spending power.
If the public overspent, the swelling of inflation could be curbed by
higher interest rates. It was within the hands of politicians, not God,
to manage supply and demand.

People wanted the moon, said Keynes, and governments were
telling them 'that green cheese is practically the same thing'.[32] One
remedy for reducing unemployment, he joked, was for the Treasury
'to fill old bottles with bank notes, bury them at suitable depths in
disused coal-mines and . . . leave to private enterprise on the well-
tried principles of *laissez-faire* to dig the notes up again.'[33] He was
out to demolish conventional economics including, he assured
George Bernard Shaw, the foundations of Marxism.[34]

Keynes was not acting alone. Cambridge colleagues helped tweak
the General Theory and his favourite pupil, Richard Kahn, is
sometimes credited with co-authorship for having invented in 1931
a multiplier device by which the method could be accurately
applied. It took Keynes five years to put his hypothesis into print, in
which time proof of its validity was building up. Its publication in
three hundred and eighty-four pages, four equations and two curves
marked a watershed in the way economics were practised and the
world was run. 'Never did a book fall more quickly and more
completely into the hands of summarizers, simplifiers, boilers-
down, pedagogues and propagandists,'[35] wrote a Cambridge
disciple.

The *General Theory* had the great merits of readability, rationality
and of being exactly what every humane politican wanted to be true.
Franklin D. Roosevelt's New Deal in the United States was starting
to show – with some help from Keynes who advised the White
House on occasion – that governments could relieve misery and
spend their way out of recession. Hitler's programme of public
works and rearmament was ending Germany's slump. Britain had to
respond. In February 1937, Neville Chamberlain announced
borrowings of four hundred million pounds over five years for arms
manufacture to counter the German threat. Labour, committed to
pacifism and suspicious of Keynes on personal and political
grounds, was inclined to object. But Hugh Dalton, its economic
expert, had read his *General Theory* and talked his party around.

From that point on, Keynes was the guiding light to governments of every complexion. Roy Jenkins, a Labour Chancellor of the Exchequer, called the *General Theory* 'the most important book of the past hundred years'.[36] Even when Keynes seemed discredited in the 1970s oil-fuelled crisis, wise men like John Kenneth Galbraith maintained that Keynes was still right in principle. What had gone wrong was the perversion of his ideas by insipid leaders and greedy trade unionists who claimed a 'right to work' and full employment, while giving little in return.

At the start of the next century, it was too soon to pronounce Keynes dead – for even if his Theory was disputed, the institutions he invented continue to dominate our fiscal and cultural skylines. In 1944 Keynes laid the foundations of the International Monetary Fund and the International Bank for Reconstruction and Development, two aids for helping impoverished nations spend their way out of trouble. The next year, he instituted the Arts Council of Great Britain and the Royal Opera House. All four bodies were fashioned conspicuously in his image.

In Keynes, as in all men of imagination, personal proclivities and prejudices dictated the course of his ideas and the colour of his legacy, intellectual and institutional. One editor of *The Times* and chairman of the Arts Council[37] has argued that Keynes's sexual orientation was responsible for his rejection of the gold standard. Bertrand Russell saw him as a Cambridge cleric, out to redeem the world for academic purity. Some regard Keynes as an Establishment insider, others as a subversive intruder. The extent to which his character formed his economic thought continues to arouse heated debate. Little consideration, however, has been given to Keynes's private, even selfish, grounds for reforming the arts and founding a Royal Opera House. To understand his contributions to the arts one needs to trace the complicated and contradictory desires and talents of this 'practical visionary', the subject of more books than any Englishman of his time[38] except Churchill.

In many of his public deeds, and especially in the arts, Keynes was alert to his own self-interest, yet egotism drove him to ever-greater acts of public benefice. He was tugged in two directions, and over-compensated in both. He was, said his biographer, Robert Skidelsky, 'a buoyant and generous spirit who refused to despair of his country and its traditions, and offered the world a new partnership between government and people to bring the good life within reach of all.'[39]

*

That Keynes was extraordinarily clever was never in question. The eldest of three bright children,* born in June 1883 to a lecturer in moral science and his wife, a future mayor of Cambridge, Maynard (his mother called him John) outshone all other dons' sons and mentally outstripped his bodily development. He grew up weak, lanky and, in a six-year-old self-appreciation that never altered, 'remarkably ugly'.[40] Aged eight, he was taken with his brother to be surgically circumcised, apparently to stop them masturbating. He kept a home in Cambridge all his life and dearly loved his parents, visiting or writing to them weekly and consulting his mother on all matters of well-being, accepting her choice of cardiologist when his health began to fail. It was as much for her vanity as his own that he accepted the barony that came with the CEMA chairmanship.

Winning scholarships to Eton and King's, Keynes discovered a gift for making profound and lasting friendships. In Cambridge, he was elected to a secret intellectual society, The Apostles, which took in one or two of the sharpest undergraduates each year. Here, he met the future writers Lytton Strachey and Leonard Woolf. Together, they formed the nucleus of what became known as the Bloomsbury Group, a gathering of free spirits that embraced Strachey's lover, the artist Duncan Grant, Grant's mistress Vanessa Bell, her art-critic husband Clive Bell and her celebrated sister Virginia, who married Woolf.

Other affiliates included the novelist E. M. Forster, Strachey's brother, James, and Virginia's brother, Adrian Stephen (whom Grant seduced), the painter Roger Fry (who loved Vanessa Bell and Strachey's sister, Phillippa), the novelist David Garnett (who married Vanessa's daughter) and the painter Dora Carrington, who was suicidally infatuated with Strachey.

Bloomsbury was both a physical habitat and a pervasive state of mind. Much has been made by literary gawkers of its inextricable sexual entanglements, but any loosening of Victorian corsets must be viewed in the context of the group's general ethos, which was hedonist, separatist and supremacist. As admirers of the Cambridge philosopher, G. E. Moore, Bloomsberries were dedicated to the pursuit of a 'good life', sampling whatever took their fancy but

---

* his brother, Geoffrey, became an eminent surgeon; his sister, Margaret, married Professor A. V. Hill, secretary of the Royal Society

refraining from defining 'goodness' or applying rules. Life was a grand experiment in which friends had to be allowed to make mistakes, even when lives were ruined or put at risk. The pleasures of human intercourse and the enjoyment of beautiful objects, were the highest reward, the ultimate good.

For all their high mindedness, Bloomsbury talked low and dirty. When Strachey saw a stain on Virginia's skirt, he asked her loudly if it was semen. 'One can talk of fucking & sodomy & sucking & bushes all without turning a hair,'[41] wrote Vanessa Bell, appreciatively, to Keynes. They saw themselves as being above convention, rejecting religious morality and striving for the betterment of the species. 'In or about December 1910, human character changed,' wrote Virginia Woolf.[42] What united Bloomsbury was a sense of its collective superiority and a contempt for people of lower brows and staider ways.

Sexuality was a glue that bonded the group and sealed its intimacy. Most of the men were primarily homosexual, an affinity that placed them at odds with propriety and the law. Bloomsbury made of their sexual predilection an élitist distinction, espousing a 'Higher Sodomy' that, on physical and ethical grounds, affirmed an elevated set of tastes and values – 'buns, buggery and higher thinking', in the definition of one scion.[43]

Hampered by a lack of physical allure (or sense of self-loathing), Keynes formed a passionate attachment unrequitedly to a Cambridge freshman, Arthur Hobhouse, before bedding the artist Duncan Grant, both objects of Lytton Strachey's desire. When unhappy in love, or out of it, Keynes indulged in casual pick-ups. Homosexuality for Keynes was a code of conduct and a cocking of snoots at the society he served. A physical and spiritual ambivalence ran through the course of his public life.

On 1 August 1914, three days before Britain declared war on Germany, Keynes was approached by a Treasury acquaintance, Basil Blackett, with a request 'to pick your brains for the country's benefit'.[44] Five months on, he joined the most rigorous, secret and powerful Government department and rose so smoothly through its brainy ranks that in March 1919, aged thirty-five, he was sent as the Treasury's chief representative to the Paris peace conference. During the War, Keynes financed the military effort by day and talked pacifism with Bloomsbury at night. His friends were conscientious objectors and he supported them with advice and money, some of it in public commissions. Russell gave up his Cambridge rostrum and went to jail for his beliefs; Keynes kept quiet and made a great career. Nimble-minded and none too fastidious, he papered over the schisms and kept soul and reputation intact. At the Paris peace conference he opposed punitive German repayments; on losing the argument he left the Treasury and published a searing indictment of the peace treaty,[45] recovering self-respect.

While struggling to reconcile conscience with career, Keynes lost sight of the niceties that separate public and private business. When he became rich after the war, it was whispered that Keynes had used Treasury inside knowledge to make his fortune on the Stock Exchange. Keynes's accounts show that he negotiated a thousand-pound overdraft at Barclays days before war broke out and invested half of it in shares. He borrowed another thousand from Roger Fry as speculative capital. During five years in Whitehall, his assets increased eightfold to £16,431,[46] a tidy sum for a civil servant, worth quarter of a million in end-of-century values. There is little doubt that Keynes speculated during the war, albeit prudently, in modest amounts and without necessarily misusing privileged information. It was not, at the time, illegal for a Treasury official to play the markets, although it might have been regarded as improper for a man whose ministerial advice could affect the value of currencies and stocks. Keynes, it seems, refused to recognize the distinction between personal and public interest.

Slightly more compromising was the role he played in helping to acquire for the nation part of the estate of Edgar Degas, who was both an important Impressionist and an astute art collector. A catalogue of the Paris sale of Degas' estate in March 1918 had fallen into the hands of Duncan Grant, who 'suggested to Maynard that he should get the money from the Treasury to buy some of these pictures for the National Gallery.'[47] Anxious to recover Bloomsbury esteem, Keynes wired back: 'Money secured for pictures.' He had persuaded the Chancellor of the Exchequer, Andrew Bonar Law, to release 550,000 francs, equivalent to twenty thousand pounds, on the twin grounds of enriching British art and helping the French balance of payments. Heading for Paris on Treasury business, Keynes took along Sir Charles Holmes, director of the National Gallery, who shaved off his moustache and wore glasses to avoid recognition by art dealers. On the morning of 26 March, with the sound of German guns grimly audible and Debussy's death the night before casting a deeper pall,

Keynes and Holmes pulled off one of the great auction-room coups. Outbidding the Louvre for a Delacroix, they also picked up Manet's *Execution of Maximilian* and works by Corot, David and Ingres. Holmes, according to Keynes, turned down a Cézanne and two El Grecos and came home with quarter of his allowance unspent. The canny Keynes picked up for himself Cézanne's *Apples* for £327, as well as two pictures by Delacroix and a female nude by Ingres.

'As Holmes had a prejudice against Cézanne, no conflict of interest had arisen,' concludes Keynes's biographer,[48] but the position was not quite so pure. Holmes may have shunned Cézanne, but no curator would fail to spend an open cheque unless the Treasury man at his side was murmuring caution. Nothing can be pinned on Keynes, but he would never have owned the Delacroix he coveted had the Director of the National Gallery sensed a competitive ardour. Keynes had gone to Paris on public business and came back with the basis of an opulent private collection (which, by the time he was finished, included four Cézannes, two Braques, a Matisse, two Picassos and Georges Seurat's 1884 study for *La Grande Jatte*). He may not have traduced his position, but he left office much richer than he entered, and with no sense of having bent the rules. He managed, like many of fewer scruples, to convince himself that what was good for Maynard Keynes was good for the nation – a perception that would guide his intense involvement with the performing arts.

Apart from a love of fine art and books Keynes, along with most of Bloomsbury, had little time for the lively arts. Theatre they made mostly for themselves in post-supper *tableaux vivants* and charades. Music was not part of their insular Englishness. No composer of note visited Gordon Square. Virginia Woolf was bored witless at Bayreuth. Keynes in 1907 showed complete lack of enthusiasm when Grant secured tickets for Wagner's *Ring* cycle.[49] War, however, can alter the most settled of habits.

In the autumn of 1918, the exiled Serge Diaghilev introduced his latest troupe to a London public whose liking for dance he had cultivated in four vogue-making visits before the War. Keynes joined the rush for tickets. 'There is no genius in it this year,' he reported to Grant. 'The leading lady, Lopokova, is poor. But the new Nijinski, Mr Idzikovsky . . . has a charm or two.'[50]

Backstage, Keynes and Grant were introduced to the monocled

impresario. At a party given by the scandal-seeking Sitwells, Keynes met Lydia Lopokova, who let him pinch her legs to feel how strong they were. On Armistice Night he met her again and revised his first impression. She was a bubbly dancer with a prodigious technique, twenty-six years old and unhappily married to Diaghilev's Italian business manager, Randolfo Barocchi, from whom she was plotting escape. Her disappearance in July 1919 was the talk of the town, noticed even by Virginia Woolf. Lopokova fled to America for eighteen months, rejoining Diaghilev in Paris and returning with him to London at the end of 1921 in Tchaikovsky's *Sleeping Beauty*, re-scored by Igor Stravinsky and retitled *The Sleeping Princess* because, said Diaghilev, 'Lopokova is no beauty.'

The show was no hit either, but Keynes, who had not seen Lopokova or anyone half as good for three years, was smitten. He watched her night after night in the near-solitude of half-empty stalls, until the run was cut short in February 1922 as Diaghilev ran out of funds. *Sleeping Princess* left such an impression on Keynes that he demanded it for the reopening of Covent Garden in 1946 and invoked its Good Fairy in the last speech of his life to an audience of astonished financiers. Lopokova was now at the centre of his turbo-charged thoughts. Erotically, he was still sharing with Lytton Strachey and E. M. Forster the affections of a Cambridge under-graduate they called 'Sebastian' (his given names were Walter John Herbert Sprott), but the lure of Lydia proved irresistible. He was becoming hopelessly 'entangled', he told Vanessa Bell. She flashed back: 'Don't marry her . . . she'd be a very expensive wife and would give up dancing and is altogether to be preferred as a mistress.'[51] Lytton Strachey called Lopokova a 'half-witted canary' and Grant declared the couple 'utterly unsuited'.[52] Virginia Woolf predicted that Keynes would be reduced to talking in words of one syllable.

Keynes married Lydia the following year, once she had finalized her divorce from Barocchi, and they lived blissfully ever after. Some Bloomsberries believed that theirs was a sexless *marriage blanc* but their correspondence contains much kissing and 'gobbling' and marks of mutual physical infatuation. There was even talk of procreation, and hints of a miscarriage.

'Bloomsbury often missed the point,' wrote the ballet historian Richard Buckle,[53] and never more so than in Lydia's case. The evidence of their eyes should have shown Bloomsbury that she brought Keynes not only domestic happiness, but elements of lightness and laughter that he missed in his cerebral existence. She called him 'Lank' and thought him beautiful; he called her 'pupsik' and 'darling talky'.

'What are you thinking about?' he once asked her.

'Nothing,' said Lydia.

'I wish I could,' remarked Keynes sadly.[54]

And that was her gift to him. She introduced Keynes to a life out of mind and an art that was pure escapism, appealing to all the physical senses and none of the braincells. 'I . . . fluctuate with my hand on any soft skin that belongs to you,' she cooed, 'when you are not intelectual (*sic*) i.e. in the evening.'[55] He in return gave her adoration if not total fidelity. He continued to lust after young men, groping the lissom Frederick Ashton and a fellow-dancer when they came to dinner in Gordon Square while Lydia was 'twiddling her thumbs inside'.[56] His devotion to her, though, transcended such aberrations. For quarter of a century, the desire to please her and promote her art was uppermost in his mind. From the day they married, Keynes became the driving force behind the advancement of English ballet.

'There will be no more dancing, that is all over now,'[57] Keynes's prim sister told the press on their wedding day, but Lydia was not ready to become a housewife. She danced five roles for Diaghilev that autumn and starred in *Pulcinella*, the new Stravinsky-Massine ballet, the following year. At thirty-five she turned out for Diaghilev before the King of Spain, then in 1929 she danced in an early British sound film, *Dark Red Roses*, with George Balanchine and Anton Dolin. Keynes bought an estate at Tilton, on the edge of the Sussex Downs, where Lydia shocked passing ramblers by sunbathing nude in full view of a public footpath. He longed for her to shine before the whole world and encouraged her to take elocution lessons so that she might recite Shakespeare, opposite Michael Redgrave in a staging of the dramatic ballad, *A Lover's Complaint*. Cressida was to have been her next role but then Diaghilev died, in Venice in August 1929, and the crisis in ballet overrode personal ambitions.

Someone had to fill the vacuum, especially in England where the Russian adventurer had cultivated a taste for dance but erected no framework on which it might grow. A committee was formed by two ballet critics, Arnold Haskell and Philip Richardson (founder of *Dancing Times*), together with the music critic Edwin Evans, the ever-enterprising Ninette de Valois and the hyperactive conductor and composer, Constant Lambert. They called themselves the Camargo Society, after an eighteenth-century Belgian dancer, and put on three or four ballets a year in West End theatres on empty Sunday nights and Monday afternoons. Lydia was co-opted as choreographic adviser and assumed 'real impresarial power'[58] by bringing on board as Treasurer the foremost economic thinker in the western world.

Lydia danced and acted in the opening production, *Beauty, Truth and Rarity*, to her husband's delight, although her quirky Shakespeare and Milton recitations drew mixed reviews. She went on to dance William Walton's *Façade* opposite Frederick Ashton – whom she advised to hang up his pumps and become a choreographer – and in Lambert's colourful *Rio Grande*, 'divinely',[59] as Queen of the Whores. 'On all occasions Lydia Keynes was our most outspoken member,' wrote de Valois,[60] whose arch-rival, Marie Rambert, was in the process of founding a Ballet Club at the tiny Mercury Theatre in Ladbroke Grove with the help of her playwright husband, Ashley Dukes, and a who's-who subscriber list topped with serene impartiality by Keynes and Lopokova, Lady Diana Cooper and the sculptor Jacob Epstein. Rambert, known as 'Mim', was a polyglot Polish-Jewish teacher of poor technical skills but possessing an uncanny eye for talent. She spotted and nurtured the gifts of Frederick Ashton and Agnes de Mille, to the envy of de Valois who shamelessly lured Rambert's stars to the Camargo and Vic-Wells. There were, sensed the visiting balletmaster Lincoln Kirstein, 'many factions at odds here',[61] with Keynes and Lydia ranged with de Valois against Rambert, and sometimes vice-versa. Alicia Markova and Anton (Pat) Dolin broke away to form a company of their own.

There was no shortage of ideas or opportunities. Everyone had the feeling they were inventing an English art that might, in time, challenge the half-exiled Russian ballet for world supremacy. All they lacked was money, and Keynes took care of that. He took a begging-bowl to his friend, Samuel Courtauld, and dipped from time to time into his own pocket. He was, said de Valois, 'quite masterly and, when necessary, equally ruthless'.[62] In 1935 Keynes booked two Camargo performances at the Royal Opera House for delegates of an international economic conference, Markova starring in *Swan Lake* and Lydia in *Coppélia*. 'A large sum of money was raised and the Camargo Society closed down after its five years of work – with all its debts fully discharged,'[63] reported de Valois. The Society had served its purpose, sounding the dawn chorus of English ballet and furnishing it with precious experience and repertoire. Two beacons for the future were Ashton's arrival as an exotic choreographer in Lambert's *Rio Grande*; and *Job* with music by the premier English composer, Vaughan Williams, choreographed by de Valois and conducted by Lambert, with Dolin as Satan and a synopsis by Keynes's surgeon brother, Geoffrey.

With the Camargo's liquidation and Lydia in her forties, Keynes cast around for another frame in which to exhibit his trophy-wife. In Cambridge, where he had restored the King's College finances, there was a plot of land left over from a student hostel he had built. The town had ten cinemas and no theatre. Keynes proposed to redress the omission by erecting an Arts Theatre, largely at his own expense, on the vacant plot. He involved himself in the tiniest detail, inspecting everything from pageboys' uniforms to the dressing-room floors. The house opened on 3 February 1936, a day before the *General Theory* was published, with a gala performance by the Vic-Wells Ballet, followed in the third week by Lydia playing Nora in Ibsen's *A Doll's House* and Hilda in *The Master Builder* – to the wry approval of Virginia Woolf ('Lydia very good') and the acute embarrassment of the philosopher Isaiah Berlin, who earned 'a rather severe look'[64] from Keynes.

Lydia made further appearances in Cambridge and London in Molière's *The Misanthrope*, and her farewell in *On the Frontier*, by W. H. Auden and Christopher Isherwood. There was nothing more Keynes could do for her, nor was he any longer in a position to promote her cause as vigorously as before. In May 1937 he collapsed with a severe cardiac infarction. Consultants failed for a whole month to detect a swarming colony of mouth bacteria that were eroding his heart valves and closing up arteries. The infection, exacerbated by heavy smoking, condemned Keynes to a life of invalidity. Lydia nursed him like a hawk, rushing in to press ice-packs to his chest in the middle of lunch and driving away visitors who were likely to tire him. Keynes submitted happily to a kind of second childhood. At fifty-four, he did not need to work again. His investments were worth £506,450 – around sixteen million pounds in modern values – and his *magnum opus* was endorsed by all political parties. Yet, feebly as his heart beat, Keynes's brain was busier than ever.

When war was declared in 1939, Keynes convened in Gordon

Square a group of veterans of the First World War administration who 'denounced the Chamberlain government's lack of coherent policy, criticized the dispersal of Whitehall departments to the provinces and devised alternative strategies for prosecution of the war.'[65] No sooner did Churchill become Prime Minister than he hauled the 'old warhorses' back to the corridors of power. Keynes, having written a pamphlet on *How to Pay for the War*, was given exactly the same job as before – the external financing of the war. He was made officially an Adviser to the Chancellor of the Exchequer, but his brief ranged over any issues he cared to address, from Indian sterling balances to domestic coal supply. He was he liked to say, 'just Keynes', a man anyone could turn to with their problems. He became a Director of the Bank of England, a Trustee of the National Gallery and ultimately the man in charge of the nation's arts. When the United States entered the war, he emerged as Britain's chief negotiator of credits and co-operation, spending extended periods in Washington and at the Bretton Woods conference designing the post-war world. Lydia accompanied him everywhere, lightening his load with kisses and chatter and seldom straying from his sight. Amid the pressures of saving his country from ruin and foreign domination, Keynes reserved a corner of his mind for erecting an eternal edifice to his Lydia and her art.

As chairman of CEMA, Keynes did not disguise what Mary Glasgow tactfully described as his 'strong predilection in favour of the ballet'.[66] Under prim Tom Jones, CEMA had not funded opera and ballet; if the moneyed classes wanted such extravagances, they could find the resources to pay for them. Under the theatre-owning Keynes, the climate changed. First Keynes brought the Vic-Wells under CEMA's umbrella and sent the Ballet Rambert off on regional tours. Then he moved heaven and earth to repatriate the war-stranded dancers of Kurt Jooss from South America and release their master from internment as an enemy alien. Amid tense negotiations at Bretton Woods, he slipped a note to the Soviet delegation asking them to send the Bolshoi and Kirov Ballets for a London season, a request he then got the Foreign Secretary, Anthony Eden, to repeat in Moscow. In New York, Keynes went to the Metropolitan Opera and met, through Lydia, a clutch of Diaghilev survivors who urged him to assert in England the primacy of ballet over opera. He did not, in truth, need much persuasion. Backstage at the Met he renewed contact with Sir Thomas Beecham, who was conducting operas on two rehearsals, divorcing his first wife and staying half a step ahead of his creditors, slipping out through kitchens and back doors to avoid process servers. Beecham reminded Keynes of the arrogant supremacy that musicians arrogated to their art above all others. In the theatre, Keynes was, according to his CEMA drama officer, 'never more than an amateur, with all the tendency of the amateur to dogmatize, much to the irritation of the professional.'[67] In ballet, however, he was, in Ninette de Valois' words, 'a dedicated follower . . . an awesome chairman, a man of sudden dramatic decision, yet possessed of an unblushingly warm heart.'[68]

In the mental compartment reserved for his passion, Keynes had cause for concern that the huge strides made by English ballet in the previous decade were about to be lost in the privations of war. When the theatres shut down, Markova, Dolin and the choreographer Antony Tudor took up offers in America and de Valois was distracted by domesticity. Her husband, a country doctor, was short-handed in his practice. 'Ninette – *wonderful* Ninette – said that a woman's place is in the home and she went away and disappeared,' sniped the sharp-tongued Ashton.[69] Having regrouped the Vic-Wells under his own leadership, Ashton was unwillingly conscripted into the Royal Air Force. With most of its male dancers in uniform, English ballet now fell under the charismatic spell of Robert Helpmann, a witty and outrageous Australian with talents as a Shakespearean actor and a propensity for importuning attractive young men: not, perhaps, the ideal builder of a national art. Even with 'Madam' back from her surgery, the future of English ballet was parlous during the War and Keynes seldom allowed it to slip from his mind.

Opera, all the while, was making a nuisance of itself through the auspices of a National Council of Music, formed by the Glyndebourne owner, John Christie. In six halcyon summers of fading peace, Christie had set new benchmarks for operatic production in England through the rigour of three Hitler refugees: director Carl Ebert, conductor Fritz Busch and administrator Rudolf Bing. Having shut his festival for the duration and dispatched his wife and children to safety in America, the bluff, eccentric Christie had little better to do with his time than bombard the authorities with ideas for a post-war musical utopia. 'I want to crystallize the National Conscience by giving it a constitution and a home (Glyndebourne),' he wrote to the Minister for Aircraft Production, Stafford Cripps, having been brushed off by other politicians. 'The Slums and Poverty of the past would not have been tolerated if the National Conscience had been made aware of these problems,' he ranted. 'We want a better World and we offer service.'[70] Cripps, a future Labour Chancellor, said he was 'extremely interested' and advised Christie to discuss his ideas with Keynes, which was the last thing either man wanted.

Keynes had loathed Christie ever since they were boys at Eton, 'an ancient, implacable hatred'.[71] As near-neighbours in Sussex they avoided each other's eye on the platform of Lewes station and 'pointedly entered different compartments'[72] on the London train. Keynes occupied a realm of ideas and ballet, Christie a vista of farmland and opera. The supreme provider for arts made short shrift of the landowner's submissions. Through the gruesome medium of CEMA's music officer, Steuart Wilson, an English tenor who had once sung for Christie but was not considered good enough to be cast in Ebert's productions, Keynes flatly refused the Glyndebourne Festival access to public subsidy – a fiat that has been upheld by Arts Councils ever since. Personal animus motivated this decision, but with Keynes the personal was indistinguishable from the public: *l'état c'est moi*. He was, come what may, never going to allow the alien and self-interested opera world to leapfrog over his beloved ballet just as the grail of a permanent home came within his grasp.

It is not entirely clear from a wealth of self-congratulatory documentation who first cottoned on to the possibility that Covent Garden might become a state-funded public opera and ballet theatre. Kenneth Clark, who deputized as CEMA chairman in Keynes's absences, claimed credit for this and most other CEMA successes. Keynes seems to have been slightly slow off the mark, pardonably enough given his murderous workload. Once apprised of the opportunity, however, he seized it with terrier-like tenacity and restless ambition. 'The climax of his work for the future came with the opening of the Royal Opera House, Covent Garden,' summarized Mary Glasgow. 'It was a kind of symbol of what he stood for, and an earnest of what he hoped would be realized.'[73]

The Royal Opera House, owned by a property company, had been leased as a *Palais de Danse* to Mecca Cafés in December 1939 for a period of five years, with an option for renewal that Mecca, for its part, was keen to secure. The chairman of Covent Garden Properties

Ltd, Philip Hill, was caught in two minds. To a landlord, Mecca were reliable and responsible tenants who paid a commercial rent. Hill, however, was a sentimental opera lover who had sat on Beecham's opera board in the 1930s and longed to see the house restored to its traditional function. He confided his dilemma to Harold Holt, Beecham's concert agent, who was unable to help but directed him to Leslie Boosey and Ralph Hawkes who ran a music publishing company.

Boosey & Hawkes had urgent need for an opera house. During the war they had come into possession of a clutch of enemy properties and copyrights, including the complete operas of Richard Strauss. On a second front, they had acquired the Paris-exiled Belayev Editions and were negotiating for Serge Koussevitsky's Editions Russes de Musique, commandeering the major copyrights of Russian opera from Mussorgsky's *Boris Godunov* (in Rimsky-Korsakov's orchestration) through to Prokofiev's *Love for Three Oranges* and Stravinsky's *Oedipus Rex*. All they needed was a stage on which to perform them.

Boosey & Hawkes had, in the phrase of the times, 'had a good war'. Aside from publishing music, they had an instrument-making factory at Edgware, on the north-western edge of London, which had been converted for the duration to the exigent manufacture of armaments. Making guns was much better business than making music, and the partners were faced at the end of the war with an unseemly level of profits. Leslie Boosey, it is related, said to Ralph Hawkes: 'some of this money belongs to the nation – we must put it towards the public good.'[74] When Hill came by with the Covent Garden lease in April 1944, they bought it without much thought for cost or practicalities. Their simon-pure intent was 'to secure for Covent Garden an independent position as an international opera house with sufficient funds at its disposal ... giving London throughout the year the best in English opera and ballet, together with the best from all over the world.'

Mecca were outraged at the loss of a nice little dance-hall. On reading Boosey's statement, the directors rushed to law, arguing that the publishers, having no experience as opera and ballet producers, had obtained the lease under false pretences and were liable for Mecca's losses. Boosey and Hawkes went rushing to CEMA, where Kenneth Clark received them with open arms and offered to take over the house. 'I immediately wired to Maynard Keynes at his

arboreal conference and received his enthusiastic assent,' Clark
wrote. 'I then referred the project to the Treasury. I told them frankly
that I had no idea what it would cost, but that state operas on the
continent were known to be very expensive. My enthusiasm must
have melted their hearts, and they agreed.'[75] Thus, on a whim and a
prayer, did Covent Garden become a state concern.

Clark's motives were not entirely impersonal. Immensely rich and
barely forty, he had decided to leave the National Gallery and was
casting around for a bigger role, perhaps as successor to Keynes in
one of his many public capacities. He had put Keynes on the board
of his Gallery, and expected reciprocity. Mad keen on opera and
ballet, Clark coveted the running of Covent Garden for himself – but
Keynes's desire was stronger.

Although absent in the United States between June and August
1944, and again between September and December, Keynes decided
to chair the Covent Garden Committee himself. He brought on
board his friend Samuel Courtauld and his CEMA official Steuart
Wilson, as well as Clark, Boosey and Hawkes. For musical know-
how he recruited the Cambridge scholar Edward J. Dent, who also
advised Sadler's Wells; the dull Royal Academy principal Sir
Stanley Marchant; and the composer William Walton who was
having an affair with Clark's wife, Jane, with the full consent and
encouragement of the National Gallery director who was himself
philandering with, among others, Frederick Ashton's newly-wed
sister, Edith. A cosier set-up for running a public company could
scarcely be envisaged: yet there was nothing furtive or corrupt about
these arrangements. They merely reflected the English way of
making things work, through committees of the great, the good, the
rich and the sycophantically well-connected, looped around old-tie
networks of public school, Pall Mall clubs and private sports and
pastimes.

Objections to the scheme came not from public watchdogs but
from two losers who had been pointedly excluded. Christie attacked
the Covent Garden Committee in letters to the press, the Chancellor,
and anyone who would give him the time of day. 'Keynes refuses to
see me,' he wailed.[76] He applied to buy the building from Hill and
caused enough trouble for Hawkes to urge Keynes to co-opt Christie
on to their committee, if only to shut him up. Keynes, however, was
in no mood for conciliation and allowed his lackey Wilson to goad
the wounded Christie. Beecham, meanwhile, waited in America for

a call from Covent Garden – if not to run the house he knew so well then at least to be chief conductor. He waited in vain. 'They never came near me,' he told his biographers, uncomprehending and bleeding from the worst blow ever inflicted to his splendid pride.[79]

Cast out from Covent Garden, Christie and Beecham formed an anti-Keynes alliance, but soon fell out. Beecham huffed off to form yet another London orchestra, the Royal Philharmonic, and Christie reopened Glyndebourne without him. Neither gave up their smouldering claim to Covent Garden, but both recognized that the battle had been lost. 'Today,' intoned Beecham in September 1946, 'after seven years of operatic deprivation, we are in a pitiable plight. The newer public in this country, mysteriously and miraculously expanded to unprecedented dimensions, has little knowledge of the works of the great Masters, and none at all of a high standard or even correct method of performance. We have touched rock bottom.'[77]

Keynes had got his way again. Before leaving for America to shape the world's financial future, he took steps to secure the operating mechanism of the Royal Opera House. A general administrator was sought by traditional who-do-we-know? methods. David Webster was a Liverpool department-store manager who had kept the local orchestra alive through the war. Clark spotted him first and Holt vouched for his ability, but it was Hawkes who approached Webster, on the recommendation of his man-about-town cousin, Anthony Gishford. Publisher and shop-manager saw eye to eye over lunch at the Ritz Grill and Keynes warmed quickly to the practical, unflustered Webster, endorsing his appointment in July 1944. Gishford, by way of reciprocity, was appointed Public Relations Officer to the Royal Opera House.

All that remained was to organize a season. The Allies had landed in France, the war could end at any moment and it was imperative that Covent Garden should open before the Treasury relented. An opera and ballet company had to be built, borrowed or stolen. Acting under time pressure, Keynes took the felonious option. With Lydia at his side, he urged Ninette de Valois to transfer her troupe lock, stock and tutus, from Sadler's Wells to the Royal Opera House. 'I should expect that Ninette would like to come to Covent Garden,' he told Webster,[79] but de Valois was unwilling to risk fifteen years' effort and a loyal audience in a rash move to an unconstituted new venue. Although tempted by the glamour and centrality of the Royal Opera House, she feared its vast, unmapped emptiness. It was, she said, like being 'given Buckingham Palace, a few dusters and told to get on with the cleaning'.[80]

While de Valois dithered, Hawkes sounded out her choreographer, Frederick Ashton. 'If you won't,' Ashton told de Valois, 'I will.'[81] When Madam finally assented, the Sadler's Wells Governors screamed blue murder. Tyrone Guthrie, the company administrator, threatened to book the Drury Lane Theatre and perform in competition on the ROH doorstep. Guthrie preyed on Madam's well-founded fears, telling her that Covent Garden was 'an artistic graveyard' with a knack of 'swallowing up all but the most powerful and penetrating performers and performances'.[82] Dent, sitting on both boards, plotted merrily with and against Guthrie for maximum personal advantage.

It required a Keynsian device to settle the matter. Hanging around with fellow-peers in the House of Lords lobby while waiting for the King to open Parliament, he sidled up to the half-deaf Sadler's Wells chairman, Lord Lytton, and made him a whispered offer which he followed up with 'a brilliant memorandum'.[83] Lytton, a man of his word who was embarrassed to be thought hard of hearing, stood by whatever Keynes said they had agreed. In November 1945, *The Times* announced the transfer of the Sadler's Wells Ballet to Covent Garden under the headline, 'A Marriage Has Been Arranged'.

The deal that Keynes struck made creative use of his unchecked powers as chairman of both CEMA and the ROH. In exchange for sending its ballet company to Covent Garden, CEMA would pay Sadler's Wells a transfer fee of £15,000, plus a £5,000 top-up to de Valois' ballet school – a bribe by any other name.

On 20 February 1946, the Royal Opera House reopened in the presence of the King and Queen and an audience, 'most of whom were of Keynes' own choice',[84] in a programme that the chairman had picked on personal, sentimental grounds. '*The Sleeping Princess* should make an excellent start,'[85] Keynes instructed Webster. And so it did, with choreography by Ashton, splendiferous sets by the fashionable Oliver Messel and the effulgent Margot Fonteyn in the stellar role. Queen Elizabeth complained that there was nothing to eat in the Royal Box. 'Rationing, your Majesty,' they apologized.

'In my grandmother's Edwardian days,' noted Randolph Churchill, Winston's son, 'the Opera House admittedly presented as brilliant a spectacle as could be found in Europe – two tiers of boxes running all round it, replete with beauty and fashion. The women wore tiaras; the men kid gloves . . . Now the new management has restored the beautiful auditorium almost to its old splendour – not quite, for though the gold and crimson may have returned, the boxes have shrunk to a mere dozen or so on one tier only; and though the audience, headed by the King and Queen and the Prime Minister, contained figures of every known form of distinction, they were not on the whole much to look at; for nowadays nobody has any clothes worthy of the name. It was an "austerity" opening.'[86]

Keynes, while waiting to greet the Royals, suffered a mild heart attack and was hustled away to his box, leaving Lydia and Webster to do the bowing and scraping. 'He soon recovered and was able to watch the ballet,' recalled Ashton, 'while Lydia and I smoked cigarettes on the floor of the box undisturbed, until the house fireman arrived and told us to stop.'[87]

'He heard Tchaikovsky's splendid trumpets which he knew so well, and the march proceeded. He was still feeling tired, and he closed his eyes,' noted Keynes's economist friend, Roy Harrod. 'He thought of Diaghilev's production. There had been a princess, so light and quick, so charming and piquant, so gay and unexpected. His whole being had been filled with joy and exhilaration . . . That other performance had cast its spell upon him and determined his future course of action. It was a pleasant thing to be able to look back on one's life and find in it symmetry and purpose fulfilled.'[88]

Kenneth Clark, who shared his box some nights later, saw Keynes jump when a man in a black cloak passed through the door with a finger to his lips.

'Who is that?' demanded Keynes anxiously.

'That was Death,' said Clark.

Weeks later (and not the next day, as Clark fancified), Keynes was dead. He had just got back from America for the sixth time in as many years, having agreed a ruinous deal for the repayment of Britain's war debts, when the fatal heart attack struck as he rested at Tilton on Easter Sunday. Keynes was six weeks short of his sixty-third birthday; both of his parents attended the funeral.

Foreshortened as it was and widely mourned, few modern English lives have been more richly fulfilled in love, wealth and lasting achievement. No economist ever achieved such mesmeric influence over politics, art and society. Few scholars became so rich. And rare is the public figure in any sphere who enjoys a love as profound as the marriage between Maynard and Lydia Keynes. After his death,

Lydia wore his pyjamas for years – then threw them away. 'When Maynard died I thought I could never live without him, and I suffered a lot,' she said in 1951. 'But now I never think of him.'[89] She did not read his books and after his death seldom attended Covent Garden. Yet it was in tribute to her, above all other motivations, that he had restored the Royal Opera House as a centre of classical ballet.

Had Keynes cared about opera, he would either have struck a deal with Glyndebourne, or incorporated one of the established opera companies, Carl Rosa and Sadler's Wells. By shunning Christie, being 'rude to Rudi'[90] Bing and banning Beecham, he autocratically excluded every available English source of opera. Christie reopened his festival; Bing founded the Edinburgh Festival before heading off to run the Metropolitan Opera; Beecham immersed himself in orchestral politics; and Covent Garden entered the age of state opera innocent as a choirboy.

'It has never been clear to me,' wrote a future chairman of the Royal Opera House, 'whether the question of the Sadler's Wells Opera Company also being transferred to Covent Garden was raised or, if it was, why it was not pursued . . . Much time could have been saved and many subsequent difficulties avoided.'[91]

Unpublished documents show that the question was raised, in fact, only to be fudged, prevaricated and finally quashed. Guthrie, as late as February 1945, was expecting Covent Garden to take both ballet and opera companies from Sadler's Wells.[92] Discussions along those lines continued for several weeks more, but it appears that Keynes was merely stringing Sadler's Wells Opera along as a cover for his main agenda: to open Covent Garden with ballet on top. 'So far as opera is concerned,' he had told Webster four months earlier, 'I expect it is wise to keep Sadler's Wells away from Covent Garden until they are much stronger . . . About the ballet, on the other hand, I feel differently.'[93] His pro-ballet prejudice was no secret at Covent Garden. In a solemn eulogy to Keynes, his co-directors referred to it with a hint of irony as 'the art he loved *perhaps* beyond others'.[94]

As for opera, that was a necessary adjunct that could wait its turn and trust to fate. 'I think it was a mistake,' reflected Guthrie, 'that public money was used to found at Covent Garden another opera company, thus dividing in two the available funds, talent and support, which were barely sufficient for one. I do not know who was responsible. Neither I nor Miss Cross were consulted; we were presented with a quietly accomplished fact. At the time I was too much exhausted either to object or to grasp its implications for the future of opera in Britain.'[95]

Arrogant, intolerant and remorselessly self-serving behind a façade of charm and wit, Keynes founded the Royal Opera House with utter disdain for cultural and constitutional proprieties. By reversing the subordinate relation of ballet to opera, he implanted eternal enmity between the two arts, uglier than in any other opera house. By appointing a committee of cronies, he exposed Covent Garden to accusations of élitism. And by acting as chairman of both CEMA and the ROH, giver and receiver, he locked Government and Covent Garden into an oppressive intimacy that verged on perpetual corruption.

Keynes was the only man in England who could have created an opera house in the tense hiatus between two wars, hot and cold, conventional and nuclear. His monument endures, but the victory he claimed for his beloved ballet was pyrrhic. In the roars of first-night applause the recipe for lasting conflict was writ large.

CHAPTER 3

Enter the Leader
(1946-47)

AMONG PHYSICAL MEMORIES, the one that lingers is the smell. Not the sight of the ravaged city, nor the sound of its damaged engines, nor the touch of rough textures, nor the taste of food processed and spammified almost beyond salivation. It is the smell that most survivors recall – of bodies and clothes unwashed or rinsed in foamless soap; of decomposing foodstuffs sold as fresh; of fetid air, fed by the foul breath of poor diets and damaged digestions. Far from the heavenly dawn depicted by Labour nostalgists, London stank and festered in the birthpang years of the welfare state.

Few districts reeked higher than Covent Garden, where the capital's fruit and vegetable market thundered around the clock and there was neither the available manpower nor the municipal will to clean up and hose down. The market was a world unto itself, a square half-mile where whole harvests were sold on a handshake and stalls passed from father to son for five generations. Under the eye of Bow Street police station and magistrates court, where the most notorious villains were brought for arraignment, the market laid down its own laws and set the tone for the district, its porters and costermongers whistling lascivious comments at petite sopranos and ballerinas scuttling along to rehearsal. To have instituted amid such noxious, leering mayhem a royal opera house, replete with powdered flunkeys and velvet seats, was an act of dottiness or negligence that only the English could have committed in the grave extremity of their post-war circumstances.

In June 1946, rationing was extended for the first time to bread, at nine ounces a week for adults. The country embraced ever deeper privations, as the bill for Keynes's final American deal fell due. 'Our present needs are the direst consequences of the fact that we fought earliest, that we fought longest and that we fought hardest' commented the *Economist*. 'In moral terms we are creditors; and for that we shall pay $140 million a year for the rest of the twentieth century. It may be unavoidable; but it is not right.'[1]

The national mood was turning grumpy, yet there was no objection to the expensive reopening of the Royal Opera House – an acquiescence that can be largely attributed, in part, to a compensatory sense of moral superiority that swept the country. England might have lost its wealth and might, but it could still put on a show for all the world to envy. When, with personal taxes at record heights, the Government authorized local councils to raise sixpence on the rates for arts subsidy, there was again hardly a murmur of demurral.

On 29 September 1946, the BBC inaugurated its high-brow Third Programme with a concert of all-English music, the oldest by Purcell, the newest a world première from Benjamin Britten. Ruined as it was, the country fell back on culture for comfort and joy. Novels sold out within hours of publication. Galleries were packed. Public performance flourished in every form. To meet surgent demand, new orchestras – the Philharmonia and Royal Philharmonic – and a welter of private opera and ballet troupes were formed to augment and challenge state-supported ensembles. Jay Pomeroy, a Russian-born Jewish entrepreneur with a soprano mistress, put on 607 nights of Italian opera at the Cambridge Theatre and made no secret of his aim to take over Covent Garden, going so far as to usurp its aims of building 'a permanent Opera Centre' and training British artists to international standard. The one commodity in London that was not rationed was music, and for many Londoners it was the one relief that kept them going. 'You could always get in, even on first nights,' recalled an avid night-outer. 'It was never hard to get tickets, there was so much going on.'[2] Half-a-crown bought a place in the Covent Garden gallery, 13/6d a seat in the front stalls. Escape from the stench of reality was cheap and easy.

Those with connections scorned the transcendence of art and sought more privileged sanctuaries. Cecil Beaton, the society photographer and designer, talked his way into houses where they drank pre-war Château Yquem and served *marrons glacés* with fresh pineapple. Cyril Connolly, the *bon-vivant* literary editor, spent his summer in France, sponging off the Rothschilds and Lady Diana Cooper, wife of the British ambassador. Arthur Koestler, polemical journalist, lunched in Paris with Albert Camus and André Malraux. George Orwell, England's literary conscience, betook himself to the windswept Isle of Jura, where he composed *1984*.

But for homecoming heroes, escape began with a night at the theatre. Swapping rumpled uniforms for a three-piece demob suit and porkpie hat, they rushed to the box-office and remembered the rewards for the rest of their lives. Denis Healey, a future Cabinet minister, took his fiancée, Edna, to see Laurence Olivier in 'a stupendous double bill'[3] at the Old Vic, followed by a Myra Hess Beethoven recital in the National Gallery. Denis Forman, future head of Granada Television, sneaked into trade previews of every new film. Alan Jefferson, a future opera critic back from peace-keeping duties in Palestine, went straight to Covent Garden to see *Sleeping Beauty*. He went three times more to catch every change of cast but one – Fonteyn, Pamela May, Moira Shearer and Violetta Elvin, then known as Prokhorova; Beryl Grey he found unappealing and gave her a miss. The cost of Oliver Messel's £12,814 production – more than quarter of a million pounds in millennial values – was fully justified by economic utility. The sets were seen in 222 performances over six seasons, leaving an indelible imprint on the minds of a newly-civilianized conscript generation. *Beauty* defined the rebirth of British ballet, a benchmark for future attainments.

A chance to compare it with the world's best soon arrived when Covent Garden invited the Ballet Theater of New York to fill out the last two months of its inaugural season. The Americans danced *Les Sylphides*, followed by Jerome Robbins' choreography of *Fancy Free*, at which the Fourth of July gala première was conducted – at the insistence of his publisher, Ralph Hawkes – by the young composer in person. Leonard Bernstein never raised a baton again at Covent Garden as long as he lived. He came to hate London that cold, wet July of 1946. Foreigners were unable to obtain clothes coupons and he could neither buy himself a sweater nor warm himself on manly flesh picked up off the meat-rack around the emblematic statue of Eros. 'I've worn out Piccadilly in invitation and rejection,' Bernstein told Aaron Copland,[4] flying home the morning after his sole appearance.

Four of the American ballets were choreographed by Antony Tudor, who returned to something less than a hero's welcome. Snubbed in the Crush Bar as a war escapee, he was cold-shouldered by de Valois and Ashton who feared the depth of his intellect.

'Neither Fred nor Ninette spoke to (him),' said one witness.

One night in the crush bar Alan Jefferson, who went to see just about everything at Covent Garden that year, was approached by a portly man of obvious authority. 'I have seen you here before,' said David Webster. 'Will you also go to the opera?'

'Not if it's sung in English,' replied the young buff. 'I can't bear all those syllables left hanging over the end of lines.'

Webster turned on his heel and walked away. He was irked by the comment not because it was unfair but because it touched upon his own crisis of conscience. He had accepted a mission from Keynes to assemble an opera company from native resources, singing in the vernacular. But Webster was a nightingale fancier, smitten by superb voices. Among the greatest nights of his life he numbered a Covent Garden *Otello* on 6 June 1937 when the inimitable Giovanni Martinelli, months short of his sixtieth birthday, sang the title role opposite the Norwegian soprano Eidé Norena and the American baritone Lawrence Tibbett. How could he find or raise such voices in these sceptred isles? More agonizing still, he knew that the new crop of singers in Italy, Germany and Austria were available for little more than the price of a pack of cigarettes, while he was con-scripting inferior English singers to chew a clumsy text. Webster had entered into a Faustian pact. In order to fulfil his dream of managing an opera house, he had mortgaged his soul to the cause of English singing. How to pay lip-service to mediocrity while aiming for excellence would take all of his ingenuity and the rest of his life.

He faced an immediate challenge from the Cambridge Theatre, where the piratical Pomeroy was presenting Mariano Stabile, Giuseppe Taddei and his own mistress Daria Bayan, affectionately known as 'Dascha'. Never one to miss a trick, Pomeroy employed Diaghilev's designer, Natalia Goncharova. For 1946, this was a starry line-up and one that threatened to out-sing the Royal Opera House on its very doorstep.

As a makeshift counterweight, Webster imported the San Carlo company from Naples to give the first post-war operas at Covent Garden. The San Carlo had been popular with British forces who overran the port-city in September 1943 and contained two stunning young tenors in Mario del Monaco and Luigi Infantino. Alone, they were not enough to outgun Stabile and Taddei, but Webster played his trump with a sensational late announcement that the immortal Beniamino Gigli would join the company for four performances –

two *Bohème*s and two double-bills of *Cavalleria rusticana* and *I Pagliacci*. Gigli had been a huge star in England before the war. Hurriedly cleared of fascist collaboration, he came to introduce his lovely daughter, Rina, to his loyal London public. All-night queues formed on Floral Street and there were scuffles for the last tickets. Few in the audience seemed to mind that the performances were barely rehearsed and feebly conducted, or that Rina Gigli was never going to make the big time, except in her father's fond imagination. Gigli was back, and that was all that mattered to long-deprived English opera buffs. His recruitment was a master-stroke by David Webster, the first sign that this roly-poly northern shopkeeper had the makings of a world-class impresario.

Approaching strange men in public places was something David Lumsden Webster did every day of his professional life. As manager of the Bon Marché department store in Liverpool, he was regularly to be found patrolling the main floor, eyeing up customers and chatting them up, eager to anticipate the public's tastes and fancies. As he walked through the store, adjusting display units and praising his staff, his hand would snake out as he passed the confectionery counter and pop a pair of chocolates into his mouth. Webster was not a man to deny himself instant oral gratification.

The love of good things told quickly on his physique. Webster was plump, jowly and bald, with a spatter of dandruff on his shoulder; he was lucky not to live in an age when appearance counted above achievement. Nor did he attempt much by way of diet or sartorial camouflage. David Webster won the confidence of the middle-aged Masons and Rotarians who rule life in provincial cities by looking exactly like one of them, down to the last rumple. His store, on the other hand, was the last word in elegance, much smarter than the neighbouring branch of the John Lewis chain into which it was ultimately amalgamated. Bon Marché, recalled a young shopper, 'was the local fashion house; Lewis's was cheapjack by comparison.'[5] Webster, who rose to General Manager at the age of twenty-eight on a splendid salary of £7,000 a year, had created the most exciting emporium in the English northwest. He was a brilliant organizer with a ruthless streak. 'It's all right to stamp on other people,' he once said, 'til you get to the top. Then you can stop.'[6]

Running a provincial store was never going to satisfy so agile an operator or slake so hungry an ambition, but the opportunity he craved was slow to arrive. A commercial traveller's son, born in Dundee in July 1903, David Webster was raised in a Presbyterian tradition that left him thirsting for glamour and a sniff of grave sin. As a boy, he saw Pavlova dance. As a youth, he hung around stage doors for a glimpse of the great. He read economics as a scholarship boy at Liverpool University and joined an amateur dramatics society before forming his own. He was a decent actor and a dull director who derived most fun from giggling away over 'naughty' revues that he wrote with a friend in his lunch break. Getting to meet John Gielgud and Frederick Ashton were the triumphs of his young manhood; some said he was never really young.[7]

As general manager of Bon Marché, and later of the more important Lewis's, Webster was a figure of local substance. He was elected treasurer of the chamber music guild and on to the board of the Liverpool Philharmonic Society. In committee, he was industrious, quick-witted and hyper-sensitive. A request from the chairman to see his audited accounts was all it took for Webster to threaten resignation. People walked around him on egg-shells; he was too useful to lose.

In June 1939 the Philharmonic Society reopened its concert hall, which had been destroyed by fire, with a gala concert conducted by Sir Thomas Beecham. The hall was an art deco marvel, a shining white landmark in a begrimed port city. It was cleverly designed to accommodate concerts and cinema shows, something for highbrows and low. Three months after the hall opened, war was declared and the Society voted to disband the orchestra and shut the hall. Webster demurred, arguing that music and movies would be needed more than ever in times of stress. Elected chairman, he put the orchestra on a formal contract and reinforced it with London players, among them Anthony Pini as principal cello, Reginald Kell on first clarinet, the oboist Leon Goossens and most of the BBC's evacuated Salon Orchestra. Henry Holst, once Wilhelm Furtwängler's concertmaster in Berlin, became leader. 'Before Webster,' said a freelance musician, 'the Liverpool orchestra was a fiction – they were just boys bussed in from Manchester for the night.'[8] Webster put on thirty-two concerts in the first wartime season. He declared evening dress non-compulsory and threw open the doors to factory workers and servicemen, leading a minor revolution in English social mores.

At the front line of the economic war, its docks pulverized by air raids and its shipping decimated by submarines, Liverpool cried out for musical consolation. Webster, resisting easy populism, insisted on challenging audiences with works that pointed ahead to post-war renewal. Béla Bartók's Concerto for Orchestra received its first UK performance in Liverpool and Michael Tippett's first symphony its world première. The Liverpool orchestra, historically overshadowed by Manchester's Hallé, began to attract national attention. It made records for EMI, including Benjamin Britten's *Young Person's Guide to the Orchestra*, and made its début in London at the BBC Proms. Webster, in musical circles, was regarded as a rising force.

When his store was bombed, he did not have to look far for gainful employment or suffer, like Ashton, the dread hand of the draft board. Requisitioned by a friend in the Ministry of Supply, he was sent around the country to report on production targets. He began meeting serious businessmen, one of whom, Sir Robert Barlow of the Metal Box company, nominated Webster as his successor. He had just signed a contract with Metal Box at £10,000 a year, when Ralph Hawkes took him to the Ritz and hooked him on the Covent Garden line. Webster hesitated, tempted by the glamour but worried about the salary drop. The more he fretted, the more Hawkes pressed. Webster was perfect for the position: a successful executive with a passion for music and a knowledge of stagecraft who had cleverly rescued an important musical organization. That he had no direct experience of opera and ballet was immaterial, even a positive advantage.

For David Webster possessed a superior quality in the eyes of Hawkes and his colleagues. He was, in the most English sense of the word, an *amateur* – an attribute that could qualify him to captain the national cricket team, and hold the highest office in English arts. David Webster had reached the top: he could now stop stamping on people. 'He came to see me just before he took the job,' recalled Delia Barnaby, deputy music critic on the Liverpool *Daily Post*.* 'I said, "Will this mean big cigars?" He said, "might be". He had a nice sense of humour.'

All his adult life, Webster had been drawn to London like a kid to a sweetshop window. Living with his mother in Sunnyside, a blameless middle-class suburb, he hungered for glitter and guilt. Often he would rush from work to catch the 4.10 to London, change

---

* she wrote under the pseudonym of Norman Cameron, because Liverpool in those days did not trust a woman's musical judgement

clothes in the train toilet, arrive in time for curtain-up, dine afterwards at the Café Royal or the Savoy Grill, and ride the overnight sleeper back home, sauntering into the Bon Marché for breakfast. He once made the round trip five nights running to hear Arturo Toscanini conduct the BBC orchestra at Queen's Hall.

Webster's companion on these jaunts was a young man he had met at a Berkeley Square party in 1931 and promptly recruited on to the Bon Marché payroll. James Cleveland Belle became David Webster's lover and lifelong companion. The intrusive severities of an English law which punished homosexual acts with months of imprisonment forced them to dissimulate – a habit so powerful that Jimmy, even in the liberal 1970s, deleted the specifics of their conjugality from the manuscript of Webster's posthumous biography.* In London, and on summer holidays in Salzburg and New York, the two men enjoyed the freedom of anonymity and the thrill of a chance encounter in a public place, for neither held much with sexual fidelity. In Liverpool, however, they felt inhibited and afraid. Webster, a self-made man, had enemies in high places who wanted to bring him down. 'I had a great friend, Dick Bishop, who was prosecuting solicitor for Liverpool Police and was gunning for David Webster, trying to catch him out,' recalled Delia Barnaby. 'One day at lunch Dick said to me: "David Webster is shaking in his shoes in an absolute panic. He thinks we are going to close in on him, and we are."' Although reluctant to leave his mother, Webster knew he had to escape. The options before him were jail, Metal Box or Covent Garden. He chose Covent Garden.

In August 1944, Webster was given a desk and a telephone in Boosey & Hawkes's offices at 295 Upper Regent Street and told to organize a National Home for opera and ballet. Over the next eighteen months he assembled the entire enterprise from scratch. Stagehands, carpenters and wig-makers had to be hunted and hired, an orchestra, soloists and chorus auditioned, a management structure invented and a purpose defined that would unite 500 men and women in a new-born cause. The legal status of the company and its charter had to be formulated, and the views of eight independent-minded directors taken into consideration. Six different trade unions

---

* Montague Haltrecht, the author, was allowed to retain half-a-dozen veiled references to homosexuality. Jimmy, he discovered, was worried what his nephews might think of his past

had to be consulted and appeased over pay and conditions. Workshop and storage buildings had to be inspected and purchased. A financial plan was required. The Arts Council demanded to be kept informed; the BBC needed to be bullied into making a commitment. All of these issues and more were dealt with by Webster shrewdly, calmly and for much of the time single-handedly. His work did not go unnoticed.

The first task of a successful executive is to earn the trust of his board. Webster showered his directors with a disarming mix of magisterial memos and warmly personal notes. Keynes, often cruel to underlings, was impressed by Webster's eye for detail and ear for scandal. Their correspondence, always formal in address – 'Dear Lord Keynes', 'Dear Webster' – grew cheerful and chatty. Under the heading 'Gossip',[9] Webster kept his absent chairman amused with theatrical tittle-tattle. Keynes, in turn, trusted Webster to look after his aged mother on her first visit to the Royal Opera House; when the retired Mayor of Cambridge mislaid her spectacles in the chairman's box, Webster made sure they were found and returned.[10] Despite a twenty-year age difference and unbridgeable barriers of class and brain, the two men found mutual affinities that enabled them to collaborate on level terms. 'Both,' suggests Webster's biographer, Montague Haltrecht, 'were physically unattractive homosexuals. Keynes would have seen in Webster a fellow-sufferer, a man struggling with secrets and disabilities. Webster, for his part, was undaunted by Keynes's fame, knowing that the great man was vulnerable to the same pressures as himself.'[11]

It was on the rock of Keynes's support that Webster established his authority at Covent Garden, a dominance that would hold sway for quarter of a century. The General Administrator held a menial title and a deferential attitude to famous persons, but Webster made sure that no other person held anything resembling executive power in his house. He was the source of all decisions, the address for all complaints. He let it be known among staff that he could be found on a Friday lunchtimes at the bar of a pub some distance away, behind the Piccadilly Theatre, where anyone with a problem could stand him a drink. He instilled a spirit of shared enterprise, *esprit de corps* and paternalist care. The attentive habits of a good shopkeeper never fully quit his soul.

Alert and obsequious, sharp-eyed and convivial, Webster could not escape his original calling. He longed to shine in his own right, to rub shoulders with twinkling stars and, by rubbing, to promote his own worth rather than his merchandise. He loved taking curtain-calls to make 'an important announcement' to beaming audiences. But the only limelight that came his way was the afterglow of great artists and famous men. The more he craved recognition, the more he needed to cultivate his superiors and mimic them, indulging to the full his shop-floor instinct for snobbery. His first home in London was a suite at the Savoy. He went on to rent and then buy, with Jimmy, a flat in stately Weymouth Street, where they gave formal dinners for those he sought to impress, with his celebrity friends John Gielgud and the playwright, Terence Rattigan, in regular attendance. Webster name-dropped furiously to impress his staff.

When he took possession of Covent Garden from its Mecca tenants on 22 October 1945, Webster's first priority was to pick an office. He chose the biggest pair of interconnecting rooms in the building, and planted his desk at the far end of the inner chamber. The outer room was occupied by a horn-rimmed Scottish secretary, Miss Muriel Kerr, who guarded his door with a baleful glare. Stars were ushered in and gushed over, but most mortals who needed David Webster were made to approach him as foreign ambassadors once approached Mussolini, taking a long, lonely walk down an acre of carpet before reaching the great man at his desk. With lowly envoys, Webster would not even look up from his paperwork. 'What is it?' he would snap, leaving the visitor feeling like a gnat on the Duce's epidermis.

Barely had he been appointed than the board began pressing Webster to appoint an artistic director for the unformed opera company. The ballet had a surfeit of artistic directors – de Valois in charge of policy, Ashton of choreography and Lambert of anything to do with music – and the General Administrator was allowed no say in its programming. All de Valois would let him do was co-ordinate dates and accept her *faits accomplis*. Webster was determined that the opera company should stay under his control, reflecting his own ideas and imagination. So he played for time, refusing to let a conductor into the house until he had established a chain of command in the opera company with himself at the helm.

The kind of man he needed was a knowledgeable mechanic who would look after the nuts and bolts of the orchestral engine, a man rendered so insecure by temperament or situation that he would be eternally grateful for the job, and for Webster's protection. Assembling an ensemble from scratch was beyond the capabilities of a shopkeeper who could barely tell a *spinto* from a spinet. But Webster had learned enough in Liverpool to know that if a high-profile maestro was engaged, his own role would be reduced to the shadows and shallows of general administration. What he required was a musical cipher. He would then have to persuade knowledge-able connoisseurs like Keynes, Hawkes and Clark, as well as the expert musicians Walton and Dent, that such a cipher was not only the best option locally available but also in the company's best interests. The appointment of Covent Garden's first Musical Director was a process that reveals Webster at his most machiavellian.

After a delay, during which he scaled down the job title from Artistic Director, Webster in April 1945 produced a brilliant report which combined the appearance of impartial observation with a slash of character assassination to discredit the candidates he deemed undesirable. Headed 'Conductors for Covent Garden', and never previously published, the three-page memo listed eight candidates in capital letters and no particular order of preference, with Webster's personal favourite carefully camouflaged in the middle.

BEECHAM, Webster began, 'is the obvious name that comes first. There is no doubt that he is the greatest conductor we have produced, and the only first-class conductor of Opera. His drawbacks are, first, that he is not content to conduct, he must also produce . . . then he would like to conduct the whole enterprise, and as an administrator he is unsuccessful.'

This was neatly put. Beecham's claims were irrefutable and Keynes's committee were united in wanting to keep him out. Webster gave them grounds for rejection by implying that Beecham, now sixty-six years old, would seize control of the house and ruin it. Webster had talked to Beecham 'and intimated to him that as we are anxious to build up (a public) institution, he might find that limitation dull.' Beecham was 'not being offered very much work in America' and that 'notwithstanding his artistic success' Edward Johnson, the Metropolitan Opera manager, had found him 'unsatisfactory, and it is rumoured that he is not being engaged again'.

This was, at best, half-true. Beecham had a new agent in America and no shortage of concerts. He had fallen out with the Met, which prized singers above conductors, and was hankering to come home. To suggest that he was on the skids, as Webster did, was a malicious falsehood – but it was exactly what Keynes and Co. wanted to hear. 'The greatest conductor we have produced' was, on the basis of Webster's biased assessment, shut out of Covent Garden with a collective sigh of relief and without so much as the courtesy of an interview. This was unwise. A better judge of conductors would have known that Beecham would not lie low or fade away. Within months, he was back in London, forming a new orchestra and making mischief for Covent Garden – a course he pursued with unremitting malice to his last breath, sixteen years hence. Webster had made a mortal enemy, a man with mysterious connections that reached into the heart of the British establishment and up to the very Throne. He might easily have persuaded Beecham to accept an honorary title at the Royal Opera House with an occasional opera to conduct, but Webster did not want the old magician to cross his threshold. By excluding Beecham, he exposed Covent Garden and himself to attacks on their most vulnerable parts.

Webster's second target for demolition was John Barbirolli, back from seven lean years with the New York Philharmonic Orchestra and now revamping the Hallé. BARBIROLLI, Webster noted, 'is liked by musicians and by singers of this country' and 'is probably the best orchestra trainer resident in this country'. His credentials were outstanding. Webster might also have added that Barbirolli was ambitious, energetic, co-operative, good-looking, experienced in opera, untouched by scandal and just forty-five years old. He was a compelling candidate, almost without fault.

So Webster proceeded to disable him in a single, innuendo-laden sentence. Barbirolli, he wrote, 'has an odd flair for personal popularity, which is inclined to have difficult repercussions for the organizations for which he works.' This was meant, and understood, to imply that Barbirolli was an ego-driven narcissist of alien extraction ('flair' being English code for foreign) who would ensure that any credit for restoring Covent Garden would come his way, outshining the committee and General Administrator. He was neither servile nor malleable. 'His taste in interpretation is often doubtful,' added Webster, implying that this avid interpreter of Elgar and Vaughan Williams was a bit too dusky to pass muster at Covent Garden. The smears did their work, for Barbirolli was never offered the job. (Soon after, he turned down six thousand pounds a year to conduct the LSO.)

Malcolm SARGENT was easily dismissed. 'His reputation in London,' noted Webster, 'is perhaps not so high as it was before the war, probably because he conducts mainly in the provinces (Liverpool Philharmonic Orchestra) . . . and has been conducting too much.' This was wickedly disingenuous. It was Webster himself who had engaged and over-worked Sargent in Liverpool, at the cost of his London reputation. He owed the conductor a fair hearing at Covent Garden, but Webster was not a man to remember his debts.

Albert COATES, who had directed pre-war seasons in St Petersburg, Berlin, Vienna and New York was written off by Webster as too old and in 'doubtful' health. Aged sixty-three, Coates migrated soon after to South Africa, where he conducted the Johannesburg Symphony Orchestra for seven formative years.

The next candidate required diplomatic handling. Constant Lambert, music director of Sadler's Wells ballet, was esteemed by Keynes as 'potentially the most brilliant person I have ever met'.[12] De Valois saw him as 'our only hope of an English Diaghilev'[13] and William Walton, a committee member, was one of his oldest friends. The first Englishman to compose symphonic jazz, Lambert was also an influential essayist and wit, author of the much-read *Music Ho!*, successful in almost everything he touched.

At the ballet, he had educated Ashton in music and nurtured Margot Fonteyn, both culturally and as her first lover. As the central figure in a bohemian circle novelized by Anthony Powell in *A Dance to the Music of Time*, Lambert introduced body-conscious ballet folk to a Fitzrovian warren of ideas, where his painter and poet friends were reciprocally drawn into an awareness of dance. An enemy of romanticism and all things German, mildly anti-Semitic and anti-modern, Lambert adored French forms, foods and finesse. Lame from boyhood operations and often in pain, he sought oblivion in the lap of teenage girls and hard liquor. The sculptor Elizabeth Frink once left Lambert slumped senseless across a bar as she went to a concert at which he was supposed to recite Walton's *Façade*. To her amazement, Lambert walked on stage a few minutes late and gave an immaculate performance. His friends viewed his addictions with amusement. Webster, who disliked and distrusted Lambert, could not risk affronting his supporters.

He delivered a verdict that was curt, factual and damningly

neutral. LAMBERT, began Webster, 'is a very considerable musician'. He had, however, conducted very few operas. 'The internal politics of Sadler's Wells,' insinuated Webster, 'resulted in the fact that although they have had no conductor for years of Lambert's quality, he has never been offered an operatic performance.' He added that Frank Howes, reactionary music critic of *The Times*, 'had the highest opinion of Lambert's possibilities,' and left it at that. Lambert's friends on the committee may have appreciated Webster's discretion in overlooking his riotous personal life; and were probably right in rejecting him for the post. 'Lambert was an excellent ballet conductor when sober,' recalled a Sadler's Wells horn-player, 'but nowhere near as good in opera.'[14] To put it bluntly, said another orchestral musician, 'he was incapable of following a singer or instrumentalist in a *rubato*'.[15]

There were three names left in Webster's hat. Karl RANKL, he suggested, 'is the most likely foreigner resident in England for a high place at Covent Garden. I have had personal experience of his way of handling English musicians and he is very good at the job.' Although the name and track record of this Austrian exile, forty-six years old, were virtually unknown, Webster did not elaborate.

Casting his gaze abroad, he proposed Bruno Walter as the only alien star worth considering. Now in his seventieth year and living in the United States, Walter had been sacked by the Vienna State Opera when the Nazis took over in 1938. He had previously directed the great opera houses of Munich and Berlin, and was a compelling symphonic conductor. WALTER, said Webster, 'is greatly loved in this country and he in his turn loves working here . . . He is good to work with and his presence at Covent Garden would give the whole scheme some cachet.' He could not, however, at such an age be expected to form a company. Walter should be invited only as an honoured guest, Webster felt. Walter felt otherwise, demanding to know who would be training the chorus and orchestra before accepting an engagement. He never conducted again at Covent Garden, though he did make one decisive intervention in its future destiny.

Walter's nomination as the sole overseas candidate exposed the depths of Webster's ignorance or guile, for there were half a dozen other exiles he should certainly have mentioned. Chief among them was Otto Klemperer, 60, architect of Berlin's ground-breaking Kroll Oper and now penniless in New York – as was Jascha Horenstein,

47, formerly of Düsseldorf. George Szell, 48, once of Berlin and Prague, and Fritz Reiner, 57, of Budapest and Dresden, held positions with US orchestras but were open to overtures. Erich Kleiber, 55, former head of the Berlin State Opera, was mouldering in Buenos Aires. Any of these masters was capable of raising an opera house from the foundations up, yet none was considered for Covent Garden – either because Webster had not heard of them, or because he feared their competence and charisma.

The last name on his list was an Englishman working abroad, a quiet fellow who had conducted many operas for Beecham before taking on orchestras in Rochester and Cincinnati. Born into a musical family of Belgian descent, Eugene Goossens was fifty-two years old and looking for a career move after making the awful misjudgement of refusing to pay commission to his all-powerful US manager, Arthur Judson.[16] He was finished in America and dying to come home, where his parents still lived and his oboist brother and harpist sister were active in the London orchestras.

GOOSSENS was thus both qualified and available – a bit too available for Webster's liking. 'He has been conductor of the Cincinnati Orchestra for some 15 years. The fact that he has stayed there so long makes it clear that he has been very satisfactory to Cincinnati, but it might be criticized on the grounds that if he were really first-class he should have gone to a better orchestra,' was his assessment. Given the restricted choice and the urgent need, however, Keynes and his colleagues ordered Webster to engage him without delay. Ralph Hawkes had sounded him out some weeks beforehand, and Goossens had informed his parents that he expected to accept the offer. 'I'll be returning,' he wrote, 'in the most dignified and important role I could possibly return to: something which I think would make you very proud of me – at last!'[17] There was a servile flaw in Goossens character, a damaging weakness that was not publicly evident but which might have been picked up by Webster's man-watching sensors.

Whatever his instructions, the General Administrator was in no rush to issue a contract. In June 1945, three months after hearing from Hawkes, the conductor complained of lack of progress. When summer passed without further word, he agreed to conduct in Australia. In March 1946 after eleven months of inaction from Webster, Hawkes cabled a warning from New York: 'We shall lose Goossens unless we can come to brass tacks immediately. After consultation with Keynes who has spoken to Goossens on telephone I am offering him definite engagement for two years from July at five thousand pounds per annum. He cannot cancel Australian engagement thus arrival London earlier than July impossible. Most important reach provisional conclusions about operatic repertoire before he leaves for Australia.'[18]

A week or so earlier, Webster had sent formal proposals to Goossens couched in terms that were, perhaps, intentionally unappealing. 'Anything that we do by way of opera has more or less to be from scratch,' he wrote. 'Not that England is entirely devoid of good singers, but there are naturally few of them and those few, for obvious reasons, are not well schooled in Opera.' Nevertheless, the company would have to 'give every encouragement to the British artist and consider him first . . . We also intend giving every encouragement to British composers.' It read like a recipe for vocal mediocrity.

All operas would have to be sung in English because 'opera has never really prospered anywhere unless given in the language of the audience attending the performance.' Some of the conducting might be given to Lambert, Sargent, Barbirolli and 'a newcomer here, a Czech named (Walter) Sus(s)kind'.

Webster went on to outline administrative procedure. 'The general direction of the company would be in the hands of yourself and the principal producer, with myself in the Chair.'[19] In other words, every artistic decision would have to be approved by Webster before it went to the board for modification and authorization. No opera director in the world operated under such restraints, and Goossens promptly rejected the proposal on almost every count.

He pointed out that the Met gave opera successfully in the original language; that Covent Garden had only ever flourished with big singers, albeit foreigners; and that you cannot make bricks without straw. Above all, he objected to Webster's triumvirate. 'With regard to the directorial set-up, I am a little inclined to view with misgiving any divided authority. Blame for the shortcomings of a production as well as credit for its good points should fall on the shoulders of a single individual – the artistic director . . . Webster's letter has finally made me realize that I cannot safely undertake the responsibility for a project the artistic outcome of which I cannot foresee.'[20]

Goossens had left the door open but Keynes, incensed by what he saw as ingratitude, told Webster to appoint a more pliant conductor

– adding that if the new man failed 'in the first six months, we shall get rid of him and let Goossens take his job.'[21] Webster was 'delighted'[22] and engaged his privately preferred choice, Rankl.

However, while pleased by Goossens' withdrawal, Webster could not forgive the snub. Goossens sailed for Australia where he served as director of the New South Wales Conservatory and conductor of the Sydney Symphony Orchestra. Whenever he spotted a promising singer, he sent the youngster straight to Webster as a personal favour, when he could have directed them just as easily and perhaps more profitably to an American or European opera company. The kindness was not reciprocated. Whenever Goossens or his agent asked if he might guest-conduct an opera at Covent Garden, Webster's reply was always in the courteous negative.

By 1953, Goossens was almost begging: 'Dear friend Webster . . . This is just to let you know that I would welcome an invitation from the Covent Garden authorities to take charge of some opera performances at the old Theatre in which I formerly appeared so frequently . . . A lifetime's experience of opera is still in me, as befits one who has directed at different times close on sixty operas . . . I venture to think that the press and public would display some interest in my reappearance.'[23] Webster replied that conducting arrangements for the next season were 'almost complete', and offered him free tickets instead. The following year, he proposed Goossens as chief conductor of the ballet, an insult to a musician of his stature.

Goossens was thrown out of Australia in January 1956 after being caught – or, more probably, set up – with a thousand items of pornography in his luggage. The Governors of the BBC reviewed his case and gravely resolved to allow him to conduct their orchestras 'after a suitable interval'. At Covent Garden, however, any engagement was out of the question. Goossens, naïve to the last, could not believe that Webster had ordered his exclusion and continued to address him pathetically as 'Friend'. His final letter, thanking for some tickets, sighs that 'visits to Covent Garden arouse in me an almost unbearable nostalgia'.[24]

Wise as always after the event, Kenneth Clark lamented the dreadful error in his memoirs: 'David Webster didn't really know the field [of conducting] and would not turn to anyone who could advise him in case he would be overshadowed. He chose as Musical Director a minor figure named Karl Rankl and for some years we put on performances which varied between mediocre and bad.'[25] Rankl's appointment was announced on 16 June 1946, together with details of the company's curtain-raiser, Purcell's opera, *The Fairy Queen*, conducted by Lambert. Gushing news like a punctured hosepipe, as if to divert pressure from a faulty headpiece, Webster also let it be known that the choreographer Frederick Ashton was to be 'production consultant' to the opera company, though Ashton's knowledge of opera was limited and his experience non-existent. Ashton had lately created *Symphonic Variations*, the deepest and most enduring of his ballets.

'Who on earth is Rankl?' demanded the press. *The Times*, in a well-briefed leading article, bemoaned the exclusion of Beecham and 'certain other musicians working in America', but hoped that 'Mr Rankl's experience in the direction of half a dozen (*sic*) continental opera houses (would) qualify him for the great task.'[26] Rankl's credentials were taken as read. Little more was known about him in England where he had conducted barely a dozen concerts, but in America some émigré musicians were 'highly amused' when they heard of his sudden eminence.[27]

The fourteenth child of a subsistence farmer from Gaaden, near Vienna, Rankl had served in the trenches during the First World War before being invalided out to study with Arnold Schoenberg, himself newly demobbed. Among the destitute of a defeated nation, Schoenberg's pupils were the poorest of the poor. He taught them without charging a fee and they repaid him by performing all manner of musical drudgery, from selling tickets at his 'private' concerts to making piano reductions of his unplayed scores. When a wealthy patron offered a donation, Schoenberg thanked the 'dear, kind lady' and said he was sending her gift to two young disciples, Hanns Eisler and Rankl, 'both as poor as they are gifted, as ardent as they are sensitive, and as intelligent as they are imaginative'.[28]

After a spell as repetiteur and chorusmaster at Vienna's Volksoper under the crusty Felix Weingartner, Rankl served a traditional musical apprenticeship as conductor in the provincial towns of Reichenberg and Königsberg. He rounded off his training with three years as Otto Klemperer's assistant at the Kroll Oper in Berlin, birthplace of operatic modernism. In 1932, he was named music director in Wiesbaden, one of Klemperer's former posts; but when the Nazis seized power he refused to live in Germany. Graz in his home country gave him the running of its opera house for the next four years. In 1937 he succeeded Szell at the German-language opera house in Prague, a small company in a great musical city. Months later, the German army marched in. Linked to left-wing causes and married to a half-Jewish wife, Adele Jahoda, Rankl fled to England.

The outbreak of war left him stranded and penniless, living on two pounds a week from a Czech charity. In the five years until he obtained a work permit, he was put up in a spare cottage by the Oxford classicist Gilbert Murray, while his wife knitted small items for sale. When officialdom finally relented, he stood in at short notice for two London concerts and was engaged by the Liverpool Philharmonic, where he impressed Webster. After the war, he was invited to audition for the two Australian jobs that were being offered at the same time to Goossens and Lambert. Unable to get travel papers for Adele, Rankl refused to travel alone; when the plane he was booked on crashed en route, Rankl saw it as a mark of providence. Two weeks later, Webster offered him Covent Garden.

In technical respects, he was well qualified. Rankl knew the workings of an opera house inside out and was a good judge of singers and musicians. His ear was acute and his repertoire broad. He knew how to schedule rehearsals and plan a balanced season. He had a well-stocked mind, and was open to new ideas. He 'had a very high opinion'[29] he told an interviewer, of Walton, Britten, Bliss and Vaughan Williams. A high-domed little man in rimless glasses and bow-tie, Rankl looked the part of a central European intellectual as depicted by Christopher Isherwood in *Prater Violet*: ferociously intelligent, professionally stringent yet privately gentle and vulnerable. 'He frightened a lot of people,' said one of his singers, 'but I got to know he liked animals, and I thought if he liked animals there must be a kind side to him.'[30]

Rankl's drawbacks became apparent only when he began to conduct under pressure. He was the kind of conductor who, when unsure of himself, could not leave well alone. He felt the need to indicate every semi-demi-quaver and would work himself into a lather in the quietest passages. He disturbed the audience without greatly elevating the orchestra. When things went wrong in rehearsal, he did not thunder – he nagged. His friendly beam turned fractious and he lacked the native wit to jolly musicians back into good spirits. He spoke a clipped English, rendered directly from the

German. 'Oh, those swine!' he would shout, not realizing how much uglier the word sounded to English ears. 'Rankl was a sweet old thing but a bit of a martinet,' said his assistant conductor, Peter Gellhorn. 'I don't think he wanted to be. He felt always up against it.'[31]

Instead of easing with achievement, his anxiety escalated. 'It was not until he had been stretched beyond his capacity and endurance that he became the frightening hysteric we were later to see,'[32] reflected one musician. At the end of the first season, several players left the orchestra, unable to bear the atmosphere. Rankl tried to mend fences, inviting musicians to a Christmas party at his home in Acacia Road, St John's Wood, where they met his stately wife, Adele, and her 'adopted daughter', a newly-arrived Austrian girl called Christine. This set-up was too continental for simple English folk to fathom, and after a while it got too much for Mrs Rankl, who left to live with her sister in the West Country. Some years later, Karl married young Christine.*

There were social barriers, as well as linguistic and cultural ones, that Rankl could never overcome. Raised in a country where seriousness was a virtue and flippancy a sin, he had no small talk and could not make conversation with Covent Garden grandees. The convivial Clarks threw a thank-you party for him at the end of his first year. 'I am sorry you couldn't come to the Rankl party,' wrote Clark to Webster. 'I hope he enjoyed it – I couldn't tell.'[33] Rankl was the very antithesis of Lambert, who fizzed with bottled bonhomie. The two chief conductors detested one another on sight.

Nevertheless, Rankl's single-minded, strait-laced dedication was precisely what Covent Garden needed. He had six months to form an opera company, and he went at his task with a determination that more famous maestros might not have matched. Between May and early August he held auditions in the crimson-and-chandeliered Crush Bar at Covent Garden and in large halls around the country, extending the search in a quick summer trip to America. Around two thousand singers were heard, among them postal clerks, milkmen, housewives and farmhands. Few had ever sung for money, or could read a score. From these raw voices, Rankl signed up chorus singers for eight pounds a week, and soloists for forty, which seemed like a

---

* Adele Rankl refused to grant him a divorce, and he remarried only after her death in 1963 (Information from Mrs C. Rankl)

fortune. 'I thought I was a millionairess,'[34] said Constance Shacklock, a farmer's daughter from Sherwood Forest, who was taken on for secondary mezzo roles.

Webster played a full part in the search, relishing his opportunity as a talent-spotter. The untrained bass singer Ian Wallace found himself facing the former shopkeeper and a lady he introduced as 'Madame Gerhardt'. Wallace had never heard of the celebrated lieder singer and bluffed his way well enough through two arias to be called back for a further audition with Rankl. Second time round, his enthusiasm did not compensate for a sound that was deemed 'too small' for Covent Garden.

During an audition in Leeds, a Harrogate organist with handlebar moustaches, Douglas Robinson by name, was appointed Chorus Master, a post he held until 1974. At the same session Rankl met an ex-Berliner, Peter Gellhorn, whom Webster had seen working with the Carl Rosa Company. Rankl appointed Gellhorn Head of Music Staff. Norman Feasey, a pre-war Covent Gardenite known as 'the Reverend' returned as Chief Repetiteur, and Reginald Goodall, a bespectacled conductor in his mid-forties, was poached from Sadler's Wells for thirty-five pounds a week.

There was a rush of qualified refugees for the job vacancies but the order was out to buy British. Webster noted that 'apart from Mr Rankl, Peter Gellhorn would be the only foreigner on the musical side'.[35] The fact that both men were naturalized UK citizens was immaterial. It was a matter of island pride that Covent Garden should be crewed with native stock. Rankl, the day their papers arrived, told his wife, 'Liebchen, we are British!' She was promptly dubbed 'the British Liebchen'.

At the opening rehearsals, hardly anyone had ever seen or heard the operas they were meant to be performing, so limited had been the English exposure to opera before the war. Rankl could take nothing for granted; he had to teach the art from scales up.

An orchestra of sorts had been put together by Lambert putting the word around the public bar of The George and other watering holes that there were jobs going at eighteen quid a week in a new band under his cheery baton. Only twelve members of the orchestra had ever played opera before, and the leader, Joseph Shadwick, was so unsuited to the task that he departed after only one season.

There had been no provision for such an orchestra in the original Covent Garden scheme. 'Our plan,' Webster reminded Keynes, 'was to use one of the existing (London) orchestras for the Covent Garden work, but this has not proved practicable. In any case, demobilization has changed the personnel picture and we find that we can form our own orchestra. Constant is convinced that its quality will be high.'[36]

The cost of the orchestra was enormous, over £70,000 a year, but Webster hoped to earn back some money from commercial engagements. Lambert assured the BBC 'that he was trying to make Covent Garden orchestra into a thoroughly efficient and coherent entity, and with that in view he hoped to get them concert and recording work in due course apart from their work in the pit at Covent Garden.'[37] But this was either drunken talk or dangerous self-delusion, for there was no chance of Covent Garden attracting the calibre of musician that played in the London Symphony Orchestra, London Philharmonic or BBC Symphony Orchestra, let alone the golden-handshake Royal Philharmonic and Philharmonia orchestras that Beecham and EMI's Walter Legge were forming from the best demobbed bandsmen. If a musician wanted excitement, he went to work with Beecham, Toscanini, de Sabata and Celibidache at one of the self-employed bands. If he wanted security, he signed up with Boult for a BBC pension and paid holidays. At Covent Garden, all that was on offer was a ten-month contract under conductors of choleric instability. Man for man, Covent Garden was the weakest of London orchestras and remained so. To make up numbers, Shadwick went looking for women players, incurring a reprimand from his union.

Lambert had first crack at the orchestra. After leading it in the curtain-raising *Sleeping Princess*, he set to work on a dazzling venture that would open the new era of opera at Covent Garden. The two hundred and fiftieth anniversary of the death of Henry Purcell had fallen in 1945, and Lambert came up with the idea of reviving his famous but unfamiliar masque, *The Fairy Queen*, as a full-blown three-act opera. Purcell, declared Lambert, 'is by general consent the greatest of English composers and is considered even by those Continentals who still imagine England to be *le pays sans musique* as one of the great classical masters.'[38]

By cutting screeds of Shakespearian dialogue, the masque was kept to an endurable three hours. Professor Edward J. Dent helped modernize the instrumentation. The designer was Lambert's flat-mate, the artist Michael Ayrton; the choreographer was Ashton and the producer was Malcolm Baker-Smith, an associate of the French cinema director, René Clair. *The Fairy Queen* was not an opera but it was about as English as could be, representing a combination of all English arts, a Restoration-era *Gesamtkunstwerk*. To make up for a lack of celebrated singers, or much strong stuff for them to sing, a full galaxy of dancers was trotted out, headed by Fonteyn and Helpmann and augmented by Beryl Grey, Michael Somes, Alexander Grant and the ominously popular Moira Shearer. 'The Sadler's Wells Ballet (Director: Ninette de Valois)' took top billing, above 'Soloists and Chorus of Covent Garden Opera.'

Lambert had invested six months of his short life in *The Fairy Queen*, only to find that Webster was scheming to replace him with Rankl. Webster was not prepared take risks with his opening night, and could not be sure that Lambert would turn up sober. He was forced to back down when Ashton, Ayrton, Helpmann and Baker-Smith wrote an emphatic appeal on Lambert's behalf, backed by a veiled threat of mass resignation:

> The fact that *The Fairy Queen* is more ballet than opera and that the vast majority of the action is choreographic and devolves upon the ballet company, who have worked under Mr Lambert's music direction for many years, indicates that they would be likely to perform with greater confidence under a conductor so experienced in this medium as Mr Lambert.[39]

The opening, on 12 December 1946, was dutifully received. The production was revived once, in 1951, and never again.

Downcast and disillusioned, Lambert slumped into decline. Although newly in love with Isabel Delmer, estranged wife of a war correspondent and former mistress to Miro, Epstein and Giacometti, he went from booze to bust. Between acts of *The Fairy Queen*, he would nip out for a large gin, no tonic. In one pub, he was seen to spend half his weekly pay packet. After a holiday with Ayrton in Italy, he returned to conduct *Turandot* and had a terminal ruction with Webster. The morning after his last scheduled performance, 2 July 1947, Webster gave him the choice of resigning, or getting fired. Isabel, who married him in October, concurred that 'his physical and mental state at this time was such that he could not be relied upon to give *consistently* good performances.'[40]

In his resignation letter, Lambert said he intended to spend more time composing and 'will obviously be unable to give the hundred per cent support to the ballet which I have been able to give in the past.' Webster's reply was gushingly and ungrammatically insincere: 'The Sadler's Wells Ballet owes you an enormous amount of credit for the work they (*sic*) have done. Certainly, no ballet company since Diaghilev has had such an outstanding list of musical works in their repertoire, and as far as English composers are concerned I am quite sure that they have never had such an innings with any other musical institution. It does you enormous credit... I personally am extremely happy that it is likely you are going to do more composing and I am sure the whole musical world will be glad also.'[41] Webster could afford to be generous, having got rid of an enemy at no personal cost.

Lambert never conducted opera again at Covent Garden. De Valois continued to book him for her ballets, and named him artistic director of her second company, at Sadler's Wells, at a paltry five hundred pounds a year. He would merit a footnote in England's cultural renaissance, but no memorial in its central edifice. On 15 August 1951, after conducting *Rio Grande* at the Proms, he collapsed in the street and had to be helped home. Some nights later he woke up delirious, raging against Webster and his interference in *The Fairy Queen*. 'Don't let them take me away,' he pleaded. Rushed to hospital, he died the next morning, two days short of forty-six years old.

The cause of death was broncho-pneumonia and diabetes mellitus. Had the latter condition been diagnosed sooner, it would have been treated with insulin injections and noted as the main cause of his alcoholic thirst. The composer Dennis ApIvor, who observed Lambert with the eye of a qualified physician, believed he drank to stave off boredom. This being England, nobody told him he was killing himself or needed to see a doctor, because what a man drank was his own business – and, anyway, Constant was such fun when drinking. Even Dr ApIvor admitted that 'the volatile and uproarious side of his company, of which I have never seen the like, was probably at least fifty per cent of himself.'[42] Isabel went on to marry Lambert's best friend, the composer Alan Rawsthorne. Both would contribute to Ashton ballets, but neither was engaged by Webster for the Opera. Nor was any tribute to Lambert permitted at Covent Garden. Lambert, said the novelist Anthony Powell, had 'a touch of genius' – a quality too dangerous for David Webster. Constant

Lambert was the first but would not be the last conductor at Covent Garden to collapse in a gutter and die in disgrace.

The winter of 1946-47 was the worst for half a century, vicious winds whistling through the blitzed-out city and a frost piercing its shattered defences. The Thames froze at Westminster Bridge and fuel shortages, causing frequent power cuts, meant there was no relief from the cold either at home or at work. In the warren of Covent Garden's rehearsal rooms and offices, the lights came on for only two hours a day. The cats in the neighbouring market turned feral with hunger. A chorister who stopped to stroke a passing puss was warned she could get her hand bitten off.

The gloom was as pervasive as the cold. Winston Churchill talked of an Iron Curtain dividing Europe. Many awaited the imminent outbreak of a nuclear Third World War. In the literature, the art and the music of that winter, it is hard to find a single note of hope. Vaughan Williams, who so often caught the national mood, was at work on a sixth symphony which would end in hushed despair.

The only happy faces belonged to the 'spivs' and black-marketeers who ran a racket in scarce commodities, turning an overwhelmingly law-respecting country into a society that condoned law-breaking when it eased officially-imposed deprivation. Like America under Prohibition, England during post-war rationing underwent profound changes in its character and conduct.

On these dark, cold and fearful mornings, Karl Rankl set to work creating an opera company at Covent Garden. The forces at his disposal did not inspire confidence. 'A good many of the men were just out of the forces,' recalled a chorister. 'One was lame, one scarred by burns and all of us were poorly dressed. I was wearing a coat my mother had made me out of an army blanket. We didn't look very well fed either.'[43]

The first production for this pallid and bedraggled assembly was a sun-kissed *Carmen*, the most popular and passionate of operas and the one least suited to the conductor's temperament. Pedantic and bloodless, a counter of crotchets and stickler for formalities, Rankl beat his way metronomically through Bizet's blazing love-tangle. An English pre-war mezzo, Edith Coates, sang the heroine and an Australian ex-policeman, Kenneth Neate, was Don José.

The Queen and several Cabinet ministers turned out for opening night, 14 January 1947. They cheered the ballerina, Beryl Grey, and little else. Apart from the establishmentarian *Times*, which proclaimed a success, the reviews were as grim as the weather. A sour pack of critics found little to praise apart from Edward Burra's set and costumes, and the capable stage direction of Henry Cass. Before the war, Covent Garden had not bothered with production. No director was listed on playbills and any shifting around was left to the stage manager, who chalked crosses on the floor where singers were supposed to stand. The noticeable difference at the new Covent Garden was that designers and directors had been recruited from the thriving theatrical world to enhance the operatic experience. Otherwise, comparisons with pre-war performances were overwhelmingly unfavourable.

Carmen was followed by Massenet's *Manon*, a relative novelty to English audiences, conducted by Goodall, adroitly directed by Ashton and beautifully designed by James Bailey. The singing was the let-down once again, with the main roles taken by an American, Virginia MacWatters, who was pretty but slight, and a venerable English tenor, Heddle Nash, who was born in 1894 and sounded woodenly Victorian.

And so the season wore on, with few magic moments apart from the return of Eva Turner as Turandot, a role she had made her own at La Scala and was now required to relearn in English. 'I pray it goes well,' she told a friend.[44] The rest of the programme was a line-up of inspired amateurs and tired professionals. 'I am shocked that singing of that order can survive the first week of rehearsal in a respectable opera house,' griped the *New Statesman*'s Desmond Shawe-Taylor of some roles in *Der Rosenkavalier*. 'Who has the power of veto at Covent Garden and why wasn't it used?'

On 1 April 1947, Rankl mounted the conductor's box to rehearse the third act Pantomime in *Der Rosenkavalier*, beating two to the bar. David Franklin, singing Baron Ochs, recalled the ensuing embarrassment:

He raised his hands, looked around expectantly and plunged into his downbeat. With completely deadpan faces, the orchestra played the prelude to *Carmen*. Rankl . . . snatched the music from Joe Shadwick's stand – Joe led the orchestra. 'But this is *Rosenkavalier* that you have,' said Rankl, 'why you play *Carmen* – why?' Joe explained to him that on All Fool's Day we play jokes on our friends. If only Rankl had had the wit – or the humanity –

to realize it, the important word was 'friends' . . . But Rankl told Shadwick not to be silly. 'Rehearse properly,' he said angrily. . . Fifteen minutes later, when he stopped them to clear up some problem in the score, he turned to Shadwick and said anxiously, 'When I come into the pit tonight to conduct *Magic Flute*, what will you play?' 'For God's sake,' said Joe, 'we shall play the *Flute*, of course. This was just a joke.' 'A *joke*?' said Rankl – he couldn't believe it.[45]

In the coffee break, Constance Shacklock overheard him asking a fellow-immigrant, 'what is April Fools, Gellhorn?' On another occasion, as Rankl began his rehearsal, the band struck up 'Happy Birthday!' 'What are you doing? This is not our music? What is this?' he cried. Someone explained patiently that it was a tune rendered affectionately on birthdays. It was 1 October and the band wanted to salute their conductor but Rankl, apoplectic, could not accept it.[46] To him the opera house was a place of service, solemnity and decorum, a temple of the arts. When a large Welsh chorister, arriving late, walked into rehearsal in his outdoor clothes, Rankl rushed up and ripped the hat from his head. For a glowering moment, the two men almost came to blows; neither could understand why the other was so angry.

The bitter, irascible Rankl scarcely resembled the leader of men whom Webster had described to his committee: 'I have had personal experience of his way of handling English musicians and he is very good at the job.' Rankl smoked a pipe and went to cricket matches at Lord's in the hope of penetrating the mysteries of Englishness, but he never learned to relax and form working relationships. He believed fervently in the viability of English-sung opera and the trainability of English singers, but he lacked any powers of public persuasion and was too shy to expose himself to press interviews. Beecham branded Rankl's appointment 'the mystery of mysteries' and his toadies wafted a stink of venom around the press.

'We felt the press had their knives into us from the beginning,' said Gellhorn. 'Nothing we could do was right, and both Rankl and I worked so hard, conducting three or four nights a week. Sunday mornings, I would lie in bed until lunchtime, exhausted.'[47] Rankl kept saying that their efforts would take years to be recognized, but the opening season was a write-off and the public was drifting elsewhere. Covent Garden Opera drew a sixty per cent attendance, an average of twelve hundred spectators a night.

Yet the Arts Council kept faith, more than doubling its grant to £55,000, and some critics knowingly suppressed the deficiencies in service of what they saw as a greater public interest. 'I thought that some of my colleagues ... should take a longer view,' said Frank Howes of *The Times*, 'even if in detail there was truth in what they were saying. And I think now that the start was right.'[48]

Even in a false dawn, Covent Garden was not without friends. The trustees were astonishingly well-connected and they pounded their address books tirelessly. Clark, in particular, preached the cause around his circle of political, commercial, artistic and sexual conquests. He was forever badgering Webster for free tickets to give to contacts who might be 'valuable allies from many points of view, as well as being charming people' – the targets in this instance being Sir John Anderson, the Independent MP, and his charming wife, Ava. Sir John was not so much a household name as a backyard fixture, his 'Anderson Huts' having sheltered many British families during the terrors of the Blitz. He had served as Home Secretary and Chancellor of the Exchequer under Churchill, and was retained as a nuclear weapons adviser to the Labour Government, with a private secretariat in the Cabinet Office. 'If you could let me have two tickets,' suggested Clark, 'I think it would repay us.'[49]

There had to be a quid pro quo. In return for free seats, the Royal Opera House amassed a list of powerful people who could be called upon in time of need to press its case with Government. Covent Garden became a professional player of the English game of grease-and-favour, always getting more than it gave.

Adversity, as Churchill discovered, brings out the bulldog in the British. The more Covent Garden got bombed with bad notices, the greater was its collective tenacity. 'Everyone, from the top to the bottom, was fired with a deep sense of enthusiasm which it was impossible to ignore,' said the bass-baritone, Michael Langdon. 'I was immediately caught up by it, and it quickly changed from being just a fill-in job to being something I was desperate to do. Above all there was a tremendous amount of fun in what we were doing.'[50]

'We were building a British opera company,' declared Constance Shacklock. 'We were working as a team to build something of value, something the country could be proud of.'[51]

'It was a very special time,' recalled Iris Kells, a chorus girl who was promoted to soloist. 'So many had been in the War. Some of us who were very young were helped along by pre-war singers. Everybody pulled together.'[52]

'The chorus rehearsed in the girls' dressing room at the top of the building, up four noisy flights of concrete stairs,' reminisced Irene Thomas, who went on to amaze the nation with her erudition as a radio panellist on *Round Britain Quiz*. 'There was no proper chorus rehearsal room. We sat in a clutter of make-up boxes, crinoline frames, wigs, mirrors, shoes and dress-rails with Robbie (Douglas Robinson) and the pianist wedged in the corner. But we didn't mind the discomfort . . . we began to forge a company spirit.'[53]

There were rough pubs in the vicinity that opened for market porters at six in the morning and held Last Drinks for singers until after the final curtain. The Nag's Head, opposite the stage door, was a ready haven for the desperate. Its landlord, Wally Pack, was a retired boxer and his wife a mother-surrogate to the homesick, and around the bar there would usually be an old-timer or two from the Beecham era, eager to trade gossip for the price of a scotch. For more substantive nourishment, there was a greasy spoon café in Floral Street that did not look too closely at ration coupons. Deprivation meant that few could afford to be over-fastidious. One prop-boy used to collect fag-ends after the Smoking Chorus in *Carmen* and re-roll them for resale to the cast. Some men from the market doubled as extras in crowd-scenes, others earned a bit on the side helping out as scene-shifters. Michael Manuel, whose father owned a fruit-and-veg stall, was taken on to the staff and became stage manager for the ballet.

A community of allsorts began to emerge, studded with the kind of characters that make every theatre and circus seem larger than life. There was 'Bogey' Ballard, the veteran chief machinist, who knew all the secret passageways in the building and had a horrible knack of turning up on an overhead gantry, shouting 'I heard you!', just as people were disparaging him. There was a stage electrician called Norman who used to pull on rubber gloves and hold together two live wires to produce the lightning-flash in *Don Giovanni*. Sergeant Martin, the moustachioed chief commissionaire in his long red coat with gold buttons, was a sentimental soul who held tickets for the best shows for his wartime commanding officer in the Scots Guards. The repetiteur Eric Mitchell, a former Royal Marine, came to work each morning in black coat and striped trousers. Michael Wood, the beanpole press officer, would walk to the office with a tiny fox-terrier called Henry – unless it rained, in which case he sent the dog ahead by taxi. Wood had his shoes polished to a high gloss three times a week by his former Army batman.

The combination of grey deprivation and lurid eccentricity, external assaults and internal solidarity, created a remarkable sense of unity and purpose. And once the company began touring the country, sharing bedrooms in shabby digs and jokes about their landladies, the cohesion bonded into something far stronger than a place of employment and entertainment. 'We were like a family,' said the stately Shacklock, who stood out for her glamorous, home-made hats. 'I knew every member of the chorus by name, and the ballet too,' she said; fifty years later, she still saw some of them for lunch.

'The great thing about the Garden was the touring,' added Iris Kells, 'it built the company and brought us together.' 'We played cards with the orchestra,' remembered Irene Thomas, 'pontoon, with a suitcase-top as a table.'[54] Some returned from tour newly in love. Irene fell for a Welsh chorister, Eddie Thomas; Kells wed a repetiteur, Leonard Hancock. Shacklock fell for Eric Mitchell when he coached her as Brangäne in *Tristan and Isolde*. They married at the end of the first season in a registry office. Mitchell, whose first marriage had broken up in the war, could not be entered in holy matrimony by the Church of England in the Kensington church where he served each Sunday as organist. Such were the rules that earned England its reputation for bifocality, but few contested the *status quo* at this time, and the Mitchell couple were content to receive a private blessing from their parish priest.

Greater and more lasting than the roll of romantic couplings at Covent Garden was the emergent collective ethos. It pervaded the company from top to pit and must be regarded as David Webster's supreme achievement, arising from his concern for staff welfare, a quality that was rare in class-ridden British industry, outside the Quaker factories and the paternalistic Jewish stores of Tesco and Marks & Spencer. Most chief executives held themselves aloof, descending once a year to join the workers for Christmas lunch and hand out the annual bonus. Bosses were addressed as 'Sir' and subordinates by surname.

Webster, by contrast, was a caring and visible administrator. He was not readily approachable inside the opera house, but would strike up a conversation with any employee who encountered him on the street or in a pub. He usually remembered their names and, if he forgot, called them 'my dear chap'. He was not a daunting figure either in height, dress or demeanour, and seemed to court affection rather than respect. 'In the main, he earned the loyalty of his staff for he brought great dedication to his job and he had a generous nature,' wrote a future chairman, 'although he found it almost impossible to go backstage after a performance to say, "Well done". Why this was, I never discovered.'[55] Some put his reticence down to a natural shyness, which turned to an 'obsessive secretiveness'[56] as his company came under pressure.

Like many gay men, he may have longed for a family of his own and at Covent Garden he created a surrogate of sorts. 'Do you know,' he once reproached the Welsh baritone, Geraint Evans, 'you've never invited me to your home.'[57] To members of the company, this fat, bald, florid little man was a fatherly rock of solidarity.

'Webster was always there for the singers,' said Iris Kells. 'We had very few problems. I don't remember being angry at anything.'

After Keynes, Kenneth Clark thought he deserved to become chairman of the Arts Council, or Covent Garden, or both. He had deputized during Keynes's long absences and knew all the right doors to knock and all the right men to lunch along Whitehall, which perversely worked against him. What Whitehall wanted was to put the genie back in its box. Keynes, with his fluid mind and stealthy charm, had set up a state-funded Arts Council and national opera house that operated at arm's length from the proper authorities. It was time for the Civil Service to claw back control, offering Clement Attlee's hard-pressed Cabinet the means to renege on promises and curb the costs of Keynes's folly. The twin crowns of the arts kingdom were now in the gift of the Prime Minister, acting on the advice of officials who drew their recommendations from a list of the Great and the Good who could be relied upon to show 'worthiness, soundness and discretion' – any quality, that is, except bold imagination. These were the curbs that Whitehall sought to impose upon the arts, and they concurred more or less with the needs of Attlee's Cabinet.

Contrary to popular myth, the architects of the welfare state were no keener on supporting the arts than the most reactionary of Tories. The Labour Government was composed of social reformers, trades union organizers and political strategists, few of whom felt much concern for culture. Their objective was equalization of opportunity in a post-imperial state, an aim that was annoyingly delayed by war debt, a mutinous workforce and the ever-spiralling cost of nuclear defence in the face of a perceived Soviet threat. They had neither the resources nor the inclination to foster the arts as a source of hope and revival. Some ministers regarded the arts as a niggling distraction, others as a necessary palliative: socialist bread and circuses. Either way, the arts needed to be yoked to the machinery of government.

To head the Arts Council, Whitehall and the Labour Government selected a retired officer of the City of London Corporation's Drapers' Company, a man who had sat for years half-noticed as vice-chairman of the Old Vic and Sadler's Wells. Sir Ernest Pooley was six months short of seventy years old and, in Clark's words, 'having no interest in the arts, he could be relied upon not to press their claims too strongly.'[58] Mary Glasgow, the Council's secretary-general, refused to mask her contempt for Keynes's successor and paid for it with her career; Pooley replaced her in 1950 with W. E. Williams, one of Tom Jones's antedeluvian Taffia. In her memoirs, Glasgow reported that she was once told by a drunken civil servant that Pooley was a 'safe little shit' who would not demand money or make trouble because 'we've got something on him'.[59] Whether or not there is substance to this rancorous aspersion, implying sexual (specifically, homosexual) scandal, the grey-faced Pooley chaired the Arts Council for seven lean years; at the end of which, he was created a baronet and got married for the first time, to an old chum's widow.

Under his aegis, the Council's grant rose from an initial £235,000 to £575,000 in 1948, at which point Pooley decided that state benefice had reached its natural limits. 'We don't need any more,' he said, 'an increase will only get us into trouble.'[60] By the time of his departure in 1953, the grant was just £675,000, which included a Coronation year bonus. It is hard to avoid the conclusion that Pooley had been picked to curb the resurgence of British arts, and he did his level best. Subsidy for the arts, he once wrote by way of self-epitaph, 'is frequently both unnecessary and undesirable'.

With the Arts Council emasculated and ruled by a Sadler's Wells man, Covent Garden found itself dangerously isolated. The Trust, alarmed, set out to find a champion whose name would conjure up a

Keynesian measure of awe, not so much from the general public as among the handful of senior mandarins and politicians who had to approve the appointment. Clark might have made a fine figurehead, but in the corridors of power he was dismissed as 'lacking bottom'. What was needed was a man of irresistible intellect and outstanding public service whose word was law in Whitehall. The ideal candidate was found, selflessly or unwittingly, by Clark himself when, in March 1946, he procured a pair of complimentary ballet tickets for the 'valuable' Sir John Anderson, 'who was, in the opinion of Whitehall, the greatest administrator of his day'.[61]

Anderson's public life had been so rich and eventful that he had never spared a flicker of interest for art. 'Administration he was born to and the art of government came not unnaturally as a corollary . . . the arts had never been specifically within his field of operations,' wrote his admiring biographer.[62] 'His knowledge of ballet and opera was minimal, and he did not pretend otherwise,' said a Covent Garden subordinate.[63] A stationer's son from Edinburgh, Anderson excelled in mathematics and philosophy and spent a post-graduate year in Leipzig presciently studying the radioactive properties of uranium. He came top in the Civil Service exams in 1905 with the second highest score in history and was put to work in the Colonial Office, reforming West African currencies. By thirty, he was developing a visionary health insurance system. At thirty-seven he became chairman of the Board of Inland Revenue and, at forty, permanent under-secretary at the Home Office, where he planned the emergency supply and transport mechanism that broke the 1926 General Strike. In between, he had acquitted himself with courage in Dublin during the settlement of the Irish crisis.

He was sent out to settle Moslem-Hindu riots in Bengal in 1932 and escaped an attempt on his life. Six years later, he declined an appeal from Chamberlain to become High Commissioner in strife-torn Palestine, settling instead for a sinecure as an independent MP, representing Scottish Universities. Within eight months he was brought into Chamberlain's Cabinet to organize London's defences. Churchill admired his analytical mind and capacity for hard work, promoting him to Home Secretary and then to Chancellor. He left Anderson in charge of the country when he went abroad, informing the King: 'It is the Prime Minister's duty to advise Your Majesty to send for Sir John Anderson in the event of the Prime Minister and the Foreign Secretary being killed.'[64]

Civil servants called him 'Old Jehovah' and deemed him infallible, albeit self-righteous and woodenly humourless. Anderson had 'without question the most acute brain in Parliament,' said one official. He was 'the only member of the Government able to talk with eminent scientists on equal terms. Scientific papers, consisting mostly of formulae, passed through our office, intelligible only to the Chancellor.'[65] Under Attlee, his command of nuclear technicalities remained indispensable.

In 1946, Anderson took on the chairmanship of the Port of London Authority, an economically sensitive hotbed of industrial unrest, and put his high mind to augmenting his index-linked pension with some rewarding City directorships. In any national crisis, whether flooding in East Anglia or a row with the Russians, someone would send out a call for Anderson and the Solomonian Scot in his high-winged collar would arrive to give solemn and impartial judgement. The initials 'J.A.' on an official memo were enough to put any issue beyond debate. 'Looking back,' wrote a senior colleague, 'I cannot think that he ever made, or caused to be made, a wrong decision.'[66]

In private life he was punctilious and dour. Mourning his beloved first wife, who died during a cancer operation in 1920, he betrayed no emotion at her funeral and required their two tiny orphans to shake hands politely with all present. Falling in love with a Foreign Office widow during the London blackout, he addressed the object of his affections as 'Mrs Wigram' until their marriage. It was mostly to give the French-educated, piano-playing and slightly frivolous Ava a chance to play the grande dame that he was tempted by the Covent Garden chairmanship, though he recalled that it was his assent as Chancellor of the Exchequer which had allowed Keynes to conceive the Royal Opera House project in the first place.

Before accepting the chairmanship, he wanted to be sure he was in possession of all relevant facts. He pressed Webster for details of cash flow and trade conditions. Webster replied that funds were running low, and that Swedish Opera received some ninety-two thousand pounds a year,[67] almost four times as much in state grants as Covent Garden did. Armed with these figures, Anderson wrote to his successor as Chancellor, Hugh Dalton, in a tone so peremptory it sounded more like a military ultimatum than a civil request.

'My dear Dalton,' he began, 'When I mentioned to you a week or two ago that I had been invited to become Chairman of the Covent

Garden Trust in succession to Keynes, I said that I would not feel justified in accepting the suggestion unless I could be assured that the project had been placed on a sound financial basis.'

He was not, he stressed, asking for more money than the Budget had allocated. That would be presumptuous and unprocedural. What he wanted was a copper-bottomed statement of commitment to Covent Garden. 'I want to be assured on two points,' he wrote. 'First that in expressing your offer in terms of so much a year "for the quinquennium" you do not in any way rule out the possibility of a larger payment in certain contingencies before the end of that period and, secondly, that you recognize in the arrangements now contemplated that the State will be assuming a definite obligation to see to it that, subject to others playing their part, Opera will not be let down.'

He went on to berate Dalton for refusing to grant tax relief on gifts to the arts, a veto which (according to Webster) had cost Covent Garden a twenty-five thousand pounds annual donor whose income was subject to 97.5 per cent tax. 'I ask you, therefore,' concluded Anderson combatively, 'to review your attitude in the light of these observations . . .'[68]

No ordinary citizen writing to the Chancellor in such forthright tones would expect to receive more than a dusty reply. But Anderson was no ordinary citizen. He was a supreme civil servant and former Chancellor of the Exchequer who knew that the response to his letter would be drafted not by the man who signed it but by senior Treasury officials whom he had personally raised and trained in the epistolary and administrative arts. The reply was, in effect, preordained by the precise formulation of Anderson's demands, and he did not have long to wait to receive it.

Five mornings later, he sliced open an envelope and read with dry satisfaction a crested document greeting him as 'My dear Anderson'. Dalton began by reiterating the procedure that Anderson had himself put into practice: 'The assistance which the Covent Garden Trust receives from the Treasury will, of course, come to it through the Arts Council,' wrote Dalton. 'You will understand that in general I should wish the Council to feel themselves responsible for the allocation of the funds which Parliament puts at their disposal, and to plan their work ahead in the expectation of an assured but limited grant.'

The commitment Anderson sought was carefully worded in the

language of mandarins, so carefully that the key words have to be emboldened for non-officials to grasp their import.

'I recognize, however,' continued Dalton, 'that the magnitude of the Covent Garden undertaking and the difficulty in present circumstances of estimating its future needs places it in **a special position**, and that the State will be assuming **a definite obligation** to see to it that, subject to others playing their part, **Opera is not let down.** I do not therefore rule out the possibility that **the fulfilment of this obligation might in certain circumstances make it necessary to increase the Treasury grant** to the Arts Council still further than I undertook in my letter [to Pooley] of July 15th. It would, I think, be agreed that these circumstances would not be held to have arisen unless in any year the Trust could show a need for a grant from the Arts Council of an amount exceeding £60,000.

'I am sending a copy of this letter to Pooley.

Yours ever,

Hugh Dalton.'

Anderson was not a man to whoop for joy, but he instructed Webster to inform the Trustees that he regarded 'the terms of the reply as satisfactory' and was now prepared to accept their invitation to become chairman. He was so pleased with the letter that 'he used always to carry (it) about with him in his pocket, taking it out and brandishing it when the need arose.'[69] In his mind it amounted to a constitutional guarantee of Covent Garden's centrality and an irrevocable pledge of financial support. For while he acknowledged that, in theory, 'no Chancellor could commit his successor, the whole history of practical politics was based on the fact that he did.'[70] Anderson held Dalton's letter to be 'morally binding on all future Chancellors';[71] it meant that 'you can close Covent Garden, but you must not starve it'.[72]

This may sound impossibly naïve to post-modern ears which have grown accustomed to senior civil servants being 'economical with the truth', but that is more a measure of how much England has changed in the second half of the twentieth century than a mark of Anderson's gullibility. He belonged to a school which held that government is conducted on a basis of trust and continuity, where an Englishman's word is the bond that ties the hands of future generations and prevents them from disrupting the smooth running of the country. Anderson would himself have cause to be disappointed with the way the rule was applied to Covent Garden, but both he and his immediate disciples upheld the need for a British government to stand by its word, whatever the cost. The retreat from that red line took place only when the country went bust a second time, after the Suez disaster and the loss of empire.

In Anderson's eleven years as chairman of the Royal Opera House, the Treasury developed a resistance to Jehovah's thunderbolts and yielded less than he demanded. Nevertheless, Anderson's letter of intent was a landmark in the company's self-perception. It gave an immediate boost to internal confidence, followed by a lasting glow of self-importance. 'Under the shelter of John Anderson's unshakeable stature the venture of British opera grew lusty and acquired stability,' wrote his biographer. Anderson proved, as expected, a redoubtable chairman. His mastery of any problem from both sides of the argument was an intellectual tour-de-force. He listened closely to unwelcome opinions and delivered judgements that sounded irrefutable. His readiness to delegate had been a feature of his career, and he made no exception in this non-executive role. Ava loved foreign travel and Anderson was content to leave Covent Garden in Webster's hands for long periods, with Clark occupying the Royal Box as deputy chairman.

Webster was not the sort of man Anderson would have chosen to run a Treasury department but, once convinced of his competence, he let him carry on with very little interference. Webster never achieved the cordiality with his second chairman that he had enjoyed with Keynes, and his attempts to charm Ava were lost on a lady who fawned on minor royalty and restricted her contacts with his office to ticket requests. Her husband quickly put a stop to the random leakage of free seats. 'I think there might be something to be said for giving tickets out occasionally to members of the Labour Party,' he suggested, 'but their distribution would have to be in accordance with some plan.'[73] In the mind of a born bureaucrat, there had to be a plan for everything.

Anderson attended opera and ballet dutifully, without displaying any sign of pleasure. When his wife complained about a bad performance, he would reproach her mildly: 'Now, now, Ava, you must remember they are doing their best.'[74]

He was scrupulous in separating his role as a Government adviser from his activities at the Royal Opera House, and every few months his clerk at the Cabinet Office would invoice Webster's secretary, Muriel Kerr, for the sum of one pound to cover Anderson's use of Government postage and stationery for Covent Garden matters.

He ordered formal minutes to be kept of all board meetings and, since the company was publicly funded, felt they should be taken by a qualified civil servant. The Treasury, anxious to keep tabs on its money, supplied a senior official called Denis Rickett, formerly Anderson's confidential assistant on nuclear weapons and soon to become principal private secretary to the Prime Minister, Clement Attlee. Rickett was far too elevated to take physical notes of board proceedings; he left that to his assistant, Miss Bevan, who scribbled away in shorthand and submitted a draft that the senior mandarin then edited into official language. 'There would be vigorous arguments at these meetings and voices were raised in anger,' said an Arts Council observer, 'but if the Board failed to agree on a proposal all that would ever appear in the minutes is the Cabinet phrase: "The Board took note . . ."'[75]

Rickett, who went on to become vice-president of the World Bank, was the first in a distinguished line of Whitehall grandees who took an afternoon off each month to serve as Secretary to Board of the Royal Opera House. No payment was involved, but the officials could attend opera and ballet whenever they liked and more often than some were able to afford on a Whitehall salary. In exchange, Covent Garden gained an invisible friend at the heart of Government and, sometimes, at the Prime Minister's right ear. Its relationship with the Treasury was formally defined, black on white, as *a special position* with *a definite obligation*.

The document that declared these terms grew frayed in Anderson's breast pocket, and a spare copy was kept in the Covent Garden archive, albeit under lock and key. The Royal Opera House did not want the world to know of its unique access. Twenty years after the Dalton letter had been made public in Sir John Wheeler-Bennett's biography of Anderson, the copy that was kept at Covent Garden was still withheld from researchers. 'If to be used publicly,' said a note on the file, 'John Tooley [general director] should agree.' It was only in January 1982 that the letter was finally released to BBC Television for a *Panorama* programme on opera funding.

This discretion was not casual or excessively cautious. It amounted to a tacit recognition by Covent Garden directors that their

links with Government were too incestuous to warrant critical
scrutiny. The cosiness established by Keynes and Anderson
persisted and thickened until the tensions inevitable in an illicit
relationship finally erupted in an explosion that almost wrecked the
Royal Opera House and set England's performing arts back fifty
years, all the way back to the bleak beginnings.

CHAPTER 4

Overture and Beginners
(1947–51)

AMID THE PRIVATIONS of the period, it was not easy to notice that something new was being born, a new nation, a new place in the sun. To returning soldiers and militant workers, the war seemed a wasted effort, the Labour Government a let-down. Class consciousness still segmented the country into unwalled ghettos. A man's station in life was determined by the twang of his accent and the cut of his suit. England had not changed in any of its timeworn ways, except for the worse. Women, who had seized the work-bench during the war, were sent back to hearth and home. Universities made a show of opening their portals to returning heroes, but most students were middle- and upper-class products of prohibitively expensive 'public' schools or rigorously selective grammar schools. The route to a worthwhile occupation was restricted by class and upbringing.

Where one lived was policed by price and prejudice. A frock-coated estate agent in Belgravia would never show properties to a cash-flush street-trader; a Birmingham landlord did not rent rooms to blacks, foreigners and unwed couples. Wages were fixed by an owners' cartel, or a union rate; profits, on the other hand, were untrammelled. Income tax was deducted at source from the working man's weekly envelope; businessmen paid no tax on their off-shore accounts and investments. Industrial inaction, the revenge of the underclass, hit the poor before rich. Rationing, the white flag of economic defeat, was bypassed by the luxuried classes.

Most British homes had no telephone or refrigerator; many had no bathroom and only an outdoor toilet, often shared with neighbours. Fewer than one person in twenty owned a car. Promises of a better tomorrow sounded hollower by the day. A cloud of disillusionment settled across the country as its pivotal decade drew to a close.

'Left governments,' wrote George Orwell in March 1948, 'almost invariably disappoint their supporters because, even when the prosperity they have promised is achievable, there is always need of an uncomfortable transition period about which little has been said beforehand.'[1] These hidden costs of Socialism, added to the debts of war, had ruled out the bestowal of any peace dividend.

Yet events were taking place, within and beyond the island that, between the watery summers of 1947 and 1948, would alter England for ever, both materially and in its battered self-perception. The Empire, which for two hundred years had stoked the nation with mineral wealth, fresh markets and false pride, was about to be dismantled. On 15 August 1947, the union flag was lowered in New Delhi and the subjugated sub-continent partitioned into two states, India and Pakistan. A rage of bloodshed ensued between Hindus and Moslems, a holocaust unleashed by the cavalier incompetence of the viceroy, Lord Mountbatten, and the precipitate haste of the British people to be shot of their past.

In January 1948, Mahatma Gandhi, man of peace, was shot dead while at prayer. That same month, Britain withdrew from Burma. In March, civil war erupted in Malaya. In April, British forces pulled out of Palestine, leaving Jews and Arabs to fight out an unending war. East of Suez, England was speedily ending its dominion.

In Europe, Stalin solidified his eastern bloc with a putsch that in March 1948 ended democracy in Czechoslovakia and precipitated the shocking murder of Jan Masaryk, thrown from a high window of his Foreign Ministry in Prague. The Americans, alarmed at the spreading Soviet hegemony, began pumping Marshall Aid into western dependancies before the month was out. Luxury goods long absent from London appeared in Hamburg shop-windows, to the amazement of British squaddies. The status of their nation was slipping before their unbelieving eyes. Heroism and imperial power had given way to retreat and recession. Despondency set in, akin to defeat. Something had to be done to restore national self-esteem. It was not enough to build quarter of a million homes and announce educational reforms, as the Labour Government was doing. England needed an ideal, a New Jerusalem, something to love and believe in.

On 5 July 1948, that shining icon was unveiled by Aneurin Bevan, minister for health and housing, by the symbolic act of handing the keys to Park Hospital in Trafford, Manchester, to a delegation of doctors, nurses and public administrators. The National Health Service, harbinger of hope, had been born.

Bevan, a self-educated Welsh miner who went down the pit at fourteen, was the only member of Attlee's Cabinet of Old Etonians and union barons who could have prevailed against the combined resistance of the medical establishment, the pensions and insurance industry, the Treasury, the Tories and some of his fellow-ministers. It was a blazing achievement, the greatest by any politician since Lloyd George's social reforms of 1908, and made all the greater by the marginality of its inceptor.

Bevan relished opposition more than he enjoyed government. During the war he had refused to join Churchill's coalition, defending the right to criticize even in a national emergency. A blazing demagogue with a scathing tongue, married to the turbulent and beautiful Scottish MP, Jennie Lee, Bevan lambasted the Conservatives as 'lower than vermin'. To the landed gentry and the Tory press, he was the mouth-frothing hate-figure of a socialist regime that was reducing Great Britain to dull conformity. In every important decision of state, he put principle above practicality.

Bevan envisaged the National Health Service not as a poultice for the poor but as a provider of 'the most up-to-date' medical care for every citizen, 'irrespective of means, age, sex or occupation'. The Service was to be 'comprehensive and free of charge'. Its scope exceeded any system attempted in the most caring and paternalistic of societies, more catholic even than the cradle-to-grave nanny-states of Scandinavia and the Netherlands. Bevan freed hospitals from local control and smashed the resistance of family doctors by bribing senior consultants with honours and bonuses. No one was obliged to join the NHS, but ninety-five per cent of the populace registered within two months, along with nine out of ten GPs.

The dawning of the NHS changed the habits of the nation. Women who formerly had babies at home because they could not afford a hospital bed, now gave birth in state-sheeted safety. No one was now too poor to see a dentist or have an eye-test. No one had to ignore an ache until they could pay to have it examined. A goitred mendicant could be attended by the King's personal oncologist. At dinner one night, Bevan declared, 'tomorrow, thirty thousand people will hear who cannot hear today'.[2] He had spent all week assessing every available hearing-aid, before choosing the most expensive.

Nothing was too good for the national health. Even the rich, who saw private specialists, rushed to an NHS hospital if they had anything seriously wrong. The charitable nature of lower-order health care was consigned to the past. The National Health Service, said a Labour MP half a century later, 'marked the introduction of Christian values to English public life'.[3]

It was Labour's supreme accomplishment, immunized by public affection against future restraint. Bevan dreamed that costs would fall when the nation became healthy, its ailments cured. He later said, 'we shall never have all we need,' but he was building Utopia, not a budgetary formula. As British medicine ventured into heart transplants, test-tube babies and hip-replacements for the over-eighties, the bills ran into billions and the NHS became Europe's biggest employer, an over-centralized, cash-guzzling monster. But such was its iconic status that it became politically untouchable. Even the free-marketeering Margaret Thatcher was made to proclaim, 'the National Health Service is safe in our hands'. The NHS was the first emblem of post-war England, the crucible of a 'caring' society whose soothing unguents replaced the pomp and circumstance of imperial grandeur.

Thus it was that between the summers of 1947 and 1948, England retracted its horizons and became another country – a nicer country, some said, though one still far from self-knowledge and inner peace. Bevan's hall mat was filled each morning with hate-mail; he was jostled in the streets by hoodlums roused to outrage by the Tory press and elderly colonels wrote to *The Times* that the country was going to the dogs. But in the seminal summer of 1948, England's cricketers were thrashed by Don Bradman's Australians by four Tests to nil, and even diehards had to admit that the imperial lion was looking toothless and in need of a new coat.

Germany had begun its economic miracle and Europe was talking of unity. England, for its part, set off on a solitary voyage of self-discovery, a search for creative purpose that would supplant the 'civilizing' goals of building and ruling an Empire. The NHS represented social justice and scientific progress as putative goals, but the national aim remained uncertain. What would become of England when the last patch of red was gone from the atlas and the powers denied her a seat at the table? Did the Old Country have anything left to offer the world? Had the war been fought in vain?

One answer, for those who kept a finger on the national pulse, came where it was least expected – in an art where no Englishman had excelled for two centuries and a half, an art dismissed by the greatest of English dictionarists as 'an exotick and irrational entertainment'. On 7 June 1945, a month to the day after peace returned to Europe, Sadler's Wells reopened with a new opera, *Peter Grimes* by Benjamin Britten. The composer was very young, just thirty-one, but not wholly unknown. Before the war he had produced a piano concerto at the Proms and a suite of string variations at the Salzburg Festival. Moving to America with his companion, the tenor Peter Pears, he wrote a mid-Western Singspiel, *Paul Bunyan*, with a text by the expatriate poet W. H. Auden. He received more commissions and was widely performed, but Britten was beset by feelings of guilt and longing. Pears, browsing in a second-hand bookshop in Los Angeles, bought him an 1851 edition of the poems of the anti-romanticist George Crabbe (1754–1832). Some days later Britten read a magazine article by the novelist E. M. Forster, beginning with the words: 'To think of Crabbe is to think of England.'[4] 'I suddenly realized where I belonged and what I lacked,' he said.[5]

Peter Grimes relates the torments of a strong-willed fisherman, hounded by his village after the death of an apprentice boy at sea. It had nothing to do with war, victory, democracy, reconstruction, or any other burning issue, except in the most ethereal and generalized sense. Where others wrote for the here and now, Britten dared to compose in a time and place all his own. He wrote swiftly and surely, the opus number, thirty-three, being greater than his age.

At Sadler's Wells, disgruntled singers declared the work 'a piece of cacophony' and sent an Equity trade union deputation to the governors to complain about Britten's 'excessive' publicity. The rebels demanded a democratic say in the company's repertoire. Joan Cross, chosen by Britten to sing the sympathetic schoolmistress Ellen Orford, resigned as company director. The baritone playing Captain Balstrode jumped ship with six weeks to go, declaring the music 'outlandish'. The hostility arose, it seemed, less from the music than from an awareness that the composer, tenor, conductor, Reginald Goodall, and producer, Eric Crozier, were all con-scientious objectors who had sat out the war, and that two of them were blatant homosexuals. A demonstration was threatened for opening night. 'Whatever happens,' said Tyrone Guthrie to Joan Cross in her dressing-room, 'we were absolutely right to do this piece.'[6]

When the curtain fell, the opera was greeted with total silence – a full thirty seconds, according to one report. Then the house erupted, and the curtain-calls were too numerous to count. The audience, wrote Crozier, 'did not know what had happened nor how they could have been so deeply affected'.[7] Over the following days, reviewers pronounced *Grimes* 'a work of genius',[8] 'an astonishing work'.[9] For the next three weeks, the doyen Ernest Newman wrote in the *Sunday Times* of nothing but *Grimes*. An American in London, the distinguished literary figure Edmund Wilson, wrote in his travel diary:

> By the time you are done with the opera – or by the time it is done with you – you have decided that *Peter Grimes* is the whole of bombing, machine-gunning, mining, torpedoing, ambushing humanity which talks about a guaranteed standard of living yet does nothing but wreck its own works, degrade or pervert its own moral life and reduce itself to starvation . . . you feel that you are in the same boat as Grimes.[10]

Every critic seemed determined to find metaphors in an opera that was emotionally as cathartic as it was tonally conservative. The much-touted modernism of *Peter Grimes* lay not in the music – 'it's full of howlers,' the composer sighed in later years – but in an ice-breaking presumption that art could psychoanalyse the English condition, and that England might be redeemed through its arts. 'It looks as if the old spell on British opera may be broken at last!' rejoiced Britten.[11]

Acclaim, however, did not quell the storms. Although *Peter Grimes* would be sung over the next four years on twenty-five foreign stages from Budapest to Los Angeles[12] and became the most performed of post-war operas, petty resentments persisted. The safety curtain was brought down early one night, cutting short the ovations. A BBC broadcast could not be recorded for posterity because the Sadler's Wells orchestra demanded extra money. A studio recording, paid for by the British Council, was cancelled when the company voted to tour Germany instead. After nine packed performances, Britten withdrew the work from Sadler's Wells. Guthrie resigned the day the season ended. Cross, Pears and Crozier followed soon after, forming an English Opera Company to produce Britten's forthcoming works in a joint venture with John Christie of Glyndebourne.

For Covent Garden, the sight of England's ascendant composer linking arms with the arch-enemy at Glyndebourne was life-threatening. If English opera was experiencing a rebirth, parturition could not be allowed to occur in a Sussex country barn. The Royal Opera House had been created, at public expense, to be the acme of national activity in the lyric arts. If the most thrilling new operas were appearing elsewhere and at no cost to the tax-payer, its existence would be foreshortened.

The ROH could, of course, call on other composers, from the genial Vaughan Williams to the languid William Walton who sat upon its Trust. But Britten had, with *Peter Grimes*, vaulted over all English composers, past or present. He was the man of the moment, a musician who transcended the musical ghetto and spoke to the heart of the nation. Unless it could accommodate Britten, Covent Garden could not expect to sustain its centrality, or indeed its survival.

Coming to terms with Benjamin Britten was never going to be easy. A hyper-sensitive soul who viewed the adult race with suspicion verging on contempt, he reserved a special loathing for large cities, long lunches and anything resembling the established order. Politically, he sympathized with the Moscow line on most issues. Professionally, he formed warm and fruitful relationships with writers, directors and many musicians, only to drop them without a word if he felt slighted, or found their usefulness had expired. Colleagues treated him like unwrapped nitro-glycerine. The only man who felt comfortable with Britten was his lifelong lover Pears, a slightly reedy tenor capable of astonishing on-stage intensity and groundless off-stage hatreds.

The Royal Opera House, whose very name resonated with rotten metropolitan privilege, was anathema to Britten. His publisher, Hawkes, was careful not to press its cause on the tetchy composer and Webster, who had commissioned *A Young Person's Guide to the Orchestra* for Liverpool, had no choice but to smile at Britten and say nothing about Christie.

On 12 July 1946 Britten's chamber opera, *The Rape of Lucretia*, began a two-week run at Glyndebourne before going on tour. It contained some of the most beautiful music he ever wrote and featured the operatic début of Kathleen Ferrier, a Blackburn telephonist whose rich contralto voice had enthralled factory audiences during the war. Out of costume she was plain 'Kath', beloved by all. She shared the role with Nancy Evans, wife of the record producer Walter Legge. Both needed a 'great deal of rehearsal before we could achieve [Lucretia's farewell] without bursting into tears'.[13]

Orchestral players found themselves dabbing their eyes and critics fumbled for superlatives. Howes in *The Times* predicted that Britten might 'lift opera out of the dead end in which it has been stuck since the death of Puccini'. There were some dissenters, however. Beverley Baxter, a Tory MP writing for the Beaverbrook press, 'longed for the orchestra to go out and have a drink so that we could hear the words'.[14] William Glock, a future BBC boss, called for 'a re-writing of the whole opera'.[15] Desmond Shawe-Taylor deemed the *Rape* 'less successful'[16] than *Grimes* and, with a year's hindsight, summarized a consensual view that it was flawed by Ronald Duncan's pretentious poesy and by a moralizing Christian ending that sounded both anachronistic and insincere. On tour in Edinburgh, Glasgow, Manchester, Liverpool and Oxford, the *Rape* played to half-empty houses. Christie complained there was 'no music in it'[17] and claimed he had lost eleven thousand pounds; the Arts Council gave him three thousand in compensation.

Britten made no effort to reassure his patron. In October, he declared independence from Glyndebourne, agreeing to return the following summer as a 'guest company' with a revival of the *Rape* and the première of *Albert Herring*, a laconic variation on English rural life. Directed by Frederick Ashton, who disliked Pears and loathed his voice, *Herring* was a tense affair. 'Ben wouldn't speak to Christie or allow him inside his own theatre,' said Ashton. Christie 'hated Ben's music and said so out loud,' reported the opera's designer, John Piper.[18] 'This isn't our kind of thing, you know,' Christie told his guests on opening night,[19] heaving a huge sigh of relief when the composer huffed off to found his own festival at Crabbe's fishing village of Aldeburgh. In 1948 his were still the only new operas seen in England since the war.[20]

Britten now flung down a gauntlet in the direction of Covent Garden, in the manifesto of his English Opera Group. 'We believe the best way to achieve the beginnings of a repertory of English opera,' said Britten, 'is through the creation of a form of opera requiring small resources of singers and players' – the antithesis of Webster's 500-strong payroll. Webster, timing his approach to perfection, took Britten to lunch with Karl Rankl a week later.

Dispensing with courtesies he got straight down to business, asking Britten to write a large opera for Covent Garden, offering a revival of *Peter Grimes* and assuring him that his friends Pears and Cross would be welcomed in the main roles.

'So far as the possibility of your Company finding a home at Covent Garden is concerned,' Webster summarized, 'neither of us can see anything against this, indeed we would be delighted to welcome you here, and to pursue enquiries to make that possible if you, on reflection, say so.

'We would like to assure you that no one connected with us would feel anything but the strongest desire to help and to co-operate with you in any plans you have for your Company . . . Both Karl and myself, however, would very much appreciate being taken into your councils and your discussions, completely unofficially, and we will willingly arrange as I have said as far as is possible for you having the use of any of our artists, or anyone you want . . .

'You need, I am sure, no assurance that both Karl and I feel most warmly to you personally and to your very great talents, and if there is anything that we can do at all to help you to realize your own ambitions for your Company, you have only to ask us.'[21]

The line had been baited and the fish was tempted. In November 1947 Covent Garden put on a new production of *Peter Grimes*, rejecting offers from a desperate Sadler's Wells to buy its original sets at half-cost (£1,050) and borrow half its chorus.[22] Rankl conducted the opening performance, but thereafter gave way to the expert Goodall. With Pears and Cross in the roles they created and stage direction by the steadfast Tyrone Guthrie, the opera was cast for safety. It lacked the shock of novelty yet, on a larger stage, seemed all the more momentous and, on opening night, was augmented in its sea-fog atmospherics by a fortuitous London pea-souper that penetrated every corner of the house.

If Britten could be induced to write a successor, there was every chance of Covent Garden achieving world renown. Yet, despite the accolades, doubts persisted about general standards of performance. Britten, dropping in on a second-cast night, dashed off a furious letter to Webster: 'I went to Covent Garden to see a performance of 'Grimes' recently and I must frankly say I was shocked by it, and I feel that to take the work abroad in this condition would be to its detriment and incidentally to the detriment of English Opera itself. The reasons, I think, are three: 1. Under-rehearsal; 2. A disregard of

dynamics and expression marks that has grown up; 3. Miscasting
. . . I hate to say this, but I feel that unless you can do something
about the performance I shall feel strongly inclined to put pressure
on my publishers to make the tour impossible . . .'[23]

Webster was unperturbed. With Glyndebourne out of the way,
there was nowhere else for Britten to take his operas unless he
wanted to save them for his Aldeburgh outpost. Britten was
important to Covent Garden but no longer essential. Covent Garden,
on the other hand, was now the only place where an English
composer could find a fitting home.

Webster did not bother to acknowledge Britten's asperities. Five
weeks later, he sent him a warm note reporting that '*Peter Grimes*
and the Company have had a great success both in Brussels and in
Paris. The Queen of the Belgians was at the first performance.'[24]

In the widening search for a world role, the English fell back on
language. England had given the world the most flexible and utilized
of modern tongues. English was the *lingua franca* of aerodynamics
and air traffic control. It had replaced German as the vernacular of
physics, psychoanalysis and biblical exegesis, and was taking an
unassailable lead in the uncharted infinities of computer science and
space research. It was the resolvent language of the United Nations,
the basis of international law. French and Italian might determine
couture and cuisine, and Russian was the rhetoric of occupied
Europe and dialectical materialism, but English held sway in
finance, technology and the horizons of unfolding knowledge.

It would be ridiculous to pretend that the ascent of English was
due to anything other than the military and economic might of the
United States. Nevertheless, the island that invented the language
maintained an arm-lock on its usage and development, both as
keeper of Shakespeare's chalice and as a prolific source of popular
literature. The world's top-selling children's author, Enid Blyton,
wrote the King's English, as did the most widely-read crime writer,
Agatha Christie. George Bernard Shaw was the most performed
living playwright. Winston Churchill, idle in opposition, was writing
a *History of the English-Speaking Peoples*. T. S. Eliot, who received
the Nobel Prize for Literature in 1948, had chosen (on the advice of
a fellow-American, Ezra Pound) to spend his creative life in
England. P. G. Wodehouse and Noël Coward were the living arbiters
of English wit. Hollywood actors and Ivy League preppies adopted

Oxford accents and wore Savile Row suits. The BBC was the world's most trusted provider of news and information.

With a grip on the American imagination and the currency of mass communications, it was just possible to envisage that England might regain by language the influence it was losing with empire. Those who turned politically rightward favoured a North Atlantic union of English-speaking forces in which England supplied the lexicon of leadership. Leftist thinkers preferred an English-speaking Commonwealth of nations that would unite the scattered shards of Empire and follow the stately procedures of the mother of Parliaments. Either way, the English language appeared to be England's best hope of resurgence, its premier asset.

The supremacy of the King's English was so taken for granted that it was scarcely debated as a cultural issue. Any institution that represented national aims needed to conduct its business in English – the more so if its art-forms had originated in another tongue and place. Italian and German, the parlance of opera, had been reviled for six years as enemy dialects. The Royal Opera House could not be their beachhead in Britain. 'The operas will be given in English,' affirmed Webster in a mission statement to the Arts Council.[25]

The question of opera in English had always been a shibboleth of privilege. The nobility and *nouveau riche* in the nineteenth and early twentieth centuries went to Covent Garden to hear foreign stars sing in foreign tongues. The lower classes made do with cut-price opera in English from Carl Rosa's touring troupe and the Sadler's Wells missionary ensemble. Miss Lilian Baylis wanted her visitors to understand what they heard on the opera stage. She found an ally in a crusty Cambridge professor, Edward J. Dent, who became her most fluent translator.

Dent was a recognizable English type: a bachelor misogynist, born into Yorkshire gentry but living on reduced means, an amateur at everything, fixed in his scholarly prejudices. 'One must look at things from an historical point of view,' was his stock phrase.

As a young Fellow of King's, Dent had planted in E. M. Forster's mind the plot for *A Room with a View*; he is immortalized in Forster's first novel, *Where Angels Fear to Tread,* as the pallid hero, Philip Herriton, who discovered the sap of life on a trip to Italy. Dent was tempted by foreign pleasures, but returned to spend his life in Cambridge, producing learned studies of Scarlatti and Mozart and English librettos for Miss Baylis's operas. Some of his translations were flecked with naïvety, or mischief. His finest line, from Tchaikovsky's *Eugene Onegin*, was, 'Balls in the country are quite a sensation . . . ,' which the chorus used to sing with unusual gusto. Still, beside the general run of opera translations – which, for example, had Colline, needing a shave in *Bohème*, sing: 'The first chance I get, I will scrape acquaintance/ With a beard eraser' – Dent's texts were fluent, musical and even witty.

His outlook was also redeemingly uncloistered. Although he loved Mozart above all composers and played a vital role in his English revival, Dent was an aficionado of modern music, a friend and biographer of Ferruccio Busoni and founder-president of the International Society for Contemporary Music. He was a born committee man. Although infirm and going deaf, he agreed to join the Covent Garden Trust with a view to sabotaging it on behalf of Sadler's Wells. 'I said to Webster,' he reported after a first meeting, 'I wished he could scrap the whole thing and make an entirely new interior out of it, without boxes, on modern democratic lines.'[26] As Sadler's Wells began to crumble Dent, mindful of his translator's royalties, set out to cultivate Webster and define new roles for both houses – both of them singing off his copyrighted sheets. It was Dent who proposed that Covent Garden should be reserved for 'grand opera' and Sadler's Wells for 'opéra comique', a distinction that endured in principle for the next half-century. With unerring self-interest, he also proposed they should jointly publish opera librettos in English.[27]

With Webster, Dent soon found common ground. 'He is rather fat and prosperous looking, not unlike John Christie,' he informed Clive Carey, the Sadler's Wells manager, 'but whereas Christie has the "powdery" pink and white surface of a Raeburn, and looks so Victorian that you almost think he's got mutton-chop whiskers, Webster is pink with a high polish, and ought to be Lord Mayor of some big provincial town.'[28]

Webster encouraged Dent to believe he was a man after his own heart, committed to the performance of opera in English and the creation of an indigenous repertory. Webster was also anxious 'to secure the adoption of standard English versions by schools, teachers and opera companies throughout the English-speaking world'[29] – in accordance with the national agenda.

Amid the debris of an ill-attended opening season, however, Webster was plotting a retreat. 'One of our biggest drawbacks appears to be that we are performing in English,' he reflected at the opening of the 1947-48 season, '. . . it seems incredible that certain sections of the public view opera in English as inferior to opera in foreign languages.'[30]

Early that year, the Austrian legation in London had proposed that the BBC's Third Programme should bring over the Vienna State Opera for a series of live broadcasts. The BBC asked Webster if he might stage the operas and Walter Legge at EMI if he wanted to record them. 'Of course we'll put them on,' cried Webster.[31] Unheard for eight years, the Viennese possessed the world's finest ensemble, albeit one which had embraced Nazism with unexampled enthusiasm. In June, Webster flew to Vienna with contracts for seventeen performances of *Fidelio, Don Giovanni, The Marriage of Figaro* and *Salome*. In September, the Vienna State Opera arrived at Covent Garden to be met by angry demonstrators – not, as feared, concentration-camp survivors, but members of the Musicians' Union, protesting at the engagement of the Vienna Philharmonic Orchestra in place of their Covent Garden pit band.

It did not take more than a minute of Overture to underline the qualitative difference. 'It was a standard of performance people hadn't heard here for years,'[32] exclaimed a BBC official. The celestial voices of Maria Cebotari, Elisabeth Schwarzkopf, Irmgard Seefried, Hilde Gueden and Sena Jurinac, followed by the rippling eroticism of Ljuba Welitsch as Salome, were the talk of the town. Hans Hotter was the Count in *Figaro*, Julius Patzak the Florestan in *Fidelio*, Anton Dermota the Ottavio in *Don Giovanni*, each unequalled in his role. The exiled Richard Tauber was reunited with his former colleagues, singing Ottavio in the last opera of his life before entering hospital with a fatal illness.

Rankl was to have conducted *Figaro* but proved incompatible with the Viennese. Josef Krips took the baton in Mozart, Clemens Krauss in Strauss and Beethoven. Webster scuttled around back-stage signing up young singers. He bypassed Cebotari, Hitler's favourite, and for unaccountable reasons the lustrous Jurinac, who went to Glyndebourne. But in scooping up the cream of Vienna, Webster altered the character and purpose of his company. Gone was the determination to promote 'the British artist'. Covent Garden would become a multinational company, still singing in English to be sure, but not for long.

Hotter returned to sing Hans Sachs in English in *The Mastersingers*, the first Wagner opera since the war (the chorus line 'Honour your German masters' was tactfully amended to 'your noble masters'), followed by Wotan in *The Valkyrie*. His diction was so mangled that Webster and Rankl, without reference to the Trustees, reverted other operas to their original language.

In February 1948, German rang out, harsh and guttural, from the stage of the Royal Opera House, Covent Garden. The opera was *Tristan und Isolde* and all eyes were on Kirsten Flagstad, the magnificent. Flagstad, who had first appeared in 1934 and spent the war in her native Norway, was desperate to sing in London again. Her husband, Henry Johansen, had been arrested as a Nazi collaborator and died in jail awaiting trial. Her American engagements were cancelled; 'we really needed those concerts and the money,' she sighed.[33] More than the income, she physically needed to sing. A heavy-boned, placid woman, apparently without nerves, she would sit knitting and sipping stout in her dressing-room until the stage-call came to go out and die. 'Apart from my work, I am just an average woman,'[34] she said, and meant it.

Her return was a revelation. 'She walked into rehearsal at ten in the morning, folded her arms across her chest and sang full out. I had never heard any sound like it,' recalled Iris Kells. Out in the market, porters stopped in their tracks when Flagstad let rip with 'Tristan, Geliebte!' Her first Tristan, August Seider, was overwhelmed. He was replaced by the resonant though diminutive Swede, Set Svanholm, who reached Flagstad's midriff.

Riding a taxi to work, she often gave a lift to walking choristers and showered many kindnesses on junior colleagues. 'What I loved about Flagstad was that she never made me feel a little secondary artist,' said the fast-maturing Constance Shacklock, who became her constant companion. 'In three months, I didn't know my own voice or my own self. I just wanted to be like her.'

Her attitude was not shared by other imports. Hotter was polite but superior. Schwarzkopf could learn a role in perfect English at twenty-four hours' notice but 'was not particularly friendly'.[35] She had left Vienna and moved in with Legge, joining Covent Garden on sixty pounds a week, which was fifteen pounds cheaper than native principals. Her Aryan beauty and silvery voice won public and critical acclaim.

In addition to Germans, Webster also bagged a brace of Italians –

Paolo Silveri of the San Carlo company and Elda Ribetti, who had married an Englishman. Neither did much for morale and their first appearance in *Rigoletto*, was deemed 'a stupid misuse of public money'.[36] English amateurism could be tolerated, but adequacy and arrogance were unacceptable in foreigners.

As the English lines of his company blurred, Webster was hustled into an unnaturally bold move. A reflective man, known to his board as the Arch Procrastinator, Webster liked to put off major decisions until the problem had gone away or the outcome became inevitable. He was on the way to assembling a professional opera company, but he had yet to imprint his own aesthetic preferences on the enterprise. What Webster loved above all was glamour. He needed to reinforce Rankl's tetchy and tunnel-visioned artistic leadership with a real innovator, preferably an Englishman.

In the autumn of 1947, Webster removed Frederick Ashton's name as Production Consultant from opera playbills, having received a visit from a young job-seeker. Peter Brook had directed a quick and witty *Love's Labours Lost* at Stratford-upon-Avon, followed by a hotly disputed *Romeo and Juliet*. He was being spoken of in some quarters as the white hope of English theatre, and was all of twenty-two years old. Webster, impressed, offered him a job, recanted, kept in touch and finally told the Trustees that he wanted a Director of Productions, a title Brook had invented on the spur of the moment. Webster told them that Brook had 'a first-class musical mind' and was Britain's brightest theatrical spark. His encomium was approximately half-true.

The son of Latvian-Jewish radicals who came to England and invented a popular laxative, Brooklax, Brook grew up in suburban Chiswick with a burning fascination for footlights. At Oxford, he started a University Film Society and directed his first movie. At twenty, he was putting on shows in Birmingham and the West End. He despised the 'niceness' that emasculated contemporary English drama, dominated by Rattigan and Coward, and was drawn more to the caustic absurdities of Cocteau and Anouilh. His directorial style turned dangerously improvisational. Before going to Stratford to direct *Love Labour's Lost*, he recalled,

I worked it all out beforehand, every move, with little arrows on pieces of paper. Then the first rehearsal began and I gave out the instructions. Everyone obeyed, but I looked and suddenly realized, 'This is dreadful. Stop, start again.' My plans were no good because they were plans. From that day onwards, I never prepared anything in detail.'[37]

Brook breezed into the Royal Opera House with a brief to shake up its opera productions, which he found 'unbelievably bad'. He had taken piano lessons as a boy from a former teacher at the Moscow Conservatoire, but had limited knowledge of grand opera and no love of its mannered ways. 'I entered the opera with one simple aim,' he wrote, 'to give this sleepy, old-fashioned institution a series of shocks that would jolt it into the present-day world.'[38]

He ran up against the rock of reality in the shape of 'Bogey' Ballard, the wing-collared, octogenarian backstage boss who ruled the bowels of the house. Brook ordered a change of scenery for *La Bohème*; Ballard insisted on doing things the way Mr Puccini had instructed him. Brook went to Webster, suggesting that Ballard should be considered for gentle retirement. Old Bogey, however, was the only man who knew where anything was kept backstage. Decrepit as he was, Ballard outlasted the upstart Peter Brook.

The first production by the new director was Mussorgsky's *Boris Godunov*, an epic work that appealed to Brook's Baltic blood and his love of filmic crowd scenes. Unable to find an English designer who felt the same way, he borrowed a Russian, Georges Wahkevitch, from Roland Petit's Parisian ballet company. *Boris* was a striking success, diminished only by Silveri's tameness in the title role. A year later, when the Bulgarian Boris Christoff made his début, the opera glowered with menace. Christoff and Brook were at each other's throats until the very moment the curtain rose.

Like any young lion let loose in a flamingo pool, Brook wreaked havoc among the singers. No respecter of vanities, he yelled at German sopranos like a Gauleiter, commanding their unquestioning obedience. Some he rejected as too fat or ugly, not normally an impediment to operatic success. He encouraged the sexy Ljuba Welitsch to vamp up Musetta in *Bohème* and steal the show from Schwarzkopf's Mimi. He let off fireworks in the finale of *Figaro*. Some believed he mistook it for another opera, perhaps Strauss's *Ariadne auf Naxos*. 'Peter Brook was different,' commented one singer. 'Whatever else could be said of him, he was different.'[39]

His shortcomings were nakedly apparent and loudly bemoaned.

His musical knowledge was limited and his improvisational style was readily mistaken for indecision. A last-minute change of mind could upset fifteen soloists, two hundred men and women in the *Boris* chorus and a ninety-strong orchestra. Unable or unwilling to act out roles, Brook used verbal imagery that went above the singers' heads. 'Finding out what he wanted was very hard work,'[40] said David Franklin, who sang Colline in the cat-fight *Bohème*. 'I don't believe he had listened to the piece before he produced it,' was Gellhorn's impression.

'I never had the four principal men together in rehearsal at the same time,' Brook complained of that production. 'If three of them were there, the fourth was inevitably away – not resting, as was always claimed to be so important for the voice, but flying to Paris for a quick morning recording, or to a provincial German city to snap up an extra fee for a recital. Instead, a stage manager would stand in for the missing character, holding a large score and enthusiastically singing out-of-tune Lancashire Italian.'[41]

Brook did not disguise his contempt for antideluvian backstage crews and pompous prima donnas. He sought to empower lesser artists by giving choristers and understudies an evening off and two free tickets in exchange for a written report of their impressions. Ninette de Valois and Frederick Ashton were not amused when chorus singers found fault with their ballets, and the initiative was discontinued.

Brook was determined, as Mahler had been in Vienna, to eliminate sloppy traditions. When he cut out the sordid bit of stage business in *Figaro* where the Count rests his hand on Susanna's bosom, Rankl objected, saying he could not conduct to any different action. Brook stood his ground, and Rankl became his sworn enemy. By the time they collaborated in *The Olympians* by Arthur Bliss, Covent Garden's first commissioned opera, the director of productions and the musical director were no longer on speaking terms.

Senior critics, too, resented change. Ernest Newman, aged eighty, grumbled that *Boris Godunov* 'touched for the most part the lowest depths to which Covent Garden has yet fallen'.[42] Newman, on the other hand, adored *The Olympians*, proclaiming Bliss to be England's Verdi and J. B. Priestley his Boito. The opera, a vain attempt to reflect England's hosting of the 1948 Olympic Games, had ten half-sold performances and four on tour before vanishing forever.

Brook provoked a clash of antipodal cultures, New English Theatre versus Old Fogy Opera. The climax came with *Salome*, for which Brook ordered designs from Salvador Dali, the Spanish surrealist. The shimmering 'Palestinian night' of Richard Strauss's score was to be represented by the spread tail of a giant peacock – across which Dali, until Brook dissuaded him, proposed to parade a flying hippopotamus. The costumes were grotesquely uncomfortable even after adaptation by London seamstresses. The pouting Welitsch refused to wear hers and Shacklock, as Herodias, appeared to be entombed in a yellow tent. 'I did not set out to shock,' said Brook. Dali stayed away.

On 11 November 1949, a Friday night, Welitsch earned tumultuous acclaim as the sexiest Salome in memory. 'Salome Lost 7 Veils But She Won 14 Curtains' ran the *Daily Herald*'s headline.[43] Rankl did not come out for a curtain call and Brook faced scattered boos. 'Rankl on the first night refused even to talk to Brook,' recalled Peter Gellhorn.[44]

The heavyweight press, sensing dissension, fomented a full-scale theatrical scandal. Newman, in the sombre columns of a Remembrance Sunday newspaper, denounced 'the most miserable *Salome* I have ever heard,' and demanded to know 'how much longer the London opera public will be expected to tolerate performances and productions at Covent Garden that are for the most part an affront to its intelligence. How long, O Lord, how long, we ask.'[45]

Brook was sacked the next morning – 'I was out on my ear'[46] – and the Director of Productions post was abolished. Salome was taken off after six performances and the sets were jubilantly smashed up by stagehands, acting on Bogey Ballard's orders. On the verdict of two octogenarians who knew little of the world beyond music and opera, England's most brilliant theatrical animator was thrown overboard. *Salome* may have been a mistake and he had made other errors of inexperience, but Brook brimmed with ideas. There is no telling what he might have achieved had he been granted another two years at Covent Garden.

Over the next half-century, Peter Brook became the guiding light and inspiration to every significant British director, from Peter Hall to Deborah Warner. His nine-hour production of the Hindu *Mahabharata* was one of the wonders of the modern world. His Stratford *King Lear* with Paul Scofield in 1962 was a milestone in Shakespearean interpretation and his account that year of *The*

Persecution and Assassination of Marat, as performed by the Inmates of the Asylum of Charenton under the direction of the Marquis de Sade amounted almost to a theatrical rebirth. He took eleven actors on a ten thousand-mile village trek across Africa. He visited Cuba and mounted fiery denunciations of the Vietnam War. In 1967, Brook moved to Paris, establishing an International Centre for Theatre Research and an ever-evolving, borderless culture at the Bouffes du Nord theatre. He never returned to Covent Garden.

In a choice between talent and tradition, the ROH settled for ritual. The company, young as it was, was already too arthritic to experiment in any form that challenged the restrictive, predictable disciplines of singing and dancing. In any artistic revolution, Covent Garden occupied the rearguard. Its stage directors, after Brook, would not frighten the horses, the singers or the Lord Chamberlain, who vetted all productions for nudity and profanity. Rising costs, antiquated working methods and unworkable ideals had led Covent Garden to plump for safety, stasis and compromise. Noël Coward, watching a *Bohème* with Victoria de los Angeles, found the production 'disgraceful' and the tragedy 'hilarious',[47] so flaccid were the company's theatrical values.

Gone was the blazing commitment to Englishness, the English language and an English *Gesamtkunstwerk*. Covent Garden was on the way to becoming just another opera house, a prospect which opera and ballet lovers viewed as a healthy sign of normality and other arts regarded with distaste and detachment. Covent Garden was the agent of its own isolation. It remained to be seen whether the country would support the self-regarding citadel of a pair of costly minority arts.

The first alarm sounded just before the start of the second season when Webster diffidently warned his chairman of impending embarrassments. 'I am especially sorry that we may have to go to the Treasury again this year,' he wrote, 'I was so hoping we could put off the second visit until next year. I thought we would have at least £30,000 against contingencies, but the slump has deprived us of most of this. I am sufficiently optimistic to believe that we shall do better in the Autumn, but that is mere belief.'[48]

If he anticipated a sharp intake of breath, he need not have feared. Sir John Anderson was too seasoned an administrator to be upset by budgetary vacillations. His life had been dedicated to oiling the

wheels of government and shielding officialdom from the consequences of its dutiful errors. He was the problem-solver *par
excellence*. A man who had held the nation's purse-strings in a war
of survival was not going to be daunted by the petty difficulties of a
place of entertainment. Nor was he concerned by the niceties of any
'arm's length' principle. He demanded a complete breakdown of
costs and Webster, ever the perfect shopkeeper, reeled it off in a
dictated memo, probably without having to look at the ledgers.

It cost, he reported, precisely ten pounds less than six thousand a
week to keep the lights on at Covent Garden. The electricity bill
came to £75. Stage hands and stage management earned £445. The
ballet management cost £275, the musical conductors, repetiteurs
and pianists £340, wardrobe and dressers £170. The chorus were
paid £615, the ballet dancers £810 and all the opera soloists together
eleven hundred pounds. By far the largest expense was the
orchestra, assembled by Webster and bleeding his company at the
rate of fifteen hundred and sixty pounds a week, or more than a
quarter of its total outgoings.[49]

This was obviously the key area for making economies. The
musicians were on ten-month contracts and could be dismissed
without penalty at the season's end. The orchestra was, by common
consent, unimpressive. Yet neither Webster nor Anderson apparently
thought of reducing or replacing the orchestra, a move which would
have staunched the company's deficit at a stroke. For Webster,
cutting the orchestra would have meant an admission of error and a
sticky negotiation with the irascible Rankl. For Anderson, it would
have gone against the grain to disestablish part of an organization
and undermine the status quo. The orchestra was thus left
untouched, storing up problems for the future.

Anderson's response to the crisis was twin-track. For ready cash,
he negotiated an ROH overdraft with Sir Jasper Ridley, chairman of
Coutts, the exclusive little bank where the Royal Family kept their
chequeing accounts. For longer-term stability, he went to see the
Chancellor of the Exchequer. The arts-friendly Hugh Dalton had
been forced to resign in November 1947 over an inadvertent leak of
Budget details and his successor, Stafford Cripps, was austerity
personified. Anderson, however, prepared his ground assiduously
with Treasury officials and came away with gold. In January 1948,
Mary Glasgow at the Arts Council heard from a Treasury colleague
that 'when the Chancellor saw your Chairman and Sir John

Anderson, he said that he proposed to ask Parliament to vote £550,000 as a grant for the Arts Council, of which £120,000 would be earmarked for grant to the Covent Garden Trust and would not be available for other purposes.'[50]

Problem solved, or so it must have seemed. In exchange for no extra undertaking on its part, Covent Garden had received a quintupling of its original allowance – along with a direct line to the privy purse that bypassed Arts Council providers. The Anderson deal was not merely high-handed but improper, violating the terms of a Royal Charter. Christie, who knew Cripps, resumed his epistolary attacks on the ROH. He demanded a triple merger of Covent Garden, Sadler's Wells and Glyndebourne. When that was ruled out, he called for panel of professionals – Walton, Legge, Rankl – to take charge of the ROH's weak casting and repertoire, pointedly excluding Webster.

Cripps, mildly concerned, summoned Anderson who assured him that the future health of the ROH was 'more important than any temporary fluctuations in the standard of performance'. This annoyed the crusty Chancellor, who demanded a written report, with specific recommendations for artistic improvements. Anderson set up a sub-committee, which conceded the inadequacy of some productions and the need for appointing an artistic adjutant to the General Administrator. This clipping of Webster's wings seemed to reassure Cripps, who then authorized an even greater gift.

The five-year lease on the building held by Boosey & Hawkes was due to expire at the end of 1949 and the impresario Jay Pomeroy, whose West End opera season was going well, put in a bid for a new forty-two year lease. Leslie Boosey rushed in alarm to the Arts Council. The Government was alerted and in August 1948 a compulsory purchase order was issued, acquiring the Royal Opera House on behalf of the Ministry of Works. This brash intervention in the open market drew bitter criticism in the Tory press, which condemned the purchase as an act of state theft. Boosey, withdrawing quietly, was landed with a £180,000 Ministry of Works bill for 'dilapidation'.

The stage was set for the grand master of malice, the easily-goaded goatee, to deliver his show-stopper. In January 1949, Sir Thomas Beecham addressed the annual conference of the Incorporated Society of Musicians, a grass-roots organization volubly dismayed at the rising numbers of foreign singers at Covent

Garden. Deeming the moment propitious for a full-blown barrage at his enemies, Beecham took his standard precaution of inviting the national press to Brighton to savour his coruscating wit. He began, quietly enough, by asserting that no member of the Covent Garden Trust 'knew anything about opera or had any practical experience of it'. He accused Leslie Boosey and Ralph Hawkes of profiteering from the enterprise, and then turned his fire on the artistic leadership:

> The appointment of an alien, and especially one bearing a German name, to the post of musical director of the British national opera is so incredible that I have from time to time to remind myself that it has actually happened and is not some fantastic dream. It must be, I think, because the hapless set of ignoramuses and nitwits who conspired to bring this about – this disaster – were under the impressions that the functions of a music director in an opera house were of such exotic, intricate and profound a nature that only a person of the sublime intelligence of a Teuton could grasp and manipulate them.

This was classic Beecham – irony wrapped in ridicule and a dubious cloak of patriotism, brilliantly extemporized to produce a roar of laughter and a spatter of morning headlines. He avoided mentioning Webster by name, but castigated his casting and repertoire with the authority, and despair, of a man who had achieved greater things:

> In the bad old days (said Beecham) it used to be our practice to put the horse before the cart and to discover what vocal resources we had at our disposal, and to make our choice of works accordingly. The modern practice it would seem is to select the work and afterwards discover that we have not the singers to take part. That is but one of the symptoms of comparative insanity which prevails in that unfortunate institution and among its backers.

Beecham demanded a public inquiry into this 'strange and un-English way of doing things; let them see the evidence of how the vast sum of £100,000 has been spent in one year with so little to show for it.'[51] Boosey, incensed, reached for his lawyers. Rankl told *The Times* that he 'never replied to any public criticism'. Anderson reached for his pen and composed the dustiest of public-servant replies:

> I have read the remarks attributed to Sir Thomas Beecham with surprise and regret. Sir Thomas's eminent services to music are well known but unfortunately his great gifts are associated with other characteristics including as he has demonstrated again and again an unbridled tongue . . .
>
> As regards Dr Rankl, the musical director, it was necessary in the unanimous judgement of the Trust to have in their possession someone with extensive practical experience of the day-to-day working of an opera house . . . The Trustees have the highest admiration for the manner in which he has addressed himself to his task.
>
> The fact that since the beginning of the present opera season audiences at Covent Garden have maintained an average of nearly ninety per cent of capacity justifies the inference that the public are far from sharing Sir Thomas's dissatisfaction.[52]

Back in Brighton, rebuttal came from an unexpected quarter. Steuart Wilson, ex-singer and Keynes's CEMA sidekick, now Director of Music at the BBC and a member of the Covent Garden Trust, delivered an apparently spontaneous counter-blast. He dismissed Beecham as 'irresponsible and foolish' and claimed, untruly, that the great man had never shown faith in English singers. As for allegations of waste, Covent Garden had a payroll of 599, two hundred fewer than the Paris Opéra, which received five times as much state subsidy.[53]

Beecham returned to the subject some days later in the *Daily Telegraph*, but sounded subdued and especially keen to exempt Webster from blame:

> For the Administrator of this pathetic fiasco I have some compassion. Not so long ago he publicly stated that owing to his inability to find English singers who could fill competently many of the roles in the operas being given at Covent Garden, he had been forced to import a necessary contingent of foreigners. Since then the influx of the alien element has increased, to the manifest chagrin of scores of native vocalists who consider, rightly or wrongly that there is no justification for this invasion. Anyway, it

can be disputed by no one that if we cannot have opera in Covent Garden represented fittingly without the regular appearance of non-British artists in the principal roles, the case for National Opera in this theatre is blown sky-high.[54]

All Beecham wanted was an opportunity to vindicate past glories. Over the following months he cultivated John Denison, the Arts Council's music officer, with a proposal to put on a summer season of operas – two at Covent Garden and one at Sadler's Wells. Denison showed Beecham's letter to Webster – 'I'm treading very carefully, because there will be a delicious rumpus if these negotiations come to grief!'[55] – and the General Administrator sent back a signal that Beecham would be welcome to conduct at Covent Garden, whenever and whatever he liked. Beecham demanded *Meistersinger* with twice the normal chorus, regardless of cost. Webster coolly acquiesced. An influential antagonist had been judiciously neutralized, for the time being at least.

Pomeroy, too, withdrew from the fray, ruined by a devastating bill for three hundred thousand pounds from the Inland Revenue, one of Anderson's former fiefdoms. His retirement meant that no rival opera would play against Covent Garden in the West End. In a bitter parting shot, Pomeroy declared: 'Opera becomes its superlative self only when its ingredients – music, singing and acting – speak with one voice. At Covent Garden, these more often than not are not even on speaking terms.'[56]

Christie also retreated, preoccupied with reopening Glyndebourne in July 1950 and shuttling its productions back and forth to the newly founded Edinburgh Festival. He lost Rudolf Bing to the Metropolitan Opera and, in successive summers, Fritz Busch and Audrey Christie to fatal illness. Vittorio Gui conducted, Sena Jurinac sang and Glyndebourne regained its summer role, separate unto itself.

Covent Garden had survived its winter of political and cultural discontent. Attendances were rising and there was evidence of a committed audience forming around the house as it had done two decades earlier at Sadler's Wells. A monthly *Ballet* magazine, edited by a perceptive aesthete Richard Buckle, had expanded into *Ballet and Opera*, the latter half edited by the King's nephew, the Earl of Harewood, who had mastered the history of opera while in German wartime custody. The journal was sparky enough to receive libel writs from Beecham. By the end of 1949 its two halves were serving separate readerships and split apart. Harewood, who had just married Marion Stein, daughter of Britten's editor, appointed an opera-mad North London schoolmaster, Harold Rosenthal, to edit *Opera* magazine, which became a cheerleader for ROH plans and aspirations.

As a further bolstering of public support, Anderson and his Board (the Trust had been disbanded and reconstituted with the change of property ownership) renewed Webster's contract and fulfilled their pledge to Cripps to repair artistic inefficiencies by appointing a Deputy General Administrator. He was none other than Steuart Wilson, newly knighted and signing himself on all occasions 'Sir Steuart'. Wilson had spent two and a half years at the BBC, making no mark on the Third Programme but vengefully procuring the removal from the BBC Symphony Orchestra of its founder-conductor, Sir Adrian Boult, whose sin, it seemed, had been to take in the wife and four children that Wilson, an avid womanizer, had abandoned in 1932. Wilson promised to replace Boult with John Barbirolli; he failed, and the BBC were landed with Malcolm Sargent. Waspish, snobbish and untrustworthy, Wilson's enforced retirement at the statutory BBC age of sixty was a cause for musical glee – until it was learned that, by calling on old friendships with Professor Dent and other trustees, he had wangled himself a job at Covent Garden. 'I can't understand how Webster ever let him across the threshold,' said his Arts Council successor.[57]

In October 1950, Wilson had his favourite settee, wooden arm-chair and easy chair delivered to Covent Garden by BBC van. He was to be paid £2,500 a year for unspecified duties, and would be allowed to continue teaching, writing and broadcasting, 'subject to the agreement of the General Administrator'. He was recruited mostly for show, to reassure the Chancellor and deflect press criticism. 'His name from the public relations angle is extremely useful to us,' Webster assured Rankl, 'and his direct standing in the musical world is considerably greater than mine.'[58]

Wilson, however, had few friends in Whitehall or Fleet Street and was remembered by the musical public, if at all, as a reedy tenor well short of world class. He did little to raise confidence, outside the house or within. He was a stranger to loyalty and prone to deception. Webster, agreeing to his appointment, must have forgotten the afternoon in 1947 when he returned to the office one day to find

Wilson going through his drawers. Caught red-handed, the interloper had a ready excuse:

> Dear David,
> I am afraid that I inadvertently left you somewhat in the dark. At the Trustees meeting, when you were ill, it was agreed between Sir John and myself, that a summary of accounts should be presented to the Arts Council at the Council Meeting on September 25th and that I should get a break down of certain production figures but not circulate them until Sir John had approved. It was in the middle of this that you found me with Lund [the finance officer] and I completely forgot that you had not been at the meeting and had no idea what I was after.[59]

Intrigue entered the premises with Wilson; no one quite knew whom to believe. He would summon singers to his home for private coaching; those who refused had reason to fear that they could lose roles. His rejections were poisonously hurtful. 'You tackled a big hurdle the other day to convince us that you could go beyond what we all thought were limitations in your casting, and I am afraid you didn't convince us, though we would have liked to be convinced,' he told a chorus singer auditioning for solo parts.[60] 'I don't suppose that you have for some time thought that your position at Covent Garden was entirely satisfactory to you or that you were making good enough progress yourself,' he told a bass singer. 'As far as our company is concerned I think I must tell you candidly that I don't see a future for you . . . So I advise you to give up the idea of a career in singing as your livelihood and to return to what you were doing before the War, which I gather was an accountant . . .'[61] Sitting in judgement over England's new artists was an embittered ex-singer who had himself demonstrably failed to break into opera.

Wilson's appointment and Beecham's appeasement did not resolve the company's problems. They merely postponed the day of reckoning, which was Webster's way of coping with crisis. Beecham made a triumphal return in 1951, conducting *Meistersinger* to roars of acclaim from the old press codgers, who mostly chose to overlook his waning powers of concentration. In the middle of the second act Beecham went off into a reverie and, with the singers improvising for all they were worth, loudly expostulated, 'Good God, where are they?'[62] Blom, in the *Observer*, tactfully remarked: 'There were two good performances – one on stage, the other in the orchestra – which would not quite go together.'

On their way home from the 1950 Edinburgh Festival, the La Scala company stopped at Covent Garden and, under the baton of Victor de Sabata, showed up more of the local shortcomings. Renata Tebaldi and Tito Gobbi made their mark as ascendant stars and the orchestra was resplendent. Artistically, Covent Garden was a long way from its objectives, and financially its troubles were increasing by the month. A five-fold increase in state funding had been followed by a five-year freeze. Its roof leaked and its backstage was a danger to life and limb. Into the Treasury came a new generation of officials who knew not 'Old Jehovah', and Sir John Anderson's approaches fell on deaf ears.

Other arts were clamouring for money and Sadler's Wells Opera was clambering back to form under a trained pianist and former Treasury clerk, Norman Tucker, who had worked in Anderson's office during the war and knew his way around Whitehall. Tucker refreshed the Wells with English-sung British premières of unfamiliar Verdi – *Simon Boccanegra*, referred to by its conductor as 'Buck-nigger' – and the completely unknown Janáček, in the form of a heart-rending *Katya Kabanova*, sung by Amy Shuard and conducted by a Prague-taught Australian, Charles Mackerras. The Sadler's Wells Theatre Ballet, reconstituted by Ninette de Valois under her assistant Peggy van Praagh, took on a life of its own. A young South African choreographer, John Cranko, produced a startling *Beauty and the Beast* and in April 1950 the elegant Svetlana Beriosova joined the company from the Metropolitan Ballet, New York. To the dismay of de Valois, critics like the *Observer*'s Richard Buckle favoured the underdog company with its fresh crop of legs to the respected pillars at Covent Garden. Another South African, Nadia Nerina, technically the best dancer in town, was poached by Covent Garden, as was the fast-rising Kenneth MacMillan. Sadler's Wells formed reciprocal ties with Lincoln Kirstein at New York City Ballet and was fulfilling a vital function as the nursery of British dance.

Covent Garden could no longer justify its claim for one-fifth of Arts Council funds, especially when the Council chairman, Pooley, had sentimental ties to Sadler's Wells. The Royal Opera House was being bled white by its inconsistent and painfully vulnerable opera company. The one factor which kept Covent Garden in credit was its ballet company, which not only produced a small nightly surplus but was starting to earn decent sums abroad. Webster, escorting its first American tour, sent a jubilant message to Anderson, to be 'passed on to the Chancellor'. In seventy-four performances over nine weeks, he reported, the Covent Garden Ballet had been seen by 225,000 people and received by the President of the United States and the Governor-General of Canada. It had also achieved 'the means of bringing back seventy-five thousand dollars into this country',[63] no mean amount when the Bank of England's hard-currency reserves were critically depleted. With the best ballet in the world, Covent Garden might somehow keep the wolves from its door until the country was prosperous enough to afford greater subsidy.

'It was always the ballet that bailed out the opera,' said Ninette de Valois, late in her centenarian life. 'They'd send the ballet away on a huge tour of the States and we'd come back with a lot of money to run the opera company. You can tour ballet easier than opera. They can't stand the change of climate, the rough and tumble. The voice doesn't stand up to it like legs and feet.'[64]

Madam had succeeded beyond mortal expectations. Under her iron rule English ballet had advanced, in twenty years, from nullity to world conquest. Its début at the Metropolitan Opera House on 9 October 1949, was a landmark in dance history, 'one of the most brilliant ballet openings New York has witnessed in this genera-tion'.[65] New York did not lack for good ballet. In George Balanchine, it had a Diaghilev choreographer who, backed by the monetary and organizational muscle of Lincoln Kirstein, founded New York City Ballet and other troupes. In Martha Graham and Merce Cunningham, Manhattan saw a pair of modern dance-masters, working in a notably American idiom with such forward-looking composers as Aaron Copland and John Cage. The balletic future belonged, it appeared, to the nuclear superpowers who had carved up the dance map between American adventurism on the one hand and hardline Russian traditionalism on the other.

Beside these behemoths there seemed little space for a third force, yet the newcomers of English ballet aimed to show something more than virtuosic novelty. Their repertoire was rich and self-wrought. Their style was discreetly distinctive. Their determination was immense. 'We feel that all the eyes of London and New York are upon us,' said Madam.[66]

When the curtain fell on *Sleeping Beauty*, the first uncut version of the ballet New York had ever seen, the Met exploded. Robert Helpmann heard the applause erupt 'like the sound of a gun'.[67] 'Everyone was hysterical,' recalled Margot Fonteyn. 'Crowds tried to reach the dressing-rooms; the doormen panicked . . . I felt like a person reprieved from the gallows.'[68] De Valois wrote: 'perhaps we shall never experience such a triumph again'.[69] The volleys of acclaim grew from one town to the next. Years later, the *New York Times* critic, John Martin, decided that the inaugural English tour represented 'the greatest opening of the popular audience the ballet had ever known in this country'[70] – a turning-point in American culture.

'That a dancing troupe from Paris would prove to be exhilarating and sexy was somewhat to be expected,' wrote *Variety* in a front-page splash. 'But that a ballet company from stolid Britain, the land of mutton and ale, of tweeds and Scotch whisky, would prove to be exotic and glamorous, was a complete surprise.'[71] Everywhere the dancers went, they were treated as heavenly guests. Some had not seen so much food, drink and leisured abundance since childhood.

Not everything they danced was instantly enjoyed. *Symphonic Variations*, the most thoughtful of Ashton's ballets, was written off as 'watered Balanchine' and De Valois' English *Job* drew a total blank. But America was bowled over by a troupe which tore the heart-strings in *Swan Lake* and could also tickle the ribs in *Façade* and *A Wedding Bouquet*, drily narrated by its conductor, Constant Lambert. This was an ensemble of all-rounders, a family of talents, and a source of boundless invention. America urgently demanded its return the next winter. Over the next three decades and more English ballet became a biennial fixture on the American entertainment scene. Against all odds, England had been granted a seat among the balletic superpowers.

Webster was entitled to a share of the laurels. He had purposefully lured the New York promoter Sol Hurok to Covent Garden's opening night in 1946 and then refused several invitations until Hurok procured the Met and accepted each and every one of Madam's demands. 'What made the whole business difficult,' said Hurok to Webster and De Valois, 'was that you were talking with two heads but one voice.'[72] A flamboyant Russian-born Jew who billed his own name bigger than his artists, Hurok had proposed the usual cuts in *Beauty* and sought to downplay the unknown Fonteyn in favour of the lovely Moira Shearer whose Powell-and-Pressburger film *The Red Shoes* had played fifty-seven weeks in New York. He even talked of replacing Fonteyn altogether with a US-based Russian ballerina. But Webster backed his ballet director and Hurok finally doffed his wide-brimmed fedora to the adamant woman he addressed, in a Russo-Brooklyn accent, as 'Madame de Vulva'.

Her obstinacy would be vindicated by the finest performances anyone had yet seen from Fonteyn, and by a public reaction that stopped two shrieks short of hysteria. 'I think we made it,' Fonteyn cabled her mother coolly. Weeks later, she was on the cover of *Time* magazine, a world star. At first, said Madam, 'it was only Margot . . . They didn't really see beyond her or the *Sleeping Beauty*. Then later they started to accept the choreography of the country.'[73]

Margot, for Madam, had always been the means to her end. English ballet needed a home-grown star, and she had sensed at first sight that Margot was just the star it needed. A fifteen-year-old girl called Peggy Hookham, part-Irish like herself but also English and Brazilian by descent and complexion, had applied to join her ballet school in 1934. Stage-named Margot and taking her mother's maiden name of Fontes, later Fonteyn, she appeared late in 1935 as the bride in Ashton's first Stravinsky ballet, *La baiser de la fée*, and as Odile in an almost-new *Swan Lake*. Alicia Markova was pirouetting out of the company on a high pointe, refusing to play ensemble parts, and Fonteyn slipped sweetly into her roles. One night she played a child whore in *Rio Grande*, the next a twinkling fairy. Having promoted her in an emergency, De Valois protected her from rivals and self-doubt. 'And some have greatness thrust upon them,' was her cabled exhortation to Margot on an early opening night.

Ashton defined her style and Lambert, her secret lover, drew out a piquant eroticism, but Fonteyn was always Madam's creation and fondest hope. 'Margot was her favourite,' said Moira Shearer, the Scots redhead whose cinematic appeal outstripped Fonteyn's stage-bound fame. 'I wasn't one of her girls. She called us all by our surnames, except Margot. After my first *Giselle* in 1948, Miss de Valois came round to my dressing room, screaming at me, purple in the face. She said, who taught you those things? I said, Madame Karsavina. At which point she went white in the face. The next I heard, Margot was taking lessons from Madame Karsavina.'[74]

'Margot had every first night, of every season, every production,' lamented Nadia Nerina with pardonable hyperbole. 'It was very frustrating for other ballerinas.'[75]

Nevertheless, after a decade at Sadler's Wells, Fonteyn's fame was confined to the ballet. She was skin-tight gorgeous, extensively photographed and elegant to a fault, but not quite a public figure. Three post-war factors transformed her status. The larger stage at Covent Garden endowed her with a degree of grandeur that made her seem larger than life and attracted an upper-class fan club. Fonteyn was the first member of the company to acquire snob appeal. 'I am afraid that as Margot is not dancing that evening, it is very difficult to make people buy expensive seats,' explained Kenneth Clark's wife, Jane, to Webster in May 1948. 'The first question everybody asks when we talk about this is what Margot is dancing. If I had known at the meeting, when the date was decided, that she would be in Paris, I should have protested very strongly against having the Gala evening without her.'[76]

What she was doing that springtime in Paris was enjoying her second lover, the dancer-choreographer Roland Petit, who taught her how to dress at Maison Dior and teased out a vein of seductiveness in her gestures. She had her nose surgically reshaped and luxuriated in new-found physical confidence. 'In Margot's life, I was just the person who, at the right time, opened the door,' said Petit.[77] It was American critics who first commented on her lack of English 'thinness and meagreness of temperament'.[78] Transatlantic triumph completed her five-year ascent from English all-rounder to world champion. Margot Fonteyn, as Madam had foreseen, was a human blank page on which history could be written.

She repaid the company's faith with due servility. Her weekly wage in 1950 was £100, thirty per cent higher than any opera singer but well below her escalating market value. La Scala offered her £150 a week to appear in Milan. Hurok dangled six hundred dollars a week for a US tour, more than twice her Covent Garden pay. But Fonteyn was a company girl, body and soul. When she needed to be with her lover, she politely requested leave of absence. When injured, she accepted half-pay. She lived with her mother and had few friends or interests beyond the ballet.

In 1953, fearing she might be lured away, Webster increased her US touring fee to twelve hundred dollars a week, four times her home salary. It was only after her marriage to the Panamanian diplomat Tito de Arias in February 1955, that Fonteyn evinced a need for pecuniary recognition. By 1962, she was making £400 a night at Covent Garden and $24,600 for thirty-six US appearances – all payments being made to a tax-sheltered Panamanian company, Diana, S. A., as befitted her elevated social status and her exceptional position at Covent Garden.

No other dancer had remotely the same allure. Shearer, a shy girl who disliked the bawdy side of ballet life, was dismayed at seeing life-sized effigies of herself outside cinemas where *The Red Shoes* was still showing. She had outplayed Helpmann in the film and was never forgiven for it by the Sadler's Wells old guard; when she stepped out in the title role on the first night of *Cinderella*, not one member of the company wished her luck. In America, she was content to let Fonteyn hog the limelight and shared her sleeping quarters on the company train without complaint. Newly married to the writer Ludovic Kennedy, she soon fell pregnant and retired from the stage, naming Fonteyn as godmother to her eldest daughter. The company's other principals, Beryl Grey, Pamela May and Violetta Elvin, did not presume to contest Margot's supremacy, knowing that Madam would tolerate no challenge.

The male dancers were of lesser calibre. Helpmann, Fonteyn's regular partner, failed to cover up low leaps and weak technique with comic winks and thespian skills. 'He was a pretty poor dancer, but a marvellous mime,' was the collegial verdict.[79] His place was taken by Michael Somes, a large-boned Devonian whose marriage to a fellow-dancer, Deidre Dixon, almost broke Frederick Ashton's heart. Ashton had been smitten with Somes since 1934, but the sexually ambivalent, emotionally repressed Englishman had a mind of his own and a temper to match. On stage, he caught and supported Fonteyn.

If Margot was the magnet for English ballet, Ashton was its creative mind. Most people were drawn to ballet to see beauty, whether of half-naked young bodies with exaggerated cod-pieces and visible bottoms, or of the chaste co-ordination of music and movement. Ashton added an unsought bonus: the prospect of cerebral stimulus. Ashton ballets tended to deal with adult issues rather than nursery stories. *Symphonic Variations* (1948), an abstract for six dancers to music by César Franck, contemplated the state of religious faith, sexual love and English pastoralism after the savagery of war. Liberated by Covent Garden's great spaces from the constraints of the Sadler's Wells stage, Ashton daringly stopped his dancers dead-still, arousing trains of thought about the individual's place in a fast-moving world. It was the first unqualified masterpiece of English ballet, wearing its seriousness without solemnity, its beauty without preening.

His next work was a failure, depicting Richard Strauss' *Don Juan* (1948) as an anti-hero, his virility weakened by austerity, the flaccid Helpmann almost scissored apart by a flying Fonteyn. In Prokofiev's *Cinderella* (1948), the prime roles were given to the Ugly Sisters, danced by Helpmann and Ashton himself with seditious disdain for fairytale endings. Ravel's *Daphnis et Chloe* (1951) he redeemed from romantic excess and presented as a conflict between corporeal and spiritual love. *Tiresias* (1951) touched on the insoluble conundrum of whether men or women get more out of sex. *Sylvia* (1952), with music by Delibes, was a soppy anachronism, written to please Fonteyn's American fans; but most Ashton ballets flung barbed questions at an increasingly receptive audience.

The choreographer had somehow reinvented himself as chronicler of modern England. He made the ballet intellectually respectable, and far more innovative than hidebound opera. Going to the ballet became as much an essential of civilized metropolitan life as reading the latest Graham Greene novel, seeing the new Terence Rattigan play or hearing a Britten première. Ashton was the engine for a ballet of ideas, making a sensual art socially relevant.

This amounted to a sensational leap, for the man as much as for the art. Ashton had grown up half-wild in a South American outpost and achieved little by way of formal education. He was physically lazy and did not seem always to know his own mind, but behind the slack exterior there ticked a busy intellect, allied to a comic streak that could send stiff-lipped royalty into fits of mirth. A voracious reader of classical and modern literature, Ashton infused his ballets with cultural allusions and confused dancers with ideas well above their heads. He could reduce them to tears with his turns and twists, but mostly cajoled them into position. He was exacting rather than tyrannical, and much loved.

Ninette de Valois was a more daunting proposition. 'She was awful to rehearse with,' said Shearer, 'she tore us apart down to the last toenail. But when it came to the performance it was clear that she had seen everything clearly in her mind – unlike Fred, who often seemed to improvise.' As a choreographer, Madam was approaching her nemesis. In 1950 she fashioned a *Don Quixote* to music by the modernist Catalan exile Roberto Gerhard. It was her first ballet in seven years and, as it proved, her last. Although respectfully received at Covent Garden, and despite brave performances by Helpmann and Fonteyn, the ballet bombed in New York. 'After the third of its five scenes, two or three dozen patrons rose from their orchestra seats and, with no apparent attempt to be covert about it, walked from the auditorium. From then until the end, departing figures provided an unbroken counterpoint to the movement on the stage,' reported *Musical America*, its critic, Cecil Smith, adding that 'the débâcle was of Miss de Valois's making . . . neither madness nor fantasy was evoked by the choreography.'[80]

But her appetite for achievement was unspent and, if her creative contribution was at an end, her energies could be applied all the more vigorously to imperial administration. She was in charge of two national companies and the ballet school that fed them with fresh recruits, a position of unparallelled authority. 'She was a very powerful woman,' said Shearer, 'almost a Hitler in her way of running things – though that may have been a good thing at the time. Ninette de Valois was, to me, the antithesis of Diaghilev in running a company. He was entirely generous, and she was closed.'

Others saw her in a gentler light, recalling that she was often racked by arthritic pain. 'She overcame personal feelings,' said Diana Gould who danced for de Valois before marrying the violinist, Yehudi Menuhin. 'To me she was helpful and kind and understanding.'[81]

There was something incorporeal about Madam, as if she did not fully belong to a race of flesh and blood. In an art that glorifies the human form, she dressed in shapeless jackets and skirts, swinging a bulging handbag. Even in her dancing days, she was not one to undress before others or expose bare skin on stage. Where many dancers hopped in and out of each other's beds like overfed rabbits, Ninette de Valois was impervious to lust and untouched by scandal. So detached did she seem from her own physicality that dancers stood before her as if before a heavenly throne. One dancer was fascinated by the contrast between Madam and her brother, the ballet photographer Gordon Anthony. 'Like many ballet fans and hangers-on, he was a tremendous pooftah. Gordon was completely effeminate, while she must have come out with all the male genes in the family.'[82]

'You were either petrified, or you adored her,' said Antoinette Sibley, a pupil at her school. 'She really liked naughty people, and I adored her. I answered her back. Someone like Anthony Dowell, who was reserved and trying too hard, had it much tougher.'[83] Madam had expanded the school in 1947 into a full-scale curricular establishment, taking children from nine years old to university entrance. The first intake were all girls, paying fifty-five guineas a term. A dozen boys were added the following year, most of them on scholarships. 'Madam only took (whom) she wanted and she had an incredible eye,' said one of the teachers.[84] She valued an all-round education and would not accept pupils into her companies until they had passed their School Certificate (GCSE) in at least five subjects. Sitting at a long table, flanked by satraps, she delivered snap verdicts on her charges – this girl bound for glory, that one for university.

She brooked interference from no one. Having loaned Beryl Grey to dance in *Carmen*, she withdrew her one night without notice, over the conductor's objections. 'There was no talking to her,' he sighed.[85] When Webster asked Moira Shearer and her husband to suggest a ballet synopsis to Covent Garden, their plot was dismissed unread by the ballet sub-committee because, said its chairman, Kenneth Clark, 'Ninette naturally feels that any new ideas for a ballet should at an early stage have been submitted to her.'[86] Webster, said his secretary Muriel Kerr, was 'terrified' of Madam and jumped out of his skin when her presence was announced in his vestibule.[87] She attacked him for being 'pro-opera' and fought by all means, fair and foul, to uphold the primacy of ballet at Covent Garden. But she knew that ballet needed to batten on to a thriving opera company to sustain its profile and employment and she was prepared to concede, when pressed, that Webster had his uses as 'a good businessman'.[88]

As the decade ended, the mood curdled. The Labour Government, having weathered economic woe and achieved most of its objectives, trod on a national corn when, in September 1949, Stafford Cripps devalued the pound from four dollars and three cents, to a paltry two dollars eighty. The measure was meant to revive British exports and it succeeded in due course. But the public recoiled in outrage at the humbling of their currency. England evinced an irrational pride in the solidity of sterling. The first Labour premier, Ramsay MacDonald, had sacrificed his last claim to be the people's choice by suspending the gold standard in 1931, causing the pound to lose twenty-five per cent of its value in a week. Now Cripps shrunk sterling by one-third overnight and the backlash was felt by every MP. Never having lost a by-election since the war, the Government saw its support plummet in constituency soundings. In February 1950 Attlee decided to cut and run ahead of a tough Budget, calling a snap election.

He almost lost. A politically oriented advertising campaign by 'Mr Cube', emblem of the sugar monopolists, Tate & Lyle, swayed voters against further nationalizations. Churchill talked of 'setting the people free' under the Conservatives and Labour lacked a counter-punch. Attlee was visibly weary, Cripps was dying of intestinal cancer and the rest of the party were gearing up for a succession struggle between power-clinging pragmatism, represented by Hugh Gaitskell, and the impractical idealism of Aneurin Bevan. Labour scraped home by a wafer-thin majority of eight seats and the post-war agenda was pulled to a stuttering halt.

Unheeded by politicians, the reversal had been foretold in art. George Orwell, in his *1984* valediction, portrayed a futuristic totalitarian state in drab colours that belonged, all too familarly, to 1940s Britain. Any extension of socialism was, inferentially, a threat to liberty. The menace was underlined by massive Communist advances in Europe and China. Intelligent support for any form of Marxist praxis was discredited by Arthur Koestler's influential polemic, *The God that Failed*. Socialism in England had gone as far as it would go.

A nation that boasted of equanimity was mired in misery. Francis Bacon, the finest painter to arise since the war, depicted only suffering and despair. Dylan Thomas, the popular poet, wrote of death and mourning. Graham Greene, the mainstream novelist, wrote of the death of love.

Hopes of creative renewal were scorned by the elysian T. S. Eliot who, in the year of his Nobel Laureateship, gave vent to a bitter diatribe that proclaimed the death of civilization:

> We can assert with some confidence that our own period is one of decline; that the standards of culture are lower than they were fifty years ago; and that the evidences of this decline are visible in every department of human activity. I see no reason why the decay of culture should not proceed much further, and why we may not even anticipate a period, of some duration, of which it is possible to say that it will have *no* culture.[89]

Cyril Connolly, whose literary magazine, *Horizon*, had thrived on wartime intellectual ferment, accused the Government of doing 'practically nothing' to help advance the culture. In 1949, he closed the magazine, citing public apathy and a dearth of talent. British cinema turned insular and escapist in a succession of stiff-lipped comedies and war films. English theatre was numbingly polite. The belief that art could rebuild society was fading, and the artistic ventures founded upon this faith were shaken in their very purpose.

At Covent Garden, the worm turned during election month. The commitment to Englishness was weakened yet again and Webster was ordered to summon as many foreign conductors as were needed to bring the opera company up to standard, its existence to be justified by excellence alone. This meant telling Karl Rankl that his job would be abolished. Erich Kleiber had been booked to help out around the sensitive Christmas period. Rankl, who had been assured by Webster that things were improving, was stunned – both by the notice of dismissal and by a crippling anxiety of what might transpire if a celebrated conductor like Kleiber occupied his place in the pit. He loathed Kleiber with a venom that was both personal and political. Kleiber had clung to his post in Berlin for two full years of Hitler's Reich, while Rankl quit Germany the day the Nazis came to power. 'He was a wicked man,' said Rankl of Kleiber.[90]

'I was surprised at your views on Kleiber,' replied Webster with calculated disingenuousness. 'He seems to be one of the few people who share our views – he is all for encouraging local singers and he has done a great deal of this kind of work in South America. He believes in opera in English with the kind of exceptions we have already made . . . (and) he speaks well of you.'[91]

Rankl replied, within hours, in an agitated handwritten note:

'Dear David,
    I have read your letter very carefully. The only question I should like to ask is: Are you presenting me with a *fait accompli*, or are your proposals still open to a discussion between ourselves?'[92]

Webster's response was unyielding:

'My dear Karl, The principles in my letter are beyond discussion. . . The office of Musical Director will cease after the 1950-51 season. This is also beyond discussion.'[93]

A more confident, less naïve musician than Karl Rankl would have resigned there and then. His contract stated unequivocally that no musician or singer could be engaged or dismissed without his written consent. By hiring Kleiber behind his back, Webster had committed a flagrant breach of contract and Rankl would have been within his rights to sue for exemplary damages through his eminent firm of lawyers, Rubinstein Nash. He was inhibited by two concerns: a refugee's insecurity, and a deep-seated commitment to the singers and musicians whose talents he had discovered and nurtured. Unable to afford legal action, and impelled by forlorn ideals, Rankl took up his baton for the transformatory season of 1950-51.

He opened with the stomach-churning obligation of a *Flying Dutchman* produced by 'Mephisto' Heinz Tietjen, artistic director at Bayreuth during the Hitler era, upon a set by Emil Preetorius, Goebbels' favourite stage designer. Clemens Krauss, music director in Hitler's Munich, was due later in the season, and one of the new singers, Frederick Dalberg, was a Newcastle-born bass who had changed his name from Dalrymple and plied his trade in Germany during the war. In place of purified Englishness, Covent Garden was leading the way in the appeasement of Nazi sympathizers.

'I see Tietjen's been here,' was Kleiber's comment on entering the auditorium.

'How did you know?' said Rankl, astonished.

'Speakers and microphones everywhere,' said Kleiber. 'Tietjen was always spying on his staff.'[94]

'I felt terribly sorry for Rankl,' said a stage manager. 'He was on his way out and, as well as Kleiber, all these Nazis were coming to Covent Garden. That must have been a bitter taste.'[95]

Rankl's revival of *Salome*, on sets rebuilt from the jettisoned *Olympians*, got the new season into its stride. *Tosca* directed by Christopher West, a former Brook assistant who stayed on as house producer, augured well, despite the unscheduled posthumous reappearance of the heroine, Hilde Zadek, who bounced back into view after landing from her suicide leap on to an oversprung mattress. Rankl and the orchestra seemed to be growing together in confidence, until Kleiber arrived and put the art of performance on an altogether different plane.

Erich Kleiber had earned his spurs not as a provincial conductor in Graz but as head of the State Opera in Berlin for twelve years, resigning in protest against the Nazis' ban on his projected première of Alban Berg's *Lulu*. Married to an American, he had spent a sedate war at the Teatro Colon in Buenos Aires and, on a return trip to Europe was approached by Webster with a princely offer of two hundred pounds a night to conduct at Covent Garden.

The ovation that erupted as he entered the pit to conduct *Der Rosenkavalier* on 6 December 1950, was 'like the cheers of a beleaguered garrison at the sight of the rescuing force.'[96] A schoolboy in the audience felt a 'perceptible difference'.[97]

'Kleiber made me blossom,' declared Constance Shacklock, who sang Octavian. 'He had a way of bringing out the best in everyone. Rhydderich Davies, the Welsh boy, very beautiful voice but not particularly musical, was playing the Attorney and there is one point where he is talking to Baron Ochs and says 'May it please – (pause) – your Lordship . . .'

Kleiber shouted up to him in rehearsal: 'My boy, why do you think Strauss wrote those rests?'

So Rhydderich said: 'I haven't a clue, Sir.'

He said: 'Well, Strauss was an asthmatical – gasp – old boy. Try it again.'

Well poor old Rhydd nearly choked himself.

'Sorry, sir, can't do it,' he cried.

Kleiber said: 'My boy, you can do it. You're an artist.'

There was dead silence. We were awestruck.'

A back-desk cellist was overheard saying, 'I wouldn't have believed I could enjoy a Saturday morning rehearsal so much. And he finished half an hour early.'[98]

Der Rosenkavalier was followed by Tchaikovsky's *Queen of Spades*, *Rigoletto* and *Carmen*, the conductor's appeal spreading like fire both within the company and beyond. Though his American wife, Ruth, liked to kick up a fuss over imagined slights and Kleiber himself would threaten at times to catch the next plane to Buenos Aires, for performers he could do no wrong. 'He was always on our side,' said an orchestral player.[99]

'He was a dear man,' smiled Shacklock. 'He always came to see you before you went on stage, to say: just watch that little note there. As if of all the thousands of notes in the opera, this was the one that mattered. He used to knock and walk in, didn't wait for an answer.

Well one night I was late getting ready. I was decent, but not fully dressed. When he came in I protested, "Herr Kleiber!"

"It's all right my dear," he said. "Firstly, I'm short-sighted. Secondly I'm married. And thirdly, I like what I see . . .'"

'We must do everything in our power to keep him here,' Kenneth Clark told Webster. 'He has made an immeasurable difference. But when all is said and done he couldn't have used the instrument unless Rankl had created it.'[100]

The humourless, unflirtatious Musical Director had, rather nobly, introduced Kleiber to the orchestra before scurrying away to nurse hurt feelings. 'Kleiber got six rehearsals for *Carmen*, which had been in repertoire for three years, while Karl was doing a new *Götterdämmerung* and praying for every rehearsal he could get,' said Christine Rankl.[101] When he came on one night to conduct *Fidelio* and was greeted by shouts from the audience of 'We want Kleiber!', his pride was wounded beyond repair. The news that Kleiber had been booked for *Wozzeck* the following season, an opera that Rankl coveted for himself, was the final straw.

During parallel rehearsals – one at Covent Garden, the other at Kingsway Hall, Holborn – a dispute broke out as to which conductor had first call on the orchestra's two regular trumpeters. Had Webster been around, matters might have been smoothed over, but the General Administrator was in America with the ballet and the problem fell into the domain of his officious deputy, Sir Steuart Wilson. The double-booking had been Rankl's fault, arising from his refusal to help scheduling Kleiber's rehearsals, but Wilson's pompous handling turned a slight scratch into gangrenous wound. 'I again told him that if he would not accept responsibility for Kleiber's rehearsal somebody must, and that it was now important that I should do so,' reported Wilson to Webster in America. 'I therefore regard Rankl's refusal to co-operate in any way, even under protest, in this matter of the rehearsal as being a definite challenge to define the authority of the Musical Director, and I equally definitely take up the challenge and say that he voluntarily abdicated his rights by refusing to co-operate.'[102]

Wilson sent Rankl an ultimatum: 'Will you accept as a compromise that you end your rehearsal at 12.30 p.m. and let all the orchestra go including the two trumpeters who will be here at 12.40?'[103] Rankl acquiesced, but came home and told his young girlfriend that he could not take much more. 'Throw the job in their faces,' she said, 'I'd rather have you alive than dead.'[104] On Webster's return, Rankl formally resigned 'from all my positions with the Covent Garden Opera Company'[105] from the end of July. Since his contract expired on that date and was not to be renewed, his gesture was as toothless as his humiliation by Wilson had been pointless.

A resignation statement was issued, at Rankl's request, because (as Webster told his chairman) 'he has to find work for himself and finds the matter a little delicate without some announcement having been made.'[106] No reason was given but Rankl was thanked by the Directors for his 'immense pioneer work in the formation and training of principals, chorus and orchestra'.

The remainder of his tenure was not so much regretful as pathetic. He conducted *Parsifal* and the *Ring* with considerable panache, to the point that one loyal staffer felt that 'there hasn't been anything better'[107] since his *Götterdämmerung*, with Flagstad as Brünnhilde. On the last night of June, Flagstad and the conductor bade farewell to Covent Garden with *Tristan und Isolde*. Flagstad took twenty-one curtain calls, but there was no tribute to Rankl. Three and a half weeks later in Liverpool, Flagstad made her final operatic appearance and David Webster walked out in front of the curtain in his home town to salute her career. He went on to raise a round of applause for Shacklock who had that night sung her fiftieth Brangäne. But not a word passed his lips about Rankl, who had just given his last performance with the company he had created. 'I wanted to call out, "what about Rankl?",' recalled the bass singer Michael Langdon, 'but I lacked courage. I was young and had my future to think of; I kept my mouth shut.'[108] Rankl was given a lift back to his hotel by a new member of the music staff, Emanuel Young. In the car, he burst into tears.

He was rapidly erased from Covent Garden memory. Hard-up and out of work, Rankl wrote to Webster in September wondering when he could expect the 'handsome cheque' he had been promised if he went quietly. A settlement of one thousand pounds was eventually paid into his account, small recompense for five formative years. He invited Webster to his opening concert as chief conductor of the Scottish National Orchestra the following winter; Muriel Kerr sent personal 'congratulations on your appointment in my home country'[109] but no one from Covent Garden attended. The following year, his name was left out of a Covent Garden history, provoking a protest from Clark and a libel threat from Rankl. 'I am naturally sorry that you should be upset by the omission,' Webster wrote. 'There was no wish either to hurt you nor to omit your name from any place where it should appear. The brochure was intended primarily to be a piece of publicity for the Coronation Season.'[110]

The more the Royal Opera House improved, the more eager Webster was to eradicate traces of Rankl, who now seemed too insignificant to have been associated with so exalted an institution. He remained fond of 'dear Karl' and fretted about his unemployment after his Scottish position folded, volunteering to 'write to a few people to see if they can do anything about him . . . freelance conductors at a reasonable price are not as common as all that.'[111] But he never asked Rankl back to conduct at Covent Garden. As far as Webster was concerned, said Peter Gellhorn, who left the company for a better job at Glyndebourne, 'when it was finished, it was over – he didn't want to know you.'

Rankl might have been the wrong man for the job, but he did more than anyone could have expected from a smalltown *kapellmeister*. The visiting conductors Clemens Krauss and Rudolf Kempe praised his chorus as the best in the world, and some of the singers he discovered and trained were soon taking wing, Shacklock to Moscow, Geraint Evans to La Scala and the Met. 'That first five years of discipline with Rankl is something I'll always be grateful for,' said Shacklock. But Covent Garden, along with the rest of Britain, was keen to cover up those dedicated, stumbling beginnings and stride ahead to a less principled, amnesiac future.

CHAPTER 5

First Act, Forbidden Acts
(1951–59)

THE REBIRTH OF the nation was marked ceremonially on 3 May 1951, a wet Thursday of scurrying morbidity. On a patch of reclaimed marshland on the south bank of the River Thames, diagonally opposite the Mother of Parliaments, the Festival of Britain was opened by the Archbishop of Canterbury, Dr Geoffrey Fisher, who proclaimed a 'belief in the British way of life' and a hope that 'we may continue to be a nation at unity with itself and of service to the world'. National self-reconsecration was the refrain of the Festival Exhibition, which 'unfolded the tale of the continuous impact that this particular land has made on this particular people, and of the achievements that this people has continued to derive from its relationship with the land.'[1]

The particularity was significant. As patriotism was the last refuge of a scoundrel,[2] so insular nationalism had become the rallying cry of returning heroes. 'The belief that Britain will continue to have contributions to make in the future is founded on two factors,' quavered the Exhibition guidebook (price 2/6d), 'the People of Britain and the Land of Britain.'[3] An echo of Goebbelsian rhetoric, *Ein Volk, Ein Land*, pervaded the undertones. 'The "People of Britain" Pavilion shows how the British stock was blended,'[4] explained the guidebook, adding a thoughtful disquisition on 'the problem of space' – or *Lebensraum*. The nation was turning in upon itself with a celebration of Merrie England that was both surreal and anachronistic. A pylon stretched pointlessly into the sky, symbolizing the Vertical Future. A Milk Bar proferred the delights of arable farming. Foreign foodstuffs were banned from the site. English wit and self-mockery were conspicuous by their absence.

The Festival had begun as an open letter written to Stafford Cripps by Gerald Barry, editor of the *News Chronicle*, in the roseate dawn of September 1945. Barry drew attention to the approaching centenary of the Great Exhibition of 1851 in which Britain at the pomp of empire had displayed its wares and vitality to the world. The anniversary, he suggested, offered an opportunity for the nation to affirm to the world and to itself that it had weathered the war and was poised to invent a better future. Cripps was unimpressed, but his Cabinet colleague Herbert Morrison, Lord President of the Council, leaped upon the concept and made it flesh.

Morrison, a muscular London politician who mysteriously destroyed most of his personal papers, longed to leave a national monument. The Festival became his pet project. Using his clout at Party headquarters, he extracted from the Treasury a huge budget of twelve million pounds, reduced to eleven million in the 1949 devaluation crisis. He made Barry director general and surrounded him with a council of cultural eminences: Kenneth Clark, T. S. Eliot, Malcolm Sargent, John Gielgud. Under Tory attack for extravagance, he appointed as chairman Churchill's wartime chief of staff and close friend, General Lord Ismay.

At the centre of the site was its only permanent edifice, the Royal Festival Hall, commissioned by the London County Council to replace Queen's Hall, which had been bombed to rubble on 10 May 1941. Acclaimed as a marvel of modern architecture but acoustically dull, the brave new concert hall was ringed by temporary pavilions and a Dome of Discovery, displaying varied aspects of British life and endeavour. Surfaces were painted in gaudy hues of red, white and blue and futuristic designs offered a respite from a decade of utility products. The catering was reassuringly awful. Anyone who ordered wine was poured British sherry by a 'slatternly'[5] waitress.

Elsewhere, the Festival sprouted a funfair in Battersea Park, a pageant in Cardiff, an exhibition of Industrial Power in Glasgow, an opera in Liverpool and a festival ship that stopped at major ports. 'I want everyone in Britain to see it, to take part in it, to enjoy it,' said Morrison. 'I want to see the people happy. I want to hear the people sing.'[6] By the time the pavilions were taken down in October, eight and a half million people had visited the site, equivalent to one-sixth of the country's population. 'You came away feeling you could dance like (Gene) Kelly,' said the budding playwright Arnold Wesker, 'and, for a few moments, along the road, with one's friends, you actually did step more lightly and leap a little.'[7]

The press played up the general jollity and Morrison, who skipped an important ministerial meeting of the Council of Europe to show the King and Queen around his creation, was popularly rechristened 'Lord Festival', an appellation that impressed his power-conscious grandson, Peter Mandelson. 'The Festival has been a good thing for all of us,' intoned Archbishop Fisher at the closing ceremony, 'it has been a real family party.'

This airy platitude was vaguely incontestable, but the family party was a dubious choice of phrase. For the Britain that the Festival purported to represent was no longer a family affair. The war had destroyed its cultural homogeneity and the peace its racial purity. Some sixty thousand Hitler refugees, mostly Jews, had arrived before 1939 and an equivalent number followed after 1945. Their cultural impact was explosive. The art publishers Bela Horovitz and Walter Neurath revolutionized dowdy British book design. The music publishers Ernst Roth, Erwin Stein and Alfred Kalmus nurtured young British composers to world fame. Bauhaus-trained architects mocked mock-Tudor semis and altered the urban landscape. Nikolaus Pevsner chronicled *The Buildings of England* and redefined *The Englishness of English Art*. Karl Popper and Ludwig Wittgenstein, Isaiah Berlin and A. J. Ayer, revitalized Oxbridge philosophy. Alexander Korda breathed life into British cinema. Elias Canetti contemplated a cerebral novel that would win him a Nobel prize. Lucien Freud was emerging as the country's most original portraitist. None of these trends or individuals were reflected in the Festival of Britain, which celebrated as restrictive and mythical a vision of national conformity as any Nuremburg Rally.

Nor were Jews and European *émigrés* the only outcasts. An employment boom brought about by the National Health Service and the nationalization of transport had created a sudden need for more nurses, midwives, hospital ancillaries and bus drivers than were locally available. The NHS and London Transport placed job adverts in West Indian newspapers. Young men and women, raised to admire the Mother Country, rushed to apply for positions, many of which offered vocational training. The first 492 immigrants disembarked at Tilbury in June 1948. Wearing thin suits and jaunty hats, they expected to be welcomed, or at least tolerated, by the country they had come to help.

Instead, they faced a brick wall of medieval primitivism and prejudice. Eleven Labour MPs signed a letter of protest to the Prime Minister and a Cabinet committee was formed to examine 'ways which might be adopted to check the immigration into this country of coloured people from British colonial territories'. Landlords put up signs saying 'No Coloureds'. The newcomers were appalled by damp and filthy accommodation. Many houses had no bath or shower. Some used the bathtub for storing coal.

At work, immigrants were shunned or abused. The first black copper in the Metropolitan Police was so ill-treated by colleagues at Bow Street station, opposite Covent Garden, that he recalled crying himself to sleep at night for a whole year. In hospital, patients would shout 'get your black hands off me' at nurses and porters who were trying to look after them. The Festival of Britain turned a blind eye to the fast-changing demographic map of Britain. The Land and the People were a tight little item that excluded aliens from arcadian bliss. Seen with half a century's hindsight, the Festival was aimed at the nation's narrowest instincts, and was thus successful beyond measure.

Morrison was promoted in March 1951 to Foreign Secretary, in place of the dying Ernest Bevin, but Labour was too far gone to be resuscitated. A month before the Festival opened, the party was split down the middle by a blazing Cabinet row between Aneurin Bevan and the pragmatist Chancellor, Hugh Gaitskell, successor to the dying Cripps. Bevan loathed Gaitskell with a passion that was as much physical as political. He called the Chancellor 'a dessicated calculating machine' and his supporters reviled 'the prim set of his mouth (that) seemed to symbolize the primness of his political views'.[8] Gaitskell despised Bevan as a dangerous windbag, and goaded him into action by imposing charges for NHS spectacles and dental care in his first Budget, supposedly to help pay the costs of the Korean War.

It was not the money, thirteen million pounds, that mattered to either man, but the principle and the personal. Bevan objected to any charge for NHS services as a breach of faith, and to British participation in the Korean War as an act of American toadyism. Gaitskell wanted to reinforce the Atlantic alliance with an extra £690 million of rearmament spending, and to bring the NHS back under Treasury control.

When he refused to back down on the charges, Bevan resigned

from the Government, taking with him Harold Wilson, President of the Board of Trade, and John Freeman, a junior minister. When Attlee called a snap election in September, Labour lost by seventeen seats. It hardly mattered that they mustered 176,000 more votes than the Tories and a forty-nine per cent share, higher than in 1945. The vagaries of the first-past-the-post system had produced a result that reflected public sentiment and put paid to a clapped-out administration.

Apart from promptly bulldozing the Festival of Britain site and leaving it derelict for a decade, the Tories neither turned the clock back nor moved it forward. 'Steady as she goes' was the motto, with R. A. Butler as a conciliatory Chancellor and an apolitical Minister of Labour, Walter Monckton, who did his best to befriend the trade unions. 'Little had actually changed,' wrote a Labour historian, 'Attlee's patriotic socialists gave way to Churchill's social patriots.'[9] The ruling dogma became known as 'Butskellism', a centre-ground consensus that bogged the 1950s down in a mire of political stagnancy. Mounting social and industrial disasters were swept, along with any pretence at idealism, beneath the Plimsoll line of both main parties. Wages were allowed to rise at three times the rate of production. Quick-fix housing began to uglify cities and destroy communities. Future leaders would deride the period for its 'retreat from reality'.[10]

The Royal Opera House had a small part to play in the Festival of Britain, and played it shabbily. In 1948, Webster had endorsed an Arts Council scheme to commission new operas for the Festival and stage them at Covent Garden. Dozens of anonymous submissions were read by a selection panel comprised of Constant Lambert and Edward Dent, representing the ROH, Steuart Wilson and Lawrance Collingwood of the BBC, and Eric Walter White of the Arts Council. White was the only member who knew the composers' identities, and he acted with 'great discretion'.[11] There was consternation when the victors were named, not least from Lambert, who found he had chosen *Deirdre of the Sorrows* by his arch-enemy, Karl Rankl. 'By God, I hate that bastard's guts,' he exploded, 'but it's still a good score and my word stands.'[12] The other winners were *Beatrice Cenci*, by Berthold Goldschmidt; *Wat Tyler*, by Alan Bush; and Arthur Benjamin's *Tale of Two Cities*. The composers received an award of three hundred pounds in exchange for granting the Arts

Council the right, for the next two years, 'to nominate the first production'.[13] The Council would 'do its best to bring about' a production, and the composers were led to understand that it would take place at Covent Garden.[14]

Then the back-tracking started. Someone noticed that the operas picked to celebrate the Festival of Britain had been written by three foreigners and a Communist. The Royal Opera House smartly withdrew and the Arts Council blushed deeply and did nothing. Bush, the moment his two-year clause expired, sent his insur-rectionist epic to the German Democratic Republic where it appeared in Leipzig in 1955 and remained for decades in the repertory. Benjamin, an Australian, had his Dickens melodrama broadcast by the BBC in 1953. Goldschmidt, a German refugee, was allowed to conduct selections from *Beatrice Cenci* on the Third Programme for his fiftieth birthday that year. Dismayed by Covent Garden's disregard for its commitments – an Englishman's word was, after all, supposed to be sacrosanct – Goldschmidt wrote a letter of protest to *The Times*. The result was that he was shunned by the English operatic establishment and had to wait until 1994 to see *Beatrice Cenci* triumphantly vindicated in Berlin and successfully recorded by Sony. Rankl's *Deirdre* never got that far. His appeals to Webster went unanswered, despite testimony from singers that the opera was performable. After his death in 1968, Rankl's widow placed the score for safe-keeping with an archive in Graz, where it languishes unsung to this day.

In place of the victorious alien operas, Webster put on the tepid première of Ralph Vaughan Williams' *Pilgrim's Progress*, more sacred oratorio than grand opera, and no fewer than nineteen performances of *The Bohemian Girl* by Michael Balfe, a Victorian pot-boiler that had faded from all living memory except for Sir Thomas Beecham's. Opening in Liverpool, where it was billed as the Festival high-point, the opera earned Beecham £150 a night conducting fee, plus 3.5 per cent of box-office takings as a royalty on a performing edition in which he questionably claimed copyright. This torpid anachronism then vanished once again into a mist of its mediocrity. Webster, unable to attack Beecham, avenged himself on the innocent producer, Dennis Arundell, who was blacklisted at Covent Garden.

To an introspective ROH, the Festival of Britain had been an unwanted distraction. Covent Garden was preoccupied with an internal struggle. The Board demanded a new music director. Webster was determined to delay any appointment for as long as possible in order to extend his own authority. Having attended many auditions, he considered himself a connoisseur of singers and a master of casting and looked forward to a period of grace unhampered by a resident conductor. He decided to buy time by seeking a partial replacement and wrote to Sir John Barbirolli in Manchester, asking him to lunch. Barbirolli, whom Webster had spurned in 1945 as too vain, replied warmly: 'As you know I am not much of a luncher, but if you would like to give me a sandwich and a whisky and soda it will be very nice.'[15]

News of their meeting leaked to the press, and Barbirolli was besieged – 'they even got into his hotel bedroom'.[16] Two days later, it was announced that Barbirolli had 'accepted an invitation to be Guest Conductor with the Covent Garden Opera during the 1951/52 Season. The acceptance of this invitation will not involve curtailing his services with the Halle Orchestra.' Both men got what they wanted out of this arrangement and emerged the best of friends, signing their future letters 'love and best wishes'. Webster increased his power and Barbirolli strengthened his hand in contract nego-tiations with the Halle, while securing top whack at Covent Garden – two hundred and fifty guineas for each first night, and one hundred and fifty for subsequent performances.

He opened with *Turandot* and *Aida*, and was not seen again that season. Next year, Barbirolli repeated the same operas, followed by *Bohème*, *Tristan* and two nights of Gluck's *Orfeo ed Euridice* built around the family-favourite contralto, Kathleen Ferrier, who was making her ROH début at the age of forty. Ferrier had breathed new life into the baroque opera at Glyndebourne and her rendering of 'What is Life to me Without you' was reputed to melt granite. But she had undergone a serious operation and Frederick Ashton, who directed and choreographed the production, took care to spare her unnecessary effort. Webster was among the handful of people who knew the gravity of her condition and his decision to authorize the production was a calculated and compassionate risk.

The Sunday before opening night, when his faithful designer Sophie Fedorovitch failed to turn up for the pre-dress rehearsal, Ashton sent an assistant round to her studio. Sniffing gas, he let himself in with a spare key and found the designer prone beside her bed. She had been dead for two days, poisoned by an accidental leak.

During the week, Buckingham Palace announced that the King was gravely ill, and the nation prepared to mourn.

Ferrier, before going on stage, gave Barbirolli a set of blue-enamelled cuff-links and a loving note thanking him 'for making an Orpheus dream come true – and for many other blessings spread over the last three years'.[17] On the second night, 6 February 1953, she made an awkward move and broke her hip in several places, the bone weakened by cancer. She sang out the second act leaning on a stage prop and took her curtain calls on the conductor's arm. 'I shall never forget,' said Barbirolli in a memorial tribute, 'the impish glee with which she literally purred over one of the critics' comments that her movements were an object lesson even to the Sadler's Wells Ballet.'[18] Seven months later, Ferrier was dead.

Barbirolli conducted three listless productions the following season, and nothing more. When Webster half-heartedly raised the vacant music directorship, Barbirolli changed the subject.

Kleiber was the next candidate, but he was both costly and capricious. On his return to Covent Garden, Kleiber restricted himself to eighteen performances of four operas. His involvement climaxed with *Wozzeck*, the atonal opera he had brought into the world more than quarter of a century before, and which was being staged for the first time in Britain. Its tale of a war-weary soldier, brutalized by his officers and comrades and idly betrayed by his mistress Marie, was more topical and radical than any play in the West End, but Kleiber knew the immensity of effort it required. He sent for Reggie Goodall, who had been sacked from Covent Garden after poor reviews and got him to coach the cast for four months and start training the orchestra. Kleiber himself called nineteen sectional rehearsals. 'Just think you are playing a Haydn symphony,' he told the orchestra.[19]

The six performances of *Wozzeck* were poorly attended and deeply perplexing to reactionary critics like Frank Howes who told *Times* readers how 'nasty and depressive it all is'. But the collective achievement surpassed belief. The cast of mostly staff singers hit the toughest passages with stunning accuracy. The antediluvian mechanisms and antiquated backstage bosses coped with fourteen scene changes in under ninety seconds. And the orchestra played for the first time like a frontline ensemble, equal to any task a composer could throw at it. The half-empty house was dotted with enthusiasts who came night after night to experience a work, which as Philip

Hope-Wallace wrote in the *Manchester Guardian*, 'seizes the imagination by the short hairs of the scalp'. *Wozzeck* was the moment Covent Garden came of age and Hope-Wallace credited the transformation to 'Dr Kleiber, a great artist'.[20]

Kleiber, however, was fed up with foggy London winters and fretting for continental activity in Berlin, Vienna and recording studios. He found fault with Webster and became unpredictably perverse, perhaps a symptom of impending illness. After a gripping *Elektra*, directed by Rudolf Hartmann of Munich, Kleiber left London on the eve of the Queen's Coronation, and never returned. Two and a half years later, on Mozart's bicentennial birthday, he was found dead of a heart attack in the bath of a Zurich hotel suite.

Apart from Barbirolli and Kleiber, there was no conductor with strong claims to be the next music director. The names that came Webster's way were ridiculously inapposite. Steuart Wilson volunteered two Englishmen: Anthony Bernard, a sixty-year-old former Shakespeare Theatre conductor, and John Pritchard, aged thirty, who made a messy début in charge of Professor Dent's new translation of Verdi's *Masked Ball*. William Walton, from the boardroom, nominated Harry Blech, a violinist who had formed his own chamber orchestra, the London Mozart Players. The half-deaf Dent, despairing of conductors, told Webster that what he needed was an artistic director and the best man for the job was Aladar Toth of Budapest Opera. Toth, said Dent, spoke 'practically no English' but was 'keenly interested in Purcell' and had put on a *Peter Grimes* 'which was far better in every way than either of the London productions'.[21]

The more far-fetched the suggestion, the more it suited the General Administrator, allowing him time and licence to play fantasy opera and book the conductors and singers of his dreams. Not all of them responded. Early in 1953, he made strenuous efforts to attract Wilhelm Furtwängler for *Meistersinger*, but the Berlin conductor, never the most decisive of men, was unmoved by the proffered honour and died before much progress was made. Each such demise or refusal enabled Webster to convince his board of the lamentable lack of conductors and music directors, and thereby to strengthen his grip on artistic planning.

An intriguing solution was forming in his mind. In the autumn of 1951, Benjamin Britten completed his first Covent Garden opera, *Billy Budd*. He nominated the Austrian conductor Josef Krips to conduct the première on the strength of a fine *Rape of Lucretia* at Salzburg but Krips, receiving his copy of the score six weeks before opening night, declared the photostats unreadable.

Mistrusting other maestros and bypassing the fractious Goodall, Britten asked Peter Gellhorn to commence rehearsals and finally decided, 'however reluctantly'[22] to conduct the run himself. 'He certainly knew his job,' said one orchestral player. 'He also had the ability, unusual in a composer, to explain to us clearly in words what he required from us in music.'[23] Webster, rather meanly, paid him just five hundred pounds for four performances and much preparation.

Britten grumbled about 'the size of the house, state of company, lack of co-operation'.[24] The disorderliness of a grand opera house offended his prim nature. Two months before opening night there was still no singer designated for the title-role until Webster, on an American trip, saw a blond, broad-chested California baritone, Theodor Uppman, and signed him to play Herman Melville's innocent ship-boy, hung at the yard-arm after a murder at sea. 'The fact that an opera is in English does not make it easy to cast,' he told the Ministry of Labour, after protests from the actors' union, Equity. 'I would say categorically that there is no Englishman who is suited to the role of Billy Budd.'[25] Pears played the hapless Captain Vere and Frederick Dalberg the evil Claggart.

Expectations ran impossibly high, for not only was *Budd* a reprise of powerful *Grimes* themes of death and guilt on the high seas but it introduced, as co-librettist with Eric Crozier, the novelist E. M. Forster, who had never written for the stage and had produced no large work since *A Passage to India* back in 1924. 'I feel confident that *Billy* will make all Ben's operas until now look like experiments leading to the first of his great mature works,' wrote Crozier to his future wife, Nancy Evans. 'It will be a tragedy if Morgan does not live long enough to write other works for him.'[26] Forster, happily, enjoyed an Indian summer after *Budd*, but did not work again with Britten. As for the opera, it split opinion from the start and stirred more disquiet as it matured.

The morning papers recorded a 'torrent of applause', but Ernest Newman in the *Sunday Times* derided the libretto and discerned no musical progress on Britten's part; woundingly, he likened the finale to *H.M.S Pinafore* by Gilbert and Sullivan. Younger critics like Desmond Shawe-Taylor and Philip Hope-Wallace damned *Budd* with faint praise. In the *Manchester Guardian*, Hope-Wallace argued that the opera had been dramatically undermined by Britten's decision to give 'the moralizing tenor part' to a non-protagonist, Captain Vere. 'This gives the opera a core of almost German earnestness . . . (and) has the effect of weakening the natural hero Budd and the villain Claggart in spite of their monologues and self-revelations, into little more than abstractions of good and bad,' he observed.[27] Twenty-seven years later, the same critic was 'over-whelmed' by a Covent Garden revival of *Billy Budd* and wondered whether his first response had not been swayed by over-zealous interpreters. In the 1980s, critical wisdom graded *Budd* as second-rate *Grimes*, most tellingly in a television survey of Britten's work.[28] The tide then turned, but commentators could not agree about the meaning of it all. Reviewing a Welsh production in 1998, Michael Kennedy saw the opera as 'the conflict between public duty and private sentiment at a time of national danger'.[29] Peter Conrad, con-versely, noticed 'sweaty bonding rituals of mateship' and applauded the opera for showing 'how homosocial behaviour on board ship approaches but tactfully avoids homosexual declaration'.[30] It was as if two seasoned critics had been watching separate shows, so richly contorted were the possibilities embedded in *Budd*. On the opening night, it was the astute Kenneth Clark who observed that this was 'one of those masterpieces that change human behaviour'.[31] Noël Coward, on the other hand, left the theatre unmoved.[32]

The verdict that mattered was delivered by the opera circuit. Unlike *Grimes*, which circled the world, *Budd* with its single-sex cast was shunned. In Germany, a cut version was staged at Wiesbaden and fast forgotten. Apart from a television airing on NBC in 1952, *Budd* was not seen in America until 1970, by which time Britten had reluctantly halved its four acts, reducing three intervals to one. The original *Budd* was not revived until 1997.

The flaws revealed or perceived in *Budd* gnawed away at Britten's ever-fragile confidence and increased the stomach-churning anxiety that gripped him when he was required to conduct on big occasions. He thanked Webster for his support and looked forward politely to further collaboration,[33] but his first loyalties lay with Aldeburgh and the English Opera Group. Beyond his gaze, meanwhile, powerful forces were conspiring to raise him to high office. Harewood, smitten by *Budd*, arranged with his father-in-law Erwin Stein, who was Britten's editor at Boosey & Hawkes, to nominate Britten as the next music director at Covent Garden. Webster leapt at the idea, not least because Britten would be a non-executive music director who conducted only his own works and maybe a Mozart or two, leaving the General Administrator to select other conductors and casts. But he anticipated boardroom opposition, knowing that Leslie Boosey would not want Britten to be distracted from composing and that William Walton was seething at the praise and favours being showered on his rival.

Walton had entered the war as England's rising composer and ended it an also-ran. Kept in comfort by his mistress, Lady Wimborne, until her death in 1948, he married a young Argentine beauty soon after and was struggling to make an opera out of Chaucer's version of *Troilus and Cressida* while setting up home in exile on the Italian island of Ischia. Although constitutionally lazy and not given to malice, he had blocked a British Council recording of *Grimes* and liked to moan about Britten and his 'coterie'.[34]

Webster, faced with opposition, took his usual course of doing nothing until, nagged by Harewood, he neutrally raised the proposal with the board. Boosey, predictably, declared that Britten was a professional composer who should be absolved from practical duties. Walton, at his last board meeting prior to emigration, wondered whether Britten would be prepared to conduct *Troilus*; Harewood said he would. And there the matter rested. Britten himself was lukewarm to the idea. He would only take the post, he told Webster in November 1952, if he could bring along his English Opera Group. They would be regarded as a clique, warned Webster. A clique, said Britten, was the only way anything got done in music; he hated having to deal with strangers at the best of times.[35]

He was, by now, deep into his next Covent Garden commission, an opera proposed by Harewood and dedicated 'by gracious permission to Her Majesty Queen Elizabeth II, in honour of whose Coronation it was composed'. Harewood, about to be employed by Webster 'in a general kind of capacity',[36] wanted something 'appropriate' for his maternal first cousin's ascent to the Throne, securing the consent of his paternal second cousin, Sir Alan Lascelles, who happened to be the Queen's Private Secretary. Small world, the English aristocracy.

On a skiing week in Austria, Harewood discussed with Britten and Pears England's deplorable lack of a national opera, in the way that Italy had *Nabucco* and Germany *Die Meistersinger*. Britten rose to the bait and conversation turned to the glories of the first Elizabethan era. Harewood proposed Lytton Strachey's history of *Elizabeth and Essex* as a plot, recounting how the Queen's love for a courtier led to his execution. Britten imagined a synthesis of Tudor polyphony with the post-tonal chords of a New Elizabethan era. He chose as librettist the South African-born Bloomsbury poet William Plomer, a circumspect friend of E. M. Forster's. Webster told them to write as large as they liked, confident that any deficit would be covered by an extra Treasury grant for the Coronation.

The first objections were raised by the Sadler's Wells Ballet, which kicked up a fuss at being denied the chance to strut its stuff before the new Queen. Ninette de Valois demanded *jus primae noctis* – either a new ballet performed before *Gloriana*, or a full evening of dance. In the Covent Garden boardroom, ballet backers battled opera buffs. 'O David – dear David – Can nothing be done to stop K. Clark's silly mouth?' wailed Britten to Webster. 'I have, five minutes ago, received yet *another* message from my lord of Upper Terrace about the Ballet v Gloriana situation (it was thru 'the usual channels', of course). I am now informed that there is going to be a short ballet on June 8th *before* poor old Glory Anna. Just like that. Now if anything fresh was settled at your last Board meeting – please can *you* tell me direct and not have just any old trustee sending messages. Anyhow, you know that only over my dead body, dead opera too, will there be a ballet before *Gloriana* that night . . . Excuse scribble, please, but I'm still shaking with temper! love – Ben.'[37]

The composer eventually agreed to write ballet scenes that would be choreographed by the 25-year-old John Cranko, for whom he felt a budding affection. John Piper, his favourite artist, was engaged to design the sets; the director was the EOG's Basil Coleman who had served him well on *Budd*; Joan Cross agreed to play Elizabeth and Pears was to be Essex. Surrounded by friends, Britten composed at high speed, as many as twenty-eight pages of full score in a day. His only discomfort was the conductor John Pritchard, selected by Webster after Britten declined the baton. Pritchard was often late for rehearsals and did not appear to have mastered the score. His lover and agent, Basil Horsefield, had been known to stand in for Pritchard when the conductor was delayed, earning them both a sharp rebuke from Webster.[38]

As *Gloriana* reached completion, clouds gathered. A circle of young critics and acolytes had published during the winter an adulatory survey of Britten's life and works[39] which inflamed envy in musical rivals and pursed many lips for reprisal. In the Coronation Honours List, Britten was created a Companion of Honour, an unusually exalted tribute for a man under forty. English mediocrity awaited its day of reckoning. A coalition of rebuffed composers and sceptical critics murmured together in pubs. Walton whispered to Rawsthorne, who moaned to 'Twelve Tone Lizzie' Lutyens, who drank daily at the BBC. Lutyens dismissed Britten's music as 'brilliant journalism'. To appease the chief moaner, Webster asked Walton to write a Gala reorchestration of the National Anthem, thus annoying Britten.[40]

Adding to his own woes, Britten swelled the enemy ranks by shedding friends and allies without a word of explanation. Tenors who sang higher or better than Pears were made to feel unwanted. Conductors who were over-applauded were not reinvited to Aldeburgh. The tense atmosphere at Britten's festival recalled the fickleness of the Elizabethan Court, where yesterday's golden knight was tomorrow's grim beheaded.

On 2 June 1953, Queen Elizabeth the Second was crowned with pomp imperial in Westminster Abbey. The Conservative Government spent a million pounds on the festivities, aiming to fortify national unity and display England at its most arcadian. Coronation mugs sprouted in every market and food rationing was eased by an extra pound of sugar and four ounces of margarine. The Queen entered the Abbey to the chords of Walton's *Orb and Sceptre* before taking the oath and hearing the surge of Handel's great chorus 'Zadok the Priest' as she was anointed. The first Coronation on live television was watched by twenty million people, more than half the adult population, many of whom purchased a set for that purpose. Almost twelve million tuned in to the radio. Hundreds of thousands lined the processional route. It was the first occasion since the war and the last for forty-four years in which the nation acted in unison. On the morning of the Coronation, *The Times* reported that Sir Edmund Hillary and his sherpa guide, Tenzing, had reached the summit of Mount Everest, supposedly the world's highest peak. England ascendant was the motif of Coronation week. Even at cricket, the national game, there were signs that England was about to regain the Ashes, ending twenty years of Australian dominance.

Six days after the Coronation, *Gloriana* received its première at

Covent Garden before the new Queen and an audience comprised of the highest in the land. The Court and *corps diplomatiques* turned out in force. Evening dress and full decorations were *de rigueur*, the top seats cost six guineas and the interior of the theatre was redecorated for the occasion by Oliver Messel, the Royal Box lined with a cloth of gold. All eyes were on the new Queen and the Establishment felt obliged to attend, either out of a sense of duty or nagged to distraction by the socially-mobile wife of the Covent Garden chairman, Sir John Anderson, himself lately ennobled as the first Viscount Waverley. 'That tiresome, pushing little Lady Waverley was still wriggling her way up the ladder,' noted Cecil Beaton, who was taking photographs at the Palace; 'with her innate vulgarity of yellow, frizzy musical comedy curls and sycophantic flattery, she stuck out a mile.'[41]

The failure of *Gloriana* was rendered almost inevitable by the status of its audience. If the invitation list was inappropriate, the offering was doubly so. Harewood's presumption that the avowedly unmusical new Queen, fresh from her Abbey ordeal, would want nothing better than to spend two and a half hours watching a modern opera was wishful, to say the least. Britten, too, was not without blame. His opera creaked with Plomer's archaisms, assumed a detailed foreknowledge of Tudor history and portrayed the Queen as cruel and capricious, not what was expected in Coronation week. It was a warm night, and Covent Garden was airless. Starched collars wilted with perspiration and yawning broke out in the stalls. Prince Philip was seen reading a green-and-white Penguin crime thriller hidden inside his programme.[42]

'Oliver Messel's decor was superb,' recorded John Colville, the Prime Minister's principal private secretary, 'and the audience – well dressed at Covent Garden for a change – matched it. But the music was above our heads and the episode depicted by the opera, Elizabeth's squalid romance with Essex, totally unsuited to the occasion.'[43]

The response was apathetic. Even those who were moved to applaud did so in a patter since many hands were white-gloved for the occasion. 'An audience of stuck pigs,' Britten called them.[44] 'One of the great disasters of operatic history,'[45] said Harewood. 'A fiasco,' said the Secretary to the Covent Garden Board.[46] The critics performed on cue. Newman in the *Sunday Times* proclaimed that 'the bulk of the music is hardly more than pastiche'. Richard Capell in the *Daily Telegraph* called it 'pageant rather than drama', and Philip Hope-Wallace in the *Manchester Guardian* found himself, at the end of the first act, 'wondering if the opera will ever get off the ground'. The reviews were by no means wholly uncomprehending, but nothing less than hallelujahs would have satisfied the Brittenites and Harewood felt so affronted that he turned witheringly on *Opera* magazine for failing to appreciate 'what the Gala stood for, how it summed up the efforts made for English opera since 1945; how, through it, the arts generally and opera particularly were recognized as they had never been before in England.'[47] The popular press renamed the opera 'Boriana'. Despite healthy attendances drawn by the controversy, the show was a write-off. 'Sic transit Gloriana,' quipped one musical journal. La Scala cancelled its intended production and the American première was done in deepest Cincinnati. The opera redeemed itself at Sadler's Wells in 1966, despite last-ditch efforts by Webster to withhold the rights from a rival company. It contains, notably in the dance sequences, some of the liveliest and happiest music in any Britten opera, but a first-night flop is hard to reverse and four decades passed before the work was considered worthy of a recording.

Gloriana set the seal on Britten's involvement with Covent Garden. He would write and conduct a ballet, *The Prince of Pagodas*, for his friend John Cranko, but no new opera of his would ever come into being at the Royal Opera House. *Turn of the Screw* went to Venice, *A Midsummer Night's Dream* to Aldeburgh, *Owen Wingrave* to BBC television and *Death in Venice* to New York. Although he had warm feelings for Webster, after *Gloriana* Britten did not trust Covent Garden to appreciate his work and protect it from the wolves. His goal was to bring art to the people at every level, from the rudiments of *Let's Make an Opera* to the moral complexities of *Peter Grimes*. Covent Garden's aim was, increasingly, to present exquisite singing for connoisseurs and the moneyed classes. The dichotomy had become irresoluble.

In reputational terms, the failure of *Gloriana* was not Britten's but Covent Garden's. It demonstrated that a company created to foster national opera was unable to accommodate the country's greatest composer. *Gloriana* had been the right opera for the wrong time and place. A prompt revival might have revived Britten's faith in Covent Garden, but the board were cowed by the Royal disgrace and Webster was constrained by their shame from making amends.

He never gave up hope, however, of securing Britten's commitment in a different capacity. Five years after *Gloriana*, Webster wrote a memo to his board about the endless search for a chief conductor. He argued 'that there is no one available or in the offing to whom we should offer the job of Musical Director of opera at Covent Garden,' but declared himself 'in favour of an approach being made to Britten under the Musical Director heading – not because I thought he would take the job but because I thought (that) out of the discussion would come some notion of how Britten could help Covent Garden.'

This was an imaginative leap on Webster's part. Attaching a great composer to an opera company, not as a conductor or for the music he might write but purely for his creative mind and refined taste, was positive thinking of a high order. Webster hastened to reassure his directors, somewhat wishfully, that 'we need not worry about the coterie aspect of Britten ... It is my strong belief that he has outgrown the coterie phase.' He added: 'To me he would be of immense value. His salary would be a matter of opinion but I would have thought about £2,000.'[48]

There is no evidence that Webster ever put this idea to Britten, and his memo received short shrift from a Board whose priorities had shifted ever further away from English opera. Relations between Covent Garden and the composer were doomed to remain sporadic, wary, and mutually unrewarding. An attempt was made to lure Britten to take part in a 1973 Gala celebrating Britain's accession to the European Common Market, but the composer withdrew on grounds of ill health, and was not greatly missed at the Royal Opera House.

The *Gloriana* debacle of the Coronation summer was quickly overshadowed by events of greater moment. Before the month was out, England was agog at news that Princess Margaret, the Queen's younger sister, was keen to marry Group Captain Peter Townsend, a freshly-divorced royal equerry. Divorcees could not remarry in the Church of England, of which the Queen was titular head, and Townsend was packed off to Brussels, leaving the Princess disconsolate and the press in clover.

More sombrely, a fortnight after *Gloriana*, Winston Churchill gave dinner at 10 Downing Street for the visiting Italian premier, made a dazzling speech about the Romans in Britain, sat down heavily and suffered a stroke. Over the next few days he lost the use of his left arm and leg and his doctor, Lord Moran, did not think he would live. Anthony Eden, his deputy, was in America recovering from a gall-bladder operation. The country was being run by senior civil servants, in consultation with the top Tories Lord Salisbury and Rab Butler and the Queen's private secretary, Sir Alan Lascelles. Remarkably, despite the presence at dinner of so garrulous a guest as Kenneth Clark, no word leaked out of Churchill's incapacity. He made a partial return to health and remained in office for two years more, persuading the country that it did not need much by way of leadership beyond a wave of the hat and a cigar-clenched grin. The absence of strategic purpose was demonstrable across politics and industry however, as Britain indulged consumer desires with half a million car sales in 1955, and self-disciplined Germany built the strongest economy in Europe. Inflationary self-delusion was the order of the British decade. The burning issues were questions of class: whether one spoke 'U' (respectable) or 'non-U' (common). The ship of state had an esteemed skipper, but there was no one plotting a course.

The absence of a driving-seat music director made no obvious difference at Covent Garden. The singing and playing continued to improve, and when the Bavarian State Opera brought three Strauss operas in September 1953, there was no rush on the box-office and no blush on English cheeks. The home company could do just as well – and went on to prove it with a run of five Strauss operas under Rudolf Kempe, a tall, reserved Saxon who became a seasonal fixture. After a wooden *Ring* fell flat under the baton of Fritz Stiedry, Kempe took over the production and demonstrated the difference a good conductor could make. The *Daily Telegraph*, under the headline 'Wagner Revealed', declared in an editorial that 'Kempe has restored the *Ring* to us. He has made the orchestra sing and removed the necessity for the singers to bellow, bark, scream or hoot.'

The weakness of the *Ring* was its lack of local content. Apart from the Czech-born Otakar Kraus as Alberich, none of the central parts was entrusted to a British singer. Webster, unhampered by Rankl, splurged his budget on foreign glamour – the magnificent Hotter, Margaret Harshaw from the Met, the Swede Svanholm, Leonie Rysanek and Hilde Konetzni. The director was Rudolf Hartmann, the Bavarian intendant. Amid roars of relief for a redemptive *Ring*, no one seemed to notice that Covent Garden Opera was drifting away from its founding objectives. Vision, rigour and principle were cast overboard. Expedience ruled an eclectic display.

It was in this period of unbridled improvisation that the legend of Webster's omniscience was born. He began to court the limelight of press interviews, assuming a paternalist *gravitas* that verged on pomposity. Publicity articles that flowed from his pen were almost unreadably stuffy. 'It may be that when it is demonstrated that there exists the possibility of operatic careers in this country this somewhat vicious circle may be broken,' is a typical sample of unpunctuated Websterian prose.[49] The frivolous side of his nature, his Pickwickian relish of gossip, was carefully concealed. To the opera public and to most of his staff and directors, Webster was a dusty figure with an uncanny command of company activity. The real Webster was revealed only to an inner circle of trusted allies who met weekly behind closed doors.

'We were an awfully close-knit bunch,' said Elizabeth Latham, who arrived from Stratford as stage manager in 1950. 'We met in Webster's office: Morris Smith and Douglas Robinson, the orchestra and chorus directors, Patrick Terry, the opera company general manager, Webster, Miss Kerr and myself – and Lord Harewood after he joined the staff. We all knew what was going on, there were no secrets. We had this thing called The Bible, which was the scheme for the whole year, and would adjust it as necessary. It seemed amazing to me then, and still does now, that the house could have been run so simply and with such little fuss. I never had a contract. We shook hands, and that was that.'[50]

Their intimacy verged on the conspiratorial. Sir Steuart Wilson, Webster's deputy, was invited to the meetings 'as seldom as we could manage'. Latham, along with the director Christopher West, the production manager John Sullivan and the rest of the weekly group were also made welcome at Webster's Weymouth Street flat, where Jimmy Cleveland Belle was a 'charming, delightful host' and Webster was seen at his most relaxed. With Morris Smith in particular, he would, it was said, 'uninhibitedly, and safely, unburden himself'.[51] Smith, a Coldstream Guards trombonist who lost his playing nerve after being attacked in the park with a parasol by a pacifist lady, let it be known that he belonged to the same masonic lodge as Webster. A below-decks tyrant, Smith gained an 'unenviable reputation'[52] among orchestral musicians whose careers were

shadowed by his blatant favouritisms. Successive conductors, and
even the chairman himself, were unable to overcome Smith's
reactionary prejudice against women players.[53] As much lackey as
bully, he would preface his more preposterous decisions with the
words, 'Webster says . . .'

The existence of an inner clique, though, barely intruded on the
daily life of the company. Latham, who balanced her career with
marriage to a Harley Street surgeon, was on formal terms with the
General Administrator. 'We were always Mr Webster and Miss
Latham,' she recalled. 'He had this extraordinary passive face. One
day he came on stage and said, I think you really deserve a rise now,
Miss Latham. You will notice it in your bank account next month.'
She was getting fifteen pounds for a six-day week – in at eight-thirty
a.m. to check the scenery before rehearsal; afternoons taken up by
paperwork; at six she raced home to bathe and change for the
performance; at midnight she locked up. Her credentials were
established not by any closeness to Webster but by her willingness
to 'take a coat off and run a flat as well as any stagehand'[54] – and by
a remark tossed her way after a week at work by the assistant chief
machinist, Ted Lilley. 'Miss,' said Ted, 'Mr Ballard says you know
your onions.' Authority in the backstage had not altered appreciably
since Puccini's day.

Among the Victorian pulleys and rat-runs, Webster had neither
command nor control. He tried in 1947 to assert his management by
appointing a fellow-Liverpudlian, Cliff Clifford, as stage manager,
but Clifford was cowed by the Ballard gang and Webster knew better
than to tangle with a bunch of swarthy lads linked by theatrical
heritage and family bloodlines. When snow failed to fall in *Bohème*,
or descended with a thump like a feather mattress, Clifford shrugged
his shoulders and blamed it on the untamed stage crew. When half
the chorus collapsed coughing and the cause was traced to dusty
floors, Clifford complained of the lack of a staff cleaner. He was a
kindly man, who let stage-struck youngsters take over his prompt
corner – 'keep an eye on this for me,'[55] he would say in mid-opera,
while he nipped across the road for a drink – but he was too weak to
last. 'I had never seen a stage so badly run,' said Latham, who
resigned after ten weeks at Covent Garden and went to work at
Glyndebourne. Her letter to Webster, outlining Clifford's shortcomings, has been removed from the files, but Clifford's contract
was not renewed at the end of the 1950-51 season. 'I am particularly

sorry that I have not been able to give you this news in person,'[56] wrote Webster, avoiding an unpleasant interview with an old provincial friend.

Latham, resuming her post in September 1951, discovered unplumbed depths of inefficiency, and worse. Wages were being paid to men who never showed up, and probably did not exist. She spotted the fraud when the company went on tour and Latham noticed that the names of her stagehands differed from those on the pay packets. 'We were working with dead men,' she exclaimed. 'We'd write ahead and ask for six hands, but when I checked the wage list none of them were the Bills or Freds we'd been given.' There was also some tinkering with expenses, with pounds fiddled up to guineas. Latham took the discrepancies not to Webster but to the company secretary, Douglas Lund. 'He was excellent,' she noted, 'like a weasel down a rat-hole.' The corruption was silently purged. No trace survives in the archives and Webster does not appear to have informed his Board, let alone called the police. Latham came down soon after with consumption, brought on by stress and overwork, and Webster assured her that he would pay her full salary for six months of recovery. 'My God,' she thought, 'just how much money have I saved them?'

Petty theft and Mickey-Mouse practices were creeping in to British industry and would become endemic in Fleet Street, but in the early 50s they were still unusual in the London theatre and unheard of at Stratford. Webster needed to hush the scandal, not because he feared for his position but because it would have dented his myth of immaculate management.

His awareness of image was ahead of its time, and his use of industrial psychology was equally advanced. 'He knew us all, weaknesses and strengths,' said Latham. His technique was to say little and do nothing, letting others assume that he read their minds, approved their actions and deserved credit for their success. It was only in the very jaws of disaster that he ever acted decisively, and such instances were so uncommon that their rarity greatly magnified the impact of his intervention.

Once, during a rehearsal of Offenbach's *Tales of Hoffmann*, he began to suspect that the conductor, Désiré Emile Inghelbrecht, retired chief of the Paris Opéra, did not know the score. A hurried check revealed that the elegant septuagenarian had never conducted *Tales* in his life. Webster, in full view of the company, sacked the

Frenchman and summoned a new member of the music staff, Edward Downes, to take over. Downes, until lately a horn player at Sadler's Wells, seized his opportunity with both hands and saved the show. Webster was credited with *Hoffmann*'s rescue, even though the problem had arisen from his own cavalier assumption that any maître from the Paris Opéra would know his Offenbach like a Stratford man knew his Shakespeare. Webster's ignorance of conducting lore was absolute, but his bold decision obscured the original error and reinforced his aura as a far-sighted, all-seeing leader of an ever-improving enterprise.

Not that conductors ranked high in Webster's list of priorities. Singers were paramount, and it was to their welfare and development that he devoted most attention. With Rankl gone and Wilson often away on well-paid lecture tours, Webster increased his involvement in the selection process. Rankl's four-cornered trawl of the kingdom had more or less exhausted native resources but a tide of hopefuls began to turn up from the dominions. Sylvia Fisher, who had sung *Aida* on Australian radio, convinced Rankl on her fifth audition to cast her as Leonore in *Fidelio*. Her success smoothed the path for many of her compatriots. Fisher's voice was extolled by *Opera* magazine as 'one of the joys of the present day'[57] and her cheerful, no-worries attitude made her the perfect company singer; she also married the company's Italian coach, Ubaldo Gardini.

Less immediately appealing, at least to the managerial and critical teams, was the New Zealander Joan Hammond, whose mannish demeanour attracted a vociferous clique. Webster was not convinced. He was looking for team players, not prima donnas. The antipodeans he hired were not the kind who answered back. Elsie Morison was poached from Sadler's Wells in 1953 and Marie Collier from Glyndebourne two years later. The tenor John Lanigan was retrieved from Jay Pomeroy's wreckage. 'I had a letter one morning from Webster, asking if I would think of joining to do *Fidelio* and *Bohème* – for me, it was heaven on earth,' said Morison, who was married at the time to a Covent Garden bass, Kenneth Stevenson.[58]

None of these recruitments, however, possessed the elusive gleam that separates the timeless artist from the merely timely. What was needed was a heavenly star, incontestable and irresistible, who would give a rocket-boost to ROH prestige and raise other singers with her to a higher plane of fame. Webster, at auditions, prayed for a Nellie Melba or a Florence Austral to ascend from the antipodes – and prayed doubly hard that she did not apply first to Vienna or New York.

The miracle he was seeking arrived in the mail one morning in the autumn of 1951, in the shape of a testimonial from Eugene Goossens who was still trying to work his way into Webster's favour. 'The bearer of this letter,' wrote Goossens,

> has a magnificent soprano voice and has done excellent work here in concert and operatic performances. Her voice is in the true Austral tradition and she made quite a sensation here recently in her creation of Judith in my opera of that name. Her departure for Europe will be a great loss to Australia for such grand natural voices as hers are all too rare nowadays.

An audition was arranged at the Wigmore Hall at 2.45 p.m. on 16 October, before Sir Steuart Wilson who gave a typically dusty report: 'Starts with a good ring in the voice. Very little stage experience *or gifts by nature*.'[59] The gangling, square-jawed Australian, three weeks short of her twenty-fifth birthday, was advised to return to her studies with Clive Carey and reapply six months later. Second time round, in June 1952, Peter Gellhorn detected an 'unusual solidity' in her voice and suggested that she might, in time, become a dramatic soprano. A third audition was held on 10 July at Covent Garden with Webster himself in the stalls. The tall girl sang 'Non mi dir' from *Don Giovanni* followed by 'Ritorna vincitor' from *Aida* and, while most felt she would at best become a decent understudy for Sylvia Fisher, Webster in his report noted: 'with work, might do better than that'.

Before the week was out, members of the music staff heard her sing Giorgetta in a Royal College production of Puccini's *Il Tabarro*, and the matter was settled. 'I got a telephone call the next day from the Garden,' recalled Joan Sutherland, 'and they said, "My dear, we have decided that you should join the Company, starting in September."'[60] She was to be paid ten pounds a week and was told to learn the First Lady in *The Magic Flute*. Sutherland made her début on 28 October and a week later sang the High Priestess in *Aida*. Four days after that, her recital début at the Wigmore Hall drew a ripple of reviews from critics alerted to her promise by Webster, who was convinced from the outset of her potential. 'This,' he said, 'is the first singer we've had here since the War who is capable of becoming a star.'[61]

But the rise of Joan Sutherland was to be slow and spasmodic. Seven years would pass before she exploded on to the world's consciousness in the Mad Scene of Donizetti's *Lucia di Lammermoor*. Time enough for various members of the Board and the music staff to question her stiff gestures and lack of conventional good looks. After *Lucia*, any fool could have spotted her star quality, but it took courage to keep faith in Sutherland for seven lean years. Webster, however, harboured no doubts. He assured Mrs Sutherland that her daughter was destined for greatness and when Joan slipped out to marry her Svengali-like pianist friend, Richard Bonynge, the General Administrator sent a huge bouquet of red carnations to the church in Ladbroke Grove and gave the young couple a reception at his Weymouth Street flat. No other young singer was so favoured. When Sutherland sent her agent, Joan Ingpen, to beg for Mondays off to have her teeth fixed, Webster's only quibble was, 'are you sure she is seeing the best person?'[62]

Her ascent was delayed by several impediments, not least the onset of pregnancy and the insistent presence of Bonynge, who whipped her off to a throat specialist at the first sniff of a cold and lobbied tirelessly for her advancement. Socially, she held herself slightly apart and shunned the coarse humour of singers. On one occasion, when Geraint Evans's hand touched her bare midriff in a *Figaro* rehearsal, she swung round and belted him across the jaw. She made another baritone swear never to relate that she had let off a thunderous fart as he clasped her to his bosom. Even as an ingenue, she assumed the *hauteur* of stardom.

The immediate obstacle to vertical progress was an historic force far greater than herself. On 8 November 1952, the day after Sutherland's début recital, Maria Callas made her first appearance at Covent Garden, with the Australian trailing her in the minor role of Clothilde, her nurse. Callas, just twenty-eight years old, was a Manhattan-born Greek who had been provoking near-riots in Italian opera houses. Outside of Italy, she was known only in Greece and South America. She possessed a twin-edged reputation, for ferociously intense performances allied to a temperament that brooked no contradiction. Frumpish yet sultry, she was married to a Verona businessman, Giovanni Battista Menenghini, whose role in life was to obstruct anyone who approached Maria, making her own recalcitrance appear moderate by comparison. Before Covent Garden came into her reckoning, she had fallen out badly with her mentor, the conductor Tullio Serafin, and turned down a début at the Met in New York.

The first Englishman to be smitten was the Earl of Harewood, who in August 1947 caught the second or third night of her Italian début in Ponchielli's *La Gioconda*, with Serafin conducting, in the Arena di Verona. Harewood was struck by the tigerishness of her delivery and undismayed by a quavery harshness that marred some high notes. Four years later, he heard her in Verdi's *Sicilian Vespers* in Florence, under Erich Kleiber, and marvelled at her enlarged authority and waistline. Webster turned up soon after with a proposal that she should embrace the role at Covent Garden in English – which was, in a sense, her native tongue. Callas laughed, and countered with an offer to sing *Norma*, in Italian. Webster murmured a noncommital approval which endeared him to Callas, who was accustomed to more emphatic, usually hostile, responses.

Bellini's little diva-pleaser of an opera had last been staged at Covent Garden in May 1930 to suit Rosa Ponselle. Dating from 1831, it was the high watermark of bel canto opera, an early-romantic school that demanded tonal beauty and exaggerated dramatics. If it took a démodé work to catch a Callas, Webster deemed it worth the risk. Meanwhile, EMI's Walter Legge had wormed his way past Menenghini to get Callas's signature on a record contract. London was about to become her stepping-stone to world fame.

Typically for Callas, between consent and consummation, lay months of vacillation. Her London agent, Sandor Gorlinsky, implored her to confirm the ROH dates. Callas demanded a six-month postponement, having accepted a better offer from Mexico City. Webster cabled her new *Norma* dates, assuring her that 'we count on and look forward to your participation'.[63] This time, Callas confirmed – for a fee of two hundred and fifty pounds a night, £100 higher than any other ROH artist, plus ten pounds a day living allowance (equivalent to Sutherland's weekly wage) and return fares for herself, husband and secretary. Webster booked her a suite at the Savoy and filled it with flowers. At her general rehearsal, the orchestra broke into applause.

On opening night, Callas's first big duet with the mezzo-soprano Ebe Stignani earned an ovation and was, against house rules, encored. When she delivered 'Casta diva', the house erupted. If ever a star was born, this was the moment. A great artist had come of age on a great stage, each enhanced by the other. All tickets for the remaining four performances were gone by morning. The first reviews were reserved, Ernest Newman grouching that she is 'slightly sub-Normal' and 'no Ponselle'. Philip Hope-Wallace in the *Manchester Guardian* struck a more admonitory note:

> Her phrasing was often memorable, arresting and even perhaps exaggerated; though she is a most musicianly singer. Yet the flawless vocal emission which is the cardinal quality called for in this exposed and perilous role was not vouchsafed. The voice is uneven. Some things, such as the gliding runs in the first scene and the attacked high notes in the second, were dazzling and amazed the audience. There were some beautiful soft phrases. But the voice did not ride the big final ensemble as it should . . . I myself cannot feel that she is more than a plausible *Norma*. The classical dimension was wanting.[64]

Even at this stage there were *cognoscenti* who voiced concern at her intensity and warned that if she carried on so recklessly she would burn out in her prime. They were stating the obvious. What made Callas so compelling was her reckless passion in performance, risks that she took half-knowing that they could destroy her voice and herself. To her overnight fans, Callas was a revelation. *Opera* magazine raved over her 'fabulous *fioriture*' and 'stupendous' top notes; she appeared twice on its cover in three months. Joan Sutherland, as Clothilde, sidled up to Callas in the wings and whispered shyly that she would like one day to sing Norma. 'Why not?' said the diva. 'It means a lot of work; but why not?'[65]

Callas went from London to open La Scala's season in Verdi's *Macbeth* and then to Florence for *Lucia di Lammermoor*, where the veteran tenor Giacomo Lauri-Volpi, who sang Edgardo to her Lucia, told the press that 'this young artist, with her ability to rouse the multitudes, may yet lead the lyric theatre to a new golden age of singing'.[66] But she was always larger than operatic life. Her visual impact was as stunning as her aural appeal and her instinct was uncanny. The conductor Antonino Votto referred to 'a unity of music, drama and movement . . . an aesthetic phenomenon'. On and off stage, she became the most famous Greek woman since Helen of Troy, a modern immortal. Quarter of a century after her death, she sold more records each year than any living soprano.

Webster, asked to sum her up in one sentence for *Vogue* magazine, reflected that she liberated opera from its inbred artificiality and raised it to an altogether higher plane. She possessed

a radiant personality steeped in music, a rare feeling for words, their meaning and colour, an acute sense of timing, an innate appreciation of line in music and movement, an ability to make an audience part of her own experience, a capacity to fuse music and drama so that an aria is not a set piece but part of a complete musical and dramatic development within which she can raise a *Tosca* to the level of classical tragedy.[67]

What Callas did for Covent Garden was to raise the English company to world rank. Although she returned only five times, in six roles, the Royal Opera House was pivotal in her life. Falling out with every other major house, she maintained tranquil relations with Webster and his staff. Legge, one of her closest collaborators, called her 'vengeful, vindictive, malicious . . . ungrateful',[68] and she did not seem to care who got caught in the eye of her storms – managers, fellow-artists, police officers, tax inspectors, politicians. Callas possessed an ego the size of Olympus and an insecurity that was never long subdued.

But most testimonies suggest she turned difficult only 'when those around her failed to show the same dedication – when people arrived unprepared or unserious, that's when she'd hit the roof'.[69] Edward Downes, who occupied the prompt box at her début and rehearsed her in other roles, remembered her as 'an exceedingly professional lady. She sang with prodigious intensity all the time. And all the stories about her tantrums, they were never involved with her professional colleagues who were doing their job. She was always there to rehearse, she always worked, there was never any shirking.'[70] A future ROH chairman who took her to lunch with his wife noted: 'what struck us most was her intensely practical and analytical approach to her work.'[71]

At Covent Garden, she threatened once to walk out of *Trovatore* after a clash with James Johnston, a Belfast tenor with his own butcher's business and a slightly whimsical attitude to work. She also blew out the conductor, Alberto Erede, for refusing to accept her tempi in the final aria. But these were rare dissonances amid general harmony. 'She and (Giulietta) Simionato were always going off into peals of laughter,' reported the bass singer Michael Langdon, who overheard them, in mid-performance, discussing the price of knickers at Marks & Spencer. In rehearsal, Callas noticed Langdon's habit of beating time with both hands, clasped behind his back. Sneaking up, she grabbed his wrists just as Erede gave his cue, giggling into his ear, 'now you won't be able to sing, will you?'[72] *Trovatore* was the third of three operas she sang in Coronation month. Her fee was now £400 a night, net of tax.

She was not seen again at Covent Garden for three and a half years, by which time she had slimmed herself down from fourteen stone to ten, telling her hairdresser she aimed to resemble Audrey Hepburn in the film *Roman Holiday*. At one stage she dyed her hair blonde. In Luchino Visconti's May 1955 La Scala production of *Traviata*, conducted by Carlo-Maria Giulini, there were gasps in the stalls at her sudden luminosity. A gorgeous Violetta had emerged from caterpillar fat, investing the role with a sulphurous passion and sickly decline that split Italian critics into warring camps. Many had never seen a more gripping account of the role; others cavilled at her gestures and complained that the voice weakened towards the end, impaired by weight-loss. Callas maintained that she made her voice sound weak to accentuate the consumptive heroine's tragedy.

The Callas that London saw in two *Norma*s in January 1957 was a fully-fledged world star. She had conquered New York and been launched, by her new friend Elsa Maxwell, into high society. The Savoy gave her 'the Callas suite' and Covent Garden paid her hotel bills, plus £500 a night.* The hotel thronged with pressmen and the performances ended with Callas and Stignani in tears, overwhelmed by the blaze of their reception.

She returned in June 1958 for a Gala marking the centenary of Covent Garden's Victorian reconstruction, followed by six *Traviata*s. She was now so expensive that Webster had to raise top ticket prices from four guineas to five, notifying his chairman of the stupendous cost of Callas:

---

* on applying for a work permit, Webster declared to the Ministry of Labour that he was paying Callas £300; he clearly did not want the Government to know how much tax money was flowing to one foreign singer

6 performances @ £500	£3,000.00.00
2 return fares to Milan	£154.10.00
Hotel for 3 people for 23 days	£923.6.10
Tax paid by us	£1,575.6.00
Total	£5,653.22.10
Cost per performance	£942.3.10

Such was the financial pressure that when the BBC's *Monitor* programme sought an interview with the diva, Webster demanded a fifty-guinea 'management fee' on the grounds that Covent Garden were paying all her expenses 'and it did not seem to me very fair to Covent Garden that the BBC should have this artist working for them at what in fact amounts to our expenses.'[73] He took steps to protect her lustre by denying her chief La Scala rival, Renata Tebaldi, the showcase of a new production. Tebaldi sang seldom in London and, though she acquired devoted fans, Webster and Harewood were wedded to Callas.

Webster bragged to his Board of his 'special relationship'[74] with Callas. She was the rock on which the case for an all-English company shattered, the pivot around which Webster was able to turn Covent Garden towards internationalism. Callas, however, was not built to last. By 1958 her voice was plainly fraying. 'Some of us remained only fifty per cent enraptured,' wrote Hope-Wallace. 'Personally, I suffered much.' Not that most fans minded the sudden shrieks. Callas could have recited the A to D telephone directory in E-flat and the house would have hung on to every Brown and Cook in the book. 'Like everyone else,' confessed a budding critic, 'I was converted to opera by Callas.'[75] Every time she sang was an act of defiance, a glove flung in the face of fate and purism. 'Opera is a battlefield,' said the living Callas. 'My weapons are my voice and my technique.'[76] Viewed in retrospect, 'filmed excerpts from Callas's performances attest to the desperate intensity with which she sought to justify opera, regardless of her own vocal or mental survival.'[77]

The fatal acts were about to unfold. On her next trip to London, in 1959, she fell for Aristotle Onassis, the Greek shipowner who coveted her glory and abused her love. Her stage appearances became infrequent as she sat by the phone waiting for Ari to call. Webster called her often, but to no avail. The dramatic finale was destined for London, but not quite yet.

Sweeping into the theatre on the eve of the 1958 Gala, Callas overheard Joan Sutherland rehearsing the aria 'I dreamt that I dwelt in marble halls' from Balfe's *Bohemian Girl*. She stopped to listen and, when told the soprano's name, remembered the ungainly Australian who had sung Clothilde in her own début, less than six years before. She praised the singing to Harewood, and then said: 'She has learnt very well how to copy me.'[78]

Sutherland, apprised of this remark, was delighted. Still awaiting her apotheosis, she took the compliment in the spirit in which it had been intended. Callas was the queen of the operatic walk, and an ambitious singer could do no better than watch, wait and try to outshine her. Sutherland and others at Covent Garden absorbed something of the Callas ardour and her bel canto repertoire, while taking care to avoid her tonal impurity. Legge warned that Callas's example could destroy the next generation of singers; in fact, all she destroyed was herself. Some months after the Gala, the critic Noël Goodwin wrote, with uncanny prescience:

> I predict that if Maria Callas, now thirty-four, goes on performing at the present rate, she will have left no professional singing voice by the time she is forty. Joan Sutherland ... will, within five years, be acclaimed as famous an international star as Maria Callas is now, but she will no longer be a member of the Covent Garden Company.[79]

*

The cost of internationalism was unbudgeted. Engaging foreign stars had been a calculated risk – vocal credibility in exchange for financial exposure – and the first part of the equation was richly fulfilled. Covent Garden was becoming known as 'a singer's house' – more than just a famous stage, it was now a place where artists came to learn their craft. By the mid-1950s, one executive observed, 'singers from all over the world would make special journeys to London to study with the staff',[80] so expert were the repetiteurs and coaches at teaching roles and getting the best out of untapped vocal potential.

Such considerations can moderate a singer's fee demands but the cumulative cost would plunge Covent Garden into an unending cycle of cash crises. When matters grew desperate Webster said nothing to his board, and tried to catch the eye of John Denison, director of music at the Arts Council. 'I got on very well with David,' said Denison, 'and from time to time he'd say to me, "perhaps you could drop round for a chat on Thursday evening?" So I would go to his flat at Weymouth Street, after supper, and we'd take a walk around the block. Then David would say, "we're running out of money, I don't think I can pay the wages next week." In the morning I'd see the Treasurer at the Arts Council and ask for a thousand-pound advance on Covent Garden's next grant. That's how it was done, no forms to fill, no fuss.'[81]

No opera house can live hand to mouth and expect to sustain high standards. In 1952, the overdraft reached £100,000 and closure became a distinct possibility unless an uninterested Tory Government agreed to increase its grant. Papers were produced showing that the French Government gave the Paris Opéra eight times the amount of Covent Garden's stipend and even the Colón in Buenos Aires received twice as much. But the Treasury argued that ROH grants had risen sixfold since 1945, well above inflation.

In February 1952, the Arts Council chairman Ernest Pooley delivered morbid news to the Covent Garden chairman, not without a wry smirk. 'Dear John,' he wrote disingenuously,

> You will be disappointed but not, I suppose, surprised, to hear that the best we can do for the Royal Opera House Covent Garden in 1952-53 is a grant of £150,000. In submitting our estimates to the Chancellor of the Exchequer we included a much higher figure for Covent Garden, and I can truly say that we represented your needs very strongly to the Treasury. However, the Chancellor has been unable to give us any increase on our previous year's grant of £575,000 for the whole of our operations and we in turn cannot improve on the sum we voted Covent Garden last year.[82]

Lord Waverley replied, in his dustiest Scottish tones:

> My dear Ernest,
>   I read your letter of 14th February to my Board yesterday. It is clear that we are confronted by a major financial crisis which will call for grave decisions in the very near future. In view of the care with which the details of our expenditure have already been examined I cannot help feeling very doubtful whether further discussions will prove profitable . . .[83]

Waverley decided not to waste his time on the Arts Council. He went into action on higher ground at the Treasury, his old department, and put in a bid for an exceptional one-off grant, half of it to pay off the overdraft and the other half for 'bricks and mortar' repairs. By summer, he had won the case and got the Chancellor to approve a £90,000 'rescue operation'. This concession was then consolidated the following year into the regular ROH grant, which rose by around sixty per cent. Even this boost, however, failed to stem the losses or guarantee financial stability. Through the 1950s, Covent Garden found itself unable to get by on £240,000 to £270,000 state subsidy, ten times its original allowance (retail prices, from 1946 to 1956, rose by just fifty per cent).

The more Covent Garden was given, the more it spent on foreign singers. The nights might glitter but by day Webster and his team wrestled with the spectre of foreclosure. In Whitehall minds, said Denison, both Covent Garden and the Arts Council were impermanent bodies that could be disestablished without fuss. The insecurity was acute. At Sadler's Wells, with no world stars, the situation was just as grim. The costs of running opera and ballet had risen 'out of all proportion to the income'. The day was gone, lamented its director Norman Tucker, 'when artists could be expected to take a kind of charitable or missionary view of their work at Sadler's Wells'.[84] Yet, as leaders of both houses would rue in later, tougher times, there was still enough cash in hand to enable them to act on impulse and recover from mistakes.

Waverley now decided to go politicking. 'When does Pooley's term end?' he asked Webster in a curt memo, before making sure that the next chairman of the Arts Council would be a trusted friend. At a meeting of the board his eye fell on Kenneth Clark, a founding father who had failed to find a role after his National Gallery era. Clark liked to say that he had only two loyalties in life – to his family and to the Royal Opera House. 'I have not only enjoyed performances there,' he wrote, 'but have developed an affection for the whole place – the auditorium, the foyer and the members of the staff, which is like a family feeling.'[85]

He was the perfect candidate for Arts Council chairman, a Covent Garden stooge, and his appointment was rushed through the 'usual channels' that Waverley was so expert at navigating. Clark's ascent at the prime of life – he was still on the right side of fifty – promised a rekindling of the Keynesian ideal of art for everyman, accessible and comprehensible. But Clark, for all his passion and erudition, turned out to be a terrible disappointment. 'I cannot say that the Arts

Council prospered under my chairmanship, or that I enjoyed my spell of office,'[86] he admitted. There was not enough money to make much difference, he complained, and the Taffia-epoch secretary-general, W. E. Williams, denied him a secretary or an office. 'K. Clark wasn't allowed to know anything,' chuckled John Denison, the music director, 'we just got on with it.'

Clark, truth be told, was easily distracted. He craved fame, and soon took on a livelier post as chairman of the Independent Television Authority. In time, he found his *métier* as presenter of the most illuminating art series ever seen on the small screen. It was as 'Lord Clark of *Civilization*' that Clark entered posterity – though without reaping the contentment that usually accompanies success. Clark was a restless man, beset by a concupiscent urge that verged on the obsessive. 'He was forever looking over your shoulder at any passing woman,' said a Covent Garden associate.[87] His conquests were numerous and he rented a flat in Dover Street for casual assignations. Jane Clark, for her part, took to the bottle.

Soon after taking office, Clark stumbled across a highly irregular arrangement. The Council and the opera house were, he discovered, employing the same accountant and company secretary. Douglas Peter Lund worked mornings for the provider of grants and afternoons for the receiver. Insiders joked that he would write a strong letter to himself demanding financial information, and then carry it from St James's Square to Floral Street on his lunchtime walk to save postage, before replying to himself in equally robust terms.

Lund had been a tax inspector in Newcastle before serving as chief accountant to the Royal Air Force in Italy, where he fell prey to the opera bug. Unwilling to return to provincial monotony, he wangled an introduction through his commanding officer to Leslie Boosey, who found him part-time work at Covent Garden, augmented in 1950 by an extra half-job at the Arts Council. Lund, known as 'Peter' at work and 'Douglas' to friends, was a cautious man who would never have taken the liberty of writing an official letter to himself. Exchanges between Covent Garden and the Arts Council were always conducted and signed by the secretary-general and general administrator. Lund, said his colleagues, merely drafted the letters, in both directions.[88]

Honest as Lund was, Clark saw impropriety in his dual loyalty. 'I mentioned to you the other day the anxiety I feel about our joint employment of Mr Lund,' he told Waverley. 'The fact that Covent

Garden and the Arts Council go halves in their Finance Officer is a matter which could be interpreted very injuriously by such a body as the Public Accounts Committee . . . We on the inside know that Mr Lund's dual role works to our joint advantage – but that could be made to look otherwise from the other side of the fence.'[89]

Waverley dismissed Clark's fears as petty niceties. As far as he was concerned, the Royal Opera House was, like the Royal Family, above reproach and answerable to no mortal authority. He had talked to Lund, he told Clark, and his 'personal feelings are that under practically no circumstances is he prepared to give up Covent Garden.'[90] So Lund was allowed to continue working for both organizations, staying with the Arts Council until 1965 and with Covent Garden until his statutory retirement in 1972. So collusory was the arrangement that when Covent Garden raised his £2,250 salary by ten per cent in January 1955, 'Mr Denison undertook to ascertain whether the Arts Council would be willing to contribute one half of the proposed increase.'[91] On two salaries, Lund earned more than either of his bosses, Webster and Williams.

In addition to his double-role, Lund also did a little freelancing on the side. When Webster engaged foreign stars, he would offer Lund's services to get them the best deal on UK taxes; as a former inspector, Lund knew all the loopholes and could make their ROH sojourn that bit more profitable. 'Perhaps you'll allow Mr Lund to present his bill for looking after Tito's tax?' Webster would remind Gobbi's agent, making sure his chief financial officer got properly recompensed. After he retired, Lund was allowed to keep an office in the Royal Opera House so that he could keep 'in touch with events and with those singers whose tax he looks after'.[92]

Everybody trusted Lund, who died in 1974 and never put so much as sixpence in the wrong column. However, where public money is being handled, it is as important for the bookkeeper to avoid any hint of suspicion as it is for the books to balance. Lund blurred the lines of state funding, casting a shadow of doubt over both giver and receiver and introducing a procedural sloppiness that would, in time, bring both institutions into disrepute. If the Ministry of Defence and Rolls-Royce had been sharing the same accountant, the implications could hardly have been graver.

So close were Covent Garden and the Arts Council, they even shared the same bank. If Coutts got fretful about Covent Garden's credit worthiness, they had only to consult the Arts Council, which bankrolled the ROH. The risk to Coutts in letting the ROH run up large debts was therefore non-existent.

To the pure, it is said, all is pure. It would never have crossed the high mind of a man like Waverley to imagine that ROH dealings with the Arts Council were intended for any purpose other than the greatest public benefit. Nevertheless, he would have been the first to acknowledge that any drift from accepted norms of public conduct can induce a laziness of mind that fosters, if not corruption, then at the very least an inferior form of governance. That Waverley, the Civil Service paragon, should have given Covent Garden the licence to break rules is a paradox almost beyond comprehension. In later years, wags would say that when public men joined the Board of the Royal Opera House, they left their brains at the door.

While Waverley played politics, Webster fixed the press. To justify hugely increased public funding, he needed to show results – and results in the lively arts are measured in high attendances and rave reviews. The press in the 1950s was overcoming its wartime complaisance and, as pages increased, starting to report closely and critically on national enterprises. Tougher verbiage came into play. A new *Tannhäuser* was put down as 'a disgrace';[93] a John Cranko ballet, with Beryl Grey and David Blair, was 'a great disappointment . . . beyond the point of no return'.[94] The grumblings of old Ernest Newman could be ascribed to geriatric dyspepsia, but the new wave of opera and ballet critics were less predictable and they were beginning to question the purpose and viability of the Royal Opera House.

Attendances started to drop, especially for routine revivals sung in English by non-star casts. A run of *Bohème* played to 54 per cent capacity on poor reviews and *Rigoletto* to 46 per cent. Webster cultivated the critics, knowing the glow a good lunch could bring to the next batch of reviews. But he needed to boost confidence in his company and was prepared to use his powers of appointment to sway leading journalists.

The placement of newspaper coverage and dining of editors was generally left to the ROH press officer Michael Wood and his Australian deputy, Bill Beresford, recruited from the *Daily Express*. When Wood went off in 1958 to manage the ballet company, he was succeeded by Beresford. He took as his deputy a girl who had come to Webster's office two years earlier, asking for a job.

'What can you do?' said Webster.

'Well, I can't sing,' said Sheila Porter, 'but I have an Oxford degree in Greats.'

The fact was not lost on Webster that Sheila was the twin sister of Andrew, associate editor of *Opera* magazine and music critic of the *Financial Times*, whose managing director, Viscount Moore, had succeeded Denis Rickett as Secretary to the Covent Garden Board. Sheila Porter was duly recruited as deputy press officer. Beresford, it so happened, lived next door to Andrew Porter on Pembroke Walk. The circle was stiflingly small.

It says much for Andrew Porter's strength of mind that he shut out all intimate connections and wrote some of the most intelligent and combative coverage of Covent Garden over the next two decades. It says just as much for Webster's delicacy that he did not, by word or wink, seek to influence Andrew Porter through his sister. 'It was never a hazard,' she maintained.[95]

The temptations resisted by Andrew Porter were, on the other hand, meat and drink to *Opera*'s editor. Harold Rosenthal had taken charge of the monthly when its founder, Lord Harewood, went to work for Webster in 1953. Rosenthal was also on the ROH payroll, earning three pounds a week as company archivist.[96] He loved being on the inside of an opera house, mingling with stars in the staff canteen. A suburban ex-schoolmaster, he was an exceptionally ugly man with a puppylike desire to please. The director Christopher West, whom Rosenthal considered his friend, quipped that he had 'a face like an arsehole turned inside out'. Others called him 'a slippery little man, so ugly you had to be nice to him'.[97]

Opera, with a circulation of barely five thousand, was acquiring a cachet as the buffs' Bible, authoritative in tone and exhaustive in detail. Many of its reviews criticized Covent Garden productions and some of Rosenthal's editorials challenged aspects of policy. But his belief in the need for a Royal Opera House was absolute and his pages were at its service. A puffy little feature introduced 'new singers at the Royal Opera House'; Sadler's Wells, Glyndebourne and the emergent Welsh National Opera were never given equal weight.

Rosenthal's presence in the Covent Garden corridors was widely resented. Beecham, in 1951, demanded his dismissal. Sir Steuart Wilson complained about 'the general position that *Opera* holds inside the House and I wish that we could make something a little more satisfactory than having their waspish attacks directed at us from the inside.'[98] But Webster was unbothered; when Rosenthal resigned in 1956 to write a glorifying centennial history of Covent Garden, he was still given the run of the house and a modest budget to purchase items for the archives.

Webster believed he had Rosenthal in his pocket. A peep of impartiality from *Opera*, an editorial in praise of Norman Tucker's reforms at Sadler's Wells, drew an enraged response. 'Thank you for your letter of October 27th enclosing the drivel which you propose to publish,' wrote Webster. '. . . As you know I have never objected and never will object to criticism either of this organization or of myself, but to propose to publish such plausible nonsense at this juncture in our careers is really going too far.'[99] Webster threatened to found a rival publication and run *Opera* out of business. Rosenthal, terrified, crawled back into line and so successfully appeased Webster that he felt confident enough, the following year, to put himself forward to succeed Harewood, who was leaving to become Director of the Edinburgh Festival. 'My dear David,' wrote Rosenthal, 'I don't know whom you have in mind as your next Controller of Opera Planning, but I would very much like you to consider me seriously as a possible successor to George. I feel that I could do the job and that my knowledge of the world of opera and its personalities is as good as anyone's.'[100]

Webster ignored the application, which was repeatedly resubmitted. He did, however, accede to the next suggestion from the insistent editor. Rosenthal was forever impecunious and on the lookout for little jobs. He offered to supply Webster with a quarterly listing of the world's leading singers and conductors, where and what they were performing and with whom. The information flowed into *Opera* from its worldwide correspondents and could be made available for a modest financial consideration. Webster, who could have read most of the information in the magazine itself, or obtained it from his fellow-intendants, decided to find value in Rosenthal's idea and agreed to pay him £250 a year in quarterly instalments.[101]

This was no small sum, enough to pay for a family holiday in a luxury resort. Rosenthal drew payments from Covent Garden for a good few years (the termination is not noted on file), at times requesting an advance for 'urgent family expenses'. His income was hidden from the contributors who supplied his data, and from the critics who might have been concerned by his conflict of interests.

Webster made no apparent use of the information he acquired from Rosenthal. He was buying the man, not the material, and seemed content with the bargain. In the struggle to sustain Covent Garden he could safely rely on the unqualified support of *Opera* and its heavily compromised editor.

An air of aimlessness set in, obscured by growing ease. Churchill finally resigned in April 1954, at the age of 79, but his heir was a man of short temper, broken health and no experience in domestic affairs. 'I don't believe Anthony can do it,' said Churchill on his return from the Palace, and Eden soon proved him right. Austerity was ending, but there was no grand design for creating prosperity. The age of anxiety had given way to an epoch of uncertainty. England was planning to muddle through.

The absence of visionary leadership can erode great institutions no matter how efficiently they are administered, and Covent Garden was not alone among the ships of state that were drifting to no obvious purpose. The BBC, the Church, the Royal Navy and the England soccer team which lost its unbeaten home record in a 3-6 defeat to Hungary were all struggling with questions of identity and strategy.

By September 1954, the doubts about Covent Garden's artistic aims were growing intense. The season opened with bad news from abroad. Benjamin Britten's new opera, *The Turn of the Screw*, was premièred in Venice on 14 September and broadcast back home over the BBC Third Programme. Despite carping from Howes in *The Times* and some indiscretions in the French press about the composer's homosexual obsessions, the public response and critical consensus were that Britten had, as the *Manchester Guardian* put it, 'created another masterpiece'.

The opera came to London three weeks later – but to Sadler's Wells, not to Covent Garden. While awaiting its turn at the *Screw*, the Wells put on (at Britten's instigation) the world première of another English opera, *Nelson* by Lennox Berkeley. It was tepidly received and soon discarded, but the spirit of enterprise seemed livelier in Islington than at the slumbrous Royal Opera House. Early Verdi was being promoted by Tucker and young conductors, like Charles Mackerras and Alexander Gibson, were given their head; Gibson would go on to found Scottish Opera. The Welsh National Opera were preparing to make their London début – at Sadler's

Wells, needless to say. The Wells had been drenched in emotion the previous spring when, for the centenary of Janáček's birth, *Katya Kabanova* was sung by a cockney sparrow, Amy Shuard, and conducted by the imposing Czech exile, Rafael Kubelik, who was about to return for a second run. The strengths of this production had led Shawe-Taylor to underline 'the paramount importance of the operatic conductor'. Webster was under pressure to act fast, or miss out.

He had been trying for years to meet Kubelik, who had flown to London in February 1948 on the day the Communists seized power in Prague. The willowy son of a legendary violinist, Kubelik had spent the first half of the war conducting opera in Brno, and the second half as head of the Czech Philharmonic. Stateless in his mid-thirties but well known in the West, he was besieged by attractive offers, accepting a guest conductorship at the Concertgebouw in Amsterdam and in 1950 the music director's baton at the Chicago Symphony Orchestra. His shiny-eyed integrity and an appetite for dissonant new music did not go down well with older subscribers and earned him torrents of vituperation from the *Tribune* critic, Claudia Cassidy. Kubelik, hyper-sensitive to personal slights, quit after three seasons and returned to London with his violinist wife, Ludmilla, who had been left partly disabled and in constant pain after being physically assaulted in Prague.

Webster was smitten by *Katya*. On 6 October 1954, he informed the Ministry of Labour and National Service that he wanted to appoint Rafael Kubelik as music director of the Covent Garden opera company for a period of seven and a half months a year. An official announcement was made the following day.

Kubelik, conducting abroad, issued a statement declaring his faith in Covent Garden's founding covenants. In Brno, operas had been sung in Czech; in London they should be sung in English by local singers of the highest quality. He was thrilled with Shuard, who quickly signed for Covent Garden, and confident he could find more like her. His second run of *Katya* was, if anything, more shattering than the first. He made his Covent Garden début weeks later, in May 1955, with a more familiar Czech masterpiece, *The Bartered Bride*, with Morison, Lanigan, Otakar Kraus and Noreen Berry in the leading roles. Smetana's opera was a perennial favourite at Sadler's Wells and Norman Tucker was left impotently fuming as Webster impudently stole his best conductor, soprano and box-office comedy.

Webster next attempted to steal Sadler's Wells new clothes with two world premières in eight weeks. First, in December 1954, came William Walton's long-awaited *Troilus and Cressida*, seven years in the making, a bid by the former ROH board member to reclaim the rank of top composer. Walton, with a librettist chosen by Lady Wimborne, wisely eschewed the Shakespearean play which depicts Cressida as a heartless tart and opted for the Chaucerian tale which shows her torn between two lovers, Greek and Trojan. However, on reading Christopher Hassall's draft libretto, Walton was beset by doubts and sent the script for a second opinion to Ernest Newman. Later in the process, he asked W. H. Auden and Laurence Olivier to tinker with it.

He was desperate for the opera to succeed and called in favours from famous friends. Olivier, for whom Walton had composed a *Henry V* film score, was named in *The Times*[102] as the opera's producer and Henry Moore, the foremost English sculptor, as its designer. The Cressida role was written for Elisabeth Schwarzkopf and Troilus for Nicolai Gedda; the conductor was to be Malcolm Sargent, who had given the storming first performance of *Belshazzar's Feast*. Of this glamorous line-up, only Sargent signed up – and his contribution was to bring the work to the edge of destruction.

Sargent had not conducted an opera in eighteen years and barely looked at the score before starting rehearsals. He refused to beat time for singers unless the orchestra was playing, ignoring a plea from Peter Pears, who sang the avuncular role of Pandarus. He tinkered with the instrumentation – 'it's my fucking opera and I'm going to write more for the second harp,'[103] exploded Walton, reversing the textual changes – and in the homebound car one afternoon the conductor tried to grope the composer's young wife.

Walton, fearing Sargent might botch the opera deliberately if he took him to task, shared his despair with the visiting Jascha Heifetz, for whom he had written a magnificent concerto. That night after dinner, Heifetz took the conductor aside.

'I gather, Sir Malcolm, that you are coming soon to visit the United States,' he remarked.

Sargent, swelling with pride that his tour should have been noticed by the greatest living violinist, murmured something about his desire to bring great music to the American public.

'Well listen here,' said Heifetz, in an Edward G. Robinson snarl.

'Unless you sit down right now and learn every note of William's opera, I shall make sure every orchestra in America knows that you are a fake who can hardly read music. Got that?'[104]

Sargent knuckled down to his task, but the opera was beyond redemption. A glittering crowd including Olivier and Vivien Leigh, Somerset Maugham, Henry Moore and Yehudi Menuhin thronged the Royal Opera House on opening night to hear Pears overcome a bout of flu, the Hungarian soprano Magda Laszlo make a goulash of Cressida's English and only Richard Lewis as Troilus fulfilling the composer's hopes and expectations. The press did their best to find rousing adjectives, and Howes in *The Times* called it 'a great tragic opera', but the public response was tepid and by the end of a broken run of twelve performances the house was half-empty.

Walton made cuts and adjustments for sundry revivals but the work never caught fire. It lacked big moments and a build-up of dramatic tension. Tuneful and antediluvian, it was old before its time. When a restoration was staged at Covent Garden in 1976, the next critical generation dismissed *Troilus and Cressida* as 'a hopeless old dodo'.[105]

These reservations were alive within Covent Garden even at the time of the première. Many staffers shared the view of Lord Harewood that Troilus was the equivalent of a 'well-made play'. They placed their faith in *The Midsummer Marriage* by Michael Tippett, which some construed as an English reworking of *The Magic Flute*.

Walton and Tippett were human antipodes, one raised in northern poverty, the other in southern comfort. Walton was blunt-spoken and uncluttered. Tippett pursued vague and esoteric ideologies. Walton had gone to war with rousing film scores; Tippett went to jail as a conscientious objector. Walton was well turned out and something of a ladies' man; Tippett was homosexual, slept in a hovel and was likely to turn up in open-toed sandals. Musically, Walton knew the value of every note and never wasted one. Tippett sprawled all over the staves and looked bewildered when told that what he had written was unplayable on strings. He devised his own librettos, which were riddled with abstruse Jungian and Hinduist symbolisms.

The opera was introduced to Covent Garden by Edward Sackville-West. Webster proposed Cranko or Ashton as director and Graham Sutherland as designer; the jobs finally fell to the house director Christopher West and the sculptress Barbara Hepworth –

not that they were able to shed much light on the composer's intentions. John Pritchard was given another chance to make a name for himself, but Tippett found that Pritchard was sight-reading, and 'Webster warned him that unless he learned the score fully he would never conduct at Covent Garden again.'[106]

While Tippett's supporters rallied behind the project, internal opposition crystallized around Sir Steuart Wilson who had warned from the outset that the opera was overlong, its story 'unattractive' and its visual aspects unclear. 'The nature of the music,' he noted, 'is difficult to describe. I have heard one act only on the piano and it appears to me on the whole to be very diffuse and exceedingly restless: every bar seems filled to the uttermost with notes. The experience I have had with Tippett's music is not encouraging from a practical point of view . . .' Tippett's orchestration said Wilson, 'is highly impractical, and requires a vast amount of rehearsal to extricate the composer's meaning . . . A great deal of time will have to be spent in straightening out the badly expressed intentions of the composer. This opinion will, I know, be corroborated by those few conductors who have coped with Tippett's major works.'[107]

Many of the cast came to share his view. 'If you are coming to ask me what it's about, don't bother,' said Otakar Kraus, who sang the King Fisher. 'I don't know who I am, and that's the truth,' said Edith Coates, described as An Ancient. 'I can only say that I know my part,' was John Lanigan's terse comment to an eve-of-première journalist.[108] When Joan Sutherland, as Jenifer, asked Tippett about the meaning of her part, he said: 'Don't worry, darling. Just sing everything beautifully and the rest will take care of itself.'[109] To the press, he responded: 'I have gathered that the singers don't see what I'm getting at, but the whole thing seems perfectly simple to me. This is a story of two sets of lovers, and their different approach towards marriage. It is a piece of depth and imagination, and it is like a crystal ball which you can turn endless ways.'[110] Some of the cast, he later said, were in tears before the première, denying the remarks attributed to them.

Sutherland and Richard Lewis as her lover, Mark, sang as beautifully as the composer could have wished – 'even if their acting was stiff'.[111] Tippett's boldness was widely praised, as was Covent Garden's in staging so perplexing an opera. The theme, said Howes in *The Times,* 'is magnificent.' But the text was called a 'hotch-potch' by Martin Cooper in the *Daily Telegraph*, 'rubbish' by Shawe-

Taylor in the *Sunday Times* and 'nonsense' by Cecil Smith in the *Daily Express*, adding: 'I consider this libretto . . . one of the worst in the 350-year history of opera.'[112] The audience split almost along generational lines, older viewers showing less tolerance for Tippett's ramblings than younger ones who sensed a raw energy in the piece. The composer himself appeared serenely untouched by criticism, and remained so three years later when his second symphony broke down in chaos a few minutes into its broadcast première. 'Sorry,' said the conductor, Sir Adrian Boult, into the live microphone, 'my fault entirely.' The BBC overrode his apology and wrote a letter to *The Times* blaming the composer.

In the course of time, *The Midsummer Marriage* acquired a cultish following and Tippett a coterie of accomplished interpreters. Three of his five operas were premièred at Covent Garden, where he was elevated, *pace* Britten, to the status of Great British Composer. Yet, despite unwavering support from the ROH and the leading German publisher, Schott, none of Tippett's operas caught on abroad or sold out at home. The German première of *The Midsummer Marriage*, in 1998, was laughed off in Munich as an English eccentricity.

Webster's intentions had been of the best, but the double première demonstrated only that the ROH was no place for new music, conventional or adventurous. The second half of the twentieth century would not yield many operatic masterpieces, but none of its few successes originated at Covent Garden, and British composers discovered that they were better off working with almost any other national company, or best of all with Glyndebourne. The creative aspect of Covent Garden's Keynesian mission died an early death in that dull mid-50s winter.

One spring afternoon, at the end of a Board meeting, Waverley cleared his throat and said, 'Webster, would you be good enough to retire for a few moments? I wish to discuss a certain matter with my colleagues.'

When the door shut, the chairman continued. 'David Webster is overburdened,' he said. 'We should find a suitable young man to assist him. I wonder if any of you has a person to nominate.'[113]

Most of those around the table were aware that Sir Steuart Wilson as Deputy General Administrator was fomenting trouble, and that he and Webster were barely on speaking terms. Wilson had formally complained to Waverley of Webster's shortcomings and now sought to address the board, threatening to go public unless his grievances were noted. Waverley stalled, knowing that Wilson was due to retire in August 1955, his sixty-sixth birthday. He was anxious for Wilson to leave without fuss and for his successor to be an aid to Webster rather than a threat. Even Lord Harewood, resourceful as he was, left Webster and Waverley with an uneasy feeling as to his larger, long-term ambitions.

'Mr Chairman,' piped up Edric Cundell, head of the Guildhall School of Music and one of the newer members, 'I am fortunate to have at my school a very able administrator, John Tooley, and would very much regret to lose him . . .'

'Cundell,' rasped Waverley, 'I am much obliged to you. Will you ask Mr Tooley to attend upon me at the Port of London, tomorrow at nine o'clock. I think we can ask Webster to rejoin us.'

Tooley thus slipped into Covent Garden like gin into vermouth. A product of Repton and Magdalen College, Cambridge, he had spent the war in the Home Counties after falling off a motorbike and being rendered unfit for action. The son of an Admiralty civil servant (Waverley, at their interview, never asked about his background), he shocked his family with talk of becoming an oboist, then a singer, before settling for musical management. Personable and quiet, married and thirty-three years old, he had no further urge to see his name up in lights, but would have appreciated a higher wage than the £1,400 he was offered. 'Webster kept salaries depressed by holding his own down,' said Tooley. 'I had a struggle to make ends meet. A lot of younger people on the staff who had children had a tough time. But Webster insisted everybody had to fall in line.'[114]

Tooley busied himself getting to know the House 'and everyone in it, Niebelheim to Valhalla'.[115] Webster was suspicious at first and refused him the title of Deputy, designating him Assistant. He kept Tooley away from his precious opera stars and used him as his go-between in an increasingly fractious relationship with Ninette de Valois. 'Tooley was Ballet,' said singers, 'we were never much aware of him.'[116]

His appointment was, however, the straw that snapped Sir Steuart Wilson's tolerance. Returning from a lecture tour to find his plea to the Board deferred and his job turned over to a stripling, Wilson resigned on 17 April 1955, refusing to work out the last months of his contract. A statement in *The Times* noted that 'when the present season ends the post of deputy general administrator . . . will be discontinued.'[117] The *Daily Mail* added that Wilson was 'withdrawing immediately on leave'. He told the paper: 'The words "withdrawing immediately" were chosen by myself. You must draw your own inferences from them.' This was unusually strong language for a public official, but Wilson would not be drawn on specifics. He said nothing further for three whole months. Then, furious at the world's indifference to his dismissal, he exploded into print in an interview with the most scurrilous of Sunday newspapers.

MUSIC CHIEF LEADS BIG CAMPAIGN AGAINST VICE

ran the *People*'s headline, and the story that followed was as explicit as the times and libel laws permitted:

A campaign against homosexuality in British music is to be launched by Sir Steuart Wilson, until last month (*sic*) Deputy General Administrator of the Royal Opera House, Covent Garden. Sir Steuart, 66, told the *People* last night:
'The influence of perverts in the world of music has grown beyond all measure. If it is not curbed soon, Covent Garden and other precious musical heritages could suffer irreparable harm.
'Many people in the profession are worried. There is a kind of agreement among homosexuals which results in their keeping jobs for the boys.[118]

In classic Sunday-shocker style, the *People* cast around for men of substance to authenticate its scoop. The best they could find was Mr Walford Haydn, 'the famous composer and conductor', who said:

'Homosexuals are damaging music and all the other arts. I am sorry for those born that way, but many acquire it – and for them I have nothing but contempt. Singers who are perverted often get work simply because of this. And new works by composers are given preference by some people if the writer is perverted.'

The newspaper then solicited and reported a rebuttal from Mr David Webster, General Administrator of the Royal Opera House:

'Music is flourishing,' he said. 'It is nonsense to say that there are jobs for the boys as Sir Steuart alleges.'

Wilson's target was unmistakable, and the report must have struck terror into Webster, coming as it did in the midst of a police crackdown against homosexual men and the places where they met. A war on 'vice' had been declared in 1953 by the Tory Home Secretary, Sir David Maxwell Fyfe, in a grotesque reaction to the Muscovite defection of Guy Burgess and Donald Maclean, whose spy ring was predominantly gay. The Metropolitan Police, for their part, were keen to improve arrest rates in order to mask a rise in organized crime and its seeping corruption of the constabulary.

The vice squad were notoriously compromised and eager to cover up with some big 'collars'. They were no respecters of reputation. Lord Montagu of Beaulieu, peer of the realm, was arrested, charged and jailed for a year for having sex in his own beach house with various men at different times. Sir John Gielgud, the greatest living actor, was grabbed in a public lavatory in Chelsea on the evening of 21 October 1953 and convicted the next morning 'for persistently importuning'. He told the court: 'I was tired and had had a few drinks. I was not responsible for my action.' He was fined ten pounds and told by the magistrate 'to see your doctor the moment you leave here'.[119] (The choreographer John Cranko was arrested in the same area, made the same excuse and received the same fine six years later, a traumatic experience that led him to consider emigration.) Britten and Cecil Beaton were interviewed by Scotland Yard.[120] Alan Turing, the computer genius who cracked Germany's wartime codes, committed suicide with a strychnine-laced apple to escape secret-service scrutiny of his homosexual life.

English hypocrisy was enjoying its high noon. At least one member of the Cabinet, the Colonial Secretary Alan Lennox-Boyd, was a practising homosexual. The flamboyant Labour MP and sometime *Express* gossip columnist, Tom Driberg, was a notorious sex-pest who preyed on young working-class males. When he was arrested in a public lavatory and convicted in open court, not a word appeared in any newspaper, thanks to a code of silence imposed by his friend, the press magnate Lord Beaverbrook. Yet it was Beaverbrook's *Sunday Express* that led the pack against less protected miscreants, demanding in Gielgud's case that the nation should 'mark its abhorrence of this type of depravity by stripping from men involved in such cases any honours that have been bestowed on them'.[121] A prominent MP could importune with impunity but the arrest of a little-known choreographer was front-page news in the *Daily Express*, which described Cranko as 'the latest on the list of famous stage names who have been found guilty of this squalid behaviour'. The paper added: 'It has become a sour commonplace in the West End theatre that unless you are a member of an unpleasant free-masonry your chances of success are often lessened.'[122]

Webster, at this time, was acutely vulnerable. Although his private life seemed a model of middle-aged respectability, Jimmy got frisky at parties[123] and Webster himself predated on fanciable youths, who were sometimes repelled by his noxious halitosis. One queenly young man, invited to dinner with Gielgud at Weymouth Street, found himself overcome by tiredness (had the wine been doctored? he wondered) and awoke on a sofa, Webster beside him and Jimmy gazing at them from an overhead gallery.[124] In London's gay underworld Webster was the butt of many in-jokes:

David Webster, in a public lavatory, whispers to the man in the next stall, 'what do you like?' There is a long pause. Then the man whispers back, 'Callas in *Traviata*.'

Webster sent Fred Ashton into a terrible tizz by threatening to seduce his boyfriend, Dick Beard.[125] On a 1953 tour of Rhodesia, he was reportedly seen in a sauna with other white men and black boys, 'red all over and looking like a boiled lobster'. According to rumour, he so injured an African boy in the act of love that the victim was rushed to hospital and Webster had to be hustled out on the next flight. No trace of any such incident exists in ROH or Government archives. John Denison, who knew Webster well, is convinced that talk of a homosexual scandal was 'all mischief that emanated from Wilson'. Nevertheless, the poison could paralyse a man's career and Webster, at the height of his power, was pursued by the same fears that had forced him once before to leave Liverpool and start afresh.

Alarmed at his exposure, ROH friends brought influence to bear. The Clarks, who knew everyone, invited the head of Scotland Yard to the opera and introduced him to Webster, believing the contact might come in useful.[126] Others moved silently behind the scenes.

Newspapers, like fish, feed off each other; a good story in one is invariably snapped up by the rest. Remarkably, however, not one word of the *People*'s charges of Covent Garden 'vice' appeared in any other corner of the British press – or ever again in the *People* itself. Such omissions are not coincidental, and while the Express group were leading what David Astor, the *Observer* editor, called a 'rabble-rousing . . . witch-hunt' of homosexuals, it would have taken more than gentle persuasion to deflect the hacks. Who called the shots and with what weapons? The finger points unerringly at Garrett Moore, Secretary to the ROH Board and, by day, managing director of the *Financial Times*.

As Waverley ailed, Moore increasingly took the chair at Covent Garden. He knew the press barons as social equals and sat on their Newspaper Proprietors Committee, which adopted a tacit code of practice to the effect that one press baron did not attack another. Beaverbrook had procured press silence on Driberg by convincing his rivals to honour the code. The FT chief, by similar means, quashed the Wilson smears as an assault on his domain. Moore was not a man to boast of conquests, but a wink of satisfaction can be seen in his memoirs when he notes that 'subsequent evidence of the (*People*'s) campaign was strangely lacking'.[127] Strangely, indeed.

It had been a close call. Any tabloid reporter in search of 'jobs for the boys' at Covent Garden need have looked no further than the inner office where most of Webster's team were lifelong bachelors. Christopher West was professedly gay; Morris Smith and John Sullivan were avowedly religious and hostile to women. 'Nobody asked if they were gay,' said Elizabeth Latham, 'one was very careful what one said and did in those days.'[128] In the so-called 'straight' theatre, Covent Garden was known as a gay house, with many of its designers and directors drawn from the unuttered community. Webster, in whose gift these appointments lay, especially favoured Oliver Messel, Michael Benthall (Helpmann's life-partner) and Peter Potter.

The theatre, by tradition, was a haven for minorities and outcasts, a place where intolerance was suspended along with disbelief. Outside, however, the atmosphere was oppressive. Although the gutter press revelled in mock-horror, homosexuality was swept under the carpet in polite society. Playwrights and film-makers skirted the subject, knowing it would not be passed fit for public viewing. The plays of Noël Coward, Ivor Novello and Terence Rattigan, and the novels of Somerset Maugham and Angus Wilson substituted man-woman euphemisms for 'the love that dared not speak its name', a love whose status had not changed since the day of Oscar Wilde's conviction. England's leading painter (Bacon), poet (Auden), composer (Britten), actor (Gielgud), novelist (Forster), and choreographer (Ashton) were all homosexual, an attribute that was unmentionable in studies of their lives and works. Forster was unable to publish his homosexual novel, *Maurice*.

Gay men developed common dialects and mannerisms. Britten, writing to Webster about a mutual friend, spoke in camp tones that he would never have used with Harewood: 'Are all things right now with Johnnie Cranko? I do hope you've had your talk with him, because the poor boy's *really* worried.'[129] Under stress, homosexuals chose colleagues they could trust. Webster favoured Britten and Tippett above all composers and John Pritchard above all local conductors. He identified Maria Callas as a gay icon, more potent than Judy Garland. It would not have taken deep investigation for the gutter press to expose Webster in their terms as an 'evil man' and Covent Garden as a 'den of vice', prompting calls for its closure. Wilson's assault had been designed to bring down Webster and the house around him. He had to be repelled, not so much for Webster's sake as for the survival of the company.

A month after his attack, the departed deputy wrote to Waverley apologizing for his comments in the *People*, 'which he said he had not authorized'.[130] The insincerity of his retraction became apparent within a year when he popped up in the *Daily Telegraph*, demanding a public inquiry into 'the powers at present wielded by the Administrator of the Royal Opera House, Mr David Webster, uncontrolled by the Board of Directors . . .'[131] The *Telegraph*, in a leading article, said the Board could 'hardly ignore the criticisms made by their former Deputy General Administrator'. But ignore them they did, in self-imposed silence, and Wilson was left to sputter off into well-deserved obscurity. Years later, in 1970, his widow approached Webster and Tooley for information for a posthumous biography. Webster said: 'He wanted my job – and Mary (his previous wife) egged him on.'[132] Tooley offered to 'help in any way I can' but when he asked to see the files, the archivist replied: 'I have had a good look through the papers which we have sorted so far and I cannot find anything of use related to Steuart Wilson's time here.'[133]

The operatic ups and downs were starting to depress the ballet. Acclaimed in America, the ballet company was losing ground at home. 'The midsummer nights in the Royal Opera House Covent Garden have been ringing to resounding cheers,' editorialized *Dance and Dancers* in August 1955. 'Well-dressed crowds have been milling around in their efforts to get tickets . . . All this excitement has not been for ballet but for the great international stars who have been appearing as guests with Covent Garden Opera.' Ninette de Valois had warned that her public was fickle and could be lured away by an Italian diva with a top B-flat, and her presentiments were being fulfilled. 'You must be *mad* going to the ballet,' was a sneer aimed at balletomanes,[134] who had little to contend in their defence.

The big ballet draw of 1955 was Richard Buckle's memorial exhibition for Serge Diaghilev, seen by 165,000 visitors in Edinburgh and London. De Valois, back in 1931, had claimed a stake in Diaghilev's legacy with *Job*, the first all-English production. Its Covent Garden revival in the summer of 1955 brought the farewell appearance of Anton Dolin as Satan, setting a symbolic seal on the formative era of English ballet. The founders were fading and their heirs lacked the same edge of vitality.

Far too much hinged on the physical endurance of Margot Fonteyn, thirty-six years old, newly married and in sight of middle age. Fonteyn stood at the summit of a stultifying pyramid. Beneath her, five dancers – Beryl Grey, Svetlana Beriosova, Violetta Elvin, Nadia Nerina and Elaine Fifield – cultivated a personal following without attaining universal stardom. Nerina, a South African, had, in Buckle's view, 'three times Fonteyn's strength and technique, but . . . never imposed herself to the same degree as Fonteyn as a personality.'[135] Fifield, an Australian who had been hailed as 'a new Pavlova' at Sadler's Wells, felt stifled by the Covent Garden pyramid and, divorcing the conductor John Lanchbery, opted in 1957 for repatriation. Moira Shearer had retired to have babies, Grey was about to go it alone, and Elvin was on the point of hanging up her shoes.

Beneath the glass ceiling of five ballerinas ranged a motley of has-beens and hangers-on who blocked the path of young hopefuls. The male leads, Michael Somes, Alexander Grant and David Blair, lacked magnetism. The company as a whole lost impetus. Peggy Van Praagh, who ran the second corps at Sadler's Wells, resigned to go freelance and eventually to Australia. Louis Yudkin, the popular stage manager, had been killed in a plane crash in Africa.

The one fruitful resource was the company's flourish of choreographers: Cranko, the young Scot Kenneth MacMillan, and the eternally surprising Fred Ashton who, however, was having a hit and miss season. Frustratingly, his best shot of 1955, *Madame Crysanthème*, with Fifield as heroine (music by Rawsthorne, costumes by Isabel Lambert), opened during a newspaper strike and sank without notices.

The fortunes, present and future, of English ballet rested heavily on the shoulders of Margot Fonteyn, who was willing as ever but weakening. She had missed five months through illness in Coronation Year and Webster reported a gloomy prognosis to the Board. 'I have been concerned about that matter myself,' said Waverley, in a rare interjection on artistic personnel. When Fonteyn returned in *Apparitions* more than fifty bouquets were thrown, house staff shouted 'Margot!' and Webster openly wept. When asked why, he replied: 'If you don't know, you don't deserve to be told.'[136]

Brilliant as she was, Margot could not last forever and there was no alternative in store. Dancers quoted a comment by the novelist Angus Wilson about 'a certain stagnation in English contemporary life', applying it to their own parlous situation.[137]

Ninette de Valois did not take criticism lightly. She went flaring onto the attack, blaming Covent Garden, the press and the public for lack of support. 'The Royal Opera House Covent Garden receives a handsome grant from the Arts Council to which much publicity is given,' she thundered. 'The grant is in respect of opera and ballet. One of its principal services to the public is that it enables the prices of seats to be kept at levels which have increased comparatively little since before the war when compared to increases in the prices of other commodities. Ballet seat prices have increased by something like 25 per cent compared with pre-war, but opera seats are at a much *lower* average price.'[138]

Madam begrudged the dollar profits that her troupe pumped into the ROH and complained that her dancers were unable to get enough stage rehearsals. Her relations with Webster soured, and Tooley shuttled curt messages between them. Yet, at no time then or ever after did she consider secession. 'I don't think opera and ballet should ever be divided,' she declared. 'They haven't been over three hundred years. Why should they now?'[139] Deep down, Dame Ninette knew that her company could not survive unattached to the opera house. Proof, if proof were needed, was supplied in October 1955 by the Ballet Rambert which was going broke on a six thousand pound Arts Council grant and launched an emergency appeal in *The Times*.

The subsidies to Madam's enterprises were not separately published, but her first troupe received a handsome share of Covent Garden's quarter-million pounds, her second ensemble got part of the hundred thousand awarded to Sadler's Wells and her ballet school was getting fifteen thousand a year 'for capital expenditure' under the dubious 1946 deal. Madam's compact with Keynes had been richly rewarded.

On 5 May 1956 she marked her company's quarter-centenary with a three-ballet evening: her own *Rake's Progress*, Ashton's *Façade* (both danced by the ageless Helpmann) and a new Ashton *pièce d'occasion*, *Birthday Offering*, that was so exquisite it outlived the occasion and entered the staple repertoire. 'There was a full house, a hum of excitement and speeches at the end,' reported *The Times* dutifully. Alexander Bland in the *Observer* warned that state patronage of ballet could give rise to 'rigidity, bureaucracy, ossification', which de Valois had managed, thus far, to hold off. But enthusiasm was scarce and it seemed that ballet was losing its iron grip on the public attention.

Three nights later, English theatre rose from its drawing-room doldrums with the eruption at the Royal Court of *Look Back in Anger*, a kitchen-sink rant against class, complacency, the men who fought the war and all the good works that followed, starting with the Festival of Britain. Noël Coward found the play 'electrifying' and Kenneth Tynan, the *Observer* critic, called it 'a minor miracle'. Its anti-hero, Jimmy Porter, spoke for a rising caste of demobbed males who had no cause to respect age and rank. 'I suppose people of our generation aren't able to die for good causes any longer,' said Porter. '. . . If the big bang does come and we all get killed off, it won't be in aid of the old-fashioned grand design. It'll just be for the Brave New-nothing-very-much thank you. About as pointless and inglorious as stepping in front of a bus.'

Laurence Olivier, watching the play, was unmoved at first, but when he returned with his filming partner Marilyn Monroe, her husband, Arthur Miller, proclaimed it 'great stuff'. Olivier went to see the playwright, John Osborne, and asked him to write him a role. In *The Entertainer*, England's most bankable actor embraced the new realism with a fervour that revitalized spoken theatre and made it again the hot ticket in town. The Royal Court, on seven thousand pounds of Arts Council subsidy, was stealing the headlines from the Royal Opera House, on quarter of a million. Angry Young Men now held the stage, and all else appeared outmoded. Osborne's success was soon matched by Harold Pinter and Arnold Wesker. Samuel Beckett was all the rage and a new wave of directors rose with the tide of modern dramatists, chief among them Tony Richardson at the Royal Court and Peter Hall at Stratford-upon-Avon. The centre of energy was shifting towards straight theatre.

If this was bad for ballet, there was worse to come. The new Soviet leader, Nikita Khrushchev, had visited London in April 1956 and, although he failed to impress either Eden or the Labour Party, the resumption of person-to-person politics permitted a semi-thaw in cultural relations. Webster, who had visited Moscow the previous winter, was suddenly rewarded with a visit by the Bolshoi Ballet, the first by any Russian dance troupe since the Revolution. As word got round, there was a rush on the box-office. 'It is doubtful,' reflected *Dance and Dancers*, 'whether in the past history of ballet in England there has been queueing for three nights to book tickets.'[140]

On the opening night, 3 October 1956, the house was crammed with the pride of British ballet: Fonteyn, Ashton, de Valois, Somes, May, Grey, Beriosova, Nerina, Fifield, Cranko, MacMillan, Dolin, Markova, Rambert, Shearer, Helpmann and several who danced elsewhere that night but rushed in to catch the closing moments. The glittering Galina Ulanova, now forty-seven years of age, and her regular partner Yury Zhdanov danced Leonid Lavrovsky's *Romeo and Juliet*. By the end, Fonteyn was in tears. She told reporters, 'I am so dazzled, so dazed. Ulanova is just indescribable. I had no idea, no conception of her. I cannot describe it. I did not watch her technique. One cannot watch technique when watching Ulanova.'[141]

Webster went on stage to interrupt the ovations, which lasted fully an hour and a half. He made a masterly speech, talking of 'the miracle that is Ulanova' and of Britain's 'affection and admiration' for the genius of Russia. The Prime Minister, sitting centre stalls, nodded approvingly. The next morning, every newspaper except the *Financial Times*, splashed the Bolshoi across their news pages. 'They're Just the Best in the World,' proclaimed the *Daily Herald* on its front page.

'What a lot we have to learn!' sighed the ballet historian Mary Clarke. 'Each night I went to the Bolshoi, I felt more ignorant and more lacking in theatre experience.'[142] Altogether the Bolshoi danced twenty-four times that month at Covent Garden and three nights in Croydon, adding *Giselle*, *Swan Lake* and *The Fountains of*

Bakhchisarai to their playbill. The ovations continued to mount and the arguments to rage, with Dolin and others rushing into print to insist that English dancers were every bit as good as the Russians. The contrary evidence was collected at the box-office, which turned in a forty thousand pound net profit from the Bolshoi month, reduced only by subsequent political complications.

After their final appearance in Croydon, the Russians were whisked to the airport to board a waiting fleet of Aeroflots. Moments after the last plane had left British airspace, radios crackled with news of a Soviet armoured invasion of Hungary, suppressing an anti-Communist uprising. Prospects of future cultural contacts receded and the Sadler's Wells Ballet, which had shipped its sets to Leningrad in anticipation of a reciprocal visit, lost eighteen thousand pounds in getting them back. British attention, meanwhile, shifted south and east to Suez, where Eden had ordered an invasion to reverse Gamal Abdel Nasser's seizure of the Suez Canal, which had been held by Britain under a dubious imperial treaty. As the nation split painfully over an unjust and unnecessary war, British ballet heaved a sigh of relief to have escaped further comparisons with the Soviet grandmasters.

The gulf between English effort and Russian expertise had been cruelly exposed, and Ninette de Valois needed to act promptly. She ordered a complete overhaul of the training of male dancers at her school and called in palace contacts to procure, in January 1957, a Royal Charter for her companies and a Damehood of the British Empire for Margot Fonteyn. The Sadler's Wells Ballet thus became the Royal Ballet, outranking the Covent Garden Opera Company. Dame Margot stood on a pedestal above all other dancers.

As for the art, there was not much more Madam could do except play to the national strengths. If the Russians had a flaw, it was the dullness of their sets and the archaic predictability of their choreography. Madam hired good designers (John Piper, Osbert Lancaster, Isabel Lambert) and gave Cranko and MacMillan a license to innovate, the latter drawing his dancers ever deeper into dark realms of suicide, rape and lunacy. Britten's *Prince of the Pagodas* on New Year's Day 1957 was followed the next season by *Ondine*, a brilliant score by a German outcast, Hans Werner Henze, who had met Ashton at William Walton's home on the island of Ischia. Together, they gave Fonteyn her most shimmering role, the pose in which she is cast in stone in a statue in her home town,

Reigate. 'The crown of our creation, the radiant centre of the whole ballet, was Margot, the *assoluta*, the frail instrument, the master's Stradivarius,'[143] wrote Henze, whose cosmopolitan charm was much in demand among the Angry Young Men of bohemian Chelsea.

British composers – Malcolm Arnold, Richard Arnell, Dennis ApIvor, Alexander Goehr and Matyas Seiber were also favoured by Madam's quest for novelty but many of their submissions were rejected by her chief conductor, who complained that 'the composers have only an imperfect idea of what a ballet score should be'.[144] The standard of ballet conducting, post Lambert, was variable. What was unchanged was the voltage of Madam's ambition. If the Royal Ballet could not outdance the blazing Russians, Ninette de Valois was determined that it should outsmart them. 'We belong to the West,' she declared in May 1957. 'To change our style would be to kill our particular individuality, and to confuse the issue of our future place in the history of dancing . . . Today it can be said that the English school has by now absorbed classicism in the main; it is moving forward to a second stage . . .'[145]

The Kubelik era at Covent Garden Opera, brief as it was, was characterized by a gleaming idealism. Kubelik was a believer in human values and human rights. His faith in mankind was pricked only by an endearing lack of self-confidence. Before *Bohème*, an opera he had never conducted before, Kubelik was seen 'simply quivering'.[146] Verismo and bel canto were not his cups of tea, but in Verdi and Wagner, Mozart and the moderns, he was deft and compelling. Polite and patient in rehearsal, his performances glowed with the incandescence of sudden inspiration. Some in the orchestra grumbled that he varied his tempi from one night to the next, but this was ever the mark of a fine conductor: to follow a fleeting fantasy and let each performance be a grand improvisation.

As a conductor Kubelik ranked, in his early forties, among the world's top names. He made records for EMI and Deutsche Grammophon and drew an ROH emolument of £6,500, necessitating an immediate increase in Webster's measly £3,500 salary. He rented a flat in Hampstead and sent his son, Martin, to a local prep school; his much-loved wife, Ludmilla, was physically incapacitated and undergoing repeated bouts of surgery.

Kubelik began in October 1955 as he intended to proceed, with a Verdi *Otello* that was meticulously well prepared and cast, for the most part, from internal resources, with the exception of the Chilean Ramon Vinay as the tragic hero and the Dutch soprano Gré Brouwenstijn as Desdemona. There was to have been a bigger star, but when Tito Gobbi failed to turn up by the end of the first week of rehearsal, Kubelik cancelled his contract. Gobbi, in his memoirs, maintained that his flight had been delayed by fog and it was all a wretched misunderstanding. Edward Downes, who was involved in the rehearsals, had a different recollection:

> Gobbi's agent, Sandor Gorlinsky, rang up to say he was going to miss the first three rehearsals because he had engagements on the Continent and had sung the part of Iago more than a hundred times. Kubelik said: Absolutely unacceptable. He asked me if I knew anyone who could learn Iago in a weekend. So I went round to Otakar Kraus's flat in Notting Hill, and taught him the part.[147]

Gobbi turned up at the theatre with his agent and lawyers. Webster summoned learned counsel. On the opening night Peter Potter, Christopher West's one-legged assistant, anticipated a scandal when he saw Gobbi and his entourage occupying a row of centre-stalls. He and Webster hopped about the gangway behind the grand tier throughout the performance. At the final curtain, Gobbi rose to his feet and cheered Kraus to the echo. *Otello* was hugely acclaimed and, in Harewood's words, 'caused virtually a change of mind in public and critics about the possibilities of the young company'.[148]

Kubelik had called a press conference some weeks before to declare his commitment to performing opera in English with native singers, dispensing as far as possible with international stars who 'come and go and have no idea of real artistic co-operation'. This statement set him irretrievably at odds with the Callas-gaping opera lobby and with star-struck members of the ROH board, but Webster lent his support and the company swelled with the confidence he instilled. 'We learned so much from Kubelik,' said Elizabeth Latham. 'He was one of the few gentlemen that ever entered the theatre, and he imagined everyone else was ticking over just as he was. I don't think he was right for Covent Garden – he was too nice.'[149]

Elsie Morison, who would give up her career nine years later to become his second wife, was captivated by the way 'he understood singers, he breathed with you'. A *Magic Flute*, staged in January

1956 for the bicentenary of Mozart's birth, exemplified Kubelik's aims. The bill was topped by Morison, Jess Walters, Richard Lewis and Adele Leigh – all home-grown, with Shuard, Iris Kells, Josephine Veasey and Joan Carlyle in the supporting roles. Kubelik had refined the concept over seven months with the producer, Christopher West, and the designer, John Piper, and even got to grips with crusty old Professor Dent, inducing him to modify the English translation. The result was a trifle over-serious, but beautifully performed and improving measurably when Sutherland and Pears replaced Morison and Lewis in the revival. Webster found the production over-rehearsed and Rosenthal complained that Kubelik's productions were hogging all the stage time, at the expense of other conductors and guest stars. 'Kubelik's almost fanatical insistence that, when he was preparing a new work, virtually everything else had to go by the board, resulted in the dullest mid-season (1956-57) in memory,' he wrote.[150]

There was also disaffection within. Shacklock, a company founder, resigned at the end of Kubelik's first season to pursue a freelance life that took her to the Bolshoi and the West End, where she wound up trilling the hills alive in *The Sound of Music*. 'I didn't find Kubelik warm,' she said. 'I can't say I didn't get on with him but we weren't on the same wavelength. And then he married Elsie Morison. We were very happy for Elsie.'[151] Fisher also quit, and others turned murmurous. Geraint Evans lost his Papageno role to Jess Walters and Adele Leigh was demoted from Pamina to Papagena. Evans took Leigh to see Webster, saying, 'it's rather disgraceful the way Adele has been treated.' Webster replied: 'I cannot interfere.'[152] (He did, however, implore Kubelik to find something for the Welshman, who 'has had no new part of any worth for some time'.)[153]

Joan Sutherland, Webster's white hope, went into a huff after falling out with Kubelik over her recitatives as the peasant girl in a *Carmen* rehearsal. She made no further headway in Kubelik's time. 'He was not much use to her,' reflected Downes, 'because he didn't understand Italian repertoire and was scared of much of it.'

On the other hand, he was quick to spot a Canadian truck-driver who, dismissed by the senior repetiteur Norman Feasey, was retrieved by Downes and coached for the king's role in an explosive *Ballo* in Maschera in Kubelik's second season. Jon Vickers was proof positive of the case for producing opera in English.

The second season also saw a thrilling but ill-attended *Jenůfa*, a mixed *Meistersinger* in which Sutherland (as Eva) refused to sing out because she felt Kubelik was letting the orchestra overwhelm her, and the first complete staging of Berlioz's *The Trojans* which sold out every seat for eight performances and sent ripples round the world as a miracle of English stagecraft, an object lesson to the French who persisted in demeaning their greatest composer.

In the huge *Trojans* cast there was only one foreigner, the American Blanche Thebom. Vickers was the male lead and, despite refusing to take much direction from the director, John Gielgud, bestrode the stage like a titan. The chorus numbered 120. 'You had to do a lot of coaxing, and try to remember their names and take trouble not to treat them like a lot of cattle,' the great actor reminisced. He also 'quickly came to realize that when the conductor comes on to the scene, he really is the boss'.[154] Kubelik insisted that *The Trojans* should be staged exactly as Berlioz intended, without cuts, gimmicks, updatings, or artificial sweeteners. The opera had never before succeeded at full length.

The only dissension arose in the boardroom, where Isaiah Berlin had been urging that 'a revival of an opera by Vivaldi would rivet international attention in a way in which *The Trojans* will not'[155] and the opera sub-committee chairman, Viscount Moore, offered to resign after Webster, without prior approval, engaged a Rumanian designer, Mariano Andreu, who was suspected to be Gielgud's lover. 'What folly on the part of anyone in Webster's vulnerable position to pick on a man whose chief qualification seems to be close personal association with John Gielgud!' exclaimed Waverley.[156]

The outcome, however, dispelled all clouds. Crabby old Dent, who supplied the translation, told Webster: 'It was a stroke of genius, I felt, to engage John Gielgud as producer. I went to several dress rehearsals and realized all along what difficulties he had to contend with, but he surmounted them marvellously, and I saw how he gradually developed the personalities of Amy Shuard, Jess Walters and A-canius, whose name I don't know but I think she is one of our own people.'[157] A voice from the past, Eugene Goossens, added his blessing: 'I have just come from *The Trojans* and I feel I must tell you – as I just told Rafael – how completely moved and overwhelmed I am by the splendour and sheer precision of the whole production.'[158] In the press, Peter Heyworth reported 'a triumph for the whole company' and Andrew Porter extolled 'a sumptuous and splendid and glorious experience'. 'It was the greatest thing we did,' said Iris Kells.

There was more to come from Kubelik, but not much more. Eager to introduce modern drama, he got Webster to nag his Soviet contacts for the rights to stage Prokofiev's *Fiery Angel* and Shostakovich's *Lady Macbeth of Mtsenk*, both suppressed by Stalin. He proposed to conduct the world première of *The Greek Passion*, by his Czech fellow-exile Bohuslav Martinů, but Sir Arthur Bliss, composer of the ephemeral *Olympians*, persuaded the Board that the score should first be 'seen by one or two competent musicians'. The authorities selected for this task were Edric Cundell of the Guildhall School of Music; John Denison of the Arts Council; and Anthony Lewis, a provincial conductor. Their reports were denigratory and the opera was dropped.[159] Kubelik also talked of staging Rankl's *Deirdre* as an act of contrition, with Morison in the title role, only to be vetoed again by the Board. The discouragements were increasing.

In his third and final season, Kubelik conducted *The Carmelites* by Francis Poulenc, twelve months after its La Scala première, and a new *Tristan und Isolde* (in German) with Vinay and Fisher, alternating with the magnificently ascendant Swede, Birgit Nilsson. The only other new show of a cash-strapped season that coincided with the centenary of the ROH building was a Verdi *Don Carlos*, produced by Luchino Visconti and conducted by Carlo Maria Giulini – an all-foreign, all-star effort with Gobbi, Boris Christoff, Brouwenstijn, Fedora Barbieri and, wonder of wonders, in the title role, Jon Vickers, made in England and the major find of the Kubelik era. The production, said Peter Heyworth in the *Observer*, would be talked of 'for years to come' – and so it was. Giulini and Visconti atttended all of each other's rehearsals, setting a moral example of artistic collaboration. Kubelik's reforms were bearing rich fruit but the Board was in no rush to support him.

Kubelik had warned that he planned his international diary a year in advance, and needed a quick decision on contract renewal.[160] No answer was forthcoming. His own resolve had been weakened by a persistent stream of xenophobic innuendos emanating from a familiar source. In June 1956, assessing an ROH ten-year report, the *Daily Telegraph* critic Martin Cooper cast doubt on the company's aims and wondered whether English voices would ever grow large enough to fill its vast stage. Kubelik, stung, wrote to *The Times* urging critics to 'ignore the snobs and instead fight for communion

between the British public and British composers and singers.'
Cooper retorted that 'these singers must be worth communing with',
and on the very same day, as if by mystic co-ordination, the arch-
meddler, Sir Thomas Beecham, reached for his poisoned pen in
support of his satrap hacks. Beecham's letter to *The Times* opened
with a swipe at the departed Rankl before pouring scorn on Kubelik:

> Now we have another foreigner in charge. But does he possess any
> of the qualifications for the creation of a truly national
> organization? It is not a question only of conducting; the modern
> world positively teems with conductors of every nationality and
> nearly all of them are highly praised by the press.
>
> What we have got to realize is that Covent Garden has neither
> accomplished the purpose for which it was established, nor is it
> ever likely to do so while it remains in the hands of those who are
> now in charge of it . . . The dignity of our nation is today at stake
> and we are presenting a sorry spectacle to the outside world.[161]

Kubelik, reading this, promptly offered his resignation, contending
'that my status as a foreigner might be regarded as a handicap to
creating British national opera'. His letter, together with a draft blast
to *The Times*, landed on the desk of Viscount Moore, who went to
the conductor and asked him to stay his hand for twenty-four hours
until Lord Waverley had time to act.

The aged chairman summoned a board meeting the following
afternoon, at the end of which he dictated a magisterial missive to
The Times, declaring that the ROH music director had resigned upon
reading Beecham's letter. 'The board have informed Mr Kubelik that
they are unwilling to accept his resignation,' intoned Waverley.
'They have assured him that he has their entire confidence and that
he can rely on their unstinted support in pursuit of the policy he has
outlined during his tenure of his present office.'

Kubelik was called to the boardroom to be read this letter. 'He
flung his arms wide apart, said dramatically "It is finished," and then
embraced the chairman.'[162] There was no more talk of walking out,
but the 'unstinted support', he found, was not wholehearted and the
critical sniping persisted. Kubelik also felt vicariously the anguish
of his dying friend Martinů, whose faith in his final opera had been
damaged by Covent Garden's rejection. In the end, Kubelik just
slipped away, saying he would be happy to return as a guest

conductor. He told Webster he wanted freedom to follow his artistic instincts, and fewer constraints from punitive UK taxes.[163] 'I don't remember why I left,' he told me years later. 'Perhaps I made a mistake. Fate is strange.'[164]

In 1961, after Ludmilla's death, he found fulfilment in Munich as chief conductor of the Bavarian radio orchestra, with which he recorded (among many indispensables) the outstanding *Meistersinger* of all time – only for a contract dispute to prevent its release. Kubelik was never a lucky conductor. In 1973 he became music director of the Metropolitan Opera in New York, but resigned before taking office when Goran Gentele, his co-director, died in a car crash. Kubelik would not fulfil his operatic ideals, but his home life was made happy by Elsie and his final years were uplifted by the velvet revolution that liberated his beloved homeland.

For a brief moment in the 1970s it seemed that Kubelik might return to London as music director of Sadler's Wells, whose manager, Stephen Arlen, was now married to Iris Kells, Elsie's best friend. Kubelik weighed the offer before deciding, wisely, not to risk further exposure to the *Opera* gang who, he felt, had hounded him for reducing Covent Garden's dependence on unruly stars. He never told Elsie his reasons for leaving London. 'He was not a person to dwell on things,' she said. 'He never held a grudge and liked to look ahead, not backwards.'[165] His ROH file has been purged of any mention of his departure.

Brief as it was, the Kubelik era at Covent Garden left a lasting lesson in leadership, both practical and moral. 'Kubelik brought real humanity to his music making,' noted John Tooley. 'He wasn't obsessed with absolute precision of playing but what he wanted was the spirit, the heart of the music, and he knew how to get there.'[166] Harewood felt uplifted by his unusual blend of sincerity and professionalism, reporting in his memoirs that Kubelik's three years at Covent Garden were 'the best of my life'.[167]

What Kubelik brought to the company is best illustrated by Edward Downes. Conducting *Jenůfa* one night in 1959, Downes suffered a haemorhage behind both eyes and was blinded. He groped through to the end of the opera and was rushed to hospital. Next day, a specialist told him there was no hope, his sight was destroyed.

'Kubelik wouldn't accept that,' said Downes. 'He sent me to three surgeons in Switzerland, one of whom operated and restored some of my vision. I was earning twelve pounds ten shillings a week and couldn't afford that kind of treatment. Kubelik paid it all out of his own pocket. He was a good man, in the true sense of the word. If he had stayed at Covent Garden, there is no telling what kind of family company we might have become.'[168]

One morning in 1956, Elizabeth Latham walked on stage as usual at eight in the morning and saw a strange man peering down at her from the gantry.

'Who's that?' she asked a stagehand.

'A spy from the union,' he whispered.

Bogey Ballard having finally retired, his powers had passed to shop stewards and union convenors who had no sympathy for the intensity of effort expected in the non-commercial theatre. Under Ballard, the stage carpenter had been boss backstage. Now, there were norms and national rules to be obeyed and a closed shop to be protected. Three rival unions – NATKE, ETU and T&GWU – fought for dominance backstage. In early 1956 the Musicians Union stopped BBC relays from Covent Garden; months later, the actors and ballet union Equity blocked the televising of *Petrushka*. 'I knew the game was up,' said Latham. 'I could see that this was not going to be the theatre I believed in, so at the end of the season I resigned.'

On one of her last nights, Equity succeeded in having an Italian, Melchiorre Luise, banned from singing the minor part of Sacristan in *Tosca*. Latham had to explain to Luise that he was being replaced on union orders with a British bass, Howell Glynne. Luise watched the opera from the wings and, after the final curtain, went on stage to congratulate his replacement. 'That night finished it for me,' said Latham, who packed her bags and went to Vienna to live with her friend, Hilde Zadek.

Similar scenes were being played out all over the land. As the industries that Labour had nationalized responded to central directives, so their employees banded for strength and protection into the embrace of increasingly powerful unions. More than fifty per cent of all male employees were union members; among working-class men, the figure was closer to eighty per cent. More and more time at work was taken up with union meetings and the number of strikes rose exponentially. Between the end of the war and 1954, two million days were lost to industrial inaction. In the next decade, the loss rose to 3,889,000. Union leaders became key players on the national stage, invited to Downing Street by Harold

Macmillan who saw himself as a 'One Nation' Tory and fostered a spending spree in the interests of social peace and electoral gain.

Macmillan, a wealthy publisher's son married to the Duke of Devonshire's daughter, was the epitome of bourgeois complacency. 'Let's be frank about it,' he told the country in 1957. 'Most of our people have never had it so good.' Two years later he was re-elected in a mini-landslide, but when the concessions he made and the debts he amassed fell due for payment he would be swept from office in an unprecendented ferment of scandal and decay.

Lord Waverley, who had devoted his life to the philosophy and practice of good governance, lived to see his esteemed Whitehall reduced to 'the management of decline' and his country embracing inflationary chaos. He underwent surgery in September 1957 and returned from hospital to deal with a threatened chorus strike. He addressed his pain and his duty stoically to the last. A fortnight before he died, Waverley summoned Ninette de Valois to his bedside, in the 'shabby gloom' of St Thomas's Hospital, south London, a former poor ward that had not been much improved upon under the NHS. He had announced his retirement and was, she recalled,

> relaxed, yet curiously excited and hopeful about Covent Garden's future. 'Lord Moore will be the new Chairman. He's the right man, is he not? I have every faith in young Moore . . .'

Even at the end, said de Valois, he saw things 'with extraordinary clarity'.[169] News of his decline was conveyed to the Queen, who brought forward the Order of Merit that he was due to receive in the 1958 New Year's Honours List. Lord Waverley, dying, was dutifully touched. 'The Civil Service,' he said, 'will be pleased about this.'[170]

CHAPTER 6

Short Interval: Champagne, Canapés and Nature Calls
(1959–60)

THE NEW CHAIRMAN was – after Keynes, Webster and de Valois – the fourth cornerstone of Covent Garden, the last of its formative figures. Garrett Moore, who had become 11th Earl of Drogheda on the death of his father in November 1957, would chair the board for sixteen years, having served it as secretary for seven. Half his working life was taken up by Covent Garden, both chronologically and in the amount of time and unpaid attention he lavished on it.

Drogheda did not take his responsibilities lightly. 'He was a restless man,' wrote the long-serving *Financial Times* editor, Gordon Newton. 'One never saw him sitting quietly at his desk, thinking. He had two secretaries, one for the *Financial Times* and the other for the Royal Opera House – he became chairman of both – and he always seemed to be dictating something to one of them. He was one of the greatest memo writers of all time. He always carried a pencil and small paper pad in his pocket. As he strode about the place, he would stop and make a note, which would result in someone, somewhere receiving yet another memo later in the day.'[1]

These notes, known as Droghedagrams, landed several times daily on the desks of Newton, David Webster and others who came within his purview. They were tartly phrased, neither critical nor peremptory but politely interrogative: had you noticed that . . .? what are your plans for . . . ? He expected immediate action. Failure to respond resulted, late the same day, in the ultimate Droghedagram: 'When do you think I will be receiving a reply to my previous notes?'

Andrew Porter, the *Financial Times* critic, would finish work around two in the morning, having written his review and checked the galleys for the last edition. Seven hours later, his doorbell would ring. 'The Droghedagrams arrived at nine,' he recalled, 'brought by a boy on a bike.'[2]

At the opera, Drogheda sat 'with a tiny torch to hand, making notes of anything that goes wrong'.[3] Whether he ever indulged his genuine love of music and dance is uncertain for he assumed a dangerously hybrid role of chairman and chief critic. Droghedagrams flowed from the Royal Box down to the prompt corner and on to the side-stage often in the middle of performances, reminding managers of their lapses and artists of his scrutiny. At a dress rehearsal he sent a note to the producer Christopher West saying: 'From now on I want all the action on the prompt side of the stage, because I can't see the other side from the Royal Box.'[4]

'He did not bide time by being either shrewd, over-discreet or patient,'[5] noted Ninette de Valois, who bore his asperities with uncommon restraint, appreciating the sincerity of his concern and attributing his agitation to their common Scots-Irish heritage.

Drogheda cherished his ancestry to the point of insufferable snobbery. In a company which held a Royal Charter and employed the Queen's cousin as its administrator's assistant, he liked to remind people that his forebear was knighted by the *first* Queen Elizabeth and his Earldom dated from an era when the present Buckingham Palace dynasty were mere Electors in some swampish German province. His bloodline was as blue as his eyes, which were piercing though warm, and he looked down an aquiline nose at most of mankind. He recognized, however, the nobility of genius and admitted the likes of Ashton, Fonteyn and Callas to his own superior caste. In art and at work, he was more meritocrat than aristocrat.

Drogheda changed the character of Covent Garden from populist to élitist – decadently, by means of social elevation; progressively, by preaching, pestering and pummelling everyone to raise their sights and achieve the highest standards. His motto might well have been, 'the best for the best'.

His philosopher friend, Isaiah Berlin, summed up Drogheda as 'a curious mixture of painstaking conscientiousness and aristocratic self-indulgence and impatience'.[6] His patrician arrogance could be charming at times, infuriating at others. He was, said a colleague, 'not an easy man with whom to communicate a view which was not wholly palatable to him'.[7] Lord Gibson, his FT chairman, called him 'a great life-enhancer – a man unlike anyone else who ever lived'.[8]

Charles Garrett Ponsonby Moore was born on St George's Day 1910 to ill-matched parents who separated when he was eleven. His father believed in public service and rose to become director general of the Ministry of Economic Warfare. His mother was devoted to pleasure and playboys; she particularly liked racing drivers and was chummy with the flier Amy Johnson. After their divorce, the tenth earl married the ex-Gaiety actress, Olive May. Garrett's upbringing was thus colourfully contrasted, mingling duty with fun, fidelity with fickleness, tradition with fashion, and high seriousness with theatrical sensation.

After Eton and Cambridge, he went to work in the City and dallied with débutantes. Keen on music, he founded a Quartet Society with a friend, Jack Donaldson, at the home of Beecham's patron, Lady Cunard. He got to know Sargent, Walton and other leading lights but seemed languidly unfulfilled. Two fortuitous meetings reshaped his life. In 1932, he was introduced to Brendan Bracken, a red-haired newspaper manager whose resemblance to Winston Churchill was so striking that he fostered rumours of his own bastardy. Bracken had built a small empire consisting of the *Financial News*, *Investor's Chronicle* and *The Economist* which, in due course, he merged with the *Financial Times*. He liked the young Lord and offered him a job selling advertising. Garrett, thrilled by the smell of print and the access it gave to world events, found his métier in newspapers.

Soon after, he found true love. Weekending at Bracken's country house, he met a pianist of arresting looks and was smitten for life. Joan Carr had fled a nightmare marriage to a palm-court violinist and was resuming her career with the help of a wealthy Jewish couple, Violet and Sydney Schiff, who had sponsored her career since childhood. Humbly born, Joan was a couple of years older than her suitor and amorously less ardent. A *roman-à-clef* about her early life suggests that she feared sexual contact after harrowing experiences of marital rape. Alarmed by Garrett's impetuousness, she 'did not know how to deal with what she had reason to call his grim whimsy'.[9] He pursued her to New York, where his persistence paid off and they married at City Hall in May 1935. Their son was born two years later. When the Blitz began Garrett, following a widespread practice among the rich and privileged, sent his wife and son for safety to the United States. He, meantime, served in an anti-aircraft regiment before being seconded by Bracken (now Churchill's Minister of Information) to assist Oliver Lyttelton, a War Cabinet member with responsibilities first for the North African front and then for the Ministry of Production.

By the time he saw Joan again, on a mission to Washington in 1942, she was romantically involved with a Frenchman who stabbed himself melodramatically in the chest when she returned to her husband. The Drogheda marriage was never a conventional relationship. He pursued beauties throughout his life, fancying his chances with the newly-wed Marilyn Monroe, who rented his house while filming *The Prince and the Showgirl*. Joan was equally sought after – 'the most seductive woman since Cleopatra' said an admirer.[10] She cultivated a circle of male friends, mostly intellectual and homosexual, such as John Pope-Hennessy, director of the Victoria and Albert Museum. 'Her quick mind, wide reading and professional talent as a pianist, allied to ethereal beauty and elegance, greatly appealed,' observed the social gadfly James Lees-Milne. 'Moreover ... her background had been fraught with penury and want, a fact which to her credit she never forgot or glossed over after marriage to Garrett had brought security and comparative affluence.'[11] 'She made you feel as if you were the only person that mattered in the world,' said a senior FT figure. 'I was totally smitten – but for her I don't think things went much further than that.'[12]

Together, Joan and Garrett made a compelling pair. Her musicianship and mental powers gave depth to his shotgun opinions and her charm unruffled many feathers that he had disordered. 'She had an amazingly well-stocked mind,' said a senior Arts Council official. 'Of course, you could talk to her about music, but she was immensely knowledgeable about art and widely read in many other fields.'[13] She sometimes griped that Garrett never read a book from start to finish, simply filleting the salient bits. Her approach was always the more substantive.

It was Drogheda's war record in Whitehall that commended him to Waverley, who grew increasingly fond of him and promoted him in 1954 from Secretary to full board member and chairman of the opera sub-committee. When Drogheda offered to resign after the *Trojans* tiff with Webster, the undemonstrative Waverley wrote him a letter of almost paternal warmth:

My dear Garrett,

I agree that such conduct as you describe is quite intolerable.

But please do nothing rash. You cannot think what a comfort it has been to me to have you as a colleague & in what is, or ought to be, a key position.

I will deal with Webster at the first opportunity.

Yours ever, Waverley[14]

Drogheda had his own ideas on how to deal with Webster, but he needed first to secure the support of his board, which he did by stacking it with friends. Out went Sir Arthur Bliss and Edric Cundell, Philip Nicholls and the Hon. James Smith, all Arts Council nominees. In came Jack Donaldson, his oldest friend who, as his wife admitted, 'was known at that time neither to the other members of the board nor to anyone else in the musical world'.[15] The publisher Mark Bonham-Carter became ballet chairman, less for his dance knowledge than for being a friend of Princess Margaret's. Thomas Armstrong, quiet principal of the Royal Academy of Music, came in to represent musical interests, and William Coldstream, head of the Slade School of Art, added visual expertise.

Not content with these changes, Drogheda added three business-men to the board – Sir Colin Anderson, who donated new lighting for the ROH; Sir Leon Bagrit, a self-made Russian Jew who had bought Kenneth Clark's house in Hampstead and filled it with fine art; and Burnet Pavitt, UK boss of the Hoffmann-La Roche pharmaceutical giant and Lady Drogheda's four-handed piano partner. The chairman intended to raise cash for Covent Garden and reduce its state dependancy. Where his predecessors were public servants and philosophers, Drogheda was an advertising salesman who harried FT guests over lunch until they coughed up, leaving his editor 'squirming with embarrassment'.[16] Even at the Newspaper Publishers Association, of which he was chairman, he would pester fellow-moguls to buy space in his paper, announcing their latest financial transactions. 'It was a bit unnecessary,' said his sometime deputy.[17]

At Covent Garden, he proceeded to soak the rich, compensating them with an exclusive annual gala and regular invitations to share his Royal Box. 'You know quite well why I want to avoid Fridays and Saturdays for first performances,' Drogheda told Webster. 'It so happens that a lot of people, including yourself, take themselves out of London at weekends, and many of them *are the sort of people that we want to be present at first nights.*[18]

Following an American model, he decided to form Friends of Covent Garden and hired a former flying ace, the Hon. Kensington Davison, DSO, DFC, to run it. Davison recruited ten thousand Friends, many of them young and impecunious. He was a tireless populist and a tenacious organizer whose influence was felt in all parts of the house. But the forming of Friends was another step in the retreat from universality. It introduced an effective class system to Covent Garden – outer circle (general populace), inner circle (Friends), Drogheda circle (exceptionally wealthy or well-connected). From this point on, rows of best seats were withdrawn from public sale and reserved for persons of privilege, or for companies who leased up to 140 seats annually under the so-called Premium Stalls Scheme.[19]

These divisions marked a turning point in the social evolution of the Royal Opera House, an abandonment of Keynes's vision of art for all and a reversion to pre-war practices. Change was inevitable, given the inadequacy of public funds to meet the company's soaring ambitions; but the barriers were offensive to poorer attenders and many began to feel excluded – the more so as ticket prices rose steadily to match the pockets of a wealthier clientele. Gallery seats trebled in Drogheda's first three years, from four shillings to twelve. Stalls seats for premium operas were priced at ten guineas and the grand tier at twenty-five guineas, equivalent to more than three hundred pounds in end-of-century values.

None of these inequities troubled Drogheda, who was a short-termist and no kind of strategic thinker. He was, however, alert to his own shortcomings and harvested the fruits of greater minds. Having brought Berlin and the LSE economist Lionel Robbins on board in Waverley's day, he later added the Oxford historian Noel Annan and the art expert Pope-Hennessy. His board meetings took on the sherry-and-rigour haze of an Oxbridge tutorial. 'It was a privilege to sit in,' said a junior staffer. 'You could not have wished for a better education.'[20]

Drogheda positively encouraged confrontation. 'We had great rows at the FT,' said Lord Gibson. 'They would usually end in him saying, "well, I couldn't possibly disagree with you on that" – which meant he had won.' At Covent Garden he bombarded Webster with impossible demands, outrageous ideas and thousands of minute observations, many of them useful and essential. Relations between chairman and chief executive were stormy. 'At times they were on non-speaks,' said one board member. 'I remember going to the Savoy Grill, where everybody who was anyone had lunch in those days, and exclaiming in surprise at seeing David and Garrett closeted at the same table. "They are making peace again," someone said.'[21]

To keep Webster on his toes, Drogheda asked Donaldson to bring on board the obstreperous record producer Walter Legge who, in addition to undermining the management, would procure the return to Covent Garden of his much-missed wife, Elisabeth Schwarzkopf. With his board in place, Drogheda proceeded to review policy. He had been warned by Isaiah Berlin that the company was running off the rails. It needed to abolish English mediocrities and revert to two periods of international opera and two slightly longer seasons of Royal Ballet. The house should shut from July to October or be rented out for the summer, 'vulgarity no object'. Berlin further urged that operas by British composers were 'to be discouraged'; they might be undertaken 'only if financially failure-proof', having been tried out at Sadler's Wells or in the provinces.[22]

This was radical and reactionary, but Drogheda was no reductionist. He intended to continue developing English singers for domestic and export markets, so long as they did not have to sing in English. His reasons, he explained, were artistic and pragmatic. 'I wanted to hear the works given as the composer originally intended,' he argued. 'Then, from the point of view of British singers, the opportunity of learning basic repertory works in the original language added greatly to their ability to obtain engagements overseas.'[23] His decision was soon vindicated as, over the next decade, a flock of Covent Garden singers made the grade at Milan, Munich, Paris and the Met. The world was shrinking and British business could no longer expect that foreigners would follow the Queen's English if it was loudly and slowly enunciated.

The retreat from the vernacular, never formally promulgated or announced, provoked some grumbling among the opera-in-English lobby but no opposition from the Arts Council which was entering one of its transitional phases. Kenneth Clark was about to yield the chair to the Tory peer Lord Cottesloe, and Taffia-Bill Williams was within sight of his pension. The House of Commons, in its first-ever debate on the arts, passed a resolution welcoming the increased popular interest in the arts and endorsing the rule 'that artistic policy should be free from Government control or direction'.[24] But there was precious little control or direction coming from the Council, which was in the process of bungling a merger of the enfeebled Carl Rosa company with Sadler's Wells, almost sinking both companies at a stroke and provoking Harold Rosenthal to devote fifteen pages of his magazine to 'The Opera Crisis'.[25]

Sensing the Council's frailty and the tide of public concern, Drogheda swooped. He ordered Webster to up the ante, telling the press that Covent Garden might not survive another year unless its subsidy was markedly increased. The deficit had reached £183,248 by mid-1959 and Coutts were getting edgy. The Chancellor of the Exchequer, Derick Heathcoat-Amory, was informally approached. He aimed to retire within two years and was thus free to indulge personal fancies. He has been described (by Roy Jenkins) as 'the most obscure Chancellor of the century', but he left two large footprints on the cultural landscape, which is two more than any of his successors.

A theatre-loving squire of slightly louche tastes, Heathcoat-Amory benignly gave the go-ahead to a long-mulled scheme to build a National Theatre on the South Bank of the Thames, down-river from the Royal Festival Hall. This was as bold a boost for the dramatic arts as the inception of Covent Garden had been for lyric theatre. The thespian sector was exultant, the more so since the NT was a pet project of the new Arts Council chairman, Lord Cottesloe, a former governor of Sadler's Wells and the Old Vic who gave it a million pounds and, when the Treasury balked, went to the Party fixer Rab Butler to get more. By the time the last coat of cement and concrete had been slapped on its grimly modern exterior, the NT had cost seven million pounds and was ready to compete with Covent Garden for cultural supremacy.

Worse, from Covent Garden's point of view, the South Bank scheme involved the creation of a second theatre to house the remnants of the Old Vic, the ascendant Royal Shakespeare Company and the impossibly cramped Sadler's Wells. 'Covent Garden said little in public,' recalled Norman Tucker, the Sadler's Wells director, 'but it was clear that the whole South Bank scheme was anathema to David Webster, his chairman Lord Drogheda and other members of the Covent Garden Board. While the Arts Council were pecking cautiously at the scheme with a marked lack of enthusiasm, the

Garden, behind the scenes at least, were definitely antagonistic, fearing, quite without foundation, a tiresome rival in the new house.'[26] Drogheda found himself on opposite sides from Oliver Lyttelton (now Lord Chandos), his wartime boss, who chaired the National Theatre and set about quietly tweaking the Government's ear.

Appreciating that Covent Garden was being downstaged, Heathcoat-Amory ordered the Treasury to come up with a better formula for funding opera. What it proposed was a new deal that granted 43 per cent of the ROH budget, with the rest to be earned at the box office. The uplift was instantaneous and unstoppable. The ROH grant shot up from £362,000 in 1958/9 to £463,000 the next year, and then to half a million. In 1962, with elections approaching, an even more generous formula gave Covent Garden a grant equivalent to 87.5 per cent of its previous year's earnings, 'without limit as to the amount payable'.[27]

This was like giving a small boy a blank cheque in a sweetshop. All Webster had to do was increase his outlay, and Whitehall would foot seven-eighths of the bill. In 1964, the subsidy reached a million pounds, more than forty times the foundation grant of eighteen years before. Amid much back-slapping, two dubious precedents had entered the relationship between Government and the arts. Covent Garden was encouraged to believe that when it ran out of cash, the Treasury would make good. And Whitehall, by treating the ROH as a special case, bypassed the Arts Council and undermined the operating ethic of Keynes's arm's-length principle. The seeds of future disaster had been liberally sown, and with the best of intentions.

The onus of justifying extra public investment fell heavily on the opera company, which gobbled up the new money and kept coming back for more. Webster entered the 1958/59 season knowing it could be his last. Mistrusted by his new chairman and maimed by the loss of Kubelik, he began thinking of changing career for the final decade of his working life. A well-connected London solicitor, Arnold Goodman, secured him a seat on the board of Southern Television. But first he had a crucial season to put on.

There were four new productions on the stocks, including the return of Callas as Cherubini's *Medée* and Kempe conducting *Parsifal*. The opening attraction, if such it could be called, was a salute to the bicentenary of Handel's death with ten nights of

Samson, an oratorio recast for the first time as opera, mutton dressed as lamb. The show, intended as an act of homage to the English choral tradition, was cast internally and promised few excitements. What transpired was that Jon Vickers, fresh from his *Trojans* triumph, took the title role by the scruff and gave an evocation of the blinded Nazarene that would have moved stone walls to tears. Twenty-seven years later, his voice gravelled with age, I saw him recreate *Samson* at Covent Garden on the tercentenary of Handel's birth – and still felt the force of his furious identification with the shackled strongman. Vickers sang four more roles that season, finishing as Parsifal and then flying off to Bayreuth to claim his rightful place on the world stage.

To Webster's relief, the Covent Garden incubator had once again come good, but even he could not have predicted the revelation that was to follow. In *Samson*, Joan Sutherland had sung an Israelite Woman whose only aria is heard near the end. She sang well and was warmly applauded. Webster would have liked her to tackle the big German and Italian diva roles, but her run as Eva in *Meistersinger* had been unhappy and her ubiquitous husband, Richard Bonynge, was steering her into the bel canto range which had reaped such dividends for Callas.

Bonynge proposed Donizetti's *Lucia di Lammermoor*. The uxoricidal opera was last laughed off the stage at Covent Garden after a Toti dal Monte performance in June 1925. The ROH music staff and opera sub-committee saw no reason to revive it, despite (or perhaps because of) Callas's evocation of the role. Walter Legge's opposition was notably vociferous. 'I remember David pushing for it really hard against several members of the board,' said Sutherland's agent, Joan Ingpen.[28] In the end, the board agreed to let Sutherland sing *Lucia,* provided it was conducted by Tullio Serafin, Callas's mentor. The director and designer was to be Franco Zeffirelli, a Luchino Visconti acolyte who had yet to make a name for himself abroad. He arrived at Bow Street to find that the man at the door, Sergeant Martin, had been one of his Scots Guards liberators in wartime Italy.

Sutherland was sent for ten days to Venice to study with the octogenarian Serafin. Back in London, she was manhandled by the director who made Geraint Evans, playing her brother Enrico, throw her repeatedly to the ground. 'Her movements on stage weren't very fluid,'[29] said Evans. Michael Langdon, singing Raimondo, felt that

Zeffirelli had spotted something 'no one realized she possessed'.[30] Serafin, in the pit, bridled at the director's veristic insistence on decking Lucia in a blood-drenched nightgown. 'Permit me to say, sir,' said Sergeant Martin to the director, 'that it's very good.'[31]

In the week of the première, the Brazilian Joao Gibin pulled out as the lover Edgardo and was replaced by the homespun Australian, Kenneth Neate. 'Is Joan going to be very good, Langdon?' fretted Webster. 'Absolutely,' cooed the baritone. 'Good,' sighed the General Administrator, 'I think so, too; I think so too.'[32] He had come close to staking his survival on her success.

Getting ready for the dress rehearsal, Sutherland was told that Callas and Schwarzkopf had come to hear her. With visible trepidation she consented to a joint photocall, pictures of which appeared next day in all the morning papers, Callas in a mink wrap, Sutherland in a flannel dressing gown. 'There were twenty-two photographers crowding into dressing-room five,' remembered Beresford.[33] According to Schwarzkopf, Callas was impressed. 'She will have a great success tomorrow,' said the diva, 'and make a big career if she can keep it up. But only we know how much greater I am.'[34]

On the night of 17 February 1959, a star was born on the stage of the Royal Opera House, an event rare and precious in the annals of art. As soon as Sutherland finished her opening scene, sitting on a rock with harp accompaniment, there were calls for encores. Between acts, Walter Legge came by to offer a recording contract, promising to telephone in the morning. Lord Harewood apologized for leaving early; he was dining at Buckingham Palace. Callas, too, reportedly left before the climax.

In the penultimate Mad Scene, having slain her new husband, running hither and thither to the mocking trills of a flute, Sutherland sang like a woman possessed, her grip on sanity flickering and fading with each swoop of the voice until, on a high E-flat, arms outflung, she fell backwards, the curtain dropped and the house exploded. 'Stay there, darling,' hissed Langdon, as Sutherland tried to rise:

> Each time (the curtain) came down she would move as if to get up, and each time I prevented her physically. 'How much longer, Mike?' she kept asking, one eye open to see if the curtain was going back again. It did – seven times, if I recall correctly. When she eventually went out to take her solo call in front of the curtain,

the house went wild and it was at least twenty minutes before we could start the final scene.[35]

The morning's reviews paled beside the night's excitements, the critics struggling to preserve critical detachment. Philip Hope-Wallace reported 'a personal triumph for the Australian soprano Joan Sutherland – a future Melba, some people would be ready to declare on the strength of her almost flawless singing of the great scene of the third act.' Andrew Porter ranked Sutherland as 'one of the world's leading prima donnas', raising the roof as no one but Callas could.[36]

Legge typically failed to phone, but an Australian heiress, Louise Hanson Dyer, booked Sutherland to sing on her L'Oiseau Lyre label, employing Decca engineers, who signed Sutherland exclusively for their firm. The BBC relayed *Lucia* live to the nation and Sutherland was courted by opera bosses from Venice, La Scala, Genoa and all the way down to Sicily. Amid the hype and glory, some wondered why it had taken so long for Covent Garden to realize her potential. Her husband suggested that she owed the company few favours. Her agent gave credit equally to Webster for persisting with such a gawky girl and to Zeffirelli: 'she was *choreographed* by him'.[37]

Overnight fame made little obvious impact on the girl they would call 'La Stupenda'. Her first decision was to take three months off, checking into the London Clinic to have her sinuses cleared, an operation which, she was assured, would give her thirty years of trouble-free singing. She returned to a world clamouring for her autograph. She sang two Handel operas – *Alcina* for Cologne Radio and *Rodelinda* at Sadler's Wells, and ended the season with four sold-out *Lucias* at Covent Garden.

Then her contract expired. 'I feel we are to blame for not having sufficient check on her activities,' lamented Drogheda.[38] Serafin suggested that she should follow one Italian-Scot heroine with another, Verdi's Lady Macbeth. Bonynge, however, insisted on Amina in Bellini's *La Sonnambula*, another bel canto role ('he has set my work back by a hundred years,' said Callas) – and that was that. 'They both knew where they were going,' wrote her biographer. 'They were going wherever Richard, and only he, said they should go.'[39]

'Everybody found Ricky difficult,' said Joan Ingpen, 'and poor Joan often didn't know whom to obey.' The following spring,

Bonynge was locked out at Glyndebourne and left banging on the auditorium door after making a pest of himself demanding that she stand centre-stage throughout Bellini's *I Puritani*. Ingpen persuaded him that in Edinburgh, where the opera was transferring, the stage was too small to accommodate his otherwise admirable idea. Bonynge was becalmed, but trouble soon flared again. Ingpen took Sutherland aside and explained that her husband's interference was damaging her career. The big Australian looked back at her with tear-filled eyes. 'If I don't do what he wants,' she said, 'he'll leave me. And I love him.'[40]

A solution was proposed by Sutherland's American agent, Anne Colbert, who said, 'if there's nothing else to do with him, let him conduct her.' 'For Joan, who did not like scenes,' noted her Decca producer, John Culshaw, 'it would mean the end of differences of opinion with strange conductors; for Richard it would mean that he would lose anonymity; and for the agent it meant a lot less trouble (they could be engaged together in what the Americans call a 'package deal') and still more money.'[41]

The only question was whether Bonynge could hack it with the baton. He made a nervous début in January 1962 with the Rome radio orchestra. Well-meaning colleagues and anxious Decca bosses urged him to take lessons with Goossens or Pierre Monteux, but Bonynge resisted options for self-improvement, apart from a few tips that he took from Henry Lewis, a former orchestral player who was married to, and conducting, the mezzo-soprano Marilyn Horne. 'I think (Bonynge) was simply unaware of his own deficiencies as a conductor,' said Culshaw, 'and strangely impervious to the shafts of irony which orchestral players would hurl at him from time to time ... (He) prevented the opera audiences from hearing Joan Sutherland with the great conductors of the age, for it soon became the rule (and there were very, very few exceptions) that to engage Sutherland you had to engage Bonynge as well.'[42]

Sutherland would not hear a word said against Bonynge. When he was booed, she stood wringing her hands in the wings saying, 'it's my fault – I went wrong in the cavatina'. They became the twentieth century's most famous operatic pairing, inseparable as Cav and Pag, forming a Melba-type touring ensemble and ending up in command of Australia's first opera house. Their huge entourage included female attendants for Sutherland and a male valet-cum-chauffeur for Bonynge, in keeping with the style of a Victorian nightingale.

Bonynge steered her into some Verdis and late romantics, but her reputation centred on bel canto. 'I think Ricky limited her,' said Ingpen, echoing a widespread sensation. Others argued that, without Bonynge, Sutherland would have languished undiscovered. 'Joan was a darling, so simple and uncomplicated,' said Adele Leigh who sang beside her throughout the 1950s. 'If it weren't for Richard, she would never have become Dame Joan.'[43]

Whatever the objective truth, Sutherland's involvement with Covent Garden ended with her apotheosis. She would return frequently as a guest artist and liked to declare that 'I have always called Covent Garden my home,'[44] but she showed little sense of obligation. 'You understand that since my very sudden "rise to fame" things have become very complex for me,' she told Webster in December 1959, turning down several roles.[45] Webster, she said, with unintended irony, 'was great at giving people confidence, certainly to me.'[46]

Her departure was a bitter blow, not just for Webster personally but for the collective ideal. Before 1959, singers who rose to fame on his stage, albeit less explosively than Vickers and Sutherland, maintained an attachment to the Covent Garden 'family'. Shacklock, Shuard, Geraint Evans and Adele Leigh enjoyed coming home as 'house stars'. Sutherland took off like a rocket and never looked back. Air travel was becoming easier, the world was getting smaller and the temptations were far too great for a singer to place sentiment above self-interest. Though she would sing a nostalgic Mad Scene at Webster's farewell and end her own career in December 1990 on the ROH stage, Sutherland would spend more of her career in the air than she did in any opera house. 'She belongs as much to Covent Garden and La Scala as she does to the Met,' noted the American singing expert John Ardoin in 1964 – by which time, she belonged nowhere. The rules of engagement were being rewritten and, as Ardoin sadly acknowledged: 'the great names of opera do not reflect the quality of an opera house'.[47] They had become the topping on the cake, the sugary sprinkling that sold the product while rotting a company's finances and fibre.

The flight of star voices from staff contracts destroyed another of Covent Garden's founding assumptions. The dream had been that a national opera company would supply its own stars from English and Empire stock. This chimera was dispelled by ease of travel and an explosion in world fees, which Covent Garden was forced to match and sometimes to exceed. The 60s were about to go consumer mad. 'There will be more food in the shops this Christmas than there has been since 1938,' trumpeted the popular press.[48] Singers were swept up by greed and by a publicity-driven need for status symbols – no longer one sports car but three. Sutherland bought a château in Switzerland, where Melba made do with an Australian ranch.

Rampant materialism ravaged the budgets of major opera houses, but the spiritual damage was greater still. The idea of opera as a collaborative act turned absurd when one soprano was paid more than the entire chorus. To the emergent Me Generation, individuality was the ultimate and community a net for losers. Against this backdrop, Covent Garden's original aspiration to artistic self-sufficiency came to seem as utopian as Nye Bevan's claim that the NHS would cost less each year as the national health improved. Opera was marching out of step with the times, and no one at Covent Garden was able to acknowledge the dysfunction, or redefine the company's purpose. This was a dangerous arrhythmia, and one that would become more pronounced as the century advanced.

At the Royal Ballet, the despondency deepened. Margot Fonteyn had murmured the dreaded r-word, and her murmurings of retirement grew louder and more insistent as a critical birthday approached. 'Margot told me quite plainly,' said John Tooley: '"Physically, I can't keep up the pace. It won't be long."'[49]

Her husband Tito Arias had returned to Panama where, politically sidelined, he plotted a *coup d'état* – his sixth.[50] Fonteyn flew out to lend support, but the *coup* was comic-opera. Arias's flotilla of armoured shrimp boats was routed by the Guardia Nacional and Fonteyn was arrested in Panama City on 20 April 1959, interrogated for two days and deported. Back in London, she changed her status at the Royal Ballet to guest artist and upped her fee. 'Guns don't come cheap,' she told her friend Colette Clark, Kenneth's daughter.[51] Even more quietly, she marked her fortieth birthday on 18 May, a date she had long set down for retirement.

She had been dancing for years on a damaged left foot and relied on sheer willpower some nights to stop her perma-fix smile contorting in anguish. The skin on her high cheekbones was stretched taut as a drum and her trim form seemed more fragile than agile. She ruled out any more *Swan Lake*s, unable to manage thirty-two *fouetté* turns on her painful left foot. Forty was old for a ballerina and Fonteyn was ready to reclaim her life; whether she would spend the rest of it with that philandering wastrel Tito was another matter, a question she needed time and freedom to contemplate.

Her ruminations plunged Madam into action and Webster into despair. Margot Fonteyn was the Royal Ballet's only star. Others in her constellation were approaching their zenith without having earned the authority and allure of a prima ballerina. If Margot quit, it would spell domestic disaster and the end of dollar revenue. All season long, the company trembled. Ashton, her creative source, alert to the shifting of sands, devised his chirpy new ballet, *La fille mal gardée*, for Nadia Nerina and David Blair. It proved his greatest success for half a decade, his signal of comic renewal.

Fonteyn, however, after the Panama fiasco stopped murmuring. Low on funds, she resolved to dance on. Not for the money, she insisted, but because there were certain things she could do which no one else could match, and because the public needed her. 'She was always loved not so much for what she did as for what she was,' noted a shrewd colleague, 'for that emanation across the footlights of a gentle, heartwarming personality which was convincing because the personality seemed so genuine.'[52]

What the year of Margot's wobbles yielded was an accelerated urgency in Madam's mind to spot a successor. In August 1959, a 20-year-old *Swan Lake* extra was summoned to the Director's office and told she was to dance the central roles of Odette-Odile on tour in six weeks' time at the Hippodrome Theatre, Golders Green, a commuter junction on the Northern Line of the London Underground. Antoinette Sibley was a graduate of Madam's ballet school, a Home Counties girl with a mind of her own. 'I felt at ease with her,' said Sibley. 'She called me Sibyl.'[53]

Her partner in *Swan Lake* was to be Michael Somes, Fonteyn's regular and the company's most rigorous trainer. Sibley was rehearsed round the clock and got through her début without incident, followed by a second performance at suburban Streatham. She then went back unremarked to the corps.

Four weeks later, she got a Saturday morning call from Somes. 'You're on tonight,' he said. Nerina was sick and she was to dance Odette-Odile at Covent Garden. 'There's no way,' said Sibley. 'I can't. No, no.'[54] Refusal, however, was inadmissible. Fonteyn, ever the team player, gave up her rehearsal time and guided her through the *fouettés*. A press conference was called to announce that Miss Sibley would be the youngest person ever to dance the role at the ROH. Even if she had fallen twice on her bottom and waltzed off with the wrong swan, she would have rated a mention in the Sunday papers. Sibley, though, was stunning, and glamorous: softer and shapelier than Fonteyn. A full hand of ballet critics phoned in raves, and several of their reviews made the front page. Next morning, Sibley could hardly get out of her house for the throng of photographers.

'Madam wasn't very pleased about it,' said her flatmate, 'because in those days the policy was that it was the company and not the individual that mattered. I think they felt that (Antoinette) had courted that publicity, which she hadn't at all, bless her heart; she'd just gone there and done what she had to do.'[55]

Like it or not, Ninette de Valois had a star in the making. Her response was to put Sibley back in the corps for six weeks before letting her dance another lead role. Then she sent her to South Africa, sharing and studying roles on tour with the experienced Beriosova, Nerina and Beryl Grey. On their return to Covent Garden, in February 1960, Sibley danced in quick succession the Betrayed Girl in Madam's version of *The Rake's Progress*, Aurora in *Sleeping Beauty*, six *Swan Lake*s and *Les Sylphides*. Beriosova said she liked her Aurora better than anyone's except Margot's, and Fonteyn herself taught her *Giselle*. Somes, whose first wife had recently died, moved in with his protégée and later married her, often reducing her to floods of tears in exhaustive training sessions. He was more than twenty years her senior but still a striking figure, the best male dancer England had ever produced, albeit now on his last legs. They made an eye-catching couple, and the romance did Sibley no lasting harm.

Nor was she the lone contender. That season, Covent Garden saw a *Swan Lake* danced by her classmate Lynn Seymour, billed as the first Canadian to dance a leading role with the Royal Ballet. Separated in age by just ten days, Seymour and Sibley shared the same teacher, Winifred Edwards, but specialized in different styles. Sibley was a classical dancer, a perfectly tuned instrument for established repertoire. The darker, more turbulent Seymour was a dramatic interpreter of new work, careering into a symbiotic though non-sexual relationship with the choreographer Kenneth MacMillan. Both dancers bristled with promise and beside them stood a third, Merle Park, two years older and Rhodesian by birth, who sought to embrace both classical and dramatic roles.

These were joyous auguries for the Royal Ballet, its first flush of renewal since entering the House. But no one knew better than Madam how long it took to make a world star, fifteen years in Fonteyn's case, and how many new blooms fell by the wayside. She glowered at the hyperbolic reviews and emphasized the need for relentless hard work. Beyond the patter of silk-shod feet, all she could hear was the ticking of Margot's chronological clock.

Webster played no part in the ballet's progress. His relations with Madam were cool and barely correct. Not one written word between them survives in the ROH archives, but a stray letter in a private collection illustrates graphically the degree to which Webster was excluded from ballet decisions but blamed for any mishaps. On tour in New York, Madam was dissatisfied with arrangements for *La fille mal gardée*. 'My dear David,' she snarled,

> I very much want an interview with you and Sol (Hurok) and will come either to your hotel or his office as soon as I hear that you can arrange it. What happened at the dress rehearsal of *La fille mal gardée* really cannot occur again – there is no Director alive that would accept that.

After a page of complaints about last-minute rehearsal changes, she launched into a series of scarcely-veiled personal threats:

> I am busy collecting a very clear picture of all the demands that are being made on my staff. If I find that anything as steep as some of the things that have already happened are likely to occur again, I promise you that I shall demand a proper hearing in their defence before I leave them. . .
>
> I tried to show you all last summer the way that you are working the Company as a whole. Before I left London, the surgeon in charge of our Company complained of overstrain. Over 200 treatments had to be given to 50 dancers during the rehearsal period. I told him that I knew I was over-taxing everyone and that I welcomed his comments.
>
> I realize that the above is irrelevant to the rest of this letter, but I mention it to show you that the *Fille* rehearsal was the straw that nearly broke the camel's back. The camel, though, was not the writer, but the spirit of the Royal Ballet as a whole.
>
> (signed) Ninette de Valois.[56]

Madam never let Webster venture so much as a suggestion about the Royal Ballet, and he feared her rare visits to his office as a secondhand car dealer fears the taxman. He remained friendly with Ashton, however, and held the purse-strings of both her troupes, after the Sadler's Wells Theatre Ballet was taken over by Covent Garden as its secondary touring company. This anomalous position exposed Webster to uncomfortable situations. At the end of a gruelling, financially successful US tour in 1964, Sibley, Seymour and Park approached him for a pay rise. 'Margot had danced the first nights,' said Sibley, 'but Lynn, Merle and I had carried the tour – we were the backbone of the company. We were very nervous about going to Webster, but I honestly believe he hadn't a clue who we were. This was the only time I ever spoke to him. Introducing us on television some time later, he couldn't even pronounce our names properly.'[57]

If the General Administrator's control of the ballet company was chimerical, his command of the opera company was now under challenge from his new chairman. Drogheda declared that Covent Garden would not be allowed to drift without a music director and that the Board, not Webster, would select and interview the conductors.

The premier candidates were Giulini and Kempe, both of whom were ruled out for knowing little beyond Italian or German opera. The next rank consisted of the Italian Nello Santi (who messed up a Sutherland *Traviata*), the Czech Jaroslav Krombholc, and the Hungarian refugee Georg Solti, who was coming to the end of a nine-year term at Frankfurt-am-Main. Solti was making a name for himself with a recording-in-progress of Wagner's *Ring* that was a marvel of early-stereo, with ear-tweaking stage effects and energized tempi. Harewood was sent to Germany to see him conduct Verdi's *Il forza del destino*. He reported favourably to Webster, who flew out and booked Solti for a December 1959 *Rosenkavalier*.

Solti's arrival at Covent Garden was hardly noticed by a press and public distracted by the return of Elisabeth Schwarzkopf, who had been absent for almost a decade. To first-nighters, her account of the Marschallin, a role she had recorded successfully and sung in sixteen productions, was a huge let-down. Andrew Porter in the *Financial Times* complained of 'artificiality', William Mann in *The Times* accused her of 'archness' and Peter Heyworth in the *Observer* ridiculed her 'toothpaste smile'. Her husband, Walter Legge, stormed into the next board meeting, demanding a motion of censure against British critics; he earned a note in the minutes stating that 'the present state of English music criticism is a national misfortune'.[58] Schwarzkopf never sang again at Covent Garden, and Legge left the Board soon after. Solti blamed Legge for wrecking his wife's performance by shouting instructions at her during every rehearsal.

His conducting was widely admired. Orchestral players told Thomas Armstrong, a member of the Board, that Solti made their fingers tingle. Drogheda was deeply moved and dismissed a counter-proposal to appoint John Pritchard as music director. He turned instead to his wife's piano teacher, a Hungarian called Ilona Kabos whom Solti had known from student days in Budapest. Kabos invited Solti to cocktails with Drogheda at her handsome home in St John's Wood. 'I was instantly attracted,' said Drogheda.[59] Solti, who spoke little English, never forgot the directness of Drogheda's greeting. 'I came into the room,' he recalled years later, 'and Garrett said: "We want you as our next music director, but we cannot pay you – we haven't any money. Oh, and you cannot say No."'

Solti, charmed and flattered, declined the offer, explaining that he did not want another opera post and was on his way to Los Angeles. 'Think it over,' said Drogheda. 'How long?' said Solti. 'Take as long as you like,' said the chairman, 'we haven't got anyone else.' The morning after his last *Rosenkavalier*, Solti flew to Los Angeles to meet his new orchestra and pay respects to the octogenarian Bruno Walter, who had been briefly considered for Covent Garden fifteen years before. Walter, to his surprise, now urged him in the strongest possible terms to take the London post. 'You have to do it,' said Walter, 'because if a generation falls out, after us, then the opera tradition won't be kept. This cannot happen. You must do it.'[60] Solti, unable a resist an appeal to his conscience, cabled his acceptance to Webster and proposed September 1961 as a starting date. Six months later, he discovered that the Los Angeles Philharmonic board had appointed a junior conductor, Zubin Mehta, without his approval. Solti tore up his Los Angeles contract and committed himself fully to Covent Garden. This was the last thing Webster wanted: an experienced, omniscient music director.

'Although I became a very great friend with David Webster later,' said Solti, 'originally he didn't want me. When Kubelik departed he felt, I'm good enough, I can do it alone. He had great sympathy towards me as a conductor, but he didn't need a music director. Cost too much money, whatever. It was basically a power complex: he didn't want to yield the power. Drogheda and the board forced David Webster to engage me, really forced him.'[61]

Sharing a car to Aldeburgh for the première of *A Midsummer Night's Dream* in June 1960, Webster did not speak a word to Solti throughout the three-hour journey. Solti volunteered to conduct the London première of Britten's new opera in a production by Webster's friend, John Gielgud. He knew how to make himself agreeable, and Webster was impressed by his musicianship. But the General Administrator was in torment. Although he had been knighted in the New Year's honours list, he felt unappreciated. Drogheda had curtailed his powers to hire and fire. De Valois was being more than usually difficult. And even on the American front which he had pioneered, Rudolf Bing at the Met bypassed him by dealing with his assistant, Tooley. Webster was fifty-seven and facing a critical career decision.

He called Arnold Goodman and asked if he could get him another job. Moments later, Goodman received a call from John Davis, chairman of Southern Television, where Webster was already on the board. Davis was looking for a new managing director. Would Webster do? said the lawyer. Delighted, said Davis. So was Webster, when Goodman passed on the offer.

Days later, Davis reported an obstacle. Was Goodman aware, he demanded, that Webster was homosexual? Not that it mattered to Davis personally, but his board would never accept a homosexual at the head of a television channel watched by women and children. The offer was summarily withdrawn. Webster lied about it to his lover, telling Jimmy that he had been unable to tear himself away from Covent Garden.[62] Whichever version was believed, he was now a life prisoner of the institution he had created.

CHAPTER 7

Act Two: Enter the Jew
(1961–70)

IT WAS CLEAR to many who were young at the time, clearer even than it would seem in retrospect, that the 60s ushered in an immense and irrevocable change in most fields of human relations. Sex, with the advent of the birth-control pill, was detached from marriage, forethought and the expectation of lasting romance. Love acquired new connotations with the decriminalization of homosexuality and the lowering of the age of consent. The price of error was reduced by legalized abortion; infants born to single mothers were relieved of the stigma of bastardy. Moral censorship eased after Penguin Books in 1960 successfully defended publishing a paperback edition of *Lady Chatterley's Lover*, overcoming the bewigged indignation of prosecuting counsel who asked the jury if they would wish their 'wives and servants' to read D. H. Lawrence's novel of cross-class couplings and Anglo-Saxon words. It went on to sell two million copies. According to the poet Philip Larkin, 'Sexual intercourse began/ in 1963,/between the "Chatterley" trial/ and the Beatles' first LP.'[1]

Yet, while the 60s are usually surveyed through smug shades of sex, soft drugs and pop songs, the loosening of stays was not the sole force of social transformation, nor the greatest. The tectonic plates of accepted conduct were shifting and relations between generations would never be the same again. Young people, scornful of elders who had acquiesced in two world wars and now contemplated a nuclear third, opted to live for today and forget about 'saving up to get married'. They left home to live alone, or informally with others. Where, in 1961, one in eight British homes was single-occupancy, by 1997 a quarter of all households consisted of one person living alone.[2] The nuclear family was consigned to the scrapheap.

Grandparents and invalid aunts were packed off to institutions, cast upon the mercies of an ever-expanding Welfare State.

Street-long communities were torn apart by high-rise architects, acting on behalf of manipulative local authorities who favoured the depersonalized tower blocks developed in Stalin's police state. The face of English urban life was being surgically restructured in fast-begrimed cement and concrete. The idea of 'community' was abolished and the word itself hijacked to imply a collectivity of interest, rather than a care for neighbours. In the momentum of demolition, a caste of property developers and asset strippers made themselves conspicuously rich. Also on the rise were new-age fashion and music entrepreneurs who pursued the spare cash in young people's pockets with an alternate vision of Arcadia. London, famed for its sober tailoring, became a Mecca of flowing peacock fabrics. Liverpool, noisiest of ports, gave birth to the Mersey Beat. Manchester, bristling with Victorian severity, nourished an ulterior media culture. The idea of England was being altered day by day.

Other western countries would be shaken by similar fissures, but the shock struck deepest in London because it was here that the 60s started to swing. Ever since the curtain rose on *Look Back in Anger*, Jimmy Porter's rage had served as rocket fuel for a resurgent English theatre, cinema and fiction. The kitchen-sink novels of John Braine, David Storey and Alan Sillitoe, swiftly filmed, vented a strikingly similar tone of pent-up frustrations. Within months of its première, the Osborne play was transmitted nationwide by Granada Television, the independent Manchester-based franchise. It scored a sixty-two per cent rating. Late in 1960, Granada brought forth two new strands of programming – a soap opera, *Coronation Street*, set in the kind of back-to-back terraces that were fast being torn down; and a current affairs weekly, *World in Action*, that tore into politics like a polecat with prey. The independent television trail-blazers – Granada, ATV, Thames – were owned by movie and music-hall impresarios of Russian-Jewish stock and manned by classless Oxbridge graduates who believed in the power of television to inform and democratize. *World in Action*'s first producer was a 28-year-old Glaswegian, Jeremy Isaacs. 'I joined Granada Television,' said Isaacs, 'because Sidney Bernstein wanted to use television cameras to reveal the democratic process to the people of this country. He televised the 1958 by-election at Rochdale when the

BBC were shit-scared of touching any electoral issue in case anything they said or did upset the parties.'[3]

At the BBC, in the autumn of 1960, a new director-general, the establishmentarian Hugh Carleton-Greene, began the process of converting a dowdy maiden aunt into a medium that reflected, and stimulated, swirling currents of public uncertainty. Social documentaries, sharper comedy and, in November 1962, the satirical lash of *That Was The Week That Was* informed the nation of its own state of flux. In November 1966, the critic Kenneth Tynan deliberately uttered the word 'fuck' on live BBC television and civilization was deemed to have come to an end. After the show, the American writer Mary McCarthy said, 'I suppose it's an historic moment.' She missed the point entirely. History was made matter-of-factly in the 60s, as one taboo tumbled after another.

In an Age of Ego, when gratification was instant and self-awareness the be-all and end-all, national ideals and enterprises were bound to take a back seat. The trick in any revolution is to stay in touch with public sentiment without succumbing to demotic pressure. The worst mistake is to turn one's back on the tide – which is what Covent Garden proceeded to do. The company was in the ascendant, but each triumph confirmed its fixity of purpose and ignored the fast-changing culture. The men who ran Covent Garden were middle-aged at a time when the world around them was young again.

Just how oblivious the company was to the risks of cultural drift is illustrated by its response to overtures from pace-setting Granada. Aware that the BBC were not screening much opera or ballet because of a never-ending fees dispute, an opera-loving Granada man, Denis Forman, suggested that the ROH and Granada should get round the problem by jointly engaging top artists to perform both on stage and in studio – thus bypassing the unions and ensuring the ROH a priceless stream of prime-time exposure. Summoned with his chairman, Sidney Bernstein, to explain the idea over lunch, Forman found himself in the Royal Box facing a formidable line-up of Drogheda, Webster, de Valois, Ashton and Professor Lionel Robbins. Their attitude could hardly have been more condescending:

They chattered endlessly about the scandals and credulities of the opera and ballet world, throwing in countless names and nicknames which meant nothing to Sidney or me. 'Have you heard who's going with Dukey for a snug week in Cannes?' one would say, and the rest would cry, 'No. Who? Who?' When the tease had run its time and the answer was given, 'Bim', they were all convulsed with laughter for several minutes. Sidney and I ate our food in isolation until coffee, when Garrett Drogheda said, 'Now, Sidney, tell us about your film idea.'

'Not film, said Sidney, 'television.' And he put me in to bat. It was clear that Webster had not read the paper and that no one else was even faintly interested . . . I was glad when Drogheda cut me short by saying, 'How interesting, but if it is about television we must of course ask the BBC first.'[4]

There were two whole seasons to run before Solti took over, and Webster made the most of his last chance to wield artistic authority. In 1959-60 he splashed out on a Zeffirelli double-bill of *Cavalleria Rusticana* and *I Pagliacci*, on Giulini conducting *The Barber of Seville*, and on a production of Verdi's *Macbeth* in which the role intended for Sutherland was taken by the cockney sparrow, Amy Shuard. Popular in the upper galleries, Shuard once swanned in to the refectory on a blistering hot day dressed in a fur coat. 'Ere, Amy,' shouted a stagehand, 'ain't yer hot in that fur?' Shuard quipped back in broadest Clerkenwell: 'Em as az furs, wears 'em.' The following year saw more of the same – a Giulini/Zeffirelli *Falstaff* with Geraint Evans in a heaven-sent role, Gielgud directing Britten's new opera, *A Midsummer Night's Dream*, and Serafin conducting *La Sonnambula* with Sutherland sleep-walking in place of the elusive Callas.

Webster was under continuous pressure from Drogheda and the Board to secure a seasonal commitment from the temperamental Greek, but Callas, torn between heart and art, was drifting in the slipstream of her shipowner lover, Onassis. London was not uppermost in her mind, and she was further troubled by clear signs of vocal decline. Walter Legge, her record producer, was powerless to make her return – but, before quitting the Board in mutual distrust, he did Covent Garden one good turn. It was Legge who urged Otto Klemperer, in his mid-seventies, to make a belated and momentous début at the Royal Opera House. Klemperer, a legend of pre-Hitler Berlin, had been retrieved from destitution by Legge and now towered over London's concert life as chief conductor of the Philharmonia Orchestra. Although maimed by brain surgery, manic-depressive episodes and such bizarre accidents as setting fire to himself in bed, he possessed so secure a sense of musical structure that players swore they could anticipate the ending of a symphony in the tempo he set for the opening bars. In Beethoven and Mahler he possessed unchallengeable authority. Even Herbert von Karajan, no respecter of colleagues, came to his Royal Festival Hall dressing room after an *Eroica* to say, 'I hope I shall live to conduct the Funeral March as well as you have done.'[5] In earlier classics he could seem exasperatingly slow, but musicians revered his fearless integrity, and feared his inflexible rigour, allied to a scathing wit.

Webster had first approached him in 1956 to conduct *Fidelio*, Beethoven's liberation opera, but Klemperer was unimpressed by the ROH production. Webster promised new sets, and Legge urged him to extend his concert-hall success to the higher-income opera house audience. Klemperer duly consented, on condition he could hand-pick the cast and direct them himself. In February 1960, Legge informed Webster that 'Dr Klemperer and I have just been discussing the necessary cast for the performances of *Fidelio*, which he will conduct at Covent Garden. What we (*sic*) have in mind is: Leonore = Jurinac; Florestan = Vickers; Rocco = (Gottlob) Frick; Marzelline = Lipp; Pizarro = Hotter; ... Minister (Eberhard) Waechter'[6] The only change to this stellar cast was the substitution of Elsie Morison for the unavailable Wilma Lipp. Webster sent Christopher West to act as assistant producer and allocated the infirm conductor a cupboard-sized changing room a few feet from the stage.

Klemperer found the conditions antiquated and dangerous -'I almost had to crawl on all fours to get into the orchestra pit,' he told his daughter, Lotte[7] – but he insisted on smoking his pipe and was, according to orchestral players, the only conductor ever allowed to puff in the pit.[8] They had trouble fathoming his downbeat and had to restart the overture several times before he was satisfied. He made an early gaffe by addressing the first horn, Tony Tunstall, as 'Mr Tuckwell', mistaking him for the famous principal of the London Symphony Orchestra, but the players were awestruck by his certitude and he rewarded the ones he liked best with interval cigarettes. They were, he said, 'no Philharmonia' but they tried hard.[9] Webster regularly came down to make sure he was content, and the singers proved accommodating, with the exception of Vickers who contested some of his tempi, though respectfully enough to avoid disruption.

Fidelio, seldom a crowd-puller, sold out within twenty-four hours. Klemperer was visibly nervous on the première night, 24 February 1961, and his spirits were not raised by an interval visit from Walter Legge who told him, '*Das Publikum ist noch ganz kalt* (the public is stone-cold).' But the woodwind chord that opens the second act emanated an irresistible tension, and the audience were gripped as if by a John Buchan thriller. At the final curtain, Webster presented Klemperer with a huge bouquet and a hand-written card that he treasured ever after. It read: 'You have conquered Covent Garden.'

Webster lost no time in booking Klemperer for *Magic Flute* the following winter with an all-British cast: Joan Carlyle as Pamina, Sutherland as Queen of the Night, Richard Lewis as Tamino, Geraint Evans as Papageno. Klemperer and West were to direct again, and Drogheda proposed Oskar Kokoschka as designer. Klemperer agreed to see the Austrian *émigré* artist in his Zurich apartment, greeting him with the cordial remark that he would have preferred sets by Picasso. Kokoschka, no less sweetly, said that he had only wanted to design the *Flute* for Furtwängler – 'and he, alas, died.' Lotte Klemperer hovered within earshot, fearing violence, but the two men had a hearty chuckle and parted firm friends and non-partners.[10] The ROH *Magic Flute* was ultimately designed by Georg Eisler, son of the socialist composer.

Rehearsals were marred by Sutherland's late arrival and grudging attitude. When the dress rehearsal overran, she returned for the finale in street clothes. Klemperer stopped her in mid-aria and asked her to follow his tempo. Bonynge, in the stalls, yelled out: 'Don't take any notice of him, Joanie. He's mad!'[11] Klemperer, whose hearing was starting to fail, apparently missed the remark. On opening night he held his beat and left Sutherland to flounder. In her memoirs, almost forty years later, she complained that his rhythm was irregular and she was advised by the orchestra leader, Charles Taylor: 'Don't watch him, Joan dear. You just go, and we'll be with you.'[12] Geraint Evans, of the same production, recalled: 'Klemperer had a fantastic sense of tempo. Sometimes it might seem to be slow, but it would always be all of a piece with the performance as he phrased it. Nor did he vary from one performance to another as some conductors do. I once asked a repetiteur to time my arias with a stopwatch at three successive Klemperer performances, and all three were exactly the same, an incredible consistency.'[13]

Sutherland left after three nights, but not before the *Flute* had been so slammed in the press that Legge, a stranger to loyalty, pondered transferring his *Fidelio* recording, which was due directly afterwards, to Karajan in Berlin. He need not have feared. In the subterranean studio at Kingsway Hall, Klemperer was unassailable and the recording was one of the greatest opera sets ever made.

His third legacy to Covent Garden was *Lohengrin* in 1963, with a German producer, Josef Gielen, recommended by Solti ('never listen to a colleague,' he told his daughter) and Régine Crespin awkwardly cast as Elsa. Despite ugly sets and variable singing, one critic hailed it as the greatest Wagner experience since the war[14] and Martin Cooper extolled 'a quite extraordinary splendour of tone and fineness of detail'.[15] Klemperer returned once more to Covent Garden, in March 1969 at the age of eighty-three, to preside over a *Fidelio* revival, six performances that sealed his mighty career in the opera house. Although his involvement was limited and late, he bestowed on Covent Garden a sense of confidence and continuity, linking it by his physical presence and moral authority to a chain of tradition that stretched back to his mentor, Gustav Mahler.

He grumbled mildly of a certain 'dilettantism'[16] which meant that everything had to stop for tea and everyone disappeared to the country for weekends, no matter what state the production was in. But he admired the company's spirit and he left behind a lasting imprint. He was, said Reggie Goodall, his repetiteur, 'a supreme musician – I had nothing but respect and devotion for him.'[17] Those who played and sang for Klemperer could never get his organic beat out of their system.

The Royal Ballet were dancing in Russia in June 1961, another of Madam's dreams come true, when news broke that would change its destiny. Appearing at the Kirov and the Bolshoi was an affirmation of Ninette de Valois's place in the Diaghilev line; she rejoiced in restoring to Russia a chunk of forsaken heritage. She was also keen for her dancers to absorb authentic Russian traditions of the kind they had gaped at when the Bolshoi danced in London.

Three days after opening in Leningrad, one of the ballerinas, Georgina Parkinson, managed to get through by phone to her husband in London. He told her that a young soloist had broken free from the Kirov Ballet at Le Bourget airport in Paris and requested political asylum. At the height of the Cold War, weeks before the Berlin Wall went up, the defection made the world's front-pages.

Nothing was reported in Russia for days until the Central Committee of the Communist Party had discussed the affair and issued a statement averring that Rudolf Hametovich Nureyev, aged twenty-three, had betrayed his motherland and run off with a Frenchwoman. The Kremlin sent a sharp note to the Elysée Palace warning that cultural exchanges between the two countries would be terminated if Nureyev was ever allowed to appear with a French state ensemble. The rest of the Kirov company flew on to London to make an acclaimed début at Covent Garden. Of the male lead, Yuri Soloviev, Andrew Porter reported that 'we have seen no one quite like him'.[18] Nureyev was not the best, nor the best known, dancer in the Kirov. Soviet ballet would survive without him.

Whether Nureyev would survive in the West was less certain. Trailed by photographers and KGB spies, he took work with the eccentric Marquis de Cuevas's travelling troupe, partnering the American ballerina, Rosella Hightower. That summer, he had a brief affair with her compatriot Maria Tallchief, before falling for the austere Danish dancer, Erik Bruhn, who became his lifelong lover. In Copenhagen he also found a teacher he could trust, the Russian emigrée Vera Volkova, who once taught Margot Fonteyn. But Nureyev was acutely homesick for his family and desperately needed to strike roots. Back in the USSR, he was put on trial *in absentia* for treason and his family were placed under surveillance. The sentence was seven years imprisonment and the secret services would be ordered to bring him back, by kidnap if necessary. Nureyev was frightened, insecure and forlorn.

Then, in October, there was a call for him one night at Volkova's flat. Would he dance with Margot Fonteyn in a charity gala at the Theatre Royal, Drury Lane? Galina Ulanova had dropped out under Kremlin pressure and Colette Clark, Kenneth's daughter, had persuaded Fonteyn that their best bet was the recent Kirov defector.

'He says he wants to dance with you,' Clark told Fonteyn.

'I've never set eyes on him,' said Fonteyn. 'Ask Vera if he's a good dancer.'

'Vera says he's adamant about dancing with you,' reported Clark, phoning back and forth to Copenhagen, 'and he's marvellous.'

'He sounds rather tiresome to me,' sighed Margot.[19]

Nureyev demanded to dance *Spectre of the Rose* with Fonteyn, but she had already assigned the duet to John Gilpin, and the Russian had to settle for a *Swan Lake pas de deux* with Rosella Hightower.

He insisted, however, that Ashton must choreograph a solo for him. Flying in to finalize arrangements, he took a taxi from Heathrow and turned up at the Panamanian Embassy, where Fonteyn and Arias had been reinstated after the comic coup. She ordered tea, five sugars for Rudolf, and took his measure between sips. 'I like him nine-tenths,' she told Colette Clark, 'but once or twice I saw a steely look in his eye.'[20] Before returning to Denmark, Nureyev attended class with Fonteyn under a false Polish name. 'You're that Russian fellow, aren't you?' demanded David Blair, who had just succeeded Michael Somes as Fonteyn's company partner. Nureyev stared him down, maintaining his fake identity. Blair never stood a chance.

The afternoon gala, a fundraiser for the Royal Academy of Dancing, was a sensational success. 'He's better than Nijinsky,' gasped the dowager Lady Diana Cooper, to her neighbour, Cecil Beaton. 'This boy,' noted Beaton, 'a peasant til he was seventeen when he won a scholarship to be trained as a dancer – looks like all the young Beatniks of today. Genius is not too strong a word to describe his quality and talent.'[21] The next morning, Ninette de Valois called Fonteyn to tell her she had engaged Nureyev for *Giselle*. 'Do you want to do it with him?' she demanded.

'Oh my goodness,' said Fonteyn, 'I think it would be like mutton dancing with lamb. Don't you think I'm too old?'[22] She was nineteen years his senior, and looked it. But after consulting her husband, Fonteyn decided that Nureyev was going to be the hottest thing in ballet and she had no choice: either dance with him, or get out. She called Madam and accepted the role. Nureyev's fee was £500 for three performances; Fonteyn was paid £400 a night. They were in no sense equals, not yet and perhaps never.

Nureyev had one reservation. Fearing a kidnap bid, he dared not stay in a hotel. Could he lodge with Fonteyn at the Embassy? She was unsure, more for reasons of state security than sexual risk. In the event, he proved the perfect house-guest, enduring a diet of English cold meats in polite silence. From their first rehearsal, though, Nureyev asserted his natural authority. 'Most of the men say "I will do it your way, how does it go?"' wrote Fonteyn. 'Rudolf, however, said, "Don't you think this way better?"'[23] No Englishman had ever handled her with such arrogant aplomb. Giselle, a role she had never fully possessed, suddenly became hers.

At Nureyev's ROH début, on 21 February 1962, there were twenty-three curtain calls. As the ovations swelled, Fonteyn plucked a rose from her bouquet and handed it to Nureyev, who dropped on one knee and lavished her hand with kisses. At that precise moment, the legend was born, stopping ballet history in its tracks and changing the course of English culture. 'If one person can come in and spoil the Royal Ballet style,' said Ninette de Valois, 'we deserve for it to be spoiled.'[24] The dream that British ballet, like British opera, could be nurtured entirely from kith-and-kin resources died that night. For the Royal Ballet to hold its own on the world stage, it would have to shed national pride and engage with the best. Nureyev was a revelation; he was also the start of a policy reversal. Soon to follow on the Covent Garden stage were his lover, Erik Bruhn, and Bruhn's Bulgarian-born ex-fiancée, Sonia Arova.

'I'm afraid I will ruin your *Swan Lake*,' Nureyev warned Fonteyn after seeing her dance with Blair. 'Just you try,' she replied.[25] There was give and take, grit and grace, in their relationship. She could defuse his tantrums with a shaft of wit, shattering the surge of violence on a surface of toughened glass. The impermeable Fonteyn became his cornerstone, and London his second home. As the French Government caved in to Soviet threats, cancelling his dates at the Paris Opéra, Nureyev accepted the title of Permanent Guest Artist at Covent Garden.

Through Nadia Nerina's husband, the businessman Charles Gordon, he found himself an agent in Sandor Gorlinsky, who managed Maria Callas and fixed him up with a tax shelter in Luxembourg. Nureyev gave little further thought to money. It was 1969 before he achieved fee parity with Fonteyn, at two thousand dollars a night. The impresario Victor Hochhauser, who managed his later tours, said: 'Rudolf was a gentleman. He was not cheap, but once we shook hands on a fee that was it – he never mentioned money again.'[26] Nureyev seldom bothered to collect his pay at Covent Garden. He sent tradesmen to John Tooley, who paid what they were owed and deducted it from Nureyev's fees. At one stage, Tooley was paying off a doctor, an anaesthetist, a firm of dry-cleaners, an irate landlord (for 'dilapidation') and a clutch of parking tickets.[27]

Nureyev was a free spirit, a roaming Tatar of Muslim and Mongol blood. He did not want to be tied down by worldly cares. 'I am twenty-four,' he declared in a precocious 1962 autobiography. 'I don't want to be told where my proper future lies, what is the "right" way to develop. I shall try to find this out for myself. That is what I mean by freedom.'[28]

For Madam, he brought a deeper form of liberation, releasing her from constant frets. Anxious about the effortless superiority of Russian ballet and the high-octane energy of American upstarts, she knew that her male dancers lacked training, technique and hunger for success. With Nureyev's arrival, her troubles were over. 'Until Rudi came along,' said one young company male, 'all a man had to do to get into the Royal Ballet was, more or less, turn up and show willing. Nureyev completely changed the pace. Where our chaps did little more than daintily hold a ballerina in the air, Rudi was macho man. He engaged with female dancers, manhandled them, threw them around. It was exciting, virile. He had worked with Russia's best and possessed a phenomenal memory. He could show you anything they did, and you could then try it yourself.'[29] Christopher Gable, Anthony Dowell, Nicholas Johnson, David Wall and others emerging from the Royal Ballet school were quick to pick up tips. 'The standard of virtuosity rose, literally, by leaps and bounds,'[30] said Fonteyn.

Nureyev, the least monogamous of men, danced with other leading ladies, notably Sibley, Beriosova, Anya Linden and Seymour, who called him 'a completely honest dancer – he won't cheat or take a cheap way out.'[31] The tension that preceded each performance, changing his shoes obsessively amid a torrent of curses until the moment came to go on stage, generated a magnetism that outshone his female, politely-English partners. 'The age of the ballerina is over,'[32] sighed Fonteyn, who alone could hold her own.

For Madam, he could do no wrong. At rehearsal he would sit on the floor, his head resting on her knee. No one could remember such *lèse-majesté*. 'If Rudolf asked for the lights to be changed, the lights would be changed,' said Sibley. 'It didn't matter that we'd all been asking, or that Michael (Somes) or the top people had all been asking for years. The moment Rudolf said it, it was done – he had that effect on Madam.'[33]

She urged him to contribute choreography, starting with a ten-minute *Corsaire* that was applauded for fully twice as long as its duration, and followed by a glittering *Bayadère*. Ashton, initially wary of competition, grew fascinated by the rippling eroticism of Nureyev and Fonteyn. In March 1963 he showcased them as *Marguerite and Armand* to the same Alexandre Dumas plot as Verdi's *La traviata*, with Somes, Fonteyn's former partner, cast incestuously as the heroine's brooding father. It was, wrote Richard

Buckle, 'romanticism to the nth degree, a Puccini opera in miniature, with music by Liszt . . . and it was only ever danced by the artists for whom it was created'.[34] Some critics condemned the ballet as 'a specimen of the personality cult', and according to Nerina 'it couldn't have been more kitsch'.[35] But it was exactly what the golden couple needed, and at just the right time.

Five weeks later they took the ballet to America, where saturation coverage and screaming crowds ushered them into a howl of fame. John Martin, ex-critic of the New York *Times*, warned that Nureyev's 'gigolo' antics would destroy Fonteyn and the Royal Ballet, but among those begging for tickets were Greta Garbo, Princess Grace of Monaco and Mrs Jacqueline Kennedy, who invited the pair (with Ashton) back to tea at the White House, where Rudolf sat in the President's chair. Madam beamed, knowing that her company had outshone the whole of American ballet and would be a fixture at the Met for so long as Fonteyn and Nureyev drew breath. Nureyev, increasingly mercurial, managed to get arrested for loitering in the streets of Toronto at three o'clock in the morning and made headlines once again. Balanchine warned Cecil Beaton that 'he is too selfish, and a dancer cannot afford to be selfish. Nureyev will end up badly, you'll see. He'll be like Pavlova.'[36] A stench of sour grapes trailed in his wake, along with a whiff of danger.

Fonteyn, said the lonely Nureyev, was the only person who truly understood him. She owed him her second life, as he owed her his second home. What the public witnessed on stage was a menopausal woman turning back the clock in lubricious encounters with a dark stranger half her age. He was her elixir of youth, and she his giver of purpose.

Their sexuality could hardly have been more explicit. Whether or not they were lovers in real life was hotly speculated in gossip columns and around fashionable dinner-tables without a shred of concrete evidence. The issue would be of no pressing interest to cultural historians had not their ardent physicality completely changed the course of the Royal Ballet's policy and identity. Fonteyn was coyly ambiguous when writing about the affair in her memoirs. 'As I was obviously very fond of Rudolf and spent so much time with him,' she wrote, 'it was food for scandal for those who liked it that way. I decided there was little I could do but wait for it to pass. The truth will out eventually, I thought.'[37]

'She must have had an affair with him,' said Nerina, 'because it showed on stage.'[38] Others, including Nureyev's secretary Joan Thring, were equally convinced that sex was 'out of the question . . . there was never any sign of anything like that.'[39] Nureyev preferred boys and had a prodigious appetite for casual sex. He was also headily in love with Bruhn. Fonteyn was fastidious, private and puritanical. On paper, they seem ill-matched, but the heart and loins are seldom ruled by logic.

'She was very sexy,' recalled Nicholas Johnson. 'I was the same age as Rudi, and I could have fancied her. In class and rehearsal, you can usually tell if two dancers have had sex from the way they treat each other. Rudi was very brutal to Margot, abused her terribly and called her all sorts of names. We all assumed they were lovers, or had been.'[40]

'In America,' said Laura Connor who toured with them in the late 1960s, 'they were never apart. He clung to her. She was his protection – he was very scared the KGB would come and get him. Margot was every inch a lady. Rudolf was a peasant. He did everything with his hands, ate with his hands, even wiped his bottom without paper. There are no physical secrets among dancers, and most of us believed that they slept together.'[41]

Nureyev himself told friends they had been lovers, but his accounts were contradictory and unreliable. The full facts of the affair, if ever there was one, may never come to light. They are, in any event, less interesting than the illusion they created on stage and the almost symbiotic intimacy they enjoyed in private. Fonteyn and Nureyev were probably as close as two human beings can get. They drew closer still after June 1964 when Fonteyn's husband, Tito Arias, was shot five times in his car while waiting at traffic lights in Panama City. Fonteyn and Nureyev had been dancing that night in Bath, where the violinist Yehudin Menuhin ran a music festival, and were returning from dinner when Diana Menuhin, a former dancer, broke the news as gently as she could. Fonteyn screamed, and ran through the hotel to an empty ballroom, where Nureyev found her and took her in his arms. Tito had been rushed to hospital but was expected to live. The would-be assassin was a political ally, Alfredo Jimenez, and press reports assumed that the attack had been politically motivated. It emerged years later that Tito, a wanton marriage-breaker, had seduced the wife of Jimenez, who shot him in a fit of sexual jealousy. Fonteyn, keeping up appearances as ever, told British diplomats that the attack was 'a put-up job' by 'three or four' conspirators whom she refused to name.[42] It is a mark of her national importance that these comments were promptly encoded and wired home to the Foreign Secretary.

Having ascertained that her husband was out of danger, Fonteyn decided to stay and dance, with Nureyev, a new *pas de deux* by Kenneth MacMillan that they were due to tour in Australia. The première of *Divertimento* was so intensely acclaimed that they danced the whole piece twice. The following day, Fonteyn flew to Panama to extricate her paralysed husband from a primitive hospital and transport him to the spinal injuries unit at Stoke Mandeville, back home. That summer Tito suffered a further collapse and almost died, losing his power of speech. His medical bills were crippling, and his children looked to Fonteyn to pay for their weddings. She had no alternative but to carry on dancing. Whenever possible, she took Tito along, feeding him solicitously, spoon by spoon. She lost none of her good humour or manners, but a steely look entered her eye and there was no more talk of retirement. She could not afford to give up, and would end up dancing longer than any ballerina in history, a career span of almost fifty years.

Her relentless, almost superhuman determination proved a mixed blessing for Covent Garden. Delighted as friends were that Margot had coped so well with tragedy, fears were voiced for the next line of soloists whose chances she was unwittingly blighting. Nerina, whom Buckle thought 'had three times Fonteyn's strength and technique'[43] saw the writing on the wall and retired in 1966, aged thirty-eight. Anya Linden, who married the supermarket heir John Sainsbury, quit a year earlier at thirty-two. Beriosova danced on langorously without ever claiming the fame she deserved. Sibley, Merle Park and Seymour would suffer collateral damage. 'I think all those three girls – Merle and Lynn and Antoinette – one day hoped to take over the company,' said Kenneth MacMillan. 'But the charisma of Fonteyn by then was so huge that it wasn't possible at that moment. And it was a shame, because it was the right moment when those girls could have zoomed up. A whole stream of dancers was eclipsed, and I don't only feel it about those three. I feel it about Svetlana Beriosova, also Nadia Nerina. But I don't know if that was anybody's fault, or if it just happened.'[44]

It was not Fonteyn's fault, said James Monahan, Park's husband, 'because it was up to the management, not to her, to see that opportunities were given to the young; and managements are – must be – inclined to favour the sure box-office success over the doubtful returns on a probationer. Yet the fact is that very fine dancers – Beriosova and Nerina among others – languished in the Fonteyn shadow and that . . . progress to the top of the Royal Ballet became discouragingly slow.'[45]

The blame for this sclerosis must be apportioned between Nureyev, for keeping Fonteyn ageless, and Ninette de Valois for cherishing Nureyev as her heaven-sent salvation and solution to all woes. Her admiring biographer explains this as 'the policy of an inspired general taking a calculated risk to improve a position'.[46] In fact, Madam was ready to give up the moment she saw her company was safe with Ashton at the helm and Fonteyn and Nureyev on stage for the forseeable future. She was almost sixty-five and longed to spend more time with her long-suffering husband of whom, by all accounts, she was touchingly fond. There were also physical causes. Her arthritis was getting worse and she was prone to migraine attacks that did nothing to soften her severe demeanour. On her last trip to America she told Drogheda that she was coming home by boat, since 'that jet migraine lasted thirty hours and I can't face another'.[47] Sibley recalls being invited with Somes for drinks at her riverside house in Barnes, only to be told they had come on the wrong day.

'What are you doing ringing my bell?' shouted Madam in her dressing-gown from an upstairs window. 'Well, since you're here, I suppose you had better come up.' They followed her to the bedroom and sat on the counterpane. Before she could even pour them a drink she had blown up at Somes, who cowered mutely beneath the storm. Suddenly, she stopped shrieking and said, 'thank you, dears, I feel much better now, the migraine has completely gone'.[48]

Three days after the première of *Marguerite and Armand*, Ninette de Valois announced her retirement, effective that summer. Her departure had been negotiated for nearly a year while Ashton, her designated successor, begged her to stay on a few extra months to allow him to remount *Romeo and Juliet* before having to shoulder the burdens of office.[49] The *Romeo* revival was the first casualty of his regime. Hearing that MacMillan had advanced on a staging of the same story, Ashton gave way with apparent good grace before starting to grumble about the chores of leadership. Madam, knowing his frailties, had installed three of her most trusted lieutenants in supporting roles. John Field, who had joined the Sadler's Wells

Ballet in 1939, was to run the touring company; John Hart, who had preceded him by a year, was put in charge of the rehearsal roster; Michael Somes became chief repetiteur. Madam insisted there should be no public farewell from the stage of the Royal Opera House and slipped away silently to look after her school, convinced that her legacy to the nation was in safe hands.

What could not be forseen was that Ninette de Valois would live past the end of the century, watching over her creation and charging into its affairs whenever things went wrong – as soon they would.

Georg Solti entered the Royal Opera House like a cyclone, a whirr of cosmic energy that brooked no resistance. 'In the German theatre where he had been working, the Generalmusikdirektor was emperor, his word unquestioningly obeyed,' said Bernard Keefe, a young conductor who had taken over Harewood's role as opera co-ordinator. 'Solti didn't find the efficiency he expected. It took him a long time to get used to the English way of doing things, where instead of giving orders you say, "don't you think it might be an idea. . . ?"'[50]

He raged against cramped rehearsal space, crowded rehearsal schedules, a phlegmatic chorus master and the absence of what he regarded as basic professional standards. 'You tell Sir Webster that this is what I want,' he would instruct the go-between Keefe.

'Hmm, I'd better think about that,' was Webster's murmured reply.

'I wanted discipline, precision; I was not used to people telling me, No,' recalled Solti. 'An opera house is like a military operation. You don't tell the general it can't be done.'[51]

He told the Board in his very first presentation that they would have to restructure the opera company, turning it from a repertory group that revived popular operas fifteen times a year with random cast changes to something resembling the Italian *stagione* system, where operas were produced with the same well-rehearsed cast and conductor for a run of six or seven performances. Webster demurred, saying Covent Garden could not afford a lot of new productions and complete restagings of old ones. Four new shows a year was the most the budget could manage. Nonsense, said Solti, and opened with ten.

There was not enough Mozart and Strauss being done, he complained. Many of the conductors were inadequate and he was not going to waste his time performing operas in English when there were not enough first-class native singers to cover all the roles. 'My God, it looks like Nibelheim!' he exclaimed on seeing the backstage offices. He told his first press conference that he intended to make Covent Garden the best opera house in the world, a dangerous boast. 'I thought there was no one there who knew anything at all about how to run an opera house,' he later said.

His high-handedness gave instant offence. William Bundy, the self-important technical director, rushed into Webster's office in high dudgeon after being ordered about his business by the hard-driving music director. 'Bill,' said Webster, 'if you're going to offer me your resignation, I have to tell you I'll accept it.' Morris Smith, the orchestral director and Webster's confidant, was outraged by Solti's demand that he should admit a few women to the orchestra. John Lanigan, the Australian tenor, christened him 'the Screaming Skull', an epithet that found its way into the satirical magazine *Private Eye*. 'He came along and made out as if we were some hick outfit,' said the conductor Edward Downes, who profited under Solti's leadership. 'But he inherited a company that was on a high, after all the hard work of Rankl, Kleiber and Kubelik. Solti just got lucky.'[52]

Internal dissension trickled out to the press room, where critics were prepared to hold Solti to his promise of world dominance. Almost inevitably, the first two seasons were an overwhelming let-down. Solti opened in September 1961 with Gluck's *Iphigénie en Tauride*, never much of a sensation, followed by a sepulchral *Don Giovanni* that was undermined by Solti's clashes with the languid director, Zeffirelli. A visionary triple-bill of Puccini's *Gianni Schicchi*, Ravel's *L'heure espagnole* and Arnold Schoenberg's scarily modernist *Erwartung* closed the season. The choice of director was inspired, but the brilliantly witty Peter Ustinov seemed to run out of ideas before the evening was over. There was polite criticism of Solti's hard-driven tempi, especially in Mozart.

A resplendent *Siegfried* launched his second season, directed by the estimable Hans Hotter and featuring Wolfgang Windgassen and Birgit Nilsson in the central roles. Solti's *Ring* recording was appearing to much acclaim, and few found fault with his Wagner nights, which continued with a *Walküre* revival. Three weeks into the season, however, Solti suffered a fiasco with Verdi's *Forza del Destino* in which the Hollywood producer Sam Wanamaker projected Goya paintings dimly and irrelevantly on to a screen above the stage and Solti's hand-picked soprano proved wholly inaudible. Outbursts of booing broke out in the main auditorium, untypically for an English audience. Solti's car was defaced and rotten vegetables were thrown as he drove away. The assaults were boisterous rather than life-threatening, but the music director did not see them that way.

A victim of institutionalized anti-Semitism in his native Hungary and then a Hitler refugee in gelid Switzerland, Solti was hyper-naturally sensitive to any hint of hostility from crowds or the organs of power. Accustomed to supportive reviews from a non-combative German press, he misconstrued the more robust notices of English critics as being personally or racially motivated. In Solti's mind there formed the spectre of an anti-Solti campaign driven by demagogic editors, disgruntled opera-goers and mutinous staff which was capable of inflicting, if not physical damage to his person, then lasting damage to his hard-earned career. Solti, to the end of his long and happy life, wore the fragility of a refugee touchingly on his sleeve.

He told his record producer, John Culshaw, that he did not know how long he would last at Covent Garden. Drogheda began urging Webster to renew his contract, which had to be negotiated two years in advance. Both sides were under pressure. Covent Garden could not afford to lose Solti after a single term without getting blighted as a company that could not keep a music director. Solti, for his part, saw London as his springboard to the English-speaking world. He did not want to leave defeated, but the noises in his inner ear could not be ignored.

England in the early 60s was gripped by racial tensions. With demand for cheap labour rising in the nationalized industries, particularly the National Health Service and transport systems, large numbers of immigrants had been arriving from Caribbean, African and Asian dominions. Averaging fifty thousand a year for a decade, the tide swelled to 136,400 in 1961 and 95,000 in the first half of 1962.[53] At the start of the decade, the Prime Minister's principal private secretary had written in his diary: 'The country is in a bad way. It is difficult to see how our economic ills can be cured and at the moment nothing that is done seems to be more than a short-term palliative. The remedy for fifty million people living in an island which can maintain thirty million and no longer leads the world in industrial exports or capital assets invested abroad is hard to find.'[54]

Racial violence erupted on the streets of Notting Hill. Oswald Mosley's pre-war Fascists reconvened as the British National Party and staged menacing rallies in Trafalgar Square. Jews, too, were made to feel uneasy. There was much adverse coverage of property barons and 'asset-strippers' like Charles Clore and Jack Cotton, who bought up small businesses and sold them off after exploiting their untapped value. The financier Freddy Greenwood achieved national notoriety when he borrowed funds from his own building society, fled to Israel and was brought back to face a jail sentence. Jews were in the news, and not in a favourable light.

Solti, looking around the Royal Opera House, saw one Jewish face – Isaiah Berlin – on the Board and none in senior management. Other races were conspicuously absent; the attitude was ante-diluvian. When the Royal Ballet toured South Africa in 1959, it deliberately omitted a South African-born company member, Johaan Mosaval. Angry fellow-dancers visited Mosaval's mother and invited her to a show they gave for a non-white audience in Cape Town City Hall. The company's policy, however, was to play along with apartheid, ignoring the riots that blew up in Sharpeville during the tour and the seminal 'winds of change' speech by their own Prime Minister which effectively ended South Africa's Commonwealth membership. So keen were the Royal Ballet to appease the apartheid regime that they asked Svetlana Beriosova to leave behind her husband, the Harley Street psychiatrist Mohammed Masud Khan on the grounds that he 'might be an unwelcome guest'.[55] Questions were asked in the House of Commons. The Opposition Leader, Hugh Gaitskell, declared that 'the introduction of racial discrimination into art and sport is repugnant to all of us' and demanded to know why it should be tolerated in a company subsidized by the Arts Council. Butler replied that this was an internal matter for the Royal Ballet; neither Government nor Arts Council had been consulted.[56] The ROH, for its part, made no apology.

Solti had no reason to be aware of this backdrop, but he felt the prejudice intuitively and experienced discomfort from both chorus and orchestra members. 'They called me a Prussian – me, a Hungarian Jew,' he exclaimed.[57] He was angry at the Home Office for putting him down as 'Georg', Germanizing his Hungarian forename, György. In contact with the press, he felt like a hound at bay. 'Solti believed the British press were against him,' said Sheila Porter. 'He was very upset by one William Mann review (in *The*

Times) and felt there was an anti-Semitic tinge to much of what was written. I heard this from his personal assistant, Enid Blech, who was also Jewish. The way Solti put it was, "They don't like me because I'm Jewish." I tried to tell him they didn't like him not because he was Jewish but because he was foreign.'[58]

When Webster and Drogheda sat him down to contract talks in December 1962 Solti 'opened by saying that after careful thought and consideration with his wife he had decided that he did not wish to continue after the (initial) three-year term.'[59] He had a lengthy list of grievances. The orchestra was beyond improvement so long as it had to play trash for ballets like *La fille mal gardée*. He needed a bigger ensemble and better players. The chorus master had to go: Robinson was 'indolent' and knew neither German nor Italian. He could not understand why both a stage director and a technical director were needed when neither Bundy nor Sullivan possessed a spark of imagination. As for himself,

his presence as Musical Director at Covent Garden was adding little to his stature. He felt unhappy about the attitude of the press . . . and felt that far too little was being done to counter this attitude and to build up his personal position . . . He had nothing to live by but his name . . . He had a duty to himself as well as to Covent Garden . . . G.S. then spoke of Andrew Porter's *Walküre* notice which had, in one respect, compared Solti adversely with Goodall. He could not understand how I, as Chairman of Covent Garden, could tolerate such a thing in the paper with which I was identified. I said that I had complained of what was written, but that I was in a particularly difficult position.

Extraordinarily, after such frank exchanges, Drogheda won him over and the conversation ended with Solti agreeing to a three-year renewal. In a codicil to his new contract, it was agreed that the orchestra would be expanded to one hundred and forty-five players. Solti, in his own hand, inserted that the chorus master must be replaced, and that the chief press officer, Bill Beresford, would either be sacked or removed from handling the opera company. Neither of these conditions was fulfilled and Solti seems to have forgotten about them once his sense of well-being began to improve.

It was not, however, the end of the state of siege that persisted with the national press. Drogheda rang the press office insistently to demand that pressure be brought to bear on adversarial critics, particularly upon Andrew Porter. 'You're a friend of his,' he told Beresford. 'You must lean on him not to write so harshly about us.'

'If I did that,' said Beresford, 'the press would lose confidence in me. You'd better speak to Sheila.'

'Why does your brother write such wretched things about us?' stormed Drogheda at the assistant press officer.

'Why does your music critic write such wretched things?' she coolly replied.

Drogheda flailed about, reluctant to confront his cherished critic. He ordered Webster to look into the efficiency of the press office, and got more than he bargained for. 'I think we should replace the woman,' said Webster.[60] Drogheda panicked: 'Please don't dispense with Miss Porter without ref'ce to me. Andrew's reaction will be very bad.'[61] A more considered note followed the next day:

> It is not simply a question of Andrew's reaction, which will surely be very violent because he and his sister are twins, but I am sure hostility and a sense of victimization will be stirred up amongst all the critics.
>
> It was probably a mistake in the first instance to take the sister of one of the leading critics on to the staff, but having done so I really think one must be more careful about laying her off.[62]

Webster, for his part, grew less concerned about press reaction the more frantic Drogheda and Solti became. When Solti approached him with a sniffy newspaper report of one of his press conferences, Webster told Tooley to send it to the lawyers, Rubinstein Nash, with a view to issuing libel proceedings.[63] Solti, delighted that someone was taking his pain seriously, let the matter drop. He warmed to Webster, who plied him with well-chosen compliments. Solti, turning fifty while guest-conducting at the Met, received a cable from his General Administrator: 'I have heard with a shock that you are daring to celebrate your extreme youth today stop nevertheless I send you affectionate greetings David.'

Solti replied:'I your youthful Music Director wish to thank you for your greetings on the occasion. They were very much appreciated.'[64]

The fondness between them grew to the point that when word arrived of his sister's death in Hungary, it was to Webster of all people that Solti turned for words of consolation.[65] Their intimacy was the more remarkable for the fact that Solti was unsympathetic to homosexuals and Webster had little time for Jews. Both knew that it was in their interest to get along, but each sensed the other's outsiderness and responded intuitively to a fellow-outcast.

The only person to leave Covent Garden at Solti's direct insistence was Bernard Keefe who, after 'a very awkward year',[66] slipped away to pursue a conducting career. 'Personal assistant: Ingpen oder andere *not* Keefe,' wrote Solti in a bilingual memo to himself.[67] He asked his own agent to become Head of Opera Planning. 'Solti got hold of me and said, you've got to come, you cannot say No,' remembered Joan Ingpen. 'So I went to see David Webster and said, I can think of all sorts of reasons why you would not want me. First, I'm an agent. Second, I'm a woman.

'David said: "Think it over, my dear, before you sell your business. Then I'll put it to the Directors. I should tell you, though, that when Solti goes, I'll defend you as best I can, but you appreciate that this job is linked to the music director's." '[68]

A self-made woman in her mid-forties, Ingpen had co-founded the Philharmonia with Walter Legge and managed the London Mozart Players before founding her own agency. She breezed into Covent Garden to find 'everything was so behindhand, they hadn't even completed the casting for the following season'. She introduced five-year planning, a Stalinist device that she later transported to the Paris Opéra and the Met, making it the industry norm.

Rival agents bridled at her elevation and two of them, Lise Askonas and John Coast, protested furiously to Webster. They had good reason, for Ingpen endorsed Solti's standards of international quality and was prone to overlook middling British singers with whom both agents were overstocked. Their protests were in vain, for Ingpen had the full confidence of Solti and Webster; their fears were also groundless for she and her singers were fastidious in an old-fashioned English way about avoiding favouritism.

'After I had been there about nine months,' Ingpen related, 'Geraint Evans sidled up to me in the canteen and said, would you like a tea? Then he said, I don't know if you've noticed but some of us, your former artists, have kept away from you for a while . . .'

Her most delicate task was to secure appearances from her former star, Joan Sutherland, who now insisted on singing only with her husband in the pit. Webster said, 'Bonynge wants to be a conductor?

Over my dead body.'[69] Solti, too, was adamant. He said, 'what am I supposed to do, engage a bad conductor?'[70] Under Ingpen's persuasion, he finally agreed to let Bonynge into Covent Garden, 'provided I am not here'.

These developments suited Webster to perfection, for he knew that Ingpen was no threat to his position and a useful ally in the taming of Solti. By charm, diplomacy and a bit of luck, he had not only regained influence in the opera company but had extended his sway to the Royal Ballet, where he overrode his old friend Ashton and took control of booking Nureyev. 'Now that he has been lifted into the rare atmosphere shared only with Callas, where he discusses his performances with you,' griped Drogheda, 'one feels somewhat in the dark: but I should like to know whether and, if so, to what extent, he will be with us through 1964.'[71] Weeks later the chairman complained: 'I have been told that Nureyev himself is very perplexed as to where he really stands with us. It seems to me that since you took over the direct negotiation with him, matters are not progressing as they should.'[72] Webster was serenely unperturbed by these blasts from on high. 'When I asked if the Board had been informed about one or other of our plans,' recalled Ingpen, 'David would smile and say, "I don't think we'll tell them about that, do you?"'[73]

The ship of state was starting to list. In July 1962, Harold Macmillan sacked seven Cabinet ministers in an attempt to shore up an unpopular Government. From then on, nothing went right for the man they once called 'Supermac'. In November, an Admiralty clerk, William Vassall, was jailed for eighteen years for passing secrets to Moscow. The KGB had subjected Vassall to homosexual blackmail and Fleet Street quivered with rumours of further treacheries.

A thick fog descended on London, the worst since the abolition of coal burning fires in 1952. It was followed by the coldest spell since 1947. Hugh Gaitskell, the Labour leader, came down with pneumonia, was admitted to the Middlesex Hospital and sent home for Christmas. In the opening days of the New Year, Macmillan's one big idea was brought down in flames by a resounding 'Non!' from President Charles de Gaulle, avenging France's wartime humiliations by denying Britain entry to the European Economic Community.

That same week, Gaitskell died of a mysterious viral infection. In a leadership poll of Labour MPs, the Gaitskellite vote split between the drunken George Brown and the dull James Callaghan, leaving the Bevanite Harold Wilson triumphant. Roy Jenkins, on the right of the party, felt 'revulsion'[74] and many centrists could not overcome their distrust of a man they blamed for Labour's fall from power in 1951. But the shrewd and self-confident Wilson overrode their reservations to ignite public opinion with promises of a new Britain 'forged in the white heat' of technological revolution. Beside his synthetic optimism, the Tories stumbled from one disgrace to the next.

In March 1963, the Secretary of State for War, John Profumo, told Parliament that there had been 'no impropriety whatever' in his friendship with a call-girl, Christine Keeler. He was lying, and two weeks later resigned. Keeler, it transpired, had also been sleeping with a Soviet naval attaché, Evgeny Ivanov. The sex-and-spies hysteria whipped up in Parliament and the press by Wilson's grubby aide, George Wigg, damaged the Government beyond repair. 'Are We Going Sex Crazy?' demanded the *Daily Herald*.

In July 1963, the highbrow magazine *Encounter* published a 'Suicide of the Nation?' issue. The following month, thieves hijacked a mail train and made off with a million pounds in used notes, entering legend as the Great Train Robbers and shattering confidence in those twin Victorian legacies, the railways and Royal Mail. A property crash brought down one of the biggest dealers, Jack Cotton. With Ian Fleming's thrillers topping the bestseller lists, the Government was obliged to admit that a former Foreign Office official, Kim Philby, had escaped to Moscow to join his brother-spies, Burgess and Maclean. A security investigation led by Lord Denning blamed the Prime Minister for his credulity in handling the Profumo affair. Macmillan, sixty-nine, collapsed under the strain and in October, from his hospital bed, resigned. Crushing Rab Butler's ambitions, he advised the Queen to appoint the 14th Earl of Hume, a Scottish landowner who had served on Neville Chamberlain's staff at the Munich Agreement. A more retrograde appointment could hardly have been imagined.

Yet when Wilson was finally elected Prime Minister in October 1964 it was with a wafer-thin majority of seven, a qualified endorsement in dangerous times. Both of the Big Powers had lost leaders in the previous twelve months – Kennedy assassinated, and Khrushchev deposed by Leonid Brezhnev and Alexei Kosygin. Britain's footprint on the world map was shrinking as its last African colonies rushed to independence. Its economy was fragile, its exports unwanted and worryingly unreliable as industrial strife took its toll on their reputation for quality and dependability. The country was like an anchorless ship, drifting between armoured continental blocs.

Culturally, however, its vitality had never been greater. Like Vienna at the turn of the century, capital of a disintegrating empire, London in the mid-60s hummed, buzzed and swung with the sounds, sights and frights of a new civilization. Sex was, as in Vienna, the fulcrum of social change and, for outsiders, the main attraction. The revolution produced a miniskirt that conquered the Paris catwalks, a mini-car that mocked American gas-guzzlers and a mini-boom in visual arts. A 'School of London' gathered around the artists David Hockney and R. B. Kitaj. Everyone wanted to have their hair cut by Vidal Sassoon and their clothes bought on Carnaby Street. British cinema flickered back to life. A National Theatre was finally formed at the Old Vic, with Laurence Olivier in charge and *Hamlet* as its curtain-raiser. For Shakespeare's four hundredth birthday, in 1964, Olivier acted his first *Othello*.

But the most powerful of magnets was the new music, which stemmed not from London but from decaying Liverpool with its idle docks, ugly housing, morbid churches and laconic resilience. In under-street, city-centre dens and cavernous clubs, teenaged frustrations found expression in a counter-culture that mimicked American hard-rock but drew its strengths from Celtic balladry and English eloquence. A group called 'The Beatles' entered the lower reaches of the top twenty in November 1962 with a single, 'Love Me Do.' Five months later they topped the charts with their second release, 'Please, Please Me'. For the remainder of the decade until their disbandment in 1970, the Beatles set the pace in a global process that turned popular culture into a generational weapon, the voice of youthful rejection and the antithesis of traditional, establishmentarian music.

The force behind the Beatles was a portly Liverpool shopkeeper with a passion for symphonic concerts and a taste for rough trade that led to him getting beaten up on several occasions and arrested in public lavatories. Brian Epstein had something in common with David Webster. In his mid-twenties, he ran a sheet-music and musical instrument offshoot of his family's furniture business, building up record sales so rapidly that, by the time he met the Beatles, he had a chain of nine shops across the city and was the biggest record retailer in the north-west. Neatly dressed and well-spoken, Epstein spent much of his time on the shop floor talking to customers. When teenagers kept telling him of 'this fab group' at the Cavern, he went down one lunchtime to hear for himself and signed the four musicians to a management contract, taking twenty-five per cent of gross receipts. Epstein cleaned up the Beatles' act, put them in suits, sacked their drummer Pete Best and signed them to EMI. Until his death of a drugs overdose in 1967, Epstein was the guiding influence of a genre of Mersey Beat that embraced, beyond the Beatles, the varied talents of Gerry and the Pacemakers, Billy J. Kramer and the Cavern's hat-check girl, little Cilla Black who, nearly forty years later, was still a popular entertainer.

A man of refined tastes, Epstein held subscriptions to the Tuesday night and Musica Viva concerts of the Liverpool Philharmonic Orchestra and became friendly with its promiscuous conductor, John Pritchard. As the Beatles took off, Epstein hired a record-counter manager from Lewis's, Peter Brown, with whom he was 'best friends'.[75] Brown moved in with Pritchard. The divergent realms of popular and serious music were joined by many such strands; the Beatles' producer, George Martin, was classically trained and the harmonic sophistication of their early LPs was supplied by soloists from the London orchestras.

William Mann, *The Times'* music critic, named John Lennon and Paul McCartney 'the outstanding English composers of 1963', extolling their 'chains of pandiatonic clusters' and Mahlerian 'flat-submediant key switches'.[76] Richard Buckle in the *Sunday Times* called them simply 'the greatest composers since Beethoven'.[77] There were dissenting voices as well, not all of them reactionary. Glenn Gould, the thoughtful Canadian pianist, dismissed the Beatles as a 'happy, cocky, belligerently resourceless brand of harmonic primitivism'.[78] Aaron Copland, on the other hand, recognized their work in 1967 as 'music of quality'.[79] Whichever view prevailed, there is no denying the grip that Beatlemania exerted on the artistic climate of their times, particularly on their home territory, without the slightest concession to cultural relativism. It was Covent Garden's great misfortune that the years of its highest attainments coincided with a pop revolution that suborned cultural values, stole press headlines and monopolized the attention of the rising generation, and generations to come.

*

The Wilson Government was not expected to be culture-friendly. Its priorities were the economy, industrial relations, education, housing and any other blight that could be lumped under its vote-catch slogan, 'thirteen years of Tory misrule'. Wilson – dynamic, quick-witted and still under 50 – wanted to be seen as another J. F. Kennedy and much play was made of his 'first hundred days'. Mistrusting his own party, he introduced to British governance the dubious feature of a kitchen cabinet, formed around his secretary Marcia Williams, the economist 'Tommy' Balogh, the party's press liaison officer Gerald Kaufman and the tale-bearer George Wigg. A taint of cronyism clung to Wilson throughout his premiership. Nevertheless, his freedom from party and Whitehall allowed this deceptive little man to move in unorthodox and sometimes imaginative directions.

Harold Wilson smoked a pipe, poured Worcester sauce on his supper and dressed like a bank clerk, but he enjoyed an occasional night out and and was mildly appreciative of culture. Taken to the Royal Ballet one night by Jack Donaldson, he recited to Ashton all the ballets he had witnessed on official visits to Moscow, reeling off a roll of dancers whom the director knew only by name. 'I liked the leader very much,' said Ashton. 'He is the first politician who has seen a ballet and remembered anything about it after.'[80]

Two days after entering Downing Street, Wilson telephoned Jennie Lee, Bevan's widow. 'I've got a job for you to do,' he said. 'Find a desk and pack your handbag.'[81] The job he had in mind was something junior in Health, but Lee opted instead for a vacancy in the Ministry of Public Building and Works (MPBW), where she set about tackling arts policy. If the Cabinet liked her proposals, Wilson promised, she would be given ministerial status.

After Nye's death, Lee had become involved with a community theatre, Centre 42, formed by the left-wing writers Arnold Wesker, Doris Lessing, Shelagh Delaney and Bernard Kops. She believed in taking arts to the people and bettering their lives. Her first year in the lower echelons of government was spent visiting arts companies and forming a dislike for the Arts Council. In the White Paper she wrote for Cabinet, she proposed a revision of the arm's length principle, breaking up the annual tango between Treasury providers and Arts Council distributors. The arts, she argued, were being absurdly funded through four departments of state. The Treasury looked after museums, galleries and the ACGB grant; the Department of Education and Science (DES) funded, for some reason, the Victoria and Albert and National Science museums; the Ministry for Housing and Local Government pumped money into municipal arts; and her own MPBW was responsible for historic buildings. Bring them all under one roof, urged Lee, away from the Treasury which was stifling artistic growth. The arts needed a large increase in subsidy, especially outside London.

Her paper was published in February 1965 under the Prime Minister's name and debated in the House of Commons. After winning a secure majority in the General Election of April 1965, Wilson, true to his word, appointed Jennie Lee as Britain's first Minister for the Arts. She was installed at the DES, out of Treasury reach, and took added responsibility for Wilson's pet project, an Open University that could provide tutorship and grant degrees to working people who had missed out on tertiary education.

Lee's arrival provoked consternation at the Arts Council, but not at Covent Garden, where the canny Drogheda had been courting the still-comely minister. A class warrior to her fingertips, Lee's every instinct rebelled at the sight of an ermined eleventh earl, but Drogheda was a strikingly handsome man with a perpetual ocular twinkle and he courted her with the chaste and yearning courtesy of a medieval troubadour. Across social barriers, they found much to like in one another. In one of her first letters from the DES, Jennie Lee thanked Drogheda for some public compliments and asked him for a breakdown of Covent Garden costs. She added, winningly: 'You have my sympathy in trying to do the impossible.'[82] Drogheda, thus encouraged, updated her on the crippling expense of closing the ROH for essential rewiring and warned that the ROH deficit was approaching £300,000. He also offered help in extending opera and ballet to the deprived regions. Whatever befell the arts under Wilson, Covent Garden had secured itself a safety-net.

Lee could not move ahead without shaking up the Arts Council. She called her solicitor, who was also her downstairs neighbour in a mansion block near Victoria, and asked if he would like to become a member of the Council. Arnold Goodman was delighted. Two weeks later she called again. Would he like to be chairman? 'It was flattering to be asked, and a job that I was very willing to do,'[83] said Goodman, eager to reap the rewards of well-cultivated connections. Cottesloe, confidently expecting a second term, was waiting to open an Arts Council meeting when a senior Treasury official arrived with a letter, telling him his time was up.[84]

Goodman would become the most influential fixer England had ever seen, chairing a multiplicity of public bodies and quangos (Quasi-Autonomous Non-Governmental Organizations) that sprang up whenever Wilson and his successors feared to grasp a nettle. He was, at one time or other, chairman of the Housing Corporation; the National Building Agency; the Theatres Trust; English National Opera; Motability; the National Book League; the Observer Trust; British Lion Films; and others too numerous to list. 'Tell them I'm on my way,' was his catchphrase. Goodman was the man for all crises, a purveyor of panaceas for people in power. The arts, in his hands, were but a means to a more exalted end.

The pudgy son of East End traders, Abraham Goodman – he became Arnold after the war – served as a deskbound Major at Southern Command before making his name as a legal firm-buster. He sweet-talked his first practice into merging with Rubinstein Nash, then stomped out to found Goodman Derrick, taking along many of Rubinstein's eminent clients. Such bustling enterprise was uncommon in the placid waters of English law, but Goodman was no common lawyer. A restless man with a nagging conscience, his corpulence belied a mental agility that could strip any issue to its particulars and rattle off a dazzling response at twice the Pitman's dictation speed. He was wasted on the law, and aspired to superior planes of intellectual and ethical activity. 'No one believes that serving the legal system is a sacred cause,' he averred.[85]

Through George Wigg, whom he had met as a colonel at Southern Command, he got to mingle with the Bevanites. In March 1957 he received a phone call from an irate Jennie Lee. The *Spectator*, a political weekly then owned by the Tory MP Ian Gilmour, had reported that three Labour luminaries had been conspicuously the worse for drink at a conference of the Italian Socialist Party in Venice. The article, written by Jenny Nicholson, wife of a Reuters bureau chief and daughter of the poet Robert Graves, was flimsy grounds for a libel action, but Bevan had suffered grievously at the hands of the Tory press and sought urgent redress. The words that incensed him were these:

And there was the occasional appearance of Messrs [Nye] Bevan, Morgan Phillips [General Secretary of the Labour Party] and Richard Crossman [MP] who puzzled the Italians by their capacity to fill themselves like tanks with whisky and coffee, while they (because of their livers and also because they are abstemious by nature) were keeping going on mineral water and an occasional coffee. Although the Italians were never sure if the British delegation were sober, they always attributed to them an immense political acumen.[86]

Bevan, who drank wine and generally in moderation, hated to be typecast as a boozy tourist on a fraternal freebie. He demanded an apology, but Goodman went one further. When Phillips and Crossman swore affidavits that all three men had been sober as judges, he issued writs for libel. Gilmour offered several forms of apology, all of them toyed with by Goodman and then rebuffed. 'I had the distinct feeling that he was whipping it up,' said Gilmour. 'I was also convinced that he knew his clients were lying. He saw it as a case that would put him on the map.'[87] After a short trial attended by intense publicity, an inept defence and a one-sided judge, Lord Goddard, the jury awarded each plaintiff £2,500 in damages, plus costs. Gilmour was shaken and Jenny Nicholson distraught; she fell sick with stress and died not long after from cancer. Goodman, on the other hand, was made.

In his diary, Crossman confessed that both Bevan and Phillips had indeed been drunk and that all three had lied under oath. Whether Goodman was aware of their perjury or not,[88] it did him no harm to be seen supporting men of power through thick and thin, truth and lies, acting for might against right. To the suspicious Harold Wilson, he possessed exactly the right qualities to be his private lawyer and personal adviser on matters.

Fearing the 'lottery of the law', Goodman liked to get his way by means of threat and bluster. In July 1964, shortly before the election, the pro-Labour *Sunday Mirror*, chasing Tory sex scandals, ran a headline: 'Peer and a Gangster: Yard Inquiry.'[89] No names were mentioned, but ten days later the German magazine *Stern* noted that Lord Boothby was 'in trouble'. The Tory peer, a long-term lover of Harold Macmillan's wife, was passing his dotage among rough boys supplied for his pleasure by the East End thugs, Ronnie and Reggie Kray. Taking Goodman's advice, Boothby wrote to *The Times* denying homosexuality and any link with criminals. Goodman then bore down upon the *Mirror* and exacted a grovelling apology, the dismissal of the editor responsible and a punitive forty thousand pounds in damages for Boothby.

The public settlement, however, was less than half the sordid story. Wilson had been informed that the *Mirror* possessed a compromising photograph not only of Boothby but also of his own ally, Tom Driberg. Fearing the electoral impact of a cross-party sex scandal, he sent Driberg to see Goodman, who used Wilson's name to bludgeon the *Mirror* into submission. Goodman, in his memoirs, omits this shameful episode, indicative as it was of his evolving *modus operandi*. It was not the majesty of the law that Goodman brandished at miscreants but (like the Kray gang) the awe of his fearsome friends. The Boothby business opened the door of his chambers to Tory as well as Labour politicians. 'It became a habit, in sticky times, for people to reach for their Goodman,' said Gilmour.[90] Edward Heath, the next Tory leader, came to confide in the lumbering solicitor, whom he had first met as a schoolboy. Another client was the Liberal Party leader, Jeremy Thorpe. The Newspaper Publishers' Association, alarmed at Goodman's assaults on press freedom, appointed him their chairman – from which position he exerted an ever tighter stranglehold on what was printed, or at his insistence not printed, about his august clientele. For the next twenty years a hand-delivered letter on Goodman Derrick notepaper carried more clout in Fleet Street than a full-blown libel writ from any other law firm.

No sooner was Wilson elected than he consulted Goodman on issues great and small, from the survival of the Royal Philharmonic Orchestra to the secession of a white minority regime in Rhodesia, where the Prime Minister's personal solicitor conducted a secret state mission without much success. The RPO's difficulties marked Goodman's first encounter with the arts in crisis. Three years after Beecham's death, the last of his ensembles was going broke and in danger of losing its title, bestowed by the crusty Royal Philharmonic Society. Wilson had been nobbled by the general secretary of the Musicians' Union, an old-school Marxist called Hardie Ratcliffe, who raised fears of string players and their infants begging for bread on the streets of London. There were also appeals from the RPO chairman, none other than the almost-disgraced Lord Boothby. Wilson got the Home Secretary, Frank Soskice, to ask the Palace for a Royal Warrant that would let the orchestra keep its name. Then he called Goodman, tracking him down in a restaurant, and asked him to apply his mighty mind to the matter.

Goodman, unfamiliar with the ways of orchestras, formed a

committee on which Ratcliffe and Sir David Webster, representing the Orchestral Employers Association, were the key members. The Arts Council's music director, John Denison, volunteered to act as secretary but was brushed aside. Goodman brought in a music-loving, newly-landed South African barrister, Leonard Hoffmann, 'to learn the ropes', as he put it. He called the first meeting at five o'clock on Christmas Eve and made it clear that his aim was to save the orchestra.[91] After that, as Hoffmann recalled, the process was little more than a financial haggle between Ratcliffe and Jennie Lee. 'Having ascertained how much money was available,' said Hoffmann, 'we simply wrote a report saying that was the amount of money that ought to be spent.'[92] The Goodman report concluded that although the RPO was under-employed, there was enough work in the capital for 'three and a half' orchestras, and the Arts Council should provide for them all.

Goodman's much-hailed solution actually resolved nothing at all. The RPO staggered along, competing for film sessions and Strauss nights with three superior rivals, themselves often short of work. Meanwhile, large parts of east and south-west England never got to hear a proper symphony concert. It would have made more sense to have recommended a national redistribution of orchestras, relocating the RPO to Nottingham or Bristol, but Goodman was not in the habit of looking beyond his brief. He was a quick-fixer, not a strategic thinker, and he left London's orchestral wounds suppurating beneath a piece of sticking-plaster, storing up venom for future emergencies. Thirty years later, the London orchestral crisis brought the Arts Council to the very brink of collapse.

The only useful outcome was a London Orchestral Concerts Board (LOCB) to keep peace between the hostile bands. Its chairman was David Webster who, behind a façade of neutrality, was secretly negotiating to employ the London Symphony Orchestra at Covent Garden. The idea was to remodel the LSO along the lines of the Vienna Philharmonic, whose members worked for the opera house but were also organized as an independent concert orchestra. A deal was struck with the LSO manager, Ernest Fleischmann, only for the players to reject the terms. Webster was disappointed but not daunted. He recognized that the orchestra he had created with such cavalier optimism in 1946 now hung like a lead weight on the ROH finances. He had no sentimental attachment to his orchestra and no fear of the Musicians Union. He wanted to leave Covent Garden on a sound financial footing and was looking further into the difficult future than Goodman dared to gaze.

As chairman of the Arts Council, Goodman posed as a lavish public benefactor. Around his council table, Goodman saw the noble head of Henry Moore, the country's foremost sculptor. Beside him sat the next Poet Laureate, Cecil Day-Lewis. Further down he recognized the great actress Dame Peggy Ashcroft, the opera administrator Lord Harewood, the historian Alan Bullock and the photographer Lord Snowdon, husband of Princess Margaret. It was an élite phalanx of the great and the good, the trendy and the ascendant. And lording it over them all was a Jewish solicitor of modest birth, an apotheosis of the English melting-pot.

In contrast to his predecessors, Goodman decided to be an executive chairman, replacing the secretary general, Nigel Abercrombie with a fellow-solicitor, Hugh Willatt. The chairmanship demanded large chunks of unpaid time, but Goodman's practice was massively prosperous, and most client problems could be resolved with one of his effortlessly threatening letters. His regular clients included the leading publishers and television bosses whom he had taken away from Rubinstein Nash, as well as some of the sharper operators in the London property market, notably Max Rayne and the swash-buckling Harry Hyams. It did not trouble Goodman that their interests clashed with his chairmanship of the Housing Corporation.

He also kept his door open to the up-and-coming. The young Rupert Murdoch was a valued client, as was Brian Epstein who employed Goodman to steer the Beatles' company, Northern Songs Limited, on to the London Stock Exchange. The result of this venture was that John Lennon and Paul McCartney lost control of the songs they were writing, which landed in due course in the lap of the American pop singer, Michael Jackson.

Goodman's attitude to money was cavalier. A collector of celebrities, he often 'forgot' to invoice influential clients. Lord Gibson, a director of the *Financial Times*, went to see him on National Trust business. After several meetings, Gibson said: 'Arnold, I really can't continue coming here unless you send me a bill.' 'Tell me,' said Goodman, hands clasped across his expansive girth, 'do I look hungry to you?'[93] It was on the arms of Gibson and his FT associate Lord Drogheda that the ascendant power-broker was introduced to the House of Lords on 20 July 1965, as Baron Goodman of the City of Westminster.

Under his leadership, the delicate fabric of Keynes's arm's-length provision was mangled and wrenched into a shapeless muddle. Instead of the Arts Council negotiating its grant with the Treasury and disbursing it after judicious discussion, the Arts Council chairman now obtained his grant from the Minister for the Arts and handed it out according to a policy they jointly devised. Goodman and Lee met for supper every Sunday night in his flat. 'They would sit on the floor examining (Government papers), and Goodman would suggest suitable memos that she might care to write to him, and suitable replies that she might care to receive from him,' reported Lee's biographer.[94] It was said that Lee knew little about the arts and relied on Goodman for guidance. The process was possibly more synergetic. Something resembling love blossomed between them. It was not sexual – 'how can I love that body?' said Jennie Lee[95] – and each had other objects of desire: hers a younger man and his unchecked power. What bound them together was an affinity of outlook and his constant attentiveness with flowers and other flatteries. What caused disquiet was the covert way in which they manipulated the arts and erased the lines that should have separated Government aims from Arts Council action. 'It wasn't Lee at all who determined policy,' said Hugh Willatt. 'It was Arnold all along.'[96]

In Lee's first two years as minister, she achieved a near-doubling of the Arts Council's grant, from £3.9 million to £7.2 million. By the time Labour were ousted in 1970, the grant had almost trebled. Goodman spread the extra money liberally, endowing rundown theatres with improvement grants and lavishing awards on little magazines and local groups. The rush of cash altered the artistic climate in Britain, encouraging fringe performers – and many charlatans – to believe that any goal was within their grasp and that the arts were now central to the national purpose. In an inevitable side-effect, much rubbish flourished and many weak companies came to believe that the arts owed them a living.

There was a paradox at the heart of the chairman's outlook. Goodman believed in excellence and argued that it should be disseminated outwards from London where the top companies were to be found. But when it came to dealing with centres of excellence, his attitude was highly equivocal. It was Goodman who proposed a forced merger between the newborn National Theatre and the Royal Shakespeare Company, a move thwarted by fierce resistance from Willatt. Towards Covent Garden, Goodman exhibited a distinct ambivalence. There were trendy voices on his Council who resented its existence. 'Foolish decisions were made like keeping Covent Garden Opera alive,' said Dr Jonathan Miller, the Cambridge satirist and physician. 'It should have been throttled, along with the world of old-boy networks, the tattered representatives of the Establishment.'[97] Goodman sympathized with such iconoclasms, but yearned with every fibre of his being to be accepted into the Establishment. Torn between heart and mind, he loudly praised the Royal Opera House while reducing its share of the Arts Council cake. Against the triple rations that he sprayed around the rest of the arts, Covent Garden received no more than a forty per cent increase in the Lee-Goodman years (£1,026,000 to £1,420,000) much of it consumed by twenty-five per cent inflation and Wilson's fourteen per cent devaluation of the national currency.

'I warned Arnold that he could not carry on throwing money at the grass-roots and depriving the mainstream,' said John Tooley. 'He replied that if we ever got in trouble he would bale us out.'[98] Drogheda became so agitated at Goodman's silky meanness that he threatened to go over his head to the Treasury and seek the restoration of a direct grant. 'If he went to the Treasury,' said Goodman, 'they'd give him a cup of tea, and that's all he'd get.'[99]

'Arnold liked to say he was a Robin Hood, taking from the rich and giving to the poor, but not too much,' recalled Lord Gibson.[100] In this golden era of British arts, Keynes's flagship suffered an insidious erosion in its finances and centrality. Goodman was no friend of Covent Garden, nor was he easily circumvented. He had the ear of the Prime Minister any evening of the week, and restricted press criticism by means of threat and bluster. At no time, as chairman of the Arts Council, did he openly express a negative opinion of the ROH. But in retirement, as Master of an Oxford college, he let slip his parvenu sense of exclusion. The Royal Opera House, said Goodman, was

> a centre of snobbery, where people go to look at and despise those who are poorer than themselves, and to admire others for being richer. *It makes no serious contribution to the arts.*[101]

Asked why he went there so often, Goodman replied: 'It is true that I maintain an outrageously expensive box at Covent Garden, which I share with five other people . . . It provides personal satisfaction to the relatively few individuals who can derive continuous pleasure from attending a succession of great operas.'[102] The Blessed Arnold might go down in cultural myth as the greatest benefactor of British arts, eclipsing even the mighty Keynes. Yet, on closer examination, his attitude was duplicitous, unprincipled and, in the long term, profoundly damaging for both of Keynes's prime creations. Despite inherent tensions in their relationship, the Arts Council and Covent Garden had shared until now a common purpose. From Goodman onwards, they sang in different keys.

A cloud lifted from the Royal Ballet the day that Madam retired. The age of austerity was over, now the fun could begin. Fred Ashton was one of the few men in the kingdom who could make the Queen Mother laugh. Where Madam ruled by fear and fanatical ambition, Fred radiated a languid charm that concealed a ferocious dedication to detail. He was flippant, lazy and frequently naughty. Dancers longed to please him, and some boys at the Royal Ballet School knew what he liked. There was no need for chaperoning because Fred was the director, and it says much for his gentle, slightly diffident nature that there were no complaints of abuse. Beside him, Michael Somes, John Hart and John Field attended to the rigours of planning and administration but with Fred at the helm a lilt of lightness entered the Royal Ballet and dancers never knew what to expect next.

'I had just danced my first *Fille mal gardée*,' related Nicholas Johnson, 'and was sitting in my dressing-room in full make-up when Sir Fred walked in. "Well done!" he said, and then he walked right past me and pee'd into the sink. Can you imagine? The great Ashton urinating in the sink where I was about to wash my face. "Couldn't hold it in for another two flights of stairs," he explained.'[103]

There was never any distance between Ashton and his dancers, but familiarity did not lessen their respect for the man and his art. 'I have never been so frightened of anyone as I was of Sir Fred,'[104] said Antoinette Sibley, who plucked up courage and went to his house in Marlborough Street to ask why he had not entrusted her with a major role. When Ashton tried her out soon after in *Les Patineurs*, Sibley froze on the night and left the stage unapplauded, but the choreographer was not unimpressed. He decided she needed a partner, and had a young candidate in mind.

The board and Webster were pressuring him to write a new ballet for Fonteyn and Nureyev, but Ashton was bored with Margot and wary of the wild man of the steppes. Despite a South American childhood, Ashton was culturally English and the best of his ballets were steeped in subtle half-tones which, he felt, no foreigner could grasp. He longed to nurture an English male dancer of undisputed world class, the like of which had yet to be seen. The boy he picked for Sibley was a vulnerable-looking lad of twenty who had barely survived the ruthless cull of the Royal Ballet School. 'To me it was a reign of terror,' said Anthony Dowell. 'There was a headmistress that really smelt fear. She knew the victims and played on me quite a bit. But I never thought of giving up. I knew it was leading to getting me on to the magic world of the stage. And I knew I was talented. I sensed that people recognized a facility.

'Madam was pretty formidable. At a school performance, *Swan Lake*, I was one of three boys and I had a certain problem with a step turning in the air. I was a left turner and I had to go to the right. She just called me down after this rehearsal and said, "look, dear, if you can't do this step I'll have to take you out of it." My world fell apart. I broke down and collapsed in a terrible dressing room in the bowels of the Royal Opera House. Suddenly I looked up and there was this person talking to me. And it was Michael Somes. I thought, crikey.

'He said, "come on, we're going to sort this out." And he took me into a practice room about the size of a cupboard, off the side of the canteen, and he tried to analyse why this step was going wrong. Sorted it out, got me doing it, put me back together, then each day he might see me round the building and say, "how's it going? let's try again." The next rehearsal, I did it in front of de Valois. She didn't say anything. I just knew I wasn't taken out.'[105] BBC cameras caught Madam putting young dancers through their paces with Nureyev in attendance. She is looking the other way when Nureyev points to Dowell and says, 'look, there's your next principal dancer.' 'Madam wasn't that keen on me,' lamented Dowell.

Dowell entered the Royal Ballet at seventeen and danced his first solo two years later. When Ashton paired him with Sibley, she was a rising star and he was prancing in the corps. 'It was Ashton who put us together,' he said. 'It wasn't accidental. With his amazing eye he knew that those were the two people to come. Maybe not – maybe he just saw that she was right for Titania and I was right for Oberon.'[106]

For the Shakespeare tetracentenary, Ashton ordered a triple-bill of two new ballets by himself and MacMillan to go with Helpmann's time-worn *Hamlet*. Ashton's contribution was *The Dream*, set by John Lanchbery to sections of Mendelssohn's music for *A Midsummer Night's Dream* and a libretto by Somes. It was a brilliant condensation, airily suggesting the familiar plot without having to follow it literally, and the starry new pair were warmly, if perplexedly, received. For what they represented was an ironic commentary to the heroic-erotic coupling of Fonteyn and Nureyev. Sibley was cocky and assertive, Dowell wistful and submissive. Their physical dialogue was knowing, sensual yet coolly in control of the sexual possibilities. Ashton had rewired Shakespeare along 60s lines of changing gender roles. *The Dream* was written off by Clive Barnes in the trade press as 'a disappointment . . . one of his second best ballets',[107] but Porter in the FT acclaimed it as 'purest lyric poetry'[108] and future scholars would recognize *The Dream* as the acme of Ashton's style. In the story of Covent Garden, it established the company's first partnership of equals, itself a sign of the times.

Sibley and Dowell, Anthony and Antoinette, would became inseparable and mutually dependent, in life as on stage. When Sibley's marriage to Somes fell apart in 1968, Dowell dispatched his maiden aunt, Joan, to look after the heartbroken ballerina. When Dowell suffered career-threatening injuries, Sibley took him to her childhood teacher, Winifred Edwards, who readjusted his horizons. When Sibley remarried, Dowell was godfather to her son. They were the model of symbiosis, the pattern for post-Margot regeneration.

Another couple was forming concurrently under more searching eyes. Kenneth MacMillan, the anguished-looking choreographer, had first paired Lynn Seymour, the lushest of ballerinas, with Christopher Gable, a nice-looking but technically limited East End lad, in a shattering 1960 ballet of rape, *The Invitation*. Liking what he saw, MacMillan drew the dancers into a clique, 'always giggling away in corners together, sharing private jokes'.[109] 'Kenneth MacMillan was always with us,' wrote Seymour. 'He looked upon (our circle) as his special little brood and we looked upon him as our precocious little boy. I saw him daily and talked with him on the phone every night, even after we just had drinks or dinner together.'[110]

Like Antony Tudor, whom Madam had evicted, MacMillan founded his choreography on the intricacies of human psychology. 'He liked to find out who in the company was having romances and would often choose to work together with two people who had just split up.'[111] Himself predominantly gay and painfully involved with one of his set designers, MacMillan was seeking variations on conventional romance. For the Shakespeare triple-bill, he cast Seymour and Gable with Nureyev in a troilistic ballet, *Images of Love,* that pitted his perfect couple violently against one another for the love of an elusive outsider. The music was ill-adjusted to the dance, since MacMillan hardly bothered to communicate with his composer, Peter Tranchell, and the press were flummoxed by Seymour's 'profane' and Gable's 'sacred' passion for Nureyev. MacMillan, meanwhile, was moving on to the highest of Shakespearean ballet summits.

Ever since the Bolshoi danced Leonid Lavrovsky's *Romeo and Juliet* in 1956, Covent Garden had craved its own setting of Prokofiev's honeyed score. The yearning increased when the Bolshoi repeated its showpiece in the summer of 1963. A plan to send Ashton to Moscow with *Fille* in exchange for Lavrovsky and *Romeo* fell foul of the diplomatic fog that descended with Khrushchev's dismissal. Ashton had already tried his hand at *Romeo* in Copenhagen; John Cranko had done another at Stuttgart.

In May 1964, directly after *Images of Love*, Seymour danced Cranko's Juliet in Stuttgart, her first overseas engagement. On her return, MacMillan told her that Ashton had given him the go-ahead to create a full-length ROH *Romeo and Juliet* for herself and Gable. 'Our three-way collaboration would be electric,' felt Seymour.[112] They rushed off to see Zeffirelli's acclaimed Old Vic production with Judi Dench and John Stride, notable for its quasi-adolescent ambience. MacMillan declared that his intended pair were even more emphatically 'the very anatomy of young love'.

There was only one snag: Seymour discovered she was pregnant. 'My life was dedicated to the ballet,' she later confessed, with self-unsparing candour. 'We could have other children, I reasoned. Juliet was mine. Juliet was the bonding of my partnership with Christopher Gable. Juliet was a priceless gift from Kenneth, glazed especially for me.' When her husband, the press photographer Colin Jones, went on assignment to Russia, Seymour took herself to a backstreet abortionist and, for the equivalent of three months' ROH pay, had the pregnancy terminated. The decision would wreck her first marriage, but worse was in store.

Ashton announced the Royal Ballet's new season with *Romeo and*

Juliet as its main attraction. To Seymour's incredulity, Fonteyn and Nureyev were billed as the lovers. Distraught, she tried to reach MacMillan, but he was not answering his phone.

> When we finally cornered Kenneth at our next rehearsal, he looked positively sickly. His sad brown eyes were embedded in deep dark hollows. The Garden had already hurt him by refusing to let him mount a ballet to Mahler's *Song of the Earth*, which he [later] staged for Cranko's company in Stuttgart. Now, with *Romeo*, he was once again up against the Establishment.[113]

Or so the choreographer felt. The reality was more enmeshed in MacMillan's inability to stand up for his convictions. He had proposed the Mahler piece in 1962 to Madam who loathed the idea, remembering that the detested Tudor had started out with Mahler's *Songs of the Death of Children*. Despite her distaste, she took his project to the board, where it met with fierce opposition from Mahler lovers, who felt that the work was perfect in itself, and that the expense of a tenor and soprano soloist was unjustified. After a heated debate, the matter was put to expert arbitration. Sir Adrian Boult, no ballet lover, ruled against MacMillan. Cranko, ever eager to pique his former bosses and please a friend, called MacMillan to Stuttgart to stage his Mahler creation. The German press raved and offers of work came flooding his way. To their credit, Drogheda and the board instantly overturned their verdict and, within a year, welcomed *Song of the Earth* to Covent Garden, with Nureyev, Dowell, Seymour and the Brazilian Marcia Haydée alternating in the principal roles. No lasting harm had been done.

With Romeo, however, the damage was deep and irreparable. Sol Hurok, the American impresario, had been griping for some time about how much more it cost him to import the Royal Ballet rather than the Kirov or Bolshoi. Moving the Royal Ballet sets alone cost twice as much, and the fees were beyond comparison.[114] Hurok carried clout at Covent Garden. On hearing that MacMillan was planning *Romeo and Juliet*, he told Ashton that while British audiences might welcome a new pairing, Americans wanted to see Fonteyn and Nureyev. Ashton and Webster apparently failed to inform the board of his veto, for neither the ROH archives nor Drogheda's papers contain any mention of it. MacMillan was simply told to replace Seymour-Gable with Fonteyn-Nureyev, and he gave in without much of a fight. His friend, the designer Nicholas Georgiadis, told Seymour that MacMillan had gone 'straight to the top, above Ashton' in his efforts to overturn the decision, but there is no evidence of any such intervention. On the contrary, Seymour now learned that MacMillan wanted to split her up from Gable, who was down to dance second cast while she danced fifth and last. This, she felt, was 'the ultimate betrayal'.[115] It took a snarl from Ninette de Valois to restore the Seymour-Gable partnership.

MacMillan's *Romeo and Juliet* opened on 2 February 1965 to a rapturous ovation and forty-three curtain calls. Fonteyn had required MacMillan to revise his young-lovers concept, which would have looked absurd on a matron of forty-five, and Nureyev gave a strangely indeterminate account of Romeo. Fonteyn confided that she could never manage one critical moment, where Juliet decides to go to Friar Laurence, which Seymour handled magically.[116] In New York, she and Nureyev were applauded for forty minutes. At Covent Garden, praise for the secondary casts outshone the première pair. Seymour and Gable were described as 'near perfect', the choreography fitting Lynn's plump form 'like a glove'. Sibley gave 'the performance of her life' alongside Dowell, who danced 'better than ever before'. As third change, Merle Park and Donald MacLeary were 'rare and memorable'.[117] MacMillan, whether out of despair or weakness, had allowed each couple to develop the role individualistically.

Seymour performed the balcony scene with Gable on television in her native Canada, and scored a notable success in several US cities. In the autumn, she and Gable danced the ballet in Rome and Milan, while her ex-husband Colin was clearing his belongings from their flat. She was seeing a thyroid specialist for her weight, a psychiatrist for depression and Winifred Edwards for moral support. The perils of *Romeo and Juliet* had brought this passionate dancer to the brink of breakdown and destroyed any prospect of a lasting duet with Gable, who gave up soon after for an acting career, appearing with the RSC in Peter Brook's production of *A Midsummer Night's Dream* and on screen in Ken Russell's *Women in Love*. The official version that 'everyone survived'[118] the Romeo fiasco did not apply to the two dancers on whose bodies the key roles had been moulded. Gable lost his patience and Lynn Seymour her innocence on the rack of Covent Garden politics.

Nor did the repercussions end with the ballet's triumph. Fonteyn and Nureyev saw *Romeo* as their ticket to freedom and loosened their links with the Royal Ballet. Ashton's directorship was also destabilized. Drogheda told Webster that the casting confusion had led him to wonder whether all was well with the company. Nadia Nerina had been to see him, terribly upset that she and Beriosova had been left out of *Romeo*. 'MacMillan had told her that he would like her to do it, *but that he had nothing to do with the casting*.' Nerina complained that 'the general state of the company's morale was low . . . that Lynn Seymour was as discontented as she was . . . (and) that everything was being done to promote Sibley in a very unfair way.' She felt the best hope for the Royal Ballet was for Fonteyn to replace Ashton as director.[119] Insuperably frustrated, Nerina quit the company and hung up her pumps.

The knives were out for Sir Fred, as they had never been for Madam. Relations with Field had soured and the administrator slipped away to run the touring Sadler's Wells Ballet. Ashton's tolerance for MacMillan was also running out. 'Fred loathed Kenneth,' said Bill Beresford. 'One night after a well-received MacMillan première, at the far end of the Crush Bar where the man who ran Moët et Chandon dispensed free champagne to senior staff, Fred moaned, "I might as well be in the gutter. The public don't respect me any more. Just listen to the way they applauded Kenneth in there."'[120]

While staging *Song of the Earth* in Stuttgart, the Scotsman was approached by a man from West Berlin and offered the ballet directorship of the Deutsche Oper. He reported the offer to Ashton, in the hope that he would be implored to remain at Covent Garden. Ashton advised him to leave, saying the experience would do him good. So, in the summer of 1966, Britain's ascendant choreographer packed his bags and left for Germany, accompanied by Lynn Seymour as his principal ballerina. 'I'll be the management in Berlin,' he told her, 'this is our chance.'[121]

The departures marked a major breach in Madam's edifice, a disruption of the seamless continuity she had sought to assure. Behind the scenes, she raged at Ashton's weakness. The director sought redemption in a new ballet, *Monotones*, after Erik Satie's *Trois Gymnopédies*. It was exquisite, as ever, and the following season he extended it with a stretch of Satie's *Trois Gnossiennes*. Dowell and Sibley stood out in a cast of six, and comparisons were drawn with his epic *Symphonic Variations*. However, with MacMillan gone, Ashton

John Maynard Keynes (1944), inventor of the cultural economy and first chairman of the ROH

Ninette de Valois, dancing *Coppelia* at Sadler's Wells

Constant Lambert, musical firebird of English ballet, before he was ejected from Covent Garden

David Webster, ROH general administrator, scouting for singers in Munich with his music director, Karl Rankl (Photo: Sabine Toepffer)

Erich Kleiber, transformatory conductor (sketch by Eugen Spiro, c. 1949)

Operatic tea break in Gaumont Cinema, Cardiff, March 1954:
(l to r) Constance Shacklock, Geraint Evans, James Johnston,
Mr Brooks (cinema manager), Sylvia Fisher

Off to Africa, 1953: (l to r) Eric Mitchell, Elizabeth Latham
(stage manager), Fred Dalberg, Joan Sutherland, Norman
Walker, Constance Shacklock, Jess Walters (photo: PA/Reuter)

Fonteyn dances with Rudolf Nureyev to Yehudi Menuhin's
violin on the night her husband was shot, June 1964
(photo: David Farrell)

Georg Solti with protégée Kiri te Kanawa (photo: Mike Evans)

Colin Davis offers his baton to the heir to the throne (photo: Friends of ROH, photographer unknown)

Solti cues in Bernard Haitink, 1987

Ashton, after being sacked as Royal Ballet director

Kenneth MacMillan, his morose successor

Anthony Dowell, future RB director (sketches by Zsuszi Roboz)

Madam, still formidably in command

Antoinette Sibley, home-grown star and Dowell's dancing partner (sketches by Zsuzsi Roboz)

ROH Chairman Sir Claus Moser (left) receives a million-pound first-instalment from arts minister Norman St John Stevas, general director John Tooley watching intently (photo: Friends of the ROH)

Last-gasp populism: Paul Findlay presents opera in the Covent Garden piazza (photo: Richard Smith)

Mary Allen, in recovery, cultivates her Sussex garden

was looking old and isolated and anxious souls on the board began contemplating his removal. The publisher Mark Bonham-Carter, chairman of the ballet committee, urged in May 1966 that John Field should be groomed as the next director. By November that year, he sounded a warning to the main board. Ashton, he said, was 'not by temperament or inclination suited to running a company'. Nor was he spending enough time creating ballets: 'in fact, we are getting the worst of both worlds'.[122] The nettle had to be grasped, he said, and the sooner the better. Webster, reluctant to move in haste, gave gentle advice to his old friend. 'Our troubles come in two ways,' he said. 'Mainly through the fact that the company feel they have no real care taken of them as individuals. Some of them refuse to go to Jack [Hart] saying "what is the use for I won't get anything even if I go". Some of them feel that his response to them is in almost all cases detached to a degree which has no personal appreciation of them as human beings . . . This lack of interest and excitement is expressed in all the little things of day to day activities. I used the phrase to you yesterday that the main company has the feeling that nobody loves them! . . . I think it is absolutely essential to the well-being of the company that we bring in to London John Field.'[123] Ashton, however, refused either to share power or to wield it and the Royal Ballet continued to grizzle as the 60s swung on.

Maria Callas telephoned Webster towards the end of 1963 and told him she was ready, after five years' absence, to return. She wanted to sing *Tosca*, and without delay. Webster had Zeffirelli, whom she trusted, about to produce *Rigoletto* for Solti in February 1964. He inserted three *Tosca*s in January and had the two casts rehearsing side by side, one in the morning, the other in the afternoon. They had six weeks in which to mount an opera and Callas, now forty, would not give an inch. Her fee was astronomical – fifteen hundred pounds a night, net of taxes, plus her suite at the Savoy and first-class return fares to Paris. She needed constant reassurance and seemed neurotically insecure about her voice, forever on the cusp of cancellation. Yet behind these anxieties lived an artist who was guided solely by her faith in art. 'I am a very simple woman,' she said, 'and I am a very moral woman. I do not mean that I claim to be a "good" woman, as the word is: that is for others to judge; but I am a moral woman in that I see clearly what is right and wrong for me, and I do not confuse them or evade them.'[124]

In rehearsal one day, Tito Gobbi, playing the cruel governor Scarpia, pinned her backwards, arms outstretched, as if to rape her. 'You want him,' Zeffirelli whispered to Callas. 'You know you want him to violate you, and that's what you can't deal with.'[125] Callas knew what she had to do. She poured herself a glass of water, drank it, stopping in mid-motion as she spied a knife on the table. As Scarpia approached again, she seized the knife, turned and stabbed him to death. No one present had ever witnessed an act of such concentrated ferocity.

On the morning of her opening night, she was running a temperature with bronchitis but for once repressed thoughts of cancellation and turned up at the stage door in good time. As she rushed into the church at the end of the first act to warn her lover of impending danger, she tore the hem of her silk dress on a protruding nail. Callas did not look down, because her character, Tosca, would never have been distracted by a torn hem. A grainy, monochrome off-air recording of the second act reveals Callas at her most luminous, ringed in waves of nervous energy, her charisma at its most compelling. A mushrooming roar of pent-up emotion greeted the final curtain, a moment when opera split the atom of physical matter. The carpers continued to carp – 'you should have heard what singing teachers were saying in the intervals,' sniffed Hope-Wallace[126] – but Callas possessed *Tosca* as no diva before or since. The stabbing, wrote Hope-Wallace, 'happened almost on the spur of the moment and took Scarpia completely by surprise! Think what that means to anyone who has seen fifty or more *Tosca*s.' Zeffirelli's production would still be in service at Covent Garden more than thirty years later.

Next morning, Webster heard from Peter Diamand, a Callas fan who was director of the Holland Festival:

After having telephoned this morning with Maria and having heard from her – and from others too – what a triumphant event last night's *Tosca* must have been, I feel the urge to congratulate and to thank you for having made this possible.

I believe I can somehow realize the great risk which you took when planning this performance: nobody could fore-tell, when you invited Maria, in what form she would be – in fact, whether she would appear at all. Many, very many, who admire Maria had become careful, even doubtful. That you felt that an artist as

Maria is worth *any* risk, – that to bring her back to the stage would not only provide her audiences with a unique experience but will also undoubtedly help her to resume her task which she, temporarily, seemed to have neglected: this deserves the greatest admiration and sincere gratitude from all who believe in opera and feel that there is no operatic artist comparable to Maria.[127]

An even richer compliment was paid by Rudolf Bing, who offered Callas six thousand dollars, more than twice her ROH fee, to repeat *Tosca* at the Met. She returned home in good spirits to sing *Norma* for Zeffirelli in Paris and resume her life in waiting for the fickle Onassis. Callas did not need British critics and French cat-callers to tell her that her top C had gone and her middle range was ravaged. She managed to record *Tosca* that autumn and sang two runs in Paris and New York, but the prospect of four more *Tosca*s at Covent Garden the following summer was suddenly too much to bear. Two days before opening night, she had not arrived at the Savoy. That evening, she rang Webster at home saying she was suffering from dangerously low blood pressure. Webster begged her to come and sing at least the last performance, a charity gala before the Queen on 5 July 1965. Out of fondness for him, she consented.

The first three *Tosca*s were sung by Marie Collier. The fourth was the last time Maria Callas ever set foot on an opera stage. With unerring artistry, and heeding no voice but her own, she ended her international opera career on the very spot where it had begun just twelve years before. There would be comeback rumours aplenty in the next few years and gossip enough to fill ten books, but the rest of her short life formed a tragic coda to the foregoing glory. Onassis soon forsook her for the widowed Jacqueline Kennedy. A recital tour with the tenor Giuseppe di Stefano verged on travesty. She declined to appear at Webster's farewell gala. 'It was always my hope that she might still return,' lamented John Tooley,[128] on hearing of her death of a heart attack, at home in Paris in September 1977, aged fifty-three.

The ROH fallout was considerable. Zeffirelli never worked again at Covent Garden, apparently unable to contemplate a reprise of his finest two hours. 'They won't come near me',[129] he complained, but over the years he rejected repeated overtures.

Marie Collier, who stood in so bravely for Callas, reaped a

whirlwind of world attention and was swamped with offers that she could neither handle nor resist. Her first loyalty, she declared, was to Covent Garden,[130] but a turbulent private life and too much travelling played havoc with her consistency. After three years of ups and downs Solti decided that her German was too poor for Covent Garden. 'You know that I admire your work in other roles,' he said, 'and I am very willing to talk to you personally if you want to see me, but I have given this matter a lot of thought, and Sir David knows and understands my attitude.'[131] In April 1971, her agent was informed that Covent Garden were replacing her in a long-planned role. Eight months later, Marie Collier fell to her death during a drunken party from a high window in Leicester Square, a few blocks away from the Royal Opera House. She was forty-four years old, and left four children.

Solti himself became embroiled in a tempestuous row with Webster. Hearing that Callas was to sing one *Tosca* for the Queen but none for the public who had queued for days to hear her, Solti demanded that she sing all four nights or none. Webster demurred. Solti went to Drogheda and said Callas was being allowed to set a dangerous precedent. 'This is not a serious opera house,' he raged, 'no serious house would allow such nonsense.' He produced a letter of resignation. Drogheda begged him to withdraw it. Solti went to the opera house with the letter in his pocket. He stayed to greet the Queen, but left before Callas began to sing.

Drogheda implored him to calm down. 'I must tell you how distressed I have been by the knowledge that you yourself have been so upset,' said the chairman, insisting that there had been no choice but to let Callas have her way. 'One must remember that extremely high prices have been paid for tickets, and as the money is to go to the Benevolent Fund we cannot possibly make refunds. One must remember, too, that the Queen agreed to come on the understanding that she would hear Callas.'[132] Webster added his apologies and Solti was appeased, though not unconditionally. 'I am very happy with your assurances that in future you will do everything to avoid this situation occurring again,' he told Webster, 'and I hope that you will understand that I feel this to be a very fundamental question in my partnership with you. If for any reason a similar situation re-occurred, the consequences must be very serious.'[133] His insistence on professionalism was absolute and he would not waste time on capricious singers, urging that even the effulgent Birgit Nilsson should be sent packing if she persisted in her unreasonable financial demands. But he was not a man to bear grudges and he seldom referred to a row once he had put it behind him.

For all the demonic energy that led John Lanigan to christen him 'the Screaming Skull', there was an almost child-like trustfulness and lovability about Solti that many found irresistible. Once he liked someone, he permitted limitless liberties. During a rehearsal in the Crush Bar, the huge Scottish bass David Ward lifted him on to the table and said, 'Georg, shut up.' Solti simply laughed. In a tricky passage of Ravel's *L'heure espagnole*, he told Lanigan, 'John, dear, I beat it twelve here.' 'Don't worry, Maestro,' said the cocky Aussie, 'I never look.'[134] Solti roared with laughter. Michael Langdon and the tenor Kenneth Macdonald were forever playing practical jokes on him. On a trip to Israel, Macdonald convinced Solti that the captain of a Royal Navy frigate wanted to give him a lift by sea from Haifa to Tel Aviv. Solti reciprocated by getting a rabbi to phone the tenor and thank him effusively for agreeing to sing in Hebrew. After Macdonald died of a heart attack during a London Opera Centre rehearsal in October 1970, Solti sent his family a cheque every Christmas.

When the young conductor Mark Elder had his wallet stolen, Solti said 'how much was in it?' and replaced the loss. If a singer that he liked got into vocal difficulties, he would ring up his fellow-Hungarian Vera Rozsa to arrange remedial coaching. John Tooley, remarried in 1968 to his former ROH secretary, Patsy Bagshawe, was invited to honeymoon at Solti's Italian villa at Roccamare.

The familial atmosphere that Solti fostered was kept warm by his trusted secretary, Enid Blech, who once ran the London Mozart Players for her husband, Harry. 'Enid held court in Solti's outer office,' recalled a regular visitor. 'She smoked cheroots, made very good black coffee and spoke fluent Italian so the continental artists were always hanging around her.'[135] Contrary to popular myth, the Solti environment at Covent Garden was unusually light and happy. It was also wide open to newcomers. Solti was always on the look-out for talent, even within his own profession, and future conductors like Elder and Jeffrey Tate owed their first steps to his patronage. 'Whatever one may think of Solti as an interpreter,' said Richard Armstrong, who went on to head Welsh and Scottish National Operas, 'one thing is unarguable: he was a fantastic opera-house musical director. He knew all the tricks, what the priorities were. All

I tried to do when I had the responsibility was to model WNO in a similar way.'[136]

At an altogether more exalted level, Solti socialized easily with the Droghedas and their friends, Isaiah Berlin and Burnet Pavitt. He was naturally convivial, curious about other people, a wry anecdotalist and compelling dinner guest. The patrician chairman was completely enchanted, almost in love.

'My dear Georg,' lamented Drogheda in the summer of 1964, 'It seems a very long time since I heard from you. I fear that I am no longer in your thoughts. This saddens me, but there is nothing I can do about it. I realize that you prefer to take other people into your confidence. It is always slightly depressing, but I must just be philosophical, I suppose.'[137]

'My dear Garrett,' replied Solti from an Israeli hotel. 'I am very sorry that you feel neglected by me, but you know very well that the contrary is true, and that you are continuously in my thoughts.'[138] 'I suspect that this is a slight over-statement,' responded Drogheda, 'but it is nice nevertheless to be told it'.[139]

The following season fulfilled all of the chairman's fondest hopes. Solti opened in September 1964 with his first full *Ring*, in a production directed by the august Hans Hotter, who also sang Wotan, alternating with David Ward. The sets were by Günther Schneider-Siemssen, and Wilhelm Pitz of Bayreuth was imported to impart fresh discipline to Douglas Robinson's chorus. Herbert von Karajan slipped incognito into several performances and emerged with Schneider-Siemssen as his Salzburg designer. Covent Garden had spotted him first.

Many of the *Ring* singers were British, several of them newcomers. Josephine Veasey, a Solti discovery, sang Fricka in *Rheingold*. In *Götterdämmerung*, ten out of thirteen roles were internally cast, including Rita Hunter as Third Norn, Collier and Veasey as Gutrune and Waltraute, Maureen Guy as Flosshilde and a Welsh newcomer, Gwynneth Jones, as Wellgunde.

The Covent Garden *Ring* was the first time Solti had conducted the tetralogy sequentially. The press reception was initially muted, but warmed up as the cycle came round again five times in the next six seasons. 'I have seen twenty-five productions of the *Ring*,' said one veteran, 'and that was the best.'[140] By the time Decca issued the first-ever recorded *Ring* in October 1966, Solti was on the point of establishing himself as the most famous living Wagner conductor.

He followed the Ring with *Arabella*, a light-hearted, often under-played romp by Richard Strauss whom the conductor had got to know and love in post-war Munich. Lisa Della Casa and Dietrich Fischer-Dieskau led a note-perfect cast. Visconti, meanwhile, presented a scintillating *Trovatore*, Gwyneth Jones dropped an 'n' from her name as it went up in lights and the Belfast soprano Heather Harper shone for Solti in a revival of Offenbach's *Tales of Hoffmann*. Both Jones and Harper were snapped up by Bayreuth and Solti took credit for developing yet another fresh strand of British singers. He also acquiesced to Joan Sutherland's return as *Lucia*, conducted by her husband.

A season which seemed to fire on all cylinders ended in June 1965 with the boldest work ever ventured at Covent Garden, the British première of Arnold Schoenberg's *Moses and Aron*. Schoenberg was box-office frostbite and the board had debated his demerits for years before Isaiah Berlin convinced Drogheda of the moral imperative. Schoenberg had conceived his opera in response to the rise of Nazism; its inarticulate hero, Moses, needs his brother Aron to convey a divine message that can neither be transmitted nor received with anything resembling total accuracy.

Solti first shied away from the challenge, then agreed to conduct on hearing that Pritchard and Colin Davis were being approached. He persuaded the composer's fierce widow, Gertrud, to agree to a new English translation, but fifteen months before the première he listened to a *Moses* recording and told Drogheda that Covent Garden could not possibly afford the rehearsal time for so complex a work. On the opera sub-committee, Sir Thomas Armstrong mounted a rear-guard resistance, protesting against noisy atonalities. It took a letter from Isaiah Berlin to stiffen Solti's resolve. *Moses and Aron*, argued the Oxford don, was 'noble, austere and uncompromising . . . a new chapter in the history of opera.' Stagings in Zurich and Berlin had given no impression of its magnitude. The first conductor and opera house to do so would reap eternal glory.[141] In a parallel memo to Webster, Berlin tipped Nino Sanzogno of Milan, and the young composers Pierre Boulez and Bruno Maderna as standby conductors if Solti proved immovable.[142] The music director, however, was back on side and ordered Edward Downes to start orchestral rehearsals fully ten months before the première.

Solti, who admitted that without an undercoat of tonal harmony he had no idea how to conduct *Moses*, demanded the aid of a visionary director. He proposed Visconti, who was busy, then Peter Brook. His third choice was Peter Hall, a storm force in British theatre who had formed the Royal Shakespeare Company in Stratford and rebased it in London. Not quite thirty-five years old, Hall commanded the respect of senior actors and the favour of Arnold Goodman. He had always wanted to direct opera and had written to Webster in 1954 describing it as 'my chief ambition in life'.[143] But apart from a 1957 dabble at Sadler's Wells with *The Moon and Sixpence*, by an ROH repetiteur John Gardner, he had yet to direct an opera. Webster offered him Verdi's *Macbeth* (1959), *A Midsummer Night's Dream* (1960), *Forza del Destino* (1961) and the sanitized *Katerina Izmailova* by Dmitri Shostakovich (1963), all of which he declined. He was on the point of rejecting *Moses and Aron* when the conductor came on the phone. 'Solti yelled at me with his engaging mixture of charm and hysteria,' recalled Hall. 'He said it was my responsibility, no, *my duty*, to work at Covent Garden.'[144]

With his regular designer John Bury, Hall overtaxed the ROH stage crew and had the obstructionist production manager John Sullivan removed. He imported live animals, including an incontinent camel from Chessington Zoo and, taking one look at the prim and proper women's chorus, engaged Soho strippers for the orgy scene around the Golden Calf. When the chorus men were ordered to strap on phalluses, the *News of the World* ran a front-page shock-horror and the Lord Chamberlain, who was responsible for theatrical censorship, was only narrowly persuaded to permit the production. The box-office was besieged by curiosity seekers and all six performances sold out.

The much-feared Mrs Schoenberg, arriving in a two-piece tweed suit in the middle of summer, pronounced the orgy too tame. Enid Blech, sensing trouble, took her shopping and returned with a Yorkshire terrier that kept the widow occupied for the rest of her visit. Solti told a press conference: 'You'll find it difficult at first, but for me, now, it is just like Mozart.' He had acquired a personal affinity with the work, both for its biblical rectitude and for the character of Moses who, like the music director, could not always make himself understood.

Moses and Aron was an unqualified triumph for the whole company, especially for Forbes Robinson and Richard Lewis, two underrated British singers who took the title roles. There were three hundred people on stage – 'more Israelites,' remarked Goodman with inverted anti-Semitism, 'than in the stalls' – and all the leading names in British arts rushed to catch the show. Among them was Karl Rankl, attending Covent Garden for the first time since his dismissal.

Webster, during the orgy scene, retreated prudishly to the Crush Bar. Solti, a connoisseur of feminine pulchritude, complained that his own head was buried too intently in the score to see anything of interest. Richard Lewis tried to punch a journalist for peeking at the strippers – whom Stella Chitty, the stage manager, covered up as they pranced into the wings. All told, this most austere of operas occasioned more fun and legends than a hatful of Italian fripperies and established Covent Garden as an international contender, equal to Vienna or the Met, just as Isaiah Berlin had predicted.

Solti glowed with delight. His octogenarian teacher, Zoltán Kodály, had come from Hungary to attend his session at the East End Roxy cinema that Webster had converted into a rehearsal hall and grandly renamed the London Opera Centre. Kodály, no lover of Schoenberg and sparing with compliments, praised his pupil's progress and Solti was 'as pleased as can be'.[145] He still found the working conditions inadequate but he enjoyed the atmosphere at Covent Garden, and his personal life had taken a decisive turn that would attach him to England for good and all.

His marriage to Hedi was coming apart. 'I never read a book before I met her, and in London she showed me which forks to use,' he confided.[146] But they had been together twenty years and his pursuit of other women placed an intolerable stress on their relationship. In her eyes, he remained the wild-eyed, half-grown Hungarian refugee who had stolen her away from her professorial first husband, a member of the Swiss parliament.

He left Hedi in their Kensington house and moved into a suite at the Savoy, where amorous whispers abounded. 'How any woman could resist him when he smiled, I don't know,'[147] said an orchestral player. It was rumoured that Solti gave white mink coats to the singers he bedded, but with modest fees and Hedi's maintenance to pay he could barely have afforded a fake stole. Promiscuity was fun, but Solti was a man who needed security. Then, one Saturday morning, a mishap at the Covent Garden press office transformed his troubled existence.

Bill Beresford and Sheila Porter had been planning coverage of the forthcoming *Ring* when Porter mentioned a young BBC television reporter, Valerie Pitts, who worked for regional news and presented the daily children's programme, *Play School*. 'Why don't I ring Val and get her to do something?' said Porter.

Pitts had an assignment that had fallen through, and a spare camera crew. She turned up at the Savoy for 11 a.m., as agreed, and hung around waiting for Beresford. He rushed in panting apologies and, leaving the crew in the lobby, took the willowy blonde presenter up in the lift to Solti's room on the eighth floor. They were not the only ones running late. 'The door opened,' said Beresford, 'and Solti stood there, his face lathered in shaving cream, naked except for a towel round his waist. I had never seen such a hairy man. His body was covered in black hair, like a bear. Very embarrassed, he asked us to wait downstairs. As we took the lift down, Val said: "Did you see all that hair on him?"'

When the television interview was over, Solti invited them both for a drink at the bar. 'Do you like opera?' he asked Valerie Pitts.

'Oh yes,' she said.

'Have you been to many?'

'No, but we just came back from holiday and stopped in Frankfurt, where we saw a dreadful thing, all about lesbians. It was by Johann Strauss.'

Solti said: 'I think you might mean a different Strauss, and was it called *Elektra*?'[148]

At this point, Beresford 'pleaded pressure of work and tactfully withdrew'. 'If Bill hadn't arrived late,' reminisced Valerie, 'I'd never have met Solti personally. He would have sat down in front of the camera and I'd have said, "tell me about the *Ring*."'[149]

Their romance was strewn with obstacles. Valerie was married, to a man called James Sargant, and Solti was not yet divorced. She was only twenty-four, less than half his age, and her upright parents in Leeds were aghast. Solti pursued her with relentless ardour, bombarding her with roses and phone calls from around the world. 'I was a laid-back English girl and he took me by storm,' she said. 'He used to say: you only have one life, you must make every minute count.' 'I had to urge Valerie to marry him,' said Joan Ingpen. 'She was sent to me by Georg to tell her why she should agree.' The couple married in November 1967 and, when two daughters were born, Solti bought a house in Elsworthy Road, Hampstead, and elected to raise his family in England. The letter from the Home

Office conferring citizenship on this eternal wanderer was framed in gold and kept in pride of place at the doorway of his studio.

When Drogheda approached him for a third contract renewal, Solti replied: 'I am only too happy.'[150] There was some dickering over how many nights he would conduct and his scale of pay over the next five years (£10,000 p.a. rising to £14,500), but Solti felt himself at home and among friends. The only reservations came from Webster, who wanted to start grooming Colin Davis of Sadler's Wells as the next music director – 'very much a change for the worse,' sniffed Drogheda[151] – and from a new board member, Professor Claus Moser of the London School of Economics who considered Solti's remuneration excessive. Drogheda, in a clinching memorandum, noted that 'it is generally agreed that Solti's presence at Covent Garden has been of enormous benefit for the standing of the House.'[152] The *Sun* newspaper captioned him: 'Solti, the Beatle of Covent Garden'.[153]

There remained, however, pockets of resistance. A small knot of opera-goers could not abide Solti's hard-driven interpretations. Some orchestral players fulminated against him for making records with the Vienna Philharmonic, arguing that much of his repertoire, 'including that wonderful Ring, was learned at Covent Garden'.[154] 'Dear Sir David,' began one anonymous letter to Webster, written in block capitals with a Willesden postmark, 'In heaven's name why don't you fire Solti? Soon no international artist will want to work with him (Vickers, Del Monaco, Birgit Nilson (*sic*) etc). Besides who wants to hear the Ring or Otello under Solti's selfish baton. Can't you fire him before it's too late? Your faithful gallerites (some of them).'[155]

The hatred peaked in July 1966, when Solti emerged from the stage door to find his white Mercedes-Benz daubed with the words: 'Solti go home'. To a Hungarian Jew who had lost relatives in the Holocaust, the assault was horrifying. Interviewed by the *Daily Express*, he exercised maximum restraint. 'It's very hurtful,' said Solti, 'not the sort of thing I'd expect British people to do.'

Drogheda reacted with sympathetic outrage. 'David told me that, after you left us last Monday and went back to your car, you found that some idiot had scrawled offensive things on it,' he wrote. 'How absolutely damnable for you. I can imagine nothing more unpleasant . . . Everything possible will be done to discern the identity of the particular idiot who is plaguing you.'[156]

A private detective, one Robert F. Forde, was engaged. He was told to keep watch on Solti's car during three *Magic Flute* nights and to mingle with the Crush Bar crowd in the intervals. Forde, with his associate, Mr K. R. Lodge, reported back that they 'did not overhear any conversations of interest to us. . . . The only jeering heard during Mr Solti's curtain calls came from a young man sitting to the left of row B, who booed once. He appeared to be alone and there was definitely no sign of an organized demonstration.' The two private eyes then searched the building for clues, but only found a rash of stickers in the gentlemen's lavatory proclaiming 'Solti must stay'.[157]

The second half of Solti's decade was more relaxed. New productions were cut to three or four a year and Solti often left the plums to his prospective successors. Contrary to the jibes, he was not a greedy conductor and he aimed for continuity. The only group he failed to impress was the critics. In Frankfurt a reviewer, once won over, tended to remain broadly supportive. In the competitive British press, critics judged each show on merit, regardless of form. The best of them could never be counted as 'supporters' in the way that sports writers supported a particular team or manager. Solti found their unpredictability perplexing, and Drogheda was driven to distraction by his own man. On reading Andrew Porter's FT account of Solti's *Ring*, he sent a memo to Gordon Newton, the editor, saying: 'It is now impossible for me to remain as chairman of the Covent Garden Opera Company and as managing director of the *Financial Times*. Would you please inform me which position you wish me to relinquish?'[158] Porter had attacked the casting of the *Ring* as 'unforgivable',[159] an imputation that drove Drogheda wild. Advised by Newton that his impulsive resignation would inflict damage on both institutions, he sat down and fired off a volley at Porter in the nastiest terms he could muster:

I would have thought that if anyone should write helpfully it is Andrew Porter. Instead of which, it seems that the presence of your sister on the staff makes you seize opportunities to be unhelpful. Apart from this, I do long for the day when you will develop a little bit of humility, and begin to question the accuracy of some of your more offensive positive statements.[160]

Porter's reply to his employer was a model of critical detachment.

'My dear Garrett,' he wrote,

I will ignore your muddled letter – the greater part of which is based on a careless misreading of my *Götterdämmerung* notice – except where it raises certain issues of principle affecting my work for this paper. You seem unable to grasp these, so, once again, I will set them out for you:

1) So long as I am music critic of the *Financial Times* its reviews will be independent and stand in no special relationship to Covent Garden . . .

2) I will not, despite your wishes, apply to you, or to my sister, for 'inside information' that has not been made generally available to all critics. I refuse to discuss Covent Garden affairs privately with my sister. She is in a position of confidence, and it is monstrous of you to propose that I should use a family relationship to take professional advantage of this.

. . . It must be plain to you what is wrong with this *Ring*, as well as the many things that are right. I hope you can distinguish between inevitable, and so forgivable, weaknesses and the wrong things, the 'bétises', that could have been right given the initial careful thought, good sense and strong direction which, on all but the musical side, Covent Garden so sadly lacks.

My tone here may sound severe (even 'offensive'). But believe me, we are working for the same end, and it is never 'helpful' for a critic to lower his sights below the Attainable.[161]

Drogheda noted in the margin that Porter had rung him 'to apologize for his letter in advance of my seeing it', but the vigour of his riposte resounds ringingly against the latterday acquiescence of many critics to the editorial priorities and media interests of their multinational proprietors.

Neither man flinched from administering further blows. 'Your arrogance and conceit are almost insupportable,' sputtered Drogheda after Porter had begun a review of Handel's *Saul* with the words, 'If Covent Garden Opera had a proper sense of its national responsibilities . . .'[162] 'What a beastly, unappreciative letter to receive,' exclaimed Porter of another memo. 'Sometimes I wonder why I go on working so hard for this paper.'[163] Drogheda signed off one vituperation: 'I am devoted to you, even though you madden me.'[164]

That sentiment was mutual. Maddening as Drogheda could be with his chivvying notes and winter-dawn phone calls, he made people sit up and take notice. There was an impresarial energy about Drogheda that raised Covent Garden from its dowdy English origins to a venue of international chic. The performers played their part in adding glamour, but it was the chairman who put fizz and pride into the company and won it a place in the sun. Isaiah Berlin, returning to the board after a three-year absence in New York, put his clever finger on the essence of Drogheda's input. 'The real point,' he told the chairman, 'is that Covent Garden has become an absolutely central part of London and, indeed, British culture. ... It is as intrinsic and traditional and national as the BBC, and that would not have happened without – as you very well know and do not need me to tell you, although I do so with the greatest pleasure – your administration.'[165] On reading this encomium Drogheda was, momentarily, becalmed with contentment.

Sir David Webster, surveying the world from the vastness of his office, had equal cause for satisfaction. The company had become the Royal Opera and he basked in reflected glory. Many of his daily dreads had vanished. Madam was off in Turkey forming a national ballet, Legge was banished, Drogheda left him mostly in peace and even the immigration officials at Heathrow airport had given up impeding his foreign singers. All a tenor had to say was 'Royal Opera House' and the gates of the kingdom swung open.

The running of the business was supervised by Tooley, his heir apparent, who made a habit of walking down the orchestral passage in rehearsal breaks and greeting everyone by name. 'You've got to be around all the time,' he said, 'talking to the players, stage crew and artists.'[166] The more Tooley was around, the less people saw of Webster, making his interventions the more momentous. Once, in the heat of a new production, the stage crew theatened to call a strike against the director. 'Someone turned to me,' recalled Ken Davison, director of the Friends, 'and hissed, "Get Webster".

'So I rushed up to his office, was let in by Muriel Kerr, and found him sitting quietly at an absolutely bare desk. He made a sign to Miss Kerr, who produced a file full of cheques which he proceeded laboriously to sign, about twenty of them.

'Then he said to me: "Now what seems to be the matter?"

'By this time I had calmed down, and told him quietly that there was a problem with the producer and the stage staff were about to walk out, and perhaps he should take a look.

'He got up, put on his coat and hat, very dapper, took his stick, and came down with me on to the stage, as if he had just come in from the street.

"Everybody all right?" he said mildly. "Anything I can help with?"

'And that was the end of the trouble. Everyone at Covent Garden trusted him to put things right.'[167]

The paternalist approach seldom failed, but Webster's was not a stable family. There were favourites and black sheep, insiders and outsiders. Those who crossed the line were ousted. Bill Beresford was called in by Webster after ten years in the press office and told 'it is time you moved on'. He was given no reason. In the mail one morning, he found a large personal cheque signed by Burnet Pavitt, a member of the board. Beresford sent it back, appalled by the patronizing gesture. His eviction, he discovered, had been wangled by Bill Bundy, the obstreperous stage boss who had Webster's ear and was also close to Sheila Porter, the deputy press officer. 'Horrendously ugly'[168] and 'a complete bastard,[169] Bundy made enemies recklessly. 'He was incredibly insecure, poor fellow,' said Tooley. One moonless night, on his way home from the theatre, Bundy was set upon and savagely beaten. His assailants were never caught; the prime suspects were members of his own crew.

Much of the early informality still prevailed. A North London schoolgirl who wrote to Webster asking if she could sketch dancers was allowed to sit in the wings any night she liked.[170] An Oxford student who came asking for a job was told, 'come and see me again next year'.[171] Hearing that Martinelli, the non-pareil pre-war Otello, was in town for the fiftieth anniversary of his début, Webster went out before the curtain and made an impromptu speech in honour of the mighty tenor. The death of Bruno Walter was similarly commemorated. It was his house, and he could do in it as he liked.

His bonhomie was disturbed only when an external foe loomed from the vanquished past, challenging Covent Garden's hegemony. The Sadler's Wells Opera had been doing well under the baton of Colin Davis and the leadership of Norman Tucker and his artistic administrator, Stephen Arlen. The company had made a successful European tour with Charles Mackerras and was nurturing new singers under the guidance of Leonard Hancock, once of Covent

Garden. Its subsidiary troupe, the old Carl Rosa, toured opera around the land.

The problem for Sadler's Wells was, as ever, its inability to make ends meet in a theatre which seated fewer than fifteen hundred. The company had to move to survive, and the obvious venue was the South Bank beside the emergent National Theatre. Tucker had put in for a South Bank plot as early as 1954. Both the Arts Council and the Tory-ruled Greater London Council were offering large grants to create a prestigious arts park, a concretization of the Festival of Britain idea. All it needed was Government approval.

Seen from Covent Garden, a transpontine, multi-disciplinary arts centre with an inbuilt opera house posed a direct threat. The matter was never formally raised and Drogheda denied employing dirty tricks, but strings were pulled to bar Sadler's Wells from the South Bank. Jennie Lee was gently persuaded that the costs would be extortionate. Arnold Goodman changed his mind. Despite GLC support and a heartfelt appeal from Laurence Olivier, Lee vetoed the South Bank opera house in order, she said, to save the National Theatre.

The decision was a recipe for planning blight. The South Bank complex arose as an unsightly, uncoordinated mess, a permanent blot on the riverscape. Sadler's Wells was almost sunk by the setback. Norman Tucker, blaming Covent Garden's 'antagonism',[172] suffered a nervous breakdown and retired. His capable successor, Stephen Arlen, was compensated by Goodman with a lease on a West End 2,900-seater, the Coliseum, five minutes' walk from the ROH. This time, Webster objected vociferously. Too close for comfort, he argued, and too large for the tender English voices that Sadler's Wells was supposed to be developing. But this was token resistance, not to be taken seriously. The underdog company moved into St Martin's Lane and Lilian Baylis's building became a venue for travelling players.

Quietly triumphant, Webster began to face the future. The death of his orchestral manager Morris Smith in October 1967, unmourned in the orchestra, was a sharp reminder that the founding fathers were fading out. Webster's term had been extended beyond the statutory retirement age, to 1970, when he would be sixty-seven. He also needed to replace Ashton, who was as old as himself, and Solti, who had accepted the conductorship of the Chicago Symphony Orchestra. Although Drogheda begged him to stay on for a further eighteen months, saying it was 'mad' to instal new opera, ballet and management teams simultaneously,[173] Webster was in a rush to settle the succession. He was not feeling at all well, and may have suffered a mild stroke. He mislaid his glasses at meetings and his speech was sometimes slurred. 'He had lost interest,' said one observer.[174] A proud man, Webster did not wish to be seen at less than his best.

His first duty was to dispose of Fred Ashton, his oldest friend in the arts. Madam had come banging around again complaining that the Royal Ballet was in disarray. Field was threatening to quit, Hart was not working out, Somes had the unpleasant habit of hitting people who disagreed with him and Ashton was his usual languid self. Ninette de Valois had never got over Kenneth MacMillan's defection to Berlin and wanted him back. MacMillan, too, was keen to return. Berlin had been, for him, a blur of drunken misery. He never managed to learn German or win public acclaim. Lynn Seymour found new friends and lovers, leaving him bitterly isolated. Egon Seefehlner, the Berlin intendant, begged Webster to take him back. 'He's drunk all the time and turns up to rehearsals in dressing-gown and pyjamas. Quite unacceptable in Berlin,' said Seefehlner.

Webster had often mentioned to Tooley, his right-hand man, that Ashton was due to retire at the same time as himself. 'Have you discussed this with Fred?' asked Tooley.

'No, I don't need to,' was Webster's reply.

'He was rather dismissive when questioned,' recalled Tooley. 'All he said was, "well of course there's going to be a change in '70, Ashton's going. You know that John, so why do you ask?"'

Tooley was given to understand that 'it had to do with something that happened in the 1930s homosexual arts scene, in which both were prominent. Ashton represented some sort of icon for David and he did not want to leave him behind. Also, de Valois was constantly saying, Fred must go. He must make room for younger people.'[175]

One morning in April 1968, Ashton was called to Webster's office and told that they would be retiring together in July 1970. 'Aren't you going to consult me about a successor?' quavered the great choreographer. Webster shook his head. 'That's all been settled,' he said.

'That was a very unhappy day,' recalled Tooley. 'I couldn't be present at the start of the disastrous meeting. When I went into the room, there was a crestfallen Ashton. He looked at me and said,

"John, I've been sacked." "Not sacked," said David, "Fred is just going with me." '[176]

The repercussions were colossal. Ashton told Somes and Hart that they were all being dismissed, and if they wanted to leave immediately he would willingly join them. He then phoned John Lanchbery, his chief conductor. 'Fred lived around the corner and would often call to say, put on the kettle, John, I'm coming over for a chat. On this occasion, I'll never forget it, he said: Put on the kettle, John, I've been sacked.'[177]

The Royal Ballet were dancing in New York when word arrived of Ashton's enforced retirement. 'We were completely shattered,' said Sibley, 'much more so than when we knew Madam was going. We were doing *Cinderella*, and everyone on stage was crying. Anthony and I had to carry that performance.'[178]

As Webster flew out to reassure the stricken dancers. Tooley pursued him with a panicky telegram:

DROGHEDA ROBBINS NINETTE BELIEVE IMMEDIATE PRESS ANNOUNCEMENT ESSENTIAL OTHERWISE SIGN WEAKNESS AND POSSIBILITY LEAKING DISTORTED VERSION STOP PHONING JOHN[179]

Nothing was announced, and the unpleasantness persisted. The Queen Mother, Ashton's friend, was notably displeased. Nureyev, who had given up pestering Ashton for choreography after going five years with only one new role, was distraught when Ashton dissolved in tears in his dressing-room. Mark Bonham-Carter, chairman of the ballet committee, feared that Ashton might take his work elsewhere, 'and while I believe we can straighten all this out eventually, the MacMillan/Ashton relationship does not help too much.'[180]

'We all blamed Webster,' said Sibley. Even de Valois let it be known that 'Webster should have changed his mind',[181] although the anti-Ashton pressure had come mostly from her. Ashton went to his grave believing Madam and MacMillan had acted in cahoots to unseat him. He never forgave MacMillan, or dared to confront the terrifying Madam. 'Fred was very suspicious of de Valois and her motives,' said Tooley. 'He was very much of the view that if it's going to be my fate to go, because that's what she wants, then maybe I have to go along with it.'[182]

Ever the artist, Ashton responded to adversity with a masterpiece. He was struck by the tragic figure of the elderly Edward Elgar, adored as England's great composer yet creatively washed up and superseded by younger men. Ashton built a flashback ballet upon Elgar's breakthrough work, the *Enigma Variations*, celebrating an idyll of youthful friendship. In Ashton's ballet, lost English values of leisure, companionship and honour shone to the fore, along with a wrenching compassion for the ageing genius who danced at its centre. Derek Rencher played Elgar, Beriosova his wife, Sibley the flirtatious Dorabella and Dowell a rumbustious architect. Staged six months after Ashton's demission, the ballet pulsated with personal resonances. 'We all knew what Fred was choreographing about,' said Beriosova, in her greatest role, 'but when he was thinking about Elgar, he forgot himself.'[183] Kenneth Clark wept at the première, telling Ashton he was 'an incomparable maestro'. Both of his remaining seasons contained significant new works, *Lament of the Waves* and *The Creatures of Prometheus*. 'I would have liked Fred to stay on for another three-four years,' confessed Tooley with the benefit of hindsight.

Solti was urged by his new wife to conduct *Enigma*. 'I kept on saying to him, go on, do it,'[184] she said. Solti explained that he hated making the music hover while the dancers did their stuff and had sworn never to conduct ballet again after working with Colonel de Basil's company at Covent Garden in 1938 and having to leave the pit at speed on the last night after forcing the dancers to follow authentic tempi. 'He loved looking at ballet,' said Valerie Solti, but in his entire decade at Covent Garden Solti never once conducted a ballet evening. Sibley, meeting him in Drogheda's box, berated him for the state of the orchestra which played beautifully for him and 'appallingly' when she danced *Swan Lake*. He smiled apologetically. As far as Solti was concerned, the union of opera and ballet at Covent Garden was an administrative convenience. He looked after the opera, and to hell with the rest.

Replacing so forthright a conductor was never going to be easy and Webster was not prepared to look far. He had earmarked Colin Davis back in 1965 and was unusually resolute in persuading the board that Covent Garden Opera needed the artistic leadership of a native son if it was not to lose sight of its founding mission. 'We all felt that we must appoint a British conductor,' said Drogheda.[185] John Pritchard, Webster's original favourite, had pitched his tent at

Glyndebourne; Charles Mackerras was deemed unready; and Reginald Goodall was too eccentric.

That left a straight choice between Davis and the house conductor, Edward Downes, who had performed wonders in revivals and brought off a tremendous staging of *Katerina Izmailova*. Downes was hard-working, plain-spoken and painfully myopic after eye surgery. Davis was regarded as the finest English prospect since the war after substituting for Klemperer in a *Don Giovanni*. Solti, who was kept fully consulted, suggested the job should be split, Downes looking after Italian and Slavonic operas and Davis presiding over Mozart, French music and moderns ('He doesn't do Wagner,' giggled Webster, 'that means we can get Kempe back').[186] Covent Garden, he warned, could ill afford to lose Downes.

The board, however, decided it had to be one or the other. The two professional musicians around the table, Sir Thomas Armstrong and Sir Keith Falkner, voted for Downes as the better trainer and all-rounder. The majority chose Davis as the better known figure. They were under time pressure to make a decision, as Davis was being courted by the Boston Symphony Orchestra. His fame was spreading fast while Downes was a well-kept local secret.

In a masterly summary by Denis Rickett, on his second stint as secretary to the board, Webster was instructed to negotiate 'an arrangement which would enable Davis and Downes to work together fruitfully and harmoniously at Covent Garden', with Davis as music director and Downes as principal conductor. That was unacceptable to the loser, who resigned from the staff and went off to establish Australian Opera in its resplendent Sydney harbour house. But Downes was too loyal and sentimental a man to turn his back on Covent Garden and returned to conduct there every year, a record he maintained to the end of the century. Goodall, meanwhile, cycled off to Sadler's Wells where he so illuminated a home-cast *Meistersinger* that he was garlanded as England's first Wagnerian, much to Solti's annoyance (the Hungarian Jew had never forgiven the former Hitler admirer his unrenounced Fascist opinions). The *Ring* that Goodall went on to conduct at the Coliseum in Andrew Porter's translation was broad and deep where Solti's was brisk and fiery, a genuinely alternative interpretation. A *New York Times* critic found it superior to anything on show at Bayreuth,[187] and London became an unexpected Mecca for Wagner worshippers. However, Goodall's Indian summer, allied to the loss of Edward Downes, left the ROH severely under-strength in the conducting department.

Davis asserted his credentials in the seasons before his accession with *The Midsummer Marriage* and *The Trojans*, removing some of the opprobrium from Tippett's opera but failing to match Kubelik's revelations in Berlioz. *The Trojans* was notable for a last-minute débutante, Janet Baker, who stepped in for Josephine Veasey as Dido and revealed a momentous talent. Baker had come up through the Glyndebourne chorus and Scottish Opera. There was now more than one way for an English singer to make a name and the new music director would need to attract and inspire the next national crop. Davis seemed to have all the right credentials. He worked easily with singers and had great respect for orchestral musicians. One morning he came into rehearsal to find the pit floor unswept. A call to Bram Gay, Smith's successor as orchestral manager, elicited the information that the cleaner was sick. Davis asked Gay to descend:

> At the pit door he offered me the choice of two brooms. He'd sent the orchestra to the canteen and the pit staff were aready moving chairs. He and I swept the floor. The message was clear. This was typical of the man.[188]

When push came to shove, Davis would always side with the working musician against the suits and allsorts of company management. He despised dilettantes and abhorred the press, even at its most fawning. When Harold Rosenthal, who had felt shut out of Covent Garden by Solti's massive competence, offered himself as dramaturg, or literary adviser, to the inexperienced music director, Davis refused to give him the time of day. As a conductor, he had few pretensions beyond solid technique and intensive preparation. 'I'm not a supremely gifted musician like Karajan, nor like Toscanini,' he said. 'I have been very, very lucky to have a balance between my brains and my feelings and my capacity as a musician. The man who is incredibly gifted from a very early age and is admired and adored from a very early age has a much more difficult time than I do . . . I know my limitations pretty well.'[189] Beyond the charming modesty was an unfathomable capacity to ignite a performance from within, until it glowed and shimmered with dramatic tension.

The only doubt about Davis concerned his solidity. At Sadler's

Wells, he had asked to be released from his contract before three years were up. There were cogent personal reasons. His fifteen-year marriage to a Sadler's Wells soprano, April Cantelo, was breaking up, and his love for their Iranian au pair Ashra Naini (known as 'Shamsi') was being thwarted by her inability or unwillingness to return to England. He moved into a dank basement, where mushrooms grew in his shoes. On leaving Sadler's Wells, he expected to become chief conductor of the London Symphony Orchestra but displayed such emotional turmoil on an Asian tour that only six players gave him their vote. He found a job with the BBC Symphony Orchestra and happiness in his remarriage in 1964. 'I set out to tame myself and to put all this energy into a more positive form,' he told the psychiatrist Anthony Clare, 'to overcome these seedy bouts of temper and rage.'[190] Devoted to Shamsi and their young family, he gave up work during school holidays to spend the time with his children. His box at Covent Garden was often given to parents he had met at the school gates. He loved to read esoteric works of psychology and spirituality and preached personal growth, seemingly at peace with himself.

Yet there was always about Davis a touch of insecurity, especially where stagecraft was concerned. Unlike Solti, who had spent his teens scurrying around the backstage, Davis was not '*un homme de théâtre*' and had no feel for thespian rituals and rhythms. At Sadler's Wells he had relied heavily upon a director of productions, Glen Byam Shaw, who 'was deeply hurt and felt badly let down'[191] when the music director upped and left. At Covent Garden, the Droghedas invited Davis to dinner with Peter Hall. 'I felt sure they would be attracted to one another,' said the wily chairman. '. . . Within days Colin was more or less saying to me that unless he had Peter to work alongside of him he did not think he could undertake the position of musical director at all. This meant creating a new post of artistic director.'[192] Davis, in a letter to Drogheda, stipulated that they should be 'on completely equal terms',[193] surrendering half of his directorial authority without a qualm. Hall, who was the most sought-after stage director and administrator in the country, had several irons in the fire, including an approach from Glyndebourne; but in March 1969 he agreed to join Davis at Covent Garden, 'with Peter on the artistic side very much the dominant voice'.[194]

All that remained was to anoint Webster's successor. John Tooley had served a patient apprenticeship since 1955. Webster was fond of him and Drogheda found him presentable. Neither wanted to advertise the post because Tooley, they felt, 'might regard the decision to advertise as an indication of a lack of confidence in him.'[195] Two board members, Annan and Moser, warned that this was politically unwise. When Arnold Goodman got wind of the handover, he demanded an open selection procedure. Drogheda refused. Goodman was adamant: 'To us it remains a simple mystery that you can contemplate filling one of the most important musical appointments in the world by the sitting deputy without inviting anyone else to air his claims. To you it remains a total bewilderment that we can think this odd.'[196]

'I saw a serious issue of principle,' noted Drogheda. 'We had taken Arts Council finance "without strings", yet now on a matter where the right course of action seemed so clear, they were putting pressure on us. I knew that Tooley might be lost to us if the humiliating process of advertising was forced upon us, and that would be a serious matter for CG. But almost more important I felt that if as a board we settled on a given line for the good of the House, we could not bow to outside pressure to take another, or rather I could not be Chairman under such circumstances . . . In the whole of my Chairmanship, this was potentially the most dangerous area of conflict with the State . . . A Labour government, determined to shatter "establishment" methods in the pursuit of "democracy" picked on CG as a test case. I thought this was illogical, impractical and unfair.'[197]

In the event, an English compromise was reached. The Arts Council held a meeting with the ROH board, which agreed to send a notice of the vacancy to a select handful of qualified individuals. In Goodman's account, 'prospective candidates were telephoned with discouraging intimations that if they wanted to apply they could but their prospects were minimal.'[198] In fact, six men were notified by letter – John Denison of the Royal Festival Hall; Moran Caplan, the Glyndebourne administrator; Stephen Arlen; the Decca *Ring* producer, John Culshaw; Peter Diamand of the Holland Festival; and the Rt. Hon. The Earl of Harewood, who had the strongest credentials and appetite for the job.

Harewood had been Webster's right-hand man before he went off to run the Edinburgh Festival. His private life had undergone a public upheaval when he left his first wife, Marion, for Patricia Tuckwell, sister of the LSO hornist. While Harewood awaited Royal assent to his divorce under a siege of pressmen, Drogheda gave him refuge in his house the night before the couple flew abroad to get married. This was a personal kindness, not a professional courtesy. He would not allow Harewood, under any circumstances, to succeed Webster.

Harewood wanted the job and began lobbying for it. Alarmed, Drogheda took Harewood to lunch and made him an offer: withhold your application, and I will appoint you to the board with a view to succeeding me as chairman. Harewood was torn. He was still on the right side of fifty and keen to run an opera house, but as chairman he could reshape Covent Garden and as a wealthy landowner he did not need the salary or the duties of nightly attendance. Upon reflection, he accepted Drogheda's offer and joined the board.[199] Those who pressed his claims to Webster's post were fobbed off by Drogheda, each with a different excuse. Goodman, who knew Harewood as chairman of the Arts Council's music panel, was told that the ROH staff wanted Tooley, and that the Royal Family were so shocked by Harewood's divorce that they might boycott Covent Garden if he was in charge. Ken Davison was told that Drogheda could not forgive Harewood for some business at the London Opera Centre that cost Joan Cross her job. Drogheda told his mistress that Harewood was unsuitable because he was bound to spend too much time on his estates, near Leeds.[200] The truth of the matter is that Drogheda never trusted Harewood and was determined to neutralize him.

Diamand, the only foreign candidate, credulously submitted his credentials to the search committee which immediately found them 'not comparable to the claims of John Tooley'.[201] He was invited to a pro forma interview at the Treasury, a matter of days before the unstoppable announcement of Tooley's succession. Honour had been satisfied, but the job was plainly fixed and a House of Commons Committee was sufficiently disturbed to call a special hearing and denounce the Royal Opera House for underhandedness – its first formal public condemnation.

As for Harewood, Drogheda had him where he wanted. When Harewood asked to be named vice-chairman, Drogheda refused but strung him along. 'So far as the chairmanship itself is concerned,' he said, 'I don't know when you would like me to disappear from the scene. My idea was that I should see Solti out, so to speak . . .'[202]

At board meetings Harewood was full of ideas and Drogheda wanted none of them. Harewood held that more operas should be sung in English and backed a proposal from Davis and Hall for a vernacular *Marriage of Figaro*. Drogheda was incensed, fearing damage to the Royal Opera's international prestige. The suspicion dawned that he might not let Harewood succeed him after all. Goodman called the Palace and asked the Queen's Private Secretary, Sir Michael Adeane, if H.M. would object to having her cousin as ROH chairman. The reply was that she would not mind, albeit 'expressed in a fashion that indicated no great enthusiasm for the appointment'.[203]

Then, before blue blood flowed, Sadler's Wells was devastated by the death of Stephen Arlen from a five-week oesophageal cancer in January 1972. Harewood was approached by the company's chairman, David McKenna, and accepted the managing directorship without delay. He resigned from the ROH board and was thanked by Drogheda for his contribution in a letter expressing hope that the two theatres would 'work closely together in what is essentially a common cause'.[204] Before the year was out, Drogheda wrote to the Arts Council chairman, 'quietly boiling over the fearful disloyalty of George Harewood in attacking Covent Garden as he did in that interview with *Time Out*'.[205] There would be further irritations.

Harewood renamed his company English National Opera and challenged Covent Garden wherever he sensed a vulnerability. He demanded ever-larger slices of the Arts Council cake, founded a sister company in Leeds as English Opera North and missed no opportunity to depict ENO as the People's Opera and Covent Garden as the crusty toffs. Drogheda, for his part, was glad to see him go. Socially, the two earls remained on cordial terms. Theirs had been a very English conflict, with no apparent rancour. In years to come, though, loyalists would wonder aloud whether Harewood might not have saved the soul and spirit of the original Covent Garden. 'This would have become a very different company,' ruminated Edward Downes, 'if George Harewood had taken over.'[206]

Exciting as these events might have looked through opera glasses, the world outside was in the final throes of 60s revolution and would never be the same again. The American war in Vietnam bred a culture of protest and narcotics. The Soviet-led invasion of Czechoslovakia crushed hopes of a nuclear thaw and spread geopolitical despair. Martin Luther King and Robert Kennedy were assassinated. Students took to the streets, their cause varying from

one western capital to the next. De Gaulle was driven from office in
Paris, Lyndon B. Johnson in Washington. Harold Wilson, briefly
boosted by England's 1966 World Cup soccer victory, was brought
low by devaluation and his inability to tackle industrial chaos.
Ireland, long dormant, awoke to sectarian violence.

As authority was mocked by its own ineptitude, the counter-
culture thrived. Rock music was the language of revolution. London
swung as never before. The Beatles disbanded, outshouted by the
next wave. Brian Epstein and Brian Jones of the Rolling Stones died
of drug overdoses. The cast of an imported musical, *Hair*, stood up
and faced a West End audience stark naked. Dramatists grappled
with *The National Health* (Peter Nichols), *The Ruling Class* (Peter
Barnes) and *Time Present* (John Osborne). Fringe theatre was the
medium for even freer forms of expression, liberated from state
subsidy and self-censorship. 'The formative stage in my career,'
wrote a future ROH general director, 'coincided with the explosive
growth of the fringe in the late 1960s and early 70s.'[207]

Amid such ferment, the Royal Opera House risked looking
irrelevant and out of touch. William Glock, newly added to the
board, brought in the radical figure of Pierre Boulez, who had
proclaimed 'burn down the opera houses!' Boulez conducted an
impressive *Pelléas et Mélisande* on an abstract backdrop by Josef
Svoboda and made a fine Philips recording, but never undertook
another ROH production. In an effort to appear with-it, two new
operas were commissioned, the first for a dozen years. *Hamlet*, by
the deadly serialist Humphrey Searle, was abandoned half-way
through its second performance when the Canadian baritone Victor
Braun declared himself unable to sing another note. *Victory*, by
Richard Rodney Bennett, who had written the delightful *Jazz
Calendar* for a Frederick Ashton ballet, was an insipid dramatiza-
tion of a Joseph Conrad story, inoffensively tonal and dedicated to
Hans Werner Henze. Neither opera filled many seats, but *Victory* at
least served some purpose as indigenous gloss on a crowning
achievement.

Solti had long talked of taking Covent Garden into Europe and the
Foreign Office were keen to establish a cultural presence in wall-
torn Berlin. In April 1970, Solti led the Royal Opera to Germany
with two Verdi productions, *Don Carlos* and *Falstaff*, which were
acclaimed, and the Bennett opera, which escaped unbooed. Solti
himself was lionized, Gwyneth Jones adored and Geraint Evans

hugely roared by a public which had known no other Falstaff except Dietrich Fischer-Dieskau. The public, said the *Frankfurter Allgemeine Zeitung*, were 'beside themselves with enthusiasm'.[208] Apart from Regina Resnik (Mistress Quickly) and Carlo Cossuta (Don Carlos), the entire cast was British. Jennie Lee cabled her congratulations – 'We are all so proud of you!' – and the company came home on a high, having scaled the twin peaks of Munich and Berlin. It had taken less than twenty-five years to go from nullity to dominance. The only regret was that Webster could not witness the triumph: he was away in New York with the Royal Ballet, trying to rebuild bridges.

'The Royal Ballet had a fantastic success,' reported Lincoln Kirstein to Drogheda, 'due I am sad to say almost entirely to Nureyev. To me he is a vulgar acrobat. Margot should really not dance, but the company and in particular Dowell, were magnificent. I saw quite a bit of Fred, who is bitter and uncomfortable.'[209] The wounds were too deep to heal.

Webster had slipped and fallen in the market the previous winter and spent a few days in hospital. He remained unwell and unwilling to face the inevitable. On 30 June 1970, Covent Garden gave him a Farewell Gala. Seven conductors and some forty soloists took part, among them Sutherland, Vickers, Veasey, Gobbi, Shuard, Jones and Evans – all his favourites bar one, the irretrievable Callas. Benjamin Britten wrote an opening fanfare, the Queen Mother and Prince Charles were in attendance and Drogheda and Ashton paid warm tribute. There was no contribution from the Royal Ballet, which was rehearsing Ashton's Farewell and nursing his grievance.

When Webster tried to address the house, he choked on his speech and left the stage whispering, 'thank you.' At a Savoy lunch given by the Friends of Covent Garden, he got up to reply to Ashton's witty speech but, after a few words, broke down and began to cry. The artists and staff clubbed together to buy him a David Hockney portrait, to be hung in the Royal Opera House, and a pair of claret decanters for his Weymouth Street sideboard. Ten months later, on 10 May 1971, on a weekend in Brighton, he suffered a second stroke and died. Many felt his life had ended the day he left the opera house.

Geraint Evans overheard Webster's name mentioned one day in a buzz of chorus room conversation.

'You were very fond of him, weren't you?' he asked the chorus.

'Fond of him?' said one man. 'We loved him.'[210]

Webster, wrote the *Daily Telegraph* obituarist, had been 'the anchorman on whom all else depended'.[211] At his Thanksgiving Service in the Church of the Holy Sepulchre, High Holborn, the choir contained a clutch of international soloists. Ninette de Valois recited a poem by Yeats, John Tooley read the Lesson, Geraint Evans delivered a moving eulogy, Davis conducted Jon Vickers in 'Total Eclipse' from *Samson*, and Solti conducted Heather Harper in the 'Liebestod' from *Tristan und Isolde*.

Muriel Kerr stayed on a while to deal with his correspondence and supervise the erection of a memorial plaque at St Paul's Church, Covent Garden. She, too, did not enjoy a long retirement. In the spring of 1975, it was said, 'Muriel Kerr went home one night, put her affairs in order, took herself to hospital in a taxi and died. That was typical of Muriel. Never making any trouble for anybody.'[212] Davis and the orchestra performed at her obsequies.

At the time of Webster's death there were fifty-one of his founding team still on the payroll, including the repetiteur Norman Feasey and a bartender, Winnie Pradier, who had served since before the war.[213] Many had stayed out of loyalty to Webster, others owed their survival to his latterday laxity. Their time was now up, and the old guard were unsentimentally dispersed.

The curtain had fallen on the opening acts at Covent Garden, and the public streamed out in search of refreshment.

CHAPTER 8

The Long Interval: Propping up the Crush Bar

(1971–87)

THE PREDOMINANT COLOUR was brown. Suits, skirts, sweaters, leather and leisurewear came in all shades from auburn to rust, with large checks and loopy patterns on an unfailingly tan background. Even theatrical sets went brown, the actors vanishing into a modish murk as directors and a looming energy crisis kept the lighting low. Just why fashion should have dictated the colour of fecal waste to be the epochal hue is a matter for psychologists to investigate. It may have mirrored economic and political pessimism as much as cultural confusion, for the 70s were a decade in which assumptions of established authority were continually under threat. Palestinian hijackers and Gulf oil producers held industrialized nations to ransom. The West Indies whipped the white Commonwealth at cricket. China detonated nuclear devices. The president of the United States, Richard M. Nixon, was brought down by two newspaper men investigating a break-in. German and Italian industrialists were kidnapped and sometimes murdered by their children's friends. The holders of power were revealed to be powerless and the organs of state cracked under pressure. It was an era of glum uncertainty.

Harold Wilson called a general election in June 1970, persuaded by the opinion polls that victory was assured. To his bewilderment, the resurgent Tories under Edward Heath turfed him out of Downing Street. Wilson's failure to curb the unions had precipitated his downfall. The number of strikes in 1970 approached four thousand. Ten million working days were lost. The Tories, in a strategy meeting at Selsdon Park Hotel, near Croydon, resolved to legislate against union power, relax controls of prices and incomes, slash public expenditure and stimulate private enterprise through a series of tax cuts. The apparatus of state health and welfare benefits, divided and often duplicated between central and local government, was to be streamlined. Hospitals and housing estates would be built on a larger, more efficient scale. Those applying for benefits would be means-tested to reduce fraud. The featherbedding of failing industries with state subsidies to stem unemployment would be phased out. It was a bold programme, misguided in parts and some years ahead of its time. It might have worked had Heath held his nerve and fulfilled his Selsdon manifesto. But within a month after taking office, the Government suffered a crippling blow. Iain Macleod, architect of New Toryism and Chancellor of the Exchequer, died of a heart attack aged 56. No other senior figure had his zeal and charisma, and the Heath regime sagged into a soggy mode of climbdown and make-do.

It would be trite, though true, to describe Edward Heath as the worst Prime Minister of the century. He came into power with the best intentions and was brought down by extreme circumstances and the prevailing wisdom of a fatalistic Civil Service whose post-imperial aim was 'the management of decline'. Heath was a self-made man of the lower middle classes. Home Counties born and bred, he had applied for an organ scholarship at Oxford, where the examiner, Dr Thomas Armstrong, steered him gently towards Modern Greats. Heath continued to enjoy music, and sailing, as his favoured recreations. On becoming Prime Minister, he was congratulated by the likes of William Walton – 'Thank God you're in!' – and Carlo Maria Giulini, who 'thanked providence with all (my) heart for having placed the reins of government of this great country in the hands of a man whose concerns and political decisions will always be illuminated and enriched by the strength of his own rich spiritual and artistic experiences.'[1] There was also a supportive cable from Sir Thomas Armstrong, retired principal of the Royal Academy of Music and Covent Garden board member.

The London Symphony Orchestra came begging the new Prime Minister to conduct an Elgar overture at its November 1971 gala, which he did to his own evident satisfaction. The Royal Opera House was more circumspect. Drogheda had lunched Heath at the *Financial Times* and found him sulky and self-centred. A lifelong bachelor with few intimate attachments, Heath preferred the anonymities of orchestral mass to the human tangles of opera and ballet. Nor was he much impressed by ermined earls and scantily clad ballet dancers. However, an appointment that he made two weeks after election drew Edward Heath inextricably into Covent Garden.

Every incoming Prime Minister reshuffles the Private Office at 10 Downing Street, 'the single most important section'[2] of the power apparatus. The Private Office is headed by two civil servants, a Principal Private Secretary and a Foreign Affairs Secretary. The relationship between PPS and Prime Minister is among the closest in government, reaching a point where 'neither should need to finish a sentence to be completely understood by the other'.[3] No person in the country has easier access to power than the PM's PPS.

The man Heath picked as his Principal Private Secretary was Robert Armstrong, a stripe-shirted Treasury high-flier – Eton, Oxford, and, by nice coincidence, the only son of his Oxford examiner, Thomas Armstrong. Charming where Heath was truculent, unflappable in times of crisis, Robert Armstrong possessed an effortless authority and the capacity to inspire affection as much as respect, both from colleagues and from Prime Ministers of both parties.

For two years, Armstrong had served as Secretary to the Board of the Royal Opera House. He warned Drogheda that he might have to miss some board meetings, but there were two junior officials, Elizabeth Beavan and Andrew Edwards, who could take minutes and he very much hoped the Board would accommodate his changed situation. 'I am delighted that you can carry on helping Covent Garden,'[4] was Drogheda's silky reply.

From now on, the ROH would be but a heartbeat away from the centre of power. Where Attlee, Churchill, Eden, Macmillan and Douglas-Home hardly noticed the opera house, and Wilson had left cultural affairs to Jennie Lee, Armstrong's Prime Ministers became dutiful attenders. Drogheda was quickly keen to ascertain what advantage the ROH could reap from its Secretary's unexpected promotion.

He asked Armstrong to procure a knighthood for Solti. Armstrong suggested that he route the request through the Foreign Office since the conductor was not a British citizen. When it came to making the award, however, he arranged for the Prime Minister to present the insignia to the conductor at a post-curtain party in the Crush Bar.

Drogheda was growing concerned about Margot Fonteyn, who had been made a Dame but had no pension arrangements.

Armstrong mentioned that there was a discreet fund at the Prime
Minister's disposal with which he could purchase an annuity for
especially deserving citizens, giving them an unofficial state
pension. The beneficiary was not allowed to know where the money
came from, and all involved were sworn to secrecy. This tidy little
Downing Street kitty was not accountable to Parliament, contra-
vening a core principle of the British constitution. Its existence,
never previously disclosed, is one of the funny little ways by which
public good could be done with a nod and a wink from the person at
the Prime Minister's right hand.

Both Armstrong and the ROH board were acutely sensitive to the
delicacy of his position. 'Robert wouldn't be addressed,' said an
official who attended board meetings for fifteen years. 'Even at
times of financial crisis, I can only recall one occasion when someone asked for the matter to be brought to the PM's attention.
"Perhaps the Prime Minister might be persuaded to look into this,"
was what was said, and nothing ever came of it. That was not the way
to go about things.'[5]

The influence Armstrong wielded was contained in the raising of
an eyebrow and a faint change of vocal inflexion. 'Yes, Prime
Minister,' could signify anything from wholehearted assent to severe
disapproval. Only an insider could tell the difference, and Armstrong
was the ultimate insider. 'Never negotiate in public,' was one of his
watchwords. Being 'economical with the truth' was a famous
circumlocution that he employed in Australia some years later, on
being sent abroad to lie for his country. Armstrong, with the classical
propriety of an Old Etonian, wrote to *The Times*[6] on the day of his
retirement pointing out that the evasion was not original: it had been
coined by the eighteenth-century political writer, Edmund Burke.

So subtle a mandarin would never betray a confidence or curry
favour, nor would the ROH board wish to discomfit him by suggesting it. It was enough to have Robert Armstrong sitting in the Prime
Minister's anteroom for Covent Garden to feel secure and looked
after. 'One had the feeling that we were extremely well protected,'
said a senior staffer. 'People in power, whether they were left or
right, knew about Covent Garden.'[7]

The incoming ROH team had much in common with the new
Government. Tooley, Hall and Davis were all southerners of modest
background, self-motivated and temperate. Hall and Davis were in

their early forties, Tooley was 46. They spoke the same language, shared the same style. MacMillan, a Scot, grew up in Great Yarmouth on the Norfolk coast and never quite got to grips with middle-class style. Even more out of step was the bluff John Field, a northerner in his early fifties.

MacMillan came home a man reborn. On his way back from Berlin, he had stopped in Munich to see some Cranko ballets and go mountain climbing with his fellow-choreographer. On the morning of their first excursion, he collapsed in his hotel room. Doctors diagnosed a severe vascular spasm, brought on by overwork and heavy drinking. He was warned to give up alcohol and never touched another drop. In London, he stayed for a while with Georgina Parkinson and her husband. Lynn Seymour, his closest friend, had given birth to twins and was still enjoying her life in Germany. A loner through life, MacMillan had never seemed more isolated.

His first act at Covent Garden was to merge the touring troupe with the main company, dismissing two dozen soloists and replacing Field's 'Number Two Company' with an experimental New Group. His stated aims were to raise standards, cut costs, and give the provinces a chance to see more stars and new work. The cull was crudely carried out and deeply destabilizing in a ballet world that had known nothing but growth. MacMillan had his known favourites and Field protected a small knot of travellers. 'There were some of us who did not fit into either camp,' lamented Wayne Sleep, a brilliant young virtuoso dancer. 'Although we were not sacked, we did find ourselves marginalized, out on a limb, working but redundant.'[8] Several dancers resigned. Those who survived were roughly treated by Somes.

Field insisted on the title 'co-director', but MacMillan refused to treat him as an equal. He was reduced to Administrative Director. Then MacMillan saw a playbill on which Field's name figured above his own and exploded with rage. Field, friendless, was forced to resign before the season was three months old. He went on to become ballet director at La Scala, Milan, and later to run the Royal Academy of Dancing. Having danced for Madam since 1939, he was banished to the fringes of memory.

In place of Field, Tooley brought back Peter Wright, a former Sadler's Wells stalwart who had worked with Cranko since 1961 and developed steadily as a choreographer under Ashton's aegis. Wright took over the burdens of administration and touring. On the main stage, MacMillan opened with a hit, importing Jerome Robbins to stage *Dances at a Gathering* with a madcap mazurka for Nureyev and Dowell that seemed to proclaim 'anything you can do I can do better'. For the New Group he engaged Glen Tetley, an ex-Robbins American whose Nederlands Dans Theater flashed full-frontal nudity on the Sadler's Wells stage and whose first contribution to Covent Garden was the ironically titled *Field Figures*, with wavy music by Karlheinz Stockhausen. MacMillan made ballets for the New Group with modern music. But the mainspring of his opening season was *Anastasia*, a three-act expansion of a Seymour showcase he had created in Berlin, the story of a woman in a madhouse who claimed she was the sole survivor of the Russian royal family.

Seymour had returned with her twins, bought a house in Chiswick and danced for Robbins. 'In Lynn Seymour we had at last a ballerina whose whole body was as expressive as a Russian's,' wrote Richard Buckle. 'She was an even more wonderful actress than Fonteyn and far more a child of the period, with an appeal which went straight to the hearts of young people.'[9] Her success was integral to MacMillan's, glossing his profundity with high charisma, and in *Anastasia* – with Beriosova, Derek Rencher, Sibley, Dowell and the cream of the Royal Ballet in support – she gave proof of her virtuosic maturity. Yet the ballet bombed. It was too long and too adhesive to the three full-length symphonies by Tchaikovsky and Martinů chosen by the choreographer. MacMillan was booed at the curtain and the press was rough. 'Little short of disastrous,' said the *Guardian*, 'dull and repetitious' was the *Telegraph* verdict. Roughest of all was *The Times*, whose critic John Percival called the choreography an 'insipid copy' of Ashton's *Enigma Variations* and Grigorievich's *Spartacus* for the Bolshoi.

Drogheda, more than usually agitated, berated *The Times* arts editor, John Higgins, a former FT man, who agreed to curb his Crankophile critic. 'If I had a bet,' Drogheda told MacMillan, 'I would put a small sum on the unlikelihood of *The Times* ballet notices continuing in the same strain; and I do not say this to you in a frivolous manner.'[10] MacMillan appreciated his concern, but was badly damaged. 'One feels so helpless in times like this,' he replied, 'and of course you can imagine how deeply depressed I am.'[11] He went to see a psychiatrist and entered three years of analysis, not a happy augury for the new era – the more so when, that selfsame month, the Royal Opera team came unstuck.

*

The handover season from Solti to Davis was dominated by the surgent energies of Peter Hall, who directed all of the new productions, one for Davis and two for Solti. Davis chimed in with a Tippett commission, *The Knot Garden*, dedicated to Sir David Webster and signifying an attempt to grapple with contemporary confusions. Tippett had discovered America and come back with a taste for jazz, gay liberation, esoteric cults and unconventional relationships. 'The new set-up at Covent Garden believes that (this) is the kind of work to coax a new and "wider" audience,' noted the sceptical Philip Hope-Wallace.[12] Tippett's plot was typically shambolic, involving a black and white male gay couple, a female freedom fighter and a black-bearded psychoanalyst singing such hip lines as 'play it cool' and 'sure, baby'.

The audience, said Hall, 'will have to participate, we must make them participate. They may scream resentfully because opera is being dragged into the 1970s. But then something will have happened. That's why Colin Davis and I feel that there could be no better work for us with which to start our adventure together.'[13]

Davis and Hall gave it their all. The director ripped out the prompt box and extended the stage over the orchestra pit to bring the young singers – Yvonne Minton, Josephine Barstow, Robert Tear – closer to the audience. Jill Gomez, as the teenaged Flora, volunteered to wear a bikini and have the top ripped off to enliven a rape fantasy. 'That's absolutely brilliant,' said Hall, but the rapist balked at his duties and only detopped her on the opening night, when a clatter of coins signified that gentlemen in the stalls were reaching for their opera glasses. Davis conducted with passion and conviction and the cast were irreproachable, but the hope of *The Times* critic[14] that the opera would receive 'umpteen' revivals was quixotic. Although foreign intendants came to view the novelty, none took it back and Tippett remained a defiantly English delicacy, his swingers' opera outdated before it was sung.

Of Solti's departing glories, *Eugene Onegin* was sung in English because the conductor and cast knew no Russian, and *Tristan und Isolde* was almost capsized by a stupendous row between director and diva. 'I threatened to leave,' said Birgit Nilsson, 'because I didn't like the terrible way the *Liebestod* was staged by Peter Hall. First it was so dark I was tripping over Tristan's body. Then Hall wanted Tristan – Jess Thomas – to stand up behind me during the last part of the scene. He had tomato juice all over him, and I got smeared with it. I looked ridiculous. Solti said I should do whatever I wanted. He would take the blame . . . Of course Solti blamed me when Hall said he didn't want to have his work ruined by stars who changed everything.'[15]

She was not alone in her reservations. Andrew Porter began his FT review: 'Poor Mr Solti! Once again a performance prepared by him with love and care, with delicate attention to detail and passionate concern for musical effect, has been spoiled by insensitive, unimaginative inscenation.'[16] Hall had cut right across the grain of Wagnerian interpretation, neither embracing tradition nor convincingly overturning it. Solti would partner him again in a 1983 Bayreuth *Ring*, at the end of which the distressed maestro said he never wanted to conduct opera again. Hall's Covent Garden *Tristan* was panned by Harold Schonberg in the *New York Times* as 'the pipsqueak posturings of a director determined to show his cleverness'. Porter called it 'cheap'.

A week into the *Tristan* run, Hall told Tooley that he was unhappy. A week later, on 4 July 1971, two months before he formally became Director of Productions, Hall asked to be released from his contract: 'I have to admit to a great mistake,' he told Drogheda. 'The only course open to me is to recognize it and to apologize to you personally and publicly.'[17] He had underestimated the amount of work involved – 'to do the job properly I would have to devote all my time to it' – and discovered that he was temperamentally better suited to festival productions than to repertoire opera. He begged forgiveness from the board, from Tooley and particularly from Colin Davis: 'He gave me half his new kingdom gladly, and it is a poor way to answer his generosity. Working with him was one of the best experiences of my life.' But nothing in the world would persuade him to stay at Covent Garden.

Drogheda was thunderstruck. It was, he would say, the bitterest blow of his chairmanship. 'It is hardly necessary for me to tell you that I was most distressed to receive your letter,' he replied to Hall. 'I played a great part in bringing you together with Colin eighteen months ago, and therefore I have a very considerable sense of personal responsibility.'[18] Privately, he could not quite bring himself to believe the reasons that Hall had given.

That weekend, the *Sunday Times* accused the board of obstructing Hall's bold plans and precipitating his resignation. Hall denied having talked to the press and reiterated his regrets: 'I can only repeat that I am very very sorry.'[19] Drogheda was unconvinced, however, and a consolatory letter from Arnold Goodman only intensified his suspicions. 'In the end,' said the Arts Council chairman, 'it may be for the best that the release of Hall's remarkable talents for full theatrical employment is of no small advantage.'[20]

On reading the words 'full theatrical employment' Drogheda smelt a rat. He phoned Max Rayne, the property developer and Goodman crony who was chairman-elect of the National Theatre. Rayne was abroad on holiday. On his return, he planned to depose Laurence Olivier from the NT helm and it did not take a genius to guess whom he had earmarked as successor. Rayne eventually returned Drogheda's call, insisting (without being asked) that his 'knowledge of what has transpired between Covent Garden and Peter Hall is limited to what has been published in the press'.[21] Over-anxiously, he also reported the exchange to Goodman who, four days later, wrote to Drogheda in identical terms assuring him that neither he nor Rayne knew 'anything' about the reasons for Peter Hall leaving Covent Garden. They protested too much.

The truth, revealed in Hall's memoirs and Drogheda's papers, confirms that Hall met Goodman at Glyndebourne earlier that summer and told him that he was unhappy at Covent Garden. The arch-fixer 'greeted the news with delight'[22] and set up a lunch with Rayne in his flat, where they offered Hall the National Theatre. Hands were shaken and nothing was announced for eight months, until Olivier was eased out. Tooley reckoned that Hall was aware of the plot to drop Olivier before he jacked in his ROH job.[23] Hall, in his memoirs, admitted that he 'behaved badly'.[24] He was, without doubt, the best man for the National Theatre, but the intrigue that took him there was more questionable than any of the Covent Garden appointments. Thanks to Goodman, Hall's transfer escaped uncensured. Thanks also to Goodman, Hall's National Theatre was awarded a giant slice of the Arts Council budget, second only to Covent Garden's.

Hall, said the theatre's historian, 'needed the National'[25] to restabilize a brilliant career that was in danger of going off the rails. Famously uxorious (he would marry five times), he craved a home he could call his own. He also coveted fame, money and fun. Before he even warmed his seat at the NT, Hall arranged to direct operas at Glyndebourne, present a weekly arts show on television and make commercials for a brand of wallpaper ('Very Peter Hall. Very Sanderson'). In an era of fiscal stringency, his consumption was conspicuous and politically criticized, fomenting unrest within his own company. He would not have lasted long at Covent Garden and both Tooley and Drogheda came round to the view that 'it is better that it should have happened now rather than later'.[26]

The abruptness of his exit, however, threw plans for the next two seasons into chaos. Hall had put himself down to direct many of the new productions. Substitutes had to be scrambled. Happily, a new staff producer, John Copley, successor to Christopher West and Ande Anderson, came quietly into his own and established an unfussy house style. By the time *Figaro* came on stage in December, Hall was barely missed. The main legacy of his brief ROH encounter was a cloud of mistrust that fell between the worlds of English theatre and opera, ending the Keynesian dream of cross-pollination. From now on Covent Garden would look mostly abroad for its directors, severing its ties with Shakespearian stagecraft.

The personal consequences were messier and more protracted. On leaving, Hall snapped a limb off the three-legged directors' table, leaving Tooley and Davis to wobble precariously. 'Colin took it very badly,' said Tooley. 'He was feeling desperately insecure, really needed every prop he could find.'[27] Never high on confidence, Davis had relied on Hall to push plans past a board whom he mistrusted and openly attacked. He possessed neither the charm nor the force of a Solti to get what he wanted. When denied, he turned tetchy and reticent. Even in repose he needed constant reassurance, supplied at first by his close friend, the ardent Berlioz scholar, critic and conductor, David Cairns. Davis, many felt, never fully recovered from the shock of Hall's abandonment and would search for years for a second Hall.

Tooley, on the other hand, showed neither pain nor discomfiture. His talent was to keep a steady hand on the tiller. In the eye of any storm, he was impervious and courteous, insisting that all was well and the show would go on. Like the captain of the *Titanic*, he confided in no one and steadfastly performed his duty. He told his wife not to get too close to anyone at Covent Garden, 'in case he had to sack them'. There was something unflappably English about Tooley's phlegm, suppressing the possibility of adversity. 'He was quite reticent about telling me if anybody was ill,' said his wife, 'he didn't want me to know.'

He trotted out an inventive lexicon of bureacratic euphemisms –
'indisposed, unavailable, unforeseen circumstances,' to cover up for
errant artists. A ballet conductor whom he sacked as a 'baleful
influence'[28] would be lauded in his memoirs as 'devoted'. There was
a rapid dismantlement of Solti aides. 'Colin and I didn't want Joan
Ingpen to go,'[29] said John Tooley. Ingpen's version differed slightly.
'I went to Colin with a list of casts,' she recalled. 'He said: "I'd like
you to leave. You're dangerous to me."'[30] Ingpen went on to become
Head of Casting at the Met, the best they ever had; Davis found the
help he needed from a German casting director, Helga Schmidt. In
Tooley's mind, the facts were rearranged to fit the image he aimed to
project of a happy family enterprise, untroubled by strife. If he could
never be the father that Webster was, Tooley cast himself as the elder
brother, the shoulder to cry on. He greeted every staff member by
name and inquired solicitously after little Johnny's eleven-plus
results or the old man's operation.

Like the politicians of his day, Tooley was not so much a leader as
a conciliator. Heath, in government, lost his resolve to confront the
unions and focused his energies on entering the European Community. He metricated shillings and pence into pounds and pee and
replaced an unpopular purchase tax with an unwelcome Value
Added Tax, fuelling inflation and stalling industrial growth. Prices
shot up by ninety per cent in the first half of the decade.[31] The miners
won a 'spectacular'[32] wage rise of twenty-five per cent after a seven-
week strike that caused electricity blackouts at Covent Garden and
across the land. Heath's attempts to enforce a prices and wages
freeze failed to appease either side of a raging industrial war. His
blustery, unapproachable personality inspired neither trust nor
warmth.

Tooley, more transparently, made himself available to all people at
all times, without giving of himself. After a bout of hepatitis, he
moved into a company flat that was ten minutes' walk from the
theatre. He could be at his desk each morning before breakfast and
seldom left the premises before the curtain went up for the second
act. 'I used to get it in the neck sometimes,' he divulged, 'when, for
perfectly legitimate reasons, I was in Zurich or at the Festival Hall,
and people in the company would say, where were you last night,
John? Pity you weren't here, rattling good performance, you missed
something.

'I was there most nights. I used to drive down to our house in

Wiltshire after the show on Friday night and I'd quite often get the train back Saturday afternoon to see the curtain up and maybe stay for one act before catching the train back. Very often I came back Sunday afternoon for a concert. It was a seven-day week. The fact is that institutions function well if there is somebody around who will give the time to drive them.'[33] 'He would occasionally have a Saturday off,' his wife confirmed.

Like Webster, he spoke no languages, but Patsy had spent three years with a United Nations agency in Rome and she made the Italian singers feel at home. Tooley displayed neither passion nor colour. He seldom raised his voice. He inherited from Webster a certain emollience, which allowed old lags and abuses to flourish. Ingpen, arriving at the Met, found tighter financial control and greater efficiency than she had left behind. Stars were paid much the same in both houses – Joan Sutherland was on five thousand dollars a night – but staff earned less at the Met and the backstage was better run. 'At Covent Garden, there was always trouble with stagehands,' she reported.

Tooley promoted William Bundy to Technical Director, in charge of all backstage operations. Bundy did not improve with age, nor did the backstage ambience. When he was finally obliged to retire at 65 in 1976, Tooley brought him back for the next six years as a freelance lighting director, regardless of his choleric disposition. 'This was a family,' said Tooley. 'If Bill Bundy blew his top, someone would rally round. The tempo was extreme. I took the view that we would get people out of their problems, and we did.' His doctrine of mutually assured assistance added a new dimension to the Websterian family myth. An organism that was always inward looking now grew dangerously inbred. People invested their entire lives in the house. Many looked no further for emotional fulfilment. Bundy's first wife, the stage manager Stella Chitty, found her second husband in the orchestra: a percussionist called Jack Wakely who, on stressful first nights, would knock on Tooley's door an hour before curtain up, spread a towel on his desk and administer a vigorous back massage to the retitled General Director. The family, in Tooley's view, was the essence of the house, a cause to be championed in its own right. Assured of its importance, it became, in parts, a breeding ground for slackness and indiscipline. In any clash between a family member and an outsider, Tooley would support his staff against all but the most exalted artists.

He missed little that went wrong, but his eye for an artist was never the equal of Webster's. His was not a quicksilver mind, and he turned for advice to the senior European intendants – Rolf Liebermann in Hamburg and Paris and Günther Rennert in Munich. Not that they could have helped him much, for his job was tougher than theirs. Where German houses would shut for a week before a new production, Covent Garden had to open every night or go bust. Where the French government always bailed out the Opéra, the ROH lived from one Arts Council grant to the next, in hope and in fear.

Tooley's was the loneliest post in operadom and he held his cards close to his chest. He gave up strong drink after his hepatitis and was to be found most intervals at the mirror end of the Crush Bar, sipping a small glass of wine and conversing with staff and patrons. He mingled with the upper classes and affected a cut-glass accent but never passed for one of the privileged. Unlike Webster, he was not a man to advertise his desires and frustrations.

'I don't think anybody ever got to know John,' said Paul Findlay, who spent twelve years as his assistant. 'What he adopted was a position where he listened. Few of his ideas were original. It was always a question of whom he had talked to last.'[34]

'He had, it was often said, a cushion-quality: the tendency to display the impression of the last chap who had sat on him,' said his orchestra manager, Bram Gay. 'It was an impression only; no one sat on John Tooley . . . He steered his own course in the end.'[35]

The inhibited, dedicated general director deserved some luck in the deadly months that followed Peter Hall's departure. He was rewarded that winter by a gift from heaven. A New Zealand soprano who had been knocking around London for three years was taken on to the staff by Colin Davis. Tested as a Flower Maiden in *Parsifal* and Xenia in *Boris Godunov*, she swanned off for the summer to sing the Countess in *Marriage of Figaro* at Santa Fe, New Mexico. She returned home to hear that Colin Davis wanted her as the centrepiece of John Copley's hurriedly recast *Figaro*. 'John absolutely didn't want me to do the part,' said Kiri te Kanawa. 'He'd seen me at the Opera Centre and knew I was a lazy, useless woman, and he didn't think I was old enough.'[36] Davis, however, was enchanted by the tonal purity of this half-Maori beauty (with whom he was once caught by his secretary wrestling on the floor),[37] and Copley agreed to start rehearsing her six weeks before the rest of the cast, led by the experienced Geraint Evans, Reri Grist, Victor Braun

and Patricia Kern. So home-made a production, designed by
Stefanos Lazaridis, would need a touch of magic to achieve ignition
and that was where Kiri came in.

'At the first orchestral rehearsal,' recalled Lilian Watson who was
making her début as Barbarina, 'when I heard her sing "Dove Sono",
it was obvious she was destined for big things. There was a rustle in
the pit as the sound hit them, an intake of breath.'[38] Victor Braun,
who bought her a drink at the Nag's Head, warned Kiri that she was
going to have a terrific success. 'Don't talk stupid,' she retorted, 'I'm
only a student – I'll do my best.'[39] She was a plain-spoken girl who
lived with her Australian husband in the stockbroker belt and
commuted daily to Covent Garden by train. There were no starry
pretensions to Kiri te Kanawa.

On the night of 1 December 1971, Davis struck up a scintillating
Figaro overture, asserting his own credentials as the finest English
Mozartian since Beecham. With 'Porgi amor' Kiri 'knocked the
place flat'.[40] Ovations mounted with each successive aria. Serene,
beautiful and tonally secure, she was framed by Davis's limpid,
unforced rhythms, so different from Solti's adrenalized interpretations. By the time she reached 'Dove sono' in Act Three the applause
was overwhelming and Davis paused to allow her a curtain call, but
Kiri had promised Copley not to break the action. Her husband, Des,
spent most of the evening in the Crush Bar, settling his nerves with
gin-and-tonics.

Next morning, the press united in proclaiming the birth of a star
– 'a teenage goddess' – in *Times* hyperbole. Philip Hope-Wallace
struck a note of caution, averring that Kiri 'is too fresh an artist' for
the Countess role and Desmond Shawe-Taylor suggested that she
was not a full-grown Sutherland sensation but a promising talent 'on
the threshold of international fame'. A day or two later Kiri was
congratulated in the corridors by one of her contemporaries, Teresa
Cahill. 'I bet Karajan will be ringing you soon,' giggled Cahill. 'He
already has,' said Kiri.[41]

For Colin Davis and Covent Garden the rewards were immense.
The new music director had staked his shirt on an ingénue and given
her perfect musical support. He could not, said Andrew Porter, 'have
made a better start' and there was much else to suggest spring in the
air. Davis launched a clearout of what he regarded as deadwood in
the chorus, orchestra and company of singers. 'Those of us who
were over fifty were gradually being phased out,'[42] noted Michael

Langdon. 'You can stay here and do nothing,' Davis told the valuable John Lanigan, 'but I have nothing for you.'[43] David Ward, the English Wotan, was pensioned off. Amy Shuard, the cockney Turandot, was cut to once a season; she died soon of a heart attack, aged fifty.

For those singers who remained on the payroll, 'working at Covent Garden had become just a job'.[44] Kiri te Kanawa, as soon as her contract was up in 1973, cut loose and joined the jet-set. Typically for her time, she showed little social or emotional attachment to the company and its members. 'I don't ever remember partying,' she said. 'It was always straight home and settle down. I had an hour and a half to travel home to Esher.'[45]

Nor did she deepen her affinity with the music director. 'Colin had a family and children,' she said, 'he didn't really have time to expand. He had a bigger life outside. For him, it was like coming into work. Tooley was a good friend to me, if you can say there are friends in this business.'

Slow and late in learning roles, she required intensive tuition, especially in German operas where she (like Davis) felt least secure. It was with Solti that she formed her warmest association, studying the Strauss heroines. 'I turned myself inside out for Solti,' she recalled. 'I knew I could learn so much from him. I used to ring up and say, can I come round for a cup of tea? His door was always open.'

Unlike Davis, who was a specialist conductor and introspective man, Solti was an all-rounder and all-too-human maestro, who chased the nubile Kiri around his studio and pinned her to the couch.

'What about Valerie?' quavered Kiri.

'She will never know,' panted Solti.

'Yes she will,' said the spunky singer, 'because I'll bloody tell her.'[46] Her finest recordings, including *Figaro*, were conducted by Solti.

Covent Garden was no longer a magnet for Anglophone singers, or even the destination of choice. Lilian Watson, who spent four years with Welsh National Opera before her ROH début, never contemplated joining the staff. 'John Tooley did his best to make you feel welcome,' she said. 'He would always be there at the start of a rehearsal period, greeting everybody by name, how are you, nice to see you. The doormen would also recognize you, which is more than can be said for Vienna. It was a good place for a British singer to come home to, but it was not home.'[47] In the modern world, there was no reason to regard Covent Garden as more than a mainline station on the singing circuit, neither a sacred cause nor a special case.

Janet Baker, another glowing attraction with deep English roots, felt much the same. She maintained a stubborn independence and, though many of her finest hours and her final nights were seen at Covent Garden, she felt no sentimental attachment to the place. 'I think the House itself is a complete coquette,' she wrote. 'She was quite prepared to give herself to the production team today, she lets the stage staff believe they own the stage: we have the dressing-rooms and that part of the stage in between the dropped curtain and the pit, and the audience is allowed the foyers and the seats. But really, she belongs to herself.'[48]

The arts under Edward Heath were pushed off the Cabinet table and into the red box of a second-rank minister, the Paymaster General. Viscount Eccles was a collector of artefacts and watercolours and a patron of the English potters Bernard Leach and Lucie Rie. A bluff, well-heeled amateur known to back-benchers as 'Smarty-boots' for his immaculate turnout, David Eccles believed the arts should help pay their own way. He introduced entry charges at museums and refused to oppose the imposition of VAT on theatre and concert tickets, pushing up prices by a tenth and more. In his second year, however, Eccles achieved a twenty-five per cent increase in the Arts Council's grant and while much of the money was consumed by stagflation it nonetheless signified an extension of Tory support for the Keynesian principle.

Having landed extra money, Eccles was not going to leave it in the lap of Arnold Goodman, whom he disliked and mistrusted. Goodman had been too close to his Labour predecessor Jennie Lee and maintained a direct line to his own Prime Minister. Eccles saw him as a threat and a snob, squandering public money on a handful of London causes. He called for the largesse to be spread among the shires, with special emphasis on amateur groups and English craftsmanship. 'We had to get rid of Arnold Goodman,' explained Eccles. 'He didn't want to do anything outside London.'[49]

'Arnold didn't want to go,' recalled his successor, 'but Eccles would not give him another term.'[50] One morning, Patrick Gibson received a call from the Paymaster General at his office in the

Financial Times. 'Your name came to me while I was in the bath,' said Eccles winningly. 'Don't touch it,' said the FT chairman Oliver Poole, on being told that Gibson had been dangled the Arts Council. Gibson, imbued with a sense of public duty and a passion for the arts, could not refuse.

No one was made happier by his acceptance than Garrett Drogheda, who counted Gibson among his most trusted associates and looked forward to a restoration of Covent Garden's preferential status. Once again, he imagined, the opera house and Arts Council would walk hand in glove to the Treasury. Gibson, however, was as even-handed as he was amiable. Over his five years as chairman, he established a doctrine for distributing subsidy more evenly around the country. As the Arts Council grant trebled – from £11.9 million (1971–2) to £37.15 million (1976-77) – the ROH share fell from twenty to fifteen per cent (£1.6 to £4.3 million). In real terms, with inflation raging and the pound unsteady, the value of its state grant declined by almost one-fifth.

'Pat Gibson was a wonderful chairman, absolutely fair at all times,' said an ROH board member, somewhat ruefully.[51] Drogheda suppressed his regrets and remained on friendly terms. 'I had no trouble from Garrett,' said Gibson. 'It was Max Rayne at the National Theatre who used to send me robust letters, ending: "However, very best regards".'[52]

There was one large trump left in Drogheda's hand. No sooner had Arnold Goodman left the Arts Council than Drogheda lured him on to the board of Covent Garden, where he served for ten years. The fact that Goodman was also a director of English National Opera and, from 1977, its chairman, did not appear conflictual to this most impartial of lawyers who, at one and the same time, represented the Conservative, Labour and Liberal party leaders. What Drogheda sought from Goodman was influence and access; what Goodman expected in return was pride, pomp and a feeling that he was central to every institution and individual that mattered.

With his usual skill, Goodman left no fingerprints. His file in the ROH archives is completely empty, cleared as if by order. His notes to Drogheda were sparing and his attendances infrequent. 'I frankly regarded the activities of the board as almost entirely irrelevant to the conduct of the opera house,' wrote Goodman in his memoirs. 'I found the discussions long-winded and rarely reaching any conclusion that was reflected in action. They bore a resemblance to an expensive engine that had no transmission to the wheels. It chugged on pointlessly at tea-time meetings where the only compensation originally was the excellent smoked salmon sandwiches. I can trace my increasing irregularity of attendance to the disappearance of the expensive sandwiches and their replacement by an inferior paste.'[53]

Goodman was being, as ever, over-modest and casual with the truth. 'Arnold's qualities were not political,' said Claus Moser. 'He occasionally brought crucial wisdom to difficult issues, such as: was this a moment when we should write to the minister? Later, when we had a threatened strike in the orchestra, Arnold was chairman of ENO. I attended his negotiations and he attended ours, and there I saw his sheer brilliance as a negotiator. He always referred to Covent Garden as "The Opera House" even when he was at ENO. But Arnold was a natural chairman – he was not made by God to sit on somebody else's board. And by the way, we never had smoked salmon sandwiches.'[54]

Goodman's chief attraction to Covent Garden was his unrivalled range of contacts. The ROH was seriously short of money. Large sums were needed to sustain the international standards that had been so painfully attained. In addition, an opportunity that loomed just around the corner would require more capital than the company had ever seen. The Government and Greater London Council were planning to remove the fruit and vegetable market from Covent Garden to the other side of the river. The market was unsightly and noisome, they said, a traffic hazard and a blight on London's tourist potential.

These were the official reasons for vacating the site. There were other, less trumpeted grounds. Britain was in the grip of a property boom as investors, fearful of industrial disorder, put their money into bricks and mortar. Contracts and kickbacks were flying like confetti, and politicians of both ruling parties became tainted. Labour's fiefdom in north-east England was comprehensively corrupted by a crooked architect, John Poulson. The Tories lost their Home Secretary, Reginald Maudling, over business deals with a property developer. The need to clear Covent Garden was dictated as much by investment potential as by any urge for modernization.

Committees had been discussing the removal of the market since 1961 and Drogheda spoke up in the House of Lords to demand a share of the free space for the Royal Opera House. He took a

Commons committee around the building, demonstrating its dangerous squalor, and he impressed on ministers the inefficiency of having operas rehearsed in an East End cinema and the ballet in a West London gym. Finally, he wrote directly to Robert Armstrong 'asking him whether he could possibly help us over the acquisition of the Royal Opera freehold,' and recognizing that 'he will probably be furious'.[55] In January 1974, just as the property boom burst, Drogheda was told that the ROH would be allowed to acquire the great Floral Hall and some extra land – but there would be no extra money for development.

This was cork-popping news, intoxicating and hazardous in equal measure. With enough room to accommodate both companies and the chance to turn a Victorian opera house into a modern marvel, Covent Garden could outshine the new National Theatre which had been built and furnished to the last teaspoon from public money. Covent Garden, however, would have to find private money, and where it might come from was unclear. The ROH board was dominated by airy intellectuals of another era, great minds and grey beards. Drogheda had recruited the groceries baron John Sainsbury, who had given sterling support to Madam's ballet school since marrying the dancer Anya Linden, but he was now the only businessman on board. Sainsbury, in his early forties, was also chairman of the Friends of Covent Garden, the 11,000-strong educational and social group whose president was Marion Thorpe, Lord Harewood's ex-wife now remarried to the Liberal Party leader. The Friends could be counted on for small change and gentle suasion, but ten million pounds would be needed for renewing the house and the need was pressing. So Drogheda did what noblemen have done since the dawn of time. He turned to his Jews.

His first lunch with Goodman as a director dealt with tapping rich Jews to support Covent Garden. Goodman himself was persuaded to donate a set of chairs to the orchestra. His friend Max Rayne sent a thousand-pound cheque.[56] Another Goodman crony, Harry Kissin, set up and chaired a Redevelopment Trust. A Danzig-born lawyer who made his fortune trading commodities, Kissin was a member of Harold Wilson's inner circle, along with the banker Siegmund Warburg and the raincoat maker, Joe Kagan. Kissin in 1973 made himself unpopular in the City by taking over the blueblood merchant bank Guinness Mahon. He earned further notoriety at the Royal Opera House by having legal papers served on him in his box one night. Drogheda gave Kissin a seat on the board but held him at arm's length, sending Ken Davison to deal with him on Trust matters.

Drogheda was not conventionally anti-Semitic in the manner of his City contemporaries. Warburg, who introduced short lunches and Eurobonds to the Square Mile, had been snubbed by the banking set and saw his firm dubbed 'the nightclub' for carrying on working past five o'clock. Jews were excluded from old firms and golf clubs. 'We can't have the likes of Paul Hamlyn in British publishing,' sniffed the patrician Harold Macmillan of a bumptious refugee.

Drogheda eschewed such prejudices. He was proud to call Solti his friend and to embrace such civilized, establishmentarian Jews as Goodman, Berlin and Claus Moser. But he was wary of self-made Jews and could not fathom their motives. 'Never forget, George,' he lectured the thrusting young chairman of Maples fusty furniture store, 'what is an Englishman's by privilege, the Jew has to acquire by merit.'[57]

George Whyte was one of a new breed of quick-thinking entrepreneurs who were shaking up the retail sector. Hungarian by birth, he grew up in the Blitz and got hooked on Covent Garden as a fourteen-year-old schoolboy on seeing the City Ballet of New York in 1946. 'Covent Garden was my alma mater,' said Whyte.[58] A well-rounded man, who studied piano and science in London and Paris, he founded his own design business, was taken over by Maples and so energized the firm that in seven years its shares shot up elevenfold. Still in his thirties, he asked if he could help the opera house.

Drogheda invited Whyte to dinner at Lord North Street with Bernard Delfont, the television magnate. Over coffee and cigars, Drogheda said, 'I wonder if you could help me with something? I've got the Queen Mother coming to this Gala and we're about six thousand pounds short. Can you think of a couple of chaps who might like to sit next to Her Majesty in the Royal Box?' Whyte, looking at Delfont, said, 'I will if you will,' and they split the bill. But when the Gala evening came around, Whyte was away skiing. He had no particular desire to meet the Queen Mum, whose views on Jews were known to be reactionary. Whyte told Drogheda he would organize a fundraising drive for the redevelopment, but would need a seat on the board to run it efficiently. Drogheda was aghast at his presumption. A seat on the board, he replied, was an honour bestowed by the Minister in the name of Her Majesty. He could not nominate for such an honour a man he hardly knew. If, after a few years of attending the finance committee and raising lots of money, Whyte would prove himself worthy as an Englishman he might, just might, be co-opted on to the board, but he could not promise anything.[59] Drogheda told Tooley: 'You must get the idea of George Whyte as a Board Member out of your system. I am not willing to consider making him a Member of the Board.'[60] Whyte, mystified and hurt, melted away. Over the next decade, he applied himself to artistic and charitable causes in Switzerland, Israel and the Far East, before making a further, equally futile, effort to save the opera house.

Salesman that he was, Drogheda was confused by altruism. A Cincinnati businessman called Corbett offered to finance a new production of Gounod's *Faust*, provided its Mephisto could be sung by the American bass-baritone, Norman Treigle. The board was torn between gracious acceptance and total disgust. Goodman threatened to resign if dollars dictated artistic policy. Drogheda asked him to draft a reply, outlining the *amour propre* of the situation. Goodman's letter to the American was a masterpiece of English hypocrisy. Having thanked Corbett for an offer which 'would make it possible for the House to have a new production', he added:

So far as Mr Norman Treigle is concerned, he is, of course, known to us, and his claims would naturally be taken into consideration for any suitable role for which he was qualified and available. We could not, of course, give any further assurance in relation to his employment; nevertheless the Board of Covent Garden will accept with great enthusiasm the proposal on your part to finance the special production referred to and we are indeed most grateful for so generous an offer.[61]

Faust was duly staged in November 1973 with Treigle as Mephisto and the Corbett Foundation paying the bills. Treigle turned out to be a heavy drinker who could not be bothered to rehearse a role he claimed to know. Threatened with the sack if he did not at least attend the general rehearsal, he turned up on crutches. Kiri te Kanawa, who sang Marguerite, was blighted by the tension and the production was roundly condemned. This did not stop the ROH board agreeing to a further gift from Corbett for Donizetti's *L'elisir d'amore* two years later. Sadly, Treigle took an overdose of sleeping pills on top of his whisky diet in February 1975, ending Corbett's involvement in Covent Garden without any point of principle having been established.

It was now painfully clear that the opera house needed new streams of funding. The state would pay the wage bill but not the costs of production. Big business was the obvious target, but there was no strategy involved. Whenever a new season was planned, members of the board and trust would ring around their friends and colleagues, soliciting funds for one show or another. A list of 'corporate members' began to appear at the front of opera and ballet brochures, and fulsome pages of thanks were offered to those 'who made this production possible'. Imperial Tobacco, hemmed with government health warnings, paid for *Un Ballo in Maschera*. Barings, the private bank, and Commercial Union Assurance under-wrote a new *Ring*. Among the steadiest donors were J. Sainsbury Limited, the supermarket chain, and the Linbury Trust of Anya Linden and John Sainsbury, which funded four new ballets in as many years. Without such gifts, the ROH would have been reduced to dull revivals. Yet, essential as fundraising had become, nothing was done to recruit the know-how and purposefulness that American opera houses brought to the serious business of raising money.

To the board's surprise, and admittedly his own, it was John Tooley who came up with the most innovative form of external sponsorship. He and Colin Davis were anxious to attract a younger audience and in the summer of 1971 succeeded in packing the stalls with young faces for a Proms week by ripping out 400 seats and charging cinema prices for *Boris Godunov*. The BBC, on this occasion, covered the deficit. The following year, Tooley persuaded the Midland Bank to fund the summer Proms, which they continued to do for quarter of a century, eager as all banks are to reach a new generation. 'John, it's good for you; it's good for us; let's stay together,'[62] said the Midland chairman, Sir Archibald Forbes.

Students would queue all night for fifty-pence tickets and Sergeant Martin, the commissionaire, crammed seven hundred bodies into the steaming arena. Dress code was suspended. 'I would wear shoes if I were you, madam,' Martin advised one flaky, long-haired blonde, 'you never know what debris there is on our floors.' The Crush Bar sold beer, coffee and rolls at street prices instead of champagne and smoked salmon. Neophytes were lured into the opera house and smitten for life, more perhaps than at any time since the opening euphoria. Tooley, in retrospect, accounted it as one of his two greatest initiatives. In 1975, he extended the scheme to ballet nights in a tent, the 'Big Top', in Battersea Park. There was a heady air of renewal about these improvisations, which persisted throughout the decade. The only objections came from Drogheda, worried about 'upsetting Covent Garden's regular clientele'.[63]

Marshalling the upper crust to support the redevelopment, Drogheda was picky about whose pockets he picked. For the launch banquet, still some years ahead, he would refuse to invite the 'wrong sort of person', ruling out many a new-money millionaire. Sir Charles Clore was one of the wealthiest men in London and a regular at Covent Garden, where he noisily appreciated good singing before departing, blonde on arm, to his table at Annabel's, the place to be seen. Clore was the country's take-over king, the first to agglomerate asset-rich businesses for no reason other than the urge to expand. 'It was a natural part of his make-up to adopt the brutal approach,' said an admirer. 'He was a zealot for money, his grasping for it was a form of gluttony, an appetite which was voracious, never satistfied.'[64] Abandoned by his beautiful wife, Clore vented his frustrations on commercial and sexual conquests. He once told Nureyev how much he admired his single-minded pursuit of wealth: was it possible that a dancer could earn a million a month, tax-free? Clore was not a subtle man, not Drogheda's type, though word was out that, in failing health, he was trying to give away much of his money.

Hearing about the appeal, Clore called his married daughter, Vivien Duffield. 'Have you been invited to this dinner at the Guildhall?' he demanded.

'No,' said Vivien, 'have you?'

'No,' said Clore. 'Pity, because I was looking to do one big thing and we could have done the whole of the development.'

'Rubbish,' said Vivien, 'we've never done anything that big.'

'Well, I'm looking to do something big,' said Clore.[65]

The price of a new building was small beer for the Clores, but Drogheda could not bring himself to ask. To let in a man like Clore would lower the tone, undoing his efforts to bury Covent Garden's plebeian beginnings. He intended to leave the opera house at the summit of society and the centre of national affairs.

Three days into 1973, the ROH mounted the opening and closing nights of a ten-day 'Fanfare for Europe', marking Britain's entry to the Common Market. Acclaimed by Edward Heath as 'our country's greatest achievement',[66] the treaty was welcomed by the business sector and intelligentsia and resented by industrial workers and empire loyalists. It was an act of disunion that inaugurated a year of insurrection as Heath's Government lost its grip on the economy and the unions rose in rebellion. But for the Royal Opera House, representing the establishmentarian view and discarding its little-England antecedents, Europe was the great leap forward. With the Queen in her Box and Heath beaming like a beacon, John Copley and Patrick Garland assembled a night full of stars in a panoply of music and drama. Laurence Olivier, Sybil Thorndike and Judi Dench gave readings; Schwarzkopf, Gobbi, Régine Crespin, Peter Pears, Janet Baker, Geraint Evans and the fresh-voiced Kiri te Kanawa did the singing. 'It was a marvellous evening,' said Heath, in a thank-you note to Kiri, 'and it was a special pleasure to see how naturally the British contribution (in which I include the Common-wealth contribution) dovetailed into the European contribution.'[67] The closing gala was built around ballet and Drogheda impressed upon Kenneth MacMillan the 'great honour that Covent Garden should have been chosen both to open and close the ten day's festivities.'[68] Little did he know that this was the last time that century the ROH would figure at the centre of a national celebration.

A quirk of fate had raised MacMillan from the sloughs of despond. Taken by an art-dealer friend, Jeffrey Solomons, to see a Clint Eastwood film, *Play Misty for Me*, he clicked with another member of the party, an Australian artist called Deborah Williams. He took her to see his ballet, *Triad*, and asked her to sail with him to America on the *QEII*, as he hated flying and was still (as he told Drogheda) 'under my Doctor's supervision'.[69] He also asked to marry her, only to discover that Williams was not yet divorced. She had come to London, working as a waitress and nanny, in order to get over a failed marriage. MacMillan's need for her was so profound that she moved in with him and he, in response, grew in strength and confidence. 'When Deborah came on the scene,' said Tooley, 'he did open up quite a lot. He found in her a very close ally and someone who was feeding him huge emotional support and was also valuable for bouncing off ideas in the way he had done with Lynn Seymour.'

The American trip was unhappy. *Anastasia* was booed and

MacMillan was hounded by Ashton fanatics. 'They followed him down the street as he left the stage door, they screamed and spat at him,' recalled Monica Mason.[70] The arrival of another Soviet defector, Natalia Makarova, added zest to the coming season. Deborah fell pregnant, Makarova danced Juliet to Nureyev's Romeo and a setting of Kurt Weill's *Seven Deadly Sins*, with the Canadian Jennifer Penney in the central role and Lynn Seymour uproariously self-parodying as Greed in one of her obese phases, kept the much-feared critics at bay. Even the death of John Cranko, who choked on his vomit after taking an in-flight sleeping pill, could not cloud MacMillan's golden summer. In August 1973, as Deborah awaited the birth of their daughter, he choreographed a three-act *Manon*. His sights were set ever higher.

Manon was overlong and undercharacterized, maimed by a mid-rehearsal injury to Antoinette Sibley. 'I never knew what her ailment was,' said MacMillan, 'I never knew and I never found out . . . I had to finish it and Antoinette wasn't around, but the whole stimulus for doing it was her.'[71] Determined to deliver on time, he created the rest of the title role on Jenny Penney and reviewers zoomed in on that central weakness. *Manon* was deemed a flop by many critics, none more influential than Clive Barnes, who descended from the *New York Times* to preview the Royal Ballet's next US tour. Barnes, a Londoner and Ashton fan, revelled in his newfound notoriety as 'Butcher of Broadway'. He attacked MacMillan both in print and on the dinner circuit and his views blighted box-office sales. Soon after *Manon* opened in New York, MacMillan learned of a plot to replace it, mid-run, with Nureyev's *Nutcracker*. 'If you take *Manon* off,' he said quietly, 'I'll put the company on a plane and we'll fly home.'[72]

As if to relieve the pressure, MacMillan conjured up *Elite Syncopations*, to ragtime music by Scott Joplin. It was one of the few ballets ever to rock the belly of the Royal Opera House with irrepressible mirth, an instant hit. When the director married Deborah, in the spring of 1974, Peter Wright was best man – a symbol of the peace that seemed to be settling on the company. Even the rumblings of Lynn Seymour, who resented Deborah and was newly pregnant herself, did not greatly ruffle the waters. Seymour went to see MacMillan's psychoanalyst and was dismayed to learn that he never mentioned her. Their detachment grew, and an altogether calmer atmosphere settled at the head of the Royal Ballet.

*

At the Royal Opera, Colin Davis was having a rocky time. After the dream start came a string of disappointments. *Nabucco*, limply cast, demonstrated that he was not much of an early Verdian. *Don Giovanni* was loudly booed. A hangover from Hall's time, it was linked to a planned Davis recording for Philips. Over lunch one Saturday, Tooley and Davis persuaded Peter Brook to direct, but by Monday morning the wily genius had pulled out. The house team of Copley and Lazarides stepped in, investing the production with trivial ideas and a squeaking metal-rod set with huge slats in the floor where singers caught their feet. The cast was weak and local: Peter Glossop, Gwyneth Jones, Geraint Evans, Wendy Fine, Stuart Burrows.

Davis, on opening night, poked his tongue at the booing audience. In a newspaper interview, he showed signs of stress. 'Are they out to destroy me?' he railed.[73] John Pope-Hennessy, queenly director of the Victoria & Albert Museum and an increasingly outspoken board member, described the performance as 'one of the coarsest . . . I had ever heard. It was badly designed, in feeble, derivative, messy sets and was produced with a hideous literalness which would have made the meaning of every syllable evident to an audience of Eskimos . . . Colin Davis' behaviour before the curtain seemed to me undignified and reprehensible .. [Davis] appears (in the few conversations I have had with him) to have the brain of a sparrow, little operatic experience and a minus quantity of taste.'[74]

Davis assured Drogheda that he was 'not in the least despondent'[75] and had found a new helpmeet in the German director, Götz Friedrich, who would produce Peter Hall's intended *Ring* and then stay on as director of productions. His arrival would necessitate a renewal of the music director's contract for a minimum eight years,[76] a prospect that left board members feeling 'very unenthusiastic'.[77] Their spirits were not raised when the experienced Czech producer, Vaclav Kaslik, stormed out before the première of *Tannhäuser* in September 1973. In a letter to Tooley, copied to every arts editor on Fleet Street, Kaslik accused Davis of being a theatrical dilettant: 'Perhaps it will be remembered that in Covent Garden my production of *Pelléas et Mélisande* ran in harmonious collaboration between Boulez and all the cast, until Colin Davis with his production ideas and demands completely broke the production of *Nabucco* and *Tannhäuser*. While Covent Garden has at the head of the artistic management such an untheatrically thinking Colin Davis there will be no place for me here.' Hours later, under invisible pressures, Kaslik withdrew his letter, having 'no desire to harm anyone's personality or integrity'. In a parting note to Drogheda he added: 'The form of communication chosen by Mr Colin Davis was extremely outrageous indeed.'[78] *Tannhäuser* was doomed. Jon Vickers had pulled out of the title role, citing blasphemy. His substitute Richard Cassilly fell sick and was replaced at the last moment by the German understudy Wolfgang Kassel, singing opposite the large American soprano, Jessye Norman. 'Do you happen to know why it was that Kassel was engaged?' demanded Drogheda. 'His voice is far from pleasing, his appearance is totally unconvincing and he is stiff and wooden in his acting.'[79] The performance did little to enhance the conductor's credentials as a Wagnerian and Drogheda decided to leave the next chairman to settle Davis' future. 'He is a strange chap!' said Drogheda to his successor, 'and all I can say to you is jolly good luck.'[80]

Drogheda found Davis opaque and ungracious. 'Colin has so often made the Board feel they had no useful part to play and were simply an impediment in his way,' he complained.[81] He also found MacMillan aloof and Tooley overburdened with detail. He was sixty-three years old and in fine health, but the fun had gone out of being chairman. The country was going to the dogs and his friends were getting out. Andrew Porter, his treasured critic, had gone to write for the *New Yorker* and his twin sister, Sheila, had quit to work for Hurok in New York after incurring MacMillan's displeasure. Drogheda's last mistress had gone off with a flashy conductor and the flunkey who guarded his box was killed in a car accident in the Cromwell Road. Covent Garden was not the same without them.

Having made his decision, he was upset to learn that the succession would not be in his gift, as it had been in Waverley's. Watched by Goodman, the board would have to follow due process. A committee was appointed, headed by Lord Robbins and comprising Goodman, Bonham-Carter and the newly-knighted Sir Claus Moser. Drogheda had a candidate in mind but said nothing for fear of prejudicing his chances. 'Garrett was one of my heroes,' said John Sainsbury. 'I was aware that he thought me helpful and reliable, but I wasn't aware that he thought of me as chairman material – only that the chairmanship wasn't falling out exactly as he would have liked.'[82]

The wheels of selection began to turn. Moser nominated Lord Annan, a Keynes protégé who was one of the best connected men in the country. Goodman and Bonham-Carter favoured the more colourful John Pope-Hennessy, who bestrode the museum world. Robbins donned a worried look and wondered whether it would be fitting for the chief executive of a publicly-funded museum to be chairman of a state-funded opera house. He wrote to the head of the civil service, William Armstrong, seeking clarification. Armstrong, the ultimate authority on mandarin law, wrote back that this would be technically improper since the money for the V&A and the ROH came from the same source. As a matter of principle, however, he added that this had nothing to do with Pope-Hennessy being a civil servant. If, for example, the committee were to pick Claus Moser, who was director of the Central Office of Statistics, there would be no grounds for objection. 'At this point,' said Moser, 'I was removed from the committee.'[83]

For six months, he heard nothing more. Then, one night at a party in June 1973, someone whispered to him that he was to be the next chairman. 'I went straight to see the Prime Minister, Mr Heath,' recalled Moser, 'and he kindly agreed – on condition that my work at the COS came first, which I assured him it would. There is no doubt that his passion for music contributed to his decision.'

Moser was 'surprised and thrilled' beyond words. Having entered the country in 1936 as a 13-year-old Jewish refugee from Berlin, he had grown used to the snubs of outsiderhood and never expected to reach the heart of the English establishment. A wartime officer in the RAF, he was mocked in the mess for being unable to play the piano without a score before him – though he could deliver a Beethoven sonata or Mozart concerto to near-concert standard. His seriousness was the antithesis of English amateurism. There was also a fun-loving side to his character, but it did not dilute the deadly earnest of his middle-European devotion to music and duty.

As an academic, said Moser, 'I never had a new idea in my life. I was a good teacher but I wasn't a great scholar. If I hadn't met Lionel Robbins, who became my greatest friend and put me on the Robbins Committee (for education reform), I would have gone on being a backroom academic.' On the committee, he met Harold Wilson who gave him the keys to the national safe. In 1957, Moser had asked to spend his sabbatical year at the Central Office of Statistics but was turned down 'because I was of German birth and this was a high-security office'. Seven years later, Wilson named him head of the COS. 'I said, "but I was turned down to work there over security clearance". He said, "well I'm asking you to run it as permanent secretary."' That, said Moser, was the moment when he felt he had been accepted. When someone described him as 'the first foreigner to head the opera house', he took it as a compliment.

'I don't know why they appointed me,' said Moser. 'There was no question that music and opera had been at the centre of my life since I was a little boy in Berlin. So if they wanted commitment, they knew they would get it. Secondly, since my profession had been statistics, economics and finance, I think they saw in me somebody who might take an interest in the financial problems. I couldn't have wanted anything more, and I worked very hard at it.'

When the board debated his appointment, the only objection came from John Sainsbury, who argued that Moser was a music buff with no concern for ballet. 'I was a dissenting voice,' Sainsbury admitted, 'in the sense that we wanted the ballet to be looked after. And maybe that did some good, actually. It made Claus try very hard to consider the ballet, even though he was an opera man. It was a fair point to make. When I was on the board I don't remember ever feeling that Claus was not doing enough for the ballet. I remember saying John Tooley's impossible, he's not giving the ballet enough stage time, but no such feelings about Claus.'

Sainsbury had not coveted the chairmanship. He was in the throes of taking his company public in 1974 and, with a young family at home, 'couldn't have entertained it at all'.[84] Moser came to value Sainsbury as 'a superlative board member, probably the most influential'. To boost the ballet, he co-opted Colette Clark, daughter of the art historian and friend of Fonteyn, as the first woman to sit on the ROH board.

Drogheda sounded content with the outcome. 'Claus seems to me an admirable choice,' he assured Pope-Hennessy, 'and I think that his very close links with Whitehall as head of the COS must be immensely valuable, with finance an eternal problem and re-development of such paramount importance.'[85] He went off on a long holiday, leaving Moser to deal with Colin Davis, which he did briskly. Davis was granted a two-year extension with no further talk of renewal until after the *Ring*. Moser also agreed to consider Götz Friedrich, the *Ring* producer, as director of productions, provided he could work within tight budgets. The general financial situation, he told Drogheda, 'terrifies me'.[86]

Securing a real-terms increase in state subsidy was no longer an option, no matter how well Moser wined and dined his political contacts. 'I used to argue that it was an honour for a government to support the arts,' he said, 'I grew up to believe that this was integral to being a decent country.' But the economy was now in freefall. Property prices crashed, taking down a small bank and undermining fiscal confidence. Fuel prices soared after the 1973 Yom Kippur War and the Government began printing petrol ration books. Some £1.2 billion was cut from public spending. The miners worked to rule, aggravating the fuel crisis. When they called an all-out strike, Heath imposed a three-day working week, then called an election under the slogan, 'Who Governs Britain?' The question itself exposed his impotence. Ministers went on the BBC's 'Today' programme, telling the nation to brush its teeth in the dark and share bathwater with family and friends. Oxford Street lit its windows with candles and storm lamps. Theatres went dark half the week.

Heath lost the February 1974 election by 297 seats to Wilson's 301. Having failed to entice Jeremy Thorpe's Liberals into a coalition, he went to Buckingham Palace to submit his resignation. 'Come along, Robert,' he barked at Armstrong after leaving the royal presence. 'I'm sorry, Mr Heath,' said the perfect civil servant, 'I must wait here for the Prime Minister.'

Wilson formed a minority Government and, in an October poll, won an overall majority of three. Having bought off the miners, he saw inflation rise by twenty per cent in a year. Unemployment topped one million for the first time since the war and the International Monetary Fund threatened to call in a loan unless savage curbs were imposed on state spending. Wilson gave up in April 1976, making way for his avuncular Chancellor, James Callaghan, but the Liberal-backed Labour Government was never stable and dying MPs had to be trundled in on stretchers to save it from defeat. Amid perpetual crisis, Covent Garden kept its contacts alive. 'Harold Wilson we only asked to ballet,' reflected Moser, 'because he only liked one ballet, so he came each year to *Swan Lake*. Jim Callaghan did his duty; Roy Jenkins and Denis Healey came more often.' Thorpe, the Liberal leader, had to retire when charged with attempted murder. He was acquitted, but ruined; his defence solicitor was, needless to say, Arnold Goodman.

The new minister for the arts was, promisingly for Covent

Garden, none other than Jack Donaldson, Drogheda's best friend. Donaldson had many friends, among them Lord Gibson, chairman of the Arts Council, who gave him land to build a house on his Sussex farm. He was not much of a minister, however, and was putty in the hands of departmental officials. 'Lord Donaldson is being paid by the tax-payer,' thundered the Heritage conservator Hugh Leggatt, 'and if he does not understand what he is talking about he should resign.' The only mark left by 'weak, tired, sweet and affectionate'[87] Jack Donaldson in three years was a Heritage Fund that he set up primarily for the purpose of giving Covent Garden a million pounds towards redevelopment. In retirement, Donaldson returned to Covent Garden to help his wife, Frankie, write a glowing account of the opera house that was published by another of his good friends, George Weidenfeld.

Gibson also returned to Covent Garden, rejoining the board after giving up the Arts Council in 1977, weary of the fruitless struggle and the gravelly zeal of his Yorkshire-accented secretary-general, Roy Shaw. Gibson preferred his deputy secretary-general, Angus Stirling, whom he hired to run the National Trust and co-opted on to the Covent Garden board. The connections between giver and receiver were still cosy, but neither man had much success in squeezing extra cash from the Arts Council. With the best will in Whitehall, there was no money to be had, and no notion of how to raise the country from its doldrums. The only sector to thrive was British pop music which, for the first time since the Beatles, captured the moment with the punk phenomenon, along with approximately one-quarter of the global music market.

The nightly news in those dark years was usually led by a live report from ACAS, the Arbitration, Conciliation and Advisory Service, which stepped into industrial disputes and came up with compromises that carefully avoided long-term solutions. The more ACAS intervened, the more disputes there were. Kenneth MacMillan, in hospital for an operation on his foot, survived a catering strike and lived on lettuce and salad cream. The National Theatre was under union siege from the night it opened in October 1976. Dissension spread to Covent Garden, where Tooley shrank from confrontation and adopted an ACAS outlook, giving ground to increasingly aggressive stage and musicians unions. The arch procrastinator had given way to the generic mediator. 'The first strike I ever saw was in Australia,' said Antoinette Sibley. 'We never had that sort of thing at the Garden. But in the final rehearsal that Anthony (Dowell) and I did of Rudolf's *Nutcracker*, the orchestra just put down their instruments in the middle and walked out.'[88]

The epoch of post-war positivism was buried on 17 July 1974, the night of Drogheda's farewell gala. Fonteyn, Nureyev, Ashton, Gobbi, Solti, Kiri, Sibley, Dowell, Makarova and Davis studded the bill. Goodman packed the brochure with adverts from his best clients, including Rupert Murdoch and his soaraway *Sun*, the proceeds going to the ROH Benevolent Fund. Jennie Lee read an interminable eulogy. 'Then Garrett spoke. He was not the least sentimental. He was the perfect paradigm of patrician ease. He was willowy, smiling, devil-may-care, casual; yet all the time absolutely controlled in what he said and his manner of delivery. Every word was audible and to the point. He was his usual mischievous self; quite cheeky to the Queen, telling her that now she had found the way he hoped she might make a habit of patronizing the opera, yet respectful at the same time. He even hiccuped into the loud speaker slung around his neck, apologizing for the surprisingly amplified sound. Now no non-gent would ever ride supremely over that sort of incident.'[89]

Prince Philip lodged a private protest over the *lèse-majesté* but Drogheda was unrepentant. He bowed to no one in his own realm, and no one would ever rule Covent Garden as he had done. He awoke next morning with 'a strange sense of emptiness'.[90] Weeks later he suffered a second shock when Gibson replaced him as chairman of the *Financial Times*. Drogheda was disconsolate. A life that had been full day and night now loomed empty. He vacated his house in Lord North Street, which belonged to the FT, and moved to the country, commuting to Covent Garden to assist with fundraising and join Moser in deputations to senior ministers. Moser counted on him to raise ten million pounds and help contest a raucous campaign by Covent Garden residents to block the project. The original scheme incorporated an underground car-port and an arched shopping arcade, not unlike Vienna's. Drogheda staunchly supported his successor. He remained an imposing figure, and when he strode through the door flunkeys scurried to obey his commands.

Asked in a valedictory radio interview if he was optimistic about the company's future, he sounded hesitant. 'It's like saying, are you optimistic about the future of Britain,' mused Drogheda. 'I . . . don't know. To say unequivocally Yes I was would be perhaps a little bit foolhardy at the present time, because there are so many divisive forces at work and we are faced with such grave economic problems here. I am quite certain that talent exists at Covent Garden, and I think it would be a major tragedy, for all the effort and work which has been put into building up the place over these years since the war . . . to say that all this is to be set to naught would be terribly sad, and I myself do not think that opera and ballet as art forms are going to die.'[91]

Moser's enthusiasm for the arts appeared insatiable. In twenty years on the board, he attended two thousand performances. His happiest moment, he said, was a compliment from Karl Böhm, the octogenarian Straussian and unregenerate ex-Nazi. Delighted to discover an English opera house whose chairman spoke German and played music, he patted his host on both cheeks and said, 'Herr Moser, sei wie Sie sind – stay the same as you are.'

With the change of chairman, Tooley had an opportunity to assert greater executive authority. He failed to do so, inhibited as much by his years in Webster's shadow as by Moser's unsuspected vigour. The erudite, short-fused academic did not tolerate fools or trust much to chance. He decided to be 'very hands-on, perhaps too much so',[92] talking to Tooley daily and meeting him at least four times a week. A gregarious man, he invited the Tooleys – along with the Gibsons, the Armstrongs and others of the Covent Garden in-crowd – to share his summer holidays at a chalet his Swiss wife, Mary, had inherited in Arosa. 'I liked John enormously from very early on and thought we got on terribly well,' said Moser. 'I said any number of times to Mary when we had difficulties, the great thing is I always enjoy going in to see John, or ringing him up and being with him.'

Tooley was more circumspect about his second chairman. Early in Moser's tenure, he reported to his assistant, Paul Findlay, that they had enjoyed a frank exchange of views. 'We agreed that we are not the same sort of person,' said Tooley, 'but we respect each other and can make a go of it.'[93]

The tide turned for Colin Davis in June 1974, not with the *Ring* but with a classic never previously seen at Covent Garden. *La clemenza di Tito* was Mozart's last stage work, shelved for a century and a half after initial success. With Janet Baker as the dominatrix Vitellia and

Davis teasing out subtleties in one of Mozart's thinner scores, the production was cheered to the echo and exported to La Scala, Milan, where Davis was hailed as a master-restorer. (Tooley was terrified that he would get booed by the notorious claques.)

Six months later came *Das Rheingold* and *Die Walküre*. The third *Ring* segment, *Siegfried*, was delayed by a year for economic reasons and the apotheotic *Götterdämmerung* was put back until September 1976. The delay worked in favour of Davis, whose authority grew through the slow unfurling. 'My God, this is going to be an appalling *Ring*,' was the initial orchestral reaction; but by the first repetition of the full cycle players found 'we believed in him; he had developed a feeling for it, and paced it well.'[94] Andrew Porter, returning from New York to review the climax, had nothing but admiration for the conductor. 'Not since Kempe in the 'fifties have I heard a *Götterdämmerung* in Covent Garden conducted with so apt a blend of naturalness and passion; with power and eloquence in the orchestral playing but no training of spotlights, as it were, on individual instrumental marvels or the conductor's artfulness; with buoyant "breathing" support for the singers, alert, not dictatorial.'[95]

The production was another matter. Porter called it 'a disaster, scenically, dramatically, and therefore – since the elements cannot be separated – musically.' Getting personal, he added: 'I think indignation is called for – indignation first of all with the Covent Garden Board of directors. Did they really sit down, talk to Friedrich, look at (Josef) Svoboda's preliminary sketches and say: Yes, that's just the kind of *Ring* the Royal Opera House needs?'[96] The notice appeared, unusually, on page three of the *Financial Times*. Moser found it 'deeply upsetting' and complained to Drogheda,[97] who shrugged wearily.

It appears that no plan for the *Ring* was ever shown to Tooley or to the Board. Friedrich was not a man who liked to be second-guessed. An apostle of the doctrinaire Walter Felsenstein, whose collectivist ideals conformed with East German Marxism, Friedrich skipped West from Berlin's Komische Oper in 1972 without appreciably altering his operatic orientation. He became chief regisseur at the Hamburg State Opera and chief proponent of the 'progressive' approach to opera production, a *Weltanschauung* that employed dark backgrounds, industrial technology, obscure dialectics and occasional political inferences. At Bayreuth, he had the chorus give a clenched-fist Marxist salute in *Tannhäuser*. 'The opera of the bourgeoisie,' he said, 'too often did, and still does, ignore true social relationships both in the works and, so far as such relationships are necessary, between stage and audience.'[98]

At Covent Garden he harangued the chorus for an hour with philosophical abstractions, but did not seem overly concerned by a loss of visual coherence from one scene to the next. Don't bother your heads with where the story takes place, he told the singers: the stage is the world and that's all one needs to know. 'To open up the drama of the *Ring*, not to encapsulate it,' was his aim. 'Not to encircle its ideas, but rather to offer them up as questions; not to iron out the variety of Wagner's thought process but to present it in all its contradictions – these are among the objects of our production.'[99] His inconclusiveness appealed powerfully to the contemplative Davis, who defended Friedrich with great vigour. 'It's all very well to say, go back and do what Wagner wanted,' Davis declared, 'but what he wanted wasn't really practical; it couldn't be done. Wagner himself wasn't successful in staging it the way he imagined it . . . So you're forced to do something else. And as the Ring is essentially an opera of ideas, it doesn't really depend on the physical facts of dragons or people riding horses through clouds. This is all poetic nonsense, and can be done only in one's own imagination.'[100]

Not everyone disliked Friedrich's *Ring*. The modernist critic Peter Heyworth found it 'the most illuminating production of the *Ring* I have seen' and Philip Hope-Wallace, who had endured more *Ring*s than any man in England, was prepared to believe that 'it may yet become clearer'. Among the cast, the New Zealander Donald McIntyre stood out as Wotan, but Helge Brilioth's Siegfried and Berit Lindholm's Brünnhilde were fast forgotten.

Those who visited Bayreuth in the summer of 1976 for the centennial *Ring*, produced by Patrice Chéreau and conducted by Boulez, brought home reports of an austere beauty and intellectual unity beside which the Friedrich effort appeared muddled and provincial. The Chéreau *Ring* would be filmed in thirteen parts and serialized on television the world over, the first known instance of an opera being made into soap. Covent Garden, meanwhile, made do with the Friedrich version for years to come, unable to afford anything better. Both Tooley and Moser counted it, somewhat ruefully, as a highlight of their epoch. Friedrich, said Paul Findlay, 'brought a level of staging we hadn't seen at Covent Garden. He unified the four works and did a lot of damage to the theatre in terms of technical time. His style of working was not what this country wanted but it was stimulating.'[101] Davis maintained that 'the Ring we did with Götz Friedrich was really revolutionary, nothing like that had been seen at Covent Garden ever before and it resulted in boos and cheers, and more boos and more cheers. But it released Covent Garden from the conventional setting, and in that sense I think we did something useful.'[102]

'Colin always needed a partner and thought he had found one in Götz,' said Findlay. Moser asked Friedrich to become director of productions. The German declined, citing pressures of work in Hamburg. They settled on a reduced role as Principal Producer for the next four years. 'Unfortunately,' noted Tooley, 'this became little more than a title, and he made no input to our deliberations on planning and casting.'[103] In 1981, Friedrich became head of the Deutsche Oper in West Berlin, a taxing position that he held for the rest of the century. He remained, nonetheless, the producer of choice at Covent Garden, even after a violent falling-out with Davis over *Idomeneo*, where the conductor bridled at his thoughts on Mozart and Isaiah Berlin in the boardroom demolished them in a devastating display of wit and erudition. The satirists at *Private Eye* kept up the attack on the interventionist director. Why did the Germans lose the war? asked the *Eye*. Because it was over-produced.

Davis, growing in confidence, turned to *Peter Grimes*, the crucible of British opera, and deconstructed it. There was too much pity, he felt, in the version enshrined by Peter Pears, and not enough anger. Davis, with a young Australian director Elijah Moshinsky, and Jon Vickers in the pivotal role, outraged the dying composer by stripping *Grimes* of his constraints. 'The violence that is overt and latent in *Peter Grimes*,' said Davis, 'the whole way that Peter defies the world – there is a famous line of his, "this is whatever day I say it is" – is the arrogance of a frantic mind which is on the edge of the abyss. Vickers was an amazing theatrical animal. He was physically frightening. He embodied for me Peter Grimes, and I have never done it since because I can't see what I can do without him. I'm sure Ben Britten didn't very much approve of what we did but it only shows that a composer doesn't always know the resilience of the pieces he has created.'[104]

'To be on stage with Vickers was fantastic,' said Teresa Cahill, who played one of the nieces. 'He gave off so much electricity you didn't want to get closer than eight feet of him.'[105]

Vickers played *Grimes* as pure monster. 'I believe Benjamin Britten saw an opportunity here,' he said. 'In his anxiety to win sympathy and compassion for the homosexual world, he plunged into the whole psychology of human rejection . . . In doing so, he created a work of art so great that to continue to portray it in this cameo, almost chamber-like way, limiting it to the experience of one man in a situation, was not doing the work justice . . . This is the story of mankind's anguish, not a human being, nor a petty little group of feminists or homosexuals or Hasidic Jews – nothing like that! It's majestic, and I don't think that it was all recognized.'[106]

The motivating force of Davis's directorship was modernization, freshening up familiar works and expanding the repertoire with novelties. He commissioned four world premières, two by rising talents and the others by established composers. *Taverner* by Peter Maxwell Davies and *Thérèse* by John Tavener were half-baked. *We Come to the River* by Hans Werner Henze aroused higher hopes, but the composer was in an ultra-Marxist phase and the outcome was pure agit-prop. Originally titled 'The General' and then 'The Privates', it was rudely referred to internally as 'The General's privates come to the river'. There were fifty-eight artists on stage, and sometimes fewer heads in the house. To cheer up his colleagues, the tenor Robert Tear announced one night that he had good news – 'they're letting them in free'. Then he added: 'but they'll have to pay to get out.'

Tippett's fourth opera, *The Ice Break*, replete with laser beams and inconsequential plot, went down no better. Tippett, whom Davis had unsuccessfully nominated for the Board, complained that Covent Garden had become a 'gala house' and was no place for a composer. Davis tried to talk Vickers and Kiri te Kanawa into reviving *The Midsummer Marriage* and Tooley was personally upset when Tippett's final opera, *New Year*, opened in Houston and Glyndebourne. If Tippett failed to match Britten's fame, it was not for want of friends at the Royal Opera House. He was, however, right to point out that the house now catered to a richer crowd and would never again entertain new work by an unproven British composer. It was in the mid-1970s that seat prices rose beyond the means of school-kids, newlyweds and pensioners. Buying a ticket to the opera was a fifteen-pound investment, as much as many people earned in a week, and a hundred times more than the starting prices. A large part of the audience became socially self-selecting, and the first accusations of 'élitism' were heard. The Board ignored the omens and pushed prices up, season by season, in order to stay solvent.

Tooley kept his door open to composers but could offer little more than tea and sympathy. He displayed no strong tastes in new music, or much else for that matter. When pressed for a preference, he named John Eaton, an American of extreme obscurity. 'I particularly regret that the commissioning programme collapsed,' said Tooley on the eve of retirement, 'and that we were unable to get the new works that were done more firmly into the repertoire; instead, far too often we had to put in pot-boilers to obtain revenue.'[107] He was not alone in this predicament. Peter Hall at the National Theatre told John Osborne, author of *Look Back in Anger*, that he would take off any new play that did not sell ninety per cent of the house. With shrinking subsidy, there was no margin for error. But Hall was able to make room for manoeuvre and it was he, not Tooley, who devised a role for the most original of English composers, taking on Harrison Birtwistle as his music director and getting him to write original music for Tony Harrison's version of *The Oresteia* and arrangements of Mozart and Salieri for the National's greatest hit, Peter Shaffer's *Amadeus*. In the realms of imagination, daring and novelty, the National Theatre outstripped Covent Garden as the Vietnamese out-thought the Americans.

Colin Davis concentrated on pushing out the walls of standard repertoire with early Verdi operas and Meyerbeer's long-unseen and unwisely resuscitated *L'Africaine*. He conducted *The Rake's Progress*, which Webster had coveted back in 1951, as well as a *Lulu* in which Friedrich's American wife, Karan Armstrong, shrieked mercilessly for three interminable acts, confirming many prejudices about the music of Alban Berg. She did herself no favours by telling an evening paper that Lulu was a girl 'who liked her orgasms', and the production was loudly deplored by the Berg scholar, George Perle. It took a further decade for Glyndebourne and the regional companies to demonstrate that *Lulu* could be sung sweetly, affectingly, and to a national television audience.

For all Davis's efforts, Covent Garden was losing creative edge. Glyndebourne, with Pritchard and Bernard Haitink in the pit and

Peter Hall as productions director, mingled sparkling Strauss and Mozart with modernist severities. Glyndebourne's *Rake* had sets by David Hockney which lodged in the memory long after Covent Garden's was forgotten. English National Opera, with Harewood in command, undertook a complete Janáček cycle, as well as much Britten, some French frivolities and one UK première that claimed world attention: the madcap creation of *Le Grand Macabre* by the Hungarian exile, György Ligeti. Mackerras was music director through much of the 1970s, followed briefly by Charles Groves, and then by a duopoly of Mark Elder as music director and David Pountney as director of productions. It was ENO that would pioneer movie-style sex-and-violence with David Alden's chainsaw *Mazeppa* and Jonathan Miller's resetting of *Rigoletto* among New York mafiosi. Harewood gave young directors a licence to thrill. ENO got talked about while Covent Garden got bogged down.

ENO's regional wing seceded in 1978 as Opera North, another hotbed of invention. Singers now had a choice between playing it straight at Covent Garden, or playing it interesting elsewhere. After five 'pretty awful'[108] years, Davis had won the confidence of the audience, only to get blocked by a conservative board. 'It's possible Colin would have liked to be more involved in the daily running of the house,' said Moser. 'He was quite good at meetings. Possibly he felt underused. Colin could take a very intelligent interest in financial problems and was more willing to discuss criticism of performances than some other people in the house.'[109]

But it would have taken a leader of spectacular energy and tyrannical disposition to turn the company around, and Davis was not that kind of man. The single most significant quality that Colin Davis brought to Covent Garden was an almost saintly degree of selflessness. Unlike most music directors, Davis was a stranger to egotism. Where James Levine at the Met excluded any maestro who might show him up, Davis set about engaging the best in his field. Claudio Abbado, music director of La Scala, led the cavalcade with *Un ballo in maschera*, disliking the orchestra but agreeing to return once it had improved. Riccardo Muti, his Milan successor, led Verdi's *Macbeth* and Bellini's *I Capuleti e i Montecchi*. Both had been offered revivals by Solti, but Davis gave them new productions. Solti himself was welcomed back seasonally. Zubin Mehta, Lorin Maazel, Haitink, Edo de Waart and Gennady Rozhdestvensky joined the roster. No opera house on earth could boast such a line-up. Under Davis, Covent Garden became the conductors' house par excellence, the place where top batons proved their mettle. 'Colin had no hang-ups about other conductors,' said Tooley, 'He was so open. When I said we ought to have Carlos Kleiber he said, yes, go get him, it'll be terrific.'[110]

Kleiber was the topping on the cake. Son of the fondly-remembered Erich and every bit as combustible, he pursued a capricious career, cancelling almost as often as he conducted and limiting himself to those few operas in which his father excelled, as if to prove some peculiar oedipal point. He had just walked out on a Hamburg *Falstaff* when Covent Garden, hit by a Levine cancellation at three weeks' notice (he never got to work at the ROH), wondered if he might like to conduct *Der Rosenkavalier*, his father's trademark opera. Kleiber hesitated, issued a catalogue of extraneous demands (including a hotel with a swimming pool, a rarity in central London), and finally turned up in the pit with a scowl on his face, as if daring anyone to compare him to Erich. When Norman Feasey, the elderly repetiteur, greeted him with 'I remember your father', Kleiber's face clouded over and he made no reply.

He devoted the first three-hour rehearsal to the Prelude, a piece of music lasting one minute and a half. Taking their seats for the next rehearsal, several players found slips of paper on their stands – Kleibergrams they called them. 'This bit I think could be more forceful and audible,' read one note. 'Many thanks and kind regards, Yours, C. Kleiber.' His rehearsals were so intense that players took hours to unwind. 'Working with him must always be an electric experience,' said the orchestral manager, Bram Gay. 'The orchestra is never relaxed. The better the work goes the greater the tension because the more fragile the creation . . . An evening with him is one of the great lifetime opportunities for self-realization; not exhausting but liberating. It is something for which we have been waiting and working all our lives.'[111] 'I have to go to the pub with some of the lads and steam off by going over the performance again verbally, over a pint,' said the orchestral leader, John Brown.[112]

After the June 1974 *Rosenkavalier*, an explosive success, Kleiber returned in 1977 for *Elektra*, with Birgit Nilsson, and in 1979 for *Bohème*. He gave no press interviews and could never be guaranteed to turn up, but the posting of his name on a playbill would cause box-office phone-lines to be jammed for hours and some buffs would cross the Atlantic on the off-chance of getting a ticket, so scarce and intense were his appearances. Kleiber never demanded a new production and stepped in twice at short notice for an *Otello* that he refashioned in unforgettable unity. On his nights off, he went to watch other conductors. 'Did you see Lorin Maazel last night?' he teased Tooley, who disliked Maazel. 'Best display of conducting you'll ever see in your life.'[113]

'Shall we do it differently tonight?' he would say on entering the pit, keeping every player on the edge of a seat. 'You dared not look anywhere but at him,' said Teresa Cahill who sang in *Rosenkavalier* and *Elektra*. 'He made tiny variations, so mercurial, always different.'[114] That Covent Garden could attract so rare a performer was a feather in its cap, much envied by the much-richer Met, where Kleiber did not appear until 1988. But Kleiber was never a part of the ROH furniture. Players were warned that he could walk out at the slightest excuse. In 1980 he declared a boycott of London orchestras after receiving poor reviews with the LSO. During his second ROH *Otello*, in 1986, with Placido Domingo and Katia Ricciarelli, he grew visibly bored. Appeals for his return were politely declined. Kleiber never conducted again at Covent Garden. He had left his mark on his father's spot, and that seemed to suffice.

Stability at the ballet was proving chimerical. MacMillan, neurotic and thin-skinned, was irresistibly attractive to the vultures who cluster around every creative being. Fearful of exposing a hint of his genuine vitality in press interviews, his public persona was that of a withdrawn, irritable, vulnerable artist. MacMillan was a thoughtful man trapped in a job that called for action. When the pressures mounted, no one in authority lifted a finger to save him.

Enmity skulked in the wings of his stage. Ashton, adored by dancers and the board, avoided contributing any new work for the first six years of MacMillan's directorship. When he finally produced *A Month in the Country*, on Turgenev's tale of a young tutor who subverts the family he serves, the press panted and fawned as they never did for MacMillan. The board, too, were thrilled that Ashton had chosen a story translated by Isaiah Berlin and music by Chopin that Berlin had suggested. Lynn Seymour danced the central role of Natalya Petrovna, with Dowell as the tutor. The ballet was ravishingly beautiful but neither physically as challenging nor emotionally as draining as *Enigma*. The response, however, was ecstatic. In New York, Clive Barnes acclaimed Ashton as 'our greatest choreographer' and Seymour received the kind of star treatment hitherto accorded only to Fonteyn. Many of the accolades were a thinly coded reproach to MacMillan, whose cable of thanks to Ashton was clipped and cold: 'Your ballet is exquisite. Thank you for doing it.'[115]

Ashton had little more to give. Frustrated by his decline, the anti-MacMillanites led by John Percival of *The Times* – 'poisonous Perce' in ROH parlance – cast around for a gladiator. They began agitating for the directorship to be given to Nureyev, whom MacMillan had neglected in his desire to advance the young pair of Waynes, Eagling and Sleep.

Nureyev let it be known that he was 'very unhappy' with MacMillan. When de Valois and Ashton were in charge, his agent complained, 'there were a considerable number of performances offered to him, and also discussions about new productions, and new works for him, whilst now it becomes an ordinary routine type of engagement.'[116] He remained the most captivating dancer in the west, an enigmatic object of universal curiosity. A reporter from *Women's Wear Daily* asked him, 'Mr Nureyev, I am sure my readers would like a word about your sex life.' Nureyev rose, put on his coat and, turning to leave, said: 'sporadic'.[117]

Fonteyn still shared his limelight. For a Friends of Covent Garden Christmas show, Ken Davison asked Ashton to dance the *Merry Widow* waltz with his ageless muse. 'You mean ballroom dancing?' said Ashton, aghast. 'But that would be impossible – you see, Margot is such a terrible dancer.' In 1976, at the age of fifty-six, she appeared on the ROH stage as MacMillan's teenaged Juliet.

Her shadow fell heavy on the company. Beriosova took to the bottle. Sibley found happiness in a second marriage and spent much of her time in consulting rooms, dogged by a knee injury. MacMillan was unable to cheer them up. He could not give dancers the sense of family and fun that de Valois and Ashton had so freely bestowed.

Against rumblings of dinosaurs and rumours of conspiracy, it seems remarkable that so sensitive a man managed to produce any new work at all. Yet in each season of MacMillan's directorship there was at least one work that stretched the limbs and the imagination in unforeseen directions. 'He felt he had to prove himself with every ballet,' explained his wife. 'There was an atmosphere of terror, a fear of failure. He was severely undermined and depressed, on medication. It shortened his life.'[118]

MacMillan's *Four Seasons*, to music from Verdi's *Sicilian Vespers* suggested by Andrew Porter, was almost too difficult for its dancers, some of whom felt it was as if they were being taught to fly. *Rituals*, set to Béla Bartók's sonata for two pianos and percussion, was derived from the kabuki and kung-fu he had witnessed in Japan. It soared way above the comprehension of *Nutcracker* critics and audiences. Percival in *The Times*, damning with faint praise, warned that MacMillan had returned to the 'confident experimentalism' of his early works. The ballet ended with Seymour, in childbirth, attended by Monica Mason as midwife, exploring uncharted areas of female intimacy.

Under pressure, often under siege, MacMillan found scant sympathy from the company hierarchy. Tooley, though he understood ballet, had little confidence in MacMillan's judgement and was not prepared to fight his cause. 'What he lacked as a creative artist,' said Tooley, 'was the true means of putting a ballet together that was consistently of a high standard from beginning to end.'[119]

MacMillan was keen to revive *The Prince of the Pagodas*, one of the company's nagging failures. Britten had fallen out with John Cranko, its choreographer, and could hardly bring himself to look at the score. MacMillan admired Britten's music and had built one of his early ballets, *Winter's Eve*, upon *Variations on a Theme of Frank Bridge*. To rescue *Pagodas*, though, he would need to make cuts and required the composer's approval. He set off with Tooley for Aldeburgh on what Tooley recalled as 'one of the most uncomfortable days of my life'.

Britten greeted them with: 'I understand you want to make cuts, which passages do you have in mind?'

Whichever page MacMillan pointed to, he exclaimed 'oh, that's one of my favourite stretches in the whole ballet.' When MacMillan asked to remove the *pas de deux* and variations from the finale, Britten snapped, 'why?'

'Because it's too much for the boy,' said the choreographer.

'Really?' said Britten acidly, 'I modelled it exactly on what Petipa did in *Swan Lake*.'

Unable to sway the dying composer, MacMillan turned to one who was dead and safely out of copyright. He decided to set Gabriel Fauré's haunting *Requiem* as a graphic protest against the horrors of war, and included it in the seasonal plans that he set before the board. To his dismay, the proposal was shot down after John Pope-Hennessy sanctimoniously suggested that misrepresentation of a requiem might offend religious feelings among the audience. The museum director seemed unaware that Fauré himself had not been in the least bit religious, and that the board was not constituted to act as a guardian of faith. MacMillan, who had been slapped down once before over *Song of the Earth*, looked to his fellow-directors for support and found none. Neither Tooley nor Davis was prepared to protest, let alone resign.

So MacMillan did what he had done before, staging *Requiem* in Stuttgart to tumultuous acclaim in November 1976, before bringing it home to a pusillanimous Covent Garden, where even sworn enemies were swayed to applaud.

'Given such criticism and administrative burdens,' wrote Tooley, 'everything was pointing to MacMillan's resignation and, in June 1977, it was announced.' Reading this typical Tooleyism, it would appear that nobody, neither Tooley nor the board, bore any degree of responsibility for his departure. MacMillan's resignation was kept under wraps until a successor had been lined up, at which point the press were told that he feared that running the company was ruining his creative flow. There was no mention of the Fauré scandal, which fuelled his decision to quit, nor of two key triggers, never previously disclosed, that directly precipitated his departure.

Early in 1977, MacMillan had to be reminded to look at his contract which was due to expire a year later. He was no good with money and not earning nearly as much in wages and royalties as Ashton who, in his time, had been Covent Garden's top earner. MacMillan's salary was £16,000, one-third less than Colin Davis's; his fee for a full-length ballet was a paltry £850. With a wife and child to support, he needed a pay rise but was told this would be untenable under the Government's income and wages freeze.

Taking professional advice, he formed a company with his wife and became its employee, asking Tooley to hire his services from 'The Partnership'. Tooley consulted the ROH lawyers, Rubinsteins, who dismissed the notion as a 'tax convenience' which breached the pay code and could get the company penalized by the Government.[120] Tooley offered MacMillan a salary of £22,500, but he was hurt by the imputation that he had been trying to cheat the system. He remembered how, as a rising choreographer, he had been forced to take a pay cut while creating *Romeo and Juliet* because it took time off from his duties as a dancer. He felt exploited by Covent Garden and unrewarded.

He was not the only one to feel that way. Nureyev, in May 1977, withdrew *Bayadère* from the Royal Ballet after finding he was being paid a nightly royalty of eight and a half dollars. Tooley, in a panic, offered him a hundred dollars, but Nureyev was hurt at being ripped off and took his work away. MacMillan did not respond to Tooley's pay offer. Added to the insult of being undervalued, the injury of being underpaid was almost the final straw.

The *coup de grâce* came from the supreme controller of British ballet. 'Kenneth came home one day,' said Deborah MacMillan, 'and said to me: "I have just been told that we're doing a new *Sleeping Beauty* and Madam will be directing it. I am no longer Director of the Royal Ballet."'[121]

Madam giveth and Madam taketh away, blessed be her name. Having sacked Sir Fred to make way for youth, Ninette de Valois now tired of MacMillan. She was almost eighty years old and racked with arthritic pain, but her vigour was undimmed and she remained the ultimate arbiter at both company and school, exercising absolute power without the burdens of responsibility. There was always, in Madam, a redeeming quality of caprice. Even at her most awesome, she could laugh at and contradict herself. An admirer characterized her around this time as 'changeable as a day in March; inflexible as a rock; irascible, benign; fiery, mild; intuitive, unaware; self-effacing, domineering; belligerent, shy; reticent (not often), voluble; arrogant, modest; giggly, dignified ... the contradictions proliferate.'[122] The danger with any such outsized personality lies with their acolytes, who seize upon each passing whim as if it were scriptural law. There was no decree from Madam that MacMillan must go; but the hangers-on, citing her desire to renew the famous *Beauty*, made common cause with the Ashton clique to undermine MacMillan's authority and enforce his resignation.

Madam's whim prevailed again when it came to a successor. Nureyev was sounded out by Tooley and seemed interested, but he needed to dance every night to stay in peak condition and would have left slim pickings for company principals. Peter Wright was also given brief consideration – too brief, some felt. The ultimate heir was an amiable outsider who had never danced with de Valois, having hitched the whole of his career to her sworn rival, Marie

Rambert. Norman Morrice had joined Rambert's school as a boy and her troupe as a dancer in 1952, spending a year in America with Martha Graham to study the advances in modern ballet. In the mid-60s, Rambert appointed him assistant director with orders to rescue her company by turning it into a contemporary ensemble. Morrice duly reinvented Rambert, leading a so-called 'dance explosion' that drew young audiences to watch works by Martha Graham, Glen Tetley, Christopher Bruce and Twyla Tharp. Graham herself helped found the London Contemporary Dance Theatre, led by Robin Howard and Robert Cohan. There was now more than one invitation to the dance, and the Royal crest looked stuffy and jaded beside the bristling upstarts.

Morrice led Rambert until 1974, when he went off to develop his own choreography. He was an appealing candidate, mop-topped in a roll-neck sweater, and any fears that he might teach the Royal radical steps were scotched at his inaugural press conference when Morrice declared that MacMillan would remain the principal choreographer. For all his modernizing zeal, Morrice was a traditionalist at heart. In a centennial radio greeting to Madam, he reminded her of the afternoon, 'just after I became director of the Royal Ballet, when you both, you and Marie Rambert, invited yourselves to tea at my flat, which happened to be in the basement of Rambert's house. I thought I was going to be grilled about what I was doing with the Royal Ballet. But when both of you arrived, you started chatting to each other and for the next two hours I was practically ignored so long as I kept the tea and biscuits coming. . . . I had you tick me off from time to time but you never held any kind of grudge.'[123]

What appealed to Madam was Morrice's determination to return her company to its roots, nurturing a new line of English dancers to the exclusion of all foreigners. 'Anyone who heard Norman speak at that time would have been swayed by him,' said a key supporter. 'The company lacked purpose and he was giving it direction for the first time since Madam retired.'[124]

Initially, it shone quite brightly. Madam's *Beauty* awoke memories of the 1946 epic with brilliant contributions from Seymour and Monica Mason, alternating as Carabosse. De Valois hopped through the rehearsals in a high orthopaedic collar and, after tripping on the studio steps, a foot in plaster. After the première, she was ordered into hospital for a week, to rest the broken foot.

'With Madam, you either survived or you didn't,' reflected

Mason, who had been terrified by Madam as a girl, 'because I saw her terrifying others.' Mason was now in her thirties and Seymour past forty. They stood up to Madam as strongminded women and she fitted the role to their distinctive personalities. 'She worked in great haste,' said Mason, 'with an ability to put in six words what I couldn't say in a hundred. There were never any doubts.' Mason, who lived in Kew, took to giving the old lady a lift home to Barnes after performances. Although her marriage broke up and she moved to the other side of the river, she continued chauffeuring Madam for the pleasure and privilege of her ceaseless conversation. One night as she pulled up outside her flat, Madam said, 'You are naughty, you know. You haven't told me you no longer live in Kew, and you're not married any more.' Mason replied, 'No, Madam, I'm not, but – this may sound like me being a total creep – I treasure every moment with you.' Madam said, 'Well I enjoy talking to you but it's out of your way and you're not to do it any more.'[125]

MacMillan, freed of the directorship, turned in his most compelling drama for years, an account of the notorious Austrian royal murder and suicide at the hunting lodge of *Mayerling*. Intensely erotic, it featured Seymour in her last MacMillan creation, with David Wall as Crown Prince Rudolf in place of the injured Dowell. The ballet was filmed for television and universally praised, but it marked an end rather than a new beginning. Morrice was keen to advance youngsters like Lesley Collier and Stephen Jeffries. Seymour found herself being passed over for her favourite roles. When her protests fell on deaf ears, she waltzed out of the company and went to Munich as director of the Bavarian State Ballet. Dowell, recovering from injury, joined American Ballet Theatre as a star replacement for Misha Baryshnikov who had defected to City Ballet.

Midway through his exile year, someone sent Dowell a clipping from the *Daily Telegraph* announcing Sibley's retirement. MacMillan, too, felt more appreciated at ABT than at Covent Garden. Jerome Robbins, who added a touch of Broadway pizzazz to the MacMillan era, never returned under Morrice. On 18 May 1979, Margot Fonteyn danced a new Ashton piece on her sixtieth birthday; five weeks later, she danced for the last time on pointe. In one short season, the Royal Ballet lost all its stars. Technically, its standards were slipping. After a US tour the ballet chairman Mark Bonham-Carter warned that they had been 'fortunate just to get away with it'.[126] Morrice, aiming to restore the company's core values, succeeded only in turning the clock back to bare rudiments.

The redevelopment appeal was not going well. At a Guildhall banquet in February 1979, Moser announced that £2,495,388 had been raised from private sources, of which the Linbury Trust had given 'by far the largest single donation'. The Government and Greater London Council had each pledged a million, but the total was barely half the initial target of £7.8 million which would pay for converting a rear extension of the opera house into rehearsal studios and dressing-rooms.

Royal help was summoned. Prince Charles, Patron of the ROH, spent three days filming what he called 'the appalling and outdated' backstage conditions. His documentary was distributed to cinemas by EMI, whose chairman, Sir Joseph Lockwood, was executive vice-chairman of the appeal. In May, BBC-1 screened an hour-long documentary about the dangerous and antiquated working conditions. Three weeks later, the newscaster Richard Baker made a televised appeal to the nation, which brought in all of thirteen thousand pounds. Prince Charles played his cello at a charity auction. Princess Margaret, always a good friend to the Ballet, went on a five-city US fundraiser and returned with half a million pounds. The kitty was still short, but there was enough in hand to start work on the rear extension. The saga of redevelopment had begun. It was expected to be completed in ten years. No one imagined it would take twice as long and cost twenty times as much.

Even at this early stage, there were fears that the company's attention was directed more towards raising money than towards raising standards. Harold Rosenthal, who loyally exhorted his readers to support the redevelopment appeal, complained of a two-tier opera house – starry international casts to impress 'potential business sponsors' and *vin ordinaire* for the rest of the time. Revivals were poorly cast and stand-ins, when needed, were flown in from Europe rather than whistled up locally. If Teresa Berganza dropped out of Massenet's *Werther*, the first-choice replacement should have been Sarah Walker or Josephine Veasey rather than an unknown and unimpressive Viorica Cortez from Paris.[127]

Tooley, in an evasive reply, admitted that financial constraints had forced him to leave many roles without a cover. 'Our aims and purposes are clear,' he protested, without specifying these noble objectives. The only justification he offered for according Covent Garden its special status was the 'quality' of its product, superior and more consistent than any other opera house. As for the redevelopment, it was being run by professional fundraisers and project managers, and did not impinge on artistic planning.[128] Everything, stressed Tooley, was under control. Even as he wrote, the country was undergoing one of its greatest political upheavals.

In May 1979, the Conservatives under Margaret Thatcher were swept to power by an electorate weary of a 'winter of discontent' in which municipal services had been paralysed by strikes, leaving refuse uncollected, schools shut and corpses unburied. 'Leicester Square is one large dump,' noted a prominent theatregoer, 'and every restaurant is approached through rubbish.'[129] In the coldest winter since 1947, domestic pipes froze and shop shelves were bare. Thatcher promised to tame the unions, reward enterprise and reduce the tax burden. She was returned with a majority of forty-three but, with the Heathite half of her party terrified of change, she proceeded cautiously at first. By abolishing subsidies for ailing industries, she laid whole towns to waste. A poignant press photo showed the Prime Minister surveying the twisted girders of a 'development site' where, until lately, a steel industry had blazed.

As unemployment reached Depression levels of three million and riots erupted in Brixton and Liverpool, Thatcher wooed working-class voters with the right to buy the homes they rented from local authorities. On the wings of a victory over Argentina in the Falklands War, she won re-election in 1983, crushing a fissipated opposition by a hundred and forty-four seats. Margaret Thatcher then proceeded to do what she wanted, routing the unions in an ugly standoff with desperate miners and reversing the public ownership of British industry by selling off the steel, coal and transport resources that Labour had nationalized. The Keynesian prescription for economic and social intervention was ripped up and ridiculed. Monetarism and market forces were the new orthodoxies.

Deploring consensus, Margaret Thatcher never seemed content unless she had a crusade to wage. One by one, she dismantled the institutions of the Welfare State, preserving only the sacred cow of the National Health Service which, she declared, 'is safe in our hands'. For her own eye operation, the Prime Minister went to Switzerland. For musical pleasures, she summered at Salzburg. For all her exhortations of national pride, she was easily convinced that other countries managed the important things much better than her own.

One of the first to recognize her exceptional determination was Sir Robert Armstrong who, sidelined to the Home Office under James Callaghan, sought out the opposition leader and invited her to the opera. Despite his early allegiance to the detested Ted Heath, Thatcher promoted Armstrong to Cabinet Secretary, head of the civil service. He remained also, with her full consent, Secretary to the Board of Covent Garden. To the access he had enjoyed under Heath, Armstrong now added real power. He was responsible, for example, for interrogating new ministers for possible security risks. Alan Clark, son of Kenneth, was summoned to his office and confronted with two files. The red file contained intelligence about the racist National Front, which viewed Clark as a potential sympathizer. Reaching for the orange file, Armstrong said, 'There are also certain matters of personal conduct . . . which could quite possibly leave you open to blackmail.' Clark, a compulsive philanderer, assured him that the girls in question were now respectably married. Armstrong gave a knowing smile and, after inquiring after Clark's sister whom he knew from the Covent Garden boardroom, sent the junior minister on his way.[130]

Authoritative as he was, Armstrong never forgot where his first loyalties lay. 'Civil servants are servants of the Crown,' he ruled. 'For all practical purposes the Crown in this context means and is represented by the Government of the day.'[131] He stood for continuity – 'I'm not sure that the underlying requirements of civil servants have changed really in four hundred years,' he told a BBC interviewer[132] – and was viewed by Lord Annan of the ROH board as one of the 'consensus men'[133] who had brought the country to its knees by yielding to union demands in the interests of peace and quiet. He was never a Thatcherite or, as the leader would have put it, 'one of us', and he was forced to submit to a ferocious review of his beloved civil service by a task force led by Derek Rayner of the Marks & Spencer department store. This dreaded unit, known as Rayner's Raiders, was out to eradicate waste, overmanning and the kind of bureaucratic circumlocution of which Armstrong was a grand master. Its chief of staff was a renegade civil servant, Clive Priestley, who quoted 'good management' manuals and employed a revolutionary rhetoric that appealed to the Prime Minister. 'If you think of the great reform movements of the past, they have all been attended by long periods of pain and agony,' Priestley proclaimed. 'The movement which triumphed is that which held power for long enough and was bloody-minded for long enough.'[134]

Throwing open his drawers to the raiders and deferring always to representatives of the Crown, Armstrong defended the traditional order with all the connections and craft at his command. He was caricatured in a popular BBC comedy series as 'Sir Humphrey', the pin-striped official who frustrates the activism of politicians. The programme was one of Mrs Thatcher's favourites; she even wrote a spoof episode herself. But Armstrong's ability to protect old establishments was strained to snapping point when the Prime Minister launched a direct assault on his favourite bastion.

The advance of Thatcherism had been greeted with dismay at the Royal Opera House. Its chairman, a Labour Party member since 1945, had clashed with Margaret Thatcher when she was minister for education in Heath's Government and he was in charge of statistics. 'I was never a friend of hers,' said Moser. 'She knew I was Labour and I don't think she liked me particularly.' Apart from John Sainsbury, a hard-line Tory, there was not a Thatcherite on the board and the need was now so desperate that Moser had to go begging, cap in hand, for an audience with the Prime Minister.

The appeal had fallen far short of its target and another million pounds was needed before work could begin on the rear extension. Moser convinced Norman St John Stevas, a royalist grandee who was Minister for the Arts, that the situation was critical and together they were granted an audience at Number 10. 'When we arrived,' Moser recalled, 'she said, "I suppose you want more money and you, Norman, can't find it somewhere else." We desperately needed money for building at the back, and we got another million pounds. There was another occasion when I went to see her with Drogheda. Mrs Thatcher, although she was very tough, was very committed to the opera house.'

More than any premier except Heath, Margaret Thatcher enjoyed going to the opera and, as Prime Minister, went twice a year. 'I remember her coming to *Trovatore*,' said Moser. 'We had a party in the Royal Box of people she knew – the Armstrongs and others. She came in looking as if she hadn't worked all day. She had read the story of *Trovatore* and asked me some detailed question about something in Act Two which I couldn't answer. We had a good evening. It ended around quarter to eleven and I said, Prime Minister

I expect you'll have to go. She said, can't we have coffee? So we all sat down and chatted away til midnight. Next morning I picked up the paper and saw that she had left at six for the Falklands.'[135]

Supportive though she was, there was nothing that irked Thatcher more than what she called 'whingeing'. Persistent financial demands from the ROH for money provoked sudden and drastic retribution. In 1982, she ordered her second arts minister, Paul Channon (Stevas had been sacked for alleged extravagance), to investigate whether the ROH was spending its public grant prudently and efficiently. To avoid suspicions of victimization, the Royal Shakespeare Company was selected for similar treatment. A sense of dread descended when it was learned that the inquisitors were to be headed by the zealous and unyielding Clive Priestley.

This was a dangerous precedent, a declaration of no-confidence in the Arts Council, whose officials attended every ROH board meeting and scrutinized the accounts. The Council, even under a true-blue Tory chairman, William Rees-Mogg, had become an object for scorn in Downing Street, a talking shop that never got anything done. Rees-Mogg, a former *Times* editor, was famed for the irrefutable logic and airy impracticality of many of his leading articles. His major policy initiative at the Arts Council was called 'The Glory of the Garden'; it advocated removing national companies from London and scattering them around the regions. Rees-Mogg and his secretary-general Luke Rittner – a shrewd Thatcherite who was mocked by arts mandarins for having no degree and only two 'O' levels – were no friends of Covent Garden. In the slipstream of the Priestley team, the Arts Council summoned Tooley, Moser and the deputy chairman, Sir Denis Forman, in May 1983 to give account of themselves. 'Claus looked defeated from the outset,' noted the V&A's Roy Strong, husband of Julia Trevelyan Oman, a regular ROH production designer.

> He was never in control of the debate, virtually at one point asking the Council to formulate policy for him . . . There was not really a voice raised in their defence, apart from the fact that we all recognized the need for a prestigious opera house and appreciated the success of the Ballet.
>
> After they left we were asked what we thought. I was beckoned to lead off and said that the rot was at the top and reflected the composition of the Board, which was by no means a consumer's

microcosm, and that it, together with the management, lacked any sense of direction. Earlier, I had drawn attention to the appallingly low morale in Covent Garden which was rotting the *esprit* of the workforce. The delegation struck one as rather helpless, arrogant and obsessed with money. Everything was put down to lack of it, not lack of ideas.[136]

Priestley, meanwhile, was going through the opera house with a fine toothcomb, with interludes for arduous trips to La Scala, the Met, Vienna, Berlin, the Kirov and the Bolshoi to compare Covent Garden with its competitors. Returning to the ROH boardroom, Priestley was greeted by the lion's last roar. Lord Goodman was aroused when Priestley handed out questionnaires for the directors to fill in.

No one present raised the slightest objection until I announced that he had no business to do what he was doing, that this was the most outrageous breach of the time-honoured principle that artistic subsidy was not related to government control. We had a rather heated scene. At one stage I informed him that after reading his questionnaire – he had come flanked by two assistants – there were in my view only six people in the world competent to answer it, and I was unhappy to say that those six did not include his party of three. Mr Priestley – an inoffensive and no doubt efficient gentleman – was clearly nonplussed by my onslaught and departed rather flushed.[137]

For the better part of a year, Tooley and Moser walked on egg-shells, encouraged only by the knowledge that Priestley was himself a theatregoer and was taking guidance from such wily professionals as Peter Diamand and Hugues Gall, head of the Geneva Opera. When the report was finally delivered in September 1983 to Thatcher's third arts minister in four years, the sybaritic and Wagner-loving Earl of Gowrie, it singled out Tooley's 'friendly, intrigue-free, supportive' management for special commendation – to the disgust of Rees-Mogg's Arts Council which wanted him sacked.

Priestley's main proposal was that the Royal Opera and Royal Ballet should be run as separate cost-centres and placed on three-year funding cycles, which would enable them to improve budget planning and avoid crises. Priestley found a creeping deficit at Covent Garden that he expected to reach three million pounds within a year. He urged the Government to write off the shortfall and raise the next grant by ten per cent, to £12.35 million. Thereafter, the funding should be pegged to inflation, not a penny more or less.

There were alternatives to increased funding, he suggested. The company could reduce the corps de ballet and opera chorus, disband the Sadler's Wells Royal Ballet, or cut back the opera to a pre-war festival season. Such measures, however, 'would write off the substantial investment of public funds that have been made over the past thirty-seven years; would reduce the value for money to be had from the very substantial grant that would still remain to be paid to the truncated ROH; and, in the case of the SWRB option, would deprive the provinces of the benefits of ROH companies.'[138]

Tooley and Moser were jubilant. 'It's very nice to be told that we are grossly underfunded,' said their spokesman. 'It's what we have been saying all along.'[139] But the Priestley Report was not a clean bill of health. The raiders found the ROH to be inefficient in many areas and urged it to cut staff and reform work practices. Some guest artists were grossly overpaid, overtime pay was out of control and there was no point in touring the Royal Opera around the country; it cost too much.

And this was where Priestley came unstuck. For Covent Garden to survive it needed to be seen as a national asset. Only one of its three companies, the SWRB, could now afford to set foot outside London and in the house itself, opera had become 'relatively inaccessible' due to high seat prices. The company could not reach more people without slashing prices, which would only increase its losses. There was little chance of reaching out through television, since one union or artist was forever in dispute over extra fees. Priestley quoted Isaiah Berlin's belief that 'opera is today, no less than yesterday, intrinsic to the culture of a developed society,' but he failed to show how opera might enrich society when it was available only to the moneyed classes in the capital area.

Like Priestley, no one at Covent Garden could see beyond the end of Bow Street. Tooley, incensed by the Treasury's refusal to scrap VAT on ROH tickets, declared that the tax would mean 'spiritual death' for the nation. His assertion sounded all the more insensitive at a time when the weekly state benefit to an unemployed couple was £47.85; the nightly cost to the state of two seats at Covent Garden was £42.00.[140] The misery was no longer shared equally, as it had been after the war. Under Thatcherism, the gulf between haves and have-nots was widening. Those who lived on state handouts could never hope to share in the nation's 'spiritual life'.

The outcome of the Priestley Report was unsatisfactory to all concerned. The Government increased Covent Garden's subsidy to the recommended £12.35 million in 1984-85, but stalled again the following year. Lord Harewood at ENO protested that his grant had now fallen to less than half of Covent Garden's. A Manchester businessman, Raymond Slater, who had spent two million pounds renovating the Palace Theatre after being promised a Royal Opera tour, cancelled a £100,000 grant to Covent Garden, along with all other arts sponsorships. Priestley became chairman of the Greater London Arts Board. Tooley brandished his report at every politician who came his way, until eyes glazed over.

Among the Priestley findings that were swept back under the carpet was his concern about a certain boardroom irregularity:

I have also recommended that the Secretariat which the Civil Service has provided to the Board since 1947 should be replaced by one formed by the ROH's permanent staff. This implies no adverse criticism of the existing Secretariat or their predecessors, but simply that an institution with an annual turnover of close on twenty million pounds should be capable of finding itself a competent Secretariat.[141]

Capable, perhaps, but unwilling to give up its agent in Downing Street, any more than the Prime Minister was prepared to tell her Cabinet Secretary, Sir Robert Armstrong, to relinquish his free nights at the opera. No further mention was made of this impertinent proposal, and for the rest of Armstrong's career and beyond Covent Garden continued to be served, free of charge, by some of the most superior officials in Whitehall.

Hardly a season went by now without the opera house having to cancel new productions for want of funds. The absence of novelty left the box office reliant on a flow of stars to entice operagoers to see an old show for a second or third time. The top-noters were never numerous, and female glamour in particular was scarce. From the very outset, Covent Garden had relied on a Flagstad, a Schwarzkopf, a Callas or a Nilsson to quicken the pulse and shorten the breath. These titans had retired and their successors were less bankable. Joan Sutherland had her fans, but the vehicles chosen by her omniscient husband were outlandish and expensive. Richard Bonynge was carving a niche for himself as a hunter of historic truffles. He retrieved Donizetti's *Lucrezia Borgia* from archival dust, followed by Massenet's *Esclarmonde*, a production that was shipped over from San Francisco at a cost of sixty thousand pounds. The diva herself was paid six thousand a night. By the second performance, she was unwell. Since there was no understudy, the rest of the cast bravely turned out in a make-do *Madam Butterfly*. There were five airings of *Esclarmonde*, which the *Daily Telegraph* called 'grotesque' and *The Times* 'meretricious'. The singers referred to it as *Excrement*, but this was the nature of diva-bait and the diva did as she pleased. In the next three seasons, she returned only once to Covent Garden.

Janet Baker retired from opera in 1981. Gwyneth Jones, another home-reared dame turned inconsistent, her screech and scoop nights saved from booing only by her regal bearing. Casting operas became all the trickier once Helga Schmidt resigned in poor health in 1979. It took five years to instal a replacement – Peter Mario Katona of the Hamburg Opera – and in that time the consistency of singing wobbled as badly as Dame Gwyneth as Desdemona.

The one stroke of fortune that befell the Royal Opera was the royal apotheosis of its prize soprano. Kiri te Kanawa had progressed through Mozart and Strauss into the Verdian roles of Amelia (*Simon Boccanegra*) and Desdemona (*Otello*), which she sang with serene beauty but no dramatic force. She was earning half a million pounds a year and, managed by her husband, Desmond, sometimes sounded less than fresh. Nevertheless, whenever she appeared in London, *The Times*' op-ed columnist Bernard Levin would clear his page of human rights abuses and bureaucratic muddle and deliver a paean of overpraise. When music critics were underwhelmed by a Covent Garden charity recital, Levin charged to her defence. 'Did you ever read such a pack of miserable, spiritless wretches as the critics who reviewed the performance in yesterday's papers?' he demanded. 'What thin and vinegary liquor has been substituted for blood in the veins of Mr Hope-Wallace, that he could say her performance of the Jewel Song failed to excite? What ailed our own Mr Higgins, a most learned and sharp-eared canary-fancier that he found the evening "a shade unsatisfying"? Failed to excite? A shade unsatisfying? I tell you, if this pair had been present at the miracle of the loaves and the fishes, one of them would have complained that there was no lemon to go with the fish, and the other would have demanded more butter for the bread.'[142]

A superior Kiri fan proved more influential. On 1 April 1981, she received a call asking her to sing at Charles's wedding. 'Charles who?' she said. The Prince of Wales, at thirty-two the world's most eligible bachelor, had chosen to marry a nineteen-year-old nursery teacher of noble birth, Lady Diana Spencer. He wanted Kiri to sing them out after the service.

The date fitted neatly in her diary. She had seven Elviras (*Don Giovanni*) and four Fiordiligis (*Cosi fan tutte*) to sing in an ROH Mozart Festival in July. Charles came to see *Don Giovanni* and found her 'wonderfully sexy and seductive'.[143] He invited her and Des back to the Palace, where she barely spoke to Diana.

On 29 July, decked out in a canary-coloured gown and cheeky, quiche-shaped hat, Kiri te Kanawa trilled Handel's 'Let the Bright Seraphim' while the ill-fated newlyweds signed the register and swanned down the aisle of St Paul's Cathedral. Seven hundred million people all over the world watched her on live television – the equivalent, said the US newscaster Tom Brokaw, of 'two hundred and fifty thousand Covent Garden audiences at the same time'.[144] The point was not lost on the ambitious soprano who, in her haste to make the wedding, had omitted to wear knickers, or so she later revealed.

Learning new roles had never been her forte and she was losing what little appetite she once felt for character growth. Rehearsing Puccini's *Manon Lescaut* at Covent Garden in May 1983, Dame Kiri (she was ennobled a year after the wedding) seemed so sullen and unprepared that the conductor Giuseppe Sinopoli threatened to walk out a week before opening night. 'He tried to get me fired,' raged Kiri.[145] The impulsive Italian was taken aside and warned that the Queen Mother was coming to the Gala performance and, unless he wagged his stick like a good boy, he would never work on these shores again. Kiri also balked at working with Götz Friedrich, whose production had been shipped in from Hamburg after Piero Faggioni's sets proved too big for the ROH stage. The second-hand *Lescaut*, was about ten boos short of a total disaster. Dame Kiri, said one critic,[146] 'had a less than comprehensive grasp' of her role.

That summer she met the sports impresario Mark McCormack on a golf course and began a new career. McCormack reckoned she would be better off singing concert arias in large arenas rather than fixed-fee operas in a two thousand-seat house. Kiri, the adopted child of poor parents, was keen. McCormack set up outdoor gigs in Australian vineyards and tennis courts. 'We made Kiri more money than she'd ever made before,'[147] he bragged. Kiri said it was 'inappropriate' to discuss her art in pecuniary terms, but from now on opera ceased to be the mainspring of her existence and she gave up learning new roles.

For want of a top soprano, Covent Garden was thrown upon the mercy of tenors. There were five lyric tenors of Mediterranean origin and comparable merit, two of whom soared above the rest. Luciano Pavarotti was a Covent Garden discovery. In 1963 Joan Ingpen, needing an understudy for the wayward Giuseppe di Stefano, checked out an all-Italian *Rigoletto* in Dublin and came home with Pavarotti and the baritone Piero Cappuccilli. The unknown Pavarotti, just twenty-seven, took over all but one of di Stefano's *Bohèmes*, as well as a television spot on *Sunday Night at the London Palladium*. Most nights he watched TV in his hotel room, understanding barely a word. Weekends he spent with Enid Blech in Sussex, where she taught him to ride a horse. He was booked by Glyndebourne for *Idomeneo* and enjoyed the company's iron discipline. Then Richard Bonynge spotted him as the only tenor tall and loud enough to look Joan Sutherland in the eye. They took him on an Australian tour, won him a Decca contract and set up his US début. From the night he hit nine top Cs in succession in Donizetti's *Daughter of the Regiment* at the Metropolitan Opera in February 1972, Pavarotti was the biggest tenor in America since Caruso. He had sung the role before at Covent Garden, but on this night the press had been hyped up to fever pitch by his personal publicist, Herbert Breslin, and Pavarotti was crowned 'King of the High Cs'. He soon had five albums simultaneously in Billboard's classical top ten.

Pavarotti was a softie at heart. He talked wistfully of his time at Glyndebourne and his early struggles as a competition singer in Wales. He cherished the memory of Enid Blech and remained friendly with the Bonynges and Joan Ingpen. But towards Covent Garden, he blanked out. In a 1995 autobiography, he gave the company one glancing mention, as if it were alien territory.

The impediment, for 'Big Lucy', was John Tooley. Pavarotti was a dispenser of bear-hugs. Tooley, emotionally inhibited, resisted his embrace. 'I had a love-hate relationship with Luciano,' said Tooley. 'He used to accuse me of engaging the "Spanish Mafia" at his expense. And of course we went for them because they were more reliable.' In Tooley's book, reliability scored higher than magic.

In preference to Pavarotti, Tooley favoured the elegant Alfredo Kraus, the thin-toned José Carreras and the glorious Giacomo Aragall, whose talents were stunted by incurable stage fright. Above all, Tooley hitched his schedules to the one tenor that Pavarotti feared as a rival.

Placido Domingo had reached Covent Garden by the scenic route. Spanish born, he was singing with the Mexico National Opera at eighteen, followed by three years in Tel Aviv and a stint at New York City Opera. He made his début in Vienna in 1967, at the Met in 1968 and at La Scala the following season. By the time he opened his throat as Cavaradossi at Covent Garden on 8 December 1971, Domingo had sung two Verdi *Requiem*s in London under Carlo Maria Giulini and Leonard Bernstein and was a fully-fledged world star.

Arriving at the start of Tooley's regime, in the very week of Kiri's triumph, Domingo chimed in perfectly with the general director's wishes. Businesslike where Pavarotti was bumptious, urbane to the Italian's abrupt, Domingo liked to say 'yes'. He was intelligent, hard-working and unfailingly punctual, a management's dream. He also knew three times as many roles as Pavarotti and could sing, apart from Italian and Spanish, in French, English, Hebrew (for Tel Aviv), German and Russian. As if this were not enough, he played the piano, conducted and longed to direct. In Tooley he found a management tutor, a confidant and friend. Seeing them together, one sensed a cautious symbiosis of two tidy men who always looked twice before putting a foot forward. Tooley would do his utmost to keep Domingo happy. When the tenor's eldest son, by a short-lived teenage marriage, was lodging in Northampton, Tooley drove up regularly to visit and report on his progress.

Domingo invested his fees in several properties, including a house in Chelsea and a flat in Covent Garden, where he or his son would stay. When vacant, he rented rooms to visiting singers. In Vienna he rented out a whole apartment block near the Staatsoper, saving the penthouse for himself.

This most organized of tenors took care to create a good working atmosphere. 'Most stars nowadays don't even speak to the chorus,' observed Constance Shacklock, whose adopted daughter sang at the ROH. 'Domingo is the exception. He knows every chorister by name.'

Tooley raved about his 'really extraordinary musicality, and his ability to use his voice to dramatic ends in a way not matched by any other.'[148] Domingo reciprocated with florid praise for the unprepossessing manager. For the rest of his career, he never missed a season at Covent Garden. Pavarotti, no fool, saw which way the scales were tipped. From the early 80s he turned capricious, cancelling as often as he sang. At the Lyric Opera in Chicago, another Domingo stronghold, he missed twenty-six out of forty-one contracted appearances between 1981 and 1989. At Covent Garden, he furnished a plethora of excuses. His father was sick; Calaf in *Turandot* was too taxing for his voice; finally, in February 1983, he telexed from Australia that he was too poorly to sing in *Tosca* – only to be snapped by press photographers on a South Sea island with a new girlfriend. He turned up for *Aida* the following season and virtually wrecked Jean-Pierre Ponnelle's new production, refusing to obey the simplest of directions. His next cancellation was *Tosca*, complaining that backstage dust at the ROH might trigger an allergy. 'I spoke to him on the phone,' said Tooley, 'and I said I want evidence of the allergy. He said, I'll get it to you. Some time later he sent me a paper from a New York laboratory which had done very serious analysis.' The final straw was a demand by Pavarotti, the morning after singing before the Prince and Princess of Wales, for a twenty thousand pound reward.

It dawned on Tooley that Pavarotti, who had a profitable sideline in open-air arena concerts, could not care less if he never sang again at Covent Garden. His booming fan club might wail, but Domingo was an acceptable substitute, ever ready to help out. Tooley would fly to the ends of the earth to squeeze extra dates out of him, and Domingo seldom refused. He owned the role of Otello at Covent Garden; also of Samson in Saint-Saëns's opera and of Hoffmann in Offenbach's. In July 1984, he led the Royal Opera to the United States with four *Turandot*s in Los Angeles, coinciding with the Olympic Games. Never had the Royal Opera known a more loyal or obliging servant. He was Covent Garden's *chanteur noble* as Anthony Dowell was its *danseur noble*.

Then, catastrophe. In September 1985, while Domingo was warming up for *Otello* in Chicago, an earthquake struck Mexico City, killing hundreds, including Domingo's aunt, uncle and two cousins in the district where he grew up. He took a private plane to the disaster zone and, in a dust-choked voice, issued a statement that wrecked the world's opera schedules. 'I am asking every theatre in the world to give me one year's leave of absence, starting immediately,' he told me down a crackly telephone. 'I expect they will make difficulties. That is why I am now asking them publicly through you: Let me go!' He aimed to spend the year giving concerts to raise enough money to rehouse two hundred families.

A week later he flew to Barletta on Italy's Adriatic coast, to shoot *Otello* in a medieval castle with Franco Zeffirelli. 'I could not abandon the film,' he said. 'A film like this costs ten million dollars to make and involves many jobs. I know live opera also costs money but . . . they can find another tenor to fill my sixty performances for a year. After that I will see where I go.'[149] On set in Barletta, he was almost unapproachable with gloom. On camera all day, he spent the evenings and half the night on the phone to opera managers, clearing his diary. The first of his relief concerts took place in nearby Bari. It raised a hundred thousand dollars but left a residue of bitterness when two sopranos pulled out of the supporting cast and Domingo's voice cracked after two arias. A party of schoolchildren gave him two hundred dollars from their pocket money.

He had not been filming for more than a week when John Tooley flew in, desperate for a word. Incongruous in a three-piece suit in the Adriatic heat, Tooley begged Domingo to reinstate his *Otello* at Covent Garden. The entire season hinged on his appearance, and the house hoped to make a profit of £150,000 by increasing seat prices for the show. 'Outrageous,' said Domingo. 'These operas are for the public. How can they afford £75 a ticket?' For two days, Tooley and Margherita Stafford, Domingo's London agent, fluttered around the fringes of the set before the tenor gave way. He would sing *Otello*, he agreed, but not in a new production. 'Right now I am not at my best,' he protested. Before Tooley left, he yielded completely.

Domingo never let him down.

But the Domingo who returned to Covent Garden in January 1987 was a changed man. His Otello was grey-toned and dispiriting. His aid efforts for Mexico sold poorly. When he announced on the Des O'Connor chat show that he was cancelling a Wembley concert at twenty-four hours notice 'because the tickets were too high,' one promoter told a newspaper: 'I want the head of Placido Domingo.' Legal action ensued, and Domingo parted company acrimoniously from his long-suffering agent. Soon after, he cancelled *Lohengrin*. The music press reported that 'the Royal Opera is at the end of its tether with Domingo'.[150] This was overstated, but an irritation had set in with the enforced Otello and Domingo found it hard to recapture his élan. 'I had a sour time adjusting myself to singing in England,' he told me. 'I was shocked, electrified, by some of the reactions. We are not machines, and we have an instrument that is very much affected by the emotions. If you are not completely happy, you cannot sing. You need your happiness to sing.' What Tooley needed was a top-note tenor, happy or not. The departure of Pavarotti and disgruntlement of Domingo were dangerously weakening the company's prospects, and his own.

The disappearance of guest artists at the Royal Ballet took a heavy toll at the box-office. After two years of purified Englishness, Norman Morrice gave in and asked Tooley to re-engage Nureyev. The wounded Tatar brooded on the invitation, telexing his assent five minutes before the annual press conference, and too late to change the printed casts. 'I am mortified by what happened,' Tooley told him. 'I could not reach Ninette de Valois, who is organizing the cast of *Sleeping Beauty* and when we eventually did, later in the day, she said that much as she would have liked you to appear she simply could not cope with explanations to the dancers and the large re-arrangement of casting which your presence at this late hour would have meant.

'I understand all of this, and I hope you will. Since things have got to this point, the last thing that any of us want is a further deterioration of your relationship with the Royal Ballet. That is not in any of our interests. Rudolf, please understand the situation, please accept my apologies for our failure to implement your decision for the reasons which I have explained.'[151] The hint of desperation in Tooley's note was unmistakable. Without a bankable star, the ballet would lose not only its overseas tours but its home audience to the sparkier Rambert and LCDT, where Seymour and Sleep were trying their hands at choreography. Nureyev, for his part, longed to return. He had been a company member of the Royal Ballet in all but name and missed its home comforts. Angry and frustrated, he told a television interviewer that 'the moment Margot ceased to dance . . . there was an incredible urge to demote me, to turn me from identity to nonentity.'[152] He went on to describe the ROH management as 'a sack of shit'.

He finally returned in March 1982 after a five-year absence, 'galumphing' (as one insider put it) comically yet charismatically through his youthful roles. He was forty-four years old and pushing himself as hard as ever. His fee was fourteen hundred pounds, a pittance compared to the four thousand paid to the baritone Geraint Evans, another fading stalwart. Nureyev was about to become artistic director of the Paris Opéra Ballet and danced only a few times more at the ROH – in 1984, 1988 and at a 1990 fundraiser for Margot Fonteyn, who was dying of cancer in Panama. Nureyev himself was by then stricken with Aids and did not have long to live. He never ceased to regret his rift with the Royal Ballet which, had decisions fallen differently, he might have led as director and galvanized in the way that he revitalized the Paris Opéra.

Other foreigners now slipped back into the schedules. Makarova danced *Giselle* and Mikhail Baryshnikov, the USSR's greatest dancing loss since Nureyev, appeared in a new Ashton piece, *Rhapsody*, to mark the Queen Mother's eightieth birthday. His American lover, the volatile Gelsey Kirkland, danced Juliet opposite the newly repatriated Anthony Dowell in a fixed-smile season marking the jubilee of English ballet. Half a century after Madam founded the Vic-Wells Ballet there was no English ballerina of world rank and only Dowell to fly the ensign among the men.

The onus of continuity lay heavily on the shoulders of Kenneth MacMillan, far more so than when he had been director. MacMillan did not disappoint. His 1980s ballets extended his skills as a social critic and story-teller. *Gloria*, using Francis Poulenc's soprano-sung setting of the Roman Catholic Mass – this time without board veto – evoked the futility of the First World War, just as Mrs Thatcher and the US President Ronald Reagan upped the ante in Cold War rhetoric. *Isadora* recreated the life and loves of the legendary American dancer, Isadora Duncan, to a new score by Richard Rodney Bennett. Innovatively, he split the title role between a dancer, Merle Park, and an actress, Mary Miller, who spoke words from Duncan's memoirs. 'Isadora', said MacMillan, 'was a more serious as well as a more tragic person than most people appreciate.'[153] He might well have been speaking about himself. 'It would be unfair to blame MacMillan for trivializing Isadora Duncan's life,' snarled Percival on *The Times*. 'She began that process when she wrote a lurid, often fictional, autobiography.'[154]

Knighted in 1983, MacMillan pressed ahead with *Valley of Shadows* – a realization of the Italian Holocaust memoir, *The Garden of the Finzi-Continis* – and *Different Drummer*, which used the atonalities of Webern and Schoenberg to rework Georg Büchner's original 1835 story of Berg's opera *Wozzeck*. He then picked up his long-delayed ambition to recreate Britten's *Prince of Pagodas*, the composer's executors having sensibly authorized his proposed cuts. None of his ballets met with instant acclaim, even within the company. It was in the nature of his art that it revealed its merits steadily over a period of time.

Morrice gave MacMillan all the support he needed, intervening to retrieve *Manon* from the scrapheap and restoring it to the staple repertoire. Lynn Seymour was still keen to bring him to Munich, but their contact ended when MacMillan slapped her face in the foyer on a Covent Garden first night after hearing her criticize the costumes his wife had designed for a new production of *Solitaire*. Morrice sought to encourage new choreography within the company, setting David Bintley and Ashley Page on the road to distinguished careers. But MacMillan was the Royal Ballet's guiding light, as Ashton had been before him, and his work was gaining favour abroad. In September 1984, Baryshnikov enticed him to become Associate Director of American Ballet Theater, with the prospect of establishing his work on a larger stage.

MacMillan was reluctant to spend time in New York without knowing how his work was being treated back home. In the rehearsal warren at Baron's Court, he struck up a conversation with Monica Mason, who was retiring early with persistent injury. 'I was friendly with Kenneth but I never had a meal with him, never went to his house, never knew him socially outside the company,' recalled Mason. 'One day, when he said to me in a corridor, "would you like to be my assistant?" I said, "yes". He said, "you're not meant to answer, you're meant to go away and think about it."'

'I said, "there's nothing to think about."'

'He said, "I'll see you in two days."'

Mason became MacMillan's eyes and ears, taking rehearsals and telephoning him daily reports – 'he hated not knowing what was going on.' Every MacMillan ballet was based on trial and error and consumed by a pervasive self-doubt. 'When he was making *Gloria*,' recalled Mason, 'he had done the *pas de deux* and we came to the first big movement for corps de ballet. He was very tense. We went into rehearsal and the miracles started happening. At the end of an hour and a half he let everybody go. He turned to me, "what do you think of that?" I'm taking notes and thinking, boys come in on the right ... do a semi-circle .. so he said, "would you say it was all right?" I said, "yes . . ." He said, "that was the worst rubbish, there is not a single thing I can keep out of today's rehearsal, tomorrow we'll start all over again." It was only on the third go that he got it.'

Upright, discreet and self-contained, Mason turned into more than a choreographer's amanuensis. Dancers came to her with their fears and niggles and she became the first port of call for anyone with an injury. Raised in South Africa, she had seen English dancers on tour as a child and all she ever wanted to do was work with the Royal Ballet. She represented its conscience and continuity.

Morrice lost credibility. He quickly set about grooming a successor. Anthony Dowell had returned from America a changed man. He had relished the limelight at ABT but recognized the grim realities of balletic business in an open market. 'The real eye-opener,' he said, 'was that they had a lay-off period and some of those dancers were serving tables in restaurants. It was tough. People were very hungry, the energy level was terrific. America opened me up as a person.' He did not have much longer to dance and wanted to recommit to the Royal Ballet.

He was given two seasons to understudy Morrice. Much of the time he spent in the rehearsal room, attacking slackened techniques. Dowell was not quite sure whether he had what it took to run a company and cast around for oracles to support his next move. He harked back to the lowest moment of his career, losing Prince Rudolf's role in *Mayerling* because he could not recover fast enough from injury. 'I was being trained back to fitness,' he recalled, 'by a wonderful lady called Winifred Edwards, who came back in her eighties to retrain me (Monica carries on Miss Edwards' traditions). Kenneth when he created a ballet had to do the central *pas de deux* and work the rest around it. I think I created one small section. I knew it wasn't ready. Miss Edwards was telling me I wasn't ready, and Kenneth couldn't wait. So I waved it goodbye, the biggest career blow I ever suffered.

'Funnily enough, after one of these training sessions we walked out and I remember crossing the road with her when out of the blue Miss Edwards said: "Anthony I think one day you should think of being director of the Royal Ballet." I didn't think it was mad, because I respected her so much. But it really shocked me and made me think.'

The crucial push came from Ninette de Valois who, in her mideighties, had just deposed the head of the Royal Ballet School – the accomplished James Monahan, former head of the BBC World Service and (as James Kennedy) dance critic of the *Guardian* – and replaced him with his embittered ex-wife, Merle Park. That kind of casting always made Madam cackle. Dowell had never been one of her favourites – 'she liked the naughty ones, and Anthony was so good,' said Sibley – but he was loyal, hard-working and above all respectful. 'I knew that she was for it – she let it be known,' said Dowell. 'Afterwards, she sent wonderful little letters of encouragement. That kept me going.'

Morrice had been due to hand over in mid-1985 but returned from a Far East tour with an attack of toxoplasmosis that caused him to take several months of sick leave. 'I was thrown in at the deep end,' said Dowell, who had just turned forty. 'It is staggering how he has matured,' said one insider.[155] Tooley relieved him of many administrative chores and Monica Mason agreed to assist him, in addition to MacMillan. 'It's quite hard serving two masters,' she reflected, 'but I was serving the company, and that's what everybody has always done.'

Some doubted whether Dowell was strong enough to impose his will. 'Anthony,' said Wayne Sleep, 'hated any kind of scene.'[156] But Ashton and MacMillan, who had twisted his body one way and another as a dancer, submitted meekly to his programming decisions. Madam was generally compliant. 'It's much harder for you, dear,' she said, 'than it was for me. I didn't have to waste time with unions and working practices and all that.' She was still 'very visible'[157] in the day-to-day workings of the company.

When Dowell put on his first *Swan Lake* at Christmas 1986, she objected loudly to the décor and lighting. 'As you get older, the eyesight goes and nothing in the show was ever light enough for her,' said Dowell. 'It obviously hit a nerve and she let fly. I just rallied and shouted right back at her.' Years later, there was a note of astonishment in his voice as he relived his resistance. It was the moment he came of age as director of the Royal Ballet, a post he would hold longer than anyone, except Madam herself.

The annual curtain-raiser for the Royal Opera was turning into a coconut shy. Bored by a lack of new productions and exacerbated by second-rate casts, several members of the press stored up their venom for the traditional coffee morning in the Crush Bar and, once the next season's programme had been distributed, let fly with all the adjectives in their quiver at the hapless trio of Tooley, Moser and Davis, sitting upon the dais. The panellists' body language invited attack. Moser would sit, arms folded and legs crossed, looking morose and away from Tooley. Davis stared down at the floor.

In fairness, there were isolated bouquets of praise. Verdi's *Macbeth*, conducted by Riccardo Muti, was considered the most exciting show in years, and the production of *Boris Godunov* by the Russian exile, Andrei Tarkovsky, conducted by Claudio Abbado, bore the unmistakable imprint of living history. Many were encouraged by the showing of a lone episode of Karlheinz Stockhausen's seven-day opera, *Licht* (Isaiah Berlin found it 'most melodious'; a friend replied: 'pure Palm Court'). A pair of rare Zemlinsky one-acters imported from Hamburg via the Edinburgh Festival showed a further spark of enterprise. On the whole, however, these glints of light were lost in the gloom and the press colloquies were dominated by cancellations, monetary losses and general moans. In November 1982, Alan Blyth of the *Daily Telegraph* and Brian Magee, a Cambridge don and future chairman of the Arts Council's music panel, demanded the head of Colin Davis. Both called for Mackerras to succeed, while others set up a clamour for Muti. Tom Sutcliffe of the *Guardian* said few tears would be shed if the opera house were shut down until its entire board and management could be replaced.

'Something old, something new, something borrowed, something blue,' quipped Sutcliffe of another meagre seasonal offering. 'Are you accusing us of disseminating pornography?' snapped Davis.

Comparisons with ENO were invariably unfavourable. Harewood had made way for a hotshot trio of Peter Jonas, David Pountney and Mark Elder who called themselves 'The Power House'. They continually renewed the stock. The spring of 1986 saw two world premières – Ferruccio Busoni's half-forgotten *Doctor Faust* in an authentic completion, and a semi-electronic *Mask of Orpheus* by Harrison Birtwistle which, many in the first-night audience felt, was the biggest breakthrough for British opera since *Peter Grimes*. The Austrian pianist Alfred Brendel went one further. He was overheard telling Sir Isaiah Berlin, as they left the Coliseum, that this was the finest English opera since Purcell's. Much of what ENO did was fresh, challenging, infuriating. Much of Covent Garden's output was stuffy, predictable and stale.

Dissent was not confined to the press. The Arts Council, itself squeezed by Thatcherite constraints, froze the Covent Garden grant with the aim, never openly admitted, of shaking out the board and management. There were also elements on the Covent Garden board who demanded change, causing Tooley no end of discomfiture. The main agitator was Sir Denis Forman who, with the Bernsteins, had made Granada the country's most watchable television station. Forman was personally responsible for one of the great serial dramas, Paul Scott's post-imperial cycle, *The Jewel in the Crown*. One-footed from a war wound and sporting red braces, Forman was a practising musician who had rescued the venerable music publishers, Novello, and published *The Musical Times*. He took a look at the ROH books and demanded radical measures. 'Forman would say, your chorus is too big, get rid of it,' recalled an eyewitness. 'This was heresy. All there was left of the opera company, after all, was a chorus and orchestra.'[158]

'Denis Forman was a great shooter from the hip,' said Tooley. 'Intelligent, well informed, passionate about opera and ballet. Often sent people off on wild goose chases.' Resentful of being bossed about, Tooley demanded a seat on the board and was refused. To his further dismay, Forman was made deputy chairman and joined Moser in dealing with the Arts Council, where Tooley was disliked.

Forman apart, most of the board were consumed by a sense of divine right. 'What one wants on a board is not a bunch of people who think the same thing,' recollected Moser. 'We had some crises and tough times, but there was a wonderful feeling of unity on the board in wanting the opera house to survive. John Sainsbury and Isaiah Berlin and Pat Gibson and Colette Clark all brought different attributes but whatever our politics we were always united, that's why we were quite powerful.'

Powerful, perhaps, but not uniformly effective. Moser had fattened the board with finance men to handle the redevelopment, which was not going well. The phase-one appeal for ten million pounds was reached only in 1985. 'The first phase ran out of money before they could double-glaze the windows,' reported a board member. 'So the loudest noise in the rehearsal room was a ghetto-blaster playing in James Street.'[159]

The next stage would cost five times as much, fifty-six million pounds, half of which would be raised by erecting an adjacent office block for sale or rent. John Sainsbury took charge of choosing architects. From an open contest, he picked a young partnership of Jeremy Dixon and Edward Jones, whose main project to date had been restoring a tree-lined Victorian street in North Kensington. Where most architects were prisoners of glassy modernism, Dixon and Jones had reconverted to early classicism. Their fervour for Inigo Jones and his designs infected Sainsbury and his conservative committee with a vision to restore the gutted market area to an imaginary splendour. Sainsbury then left the board, after fifteen years' service, to focus on the National Gallery, where he endowed an extension wing under the chairmanship of his former ROH colleague, Lord Annan. Sainsbury continued to keep a watchful eye on the Royal Ballet and was committed to be the lead donor in Covent Garden's reconstruction. When the Royal Opera and Royal Ballet were split (on Priestley's recommendation) into separate cost centres, he returned as chairman of the ballet board. In due course, he acquired a significant extraneous role as chairman of the Governors of the Royal Ballet, a group that existed and met independently of the ROH.

The board was reinforced with the likes of Lord Richardson, recently retired Governor of the Bank of England; the chief executive of Lloyd's, Ian Hay Davison; the chairman of Commercial Union Assurance, Sir Francis Sandilands; the IBM chairman Sir Edwin Nixon; and a property developer, Christopher Benson. All appointments needed Downing Street approval but, with the Cabinet Secretarys in attendance, this proved no more than a formality. The ROH board, once composed of scholars and gentlemen, was now packed with City suits. Forman, to inject a discordant note, co-opted a protégé of his, the television producer Jeremy Isaacs who had invented Channel Four (on the strength of a report by the ubiquitous Lord Annan) as an outlet for alternative and minority broadcasting. He and Tooley took against one another on sight, which is hardly surprising given the undeclared sub-text. 'I set my heart on appointing Jeremy (in John's place),' said Moser. 'When Denis and

I appointed him to the board, we shared this hypothetical thought that he could become the successor.'

Into this ferment returned George Whyte, the self-made furniture magnate whose earlier ideas had been rejected by Drogheda. Whyte, ten years on, volunteered to spend three months at Covent Garden and produce a business plan. Moser accepted his offer, but fretted that he should take care not 'to upset the staff'. Tooley sat in at the meeting, looking worried. 'I am a man who wants to provide solutions,' Whyte noted, 'but I don't believe this can work if they are processed by people who may be the source of the problems.'[160]

Whyte set about gathering information. Moser told him he thought Tooley was good with artists but weak on finance. Goodman said Moser had been a poor chairman and blamed himself for the appointment. Whyte found little communication between Tooley and Moser. He discussed artist fees with Peter Katona and was shocked to discover that conductors were being paid twenty thousand Swiss francs a night, well above the going rate in Europe. Other items of waste and inefficiency sprang to view backstage, but Whyte quickly decided that Covent Garden could not be saved by nit-picking and cost-cutting. What was needed was a new vision to raise the company's profile and finances, a strategy that combined modern marketing and merchandising methods. An independent Enterprise Board was needed to refocus the company's image and outlook. Among Whyte's ideas was a package for Concorde-class tourists, combining the Savoy and QEII with nights at the opera and dinners with the artists. The house could be utilized in summer for prestige ROH study courses in opera and ballet, a profitable and proselytizing sideline. No single scheme, and he proposed fifty of them, would raise less than quarter of a million pounds.

Whyte looked at the redevelopment and found it wanting. Half the projected cost of fifty-seven million pounds was supposed to come from the sale of new offices and shops around the opera house, to the disgust of local residents. London was basking in another of its property booms, but if prices fell before the building was finished the ROH would be left with a crippling shortfall. Whyte, in a dazzling, holistic report, urged the ROH to scrap its property deals and create an international cultural centre in the available space, funded by wealthy Far Eastern and European nations. The idea was, perhaps, quixotic – and no part of the plan could be made to work independently of the whole, but the Report deserved serious consideration. What it got from the ROH board was dead silence.

Ten months later, Whyte gave an interview to the *Sunday Times*. 'No one wants a third-rate office block that is going to be a disaster for the area, when they could have a resplendent international development,' he argued.[161] Whyte had spent £25,000 of his own money by this time. He offered to spend twice as much again on a feasibility study for the international cultural centre. He went before the Board and declared that 'at no time did I have anything but the interests of the House at heart'. They all but threw him out. He told Moser: 'You have mentioned on a number of occasions that you find my proposals attractive, on the other hand you do not wish to impede the implementation of your own scheme, which has no doubt incurred internal costs.'[162]

The Times, in a leading article, urged Covent Garden 'to market itself actively by one means or another'.[163] In a letter to the editor, Drogheda proclaimed that the main problem at Covent Garden was underfunding, and 'for this the fault rests clearly with the Government, who have so far failed to honour the recommendations of the Priestley Report.' He added: 'I do not believe sums of the order required could ever be raised through the ideas being put forward by Mr George Whyte, with whom Covent Garden first had talks fifteen years ago.'[164] Moser was never man enough to contradict his charismatic predecessor. 'One of the reasons we can't go along with your plan,' he told Whyte, 'is that Drogheda is against you.'

'These people on the Board believed they were there by God's will,' Whyte concluded. 'Apart from Forman, they were interested only in self-perpetuation and not in taking responsibility.'[165]

On 30 June 1987, Westminster City Council overruled local protests and granted outline planning permission for the next phase of ROH development, offices and all. The seeds of future disaster were being set in cement and concrete.

Internally, tectonic plates started to shift. To head the newly devolved opera company, Tooley hired Eva Wagner, dispossessed daughter of Bayreuth, who rolled up in a Porsche with her own office furniture, all glass and chrome. She lasted two years and left little impression – except on Moser, who doted on her. The reshaping of the Royal Opera would take place over and above the head of its nominal director.

Paul Findlay, Tooley's assistant, emerged as a driving force, while

Peter Katona made himself indispensable as casting director. It was Findlay who suggested live relays of opera on to a big screen in the Covent Garden piazza, the most populist venture since the Proms. And it was Findlay again who pushed for the introduction of surtitles – a running translation projected above the stage – over the objections of boardroom traditionalists and opera critics. 'I don't think one goes to the opera to *read*,' sniffed Rodney Milnes, Rosenthal's heir at *Opera*. 'What should be an act of great concentration between performers and audience is broken when the eyes flicker elsewhere. If people go unprepared to the opera, that's their lookout. Why should they spoil the enjoyment of those who do prepare?'[166] Tooley agreed to poll the audience, ninety-four per cent of whom endorsed the surtitles. 'I'm sure they are going to be very popular,' muttered Milnes, 'just like public executions.'

Findlay, a gangling man of deceptively boyish manner, was coming up as a contender. He had the support of the staff and more hands-on experience than Tooley had when he succeeded Webster, having organized and led tours of both companies to the Far East and the United States. 'I was Tooley's Tooley,' said Findlay. 'I had done everything except cook, sing and dance.' What counted now was how well he could play the board game.

The first casualty was Colin Davis. The music director had become moody and withdrawn, showing little interest in any productions but his own. One night when the singing was scrappy and the applause tepid, he told Findlay: 'I've never been music director of this place, not in the sense that Solti was. Solti did what he wanted. Whenever I wanted to do something and John didn't, he would find a million reasons why it couldn't happen.'

His relations with Tooley had cooled. 'They used to be thick as thieves,' said Patsy Tooley, 'but there weren't as many dinners with Colin and Shamsi as before.' Despite his alienation, Davis refused to give up. 'He wanted to work in London, to be with his wife and children,' said Tooley. 'Ideally he would have liked to conduct one of the London orchestras, but that was not forthcoming.' When Tooley broke the news that his contract would not be renewed beyond 1986, Davis was 'desperate'.[167] 'Colin did feel that he was asked to leave too early,' agreed Moser. 'I would have been happier to renew him than some others on the board.'

'It seemed to me a perfectly rational decision by the board,' said Tooley. 'But Colin saw it as something other than that. He felt there were knives out for him, which was absolutely untrue.'

He had been music director for fifteen years, too long by half. Had he left, like Solti, at the end of a decade, he would have departed in glory. As it was, he slunk away with a *Fidelio* in a patchwork production that was booed louder than anything since the 1973 *Don Giovanni*. Only Rosenthal found a kind word to say for the music director, postulating that the Solti and Davis eras at Covent Garden would be seen, in time, 'to be as important as were the Mahler, Toscanini and Krauss regimes in Vienna, Milan and Munich'.[168]

Tooley approached the obvious successors and was turned down flat by the first three. Muti was waiting to inherit La Scala when Abbado moved on, Abbado had his eye on Vienna and Daniel Barenboim would not work for London wages. Zubin Mehta, then head of the New York Philharmonic, was interested and thought Tooley had promised him the job, but the board cast a veto. Mehta's flying visits to Covent Garden had been marred by haste and make-do.

Tooley then suggested that they should abolish the post altogether. 'One of John's lines was, we don't need a music director,' said Findlay. 'I have been here thirty years, he said, I can handle most of that.'

When the board balked, he went looking for the conductor who would need him most. It was Moser who first approached Bernard Haitink, music director of Amsterdam's Concertgebouw Orchestra for quarter of a century and of Glyndebourne for the past decade. He had also been chief conductor of the London Philharmonic. Despite his titular authority, Haitink had always leaned heavily on artistic and administrative partners. At Glyndebourne, Peter Hall supplied the ideas. In Amsterdam they came from artistic directors. Haitink was an excellent conductor but neither an innovator nor a decision maker. When Tooley approached him, he weighed the offer, slept on it, and declined. Twice more Tooley thrust the crown upon him, and twice more Haitink refused. 'I did not think I was the man for it,' he told me at the time. 'It would drive me mad; it was a tremendous risk. But I was fifty-five and it could be my last challenge.'

When he resigned from Glyndebourne, George Christie exploded with anger, outraged that Covent Garden could poach his music director with the divine right of a medieval warlord. The press responded with joyous anticipation and relief at the ending of tedium. Haitink earned extra points by promising to ban fly-by-night stars and renew the bond between Covent Garden and the world beyond. 'There's such a gap between the *Royal* Opera House and the public and musicians outside,' he declared. 'Too much accent on this establishment thing. We must get rid of it.'[169] His inaugural production, a bleak and gripping *Jenůfa* directed by the Russian exile Yuri Lyubimov, saw the experimental introduction of surtitles on alternate nights. 'I noticed the difference,' Haitink exulted. 'The hairs stood up on the back of my neck when I felt the audience understanding every word that was being sung.' In the second act, when the foster-mother drowns Jenůfa's illegitimate baby, the sobbing in the left-hand stalls almost drowned out the cellos. Later in the season, he conducted the ballet thrillingly in a Stravinsky triple bill, the first time since Lambert that a top-notch conductor had led the dancers.

To cover for Haitink's lack of operatic confidence, Jeffrey Tate was brought in as principal conductor; he soon made way for the veteran Edward Downes, who had never been away for long. Downes had the privilege of taking over a run of *Salome* from Christoph von Dohnanyi in which Maria Ewing stripped down to the very buff for a full half-minute, against the feeble protestations of her director husband, Peter Hall. Downes, whose vision was impaired, claimed he saw sequins in her pubic hair. Suddenly, the music was looking up.

'John believed that bringing Bernard in would ensure him another period,' said Findlay. 'His biggest shock was that Bernard did not go to the wall to insist on John staying. Bernard made his point at a board meeting but would not stand up for it.' Tooley was told soon after that his term would end in the summer of 1988, a month after his sixty-fourth birthday.

'I had not expected a renewal,' he said in retrospect. 'I talked about it with Haitink, who wanted it a lot. But I said it's time for appointing somebody who would see the company through the renovation of the house.' Internally, Tooley complained he was being cut off without means of support, although the board agreed to pay him two years' severance, taking him past retirement age, and his salary was raised to a respectable £100,000.

He implored the board to replace him with an opera professional like the Anglophile Hugues Gall, or Brian McMaster who was doing well at Welsh National Opera. John Sainsbury nominated an American called Henry Wrong who was running the City of

London's new Barbican Centre, having previously worked at Rudolf Bing's right hand at the Met.

A selection panel was formed, comprising Moser, Forman, Gibson, Colette Clark and Brian Nicholson. They overrode Tooley's advice, snubbed Sainsbury's man and overlooked Findlay who was backed by most of the staff. Forman and Moser had determined two years earlier that Isaacs should succeed, and the rest of the board were in accord. 'Angus Stirling had got it into his head after the big-screen relay in the piazza that what Covent Garden needed was a television person,' said an eye-witness. 'Tooley lost his temper. "What you need," he said, " is someone who can put on a show in the house night after night." '[170]

A last-minute impediment arose. The BBC had riled Mrs Thatcher with a run of hostile programmes. She demanded the head of its director-general, Alisdair Milne. The biggest job in broadcasting was up for grabs and Isaacs was a prime candidate. He apologized to the ROH board and put in his c.v. There were two contenders of equal merit – David Dimbleby, who was backed by the BBC chairman, 'Duke' Hussey; and Isaacs, favoured by the deputy chairman and former Labour MP, Joel Barnett. When the panel hit stalemate, they reached an English compromise and chose a BBC apparatchik, Michael Checkland. He picked a deputy, John Birt, from independent television, and was deposed before long in his favour. Isaacs or Dimbleby might have spared the BBC the ravages that followed, but the Governors were too timid to choose a strong personality.

Deprived of the job he really wanted, Isaacs became available to Covent Garden on the rebound. Tooley vainly argued that he had disqualified himself by looking elsewhere, but this cut no ice with the board. Isaacs gave in his notice at Channel 4, and told his populist successor, Michael Grade: 'I am handing on to you a sacred trust. If you screw it up, if you betray it, I'll come back and throttle you.'[171] He was as different from Tooley as opera from ballet. For six uneasy months, he shadowed the outgoing general director, under the sharp eye of a new chairman.

Moser, too, had given up. He was out of tune with the times and getting nowhere with the politicians. 'The Labour years always seemed rather easier from our point of view,' he reflected. 'My last two or three years were very tough. I ended on a low.' At his parting press conference, he made a 'final and urgent' plea for more money to an unheeding Government.

Moser had intended to hand over the chair to Forman but the Granada chief was nursing a dying wife. He next thought of nominating Armstrong, who was due to retire from Whitehall the following year, but thought better of it. The next chairman had to be someone Mrs Thatcher trusted, but who could also stand up to her. The man who sprang to mind was John Sainsbury, a notable contributor to Conservative Party funds and powerful business figure. 'I had left the board and had no idea whether they would want me back,' said the supermarket chief. 'When I was approached I found it a very difficult decision, because of the pressure of my other responsibilities. I thought for some time about it and decided that I couldn't commit myself for a full term. I would only accept if they agreed that I could only commit myself to serving for two years while they found someone else.'

'John Sainsbury believed he had to get an undertaking from Thatcher that she would help,' said an ROH insider. 'He went to Downing Street and came back saying that if we doubled the box-office and sponsorship they would help.'

Corks popped in the Royal Ballet. 'We were thrilled,' said Dowell, delighted that a ballet fan would lead the board, the first since Keynes. In his opening set of accounts, Sainsbury reversed the natural order and introduced the ballet season ahead of the opera. 'Retail is detail,' he proclaimed several times daily, and he pursued minutiae with the zeal of a man who was proud to know, to the nearest hundred, how many bags of frozen peas the English bought each day. Short of temper, he brooked no contradiction and subjected staff and directors to shouting fits if they persisted in defying his will. Tooley, unaccustomed to rough treatment, was almost glad to be going. Few were aware that Sainsbury's chairmanship was short-term and stopgap.

On his last day as general director, Tooley was asked on television what had been his greatest disaster. He was stumped for an answer. There had been no failures. Everything at the Garden had been simply perfect.

Called upon to make a farewell address to the staff, Tooley turned to a close colleague and confided: 'I have been here eighteen years and it is very difficult to say what my achievements were. The only thing I can say is: I have kept this place afloat. This may sound dreadful to the outside, but anyone on the inside will know what it means.'

CHAPTER 9

Act Three, On a Spree
(1987–96)

THE SMELLS HAD gone and, with them, the character of the *quartier*. Covent Garden was no longer a market but a burgeoning tourist trap of boutiques, restaurants and faked shop fronts that concealed the superior sort of offices: publishers, property lawyers and the like. The craftsmen and artisans who occupied the less salubrious lofts were driven out by spiralling rents. Armourers, saddlers, silver-makers and many humbler guilds vanished from the district, to be replaced by chocolatiers, pizza parlours and sweater shops. The last remnants of local skills were located inside the opera house, where milliners and scene-painters rubbed shoulders with stagehands who were themselves the sons and cousins of departed costermongers. In due course, they too would be evicted, along with the police from their famous station on Bow Street – all, in some way or other, driven out by the ever-expanding opera house.

A raggle-taggle resistance movement formed. Six thousand people lived in Covent Garden and not all of them welcomed the prospect of two years' upheaval and a twenty-three million pound office block to show for it. In August 1987, two months after the ROH obtained planning permission from Westminster Council, the Covent Garden Community Association applied to the High Court for a judicial review. They argued that tenanted land which had been given to the opera house for art's sake should not be used for commercial development, and that Westminster had broken its own rules by allowing more offices in a heritage conservation area. Among the cited outrages against local history was the ROH plan to demolish the imposing Floral Hall, a Victorian crystal palace of bygone blooms, half-destroyed by fire in 1956.

As the dispute rippled outwards, new players leaped into the pond. A property company, Tottingham's, based in Columbus, Ohio, received encouragement from the ROH board to submit a neighbour-friendly scheme involving retail and residential elements. A conductor called Denis Vaughan – a former Beecham pupil who lived in a Floral Street flat opposite the opera house and waited for a ten-minute call that never came – floated an idea of linking the ROH to the Coliseum, the Lyceum and the Theatre Royal Drury Lane in an integrated performing arts village, akin to George Whyte's grounded vision. Vaughan was a dreamer whose inch-thick missives were binned unread by ROH directors, but he was tenacious, energetic and sometimes far-sighted. The only way to fund a sensible rebuilding of the ROH, he maintained, was to create a National Lottery for the purpose. Don't be absurd, he was told. Just you wait, said Vaughan.

Moser had been dismissive of protestors and dreamers. Sainsbury, alert to their disruptive potential, detailed Covent Garden's new head of public affairs, Ewen Balfour, to bend an ear to their plaints. Balfour, an engaging man from the Central Office of Information with a mystifying range of contacts in every tier of public life, drew the sting from the dissentients as the legal action took its course. Once learned counsel shuffled their briefs, matters got local and personal. The Board accused several of its tenants, restaurateurs on short-term leases, of funding the costly CGCA court action for personal gain. Attempts were made to discredit the Association's most voluble activist, Jim Monahan, an architect and son of the ex-director of the Royal Ballet School. He was alleged to have private axes to grind. Monahan said: 'My main reason for belonging to the CGCA is to continue the battle to maintain central London as a place where those on low incomes can live, and where the quality of life is not completely consumed by commercial, short-term interests.'[1]

It took six months for the review to come to court. Before Isaacs took office, he was warned that closure would have to be postponed from 1992 to 1995 at the earliest. In February 1988 the High Court ruled that Westminster had acted lawfully in granting planning consent. The CGCA appealed. In September, the Court of Appeal upheld the ruling. Leave to appeal to the House of Lords was denied. There was nothing now to stop the redevelopment from going ahead, except an attack of second thoughts within the ROH.

A new Technical Director, John Harrison, joined the company in

November 1988. He warned that the plans did not provide nearly enough space. The architects were sent back to the drawing board. A new plan was submitted to Westminster, this time without an office block or underground parking. Fifteen years of preparation and a great deal of money had gone to waste. The Royal Opera House was fifteen million pounds in the red at Coutts. The estimated cost of redevelopment rocketed from £56 million to £150 million in a year. The grim comedy was about to begin.

England in the latter half of 1987 descended from serenity to confusion. A sequence of preternatural events fell from a clear blue sky. In July, Margaret Thatcher became the first Prime Minister of her century to be re-elected for a third term. With a vast majority and little opposition, she rammed through an unfettered programme of privatizations, along with contentious reforms of the health, education and local taxation systems. Satisfaction among the propertied classes was unconfined.

In August, a gunman walked around the quiet, middle-England town of Hungerford, killing fourteen people and wounding fifteen in an unprecedented imitation of American-style massacres. On 16 October the worst hurricane on record sowed terror and havoc across the south of the country, ripping roofs off houses and paralysing rail and roadways. Three days later, the London Stock Exchange saw ten per cent of its share values wiped out on Black Monday. In November, the IRA bombed a Remembrance Day parade in Enniskillen. Two weeks later, a fire at King's Cross Underground Station killed thirty passengers and injured hundreds. Each disaster was horrific in itself; together they suggested a turning of tides, a blight on the new prosperity. In a fractious atmosphere of deepening gloom, people no longer trusted essential services or the established powers to cope with the unforeseen. The strongest leader since Churchill was also the most reviled.

Margaret Thatcher's third victory had unleashed triumphalist yelps from the newly rich. This was the age of Loadsamoney, a character minted by the comedian Harry Enfield from the yuppies and yahoos who thronged City bars and lit their cigars with ten pound notes. The yuppies were young upwardly-mobile professionals; the yahoos were brightly-coated traders who stoked a fever of speculation and walked away with six-digit bonuses. Unaccustomed to wealth, they looked for conspicuous ways to spend it. Opera, extravagant and loud, appealed. The first mobile phones went off in the Covent Garden foyer. Opera was *nouveau chic*. Record attendances were reported at ENO and Welsh National Opera, eighty-five and eighty-seven per cent respectively. Entrepreneurs got in on the act, putting on an *Aida* spectacular at Earl's Court and selling a hundred thousand tickets at twenty and twenty-five pounds apiece. The opera cost £1.5 million to produce and made a big enough profit for two of its co-promoters, Harvey Goldsmith and Mark McCormack, to attempt further ventures. At Covent Garden, Lyubimov's much-lauded *Jenůfa* had cost £529,300. It recouped £199,900 from a ninety-two per cent box-office and £150,000 more in sponsorship. The net loss was £179,400. The bulk of the costs were inbuilt: chorus and orchestra together amounted to £114,000, almost a quarter of the budget.

John Sainsbury, who knew the price of everything, gave orders to up the ante. Tickets were increased by up to forty per cent. Isaacs, a socialist and populist, recorded no objection. Paul Findlay said: 'That's the end of the opera house.' He was proved wrong, at first, as money rushed in through every door. Then, as recession gripped, top seats went unsold and the deficit grew. Worse, an impression had been given that opera and ballet could be self-financing. One Tory think-tanker went so far as to urge minority arts like opera, reaching two per cent of the populace, to shake off the shackles of subsidy and follow market forces: 'to create the kind of partnership with the British public that forty years of state subsidy have totally failed to achieve.'[2]

Such contentions were music to the ears of a new breed of Tory MPs who refused lunch at the Arts Council and privately advocated its abolition. Margaret Thatcher was herself intent on rolling back state involvement. She had ears for the likes of the conductor Lorin Maazel, a Downing Street dinner guest, who told her that London's musicians were a load of wastrels.

The portents for Covent Garden grew poorer. The new Arts Council chairman was a millionaire property developer, Peter Palumbo, who promised an increased grant but failed to deliver. Sainsbury, needing money for running costs and redevelopment, did as Drogheda had done before him: he turned to the Jews. At Glyndebourne one summer's night, he wooed Alex Alexander, chairman of Allied Lyons, to become chairman of the ROH Trust. George Christie was incensed. 'Hast thou killed and also taken possession?'[3] he raged (or words to that effect), as his chief fundraiser went the red-carpet way of his music director. For a while, the two opera companies were barely on speaking terms. Christie, as chairman of the Arts Council's music panel, was in a position to exact fiscal retribution on the ROH grant.

Alexander, a Czech-born Hitler refugee, reorganized the ROH Trust, squeezing his suppliers for donations whether they liked arts or not. He brought on board as deputy chairman the redoubtable Vivien Duffield, heir to the Clore millions, along with her friend Gail Ronson, wife of the Heron Group chairman who would go to jail for his part in the Guinness share-dealing scandal. Duffield had built a wing on to the Tate Gallery and saved a Constable for the nation, receiving no more than a cursory thank-you note from a junior minister three weeks later. 'I'd rather give the money to my East End Jews,' she told a dinner partner. 'At least they're grateful.'[4]

At Covent Garden, she demanded a say in how her money was spent. 'I was under no illusions,' she reported. 'I said I would need a place on the board if they wanted me (on the Trust). John (Sainsbury) was more pro-female than Moser. It was a seriously establishment board, nobody too brazen. They all thought I was slightly mad to undertake a job like this.'[5]

It was not in Vivien Duffield's nature to be inconspicuous. There was much muttering behind cupped hands about the '*haute juiverie*' who were taking over the opera house. It was all right for a Jew to be chairman or general director, but for rich Jews to think they owned the place was simply *de trop*, my dear. The more money Mrs Duffield and John Sainsbury pledged to the opera house, the more antagonism they aroused. 'Great credit to the generosity of these millionaires who are donating portions of their wealth to the public,' sneered Jim Monahan. 'But this is done for the public good on *their* terms . . . It is the power that such benefactors have to twist and contort public projects that is my main concern.'[6]

Two weeks before Jeremy Isaacs took over, Sir Frederick Ashton died in his sleep, a month short of his eighty-fourth birthday. The country-churchyard funeral, in late August, was ill-attended. The great goodbyes were said at Westminster Abbey in November, in the presence of the Queen Mother, Princess Margaret, peers of the realm and four generations of Royal Ballet dancers, great and small. Ninette de Valois led the mourning. Margot Fonteyn, herself near death, sent a fond eulogy from her Panamanian *hacienda*, likening

Ashton to Shakespeare 'for his extraordinary understanding of the
human heart and mind and his ability to illuminate them through his
own art form.' To many, it marked the end of an age. To Isaacs,
entering unfamiliar realms, it posed an immediate conundrum.

Ashton had named his late sister's son, Anthony Russell-Roberts,
as his executor and heir. Russell-Roberts was Administrative
Director of the Royal Ballet. A former Tooley aide, he had gone to
work at the Paris Opéra before returning as chief executive of the
RB. No one had foreseen the difficulty this could cause when Ashton
died. The Royal Ballet, which danced more of Ashton's work than
any other company, would be run by a man who earned a royalty
every time his ballets were performed. Anthony Dowell, as artistic
director, had the first and final say on what the RB would dance and
who was to appear in it, but the administrative director had an input
into the programming process and influence over the dancers whose
contracts he negotiated. In Whitehall, his position would have
required one of those moral clarifications from the Cabinet
Secretary. At Covent Garden, it became part of an uncritically cosy
set-up.

Isaacs disliked Russell-Roberts and wanted to replace him with
someone he trusted. He was warned this might be unwise. If
Ashton's heir were to withdraw his uncle's works, the Royal Ballet
would not have much to dance. The general director swallowed hard
and accepted the unacceptable.

He next tried to dismiss Paul Findlay, who had been appointed at
Haitink's insistence as Director of the Royal Opera. 'Jeremy phoned
me about a week after he had arrived and said he wanted to get rid
of Paul,' recalled Tooley. 'I told him he would lose Haitink if he did,
so he backed down.'

Isaacs and Findlay were physically and temperamentally ill-
suited. Isaacs was squat, abrasive and modernist in outlook, Findlay
was tall, courteous and traditionalist. The son of a philosophy
professor, his whirlygig outflow of ideas and activity could be dis-
concerting. Isaacs decided to second-guess Findlay with two
backstop appointments – John Cox as director of productions and
Patrick Carnegy as dramaturg. Together with Haitink and the casting
director Peter Katona, they made up the artistic directorate of the
Royal Opera, in which Findlay's voice was paramount.

Haitink was in one of his morose periods, between wives and
perpetually on the verge of resignation. Findlay calmed him down

and kept him working. 'Bernard wanted to cancel everything,' he recalled. 'He wanted to get back to Holland. Didn't get on with Isaacs. His time span for a meeting was forty minutes. One of the greatest disappointments for me as Opera Director was that he had so few suggestions to make.' His reticence was well founded. 'Lacking any distinctive taste of his own,' said Carnegy, 'Haitink became the victim of those who had to decide things for him.'[7]

Haitink encouraged Findlay to engage the best guest conductors. He also welcomed the return of Edward Downes, who would contribute the biggest repertory idea of the Isaacs decade: a cycle of all Verdi's operas, from the immature *Oberto* to a climactic *Falstaff* on the centenary (in 2001) of his death.

Findlay brought back Solti, a close personal friend, after a three-year absence. He nurtured the young Italians Daniele Gatti and Carlo Rizzi, and encouraged Sian Edwards, the first woman to conduct at Covent Garden (she joined the staff in 1988). One day, Findlay had a call from the stage door saying there was a Russian to see him. The name was unfamiliar, but Findlay came down to greet the visitor, who introduced himself as the new Director of the Kirov Opera. Valery Gergiev, thirty-five, was on his first trip abroad with a basic phrasebook, having inherited the famous theatre as the Soviet Union under Mikhail Gorbachev entered its dying phase. At the Royal Opera House, he saw a revival of Tarkovsky's *Boris Godunov*. 'I want to show that in Russia,' he declared. He could not pay a kopek, but Findlay had an idea. The BBC wanted to screen *Boris* but could not afford stage-union fees. If he shipped it to Russia, they could film it for free.

Gergiev was ecstatic. He talked Findlay into co-producing two Prokofiev operas, *Fiery Angel* and *War and Peace*, at the Kirov with British directors. During Findlay's tenure, he conducted often and brilliantly at Covent Garden – 'I have heard nothing like it since Furtwängler,' said one vocal authority.[8] Haitink told Tooley he had never heard the strings play so well.[9]

'All credit to Jeremy,' said Findlay, 'he gave me my head. I was allowed to put on ten new productions a year, after years of nothing.' Isaacs was less ecstatic. At Channel Four he had built his own staff from scratch and commanded personal loyalty. Here, he inherited inbred structures and uncongenial executives whose wages were kept on a separate payroll to prevent the lower orders from knowing what they earned. Labour relations were antediluvian. The rest of the country had ended its industrial warfare while Covent Garden was still tuning up. The orchestra came out on strike, only to be bribed back by a gift from a mysterious donor. The chorus walked out next, bitter at seeing their wages fall below ENO parity. 'We had been pushed into a corner,' said one non-activist. 'You had to be a soloist to get into this chorus, go into the Crush Bar and sing an aria to the music director before you were accepted, and do it again every two years. We sang in five languages, ENO in one. We earned less than train drivers, £176 maximum a week. They never treated us as artists. They just said, "there's no extra money". But if the orchestra came out, a week later they'd give them a rise.'[10] Backstage members of the Broadcasting and Entertainment Alliance (BETA, later Bectu), staged wildcat stoppages.

Trouble also simmered at the Ballet, where MacMillan's long-awaited revision of Cranko's *Prince of the Pagodas* was disrupted in mid-rehearsal. 'I remember being on stage,' said Anthony Dowell, 'and I was playing the emperor. Suddenly I was the only person on stage and they were having a meeting, threatening to black the first night. Monica and I had to go up and talk to the company. Wayne (Eagling) was the leader, and I just couldn't agree with all of that.'

Isaacs settled the chorus dispute to get his first season opened on time, and walked around the house radiating good will. A gregarious man with a capacious range of interests, he would stop and chat with all and sundry but, unlike Tooley, was never accepted as part of the 'family', never a 'Gardener'. It was held against him that he lunched in restaurants and only once joined the toilers in the steamy staff canteen. During intervals, he avoided the Crush Bar, disappearing with favoured guests to his redecorated office. 'This was a paternalistically run family concern,' he reflected, 'in the sense that everybody who was there had a feeling for what the House wanted to achieve. People worked in the accounts department for very inadequate pay because on the tannoy in their office they could hear the sound of a rehearsal and could, perhaps, get cheap tickets for the night. They felt that they belonged to the House and had a job there for life.

'There was no fixed retirement age. You could not get anyone out of the orchestra or chorus unless you engaged in ludicrous, protracted, undignified procedures to show them that they could not perform as well as they used to. I said, if you're not good enough, you're out. We lost that sense of family where nobody could do you any harm because you belonged. The family was broken, though, under the pressure of decades of underfunding of which the Thatcher years were the most evident. The family home, which I entered as a stranger, ended for good in the years that I was there.'

His inaugural press conference was a rumbustious affair, introducing a Five Year Plan to increase new productions, visiting companies and outside broadcasts. He specifically promised to reinstate *La Juive*, a mid-Victorian blockbuster with three strong tenors and a Jewish heroine. 'If a general director with the name of Jeremiah Israel Isaacs cannot put on *La Juive* at Covent Garden,' he laughed, 'then the job's not worth having.' He would be forced to eat those words, ungarnished.

Extrovert, extravagant and expansive, Isaacs was a refreshing antidote to the thin-blooded Tooley. His love for music blazed through every utterance, a legacy of his Glasgow childhood. 'I owe it all to my parents,' he avowed. His father, a bookish man, had a jeweller's shop. His mother was a busy family doctor who took her three sons to symphony concerts after cooking Sunday lunch and taught them to appreciate fine art by acquiring a Josef Herman oil painting, the cornerstone of Isaacs' collector's instinct for modern Scottish art. 'My great wish is that everybody should grow up in an environment where they can be exposed to what the arts can do for their lives,' he prayed. Though he forsook religious faith, he displayed a fiery adherence to his family, his Jewish heritage and certain restless ideals of education and self-betterment.

At Oxford, he was President of the Union. In television he caught an echo of ancestral values from Sidney Bernstein who 'absolutely forbade anyone to say on his channel, "I'm sorry that's all we've got time for." ' The new medium existed to spread information, and hence opportunity, democracy and equality. In *The World at War*, Isaacs reinvented the historical documentary on a massive scale, employing first-hand sources to relate the course of the conflict. At Channel Four, he had a licence to be quirky and diverse, appealing to ethnic, sexual and special-interest minorities; as the BBC abandoned highbrow viewing in a ratings war, Isaacs put out whole operas on Sunday afternoons. For relaxation, he read Greek poetry.

Sentimental to a fault, Isaacs could be brutally insensitive. He was deeply wounded by the death of a brother by a Palestinian bomb in Jerusalem and by the tragic demise of his first wife, Tamara, from breast cancer. He would burst into tears on recounting these losses.

'I was a bad husband,' he confessed to an opera house colleague. A few days later, he sacked the man without a trace of emotion.

Two years after his first wife's death, Isaacs married Gillian Widdicombe, a former *Financial Times* critic who had advised Channel Four on its opera broadcasts. A stunning beauty when young, Widdicombe snared many artistic admirers, first among them the Earl of Drogheda. She introduced the old man to her new husband, who bestowed a paternal blessing. 'Garrett became very fond of Jeremy,' said Widdicombe. 'When I asked him what advice he would give a general director's wife he said: Don't appear to know too much, they'll dislike you for it.' Widdicombe's position was doubly delicate; she was about to become Arts Editor of the *Observer* newspaper and was expected to report even-handedly on the country's costliest arts institution while married to its chief. As a token of her detachment, she engaged as music critic the repatriated Andrew Porter, who recalled a more glorious past.

Drogheda now cut a sad figure around the opera house. His wife, Joan, had succumbed to Alzheimer's Disease and he nursed her at home, refusing to subject her to the indignities of institutional care. 'Towards the end she could not remember her own name,' said a visiting friend, 'but she could sit at the piano and play a Mozart sonata, note perfect.' A few days before Christmas 1989, Joan Drogheda died. Solti, hearing the news, telephoned the ex-chairman to offer condolences. There was no answer. The earl had taken to his bed and died on Christmas Eve. 'It was like Tristan and Isolde,' said Solti, fighting back tears, 'they could not live without each other.'

A new *Ring* was needed to set the regime on its way. Haitink had demanded it as 'a crucial part of my work as music director', never having conducted the cycle before. He nominated Lyubimov as director after their *Jenůfa* triumph, overlooking his lack of Wagner experience. Isaacs, visiting the septuagenarian Russian exile in Jerusalem, was alarmed to hear that he found much of it 'terrible nonsense'. Back in the house, Paul Hernon designed a foldaway set that could be taken on the road when Covent Garden closed, to be set up before five thousand viewers in the Royal Albert Hall, or fifty thousand in a football stadium. 'We can really widen our audience appeal,' enthused Findlay.

It was not to be. Lyubimov turned up with few ideas, no German and halting English. He was mocked by James Morris, singing

Wotan, and the production attracted critical obloquy – 'lacking in motivation, unnecessarily fussy, sometimes astonishingly inept,' wrote Paul Griffiths in *The Times*.[11] *Rheingold* was saved from ignominy only by Haitink's assured conducting. It was clear after the opening segment that the cycle could not be allowed to proceed under Lyubimov, nor could it be abandoned without paying off huge casts and throwing the schedules into chaos. Helge Schmidt, Tooley's erstwhile casting director, pointed out to Findlay that Götz Friedrich was running a *Ring* in Berlin in which most of the ROH cast had already sung. It differed from his last London *Ring* in its 'concept' of an underground tunnel through which all human life flowed. 'The space is different,' said Friedrich. 'I hope it can be interesting because there are many things I want to review. It is not an emergency *Ring*.'[12]

It was more of a hand-me-down *Ring* – cobbled together, banged about and displaying little vitality. Friedrich, in middle-age, wore executive suits and delivered to budget. Haitink burnished the orchestra to high sheen, sometimes at the expense of his singers. 'I wish he'd remember we are here sometimes,' grumbled the tenor René Kollo,[13] who declined a return invitation.

The next let-down was Piero Faggioni, commissioned to produce and design a *Trovatore* on sets so flexible they could serve two other operas. The sets proved dismal and the costumes so heavy that Domingo threatened to tear his tunic off. The Spanish director Nuria Espert was brought in for *Madam Butterfly*, *Rigoletto* and a humdrum *Carmen*, featuring the stressed-out Maria Ewing, whose marriage to Peter Hall had ruptured.

Against these and other embarrassments, there were scintillating delights in each of Isaacs' first three seasons. *Un re in ascolto (A King Listens)* by Luciano Berio, premièred at the Salzburg Festival, sparkled with circus acrobatics and drew a ninety-two per cent attendance. *The Cunning Little Vixen* marked the ROH début of Simon Rattle, the rising British conductor who had fallen out with Tooley in 1979 over the apparent mistreatment of his wife, Elise Ross, cast as *Thérèse* in John Tavener's opera and then dropped. Rattle, no linguist, performed the Janáček opera in English, despite the availability of surtitles. He was loudly acclaimed, and never returned. 'He wasn't comfortable at Covent Garden,' said Lilian Watson, who sang the Vixen. 'Some of the music staff dug their heels in and did it their way. His style of working didn't appeal to them.' In addition to house recalcitrance, Rattle bridled against the snobbishness he perceived in London, ever an active deterrent for a Liverpudlian who devoted the first chunk of his career to the City of Birmingham Symphony Orchestra and the next to the Berlin Philharmonic.

Isaacs' third season produced a world première. Harrison Birtwistle's *Gawain* wove a circular spell around Arthurian legend of green knights and chaste damsels. Rough-toned at times, but also tartly tender, the opera was intended for Haitink but the Dutchman ducked out in favour of Elgar Howarth, who had premièred *Mask of Orpheus*. Peter Sellars, the Californian director, withdrew because he found the work 'anti-feminist'.

Repeated in 1994, the opera attracted organized heckling from a gang of frustrated neo-romantic composers who made more headlines by cat-calling than they ever would by writing music. Birtwistle's was a shy, stubborn, English art that drew its strengths from a rural upbringing and a fixation with Greek drama. 'I haven't invented a language,' he once told me. 'What I do is somehow joined up to something that came before it. Tradition is not aping the past but making the future. That's why I like to think that what I do is tradition.' *Gawain* was, in its way, a *Parsifal* for modern times. It did not conquer the world despite three Covent Garden revivals, but the composer's fame spread from Chicago to Berlin as a result of his ROH success. Isaacs had stuck his neck out for Birtwistle, more than Tooley had done for Tippett, or Webster for Britten, after *Billy Budd*.

He invited readers of a new daily, the *Independent*, to support young composers and librettists who were struggling to write their first opera. Close to a thousand individuals chipped in a hundred pounds each to the 'Garden Venture' and six short operas were duly produced at the Donmar Theatre. They ranged from the inept to the egregious, but the scheme drew widespread attention to the fresh water that Isaacs was trying to pump into a stagnant pond.

Downes's ambitious Verdi project got under way with *Attila*, unstaged in living memory. The production budget was just £205,000. But when staff costs and overheads were taken into account, the run of eight performances cost £1.27 million, of which £928,000 was recovered in tickets, sponsorship and catering, leaving a deficit of £344,000. It was not possible for Covent Garden to put on any kind of opera, no matter how modest, without losing large sums of money against a static public grant. Two operas scheduled for Isaacs' third season, Massenet's *Don Quichotte* and Gluck's *Iphigénie en Tauride*, had to be sacrificed on the altar of cost.

There was no margin for error, and physical safety was daily at risk in a Victorian manufactory that worked stagehands round the clock, bare-handedly hauling hunks of scenery. 'This was manual labour that was clumsy, inefficient, repetitive and dangerous,' said Isaacs. One Friday evening, working at his desk, his eye strayed to a silent television monitor on his wall. Men seemed to be running diagonally across the stage, where they were setting up that night's *Don Carlos*, the venerable Visconti production. Isaacs rushed downstairs. 'On the floor is a bloodied body,' he reported a week later. 'Over it, a nurse, a fireman and a couple of his mates are giving artificial respiration, trying to keep him alive. "Come on, Greg,"' they call to him, "keep going."'[14] It was no use. Greg Bellamy, a member of B crew, had been crushed beneath a slippage of plywood flooring. He was pronounced dead on arrival at hospital. The news paralysed the backstage. Isaacs watched as

> bells are rung to bring the audience from the bars into the theatre. I go out front to tell them what has happened, and that the performance is cancelled. Silently, they accept and leave the theatre, some donating their ticket refunds to the widow.[15]

On Sunday, before a packed house, a Verdi *Requiem* was sung for Greg Bellamy, with dancers and crewmen holding candles on stage. Agnes Baltsa, Katia Ricciarelli, Arthur Davies and Samuel Ramey were the soloists and Colin Davis came in to conduct. The takings were given to the victim's family. The ROH was fined a thousand pounds by a Health and Safety tribunal some months later, and measures were taken to minimize further risks. But in a crumbling theatre and on knife-edge deadlines it was only a matter of time before someone else got hurt. 'Greg Bellamy's death called attention, as nothing else could, to the urgent need for the redeveloped opera house,' said Isaacs.

A pall of anxiety hung over the Royal Ballet. Directly after the Ashton commemoration, the company set off in high spirits for Australia. The tour was happy and cloud-free. Only Brisbane, the last stop, posed a problem. A triple bill with MacMillan's *Rite of Spring* was not selling well. The Queensland promoter called Anthony Dowell two weeks beforehand and asked if he could substitute *Swan Lake*. MacMillan reluctantly agreed.

On the afternoon of the performance, around five o'clock, MacMillan felt unwell and went to visit a Brisbane friend, who happened to be a doctor. 'The doctor walked him straight into the hospital next door, and that's where he had the heart attack and the stroke,' recalled Monica Mason. 'It was very serious and we were terrified he wouldn't pull through. I stayed on in Australia for a three-week holiday, always phoning Deborah to see how he was. By the end of the holiday it looked brighter. I remember Deborah saying to me, "this was very serious. we just don't know how long he can survive. It can happen at any time. It could be in rehearsal with you and something terrible could happen."' The company's creative pulse was unsteady, but MacMillan was a resilient man and, without Ashton at his shoulder, was keen to get back to work.

Dowell meanwhile buckled down to strengthening the ensemble. There were some good ballerinas coming through – Alessandra Ferri, Bryony Brind, Fiona Chadwick – all home-grown products, but the icy sheen of stardom was absent. Then, two windfalls transformed the picture. Nureyev, on his penultimate visit, brought along a sleek Parisienne who had partnered him since 1984, when she was just nineteen. Sylvie Guillem had it all: glamour, beauty, *hauteur* and a gymnastic agility that defied the laws of anatomy and gravity. At twenty-three she had the strut of a champion and the nerves of an iceberg. Nureyev hoped to draw from her the elixir of youth that he had bestowed on Fonteyn, but any dreams of rejuvenation were dashed by the advance of his disease. Beside Guillem, he looked wasted and not long for this world. She, beside him, refused to be treated as an ingénue and demanded independence.

On her second trip to London, dancing *Giselle*, she was chatting to Anthony Dowell after rehearsal when he said, as a pleasantry, 'Sylvie, it would be lovely if you could give us a little more time.' Before the week was out, she was talking terms with Anthony Russell-Roberts and preparing to move in as Principal Guest Artist. News of her defection in February 1989 devastated French ballet. 'A national catastrophe,' *Le Monde* called it. Nureyev was wounded, and told her so. 'Rudolf was angry at me when I left,' she said.

'Doesn't she know I would have married her?' he told a friend.[16]

When Nureyev had got over his resentment, he gave Dowell some advice on handling his last creation. 'We were talking on the phone, and he suddenly came up with one of his brilliant phrases,' Dowell remembered. 'He said to me, talking about Sylvie: "treat with iron glove."' Guillem would be a law unto herself.

Fifteen months later, the leading man of the Bolshoi signed up with the Royal Ballet. Irek Mukhamedov was thirty years old, at the peak of his powers, and fed up with the powers that be. Communism was crumbling, but dancers were still subjected to the iron rule of Yuri Grigorovich and the company commissars. 'I was tired of being a Soviet hero, of supporting Grigorovich, the state, communism,' he explained. '. . . It was time I took responsibility for myself and Masha and the baby.'[17] Russell-Roberts met him in Vienna in an attempt to head him off from following Baryshnikov to America. A weekend in the country – at Ashton's former home, Chandos Lodge, now inhabited by the Russell-Roberts family – sealed the deal. On the Monday he met Dowell who 'liked him immediately'. Isaacs was summoned to the Soviet Embassy and rebuked for having encouraged the dancer to break his contract with the Bolshoi; defection was no longer regarded as political betrayal but as commercial malpractice.

Mukhamedov, like Nureyev, was a Tatar. Unlike Nureyev, he was house-trained. Elegant, well-mannered and generous, Mukhamedov was the ultimate dream-teamer, an artist who raised others on the wings of his own attainments. Half-clad, he was the hottest thing London had seen in tights for many a long year. All of his allure and exuberance was saved for the stage. In class, he was focused, studious and infinitely considerate. Seeing a visitor sitting with one leg extended, he quietly asked me to tuck it under the chair 'to make sure you don't get injured'. No fuss, no reproach, just the meticulous attentiveness that is the mark of all high-fliers.

'There can be resentment if the (artistic) visitors are not obviously better than our own people,' said Darcey Bussell, a rising ballerina. 'But Irek is part of the company now. He has class with the rest of the boys and they all learn from watching him.' He came, said Ninette de Valois, 'not as a distinguished visitor; he came to learn. His presence is a marvellous tonic for the company, his different style and schooling an example to everyone.'[18]

The only sour note was struck by Wayne Eagling. 'The people

who lose out from the star policy are the English dancers,' he snapped, echoing a moan that had rumbled through Covent Garden since the first foreign singers docked in 1947. 'The public should not get the idea that only big names are worth watching.'[19] Eagling left the company the following year to run the Dutch National Ballet.

With two world-beaters in harness, the extra costs approved by a balletomane chairman, the Royal Ballet recovered its twinkle. Excitement and attendances rose sharply. So did standards. Attention was finally directed to the orchestral accompaniment, which was generally appalling. The self-effacing Ashley Lawrence had been eased out as conductor in 1987; he was felled three years later by a heart attack in a Tokyo street. His successor, Isaiah Jackson from the American Deep South, made no impression on hard-bitten musicians of the ROH pit. Only when Haitink conducted – Romeo and Juliet was his second ballet – did the orchestra play as if they meant it. Jackson was replaced in 1990 by Barry Wordsworth, a solid English professional.

Isaacs now pitched into strategic restructuring. The Sadler's Wells Royal Ballet was going all over the country and going nowhere in terms of aims and identity. He proposed to rebase the company in Birmingham, where Simon Rattle's orchestra and a sympathetic city council were reinvigorating cultural life. The move was designed to appeal to the Arts Council's devolutionary demands.

Madam, who still had power of veto, was persuaded of the worthiness of the cause through a good deal of shouting into her ear-trumpet. Peter Wright, the company's quietly effective director, was warily in favour. David Bintley, his principal choreographer and intended successor, was thrilled. Reins were grabbed and roots planted. The amorphous second company finally gained a life of its own as the Birmingham Royal Ballet.

MacMillan, back at work, was delighted with Mukhamedov. 'He must remember all his mistakes,' he said at their first rehearsal, 'I will use them.'[20] He gave him a one-act ballet, Winter Dreams, and coached him steadily in the great heroic roles. He picked out Darcey Bussell for Prince of the Pagodas, spotting her potential 'far more presciently than anybody else'.[21] The ballet was riding high and MacMillan, perhaps for the first time in his professional life, seemed happy. 'We got lulled,' said Monica Mason, his assistant, 'into a false sense of security.'

*

The world was turning at alarming speed. The fortified wall that had divided Europe since the war was breached. Communism crumbled in one state after another until even the Soviet Union, crucible of working-class revolution, was abolished. The West had won the war, but dared not claim victory, military or moral. Most western economies, mired in recession and fearful of being overrun by cheap labour and products from the liberated east, erected a new wall of protectionism and xenophobia.

The arts, having sat out the Cold War, had no message for the messy peace. After the initial celebratory Beethoven Ninths in Berlin, bureaucrats set about reducing the surfeit of orchestras and theatres that resulted from German reunification. At the centre of events and the heart of European music, few tears were shed for the atrophying of culture. State-subsidized opera houses began staging commercial musicals to turn a profit. The arts establishment was too intent on survival to reflect and direct public concerns. At a time when rock stars rallied to relieve famine in Africa and film stars made political careers, the stylized, regimented, timeworn antics of opera singers and ballet dancers bore scant relevance to the burning issues of the day. The old justifications rang hollow. To the proverbial man on the Clapham omnibus, the survival of the Royal Opera House mattered less than the threatened bankruptcy of a third-division football club.

Jeremy Isaacs, faced with a funding freeze, resolved to spend his way out of trouble. He increased the thousand-strong payroll – already twice the size of Webster's family firm – by an extra hundred staff, including, and necessitating for the first time, a personnel manager. In a considerable personal coup, he persuaded Luciano Pavarotti to return after a seven-year absence, parading him at the Savoy Hotel before a ravenous mob of press snappers. The 1990 Three Tenors Concert during the soccer World Cup had led Pavarotti and Domingo to bury their rivalries above the reedy tones of José Carreras, who was miraculously recovered from leukaemia. All three now enjoyed pop-star status, earning a million dollars nightly in open-air arena concerts.

Pavarotti did not come cheap. Isaacs maintained that his fee was held in line with the prevalent top nightly rate of ten thousand pounds, but any deal with Pavarotti involved a ream of incidentals that cost several times more than his singing wage. Three or four

Concorde seats, Savoy suites, expensive gifts and sundry attentions made Big Lucy an expensive luxury that could be justified only by inflating seat prices – and thereby excluding the popular audience he had been booked to attract. Pavarotti sang fifteen performances in three productions during Isaacs' nine years. He enjoyed, to all appearances, a happy rapport with the General Director, which is more than could be said of Domingo, who complained to Tooley that he felt unappreciated. 'Jeremy didn't have much time for him,' said Tooley, 'he wasn't that interested in performers.'

Domingo had his fervent supporters, among them Vivien Duffield. 'He is the least affected of them all,' she said, 'no entourages and limos. Somebody who will give up two hours after a gruelling performance so that every single one of those little ladies who stood outside in the rain got a word and a kiss – *il faut le faire*, as they say. There aren't many in the business like that.'

Domingo sang thirty-six performances in the Isaacs period and conducted twice; he had a London property portfolio to look after and a genuine attachment to the house. When his dresser, Julio, suffered severe burns in a domestic accident, Domingo paid his medical bills.

Carreras sang eighteen times, never as impressively as before, though his female fans were legion. The cost was extortionate, and only the rich could afford to watch. 'It is against my nature to charge people *anything* to listen to music,' grumbled Haitink.[22]

As resources tightened, half a million pounds was lost each year on industrial disputes. The orchestra, perpetually murmurous, found ever more ingenious causes for dissent. Rejecting a five and a half per cent pay rise, they halted rehearsals for Meyerbeer's long-unseen *Les Huguenots* by demanding the four interval breaks specified by the composer. 'There was not one person in the management of the ROH who had a qualification in music,' said shop steward Robert Trory. The players turned up in the pit in casual clothes, distributing leaflets among the audience to explain their grievance. Isaacs took stock of the worsening situation and shut the house. It took a week of dark nights and ACAS mediation to get it reopened. *The Times*, in an editorial, advised Covent Garden to sack its turbulent musicians and replace them with one of London's underworked symphony orchestras. 'Isaacs was impossible to deal with,' said Trory. 'He only liked the sound of his own voice.'

Isaacs, hemmed in on all sides, went to the Arts Council and told them that he was prepared to run up a deficit. Unless funding was increased, he told the press, the result would be 'Armageddon'. His chairman implored Mrs Thatcher to cough up, but the Prime Minister was otherwise preoccupied. Her new arts minister, David Mellor, was keen on music but nurtured ill-feeling for Covent Garden where, he alleged, his visually-impaired wife, Judith, had been snubbed by the General Director and reception staff.

The Arts Council ordered Isaacs to balance the books or risk the consequences. Coutts made anxious noises about the overdraft. Isaacs flew to Berlin with Findlay to tell Friedrich that his *Ring* would have to be given without *Götterdämmerung*, because the rehearsals meant too many black nights. Friedrich agreed to fewer rehearsals and Findlay, rejigging the schedules, inserted twelve *Rigoletto*s and *Bohème*s to boost box-office takings.

'You bloody fool!' exclaimed Isaacs.

'What do you mean?' said his Opera Director.

'That kills Sainsbury's position with the PM,' fumed Isaacs. 'He was going to go to her and say, this theatre can't even put on a *Ring* cycle any more. That would have impressed her.'

Margaret Thatcher was on her last legs. In November 1990, six weeks before a United Nations victory in the Gulf War might have repaired her popularity, she failed to see off a leadership challenge from the disgruntled Michael Heseltine. Having ruled longer than any Prime Minister since Pitt, she was brought down by her strident opposition to European integration and her hectoring way with Cabinet colleagues. Her successor, John Major, was an unimposing man from humble beginnings who liked to go to the opera; his wife, Norma, had written a semi-official biography of Joan Sutherland. On New Year's Eve, they watched Sutherland's farewell gala, sitting with Sainsbury in the Royal Box. Major had sympathy for the Royal Opera House, and promised support.

Things were looking up, but not for the chairman. Bereft of the leader he loved, and concerned about the future of his family firm, John Sainsbury announced his resignation on 9 April 1991. Sainsbury had been an authoritarian chairman, short-fused and shouting red-faced at members of board and staff alike. His relations with Isaacs had grown tense when he found the general director cropping up as late-night television interviewer with his own BBC slot, *Face to Face*. 'Do the job we're paying you to do,' he yelled at Isaacs in full public view. 'The shouting at board meetings was unbelievable,' recalled Findlay. 'It was counter-productive.'

Where Moser liked to be liked, Sainsbury had no such need. He would turn up with his briefcase at the end of a day's work, march into Isaacs' office and demand full account of current business. For closer briefings, he summoned Ewen Balfour to report to him at Sainsbury headquarters, costing Balfour the confidence of his General Director.

'John resigned because he realized that to be a proper chairman of the opera house during the redevelopment was a full-time job,' said Vivien Duffield. 'And he wanted to apply himself to J Sainsbury Ltd. I genuinely believe that to do the job properly he felt it needed more time than he could give.'

Sainsbury reminded the board that he had agreed to serve for two years and remained twice as long. 'I stayed four years but I didn't stay for the fifth,' he reflected, 'because I had one year left at Sainsbury's and there were a lot of things that I wanted to do there.' He had created the most profitable retailer in the land and feared for its future under his techno-minded cousin, David, who was a reluctant grocer, harbouring woolly leftish views. Employees who saw the cousins pass one another in the corridor noted that their eyes never met. 'It was my life,' said John Sainsbury of the company.[23] By the time his cousin stepped down, accepting a junior minister's post in the Labour Government in September 1998, the firm had fallen far behind Tesco and there were no family members left in senior management. The provenders of the British middle classes had lost their way.

Saving the business was one pressing reason for John Sainsbury's early resignation. 'But the underlying reason,' he told me, 'was that the Government were getting more and more difficult and the squeeze on the opera house finances was terrible. I was so appalled by a Government that I supported being so mistaken about the arts in general and the opera house particularly. Palumbo had given me all sorts of reassurances but was unable to give us what we needed. The more difficult the issue, the more time one has to give to it, and I knew I could not do it. Little did I know that they would choose someone as chairman who was almost as busy as I was. I had no say in the matter. . . .'

Looking around the boardroom, the eyes fell on Angus Stirling, director general of the National Trust under Lord Gibson's chairmanship. Stirling was preparing for the Trust's centenary as a conserver of English houses and landscapes. His hands were full, but offers like the ROH chairmanship do not come more than twice in a life and he was unable to refuse. 'I should never have let Angus do it,' said his mentor, Lord Gibson.

'Angus is one of the nicest men in the world,' said Vivien Duffield. 'We never had an argument about anything. I had terrible rows with Jeremy. You'd say good morning to him, and he'd say, what's good about this morning? bloody awful morning!'

Stirling belonged to the class of Englishmen who rise without trace. After Eton and Cambridge, he had done spells in fine arts and banking before his discreet competence at the Arts Council brought him under Gibson's wing. His main attraction to the ROH board was his experience in handling public subsidy. He had connections at every level of the Council, and it was hoped that his quiet diplomacy would succeed where Sainsbury's bluster had so demonstrably failed.

These hopes were soon dashed. Palumbo told Stirling that Covent Garden deserved 'double or treble' its present grant, but he said that two or three times without delivering extra cash. The Arts Council was itself under investigation from the National Audit Office. Seeing the Covent Garden deficit reach £3.1 million, the Council ordered an inquiry by the educationalist Mary Warnock, the second such investigation in a decade. The ROH invited a parallel inquiry from the accountants Price Waterhouse. Both gave the company a generally clean bill of health and recommended a higher level of public funding. Warnock called for clearer management objectives, a break-even budget and an end to Royal Ballet touring. She warned that the redevelopment scheme would be ruinous unless the Government paid the bills and recommended that it should be shelved. The house should modernize internally and await a better day. Price Waterhouse found internal savings of one million pounds a year, adding that the company's 'sense of economy is poor'.

Nothing came of either report, nor of the new Prime Minister's avowed sympathies for Covent Garden. Major appointed his close ally David Mellor to the Cabinet as chief secretary to the Treasury, one of the most powerful positions in Government with virtual right of veto over departmental budgets. Shortly before the 1992 election, the grinning, gap-toothed Mellor arranged for ENO to be given ten million pounds to buy the freehold of its building, the Coliseum. The gift was smeared in some quarters as an electoral bribe to the arts; at Covent Garden it provoked tears of consternation.

ENO's powerhouse had run out of steam and Peter Jonas was on his way to run the Bavarian State Opera in Munich, leaving a large deficit and leaking roof to Dennis Marks, a BBC producer with no previous experience of running a theatre. His music director, equally innocent, was to be Sian Edwards. ENO, in disarray, was being richly rewarded while Covent Garden, at peak performance, was penalized on every side. 'They felt completely unloved and quite helpless,' was the view of a senior Arts Council official.[24] Suspicions of double standards were not unfounded. After the election, which Major won to general surprise, Mellor was rewarded with a job fitted to his own tastes. The Department of National Heritage brought together his love of arts, sport, travel and broadcasting. Its permanent secretary was to be Hayden Phillips, a Whitehall high-flier who was aiming for the Cabinet Office and somehow wound up on playground duty. Related by marriage to the former ballet chairman Mark Bonham-Carter, Phillips took a sceptical interest in Covent Garden and, notch by notch, tightened the Government's grip over all the public arts.

Had the new Department acted as decisively as it talked, a shaft of clarity might have pierced the muddled process of public funding and restored a sense of purpose. Instead, the Department acted as another layer of buck-passing so that nothing of importance ever got decided except under dire emergency. Whether the country needed a new opera house and how it was to be paid for and rebuilt was never debated as a matter of principle, though its exigencies crossed departmental desks on a monthly, sometimes weekly, basis. The Prime Minister, for his part, offered occasional poultices. When a Hong Kong businessman, Stanley Ho, while weekending at Chequers, expressed his desire to contribute to a British good cause, Major directed him to Covent Garden which relieved him of two and a half million pounds – saving the companies from mid-1990s insolvency.

Isaacs grew increasingly frustrated. 'I have never been in a position where I couldn't raise the money I wanted,' he told Findlay. Running a television channel, he recalled, 'we used to spend at most four weeks of the year working out a budget. Here, someone comes in to discuss budgets with me three times a week.'[25] The satisfactions of a showman were buried beneath a pile of insolubles.

He got little support from below. 'He is terribly unpopular with singers, conductors, administrators and in particular with the dancers,' noted a veteran Gardener. 'It seems that he was in New York when the Royal Ballet opened and he did not go to the first night. Having read the good notices he [told the company]: "Perhaps we can look forward to the same standard of dancing in London." I understand he was booed by the dancers.'[26]

Company members, accustomed to seeing Tooley at the Crush Bar six nights a week, complained that Isaacs was seldom in attendance. Isaacs maintained that he spent 'three or four' evenings a week in the theatre. Tooley, whose wife divorced him shortly after his retirement on grounds of 'unreasonable behaviour', served as a focus for discontent. Bewildered and embittered, he hung around the backstage and orchestral corridor, talking to 'the family', until Sainsbury pointedly told him to stay away. When Peter Wright gave way to David Bintley at the Birmingham Royal Ballet, Isaacs told the outgoing director, 'whatever you do, don't do to David what John Tooley did to me.'

Isaacs, with little to lose, decided to sweep the decks of relics of the Tooley era. He fired Ewen Balfour, ignoring a mass petition for his reinstatement, which Bernard Haitink prominently signed. Balfour was well liked. He was also well connected. Questions were asked in the House of Commons. In a political crisis, Balfour was a man to have on your side. When he left, Jim Monahan of the CGCA said: 'This is the best thing that has ever happened to us.' Balfour, like Bill Beresford before him, found a large cheque in his post, an anonymous gift from a sympathetic board member.

Also chopped were Patrick Carnegy, John Cox and Paul Findlay, the nucleus of the opera team. 'Jeremy was perfectly within his rights,' said Findlay equably. 'My contract was coming up, and he wanted to have his own man.' Findlay went on to run the Royal Philharmonic Orchestra, with Balfour as his righthand man, and later the Kirov Theatre for Gergiev.

To head the Royal Opera Isaacs brought in Nicholas Payne, a deceptively jolly Old Etonian who had put Opera North firmly on the map with modernist stagings that looked radical in London, let alone Leeds. Balfour was replaced by Keith Cooper who, at ENO, had caught the eye by blazoning a half-naked stagehand with a snake round his neck as an advertisement for *The Magic Flute*. Isaacs craved style and profile. He would get more than he bargained for.

His own contract was up for renewal, as were Dowell's and Haitink's. The two artistic directors were nodded through. Isaacs was asked to leave the room while his case was discussed. David Mellor had made no secret that he wanted Isaacs' head. The Arts Council, unable to interfere, made disapproving noises. Forman, who was leaving the board, passionately extolled Isaacs' achievements. It was a close call. By a single vote, according to an eye-witness, Jeremy Isaacs was granted a mandate to take the company through the closure period and into its rebuilt home. To balance the books, the chorus was cut from seventy-two to sixty, and seat prices were raised yet again. The top ticket for a Domingo night now exceeded two hundred pounds.

At the Westminster Abbey memorial service for Margot Fonteyn, on 2 July 1991, Ninette de Valois gave the first dull speech of her long life. The age of oratory was over. Madam now lived in a sheltered flat beside the river at Barnes, where Anthony Dowell visited her weekly to report on the ballet's progress. Her presence was no longer seen, but sensed. Many an innovative proposal would be shot down by Dowell with the words, 'Madam wouldn't like it.' To her own frustration, Ninette de Valois had become a reactionary impediment to the balletic progress she had always espoused.

For the present, the auguries were good. Mukhamedov and Guillem worked strictly apart, but the Tatar found a shining foil in the twenty-year-old Darcey Bussell when creating MacMillan's *Winter Dreams*. They came unstuck in *Manon*, where Bussell on pointe proved half a head taller than the hero, but Viviana Durante, another home-grown dancer, fitted perfectly. Her eleventh-hour insertion provoked rumours of a diva war in the popular press, always good for business. Mukhamedov danced *Romeo and Juliet* with Durante, as well as MacMillan's next ballet, *The Judas Tree*, a grim tale of gang-rape set against a backdrop of Canary Wharf, London's newest commercial development. Bussell, growing in stature, developed a stage rivalry with Guillem. William Forsythe, the American choreographer, gave them a jazzy joint showcase, *In the Middle Somewhat Elevated*. Ashley Page and William Tuckett, company members both, showed a gift for choreography.

MacMillan, at sixty-three, was full of ideas and contentment, eager to rework his life's repertoire upon the infinitely pliant Mukhamedov. 'In those last years after Fred, Kenneth felt a sense of relief,' said Monica Mason. 'He did say, you mustn't think I'm always going to be here. I'm going to retire, it'll be just wonderful.

I said, will I come round and go through cast lists? He said, maybe, maybe not.'

He intended to rework *Anastasia*, he told Dowell, 'redoing the role of Rasputin for Irek, and he was really quite fired up about how he would do it in a totally different concept.' First, however, he would restage *Mayerling*, with Mukhemadov as the homicidal Prince Rudolf. The house was packed for the opening night, 29 October 1992, and just before the curtain went up Isaacs, whose seat was directly across the aisle, moved across 'to touch his arm and wish him luck'. Many in the house that night were conscious of an extra surge of pre-performance tension. During the first interval it was clear that the company had a hit on its hands. In the second break, MacMillan went backstage and was late returning to his seat.

'I don't know why I was the one who went on the search,' said Dowell, 'but I must have picked up on Deborah's anxiety and started to look for him, went to the stage door and there heard a fireman talking of someone who had collapsed. I asked where, and I ended up in a part of the opera house where I had never been before (it was one of the phases of development where the opera got new dressing rooms, but not the ballet – surprise, surprise) and there he was, on the floor, lifeless, with a St John's Ambulance nursing person.

'I rushed back, and couldn't find my way. Finally found Deborah, took her by the hand and told her to come with me. I had never seen a dead person before and I was witnessing a terribly private moment, holding on to her while she was over the body, saying all these private things.'

A press officer, Janine Limberg, stumbled upon them and was sent to fetch Monica. The ballet was nearly over and arrangements had to be made. Rumours filtered down to the dancers as they flitted on and off stage. 'Deborah's first concern was Charlotte (her daughter) so we just got in a taxi and rushed back to fetch her,' said Mason.

Isaacs was informed. He responded warmly and impetuously. He could not allow the public to jubilate while a man lay dead, nor could he withhold information from a confused and anxious cast, Mukhemadov visibly on the brink of tears. He walked on stage, raised a hand for silence and announced: 'It is with deep sadness, and in shock, that I have to tell you that the great master whose work we have seen performed here tonight, Kenneth MacMillan, has, during the performance, suffered a heart attack and died. I ask you to stand, and to leave the theatre quietly.'[27]

This was unwise, inappropriate and, as Isaacs subsequently acknowledged, technically illegal. A death may not be announced in England until a doctor has certified it; nor, as a matter of form, should anyone be notified ahead of the next of kin. On the night MacMillan died, Isaacs gave the news to a thronged house before it was broken to the dead man's child. He argued in retrospect that the public was 'entitled to know then that in their presence a great spirit had departed, rather than reading the news of his death the next day.'[28] The public had no such right, legal or moral. What Isaacs should have announced was that MacMillan had been taken seriously ill and conveyed to hospital. Weeks later, after the first wave of bereavement, Deborah MacMillan called on Isaacs in his office and told him, in no uncertain Antipodean terms, what she thought of his conduct that night. He had made a drama out of a personal tragedy and that, in her view, was unconscionable. In the hospital, the only ones to sit with her beside the body late into the night were Monica Mason and an old friend, Peter Brownlee.

MacMillan's death gutted the Royal Ballet of its creative engine. 'Now he's dead, they call him a genius,' said Deborah MacMillan, bitterly. There was talk of appointing Bintley or Page as resident choreographer, but neither was of comparable stature. A fateful decision was taken to leave the creative post vacant. Dowell brought in Tetley, William Forsythe, Twyla Tharp and other grand names to stage one-off shows, but their fleeting visits left no residue in an organization whose glorious past dwarfed its diminished present and stunted its unseen future.

Six weeks later, the Royal Ballet suffered a second hammerblow to its morale. All summer long, the Murdoch press had been trailing the stench of royal scandal. An apparently authorized biography of Diana, Princess of Wales, serialized in the *Sunday Times*, exposed the misery of her marriage to Prince Charles, her bulimia and attempted suicide. Charles was Patron of the Royal Opera House, Diana its biggest fan. She was never that keen on opera and used to summon someone from the ROH, usually the obliging Ken Davison, to explain the plot to her at Kensington Palace two or three days beforehand. When surtitles were introduced, she dispensed with this courtesy but seldom seemed to enjoy the show unless Pavarotti was on song. The ballet, however, she adored. As a girl, she had learned to dance. As an adult she relished the physical freedom of dancers, so remote from the stiffness of royalty. She came to the ballet early and often, seldom with Charles. Her companion was more likely to be a girlfriend, dressed like herself in a mannish suit. House manager Trevor Jones, who had known her before she married as his son's nursery teacher, would admit her via a side entrance on Floral Street, incognito and unnoticed.

In happier times, Diana had conspired with the dancer Wayne Sleep to give Charles a surprise birthday gift. Each winter, Ken Davison put on a Friends Gala at Covent Garden in which ballerinas sang and sopranos danced and everyone sent themselves up something rotten. Prince Charles, as Patron, was persuaded to participate in one sketch, which he greatly relished. The following year, 1985, Diana slipped out of the Royal Box in mid-gala, changed out of her red velvet gown into a slinky silvery dress, and showed up on stage with Sleep in a funny, well-rehearsed routine to a Billy Joel song, 'Uptown Girl'.

'I said, look, it's not going to be good for you to look bad,' recalled Sleep. 'Comedy is very difficult to do in ballet terms, not to look completely cod. And she said, oh dear. But then I found out she was game to try a few things, and with honesty and fun it could work, tongue-in-cheek, very chic.'[29] Sleep was five foot two, six inches shorter than the princess. Midway through the routine he hoisted her high above his head and carried her across the stage. 'She kept looking up at Charles,' reported a press photographer.[30]

There were eight curtain calls and the audience were enraptured, all except Charles who tried to look pleased. He told Sleep that Diana was a 'terrific' dancer, but friends were given to understand that he found the dress too slinky and the act undignified. Back at the Palace he vented his displeasure. Diana was downcast.

As the marriage foundered, she increased her attendances at the ballet. She would show up spontaneously for morning rehearsals, with the young princes in tow, favouring senior ROH officials with outrageous indiscretions. Not a word leaked out, such was their affection for her. The press were on the rampage. In November 1992, the *Daily Mirror* and Murdoch's *Sun* published extracts from tapped telephone chats between Prince Charles and his lover, Camilla Parker-Bowles. On 9 December John Major told a hushed House of Commons that the royal pair were to separate. After three more years of media wars and salacious revelations, they divorced in July 1996. Diana won custody of the princes and a fifteen million pound settlement, but lost the title of HRH, Her Royal Highness. The following day she severed her patronage of almost one hundred charities and public causes. Among the six she retained was English National Ballet, testifying to the depth of her love of dance.

Having left Charles, Diana avoided the ROH. The ballet felt orphaned, bereft of its cheerleader in the Royal Box, its champion on the board and its choreographer in residence. As closure loomed, the Royal Ballet was fatally weakened.

David Mellor did not last long. The breezy, high-living Heritage Secretary had offended Rupert Murdoch by defending the BBC against the predations of his satellite broadcasting business. Mellor was easy prey. A nightclub hostess, introduced to a Sunday newspaper by a dubious publicist, confessed to having sex with the minister, who allegedly wore a Chelsea shirt and liked to have his toes sucked. When these revelations failed to procure his dismissal, tabloid hounds 'discovered' that the pro-Palestinian Mellor had accepted a paid family holiday from the daughter of a PLO paymaster. Hours after his sacking on 1 October 1992, the *Sun*'s front page crowed: 'From Toe Job to No Job'.

It was a seminal moment in public affairs. The gutter press had won a gruesome victory and politicians of both main parties cowered in fear. Murdoch's men were not finished with Mellor. Young reporters taken on by the *Sunday Times*, were ordered to 'dig dirt on Mellor',[31] *pour encourager les autres*. Media owners were flexing their pecs. The humiliation of the Heritage Secretary was the prelude to a tide of 'sleaze' that would engulf and bring down the Major Government. The downgrading of public ethics accelerated. Murdoch led the prurient pack into the royal bedchambers. His red-top *Sun* masqueraded as the *vox populi*. It mixed tittle-tattle about television soap operas with reams of sport and a generalized sneer at 'toffs'. The arts, if mentioned, were crudely derided. Subsidy was a euphemism for rich people getting seats paid for by the poor. The Royal Opera House was ripe for plucking, though not quite yet.

John Major, in his election manifesto, had promised to create a National Lottery to relieve recessional gloom. The project was entrusted to the next National Heritage Secretary, Peter Brooke, an end-of-line career politician who showed no particular enthusiasm for anything, but a dogged loyalty to his Prime Minister. It fell to Hayden Phillips, the department's permanent secretary, to make the rules by which Lottery profits would be kept out of Treasury hands and distributed to five good causes, including the arts. Phillips coined a ghastly word 'additionality', to signify that Lottery money could not be used for running costs or extant projects. It was new money, destined for new initiatives.

Denis Vaughan, prophet of the Lottery, was appalled. The operational method, he argued, was too costly; the yield to the arts would be no more than 5.6 per cent of the pot; and most of the money would be invested in buildings instead of new audiences.

'I believe,' declared Jeremy Isaacs, 'that the National Lottery was invented to find a responsible route for a Government that knew it ought to put its own hand in its pocket and pay for a national lyric theatre, but couldn't find the courage to do it.' As far as Covent Garden was concerned, it was the intended beneficiary, a view it impressed upon the Arts Council, which was designated to distribute the cash. Brooke and Phillips wanted the problem off their doorstep. The Department was under fire for a hundred million pound over-spend on the prison-like new British Library, an epic bureaucratic disaster.

At this stage, no one knew how much cash the Lottery would produce. The Arts Council guessed fifty million pounds, and formed a new department under Jeremy Newton to administer it. Peter Gummer, public relations adviser to the Prime Minister and brother of the Environment Secretary, was the supervising Council member. Endless procedural meetings were held. Entire forests were pulped into policy papers. When the balls first rolled on Saturday 19 November 1994, the Lottery overtook the football pools as the Englishman's weekly flutter. The first year's yield to the arts was £271.6 million, almost half as much again as the Council's existing budget of £190 million. The Council was left dangerously lop-sided, with more cash in Gummer's lap than in the chairman's. It was also in no position to command public confidence, having barely recovered from a crippling cock-up.

One sunny morning in July 1993, the Council's secretary general, Anthony Everitt, had summoned the press to discuss the future of the London orchestras. Funding had not flowed easier since the Goodman report thirty years earlier, and all four self-governing orchestras were in varying degrees of difficulty. The LSO, conducted by Colin Davis and resident at the Barbican, were in relative clover, having won a million pounds from the City of London to match their

Arts Council grant. The RPO, managed by Paul Findlay, were, as ever, near the breadline. The Philharmonia and London Philharmonic were, as ever, at each other's throats.

Everitt, and his music director Ken Baird, announced that the Arts Council had decided to fund only two orchestras, but could not decide which. A panel under Sir Leonard Hoffmann, Goodman's former rapporteur, would make recommendations. The officials smiled at television cameras as they delivered the death sentence on two renowned ensembles. Baird's face fell moments later when he heard the present writer denounce the deed on television as unnecessary, unworkable and an abdication of statutory responsibilities. The Council had not anticipated opposition.

Over the next five months, fur flew. Findlay pulled Valery Gergiev out of a Russian hat as the RPO's key attraction. The Philharmonia hooked Judy Grahame, the LPO's former marketing chief, to publicize its involvement with the venerable composer György Ligeti. The LPO huffed and puffed. Goodman emerged from retirement to say the Arts Council should resign. 'Orchestral music is the last thing they should be cutting,' he growled, 'it's one of the few arts we are famous for.'[32]

Hoffmann's panel split down the middle. Two members felt the contest was too close to call; three others backed the Philharmonia. Palumbo, the Council chairman, was dead set on cutting his client base. He ruled that the Philharmonia should be saved alongside the LSO, the other two could die. The LPO chairman, Elliott Bernerd, a tough property developer, refused to accept the Solomonian verdict. He called Palumbo on a Saturday night and threatened him and the Council with legal action. Palumbo crumbled and a statement was issued on the Monday that all four orchestras would continue to receive funding. Baird and the music panel chairman Brian Magee resigned, followed by Everitt. Palumbo's term ended soon after.

The next chairman was Lord Gowrie, the former arts minister. He called in Everitt's deputy, Mary Allen. 'When did you first hear of this orchestra plan?' he demanded. 'The day before it was announced,' said Allen. 'That's all right, then,' sighed Gowrie, appointing her secretary general.

Allen, daughter of a poet and actress of Irish extraction, assembled a brisk new cadre of women executives. In budget week, Allen would come in each morning at six and lock the building when she left at night. In dealing with arts clients, she played bad cop to Gowrie's good cop.

Gowrie had won the chairmanship over the Prime Minister's chum, Peter Gummer, and the piano-playing north-eastern industrialist Ernest Hall. He was a passionate Wagnerian who summered in Bayreuth and believed in the right of every citizen to see a new *Ring* twice a decade. He persuaded Sainsbury of his commitment to Covent Garden and was given to understand by Downing Street that it looked favourably on the ROH redevelopment.

Mary Allen, before her promotion, had been the Council's observer at ROH board meetings. She was alarmed at Isaacs' deficits and Stirling's indecisiveness. In two years of board minutes, hardly a single issue had been satisfactorily resolved. No theatres had been rented for the closure period. Costs were vague and programmes unplanned. Three board members – Duffield, the Labour academic Tessa Blackstone and the printing magnate Robert Gavron – pressed for action, which Stirling airily deferred.

Questions of principle had scarcely been considered. Was it in Covent Garden's best interest to rebuild a two thousand seat house when it could sell the site and build a four thousand seater, with an eye to Met-like financial independence? Why would it cost the ROH £214 million to rebuild, when Glyndebourne could knock down its old hall and build a brand new one for thirty-five million, all of it privately raised?

Allen demanded facts, not waffle. Peter Gummer, who chaired a joint AC-ROH committee to implement the Warnock proposals, warned that he could not sign a blank Lottery cheque. 'The opera house would come to these meetings, in the person of Jeremy, unable to talk in matters of detail,' said an observer. 'It was all rhetoric. It was like wrestling with jelly.'[33]

Gummer and Allen went to the Heritage Department to canvass support. 'Hayden, we need to get tough with the opera house,' said Allen, 'but we can't unless the Government are on our side.' Phillips, in classic Whitehall fashion, said: 'why don't we take it a little more gently, be a little less confrontational?'[34]

The cost had hit £214 million pounds and Stirling was demanding first dip into the Lottery hat. Isaacs, by his own admission, 'fondly imagined that I, or the Chairman, would write a simple, eloquent letter stating our need' and the Lottery cheque would arrive by return of post. When he saw the application form, with hundreds of questions and demands for professional validation, he erupted in rage and frustration.

Keith Cooper was charged with preparing the paperwork, which he did by aggrandizing his own department and distributing research tasks around the house. Cooper was a tall, engaging character who made Vivien Duffield laugh aloud and kept her abreast of internal plots, as Balfour had done for Sainsbury. He completed the application in the week that Lottery tickets went on sale. On 4 January 1995, the first working morning of a new year, Isaacs staged a glitzy photo-opportunity on the Arts Council's doorstep with two dancers, Darcey Bussell and Bruce Sansom, and two singers, Thomas Allen and Simon Keenlyside, handing in the application.

It took six months to get an answer while the Arts Council pursued due diligence, a process that Isaacs deemed wasteful. Six weeks after receiving the ROH submission, the Arts Council published the findings of a 'geological survey' into the 'provision of Lyric Theatre (Dance and Opera) in London' – in plain English, a study of how many stages the capital needed. Covent Garden, ENO, Sadler's Wells and the South Bank Centre were all putting in simultaneously for huge Lottery grants. Dennis Stevenson, head of the Pearson publishing group and a former member of the Warnock panel, was asked to report whether the theatres should rebuild, and when: it would be calamitous if they all shut at the same time. His report identified the need for a medium-sized dance house – ideally, Sadler's Wells – but indicated that there was not enough operatic demand to justify ROH and ENO running at full steam. Despite the hype of an opera boom, audiences had remained static over quarter of a century. The average age of Coliseum goers was forty-four years old, of Covent Garden audiences fifty-five. London's ballet public had shrunk from half a million attenders to fewer than 200,000 people annually. Stevenson recommended that ENO should cut back its opera output, produce large-scale dance and get out more into the regions.

As regards closure, Covent Garden deserved priority, but Sadler's Wells should rebuild first, thereby providing a temporary home and potentially younger audience for the Royal Ballet during the ROH shutdown. Stevenson was assisted in his work by three expert arts administrators: Graham Devlin, Stephen Phillips and Genista McIntosh of the National Theatre. Their approach was cool, dispassionate and non-partisan. It made a significant contribution to the planning process and was warmly received by the Arts Council. 'All options are open,' said Mary Allen, 'The only ones we will not endorse are simultaneous closure for Covent Garden and ENO, or the dismantling of either company.'[35]

The Stevenson report was ignored at Covent Garden (and in Isaacs' memoirs) and denounced by ENO's intemperate boss for its 'breathless urgency'. Marks, and ENO, were in trouble. The deficit was rising, Sian Edwards would soon resign and the Arts Council femocracy had demanded as a condition of approving Marks' contract renewal that he should seek counselling to enable him to work better with powerful women. Over the next two years, until Marks departed, ENO entered its darkest night since the schism of 1945. Audiences fell and programming stultified. Yet Government officials noted drily that, no matter how dire ENO's plight, the crisis was kept within a constitutional remit, whereas at Covent Garden, the faintest whiff of anxiety would send Stirling, Sainsbury or some shadowy official scuttling into Downing Street for succour.

Successive Heritage Secretaries were so irked by this intimacy that Hayden Phillips was ordered to investigate secret links between the Royal Opera House and the Cabinet Office. He found that Robert Armstrong, long retired, had attempted to hand over his ROH Secretaryship to his Downing Street successor, Sir Robin Butler, only to be vetoed by Margaret Thatcher. His seat went to a top Treasury man, Andrew Edwards, and nothing that Phillips could do would dislodge him. Powerful interests were protecting the *status quo* and making sure that Covent Garden was well served.

On 20 July 1995, Gowrie announced the Arts Council's largest Lottery grant – a total of £78.5 million to be given to Covent Garden, £55 million for the development itself, and £23.5 million to cover extra costs entailed during the two-year closure from July 1997. Eighteen conditions were attached to the award, at Allen's and Gummer's insistence, and Gowrie was careful to stipulate that even larger amounts were likely to be given to future regional applicants. It was an oddly defensive performance from a normally upbeat man.

Isaacs invited the press back to Covent Garden, uncorked a few bottles of wine, and was pictured on the next morning's front pages holding Stirling's arm aloft in sunlit triumph outside the Floral Hall. Gowrie was asked to justify the award in an op-ed article for the *Daily Telegraph*. The case he made was so incoherent that I, just off a flight from Australia, was obliged to produce an eleven-hundred word comment piece in ninety minutes flat. There was no question in my jet-lagged mind of opposing the grant – it was a matter of simple national interest. The ROH was the acme of British arts. Ascendant, it nurtured the broader arts economy with values and ideas. Deprived, it depressed the creative aspiration.

> In a country that does not like to give the impression of being good at anything (I wrote), Covent Garden achieves high standards almost by stealth. It is a barometer for the national culture . . . It gives London the chimera of civility and luxury that many of its hoteliers and cabbies have worked so valiantly to destroy . . . [Its] underlying objective is to entertain, to represent and, at times, to elevate the national mood.[36]

Other broadsheets generally concurred. The *Sun*, that good Friday, raised a cackle of controversy. Ever since the Lottery started, tabloid newspapers had fostered a delusion that its revenue somehow belonged to those who bought tickets – as if beer-drinkers were empowered to tell brewers how to spend their profits. Any spending on culture was élitist and snobbish. Thus did the *Sun* set upon Covent Garden:

FURY AS MORE LOTTERY CASH GOES DOWN THE DRAIN
IT'S THE GREEDY BEGGAR'S OPERA
Exclusive by Lenny Lottery

A storm erupted last night over the extra £100 million (sic) Lottery handout for opera lovers – instead of the ordinary Lottery punters. Furious Labour MP Tony Banks blasted the Arts Council for dishing out cash to 'people who never bought a Lottery ticket in their lives.' He stormed, 'Most of the millions raised by the Lottery come from working class punters. But they are getting nothing back.'

Arts Council chairman Lord Gowrie defended the payouts, insisting opera was 'not just for toffs' despite £120 ticket prices. He said, 'Opera audiences I have seen around the country are very often struggling professionals. *They are middle class people – not very rich toffs.*' He added he would have liked to have given the Royal Opera an EXTRA £10 million to help lower ticket prices.[37]

The *Sun* set up a hotline for readers to vote on whether the opera house should get a hundred million pounds, untroubled by factual precision. That day, fifteen thousand people were said to have rung the 'No' line. The next morning, the Sun resumed its attack in a telly-punned editorial: 'This Opera Windfall's* Appalling'

> Not one penny more must go to the bunch of Toscas at the Royal Opera House.
> The people's verdict in our You The Jury vote could not be clearer.
> They don't want their lottery money squandered on the minority pastimes of the well-heeled when genuine causes like medical research charities are losing out. Those who hand out lottery cash lack two things: common sense and the common touch.

No politician dared challenge the self-appointed voice of the people. The *Sun* was not read by arts lovers, but it was tamely obeyed by ministers who knew the price of its disfavour. In political circles, Covent Garden became from that day on a dirty word, never to be uttered with approbation or, if possible, at all. The new Heritage Secretary, Virginia Bottomley, just two weeks in office, said nothing. 'The lottery has been absurdly mishandled from the point of view of the public relations of government,' raged Isaacs. 'We were sitting ducks for whatever the *Sun* wanted to do to us.'[38]

The following week, the *Sun* kitted out half a dozen readers in top hats and tails and sent them for a fun night at the opera. 'The Prime Minister,' said Isaacs, 'and the secretary of state for National Heritage should have been standing on their feet saying to people, "we've brought this lottery in, it's succeeding beyond our wildest expectations . . . and hats off to the ROH which has got there first." But of course they didn't do that. They just stood back and said, "oh dear, why is Jeremy being photographed with his thumbs up?"'[39]

There was no point in apportioning blame. Lasting damage had been done to the ROH, and some of it, *pace* Isaacs, was self-inflicted.

If Nicholas Payne suffered the torments of managing opera, he hid

---

* viz. Oprah Winfrey

them well behind a fixed jollity and a hobbyist's passion for tiny details of past casting. There was much else that he kept concealed. Getting information out of Payne was as easy as getting decisions from his chairman. At Opera North, as chief executive, Payne was personally in charge of repertoire and budgets. At the ROH, he had to seek budget clearance from Isaacs, repertoire approval from the board, and date co-ordination from the Royal Ballet. His tactic was to keep all plans close to his chest until absolutely forced to disclose. This drove some colleagues to despair, and the ballet directors to spitting fury. Payne could rely on boardroom support from Isaacs and Duffield, while Dowell and Russell-Roberts went naked into the negotiating chamber and emerged skinned. Dowell muttered of a 'Capulets and Montagues' situation as relations between the Royal Opera and Royal Ballet hissed and spluttered.

'We would be asked once a programme had been planned, and sometimes printed, to make changes,' complained Dowell. 'One season we had our usual Christmas fare of *Nutcracker* and *Cinderella*, and the board said, could you put *Swan Lake* and *Beauty* in? It put enormous strains on the company. The rehearsal time got very tight, and we only just got things together. Anthony (Russell-Roberts) would come out of a financial meeting and we'd be asked to make savings, or help revenue by adding a populist work.'[40] In their last four seasons in the opera house, the ballet were allowed fewer than half as many new productions as the opera. Audiences grew weary of repetition and critics condemned Dowell for lack of imagination. His music director, Barry Wordsworth, urged him to get tough with the board. 'There would have been no point in me standing and screaming,' sighed Dowell, 'anyway, it's not my style.' He took the criticism to heart and, visibly stressed, retreated from public view. 'When you're a dancer and you read reviews, the knife goes in but you find ways of working round it,' he explained. 'When you are director, it reflects on the company and I feel incredibly responsible. I know what is good and bad, and I think we have brought standards up. If the rep has been changed it's because of financial problems, that's why.'

Payne, by contrast, radiated success. He inherited many of Findlay's best schemes, and found the music director a man reborn. Bernard Haitink, twice divorced and past sixty, had found love in the orchestra. He married the viola player Patricia Bloomfield and moved into a terraced house near Harrods, giving up all threats of resignation. 'I have changed,' Haitink told me. 'My roots are now in London. I work well here. I love the English mentality, living as an artist in a community where you can read so many press opinions, not like New York where there is only the *Times*. I admire the English for, with so little money, organizing opera groups. I admire the English singers, they are very well brought up, and the English orchestral musicians. Even if I did not work here, I would still live here.'[4i]

'Nicholas doesn't know how lucky he was that Bernard found Patricia,' said Findlay ruefully. Haitink opened Payne's era with a triumphant *Meistersinger*, deftly directed by Graham Vick on a traditionalist setting by Graham Hudson, and with two English masters, John Tomlinson and Thomas Allen, in central roles. The Wagners of Bayreuth attended; British and American singers had come to dominate their festival. Haitink exuded authority and joy. This was one of those rare opera nights where everything worked.

Haitink continued with Janáček's *Katya Kabanova*, directed by Trevor Nunn of the RSC, and effulgently sung by Elena Prokina, one of Gergiev's fresh crop. Payne indulged his sense of whimsy with Massenet's *Chérubin*, never previously seen at Covent Garden. Its English director, Tim Albery, demanded slower tempi than the Russian conductor, Gennady Rozhdestvensky, was prepared to beat. Rozhdestvensky walked out. *Prima la musica*? Not under Payne's regime, which prized deconstruction above textual fidelity. The show was predictably trivial, as was Giordano's *Fedora*, revived at the instigation of José Carreras, who sang opposite Mirella Freni, pushing sixty but vocally immaculate. Carreras looked worried. He was under police investigation in Rome for allegedly receiving secret fee boosters from the opera house. Pavarotti was appearing in the Philippines at twenty-five thousand pesos (or six hundred pounds) a ticket. Domingo pulled out of Covent Garden's *Fanciulla* in order to join the other two in Los Angeles for a World Cup concert in which they shared sixteen million dollars for record and media rights. Covent Garden, meanwhile, announced a million-pound budget cut and Isaacs vacated Webster's spacious office to make way for shops and offices at the rear of the building.

The next season was starstruck. Roberto Alagna arrived in September 1994 to rehearse Gounod's *Roméo et Juliette*, straight from his wife's funeral. Alagna, just thirty, had been discovered singing in a Paris pizza house and had lately made his mark at La Scala. Word of his bereavement trickled out, rendering his Romeo –

sung to the Juliette of the Rumanian Leontina Vaduva and watched from the stalls by his orphaned daughter – all the more poignant. 'It has the credibility of cinema,'[42] said Alagna, on seeing the video.

Backstage, he met another Romanian soprano who was rehearsing *La traviata*. Angela Gheorghiu, a rail worker's daughter, had auditioned at Covent Garden a few weeks after graduating from the Bucharest Academy. Peter Katona liked her style and booked her for *Bohème*. Solti, eighty-two and full of vigour, saw her sing Mimi and engaged her for *Traviata*, a work he had never conducted before. The director, Richard Eyre, head of the National Theatre, had never produced an opera before. 'Everybody was fresh, open to ideas,' said Gheorghiu. 'We began reading the text, each word without music.'[43]

'I never tired of watching Solti at work with the orchestra and singers,' wrote Eyre, 'punching the air, moulding, sculpting, caressing, on his toes in a half-crouch like a boxing trainer, singing and shouting like a muezzin. "Play this *forte*," he crowed to the cellos. "Break your wrists, and break my heart."'[44] Eyre, an opera sceptic, was overwhelmed.

The resultant drama was so spare and moving that BBC-2, for the first time in years, cleared its schedules and carried the opera live. Gheorghiu was an overnight star, in the same month as Alagna conquered all hearts as Romeo. They were smitten with one another. 'From Angela Gheorghiu,' glowed Alagna, 'I learned to sing with happiness.' 'It's true,' purred Gheorghiu, 'always.'[45]

Celebrity ensued, followed by notoriety. The golden pair fell out, in quick succession, with the Met, La Scala and Solti. As doors slammed, their fame grew. Not since Mario and Grisi in the middle of the nineteenth century had opera experienced a singing couple of equal calibre. Together, they were too much for the faint-hearted. Rumours suppurated around them like lava down Etna's slopes and colleagues walked on hot coals. At Covent Garden, they were proof that the old stage had lost none of its capacity to sow stardust. The spot where Callas found her voice and Sutherland her *métier*, where Fonteyn came of age and Nureyev restored her youth, possessed an alchemist's magic that was matched by no other. It was to Covent Garden that the Alagnas owed their romance and fortune.

But while stars were born beneath the royal crest, English singers for whom the theatre had been founded felt generally disaffected. A month after the lovebirds left, the Lancastrian soprano Amanda

Roocroft turned up to sing Fiordiligi in an almost home-grown cast of *Così fan tutte*, directed by Jonathan Miller. Roocroft, at twenty-eight, was growing out of Mozart and into big Italian roles. Nurtured at the Royal Northern College of Music, she was spotted by the critic Michael Kennedy and tipped as 'the soprano the world's leading opera houses would soon be fighting over'. Many did, but not Covent Garden which expected English singers to make a name abroad to prove that they were of appropriate 'international' calibre. Roocroft was well liked by Findlay and Payne, but was not prepared to wait for them to call. She made Munich her base and was effectively lost to London audiences.

Jane Eaglen, an English Wagnerian who also sang the fiercest Norma since Callas, bedded down in the United States. Bryn Terfel, the boisterous Welsh baritone, appeared twice that spring at Covent Garden – as Jokanaan in *Salome* and Balstrode in *Peter Grimes* – and then put the venue on his back-burner. He reckoned that as many Welshmen came to hear him at the Met as at Covent Garden.[46] The world was shrinking and loyalties were no longer local, but more than one singer complained that, at the ROH, patriotic pride had been displaced by the inverted snobbery of Gucci-shod cosmopolites.

The last relic of national self-assertion was to be found in the preference that Isaacs professed for British directors of post-modern tendencies. Hall was passé, Eyre and Nunn hard to fault. But what really excited Isaacs was a clever-dick director who could deconstruct a classic and make it look contemporary. It was precisely for this reason that he had hired Payne, who obliged by assigning Wagner's *Ring* not to some clapped-out German spouting Marxist dialectics but to a British director who was making real waves. Richard Jones was a respected professional who believed in the director's right to take the fifth amendment. His work was invariably dramatic but often obtuse. It included innovative open-air operas for the Bregenz Festival in Austria, Sondheim in the West End, Molière at the National Theatre, modern plays on and off Broadway and a side-splitting *Love for Three Oranges* at Opera North and ENO. Jones throughout never explained his methods or meanings.

At Covent Garden he missed meetings and was so late in delivering Nigel Lowery's designs that Haitink turned fractious. Introduced to the Jones concept by Nicholas Payne, Haitink slumped into his seat as one outrage after another was paraded before his unbelieving eyes: grotesque Rhinemaidens in rubbery breasts, a stretch limousine, an aeroplane. 'What can I say?' he moaned.

'What the director was anxious to establish was the image of time passing,' explained Payne.

'Do you think the audience will understand that?' Haitink demanded, 'even for me it's difficult to understand what he means . . . You can't just ignore everything that Wagner asked for.'[47]

Payne reported his dismay to Isaacs, who replied: 'In the last resort, if you and I are persuaded that the thing is right . . . Bernard will go along with it.' As, indeed, he did, keeping his eyes well down. Haitink was deemed the saving grace of the Jones-Lowery *Ring* by critics who split generationally over its merits. Michael Kennedy, in the *Sunday Telegraph*, wrote a protest note to Wagner in Valhalla. Rupert Christiansen, in the *Daily Telegraph*, found the production refreshingly anti-intellectual.

'There was no intention to outrage for its own sake,' said Payne, 'but there has been an intention to disturb, because we think that Wagner's work is disturbing. Beneath that, you have in Richard Jones a deeply serious director who has gone back to the text and back to what the music means. His direction is about ideas. It's not, in that sense, decorative. It's about getting to the meaning of Wagner's deeply pessimistic view of human failings.'[48]

In the teacup of British arts, a minor tempest raged. It would have quickly blown over were it not for the fact that every doubt and blunder was captured by television cameras and relayed to living rooms across the nation and, soon after, across America.

Jeremy Isaacs believed, at the very core of his being, in the power of television to uplift minds and improve the world. He had no hesitation in allowing a BBC team the run of the opera house, from board meetings to backstage dangers, with the aim of showing the extraordinary dedication practised and excellence achieved in the national lyric theatre. There was no other way of getting on television; the unions ruled out live relays and the BBC had all but given up covering the arts. To win the hearts of the nation, he aimed to appeal over the heads of broadsheet critics and tabloid saboteurs. 'Get the readers of the *Sun* on your side,'[49] urged Peter Gummer, the public relations magnate. In his eagerness to set the cameras rolling, Isaacs waived editorial approval of the project and, according to a senior member of the production team, accepted in writing that a proportion of the material filmed might turn out to be derogatory of the ROH.[50]

The series' director, Michael Waldman, had worked as a researcher on Isaacs' 1980 televisual history of Ireland. He was a trusted colleague from whom Isaacs expected the usual courtesies of contact and consultation. His confidence was misplaced. Waldman 'never came'[51] to share his thoughts with the industry veteran.

Television had changed in the 90s, its values contorted by satellite competition, confrontational chat shows and wall-to-wall sports. The story that Waldman was seeking was not the one Isaacs hoped to tell. He was competing for primetime audiences with laddish comedy, live football and topless starlets. His commitment could not be faulted: he gave up a year of his life to filming daily routines that had his cameramen aching with tedium. Out of the humdrum stuff of meetings, memos and arts politics, Waldman constructed six compellingly watchable episodes about an institution in distress.

The House commanded audiences of four million, high for BBC-2. It aroused gasps of sympathy for stagehands who risked life and limb in the cause of an art they barely glimpsed, and of admiration for the low-paid and unsung auxiliaries who laboured around the clock to put a show on stage. Given television's predilection for the exotic and unnatural, it was a fair and balanced portrait. But the television eye invariably distorts, and what lodged in the public memory was not the company's halo but its horrors.

Keith Cooper, sacking a box office manager and hurling a phone at the wall, was the unquestioned star of the series; he would be swamped by offers of marriage and other, less reputable proposals. Two barmen in the Crush Bar who had not exchanged a word for years provided an entertaining sub-plot. A stage door concierge with singing ambitions hammed it up for all he was worth, harmlessly.

The gruesome bits were the informalities. Nicholas Payne was heard complaining to Isaacs about 'the fucking rah-rahs' he had to smile at on opening nights. Isaacs was seen, naked from the waist up, dressing in black tie and yellow socks for a gala. 'Undignified,' exclaimed Joseph Volpe, tough-minded manager of New York's Met. 'What was he doing, auditioning for a Tarzan movie?'[52]

A French mezzo, Magali Damonte, hauled from cooking family dinner in Marseilles to stand in as Carmen at Covent Garden, was thrown on stage without rehearsal and left to find her own way around. The Carmen she replaced, Denyce Graves, was refused a dining table for her family because they had all been grabbed by the rah-rahs. Fiona Chadwick, a popular Royal Ballet principal, was seen dancing her last Juliet, moments after being told that, after sixteen years with the company, she was surplus to requirements.

Against the backdrop of sacrifice, high-jinks and mishaps, the board were seen languidly discussing financial crisis. 'Unless this board actually pulls its fingers out,' warned Vivien Duffield, 'we're going to lose the children's matinées.' 'The fact is,' sighed Angus Stirling, 'that we have a £2.2 million accumulated deficit and if we do not earn the money we are going to go down the chute.' Nobody seemed unduly panicked.

At the Arts Council, Isaacs, Cooper and the deputy chairman Sir James Spooner reviewed the closure plans with Peter Gummer, Mary Allen, the dance chairman Prue Skene and finance director Lew Hodges.

'The least-cost option,' said Hodges, 'would be to stop performing for two years, saving forty million pounds.'

'Ridiculous,' snorted Spooner. 'Patrons do not give money for bricks and mortar but to support their world-class opera and ballet companies. If there are no performances for two years, three years, whatever, then sponsorship will simply dry up.'

'That's like saying, fuck it, we don't want you any more,' exploded Isaacs.

No one seemed to recall that the original Lottery application made no mention of the companies continuing to perform during closure.

The House showed up many of the cracks that were surfacing in the company as it approached the dreaded date of closure with little planned beyond. Although many scenes were more than two years old by the time they reached the screen, a fatal impression was conveyed of an enterprise adrift, holed below the water line but still dancing in the ballroom and dickering on deck. The perceptual damage was irreparable. 'Fly on the wall that nearly brought the House down,' was one newspaper's verdict.[53]

From the first night of transmission, 16 January 1996, Isaacs' position was undermined. He had announced the previous spring that he would retire in September 1997, when he turned sixty-five, but *The House* and its attendant events put paid to any hopes of glory.

A month before the series was screened, relations with the Arts Council reached an all-time low. Isaacs demanded the right to 'draw down' some of the Lottery money earmarked for redevelopment. The Council replied that they could not release the funds until the ROH fulfilled the eighteen conditions of the grant, including a balanced budget and a confirmed programme for the closure period.

Mary Allen, alarmed at the lack of an integrated monthly cash flow report, put a mole into the house in the form of Richard Pulford, a former Arts Council deputy secretary-general. Pulford's brief was to report to her weekly, daily if necessary, on the company's solvency and on its progress in meeting the eighteen conditions. A man of dry wit and infinite patience, Pulford had earned his spurs in many an arts crisis. He had singlehandedly rescued local funding when Margaret Thatcher abolished the metropolitan authorities and had been joint chief of London's perpetually troubled South Bank Centre. What he found at Covent Garden was a drift into debt and a lack of clear decisions. 'A failure of senior management,' he called it. 'How the various departments have been allowed to plan on this basis is an interesting question, the answer to which must lie at the top of the organization,'[54] said Pulford.

Isaacs, facing close budgetary scrutiny, slashed the payroll. He cut a hundred jobs one week, two hundred the next. Four days before Christmas 1995 he had a meeting with the Arts Council which was 'so horrible that I have suppressed the memory, having only a dim recollection of abuse and recrimination, of men and women behaving badly'.[55]

Eye-witnesses recall that Lord Gowrie opened with a statement so airy and obtuse that, after quarter of an hour, Angus Stirling leaned across the table and said, in his gentlest voice, 'Grey, it's obvious that something is terribly wrong. Please tell us what it is.' Gowrie abandoned his peroration and handed over to Mary Allen. She reported that the Council had decided that no Lottery handout could be given to Covent Garden until its budgets balanced and its closure was acceptably planned. Sir James Spooner rose, so violently that his chair crashed to the ground. 'I have to go,' he said, 'but I can tell you this: if you want the whole thing back in your laps, we'll give it to you. We'll put it into liquidation.'

For the next two hours, one side 'hammered at the table saying "give us the cash" and the other side said, "no, we will not".' The meeting ended with an agreement to send in a team of independent accountants from KPMG. Isaacs was seen kicking the corridor wall, but progress had been made.[56] Once the audit had been conducted the only outstanding obstacle would be where the companies should perform during the exile years. Isaacs had set his face against the Arts Council's favoured option.

Sadler's Wells had been given a £27 million Lottery grant to rebuild and its chief executive Ian Albery had offered to co-ordinate his timetable to give the ROH first use of the renovated theatre from November 1997. Isaacs snubbed the offer gracelessly. 'Surely a bird in the hand is worth two in the bush?' said Albery. Isaacs muttered something about there being no restaurants in the neighbourhood. Sadler's Wells was a community theatre, drawing, as in Lilian Baylis's time, on a local audience of pensioners, school parties and council tenants. Under Albery's direction it was starting to buzz as a place for new dance. An experimental, all-male *Swan Lake*, choreographed by Matthew Bourne and starring the Royal Ballet's undervalued Adam Cooper, proved so exciting that it earned two West End runs and a Christmas show on television. Small as it was, with only fifteen hundred seats, Sadler's Wells was able to take risks. Its lottery win was resented at Covent Garden, where malicious tongues accused the Arts Council of pandering to a Sadler's Wells board member by name of Cherie Booth, Q.C., wife of a fast-rising Labour MP, Tony Blair.

The theatres Isaacs wanted to book were both in the West End: the Lyceum and Drury Lane. The latter was occuped by the long-running *Miss Saigon*, whose producer, Cameron Macintosh, refused to budge. The Lyceum's owners demanded a crippling rental and, while waiting interminably for an ROH decision, did a deal with Andrew Lloyd Webber for a revival of *Jesus Christ Superstar*.

Isaacs, while driving to work, was struck by a vacant site beside Tower Bridge. He suggested building a temporary theatre which another organization, perhaps Disney, could inherit when the Royal companies moved back home. Plans were drawn up and months slipped by. Planning permission was granted by the local authority on 18 December 1996. Two weeks later, just before *The House* aired, the scheme was abandoned for want of a willing partner. Disney were not answering the phone and the architects told Isaacs that it was now too late to erect the tent in time for the company's exile.

Visiting Isaacs in his office that week, I asked him for the fall-back plan. There was none. He seemed unfocused, his eyes straying to television monitors on the wall and his sentences drifting into thin air. He was still hoping that the temporary theatre could be built. He told the board on 22 January 'there was just a chance that the Tower Bridge theatre project might again become a realistic option'. That faint hope was extinguished when the Environment Secretary John Gummer, Peter's brother, called in the proposal for a public inquiry. Eighteen months before closure, the ROH had nowhere to go. 'The right decision would have been to delay closure, and therefore the redevelopment, until clear plans had been crystallized,' said the ROH finance director, Clive Timms. Postponement was unthinkable, said Isaacs.[57]

Anxieties flared. Vivien Duffield demanded that Peter Gummer should be brought on to the board to push things along and mend bridges with the Arts Council. Some wanted him to succeed Stirling without delay, but the rules stated that the chairman had to be a serving board member for at least three months. Gummer was co-opted in March 1996, arousing adverse press comment. It seemed improper that the Lottery gamekeeper should join the opera house poachers without breaking stride. It seemed also unwise to appoint one of John Major's closest advisers as chairman-designate when the Tory Government was on its last legs. The warnings went unheeded. Gummer's arrival coincided with the release of Lottery funds. At his first meeting, Clive Timms told the board that the costs of exile could well exceed the projected twenty million pounds. Twenty-seven and thirty-four were the figures he mentioned. An enraged Robert Gavron demanded, and received, the finance director's immediate resignation. Matters were no longer being discussed with the augustan calm of a Waverley or the detailed attentiveness of a Drogheda, a Moser or a Sainsbury.

For want of a homeless shelter, Sadler's Wells was pressed into service. 'The last time I had seen Jeremy,' said Albery, 'he told me, "Ian, don't bother, we're not coming to Sadler's Wells. We – do – not – want – to go to Sadler's Wells." '[58] Albery booked the Pina Bausch dance ensemble as his opening attraction and the Rambert company as his mainstay. Suddenly there was a call from Isaacs. 'Ian, you have to do something to help us.' Next came a call from Clive Priestley, chairman of the London Arts Board: 'You've got to help Covent Garden.' Finally, at a meeting with Mary Allen, funding pressure was exerted. Albery refused to cancel his scheduled dates and told Covent Garden they would have to fit in as best they could. Like many arts professionals, he was unwilling to grant favours to the haughty and bullying Royal Opera House.

The Royal Opera booked blocks of time at the Barbican Centre, the Royal Festival Hall and the rundown Shaftesbury Theatre on the edge of the West End. The Royal Ballet rented Labatt's Apollo in Hammersmith, six miles from its natural habitat and beside a thundering flyover. For the rest, the companies would tour Japan, America, Germany, Finland and anywhere else that would have them at short notice. In July, Pulford reported to Mary Allen that the ROH had done just enough to satisfy the eighteen conditions, though problems persisted.

Allen attended the interviews for Isaacs' successor as the Arts Council's observer. The selection process had been botched. An approach to Hugues Gall, director of the Paris Opéra, was sent to his former post in Geneva. The invitation to Peter Jonas was mailed not to the Intendant's office at the Bavarian State Opera but to the Ministry of Culture, arousing unfounded doubts about his loyalty. The only foreign applicant of appropriate calibre was Gerard Mortier, the Salzburg Festival's engagingly modernist opera boss. Mortier was asked: 'What would you do if the Government cuts the Arts Council grant and you are obliged to cut your repertoire at three months' notice?' Mortier replied, 'but this doesn't happen . . .' Someone sourly replied, 'it just has.' Mortier was asked back for a second interview. He left saying, 'all they wanted to do was steal my ideas.'

The remaining candidates were Brian Dickie of Glyndebourne and three internal contenders: Nicholas Payne, Anthony Russell-Roberts and the personnel director, Mike Morris. None inspired confidence. Payne, who had been nominated by Isaacs, seemed unwilling to answer any question that was put to him. 'If he could have said nothing, he would have,' said one interviewer.

Allen received a call from Genista McIntosh, executive director of the lately ennobled Royal National Theatre, saying she had heard the job was still open. Should she apply? With all speed, said Allen, putting her in touch with the head-hunters. The two women saw themselves as allies in a male-dominated field. McIntosh was the National's backroom girl, sorting out the nuts and bolts while Richard Eyre ruled the glamorous repertoire. A child of the Welfare

State, just short of fifty years old, she had only ever worked in subsidized theatre, first at the RSC and then at the National beside Eyre who was about to step down. She believed passionately in the citizen's right to enjoy the summits of cultural attainment but, although a Labour diehard, she took a practical view of the benefits of private sponsorship. 'Unlike some,' she told theatre students, 'I don't think the introduction of private sector funding was a pollutant.'[59]

Before McIntosh could send in her c.v., one of the head-hunters took Mary Allen aside and said: 'You could do this job. Why don't you apply?' Allen cocked her head and said she might consider it if Peter Gummer wanted her. She and Gummer had clashed fiercely at the Arts Council. In the rarified world of public relations, he did not expect a woman to overrule him and was taken aback when Allen did. Over time, they achieved a productive, if combustible, relationship.

Gummer responded enthusiastically to Allen's nomination and tried to talk her into the job. He also sounded out Stirling, who added his blessing. But Allen was concerned about leaving the Arts Council, where the Lottery Director was out of action with a broken skull and Lord Gowrie would be lost without her. She threw her support behind McIntosh who, in a sparkling interview, won over the panel, with one exception. Gummer said: 'I don't think she's good at handling stress.' It took several meetings before he was persuaded.

The announcement of Genista McIntosh's appointment on 4 July 1996 was widely acclaimed. She was a woman of proven theatrical know-how and dedication – calm, assiduous and self-effacing where Isaacs was blustery, mercurial and vain. Isaacs had been awarded a knighthood the previous weekend. Peter Gummer, ennobled by John Major, would succeed Stirling under his new title, Lord Chadlington. He was chuffed with the job, remarking that he had been going to the opera weekly for thirty-two years. He could not wait to get started.

Isaacs, however, was not the type go quietly. He had left Channel Four with a threat to throttle his successor and he did not like being cast as the villain in Covent Garden's downslide. He smarted at having to cut four operas – *Norma*, *Il Corsaro* (Verdi), *The Golden Cockerel* (Rimsky-Korsakov) and *Hérodiade* (Massenet) from his final season, leaving only two new shows: Verdi's *Macbeth* and

Palestrina by Hans Pfitzner, an eighty-year fixture in the German repertoire that had never been staged in Britain. The Royal Opera was celebrating its jubilee. Isaacs wanted to go out with a bang. In the event, he was lucky to escape with a whimper.

In the midst of his travails – with the Arts Council withholding its Lottery cheque, the Tower Bridge tent collapsing and *The House* oozing weekly into the nation's living rooms – Isaacs was snapped at seven one morning leaving the house of a senior colleague's estranged wife. A *Daily Mail* reporter asked on the doorstep if he was having an affair with Anne Dunhill, whose marriage to Anthony Russell-Roberts had broken up over his liaison with a Danish dancer. Isaacs said nothing. Dunhill, a tobacco heiress, told the *Mail* that he had been helping 'with my Latin translation'. She would later provide the paper with an amplified account and adapt her experiences as romantic fiction. 'Jeremy knew I was going to write a novel about us,' she told the *Mail*. 'It was my first time as an adultress and it was all quite exciting, rather like being a spy. I thought he had an open marriage. When he told me he didn't, I was conscience-stricken. But I persuaded myself that if it wasn't me, it would be someone else.'[60]

Isaacs held his tongue. Then, interviewed four years later about his memoir of the opera house which made no mention of the affair, he issued a snarl of defiance at the press. It was, he said 'a straight case of kiss and tell, which is a nastiness that obtrudes into British life to a degree which was unheard of thirty years ago and which is now commonplace. We all make mistakes, and that was a serious mistake on my part. I was stupid. I thought I was trying to help this woman over a bad patch. She obviously brought herself to believe it would last. But it was comparatively brief. ... It is completely behind me. Gillian has – whom I love very much – has put up with me. So it's over. Over. Finished. Gone. And yet a newspaper will leap and pay money to print it. It is – dreadful.'[61]

What Isaacs had failed to appreciate was that *Sun* and television exposure had made him a minor public figure, and hence a target for tabloid intrusion. Winning the Lottery and pulling on yellow socks for the camera had backfired in an ugly and predictable fashion, making public knowledge of a private lapse. Someone, perhaps Keith Cooper, should have warned him to watch his back. But Cooper had his hands full with a broadsheet press that were baying for human sacrifice as the price for the company's ineptitude.

Wounded and besieged, Isaacs was not alone in his plight. The tabloids, in a feeding frenzy, had staked out a dozen allegedly errant Tory MPs in their eagerness to exploit 'sleaze' and bring down an outworn Government. England at the close of the century was a snoopers' paradise, where no home was safe from long lenses and the Princess of Wales was hounded by paparazzi every hour of the day and night. She would be driven to her death. Jeremy Isaacs escaped slightly wounded to his natural habitat.

He had a television job to return to, in a production company set up by Gillian Widdicombe and producer Martin Smith five minutes' walk away from the ROH. Since the end of 1994, Isaacs had been involved in the making of *Cold War*, a twenty-four part sequel to *World at War*, and *Millennium*, a ten-part retrospect. 'I was general director of the Royal Opera House where it was agreed I could be involved in one major outside project,'[62] Isaacs explained. He credited Smith with driving the project. 'I have been there to back him up and,' wrote Isaacs, '. . . occasionally pointed the way.'[63] Widdicombe maintained that Isaacs 'hardly ever came in to the office'.[64] Nevertheless, people in authority wondered why the ROH board had allowed Isaacs to accept an absorbing extra-curricular role in the very years when all of his attention was required to steer the complex redevelopment and plan the unresolved closure period. No matter how tough conditions grew at the opera house, Isaacs kept one foot firmly in the television camp.

Genista McIntosh worked out six months' notice at the Royal National Theatre. She would take up her post in January 1997, and Isaacs was asked to leave as soon as she arrived, without so much as a day's handover. He would be paid a full salary for not working the following nine months. Stirling and Chadlington felt he was 'dying to go'. Isaacs was ambivalent. He did not like being evicted and would remain a board member until the house closed. His final half-year passed almost without incident, in a state of suspended animation. As the year ended, Chadlington noted that staff costs were half a million over budget. A further quarter of a million pounds had been lost in South America. Isaacs' last financial statement showed a deficit of three million pounds, of which two million pounds could be clawed back in identified savings. 'I feel I gee'd the place up a bit and handed it over in reasonable nick to my successors,' he said in parting.[65] 'He could have worked wonders if he had kept his mind on the job,' observed a senior Government official.[66]

Isaacs did not go gently. 'I was pushed,' he rasped in a television interview,[67] angering the rest of the board who felt he had been treated more fairly than perhaps he deserved. Months later he popped up as chairman of the London wing of the Salzburg Festival Trust, competing for donations and upmarket ticket sales with his former employer.

There were to be no ROH farewells for Isaacs, at his own insistence. He would return for the ceremonial closure in July 1997, announcing then from the stage that 'opera has a future here so long as two forces unite to defend it: the dedication of those on stage and behind who give it, and the passion of the audience – your passion – to enjoy it.'

In an open letter to his successor, Isaacs urged her to attend rehearsals, make a fuss of singers and get to bed before three in the morning. Above all, he exhorted her to innovate. 'Whatever the financial pressures that argue otherwise,' he wrote, 'it is crucial that we do not let a great lyric theatre slide, as it all too easily can, into the unthinking habit of safe repertory and safe production style. Adventure, I know, will be one of your watchwords, too.'[68]

Of the many qualities that Jeremy Isaacs had brought to Covent Garden, his dynamism had transformed the internal atmosphere and his modernist aspirations the production style. But the television know-how for which he was hired had rebounded against the institution in the most malevolent way. Television, under Jeremy Isaacs, turned the Royal Opera House into soap opera.

There was worse to come. The comic-opera era was about to unfold.

CHAPTER 10

Act Four: Where's the Door?

(January to August 1997)

ENGLAND, AT THE start of 1997, trembled on the brink of seismic upheaval. After eighteen years of Conservative rule, Tony Blair's renovated Labour Party had reclaimed the centre ground and was positioning itself to take power. Although its appeal was pitched at Middle England and its fiscal policies were prudent, Labour's agenda was radical. It aimed to set up independent governments for Scotland, Wales and Northern Ireland, to abolish the hereditary powers of the House of Lords and to rush a reluctant island into closer co-operation with Europe.

Aided by some of the best brains in the advertising and media industries, Blair employed the soap-powder trick and rebranded his party 'New' Labour. It was not so much a slogan as a statement of intent. All that was new would be hailed as healthy, useful and progressive. The old was soiled, tacky and corrupt. In the gleaming world of New Labour, the Royal Opera House and the traditional arts belonged decidedly to the old.

Genista McIntosh, known as Jenny, had one foot on either side of the old-new divide. An opera lover who bought her own tickets, she adored the excess and immediacy of live performance. Opera, she wrote, 'like all forms of theatre, is dependent for its power on performers and audience being present together in the same space at the same time to share an experience that will never be repeated again in exactly the same way. Mechanical reproductions, no matter how remarkable, cannot compare with the excitement and energy of being there, with all senses fully engaged . . . We must not breed a generation of opera lovers "spoilt" by the perfection of recorded sound . . . This is one of many reasons for ensuring that there are seats in opera houses available at prices people can afford.'[1]

As a card-carrying populist, however, she deplored the exclusivism of the house she had chosen to lead. Along with many in the arts, she had watched aghast as the company's antics brought the entire sector into disrepute. 'The allocation of £78 million to the ROH in 1995 (and their reaction to it) was probably the single most damaging event in the recent history of the arts in the UK,' she wrote. 'It gave licence to the latent hostility to art and artists that has been evident in this country for a long time.'[2]

To McIntosh and the theatrical profession, Covent Garden was no longer a flagship for British arts but a pirate vessel, afloat on the high seas and a danger to shipping. Her mission, as she saw it, was to bring the ROH back under the union flag, to tone down its élitism, renew its pact with the public and make its existence acceptable to her friends in New Labour. It was a Herculean task, but one that she approached with every semblance of confidence. A ballet board member who sat beside her at an early meeting felt she was 'thrilled about the job when she first arrived'.[3]

Equine featured and smartly dressed, McIntosh entered the opera house on 6 January and set about touring its far-flung departments. She radiated warmth and raised morale wherever she trod. 'She's lovely,' gushed one long-serving Gardener whose job would soon be abolished. Among McIntosh's first tasks would be to halve the payroll for closure, reducing the number of employees to five hundred and forty.

As Chief Executive, she entered the boardroom two rungs lower than Isaacs, who had been General Director and a member of the board. She was greeted courteously but condescendingly. Chadlington let it be known that he was in charge, while Vivien Duffield's voice was heard on all matters pertaining to money. The abrasive Mrs Duffield needed to raise one hundred million pounds in the next three years to pay for the redevelopment. 'I think people are probably scared of me,' she said, as McIntosh arrived, 'they are scared of anyone who points out what is wrong.'[4]

Tensions flared between the ROH Trust, which Mrs Duffield chaired, and the main board. She had hired Millbank Public Relations, at five thousand pounds a month 'to position the House and management team as sensitive, responsible, considerate, realistic' and 'good custodians of Lottery money'. She was not prepared to rely on Chadlington, whose company, Shandwick, flagged itself as 'the international leader in global reputation management'.

At a performing level, there was aggravated friction between the opera and ballet companies with Nicholas Payne riding roughshod over the two Anthonies, Dowell and Russell-Roberts. In talks with Sadler's Wells, Payne was team-leader with the Anthonies 'clinging on to his tails'.[5] The Arts Council had stipulated as a condition of the Lottery that ballet should have parity with opera. 'It was my impression that the interest of the Covent Garden board lay heavily with the opera company,' observed Prue Skene, who chaired the Arts Council's dance panel. Neither Chadlington nor McIntosh had a primary passion for ballet, which was squeezed at every turn. Dowell had prepared a fairly ambitious dance programme for the closure period. He emerged from the boardroom with the schedule in shreds, garnished with *Nutcracker*s and *Swan Lake*s. If he refused to accept the changes, Dowell was told, the Royal Ballet could be disbanded. 'Our priority had to be finding a way to keep the company going at full strength through the closure,' was the reason that McIntosh gave.[6]

'Anthony was absolutely suicidal,' said his friend, Dame Antoinette Sibley. 'He is fantastically loyal and would give his life for the company, but there came a point where they got to him.'

'I remember thinking, I just can't,' confessed Dowell. 'I took a walk over the Waterloo bridge because I had booked an appointment with Jenny and didn't know what to say. The responsibility was eating away at me, every day there was a new situation. The anxiety was wearing me thin. It was awful to wake up every morning nervous and dreading what you're going in for.

'Jenny was not long here, she had come in as a wonderful breath of air. I felt doubly bad at saying this to someone like her. But she was a wonderful listener, very sensible and very practical. She said to me, "this is awful, but your health must come first".'

Dowell went away to consider his position. By the time he returned, Genista McIntosh was gone.

Managing an opera house in the modern era was a high wire act with an alarming casualty toll. In the mid-90s, the Sovrintendente of La Scala, Carlo Fontana, was sacked for political reasons and reinstated after boycott threats by Pavarotti. Two music directors of the Bastille Opéra, Daniel Barenboim and Myung Whun Chung, were fired on grounds of cost and repertoire, each winning huge damages in court. Finland built itself an opera house after seventy-five years of statehood and lost both the music director and the finance director within the first season; the artistic director followed two years later. Israel created an opera house for its jubilee, performing a triple public sacrifice in the opening season of the managing director, the music director and the Mayor of Tel Aviv, who had reportedly fiddled the street-paving budgets to fund the palace of art. The Teatro Real in Madrid reopened six years late, having lost both music director and artistic director amid charges of 'rampant provincialism and xenophobia'; the Liceo in Barcelona burned down and was constitutionally restructured.

Resignations were the roughage that kept the opera machine in working order, the spice that titivated tongues between acts of art. Ruptures were routine and rarely evoked much interest beyond a claque of cognoscenti. What happened to Genista McIntosh, however, became a national issue, presenting as it did a mirror image of the spirit of the times. Shrouded in mystery and misinformation, it became the focus for two public inquiries and a political backlash that brought the ROH to the verge of abolition.

There was nothing out of the ordinary about her first two months. At the end of January, Deborah MacMillan (who succeeded Skene in the chair of the Arts Council's dance panel) complained that the dress rehearsal of *Prince of the Pagodas*, in front of a paying audience, was also the first time the orchestra had played the music in the presence of dancers.[7] *Plus ça change*. Weeks later, a crucial film section was omitted from *Anastasia*. McIntosh maintained that its absence 'did not detract from the performance'.[8]

The deficit figure fluctuated. In the absence of a finance director it was hard to know exactly how much cash was in hand. Uncertainty can breed anxiety, but McIntosh's dilemma was no worse than Isaacs' had been in his last six months without a finance director. The new chief executive appeared in February before Skene's Lottery panel, with Chadlington, to outline their plans for the closure period. Chadlington made the opening remarks, but McIntosh carried the rest of the meeting. 'The tensions between them had not yet surfaced,' said Skene. If McIntosh resented Chadlington planting himself and a secretary in an office next to hers, she said nothing. Once, when she came to the Arts Council looking wan, Mary Allen sought her out and said, 'you do know, don't you, that we'll give you any and every support that we can. Any time you need us, we're here for you.'[9] On 20 March, Allen informed

McIntosh that the Council had agreed to hand over the £23.5 million second tranche of Lottery money – on condition that it received in future 'integrated monthly cashflow' statements.[10] Members of the Council were getting edgy over the lack of clear financial information from the ROH.

At the end of March, McIntosh announced plans for the first season of exile. The best news was that Haitink had agreed to stay on as music director. 'It seems almost beyond comprehension,' noted the *Daily Telegraph*, 'that Covent Garden should have left its closure plans so late and so incomplete.'[11] Ismene Brown, the *Telegraph*'s robust dance critic, described the season as a 'betrayal' of the Royal Ballet. 'There will be six new opera productions in the first six months. And for the ballet? None.' She reported that 'wholly unacceptable pressures' had been exerted on Dowell 'to abandon by far the best option – to take the Royal Ballet to the nation's cities (agreement had even been reached with other ballet companies).'[12] Brown urged the ballet to declare its independence of the ROH management.

Internal rifts were widening. In one of two interviews that she gave as chief executive, McIntosh described the ROH as a company that had been 'put together in bits, rather than springing into coherent life like the National Theatre'.[13] She formed an executive board to pull the strands together, but her executives were disunited. Three of them – Payne, Russell-Roberts and Morris – had contested her job. 'I wish we had been more supportive as a management team when she began to feel the strain,' said Keith Cooper in retrospect. 'I don't think we supported her enough.'[14]

There was not much she could do to harmonize relations between the Board, the Friends and the fundraising Trust. Vivien Duffield, not the most reticent of activists, articulated her requirements in a stentorian tone that could chill the faint-hearted. 'Just for the record,' said Duffield, 'I never had a row with Jenny. I don't think I was ever in the same room alone with Jenny.'

In April, the country went into abeyance for a General Election. Chadlington spent much of his time at Downing Street. He urged John Major to run a television campaign depicting Tony Blair as the Devil. Major, knowing that Blair was a religious man, fastidiously refused. With his mind on impending political disaster, Chadlington eased his grip on the ROH controls.

McIntosh and Allen met in Hayden Phillips' office to survey the political outlook. An official noted that McIntosh looked thin and spent the whole meeting with her legs wound around the chair, talking slightly off the agenda.[15]

A letter written by Lord Gowrie to the *Sunday Times* kept the stew simmering. Irked by criticism of the Arts Council's handling of ROH grants, Gowrie described the original closure plans as 'quite frankly, a shambles'.[16] His criticism was directed at Stirling and Isaacs but was misconstrued as a coded attack on the new regime. Allen and Chadlington had a working breakfast on 25 April to calm the waters.

Chadlington confided that he was worried about McIntosh. As early as the second week of February, he had been warned by the head-hunter, Michael Knight, who was searching for a new finance director, that McIntosh was in 'a state of increasing personal crisis'.[17] At the end of February, she went to Chadlington and told him she wanted to leave; he gently dissuaded her. On the 27th, the board commended her 'excellent and unstinting' work. By mid-April, McIntosh felt she could take it no longer. On the 16th, she asked to resign. Chadlington urged her to give it one last try. Neither showed any sign of stress outside their private offices.

McIntosh plied an upbeat line to the press. 'Until now, everyone has been preoccupied with endings,' she said. 'I think we've reached the point when people can talk about beginnings.'[18] At a board meeting on 28 April she appeared cool and in control.

Two days later, Chadlington took Mary Allen to breakfast and confirmed that McIntosh was wobbling. Allen reacted coolly. The Arts Council had, at any given time, two or three orchestral and theatre managers who were desperate to quit and were being held in place by strong tea and sympathy. Some survived, others not. Knowing McIntosh, Allen expected her to pull through. She suggested that he should consult the Heritage Department, meaning Hayden Phillips.

In the small hours of 2 May, Labour romped to power. Key supporters, McIntosh included, were summoned by Blair's campaign manager and Herbert Morrison's grandson, Peter Mandelson, to dance the night away at the Royal Festival Hall, artistic totem of Labour power, old and new. McIntosh was unable to share the jubilation. Four days later, on 6 May, she told Chadlington that she could not carry on. He asked her to sleep on it. She said she could neither eat nor sleep; he advised her not to risk her health. The next morning she wrote a two-page resignation letter by hand from her home in Tufnell Park and had it delivered to the Connaught Hotel, where the chairman was having a lunchtime meeting. Her tone was regretful but firm; she asked to leave as quickly as possible.

Pandemonium ensued. Chadlington called Mary Allen after lunch and offered her the chief executive's job. He demanded an immediate answer. Allen was used to making quick decisions. Friends said that she weighed, on the one hand, her loyalty to Lord Gowrie and the Arts Council and, on the other, her ambition and career plan. The pay at Covent Garden was fifty per cent higher than she was earning as secretary general of the ACE, just over ninety thousand a year. She knew the parameters of the job, having scrutinized it for five years, and felt she could do better than previous incumbents. She had experience of running an arts centre at Brentford, on the western outskirts of London, and an early career as an actress. She was forty-five years old and knew that the best jobs do not often come begging.

Personal security is usually paramount in decisions of this sort. Gowrie's ACE chairmanship, under Labour, was bound to be brief; his successor might want a different secretary general. In Allen's mind, there was an additional concern. Her husband, Nigel Pantling, head of corporate finance at Hambros Bank, had been involved that spring in an ill-timed takeover bid for the Co-operative Wholesale Society, one of the Labour Party's historic adjuncts. The bid aborted and Pantling now faced an inquiry from the Securities and Futures Authority which could rule him out of City work for years. There was no imputation of dishonesty, but his earning power was likely to be drastically curtailed whatever the findings of the inquiry. The inquiry continues. A better job was an offer his wife could not lightly refuse. Taking all these factors quickly into consideration, Mary Allen accepted the job – on condition that each and every member of the ROH board separately endorsed her appointment. Chadlington began phoning them for approval.

One board member, Robert Gavron, had given half a million pounds to New Labour's election fund and was friendly with the newly installed Heritage Secretary, Chris Smith. Chadlington asked Gavron to set up an emergency meeting with Smith, that very day if possible. Smith had been a minister for half a week. A bookish man with a doctorate in the Lakeland poets, he was the first member of a British Cabinet to live an openly gay lifestyle. Before the election, he had been intensively coached by Labour veterans and former civil servants not to let himself be dominated by the Whitehall mandarinate. With these strictures possibly in mind, Smith apparently omitted to tell his permanent secretary, Hayden Phillips, that he was seeing the Covent Garden chairman on a matter of great urgency. Had Phillips known of the meeting, he would have been duty-bound to attend and might well have influenced the outcome. Instead, a junior official took minutes.

Chadlington, battered by his electoral débâcle, informed the neophyte minister that his chief executive had resigned and that he wanted to poach Mary Allen from the Arts Council, subject to Gowrie's permission. It was essential to make a rapid appointment without a proper selection process, he stressed, because of the company's difficult financial situation. Chadlington made it clear, he later maintained, that Allen might not be able to take up the job instantaneously; her availability would depend on Gowrie's willing-ness to let her go without serving notice. He emerged from the meeting under the impression that Smith was 'happy'.[19]

The official minute, submitted to a subsequent inquiry, gave a slightly different account. Smith declared himself 'extremely unhappy about many of the circumstances that had arisen', but agreed, after a long discussion, not to 'raise any further objections' so long as Chadlington conveyed his reservations to the Arts Council and the ROH Board. Smith would later tell a public inquiry that he had no idea Allen would not start work until September. Had he been told this salient fact he 'would have questioned even more strongly the circumstances of urgency which they were pressing upon me.'[20] Given that he and Chadlington were political enemies, they were unlikely to sing the same tune. The departmental record suggests that Chadlington was being frugal with the facts. However, Chadlington did not have all the facts to hand; he had no way of knowing whether Gowrie would release Allen, or make her work out three months' notice.

He reported back to Allen, who tried to catch Gowrie before he left the Arts Council that evening. She found him in his hat and coat, and booked an appointment for eleven o'clock next morning. On being told of her proposed transfer, Gowrie was shocked, bitter and bewildered – 'gob-smacked', as he later put it. He trusted Allen and, though their relationship was entirely proper, liked to refer to her as 'my working wife'. He viewed her departure as a marital betrayal. All he could say by way of blessing was, 'well, at least you're going off with a friend of mine'.

For the next five days, the entire cast kept up appearances and not a word leaked to the press. On Monday 12 May, the ROH board met at Chadlington's company, Shandwick, to ratify Allen's appointment. One member who was in America was reached by phone and told that McIntosh was leaving for the sake of her health, to be replaced by Mary Allen. 'I was presented,' said Jeremy Isaacs, 'with a *fait accompli*.'[21] He would have recommended that Payne and Morris form an interim management until a strong candidate was selected by due process. 'I was rung up in Israel,' said Vivien Duffield, 'and by that time it was a *fait accompli*.'

After the board dispersed, Chadlington spoke to Gowrie, who phoned around his Council members to tell them that Mary Allen was going to Covent Garden. The following day, Gowrie announced her departure to the press, insisting that he had 'been consulted throughout' and that the ROH 'could not have made a more appropriate appointment given the special circumstances'. Chadlington simultaneously welcomed Mary Allen's appointment, along with a new finance director, Richard Hall. He worded the announcements himself, overriding a last-minute demurral from Genista McIntosh on the reasons given for her resignation.

McIntosh, he said, was leaving 'due to ill health . . . I and all my colleagues wish her a speedy return to full health and much success and happiness in the future'. Chadlington added that he rushed the appointment through because, as he had told Chris Smith, 'we would go bust if we didn't choose a chief executive straight away . . . those who say I acted too speedily simply do not understand the financial situation of the house.'[22]

The B-word – bust, bankrupt, broke – had been uttered for the first time. It would become a refrain of Chadlington's, a thin red line of defence. Under press questioning, he admitted that the deficit had shot up to four and a half million pounds, but there was no immediate cause for concern. Mary Allen would take up her duties in September once she had wound up her former job and taken a well-earned holiday. The Arts Council met the next morning, Wednesday. Allen promptly realized that she could not give advice on anything pertaining to its largest client which she was about to join. She asked to be released immediately, but resolved, with Chadlington, to take a break in the hope of avoiding the opprobrium that had attended his own direct transfer from the giver to the receiver.

She had, in any event, been advised to take some rest after a stubborn chest infection and a debilitating course of antibiotics. Clearing her desk, Mary Allen retreated to her Suffolk cottage, where she received a warm note of congratulation and encouragement from Genista McIntosh, who was in another rural refuge, hiding from the press. Both women asked for nothing more than to lie low until the storm blew over.

But this was not to be a teacup squall. So much about the transfer was couched in the euphemisms and ambiguities of spin doctors that the public interest was piqued. Staff at the ROH, distressed at McIntosh's departure, hissed Chadlington when he gave them the news. Chris Smith, smarting from being wrongfooted in his first public act, called a departmental inquiry into the 'probity' of the Royal Opera House. Parliament was stirring and the press were up in arms. Rodney Milnes in *The Times* accused Chadlington and Allen of colluding in the removal of McIntosh and 'mounting what looks very much like a coup'.[23] The present writer, in the *Daily Telegraph*, argued that what Covent Garden needed from a new Heritage Secretary was 'a public inquiry and a new constitution to protect the house in future from the pressures that put paid to Genista McIntosh's best intentions.'[24]

Inquiries flowed hot and fast. Lord Gowrie appointed a respected lawyer, Edward Walker-Arnott, to investigate allegations of collusion. Walker-Arnott would discover 'a long history of uneasiness' between the the the Arts Council and Covent Garden, but no active wrongdoing. Barely had his inquest opened than Parliament got into the act. Gerald Kaufman, sometime press secretary to Harold Wilson and now chairman of the National Heritage Select Committee, announced that his inquiry would be held in public, with the protagonists called to account in front of television cameras. Chadlington's speed strategy had spectacularly backfired.

Doubt was instantly cast on the official reasons for McIntosh's departure. Friends and family let it be known that she was neither physically nor mentally ill, aware that any such imputation could damage her future prospects. McIntosh herself wrote to *The Times*,[25] denying reports that she had been pushed out by conspiracies or pressures. 'The decision to leave was mine alone,' she said.

In her eventual evidence before the Kaufman committee, McIntosh was gently questioned about the reasons for her decision.

'I left because I was extremely unhappy in the job,' she said. 'There is no doubt that being extremely unhappy causes one to be very distressed.'

'What was causing you distress?' asked one MP.

'It was caused partly by what I regard now, looking back, as a mismatch between me and the organization.'

Pressed again on the issue of ill health, she conceded: 'Had I continued in my job, I might well have become ill.'

In a further memorandum to Kaufman, unpublished in his report, McIntosh attempted to clarify differences of interpretation over the reason given for her departure. She had never been ill, she said, and she doubted the need to say that she was. But by the time she voiced her doubts matters were too far advanced and any delay would have caused embarrassment. Lord Chadlington was entitled to believe that, had she continued in the job, she might well have become ill; and he acted on his judgement in the best interests of the opera house. For her part, she wished it to be known that she dissented from his decision to ascribe her departure to health reasons, though not strongly enough to stop him from doing so, or in any way questioning his good intentions.[26]

No further light was shed on the matter and Genista McIntosh was allowed to leave the public arena with her integrity intact. She never said another word about her time at Covent Garden. She told colleagues, as she told Kaufman, that she found the company's structures 'diffuse' and 'fragmented'. She felt uncomfortable with internal conflicts and was unused to being shouted at by members of the board. None of this amounted to credible grounds for resignation. The mystery persists, and only a private confessor or psychoanalyst may be in possession of the full story.

The theatre closes ranks to protect its own as rigorously as the legal and medical professions. A recent Data Protection Act blocks public access to key documents in the public domain. McIntosh's associates, including ROH board members who were shown a copy of her resignation letter, sealed their lips. Nevertheless, a close scrutiny of ambient events and internal documents reveals a great deal about the motives that made McIntosh's resignation inevitable.

Word of her unhappiness percolated the upper echelons of English theatre from mid-February, when a sabotaged meeting appeared to affect her previously positive attitude. McIntosh had gone to Sadler's Wells to finalize rental contracts with its manager

Ian Albery, an ex-West End man with a strong public ethos. Albery knew McIntosh from the National and considered her 'totally honest, totally skilled'. She arrived in Islington to find two board members awaiting her. One was Chadlington, the other James Butler, a director of the accountants KPMG and a close associate of Vivien Duffield. Asked afterwards if she had not thought of attending this crucial meeting, Duffield said, 'no, I sent a strong man'.

Overcoming her surprise at being shadowed, McIntosh went into the meeting with two directors in tow. Barely had she begun to speak than Chadlington jumped in, telling Albery: 'You're negotiating with me now.' McIntosh dropped her head and said nothing for the rest of the meeting. Albery, incensed at her humiliation, exacted tough terms, some three hundred thousand pounds more than he expected to charge. 'There are many ways of skinning somebody in the theatre,' he laughed.[27] When McIntosh returned days later to sign the contracts she told him, 'Ian, you know I would never have agreed to this deal.'

It was a turning point in her relations with the board, a moment when McIntosh recognized that they could treat her like a vassal, damaging her standing in the wider theatrical world. Chadlington would later tell Mary Allen: 'I wasn't undermining Jenny, and it's terribly important they should not think I am undermining you.'[28] One of his close allies, expressing high regard for McIntosh, said: 'Peter is not a man who sits silently at meetings – he likes to get things done.'[29] To Albery, it did not look quite so amicable. 'To be treated like that,' he said, 'amounted to constructive dismissal.' Even if all the participants had taken Trappist vows – and several versions of the meeting soon raged like bushfire on the theatrical grapevine – the incident would have triggered a survival instinct in a less sensitive mind than McIntosh's. All she had to offer was proven competence. When that was overridden, her future was at stake.

Her resignation letter to Chadlington touched delicately but pointedly on such fears. She was finding the job increasingly difficult, she said, despite the board's support. Her best option, she felt, was to escape before the job overwhelmed her and affected her standard of performance. The concern she expressed was not for her physical well-being but for her professional reputation. An unhappy spell at a problem-ridden opera house would blight her prospects of ever returning to a senior position in the theatre world. When Chadlington showed her his press release, she asked him to omit any mention of health or anything else that might provoke damaging speculation. She wanted to walk out of the Royal Opera House untouched, for better or worse, and ready to resume her career. In a private communication to a close colleague, she confessed that she lacked the courage to tackle the ROH and felt that Mary Allen was being extremely brave – always a double-edged compliment.

The fuzzy reasons for her departure were nothing more sinister than an over-developed sense of self-preservation, allied to her known virtues of prudence and caution. She received a £23,000 pay-off and in August returned to her old job in the Royal National Theatre, alongside Trevor Nunn. She also joined the Trust Board of Sadler's Wells Theatre, cementing her friendship with Ian Albery. Two years later, Tony Blair elevated her to the peerage. A friend who tried over lunch, on her way to the House of Lords, to get her to discuss Covent Garden elicited nothing more than a pained and distant look.

The first three administrators of the Royal Opera House ruled for forty-two years, the fourth for just four months and a week. For the next four months, there was to be a vacuum. Lord Chadlington alternated with Sir Kit McMahon, former Governor of the Bank of England (and chairman of the ROH development board), in manning the office.

A redundancy deal was struck with the stage union, Bectu, allowing for the dismissal of virtually the entire stage and front-of-house staff in exchange for Bectu being authorized to represent clerical employees, an unprecedented concession to internal activists. Chris Smith kept well clear of the enterprise after his initial blunder, but New Labour was serving notice of future intent. Mark Fisher, the second-rank arts minister, told Chadlington publicly that he must convert the ROH into the 'people's opera house', an ominously vague term. 'My objective,' said Fisher, 'was to underline the importance that the Government attaches to improving access to the ROH, notably through more low-cost seats, more touring and use of broadcast facilities.'[30] A retroactive price tag was being pinned to the Lottery cheque, in an untested currency called 'access'.

At the end of June, as Britain handed Hong Kong back to China in an end-of-empire ceremony, the ROH deficit crept over five million pounds and members of the board were asked, for the first time, 'to consider whether the House is a going concern' – as the minutes put it[31] – or whether it should be put into liquidation. A loan of a million pounds each from two unnamed supporters (apparently Sainsbury and Duffield) staved off the need for instant action, but this was a crisis deferred, not a problem solved. Early bookings for the exile season looked gloomy, with the ballet at Labatt's Apollo running at barely ten per cent of budget.

On stage, events were building up to a dramatic conclusion. The production of *Macbeth* was cancelled a week before opening night because, amid mass redundancies and backstage wind-down, there had not been enough rehearsal time. Nicholas Payne took responsibility for a projected £200,000 loss and offered his resignation to the board, which refused to accept it. Another executive resignation could have undermined confidence and brought the house down.

On Saturday 12 July, Haitink gave a repetition of his masterly *Meistersinger* and on Monday 14th the Prince of Wales came to a closing gala, sealed with a *Sleeping Beauty*'s kiss from Darcey Bussell. The opening twirl of 1946 was a fitting farewell to the venerable old building. The Prime Minister conspicuously failed to attend. He was planning a party at Number Ten for the New Britain – a motley of fashion designers, Formula One racers, media types and rock singers, notably the Gallaghers of Oasis, who represented his vision of the nation reborn.

The next morning, the wreckers moved in. Patrons, passers-by and anyone with an eye for memorabilia were invited to take objects from the skips. Two former singers walked off with red velvet seats, which they transplanted to their television lounges.

Ten days later, the Kaufman committee held its first hearings, a fairly low-key examination of Gowrie, McIntosh and Isaacs, followed by Chadlington and the editor of *Opera*, Rodney Milnes. The sessions attracted little attention as the media unwound for the summer. A brief exchange between Kaufman and McIntosh gave some foreboding of the horrors in store. Had she, asked Kaufman solicitously, been shocked by the ROH's 'clubbiness'? McIntosh dodged the question; this was not a word she would have used. He rephrased the question. Had the clubbable atmosphere made her feel 'like an intruder?' Genista McIntosh gave an unseasonally wintry smile. 'Let's say that's not entirely unfair, chairman,' she replied.

One Friday afternoon, I went to see Solti to discuss his forthcoming memoirs. Sitting in his studio in a heavy cardigan and rollneck sweater, shivering despite the summer heat, he looked happier and more relaxed than I had ever seen him. His elder daughter, Gabrielle, was getting engaged that evening and the whole family were about to go on holiday, to his summer house in Italy. We talked about his struggles and successes, his future plans and his abiding love of women. 'Vat you want,' he upbraided me, 'I should be homosexual?'

The only worries on his mind were the general decline in musical attendances and the future of Covent Garden. He intended to do something about both issues when he got back. He was going to talk to Paul McCartney, who lived up the road, to see how they could enliven symphony concerts and he would get hold of Tony Blair to tell him he had to help the opera house. 'This can not go on,' said Solti, separating each syllable. The next morning, he left his adoptive country, never to return alive.

CHAPTER 11

Coming up for Eyre

(September 1997 to November 1998)

ON THE MORNING of 31 August 1997, the country awoke to the hushed tones of newscasters struggling to cope with the dignities of grief. Diana, Princess of Wales – 'the People's Princess' as Tony Blair renamed her that day – had been killed in a Paris car-smash with her lover, Dodi Fayed, after being pursued all month by swarms of photographers. She was thirty-six years old.

During the day crowds began to gather at the royal palaces. Many laid flowers, some wept. Diana's death had opened a floodgate of emotions. Alive, she had sought out the doomed and the deprived, visiting hospitals unannounced at the dead of night, holding hands with men who were dying of Aids. Her rejection by Prince Charles struck chords in the lives of many lone women. In her long-running media war with the Royal Family, she spoke for a new post-familial social order, while the Queen seemed locked into a rigid, failing nuclear capsule. Rejecting the dreary remoteness of other royals, Diana did workouts, took her sons to the movies and chose exotic lovers of Asian and Middle Eastern extraction. In the months before her death she had exposed herself to the war in Bosnia and waged a campaign against landmines that blew the legs off little children.

She was a wish-symbol of New Britain: liberal, multicultural and touchingly vulnerable. The stiff upper lip had given way to the brimming eye. England was acknowledging emotion. The spirit of the Blitz had dissolved in a wash of genuine mourning and sentimental indulgence, some of it resembling self-pity. The writer Julian Barnes called it 'look-at-me-grief'. Diana herself had been wealthy, white and a scion of one of England's oldest dynasties.

All week long, the crowds grew and the media were baffled. Reaction was rising from the ground up, and no one knew where it began, or might end. 'London is in a pre-revolutionary situation,' said a visiting historian. The Royal parks were flung open at night and thousands milled by floodlight at the gates of Kensington Palace, their flowers and messages piled above head height. Half a million letters were received at Buckingham Palace. The Queen was forced to break all precedent and bow to the coffin, as anti-monarchism surged and swelled. On the morning of the funeral, a Saturday, London was as still as Yukon City after the gold ran out. Elton John sobbed a song at Westminster Abbey and Earl Spencer, Diana's brother, delivered a barbed eulogy. The cortège was waved through the streets by citizens standing fifteen thick. 'Bye, Di,' they cried. Half the population watched on television. Twenty-one million copies of Elton John's song were sold in aid of Diana's charities. Cabinet ministers talked of renaming the August bank holiday Diana Day, and Heathrow, Diana Airport.

Many pontificated about changes in the national character, as Virginia Woolf had done in 1910.[1] The country, they said, would never be the same again. That assumption was partly true, but for other, political reasons. In Scotland and Wales, a devolution referendum that month dispelled the aftermath of Diana's death with a heady foretaste of independence. In Northern Ireland, the IRA had agreed an 'unequivocal' ceasefire. In London, the Prime Minister called for a new 'age of compassion'. Strangely, at a time of death, there was an intimation of new beginnings.

Coming home from Diana's funeral, I was informed of the death of Georg Solti. He had suffered a heart attack while on holiday and, chatting in bed in a hospital in Antibes, was felled by a relapse. Many in the world of music found his death at eighty-four as hard to accept as Diana's. He seemed indestructible, a force of destiny. With Solti gone, the podium lost the last of its titans.

At the next meeting of the ROH board, Vivien Duffield suggested that something should be done to commemorate Princess Diana, whose association with the ROH, 'though less than with ENB, had been considerable'. She recalled that the late princess had 'attended many performances at the House and had even danced on the stage with Wayne Sleep'.[2] The board might consider naming a ballet studio after her. They liked that idea, urging Mrs Duffield to raise funds for the purpose from the American Friends of Covent Garden.

The meeting was otherwise preoccupied with financial shortfalls and the Arts Council's preposterous refusal to show them an advance copy of the Walker-Arnott report which, it was stressed, 'had been prepared with public money'. Judging by the minutes, no board member saw fit to mention the death of Georg Solti, let alone to stand in tribute to an artist who, more than anyone, had raised Covent Garden's sights from the insular to the international.

Mary Allen turned up for work on the morning after Diana's death, refreshed and invigorated after an 'insulation' period in which she had no contact with either the Arts Council or Covent Garden. She spent the day finding her way around the warren of temporary Floral Street offices and meeting senior staff. She found the situation confusing and decided to keep a diary. Other senior staff were also keeping a private log of internal conversations, some at their lawyers' advice. The element of trust was fast evaporating. Allen eventually published her diaries; other records fell into my hands. Together, they reveal a portrait of the way capable people behave under the lash of events beyond their control and in hourly anticipation of disaster. There were few smiles, or lifeboats, to spare. At least on the *Titanic*, there had been time to dance before the men on the bridge realized that they were going down.

Allen's first priority was to redress the company's negative image. She told the flamboyant Keith Cooper that his job would be restructured to cover sales and broadcasting; a new executive would handle external relations with the public, press and politicians. Cooper was wounded but compliant. Allen's next task was to persuade Nicholas Payne of the Royal Opera and Anthony Russell-Roberts of the Royal Ballet to accept that there would have to be a unified artistic strategy, a mission foredoomed to failure. 'One of the first things Mary said to me,' Payne recalled, 'was, "you know I'm keeping a diary." I thought to myself, better be careful what you say in front of her.'

On the Friday of her first week, Allen had a two hour meeting with the finance director, Richard Hall. Expecting to see a planned deficit of £800,000 for the twenty-seven months of closure, she was shown a ten million pound black hole – on top of the existing £4.7 million accumulated deficit. The entire ROH annual turnover was only forty million pounds. 'Some mistake, surely,' she muttered, asking Hall to run another set of calculations. There was always a possibility that heads of department had slipped in extra costs between one chief executive and the next. Hall came back with the same bottom line.

There had been no mistake and, from that moment on, there would be no turning back.

The mystery of the unforeseen millions has yet to be satisfactorily resolved. John Tooley maintained that, in his time, Covent Garden had 'the most sophisticated management reporting information system in the operatic world', a cashflow control so admirable that the Met sent a man over to copy it. Jeremy Isaacs argued that he knew at all times how much money was coming in and going out, and that he left the company with 'adequate contingencies'.[3] Two teams of independent accountants had clawed over the books since his departure. The Arts Council had inserted its own monitor, Richard Pulford, to survey the balancing of budgets. Genista McIntosh had been financially competent and the acting finance director, in the year between Timms and Hall, had been by all accounts outstanding.

Yet, during the repeated crunching of numbers, a gap of ten million pounds had eluded some of the finest accountants and administrators in the kingdom – not to mention two top bankers and an accountancy firm director on the ROH board. As she wrestled with the balance sheets, Allen would uncover 'an almost total absence of proper financial information or controls'.[4] She concluded that the systems had broken down during the upheavals of closure, but this did not explain the forecasting lacunae over two previous years when Mary Allen, at the Arts Council, kept demanding firm financial targets and failed to receive them.

It would be presumptuous and pointless to attach blame to any individual for these prolonged shortcomings. In the 'diffuse and fragmented' structure of the ROH, the fault lay with the failures over half a century to weld the company into a coherent unity where ballet and opera companies talked to one another and the sundry trusts and supporters' groups worked together to a common purpose. Allen, in her first board meeting, gave a grim presentation which showed how individual departments made their own budgets and then refused to meet them. If they ran out of cash, they were used to being bailed out. In purely organizational terms, the ROH had become virtually unmanageable.

Administratively, it was years behind the times. When Judy Grahame joined as director of external relations, she found that no computer in the building could communicate with any other, because every department had purchased a different brand of software. Managers guarded their secrets and defended fiefdoms. Gardeners conspired and protected each other's jobs. Grahame, who had brilliantly repositioned the Philharmonia Orchestra during the Hoffmann process, was hard pressed to conceive an overall image strategy for an antiquated edifice that appeared so cracked and torn.

Where the money would be found to bridge the ten million pound gap was unknown. Any hopes of extra Lottery help could be ruled out. Late in August, it became clear that New Labour aimed to halve Lottery spending on the arts and divert the surplus to a sixth good cause – itself, specifically to new health and education projects. The Government was also refusing to let the ROH use money from the sale of surplus buildings for its running costs. The Arts Council was in a huff and the usual sources of spare cash – such as the benevolent patrons of the Drogheda Circle – were being stretched to their limits by Vivien Duffield's £100 million development appeal.

The board, faced with the facts, were, as Allen put it, 'terrified – like rabbits in headlights'.[5] The chairman refused to sign off the previous year's accounts since he could not confirm that the company was a going concern. It is illegal under English law for a firm to continue trading if it goes into debt and has no prospect of sufficient incoming funds. Members of the board could be held personally liable in such circumstances; they could even face criminal charges. It was suddenly no longer an honour to be on the ROH board but distinctly a danger. Faces went white around the board table as Chadlington asked for time to work on a rescue plan.

In her third week at Covent Garden, I ran into Mary Allen at a champagne breakfast in the National Gallery, after a private viewing of the Seurat exhibition. She sounded cheerily upbeat and told me how much she was enjoying the job. Her laughter rang a tone too bright, but I was dashing off to catch a flight to Washington D.C. and made a mental note to pay closer attention to Covent Garden when I got back at the end of the month.

Attention then got deflected by upheavals at ENO where Dennis Marks had resigned; with suspicious alacrity, the Arts Council gave ENO a five million pound 'stabilization' grant to pay off debts and put its house in order. The man favoured to succeed Marks was Nicholas Payne, who was fed up with Covent Garden in-fighting and preferred to run a theatre his own way, without worrying about ballets and building work. Paul Daniel, his former partner at Opera North, was to become ENO's music director and there was an opportunity to renew their dream team. Payne received a mollifying call from Mary Allen, who could not afford to lose him.

The Royal Opera season had opened quietly at the Barbican with Handel's *Giulio Cesare* and Rameau's *Platée*. Spirits rose with *The Turn of the Screw* in Deborah Warner's production, vindicating Payne's decision to branch into more intimate operas than would normally be seen at Covent Garden. Regular patrons had no trouble finding the Barbican or coping with Britten. Where they bridled was at the windswept Labatt's Apollo and the dilapidated Shaftesbury Theatre, home to a *Merry Widow* that failed to raise much of a laugh.

The pigeons were racing home to splatter ROH heads. The Royal Ballet lost £750,000 in a month and the *Widow* wept for want of stardust. Felicity Lott did her best, but the part had been cast for Kiri te Kanawa, and she had lost faith in Covent Garden, or vice versa. 'Singers are the last people that matter (there),' she told a BBC talk show. 'It has not had good management for quite a long time. The last time they called me was three years ago.'

This was a large exaggeration from an artist undergoing a painful divorce, but other strictures that she uttered rang painfully true. At Covent Garden, said Kiri, 'they have no people on the ground to help the singers. When you are giving your body (to the audience, which is what you do when you sing) you need somebody there. At the Met they still truly look after you. They have one person babysitting. We need babysitting. We need our bottoms wiped a lot and we need a lot of pampering, because we're special. We do think of ourselves as being more special than other people.'[6] During the closure, she announced her retirement from opera. She would never sing again with the company that made her. 'Covent Garden?' she said to me. 'I don't think they even know my telephone number.'

She was not the only star to stay away. Bryn Terfel made it clear that he would not appear with the Royal Opera during its wandering years.[7] The Italian mezzo Cecilia Bartoli, whose records outsold every other diva apart from Callas, was happy to sing opera at the Barbican, but not with the troupe from the Royal.[8] Pavarotti and Carreras were not interested, and only Domingo showed concern and support. The exile era lacked glamour and the public voted with its feet.

On the penultimate day of October, the Kaufman committee resumed its hearings. It could hardly have picked a tougher day for the ROH. All month long, Mary Allen had been battling with insolvency. The company had paid out £600,000 in cheques when there was only £400,000 in its account, a mishap attributed to antiquated ledger keeping. Chadlington was arranging emergency cover from a blind trust, but Allen had called in lawyers and liquidation practitioners and knew what had to be done if the creditors came pressing. At this moment there was no prospect of paying the next month's wages.

At an extraordinary board meeting on the 20th, Richard Hall and the KPMG auditor had outlined the gravity of the position and Vivien Duffield called for immediate liquidation to stop the financial haemorrhaging. A second meeting was scheduled for the afternoon of Thursday the 30th at which the company's fate would be decided.

That morning, the *Guardian* ran a front-page report saying that ROH cheques were bouncing and salaries were in arrears. Keith Cooper had categorically denied this when approached by the reporter and Robert Gavron, who was chairman of the *Guardian* and an ROH board member, hit the roof and promised to read the riot act.[9] Damage, however, had been done, and arts correspondents hovered like carrion crows as Mary Allen took her seat in committee room 15, in front of the renamed Culture, Media and Sport Committee – 'National Heritage' having been banned by New Labour as oldspeak.

Both Allen and Chadlington had rehearsed their lines at a mock tribunal earlier in the week, standard procedure when appearing before a hostile panel. Allen had been advised by Cooper to wear a black polo neck sweater, to cover up her neck which reddened when she grew agitated. She was asked by Kaufman if she wanted to make a short statement.

While Allen was speaking, Gerald Kaufman had shuffled his papers and put on a show of looking uninterested. An embittered man of caustic wit, with the clammy eye and handshake of a captive dolphin, he had been dropped without obvious cause from Labour's front bench in 1992 and at sixty-seven saw no further hope of high office. This was the nearest he would ever get to wielding power. Kaufman was an avid consumer of culture and a ticket-buying opera buff who, like David Mellor, suffered from feelings of alienation at the Royal Opera House. In plain words, he could not bear the neighbours:

There were all those people air-kissing each other (he would write in the *Spectator*); all those people rearranging their seating after the interval according to some recondite social ritual; all those people who could somehow get served when I never could in the Crush Bar – providing, of course, that they were standing at the Crush Bar at all rather than sitting at little reserved tables and ingesting cold chicken or smoked salmon.

Most aggravating of all, there were all those people who did not give a damn about the opera; who chatted to each other during the performances (and rounded on me in fury when I remonstrated) or fanned themselves distractingly with their bulkily expensive programmes; who stared at the programme before the start of a production of *The Marriage of Figaro* and exclaimed in genuine surprise, 'It's by Mozart!' What is more, the lot of them were being subsidized not only by my taxes but by the taxes of people less well-off than themselves who would never get the chance to go to Covent Garden, even if they were so inclined.[10]

For Kaufman, as he confirmed with his own vitriolic pen, this was a grudge match, a chance for the aggrieved anorak to strike back at the black-tied snobs. He was not particularly fussy where the blows landed, so long as they dented the pride of an institution he had come to need and despise. If ever a politician played to the public gallery, it was Gerald Kaufman that autumn morning.

When Mary Allen finished her statement, he ignored everything she said and launched into a languid Mancunian diatribe, his dry tone and laid-back demeanour masking the acrid words. 'It's a shambles, isn't it?' he began.

'I think that the Arts Council would be nuts to give you an extra penny until you have sorted yourselves out,' he continued. Of the present management, he added, 'You are running things incompetently and not doing your jobs.'

Allen replied as best she could, but got the worse of the exchange. Kaufman interrogated her about Genista McIntosh's departure and waved a letter, which he threatened to publish, from which he alleged that McIntosh had 'been asked to leave the opera house immediately', seemingly against her will. In the letter (which I have seen) McIntosh confirms that it was her own wish to leave immediately. Kaufman had been bluffing; he never placed this document on the open record. His aim, it seemed, was to nail a culprit for the chief executive's departure, the event that had triggered his investigation.

Allen was followed in the hot seat by Vivien Duffield, who gave as good as she got, declaring 'I don't see how any great public institution can survive on passing round the begging bowl.' Kaufman was cowed by her maternal ferocity, and any mirth rebounded against him. Jim Monahan then gave evidence for the Covent Garden Community Association, alleging without much evidence that Lottery money was being used to pay for a smart new boardroom for Lord Chadlington and his friends. The committee adjourned for a week and the press rushed off to its deadlines. The comedy in Committee Room 15 was proving a hotter ticket than *The Merry Widow*.

Downcast, the ROH team went back to Floral Street for a board meeting so surreal it could have been designed by Dali. Four members announced that they wanted to liquidate the company; the other four had no solution in mind. The meeting opened with a trawl around the table in which each and every director offered to resign, either out of regret for past negligence or out of sympathy for the embattled chairman. None of their misgivings were recorded in the minutes by Andrew Edwards, the retired Treasury official, but Chadlington asked to receive their resignations in writing so that he could, if necessary, dump them in the Government's lap.

The legal advisers then trooped in and advised that neither resignation nor liquidation would save the directors from personal consequences. If the ROH collapsed, they could be held responsible for its debts. Some, like Chadlington and Mrs Duffield, might be left after settlement with a few off-shore millions for their old age, but the composer Michael Berkeley, a recent recruit, was seen fingering his collar, fearing perhaps that his family could lose the roof over its head. Anyone involved with Covent Garden in any position of responsibility was now trapped, unable to get on with managing the crisis or to get out. As in the fall of Rome, events were mightier than the men and women in command.

There were only two options left. Either the Government could be induced to step in, which seemed unlikely, or money would have to be begged from a source whose existence came as a surprise to several board members. The Floral Trust had been set up in 1994 as a vehicle for donations from an overseas supporter. It had raised twenty million pounds, twenty-five with interest, apparently from the Sultan of Brunei's brother. England, in distress, was pumping the reservoirs of imperial goodwill. Both Prince Charles and John Major had solicited help from Asian well-wishers. The Floral Trust was created over dinner at Highgrove, the Prince's country estate.

Much of the money in the trust had already gone to the builders, but ten or twelve million pounds were thought to remain. The tricky bit was that there were five trustees, including the ROH chairman, who might refuse to surrender the money for an unforeseen emergency, aware of their fiduciary responsibility and of the interest the Charity Commissioners might take in their decisions. Chadlington would argue for the release of the remaining funds, supported by George Magan, a friend of Mrs Duffield's. But there was no telling what screws Sir Angus Stirling and Sir Jeremy Isaacs would turn on their stumbling successors in exchange for signing their reprieve. It might come down to a casting vote by the fifth trustee, Lord Carrington, the distinguished former Foreign Secretary and NATO Secretary General.

The board meeting broke up with an appeal to the chairman to raid the Floral Trust and an authorization to Mary Allen to renew the loan facility at Coutts, ensuring that the wages got paid. It would take around twelve million, the advisers said, to save the ROH from going bankrupt and the money had to be raised within a month.

Gravity turned to forced jollity as the condemned men and women rolled up two nights later at the Sainsbury Wing of the National Gallery to celebrate its donor's seventieth birthday. Lord Sainsbury, the former ROH chairman, looked as florid as the incumbent looked ashen. Mary Allen sidled up to Hayden Phillips and warned that they might need to have a word in the next few days.

Early on Monday morning, 3 November, Chadlington went to see Chris Smith. It was their first encounter since the panic session over Mary Allen's appointment and they might have been expected to compare notes before appearing the next day in Kaufman's dock. Smith appeared acutely uncomfortable. His position was under threat and he was about to take another hasty decision. Two opera houses were on fire and all the headlines were being usurped by a back-bench MP while H. M.'s Secretary of State for Culture, Media and Sport fiddled. His political advisers urged him to do something, anything; Hayden Phillips advised caution. Smith's job was not yet at risk. He enjoyed a personal friendship with the Prime Minister and could be relied upon to raise his hand in Cabinet against the ambitious Chancellor, Gordon Brown. But Kaufman was running away with his show and a weak performance before his committee could cost Smith his career.

He had to act quickly. He could not splash cash on opera without incurring the populist wrath of his party. Nor could he let the ROH founder without being implicated in the crash. His inclination was to let the company go under, proceed with the development and reconstitute a new performing ensemble in time for the opening. Hayden Phillips was of much the same opinion. They were on the point of ordering the Arts Council to stop all further Lottery payments when a fax arrived from Richard Hall, the ROH finance director, clarifying what would happen if the ROH was allowed to go bust. Not only would the main company cease trading, said Hall, but the associated Royal Opera House Developments Limited would be dragged down with it. The development would stop and the land on which it stood would fall into the hands of liquidators, to be sold to the highest bidder in order to pay off ROH debts. The Government would then be held responsible for causing one of London's prime cultural sites to be sold for a song to alien commercial interests. 'Oh, my God,' said Phillips on reading the fax. He told Smith that the Government, too, was paralysed in this situation, unable to do anything but sit tight and await developments.

So Smith did what ministers do in moments of irresoluble crisis – he asked his permanent secretary for advice, and was told to pass the buck.

Hours before entering Kaufman's chamber, Smith announced a review of 'The Future of Lyric Theatre in London'. The Government, he said, could not afford to subsidize both Covent Garden and ENO in separate homes. They should both move in to the new ROH, sell the Coliseum, and use the proceeds to pay off debts. ENO should spend more time taking its work around the country. A 'radical solution' was needed. 'I am not interested in buildings,' said Smith. 'Taking money out of bricks and mortar and putting it into artistic activity may be the best way forward.'[11]

He had asked Sir Richard Eyre, outgoing chief of the Royal National Theatre, to examine his proposal and report to him by May 1998. 'I encourage you to think freely and creatively,' said Smith in a letter to Eyre, making no secret where his preference lay. Any blame for the outcome, however, would rest with Eyre. When Mark Fisher, the arts minister, announced on BBC's *Newsnight* that Eyre 'supports our plan and will make it work', Smith slapped him down without delay. 'He said what he said, and he has been told off for it,' said the Culture Secretary;[12] Fisher was to be sacked in the next reshuffle. The whole purpose of appointing Eyre was to wash the blood off ministerial hands.

Eyre had refused three times before succumbing to the call of conscience. 'Chris did turn it on very strongly,' he explained, 'it was like being a subaltern in the First World War and being told that England Expects ... Also, having spent years banging a drum, privately and publicly, for a Labour government, it would be churlish when asked to do something for them that could provide stability for the performing arts to say, "no".'[13] Smith apart, Hayden Phillips was a close personal friend and his persuasion proved decisive.

The prospect of yet another review was greeted with despair at Covent Garden, where Eyre was remembered as an operaphobe and close colleague of Genista McIntosh. ENO's music director Paul Daniel declared himself 'greatly concerned' that the company would lose its identity and audience if it was forced to share with the ROH. He stepped up on the Coliseum stage after conducting Janáček's *From the House of the Dead* to share his concerns with the audience, who responded with roars of solidarity. Daniel cancelled all his concert dates to campaign for ENO's independence. The Musicians Union demanded an urgent meeting with Smith and Eyre. Lord Sainsbury declared that it would be 'a cause of national humilation if London should have only one opera house when every other major European capital has two or more.'[14]

Smith had won the round. Next morning, the press whistled his Eyre loud and clear, and Kaufman was outshone. Their confrontation promised rich entertainment and when Smith arrived at Committee Room 15, the overcrowding was dangerous. 'If Covent Garden could get this attendance,' carped Kaufman, 'its financial problems would be over.' The nation waited to see how hard Kaufman would press a party comrade whose elevation he must have envied.

Smith in a blue suit, Kaufman in grey, eyed one another like bantams at a weigh-in. 'I look forward to constructive and fruitful relations with the committee in the years ahead,' jabbed Smith.

'How do we get there from here?' retorted Kaufman, taking him through the process of Mary Allen's recruitment. Smith denied he had done anything to influence staff appointments at the ROH.

Kaufman read out apparent differences in Chadlington's account of their meeting.

'You, sir, are as Secretary of State, a custodian of the English language,' said Kaufman. 'Would you be good enough to reconcile these two statements?'

'I was actually very unhappy,' said Smith. 'I did indicate my high regard for Mary Allen and was extremely sorry to see her leave the Arts Council.'

Kaufman turned the questioning over to his committee. Why was the permanent secretary not present at that meeting? demanded Damian Green, MP. Smith shifted nervously in his seat and replied that an official of the department had been present throughout. Michael Fabricant MP asked why, when setting up the Eyre review, he had also announced its intended conclusion. 'This is a proposal which, I believe, could help to solve a number of long-term problems affecting the theatre in London,' said Smith. 'If Richard Eyre comes up with an alternative plan, I will listen very carefully.'

'Do I also take it,' said Kaufman, 'that, whatever Lord Gowrie may answer about funding, you are not prepared to put more taxpayers' money into Covent Garden?'

'I have no more taxpayers' money to spend,' replied Smith.

The bout ended quietly with Smith promising to 'listen carefully and seriously to your views', and vacating his seat for Gowrie, whose retirement had been announced. After desultory questioning, the ACE chairman gave way to Chadlington and Allen; the show was dying on its feet when Chadlington asked to make a statement clarifying the issue of Genista McIntosh's resignation. He was stopped by Kaufman. He then stopped Kaufman in his tracks by declaring that the ROH could go broke within days. 'Unless we can find a solution on our own, then the House will become insolvent,' intoned the ROH chairman. It was Kaufman's turn to be gob-smacked, upstaged for the second time in a day. 'I believe there is a way through,' Chadlington added. 'It is going to be difficult, but I think we have a small opportunity to get through it.'

Kaufman, conscious that any superfluous word could close the opera house, said gently: 'Are you able to expand on that? If not, I shall not press you.' Chadlington replied: 'Chairman, I would be grateful if you did not press me at this time.'

Next morning, the *Guardian* front-paged: 'Going Broke – the Opera'. Allen, expecting to find creditors at her door, slipped out of the office and made her way to a critical meeting of the Floral Trust, where tempers flared. Isaacs, according to Allen's account, was furious at being blamed before Kaufman for the financial crisis and told Chadlington that he would publicly challenge his version. George Magan had unexpectedly withdrawn his support from the rescue grant. Half-way through the meeting, Allen reckoned that they were going down. She had reckoned without Angus Stirling, one of nature's born chairmen, who allowed everyone to let off steam before steering the debate elegantly to a pre-ordained conclusion. The Floral Trust would give the ROH ten and half million pounds for running costs over the next two years, on condition that other donors continued to fund the development, and that the company remained solvent. There were to be more conditions, but the Trust was not yet ready to reveal them.

Waving the Floral Trust's piece of paper, endorsed by Stirling 'as a true record of the meeting', Chadlington rushed back to the ROH and into an extraordinary board meeting, like Chamberlain after Munich. A decision had to be made there and then, he said: either accept the rescue package or go into liquidation. In addition to the Floral money, he had a pledge of an extra two million pounds from donors who wished to remain anonymous. One identity can now be revealed. Shaun Woodward, married to a Sainsbury heiress and a close friend of the late Princess Diana, had worked on John Major's election team with Lord Chadlington and was an opera devotee – a named supporter of ENO. One million from the Woodward Trust over the next two years would tide the company over until reopening.

Chadlington went around the table seeking endorsement for his package. Most members quickly raised their hands. Michael Berkeley, who was absent, assented in writing but worried 'about throwing good money after bad'. Vivien Duffield had a shouting match with Mary Allen, after which both felt much better. Under the circumstances, everyone behaved rather well. The rescue was approved and the press were informed that the opera house had been saved at the eleventh hour by anonymous well-wishers. *Plus ça change*, said the cynics. For the rich, there would always be an opera house.

The rest of November passed in a state of suspended reality as the political and performing worlds awaited Gerald Kaufman's report.

On the 7th, Isaiah Berlin died, providentially spared from witnessing the finale of the farce. That morning, I dropped in on Mary Allen to see how she was getting on. She found me, she told her diary, 'hypnotically sympathetic, and I find myself telling him all kinds of things that I probably shouldn't.'[15] I remember thinking how pale she looked on her black leather sofa, and how brittle – a changed woman from the confident oligarch I had known at the Arts Council. We had friends in common and gossiped awhile. I caught myself choking back a question, anxious not to be told any personal confidences that I could neither report nor ignore.

Mary told me that, five weeks into the job, she had sought to resign. 'I went through a long dark night of the soul and thought, I've got to get out – anything, anything to get out of this place,' she said. Her husband and chairman talked her round over the course of a turbulent weekend. In one telephone exchange with Chadlington, she told him that she 'fully understood why Genista McIntosh had quit – I warned him we had a structural problem that no one could live with.' The chairman appealed to her sense of responsibility. 'I told her that there were five hundred people whose jobs depended on us,' he said, 'as well as donors who had given seventy million pounds to the House, and we had to do our best for them.' Had Allen quit, he told me, 'we could not have got through the past month.'

Nothing had been solved by the rescue announcement, Allen warned. 'The box office went into reverse last Wednesday,' she said. 'We gave more money back than we took in.' The details of the rescue needed fine-tuning and the Floral trustees appeared to be back-tracking. By the end of the following week, her former deputy at the Arts Council, Graham Devlin, said he could not sign the next cheque of Lottery money until he had received confirmation of the Floral Trust donation. Once again there would be no cash in hand at the end of the month to pay the wages.

The Floral conditions were stringent. In addition to cast-iron assurances of continued ACE support, they demanded written guarantees of the viability of the development and of the company after the house reopened. They intended to use the company's real estate as security for the return of their money if the enterprise collapsed. The killer clause amounted to outright interference with the company's autonomy. Stirling and his fellow-trustees demanded that a 'professional adviser' be appointed immediately 'to assist the executive team over the next four to six months'.[16] This was an affront to Mary Allen, who said she would have to resign if her authority was being undermined.

Chadlington called another emergency board at two p.m. on 19 November, announcing that the company would go bankrupt in five hours' time, when the payroll button was pressed at Coutts, unless they agreed to the Floral Trust conditions – the last of which would have to be negotiated carefully to ensure that Mary Allen did not quit. He had warned Hayden Phillips that they were on the brink of going under, and the Government had not blinked. There was no chance of an official rescue, nor would Whitehall allow money from the sale of properties to be used to run the company.

Across town, the Arts Council and the Floral Trust were eyeballing one another, each refusing, like infants behind the shed, 'to show mine before you show me yours'. Unless one fund or the other opened up by seven that evening, the ROH was finished. Richard Hall asked for, and received, permission from the board to pass essential papers to an administrator at the accountancy firm Arthur Andersen, who would take over that night if the company declared itself insolvent.

As afternoon darkened into wintry evening, accusations, bluffs and documents flew back and forth. Mary Allen phoned Coutts and asked them to delay the payroll run by half an hour, to seven-thirty. The request was highly irregular, she was told; they would do their best. She tried, and failed, to reach the Coutts chairman by phone. As the lights went out in neighbouring offices, the Arts Council and Floral Trust were still refusing to budge until each was sure that the other would move. If British generals had behaved like this at Waterloo, this cultural history would be written in French.

Five minutes before seven-thirty, Graham Devlin rang Mary Allen to say that he had released Lottery funds and she could tell the bank to pay the wages. The Floral Trust would shell out in the morning. Late that night, Allen caught a train in the wrong direction as she stumbled her way back home.

The Royal Opera House was no longer running, but reeling about, like a mugging victim, the lifeblood gushing from its head. Its direction was staggered and inconclusive. No passers-by would rush to help, and one more blow could finish it off.

On 24 November, the board accepted the Floral Trust ultimata without much protest. The trustees explained, reasonably enough, that their donor had given them plenipotentiary powers and they were obliged *to have been seen* to act properly as trustees in the event 'that things later went wrong'.[17] Everybody dealing with the opera house was now cladding themselves in legal chainmail. Mary Allen asked the board to engage a lawyer to negotiate the terms under which the 'professional adviser' would work beside her. She could not discuss the matter directly with Chadlington, as he was also a director of the Floral Trust. The ROH Trust, under Vivien Duffield, had instructed a QC to protect their position.

What the press would make of the Floral Trust gift was preying on their minds, the more so since the Trust and its donor were insisting on total anonymity. Judy Grahame accepted the external relations job that week. She told Mary Allen that, in the absence of real information, several journalists were speculating that she was having an affair with Chadlington. In fact, their working relationship had been strained to snapping point.

Copies of the Kaufman report arrived on the afternoon of Tuesday, 2 December, embargoed until ten-thirty the next morning. This was an astute publicity device, designed to procure double coverage. It allowed the press, having read the report, to conjecture its contents accurately overnight before reporting them in detail with official reactions the following day.

Kaufman's solution was comprehensive: sack the chairman, the board and the chief executive and start again. 'We would prefer to see the Royal Opera House run by a philistine with the requisite financial acumen than by the succession of opera and ballet lovers who have brought a great and valuable institution to its knees,' was one of the more eye-catching phrases. Vivien Duffield and Robert Gavron were specifically exonerated. Chris Smith was half-forgiven for failing to tell his permanent secretary that he was meeting the opera house chairman. Lord Gowrie was sent on his way with a friendly wave. Angus Stirling and Jeremy Isaacs were accused of 'disastrous misjudgements'. Chadlington was spared blame for the financial crisis but excoriated for his role in Genista McIntosh's departure and his inability to staunch the losses, 'a failure which ensured that a fragile financial position became acute'.

The most blistering criticism was directed at Mary Allen whose account of her appointment was disbelieved. 'We found Ms Allen's convoluted explanation of her actions entirely unconvincing,' said Kaufman in bold type. 'Given her experience of public office, Ms

Allen's conduct fell seriously below the standards to be expected of the principal officer of a public body whose loyalty should first and foremost be to the organization[18] which employs her.'

This was savage stuff, the kind of comment that puts people on the street and ensures they never work again. Allen stood condemned before the bar of public service, potentially debarred from public office. She had no right of appeal. Her press statement said: 'I absolutely reject and refute the criticisms about my appointment. I am angry that I have been singled out for criticism of an intemperate kind. I have been there for only three months. I have done what I could in that time.'[19]

She offered her resignation next morning at eight-thirty to a board meeting hastily convened at Shandwick. The board implored her to stay on, unanimously reaffirming 'their complete confidence' in her. She had received dozens of messages of support, including a fax from Bernard Haitink. Unwisely, she agreed to remain.

Lord Chadlington then offered to resign. To his evident surprise, the board accepted his resignation. 'He was very bitter,' observed Keith Cooper.[20] He had planned to devote his leisure years to working for a place that had given him lifelong pleasure, but he was thrown overboard in order to save the ship. Chadlington went quietly. Six months later he sold Shandwick to an American giant, denying that its weak performance in the past year had been affected by his involvements at the opera house. John Major wrote to *The Times*, decrying the need for his resignation as 'bizarre' and dismissing Kaufman's report as a 'parody' of good parliamentary procedure, 'unjust' in its tone and conclusions.[21] When Chadlington went, the million pound offer from the Woodward Trust also evaporated. 'I thought Peter was terribly good,' said Vivien Duffield. 'He loved the place, had an absolute passion for it. It was politically the wrong time. The whole thing was a disaster.'[22]

The rest of the board submitted their resignations but agreed to continue in a caretaker role under Sir James Spooner, the deputy chairman, until Chris Smith replaced them. They trooped off to the Department to see Smith, who promised to come up with an 'action plan'. He asked Mary Allen to stay on. When someone wondered why any person in their right mind would join the board of a company that could go bankrupt at any moment, and for which they might become personally liable, the Secretary of State looked confused. The game was up. He would have to give the next chairman and directors a Government guarantee that Covent Garden would not be allowed to go under.

Kaufman was jubilant, crowing his triumph in the *Spectator*. 'Had it not been for me,' he bragged, 'all [the wicked old ways] might have resumed when the House reopened . . . I do believe that the disclosures about the state of the ROH's finances emerging from our Committee proceedings did help to open Smith's eyes somewhat wider and to spur him to take action by setting up a working party on lyric theatre under Sir Richard Eyre.'[23] Kaufman's rhetoric was denounced by Chadlington as 'hysterical hyperbole'.[24] George Christie of Glyndebourne, no friend of Covent Garden's, called it 'a piece of grotesque irresponsibility'.[25] Kaufman himself protested his high intentions a mite too much. There was, however, one line in his report that rang true to all who knew the way the arts in Britain were run. 'There is no future for the Royal Opera House,' declared Kaufman, 'unless someone accepts responsibility for the sorry train of events we have described.'[26]

The Secretary of State was now back-pedalling as hard as he could to put an ocean between himself and the preposterous proposal he had made to Eyre. Paul Daniel's agitation had paid off. ENO supporters had been talking to the Blairs and Smith now said that his idea of cramming ENO into forced accommodation with the Covent Garden companies had been merely intended to stimulate discussion. 'I know that ENO has a devoted audience and many committed friends,' he wrote. 'I count myself one of them.'[27]

In mid-December the Royal Opera went to Suffolk, where Mary Allen lived, to put on Francesca Zambello's production of *Paul Bunyan* at Britten's festival stage near Aldeburgh. This little-known piece was the young Britten's first attempt at an opera, more a *Singspiel* or American musical, and it worked like a dream, transferring to the Shaftesbury Theatre as a hot Christmas ticket. Nicholas Payne's chamber opera schedule had scored another hit; he was proving invaluable to the headless ROH.

Mary Allen was being pressed by the Floral Trust to let their 'professional adviser' get started. The first investigator from accountants Coopers & Lybrand she dismissed as 'a complete Rottweiler'. She was offered a second choice, Pelham Allen, and found him sensitive and astute. She was wrestling with defining an acceptable form to their relationship when her knee gave way. It was strapped by a woman from the Occupational Health Unit but she had to hobble on a crutch to the next board meeting, which Vivien Duffield attended with her personal lawyer. The atmosphere was tense. Board members decided that they would not stay on beyond 10 January, after which Chris Smith could do his worst. Mary Allen reported that the Kaufman hearings had cost the box-office somewhere between £250,000 and £400,000. There were more lawyers and accountants in the room that day than directors and executives.

The holiday break was protracted that year, Christmas falling on a Thursday and precipitating two weeks of idleness. Mary Allen returned to the office on Monday, 5 January, to find a screed of faxes from Pelham Allen, who was settling down with the figures. He introduced himself to the board as a 'turn-around specialist' or 'company doctor', a man who spent his life bringing ailing firms back from the brink.

Allen hared off with Harvey Goldsmith, the rock impresario, to renegotiate with Sadler's Wells. 'I would never have signed such a deal,' growled Goldsmith at Ian Albery. 'I was told by my board to exact commercial terms,' said the Sadler's Wells boss sweetly.[28]

Allen was still limping heavily. 'Let me tell you about a knee operation I once had,' said Anthony Dowell at an executive meeting, describing the procedure in such gory detail that Allen's natural pallor turned ghostly white. 'That's what will happen to you if you don't get it treated now,' warned the ballet director. He recommended a surgeon who, after a scan, booked her in for a cartilage operation.

Over Christmas, she felt that something had given way inside her. 'I'd had enough,' she decided. 'There is only so much one can do.'[29] She phoned Hayden Phillips, who begged, 'Not now, please not now.' She then rang Graham Devlin at the Arts Council who said, 'Mary, I'm about to go to Florida, can it wait until I'm gone?' She laughed, and carried on working, awaiting her call from the Eyre Review. She pronounced herself confident of its outcome because Eyre's panel was being advised by Melanie Leech, a senior official in Smith's department, who, said Allen, 'is a good friend of mine'. What she failed to appreciate was that, in the maelstrom of English arts, friendship counted for naught when survival was at stake. Leech told colleagues that she avoided taking Allen's calls. Battered by Kaufman, shadowed by the Floral Trust, overshadowed by Eyre and damaged below the knee, Mary Allen clung on literally as a lame duck leader.

The two most prestigious jobs in British arts were going begging and few were tempted by the honour, or the headache. Downing Street presented Chris Smith with a list of businessmen who deserved to be rewarded for switching support to New Labour at the last election. Near the top was Gerry Robinson, chairman of Granada plc, a man widely reviled for reducing the jewel of British television to a channel of soaps and gameshows. 'It was shedding £100 million cash the year I arrived,' he explained.[30] Robinson was an expansionist. He bought London Weekend Television and Yorkshire Tyne-Tees TV and extended Granada's catering interests through a fiercely contested takeover of Trust House Forte. He also served for a while as chairman of Murdoch's BSkyB, in which Granada held an interest.

Robinson was planning further takeovers to establish Granada as the unrivalled leader in British commercial broadcasting. He was eyeing Scottish TV and Carlton, the London weekday franchise. Any such takeover would need the consent of the Department of Culture, Media and Sport, which could feel reasonably confident that he would not kick up too much of a fuss at the Arts Council.

Robinson exuded Irish charm and shrewd analysis. Privately, he loved the theatre, painted landscapes and played his children a piece of classical music before they went to bed, believing the arts to be morally improving. In commercial life, however, Robinson rode roughshod over his own predilections in his drive for growth and profitability. The ninth son of a Donegal carpenter, his personal fortune exceeded ten million pounds and he intended to retire young to enjoy it. He took eight weeks holiday a year. Robinson's plans for the ACE were to strip it down to ten members, devolve powers to regional boards and disenfranchise the turbulent chairmen of art-form panels. He would bring the Arts Council to heel and give the Government no cause for discomfort.

With the ACE under control, Hayden Phillips invited Vivien Duffield and Robert Gavron to the Department's new offices on Trafalgar Square to apprise them of the next ROH chairman. They were shown a list of three – David Davies, a businessman; John Eatwell, an economist and sometime escort of Tessa Blackstone's, the former ballet board chair; and Sir Colin Southgate, chairman of the £3.4 billion music conglomerate, EMI.

None was self-recommending. Davies was virtually unknown. Eatwell was master of Queen's College Cambridge and a Labour peer whose passion was contemporary dance. He had once left a performance of Ashton's *Enigma Variations* saying, 'we don't want more of that'. Duffield and Gavron noted that he had no experience of running a business and would be overwhelmed by Covent Garden's difficulties.

That left Southgate. A gangling man, reassuringly deep voiced, he ran a global company whose roster ran from Caruso to the Spice Girls. He had made his pile by exercising share options and attended Covent Garden frequently on EMI's £180 corporate tickets. He was acceptable, but only just. Duffield wondered if the field could not be extended. The best chairman, she felt, would be Sir Dennis Stevenson, head of Pearsons plc (Drogheda's old firm) and a long-standing Labour supporter who played the violin at night and bought more concert tickets than he ever managed to attend. Stevenson knew the opera house inside out from conducting the last review of lyric theatre, only two years before. He had also transformed the Tate Gallery in ten years as chairman. Phillips frowned. Stevenson would not do. Too independent minded, likely to make waves.

Duffield and Gavron agreed to meet Southgate and took the short-list back to the board, where it was received without enthusiasm. Someone asked to make a last-ditch nomination. What about Sir Robin Butler, Armstrong's successor as Cabinet Secretary and now Master of University College, Oxford? Surely Hayden Phillips would appreciate having an arch-mandarin at the opera. Gavron promised to convey the suggestion, which Phillips dismissed. He should have made the position clearer, perhaps. The outgoing board were not being offered a choice but an ultimatum. Southgate, who was fifty-nine, had told Downing Street that he was retiring from EMI and would make himself available full time to sort out the opera. His was an offer the board were not allowed to refuse.

Southgate's appointment was announced on the day Nicholas Payne resigned to become general director of ENO, a fresh blow to the Royal Opera. Southgate was trotted out to meet the press. He promised to make the ROH accessible to all sectors of the public. Asked whether this meant universal access, he said: 'We mustn't downgrade the opera house. I don't want to sit next to somebody in a singlet, a pair of shorts and a smelly pair of trainers. I'm a relaxed individual, but I'm passionate about standards of behaviour.'

The next morning, his comments were plastered across the top of the *Guardian*'s front page, above a photograph of a black-tied ROH gala audience.[31] A reader in Newport wrote in: 'Sir Colin Southgate has a nerve. The amount of subsidy on his ticket is more than an ordinary person's weekly wage packet.'[32] Southgate learned his lesson. From that day on, he refused to give press interviews, a peculiar reticence for the head of a public-funded institution.

Chris Smith was next up for a grilling. Gerald Kaufman called him back to tell his Committee how its recommendations were being implemented. Smith reported that 'Sir Colin Southgate has made a vigorous start,' appointing Vivien Duffield as vice-chairman, Lord Eatwell as chairman of the ballet board and Michael Berkeley as chairman of the opera board.

Kaufman opened with his customary civilities. 'Be so kind as to speak more loudly than you usually do,' he told the Secretary of State, 'you being a person of modest and retiring disposition.' Being sweet-talked in public by Gerald Kaufman was a bit like being nuzzled by a pet jellyfish.

The committee's deputy chairman, Michael Fabricant, accused Smith of 'taking the same hands-off approach that [ACE] were taking while the [ROH] was going through its problems.' Smith replied: 'I do not believe it is right or sensible for the Secretary of State or the Department to become involved in detailed managerial decisions.' 'Every time we make a criticism,' snapped Fabricant, 'you come back with *mea non culpa*.'

Two women MPs on the committee led the cries for Mary Allen's head. 'The chief executive is still there,' protested Clare Wood, 'but (she) has not made the necessary changes. We were not impressed by Mary Allen's explanation of events. The circumstances of her appointment were, to say the least, unsatisfactory.'

'Everyone agrees on that,' said Smith, 'but I had no power to appoint Mary Allen or to dismiss her.'

The chairman weighed in. He brandished a letter from Keith Cooper, revealing that the *Barber of Seville* and *Marriage of Figaro* were playing to fifty and sixty per cent houses, against a budget forecast of eighty per cent. 'That shambles,' said Kaufman, 'has continued utterly unabated and without the tiniest effort to control it.' Smith replied: 'I am not in charge of the [ROH]. I am sometimes very glad of that particular fact.'

'Much as I love this Government,' sighed Kaufman theatrically, 'we are entitled to some answers.' Smith replied that Southgate's first priority would be to satisfy himself whether the ROH was viable. 'Will he cancel the rest of the season?' Kaufman pressed. 'That is precisely a matter he wishes to look at urgently,' said Smith.

Southgate appeared to have made up his mind about Mary Allen. The music business had been a male preserve, with few women in senior positions. Allen returned two days after her operation, too soon for her own good. She had words with the finance director, Richard Hall, and decided at the same time to get rid of Keith Cooper and the technical director, John Harrison, in a night of the long knives, known as 'management restructuring'. Pelham Allen, the professional adviser, would take over finance while Judy Grahame reorganized marketing (Harrison was later reinstated). Grahame lengthened the list, dismissing the marketing director Andrew Stokes and opera press officer, Helen Anderson. Both were popular Gardeners. Keith Cooper went off to serve tables at his lover's restaurant in Shepherd's Bush, and made a documentary for the BBC. Vivien Duffield, who enjoyed having him around, turned furiously against the chief executive.

Time was running out for Mary Allen. Bernard Haitink wrote a letter in her defence to *Opera* magazine, which was clamouring for her head. 'What is desperately needed at the moment is a modicum of stability,' said Haitink. 'A third change of leadership within a year is not the answer.'[33] On 18 March, Haitink went into hospital for a heart bypass operation, putting him out of action for the rest of the season. Hours earlier, Colin Southgate had called in Judy Grahame and told her to start preparing the company's submission to the Eyre Review. He intended to propose a different structure, with an artistic director on top, followed by a chief executive. Allen's post was to be downgraded. Grahame asked him to tell the chief executive; when he failed to do so, she did. Mary Allen knew that this was the end.

For three torrid months the board and the Government had been begging her to stay; now she was cast off without the courtesy of an explanation. On 25 March she appeared before the board and resigned. The official reason was 'a growing difference of views over future plans for the organization'. Pouring herself a stiff Scotch, she cleared her desk and left.

'And then there were none,' crowed Kaufman in a paid article for the *Evening Standard*. 'With the resignation of Mary Allen as chief executive, the entire top team that ran the ROH has gone. That was what the House of Commons Culture, Media and Sports Committee insisted should happen when we issued our celebrated (notorious?) report four months ago. We were accused of going over the top. We have been vindicated.'[34]

Mary Allen responded with an open letter to Eyre, attacking the Government's 'apathy' to Covent Garden and 'the way in which such a highly trained human resource is being wasted'.[35] A few days after her departure, I took her to tea at the Langham Hotel. She had been shopping for household furnishings on Oxford Street and was preparing to get on with her life. 'I believe everything is sortable,' she said. 'There is no organization so dysfunctional that it cannot be sorted out. Two things scuppered me. The huge debt and the Kaufman Report.' She was heading for Suffolk to cultivate her garden for a while, but two years would pass before she could resume her career. Cancer, the sister of stress, struck at her breast and she underwent surgery and chemotherapy. Like Genista McIntosh, Mary Allen had entered the opera house with a buoyant reputation. Unlike her, she lingered too long and departed damaged in body and spirit.

The opera house was now in the hands of Pelham Allen until, as he put it, the board selected 'a general director of the highest artistic reputation and distinction'.[36] Richard Jarman, once of Scottish Opera, stepped in temporarily to fill Payne's shoes.

'It is symptomatic,' said Genista McIntosh in a muted side-blast, 'that the ROH was briefly run by a chief executive seconded from the accountancy partnership Coopers & Lybrand. In my view, you cannot separate managing such institutions from their artistic philosophy.'[37] The artistic credibility of the opera house was being called into question.

As if to nullify such doubts, that month the Royal Opera swept the board at the *Evening Standard*'s annual theatre awards. Sir Edward Downes, picking up the trophies, said the company had been 'run down – dumbed down – to a level that is dangerous in the extreme . . . What we are celebrating in these awards is the way the company has fought against attack. These are people who, in a damn-you-all way, have produced performances that are outstanding, despite all this. These are people who don't work from nine to five. They do it as a vocation, because this is what they have been born for, for the nation.'[38]

*

Eyre was running late and the spin doctors were getting busy. A report was planted in the *Sunday Times*, suggesting that this most public-spirited of men was about to recommend privatization. Bectu members called a protest rally and Eyre was obliged to send a private letter to Pelham Allen and ENO's Russell Willis Taylor, affirming that no one had yet been apprised of the contents of his report, 'because only I know what I intend to recommend'.[39]

While the nation waited, Chris Smith published a slim volume of essays under the title *Creative Britain*. Wrapped in blotches by the fashionable post-modernist Damien Hirst, it affirmed New Labour's faith in a 'Cool Britannia' in which shlock art, advertising and pop music were valued as progressive and profitable while traditional arts were scorned as 'unmodernized' and parasitical.

Colin Southgate flew to Los Angeles to fulfil his promise to get shot of EMI. Half his plan had already foundered. His designated successor, the diminutive American Jim Fifield, had walked away from the company with an eight-digit pay-off. Southgate headed to California to clinch a sale. He had been negotiating a takeover for months with the Canadian distillers, Seagrams, who owned Universal Pictures. When Southgate got off the plane, they told him not to bother. PolyGram, owned by Philips in Holland, had nipped in at a lower price and sold their labels to Universal. Southgate was left at the altar like a jilted bride and had to stay on as EMI chairman until he found a new successor or buyer. The unplanned distraction compounded his ROH woes and shortened his temper.

Eyre was due to report on 1 May but that week he was rehearsing the Royal Opera revival of *La Traviata* at the Royal Albert Hall. 'The reason the report has taken such an inordinately long time,' he told a *Guardian* diarist, 'is simply that never having directed an Andrew Lloyd Webber musical, I have to earn a living, which does rather interfere with voluntary work. At least you lot (journalists) get paid to write about the Royal Opera House.' Between the lines of that remark lurked a green-eyed envy for his *Cats*-rich successor, Trevor Nunn, along with a puritanical resentment of all who fed off the fruits of public-funded arts. Other asides from Eyre referred to the anomaly of Placido Domingo earning one hundred times as much for singing *Otello* at Covent Garden as the £200 paid to England's finest actors who played the role at the Royal National Theatre.

Prudish in his dislike of excess, Eyre was neither a visionary nor a stirrer, but a quiet operator who got things done and, from time to time, scored a hit. Under Eyre, the National conquered the West End with *Guys and Dolls* and staged a fistful of well-crafted new plays. It was a model company with balanced budgets. Eyre rarely rose to the bait of self-publicity. A family man, married for twenty-five years to a television producer who made *Pride and Prejudice* for the BBC, he was untouched by gossip. A book of memoirs hinted that his life was a rebellion against his Rabelaisian father, a naval officer turned farmer who voted Tory and advised his son to 'fuck his way around the world'.[40] Richard, who read English at Cambridge under Kingsley Amis, became a moral socialist. As a servant of the arts and a supporter of New Labour, he felt his report could benefit both causes.

As publication drifted into June, rumours abounded. A tip that Eyre was angling for Allen's job at Covent Garden was reported by the *Independent* ('he'd rather walk barefoot to Scunthorpe,' said his sister). Mary Allen began writing a column for *The Times*.

On 6 June, a housebound Ninette de Valois marked her hundredth birthday. 'Tell me,' she demanded, 'is there any excitement in the world?'[41] Tony Blair was collared one night at his table in a smart London restaurant, The Ivy, by the composer Harrison Birtwistle, who ticked him off loudly about Labour's neglect of the arts. 'We're getting it wrong, aren't we?' murmured Blair to the Barbican Centre manager, John Tusa, as they entered a conference hall. 'Is it a question of money?'

A day before Eyre's report came off the presses, Blair invited a small group of arts chiefs to brief him on the crisis. Over tea and cupcakes at Downing Street, one leader after another told the Prime Minister of the need for extra funding and a degree of respect for heritage arts. Eyre himself delivered a synoptic overview of the funding shortage and demanded an extra sixty million pounds. The conductor Sir Simon Rattle described the collapse of instrumental teaching in schools, a drop of 150,000 pupils in five years. Tusa spoke of the support the arts could deliver in return – and Blair seemed impressed, apologizing for his negligence and promising 'to write the arts into the core script' of Government activity. 'I think I saw a Prime Minister who does believe in the role arts can play in a civilized society,' said Sir Dennis Stevenson.[42] To muddy the waters, Downing Street spin doctors assured a *Times* columnist that Blair had merely been 'in listening mode' and had no intention of favouring middle-class habits. 'Politically speaking,' *The Times* was told, 'Covent Garden is on Planet Zog.'[43]

Southgate, taking Blair at his word, leaked a letter he had written to Chris Smith, demanding a doubling of subsidy – without which the house could not reopen. Even if every performance in the new house sold out, he warned, there would be an annual shortfall of fifteen million pounds.[44] In tone, timing, and temerity, his note could hardly have been less judicious. 'I am particularly surprised,' said Smith, 'that such a request should be made now, in advance of consideration of Sir Richard Eyre's recommendations on financial stability and planning, efficient management and value for public money. These must be the priority, before any meaningful discussion of future funding requirements can take place.'

Smith's letter was published as an adjunct to the Eyre Report, in an operation orchestrated to attract minimum attention. The report was released on a day when England's football team were playing a do-or-die World Cup tie against Argentina. The television news would run late that night, and the next morning's papers would be full of England's fate (they lost, of course). Smith's officials restricted entry to Eyre's press conference to two specialist correspondents from each national newspaper and broadcast medium.

At three o'clock in the afternoon of 30 June, the select few were shepherded into a windowless cellar-room in the Department of Culture, Media and Sport and given half an hour to read the 150-page report before questioning Eyre and Smith. Eyre appeared dour, subdued and defensive. Smith sounded petulant. 'I am glad to see we've got a full house here,' he began and, echoing Kaufmann's jibe, 'it is more than Covent Garden can manage.'

That cheap shot set the tone. 'It is our intention that the ROH should continue to receive public subsidy, and that ENO should remain at the Coliseum as its own home base,' declared Smith, nullifying his original proposal. There was little more to add. Eyre had examined all other options and found them wanting. Privatization he ruled out because it would mean writing off all the public money that had been invested over the years in Covent Garden – a weak argument, since such write-offs are inherent to every privatization. He was tempted by an idea of mine to separate the management of theatres from the running of the performing companies; he had also toyed with abolishing the Arts Council. In the end, he said, the Government had three choices – either to decide that the arts did not merit state support; or to carry on as before; or, as he would recommend, to make a real commitment on the basis of 'excellence, artistic integrity, accessibility, accountability and cost effectiveness' by greatly increasing its subsidy for the arts.

'My belief,' wrote Eyre, 'is that, at the end of this process, additional funds will be needed, if the companies are fully to deliver the objectives of the Review.' He went on to argue that 'a huge increase in funding is unrealistic', but 'a substantial increase is essential'.[45] Yet, as if to spare Smith's blushes, he portrayed Covent Garden as undeserving of the largesse he was recommending. 'I think it would be disastrous,' said Eyre, 'if the Royal Opera House were to be given special, remedial treatment.'

Eyre spoke bitterly about Covent Garden. 'It's a tragedy,' he said, 'that the ROH has been perceived as a barometer of the arts. What alarms me is that the whole world of the subsidized arts has been tainted by the opprobrium that is attached to the Royal Opera House.'

Richard Morrison, in *The Times*,[46] called the report 'a great waste: I have never read an official arts report that is so elegantly written, so full of sane suggestions and well-argued observations about the running of theatres and yet so illogical when approaching the central issues.' In the *Daily Telegraph* I lamented 'a painfully missed opportunity for which opera will pay a mortal price in the years to come'.[47] The entire sector had been hungry for challenge and prepared to respond to a new agenda; Eyre had let them down, and let the Government off the hook.

To cover their nakedness, Eyre and Smith launched into tirades against Covent Garden which they depicted as a citadel of vanity and waste. Eyre complained primly that the ROH kept two-thirds as many executives on salaries over £30,000 as any other arts company. In fact, the Royal Opera and Royal Ballet each had ten employees, including music directors, earning over £30,000. The Royal National Theatre had eight. Eyre's information was three years out of date.

Smith condemned Covent Garden for failing to submit a business plan. The ROH replied that it had a letter from Smith's office agreeing that there was no point in writing a business plan without knowing what levels of funding it could expect.

By the weekend the report was shelved. By the summer's end, it was forgotten. The newspapers were preoccupied with a soccer player, David Beckham, who was blamed for the Argentine defeat, and with the impending anniversary of Princess Diana's death. The Archbishop of Canterbury warned against a renewed outpouring of public grief. The Archbishop of York attacked those who were 'clinging to the icon . . . wallowing in her death'.[48] England was in the grip of a millennial marian cult, while older beliefs foundered for want of glamour and immediacy.

The opening pages of Eyre's report had envisaged a Utopian England in which

> our corrosive class divisions would dissolve, crime among young men would be curbed, and unemployment would be eased. Our political immaturity would be cured, our insular attitudes towards Europe and our paranoia about our national identity would be dispelled. We would put an end to our ignorance and suspicion of science, our diffidence about learning, and abolish the cultural apartheid which divides the country between those who go to galleries, theatres and opera houses, and those who feel themselves excluded from them.[49]

The way to achieve this utopia, said Eyre, repeating a Blairite mantra, was 'education, education, education'. Three days after he uttered these words, the Guardian topped its front page with the headline: 'ROH sacks head of education on first day'.[50]

Covent Garden's propensity for self-damage was not exhausted. Janet Robertson, turning up for work as head of opera education, was greeted by the personnel director, Mike Morris. He handed her a letter reading: 'I regret to inform you that the ROH has decided not to confirm your appointment.' She was then escorted off the premises. Robertson told the *Guardian* that in a previous meeting with Pelham Allen she had been told that the company's commitment to education was 'nothing more than lip service'.

Richard Eyre, approached for a reaction, purpled his phraseology. 'It makes me blind with anger,' said Eyre. 'This confirms my worst fears of bad faith and it's in a tragically time-honoured tradition of opera house own-goals. It confirms my view, which I spell out in the report, that unless there is a total change of mindset they can't survive. It appears that they have not taken on board the report. Unless they get the message soon, they will just sink into the sea.'

The facts of the matter were more prosaic than they appeared, although the handling of the affair could not have been clumsier. Covent Garden was a pioneer in arts education. The Royal Ballet toured sink estates with its 'chance to dance' programme, inspiring children of deprived backgrounds with respect for their bodies and awareness of their talent. The brightest were offered free coaching and occasionally scholarships to the Royal Ballet School. The Royal Opera tapped into London schools for child actors and choruses. It was spreading opera awareness still wider through a range of teaching aids. Its Write an Opera project had been adopted by a hundred and fifty schools in several countries. Stuffy as it was at the top, the company's roots were grassy and the singers and dancers seldom refused to give freely of their time to preach their art to bright-eyed school assemblies.

Janet Robertson had been hired by Nicholas Payne to run a vibrant department. She got off on the wrong foot with Pelham Allen, complaining about her £25,000 salary and demanding a raise. Allen felt that she lacked the right attitude and asked Judy Grahame to administer a formal warning. Resentments simmered and a decision was taken not to allow Robertson to start work.

Grahame was herself at loggerheads with murmurous staff over her sacking of two Gardeners. The Bectu representative Sofie Mason, a graduate who worked in the publications department selling advertising space in opera and ballet programmes, called a union meeting where she uttered a number of wild and unfounded allegations about Grahame. A motion of no-confidence in the external affairs director was passed. Copies of Mason's allegations were circulated to eighteen journalists. She was immediately suspended, pending disciplinary action. E-mails proclaiming 'Sofie Mason is a martyr' flew around the company and beyond. Grahame reached for libel lawyers.

The dispute was brought to Southgate, who decided that Mason had committed a dismissable offence and should be sacked. He was advised that the company could not afford more bad publicity, a probable clerical strike and £50,000 in dispute proceedings. The chairman backed down and called for conciliation. On 7 July, Mason and Bectu withdrew all allegations against Grahame, without an apology. Both sides agreed 'not to comment any further on this'.[51]

Behind the scenes, tempers seethed. Bectu claimed victory and the executive team felt betrayed. Southgate was overheard calling the opera house 'a nest of vipers'. It was an eye-opening moment that pushed the chairman towards a radical decision.

At the Kaufman committee a week later, Richard Eyre said: 'Unless the ROH regards itself as an organization that exists for the public good, and if they won't change . . . there is no justification for them to continue to receive public support.'

On 22 July, Darryl Jaffray, the ballet's education officer, was named ROH Director of Education. That afternoon, Southgate called a board meeting to deal with the financial insolubles. The time for soft shoe shuffles was over. He was ready to go for broke.

And, all the while, the opera sang and the ballet danced, in unfamiliar places and on borrowed time. I caught up with the Royal Ballet in Frankfurt, staying in one of the world's most exclusive hotels. The owner of the Frankfurter Hof, a devotee of classical dance, was putting up the dancers for the price of a Scunthorpe bed-and-breakfast. Thanks to the American choreographers John Neumeier, William Forsythe and Mark Morris, Germany was a world leader in contemporary dance, but its ballet fans hungered for the sight of a traditional ensemble dancing to a live orchestra, in place of pre-recorded tapes.

The musicians of Frankfurt had never played for dancers before and stumbled through the first act of Ashton's *Cinderella* with some alarming judders. The performance came together in the second act under the cool baton of the Royal Ballet's latest music director, a young woman of thirty-three with two small daughters at home. Andrea Quinn had inherited the baton from Barry Wordsworth, who blew out after failing to get his repertoire ideas past the two Anthonies and the ever-depressing board. 'Anthony Dowell doesn't like confrontation,' said Wordsworth, 'he can't stand up to anyone.'

'I think Andrea is on a hiding to nothing,' he added. 'She is as good a conductor as they are ever likely to get, but she'll only be good if they let her get on with the job. They have thrown out a lot of good conductors, and some[52] have died in a ditch.' John Lanchbery, another predecessor, intoned a solemn warning. 'The main thing,' he advised, 'is to fight every inch of the way against the Opera. They'll steal all your rehearsal time.'

Quinn certainly had the composure, as well as the confidence of Dowell, who warmed to her 'exciting ideas' for new ballets to music by Birtwistle and the minimalist Kevin Volans. How she would cope with the hard hats of the ROH orchestra remained to be seen. What was evident in Frankfurt, though, was that the Royal Ballet danced just as well with a strange band in the pit as they did with their home orchestra. Later in the year, they would make their first Irish appearance, at the Grand Opera House in Belfast, accompanied by the sensitive and enthusiastic Ulster Orchestra. Extraordinarily, it was the ballet's only UK residency outside London during the closure years.

The Royal Opera were also breaking new ground, ending their first exile year at Savonlinna, in the month of the midnight sun. When the sun shines, the semi-covered castle courtyard beside a Finnish lake is a splendid place to watch opera. That summer, it rained continuously and temperatures were ten degrees below normal. The dress rehearsal of Verdi's *I Masnadieri* was abandoned in blinding gales. During the performances, singers, players and audience alike were soaked to the skin. 'There was an extraordinary intimacy,' growled Sir Edward Downes, who conducted.

The following night, they gave *Peter Grimes*, unseen in Finland since 1947. The audience were gripped by the Moshinsky production, with Anthony Rolfe-Johnson in the Jon Vickers role. They leaped to their feet, roaring and stamping – 'behaving like Spaniards,' as the festival director put it. The orchestra played in shirts soaked to transparency, several men surrendering their jackets to female colleagues. 'It was sheer, bloody-minded pride,' said the conductor, Elgar Howarth. Afterwards, they cycled ten kilometres to a spartan student hostel, where no hot meal awaited them. The fortitude was admirable – but it was British grit more than company spirit. Several players, including the leader, David Nolan, were well-known London freelancers filling in for the opera tour. The myth of the essential ROH orchestra was ripe for lancing.

Offstage, Royal Opera education officers were helping twenty-eight Finnish eleven year olds to create their own *Grimes*, the first such schools project in a country noted for the excellence of its music education. On the final night, the cast gave a party for John Dobson, the veteran comprimario, who was calling it a day after playing character roles at Covent Garden since Solti's era. He was the last surviving member of the company of singers and many an eye was moist as high times were recalled. There was no one from the management team to bid him farewell, nor had any member of board came out to brave the nordic elements. The Royal Opera flew home, and on to the Edinburgh Festival, feeling chilled and undervalued.

Pelham Allen, three months into the job, was looking wan and drawn.

Having spent his working life nursing companies back to health, he told colleagues that he had never seen anything quite like Covent Garden. Normally, he found debt, fraud and neglect of duty; here, apart from some of the usual problems, there was incompetence, intrigue and external interference of every kind from politicians, the press, high society and trade unions. The staff fell into two groups – dedicated and deeply conservative, or dedicated and deeply malicious. He found the company 'virtually unmanageable'.[53]

Allen's skills did not come cheap. For its 'professional advisers', Coopers & Lybrand billed the ROH for £50,248.33 (including VAT) for the first fortnight, around five thousand pounds per working day. The charges for Pelham Allen himself were two hundred and fifty pounds an hour.[54] Things could not carry on like this for long.

On 27 July, the executive team were summoned on their mobile phones to an unscheduled meeting at EMI. They found Southgate and Allen in a fifth-floor conference room, with a war plan written out by Allen on a wall-screen. Southgate said, 'this has got to stop' and handed over to Allen, who ran through an eight-point strategy. They were about to shut down the ROH company and make everyone redundant. Orchestra and chorus were to be disbanded.

The ballet company would be kept going, if necessary by reverting ownership to the Royal Ballet Governors, whose chairman was Lord Sainsbury. However, the two Anthonies were to be dismissed and the dancers would have to agree new contracts within three months.

The building work would continue and finish in time; the Trust and Friends would be kept going as separate bodies.

An artistic director would be quickly appointed – Southgate had someone in mind – and the company would reopen in 1999, slimmed down, but with much the same structure.

All the executives enthusiastically endorsed the plan, but each and every one of them argued that the structure had to be changed. Southgate dismissed their views and charged off with Allen to see Chris Smith.

They reported back the next day, saying Smith was in agreement and would allow the subsidy for 1999 to be spent on redundancy costs. This was not enough, in Southgate's opinion, to allow the ROH to reopen in the black. He decided to resign, booking a 5.00 p.m. appointment that Thursday with Chris Smith to tell him so. At five-thirty, he showed up at the Floral Hall for a topping-out ceremony looking decidedly more cheerful. Smith had offered no more money, but had praised him to the skies. Southgate made an impromptu speech. 'And when we reopen,' he said grandly, 'all the people buying seats up there can look down on us nobs in the Floral Hall.' His executives groaned, thanking heaven that no press were within earshot.

Allen went off for a week's family holiday. He returned to find the war-plan watered down and Southgate avoiding bellicose talk. He had been advised by a close business associate to tone it down. The new strategy was called 'managed transition'. It involved calling off the 1999 performance schedule, and telling staff they would be dismissed if by January they had not signed improved contracts, surrendering extra payments for broadcasts and similar perks. The point on which Southgate now stood firm was that he would definitely resign if Smith did not offer more money in exchange for the efficiencies he was about to achieve.

At eight forty-five on Monday 7 September, Southgate and Allen went to see Smith. The figures they presented spoke for themselves. The ROH was now thirteen million pounds in debt; that sum would reach twenty million by March 2000 if performances continued. The solution was to stop and rethink. 'We have been asked to make the ROH less élitist and to bring ticket prices down,' said Southgate. 'We want to do this, but we can't without money. It's a circle we cannot square.'[55] Smith replied that he was prepared to give more money if the opera house showed willingness to change. He asked for time to reflect and promised an answer by the end of the day.

Southgate returned to EMI deeply dejected. Late in the afternoon, he was rung by Eatwell who had picked up hopeful political signals. At six in the evening, Smith sent round a letter, praising Southgate for his 'visionary approach towards securing the ROH's long-term future'. He promised more money but did not say how much.

The board gathered on Tuesday for a meeting attended by the new junior arts minister Alan Howarth. His preliminary bromides were interrupted by a raging Vivien Duffield, who said 'I've heard all this smooth talk before.' She demanded to know whether the

Government would support the company or not. Howarth said it was up to the Arts Council to decide how much money the ROH would receive. Graham Devlin said the ACE could not make that decision until the Government announced how much extra it was providing. The familiar old dodgem routine was broken up by Lord Eatwell, who said that unless an extra £5.5 million was received in December – 'not five million or five point two' – it was curtains for the opera house. Both Howarth and Devlin agreed that something of that order could be arranged, with an extra ten million the following year. Southgate smiled and proclaimed salvation.

Tough letters were sent to the Musicians Union, Equity and Bectu. The secret fallback plan was that, if agreement was not quickly obtained, the company would shut down and there would be no reopening before September 2000 at the earliest. A fallback announcement was drafted: 'The Board of the ROH today agreed to solvently wind-down its existing operation and to build a new organization from scratch.'

Staff meetings and a press conference were called around noon on Wednesday to deliver the news. The chorus took it worst, convinced they were all to be sacked; their director, Terry Edwards, had advised Eyre that there was no need to employ a full-time chorus. The orchestra were informed during *Ring* rehearsals with Haitink, whose face darkened. Bectu members gathered at Conway Hall, a relic of Victorian public-spiritedness, to hear Southgate say, 'It's hard for all of you who have given your heart and soul to this place, but it has gone from decade to decade, from crisis to crisis, and this has got to stop.' The ballet received the news during rehearsals at Sadler's Wells.

It was not so much the revised agreements that caused dismay as the realization that, once the house opened, there would be no more than two hundred and twenty performances a year, which was the most that could be afforded at present levels of subsidy. Most of the salaried artists would be on part-time contracts. 'We're being offered seventy-nine per cent of our existing salary,' said a chorus singer. 'We would become part-time but they require us to be available all the year, so we couldn't take on other work.'

The unions called it 'cultural vandalism'. Sofie Mason set about organizing a celebrity rally in defence of ROH staff. Edward Downes got up a petition that he would present at Downing Street. Nine conductors wrote to *The Times* in support of the orchestra and chorus. The letter was signed by Colin Davis, Daniel Barenboim, Pierre Boulez, Valery Gergiev, Carlos Kleiber, James Levine, Zubin Mehta, Simon Rattle and Mstislav Rostropovich;[56] three of the signatories had never conducted at Covent Garden.

This was predictable ferment, nothing to furrow Pelham Allen's brow. The two factors he was watching were the music director and the donors. Haitink's choler was rising. He demanded a meeting with Allen and the acting Royal Opera director Richard Jarman. Nothing they could say sufficed to reassure him. Haitink declared that artistic standards could not be maintained if the company stopped performing and that any gap in the performing year would cause the best players in his orchestra to seek work elsewhere. After a week of growing concern, he sent a resignation letter to Southgate.

The chairman went to see him a week later and, with the help of an EMI recording executive, persuaded Haitink to suspend his decision while he tried to salvage part of the 1999 programme. But in the week between his letter and their meeting, Haitink had spoken in Edinburgh to Hugh Canning of the *Sunday Times*. News of his resignation appeared in the Sunday paper and panic set in at the prospect of another bout of bad publicity. At the end of the month, Haitink wrote to Chris Smith offering to remain in his post in exchange for his support for reinstating a skeleton opera season in 1999. He argued that the company would lose artists, audiences and himself if it stopped performing. Smith, not wanting to be embroiled in a high-profile row, told Covent Garden to relax the total shutdown. This was the first crack in the salvation plan.

The dancers, meanwhile, had written to Lord Sainsbury, imploring him to help them in their plight. Sainsbury addressed the Royal Ballet at the end of the month and told them 'it's going to be all right'. The company wanted them to accept 36-week contracts. He backed full employment. 'As chairman of the Governors of the Royal Ballet, there was clearly a need to be very concerned at what was going on,' said Sainsbury. 'We had to get involved and say that the company needed to be looked after rather more than they were going to be, in terms of how many weeks they were going to be employed. The Governors would never accept that they should only be employed for six months of the year.'

Sainsbury let it be known that the Royal Ballet would go it alone if the ROH failed to deliver acceptable terms. Given that he was a leading donor to the ROH, his threat was twin-edged. 'In order to keep the (ballet) at the opera house,' said Sainsbury, 'we had to do some tough talking. I was wearing several hats, also as chairman of the appeal, and I was saying (to Southgate) that in no way could you expect people to give money to an opera house that was only going to function for part of the year. If that was going to be the case, I, for one, could not accept that this was the organization we were pledging money to.'

Southgate backtracked again, promising to keep the dancers on full employment and work towards a year-round programme in the new house. 'The compromise,' said Sainsbury, 'was that it was to be built up to a point where it could operate fully. It was terrible that it came to that.' A second strand snapped in the rescue plan.

Then Vivien Duffield weighed in with a letter to Southgate from her lawyers, restating the commitment of her trustees to the ROH but stipulating that the plans to perform for just thirty-five weeks a year were incompatible with the aims of their five million pound donation. Unless Southgate agreed to achieve a full forty-five week schedule for the Royal Opera and Royal Ballet within three years of reopening, there would be no further money from her trusts. There was no point in giving money to a building; it was the performing companies that she intended to support. Southgate, faced with the loss of his chief fundraiser and lead donor, caved in. Pelham Allen's rescue plan lay in ruins.

Allen had done his best. He was a good man, with good intentions, but nothing in his commercial experience had confronted him with so many conflictual forces, all shouting at the top of their voices. In the midst of a crisis meeting, with executives telling him that everything hung in the balance, he took his coat at five o'clock and said he had to go. Ninety minutes later, he walked back into the meeting. To a sympathetic colleague, he confided that he had been to a memorial service for a close relative. In the hysteria of the opera house, Pelham Allen kept his human priorities intact.

Mercifully for Allen, his time was almost up. At the board meeting of 8 September, the Board had appointed the next boss of the ROH. It had reached the decision by a circuitous route and for most of the wrong reasons. But, like a shaft of sunlight that falls upon a storm-tossed sea, it was a harbinger of calmer times, a settler of nerves.

All summer long, Southgate had been telling his board that he was going to appoint an artistic director and he had an excellent person in mind. She was Sarah Billinghurst, casting director at the Metropolitan Opera in New York, and a human barrier between its aggressive general manager, Joseph Volpe, and its music director, James Levine. Billinghurst was in her early fifties, a New Zealander who had spent her whole career in opera houses.

There were immediate objections from the usual quarters, namely Vivien Duffield. Had Billinghurst ever run an opera house? Er, no. Had she any experience of a mixed economy of state and private subvention? Also not. Did she control the Met's $163 million budget, two-and-a-half times larger than Covent Garden's? Negative.

Nevertheless, Southgate was set on having her and flew to New York to finalize details. Before he left, someone suggested to him that there was an American he should meet who could work under Billinghurst as her administrator. His name was Michael Kaiser and few in England, apart from Deborah MacMillan, had heard of him.

Lady MacMillan, who chaired the ACE's dance panel, had been catching up with old contacts at American Ballet Theater, where her husband had spent some of his happiest months. She knew Kaiser as the director who turned ABT around financially in the mid-90s after years of famine. 'They need someone like you at Covent Garden,' she told him over dinner. 'You think so?' said Kaiser.

Some days later, he called back and said, 'I want to do it.'

MacMillan said, 'You must be off your head.'

Back home, she told John Tooley, who passed his name on to a board member. Southgate agreed to meet Kaiser while he was in New York.

Neither man will exactly say what passed at that meeting, but Kaiser made it clear to Southgate that he wanted the top job and, no disrespect, would not work under Sarah Billinghurst. Southgate was smitten by a man who knew his mind. He asked Billinghurst if she would be Kaiser's number two, and she likewise refused. She had virtually cleared her desk at the Met when Southgate told her he was giving the job to Michael Kaiser.

It was at the shutdown meeting of 8 September that Michael Kaiser, under Any Other Business, walked in to meet the board. All the executives except Pelham Allen were asked to leave the room.

Kaiser turned on a beam of reassurance and within moments had the board at his feet. 'My career,' he said, 'is about finding new resources for the arts and saving money.' He was not interested in problems, only in solutions. Such positivism had not been heard in the boardroom since Isaiah Berlin was at his philosophical peak.

There was only one objection. Chris Smith, Richard Eyre, Colin Southgate and the Floral Trust had all agreed that the next boss at Covent Garden was to be an artistic director, not an administrator. Pelham Allen was present as the Floral Trust's guardian of good conduct. He had to leave the room momentarily to go to the toilet. By the time he returned, Michael Kaiser had been appointed Executive Director, reporting directly to the board.

CHAPTER 12

And so to Bed

(December 1998 to December 1999)

THE WORLD WAS in the grip of an unprecedented fit of prurience. Bill Clinton, president of the United States, had, like many who attained that office, lied and screwed his way to power. Once there, his enemies made valiant efforts to expose the lies. Failing that, they turned the spotlight on screwing.

For the whole of 1998, newspapers described the president's sexual habits in anatomical detail. He admitted, finally, to oral sex with a White House intern. Clinton survived the attempt to impeach him, but his presidency was tarnished.

A backlash was inevitable. America, in its next election, would choose between two dullards. The rest of the world was torn between its right to know and its instinct to ignore. In Russia, a drunken, incapable president with links to organized crime was allowed to hand over to a chosen protégé, rather than face investigation and trial. Germany's unifying ex-president, Helmut Kohl, was caught laundering party donations. His successor was cashiered, but Kohl escaped with a caution. The Clinton carnival had revealed limits to the embarrassment of power. It aroused a universal longing to restore purity and a presumption of honesty in elected leaders.

In Britain, Tony Blair enjoyed a higher opinion poll rating than any Prime Minister since polling began. His ministers might err, but Blair was put on a pedestal and the public willed him to be above reproach – 'you know me, I'm a decent kind of guy,' was the basis of his appeal. When his wife, Cherie, fell pregnant in her mid-forties, the event was regarded as a triumph of fidelity, decency and faith, the antithesis of Tory 'sleaze'.

Michael Kaiser stepped directly from the Clinton impeachment to the canonization of Blair. He arrived in a climate that had turned kind to leaders. Kaiser was good at making organizations work and projecting a positive outlook. He cannot, however, have anticipated the halo that would come his way as, prudently and methodically, he set about putting together again the Humpty Dumpty of English arts.

In fairness to all concerned, most of the repairs had been carried out before Michael Kaiser took up his post. In the two months before his arrival, Southgate and the personnel director, Mike Morris, hammered out union agreements and limited work-force reductions. Morris wrote off his own job.

The *Ring* resounded at the Royal Albert Hall and hundreds queued outside but many seats gaped empty because Friends and donors had not returned their allocations. Haitink grumbled that the chairman had not bothered to attend. Relations between Southgate and his deputy, Vivien Duffield, remained tense and Lord Sainsbury was keeping his powder dry. The Clore and Duffield Foundations announced a seven million pound bequest in October for educational and interactive devices to help children get more out of visits to museums and art galleries. A Jewish school in poverty-line Hackney received £400,000 for a language and technology wing. The Weizman Institute in Israel was given three million dollars for a Clore Garden of Science. Mrs Duffield refused to answer questions about the Royal Opera House.[1]

'I am not at all surprised to read that Mrs Vivien Duffield is reconsidering her donation to the ROH redevelopment,' wrote the former deputy chairman, Sir James Spooner, in a letter to *Opera* and *The Times*. 'I am sure that she and the other major six, seven and eight-figure donors (and even some minor five-figure donors like my wife and myself) feel dreadfully let down. It must seem to many that Perfidious Albion is alive and well in certain corridors in Westminster. I would hope that those concerned are, in their hearts, thoroughly ashamed of the hideous damage they are causing to two of this country's star assets and to all who work in or for them.'[2] Chris Smith said nothing, but Tony Blair told the opera director Nicholas Hytner that the money needed to regenerate the arts was 'a drop in the ocean'; the problem was, how to sell it to readers of the *Sun*?[3]

Within the ravaged company, the head of marketing, Gillian Brierley, quit after five months, complaining of lack of staff co-operation. Judy Grahame resigned, her contract paid out in full. The *Daily Telegraph*, in an editorial, wrote:

> To lose one highly respected executive in unexplained circumstances is unfortunate, to lose two sounds like negligence. Three seems reckless and four in eighteen months suggests that the organization is careering out of control. The ROH put out business-as-usual signs yesterday after the abrupt resignation of its public affairs director, Judy Grahame. Like the two chief executives and marketing director – all women – who preceded her in a rush to the door, Ms Grahame was unable immediately to give her version of events without breaching the terms of her severance agreement.
>
> However, anyone with an eye for institutional psychology must be aware that the neurosis inherent in every opera house has slipped at Covent Garden into the darker realms of psychosis. Privately, senior executives past and present describe the place as unmanageable.[4]

Nevertheless, by the end of October Southgate was able to announce that 'substantial progress had been made with artists and staff on new arrangements'. The unions claimed they had saved jobs, the management that they had cut some. Little had been resolved beyond the saving of face on both sides.

A bigger capitulation was taking place to the north. No sooner had the ROH announced cuts in its 1999 season than Ian Albery warned that without the revenue from the Opera House residency, Sadler's Wells would go bust. 'This has blown out twenty-five weeks of programming and unless something happens very soon we will be closed,' he said.[5] The rebuilt Sadler's Wells, due to open on 12 October, was also four million pounds short of its £48 million building costs.

Albery threatened to sue Covent Garden for a million pounds in lost revenue and penalty clauses. The ROH retorted that it was being made a 'scapegoat' by Sadler's Wells to divert attention from its own financial crisis.[6] The Blairs were alerted. Nobody in authority wanted to be held responsible for closing their local theatre.

On the day the Wells reopened, the Arts Council announced that it had 'secured compensation' of £1.35 million pounds for Sadler's Wells. The deal, it was reported, 'amounts to a full settlement of

Covent Garden's contract, give or take £50,000'.[7] Michael Berkeley, a member of the ROH board, gave a yelp of anguish. He admitted that Covent Garden were liable for a million but 'expressed dismay that (ACE) was insisting that Covent Garden pay a further £350,000'.[8] This seemed like punitive retribution from a Council which had its thumbprints all over the Sadler's Wells-ROH contract and bore equal responsibility for its fulfilment.* There was no escaping the conclusion that Covent Garden, far from being the flagship of British arts, was now the favourite whipping boy. Six months later, the Arts Council coughed up, without a squeak of protest, an additional six million pound Lottery grant to Sadler's Wells to cover the construction shortfall. Had Covent Garden been able to rely on such generosity, it would never have landed in the present mess.

On Armistice Day, 11 November, Chris Smith met Bernard Haitink and bowed to his terms. He also assured Lord Sainsbury and Mrs Duffield that the Royal companies would eventually return to year-round performance. The donors unstopped their cheques and Haitink withdrew his resignation, once he was convinced that the orchestra would continue to play through the following year. The consequences of this climbdown were generally uncalculated.

The orchestra was costing the company four million pounds a year. In the judgement of most conductors, it was not the equal of London's four self-employed concert orchestras, and on ballet nights it played appallingly. Approaches had been made to the RPO and one other ensemble to take over at Covent Garden if the ROH orchestra were to be disbanded. Engaging independent orchestras, free of holiday, sickness and pension costs, would have saved the ROH well over a million pounds a year.

Opera festivals like Glyndebourne and Salzburg were all the more exciting for having top-flight international orchestras playing in the pit. Newer opera companies like Los Angeles were formed without an orchestra, relying on the local philharmonic. There was no compelling reason for Covent Garden to keep its own band except for union resistance, sentimental attachments and Haitink's solidarity with an orchestra in which his wife had once played. Unwilling to grasp the nettle, Chris Smith caved in and the rescue plan was aborted. Every critical issue was fudged into a formula that allowed

* in fact, the ACE ultimately paid the £350,000 itself

Smith to release extra funds and Michael Kaiser to start work with a clean sheet.

A few days after Kaiser's arrival, we had breakfast at the Waldorf Hotel. A pale, roly-poly man in his mid-forties, Kaiser was sounding out opinion formers without taking much interest in the causes of past discomfort. His eyes were fixed on a future in which the opera house would offer access to all and the highest standard of performance. It would be a light unto the nations, developing a training programme for managers from other companies and unifying British arts behind their greatest asset. The two smaller theatres within the building would enable them to engage, for the first time, with solo and chamber performances and develop educational outreach to untold heights. 'This is a group of people that has gone through a war,' he said, 'and I want to give them hope.'

There was something admirable about his optimism, in view of the company's rampant unpopularity. Kaiser was brisk and business-like, courteous and attentive, yet he appeared self-effacing to the point that I could hardly identify a single personality trait. My mystification was widely shared. Casting around the American opera and orchestral sectors and their attendant media, I found hardly anyone who had heard of Kaiser, and the few who had met him knew nothing about him. Even in the ballet world, where he had performed most of his wonders, people described him as efficient and valuable but could not bring themselves to say what he was like. Michael Kaiser was a man without a shadow – a consultant who came to the aid of ailing organizations and left them feeling much better. Covent Garden represented the biggest challenge of his life. When his mother read the *Telegraph* headline that greeted his arrival – 'Chaos Reigns as Kaiser enters Opera House'[9] – she phoned him and said, 'have you gone off your head?'

A New Yorker by birth, he would sing in a synagogue choir on Saturday mornings and spend the afternoon watching rehearsals of the Philharmonic, where his grandfather had played. He thought of having his voice trained professionally, and thought better of it. He went to Brandeis University and MIT, and in his mid-twenties formed a business consultancy that attracted such blue-chip clients as General Motors and IBM. He sold up in 1985 and went to work in the arts, for the State Ballet of Missouri, the Pierpont Morgan Library and the Alvin Ailey Dance Theater Foundation. In 1994 he

founded his second consultancy, this time devoted to arts management. His clients included the Detroit Symphony Orchestra and the
South African government, his only overseas involvement. In 1995,
he took command of American Ballet Theater as its executive
director.

Four years was the longest he had spent in any post, and he
seemed to make neither enemies nor close friends. Deborah
MacMillan, invited to dinner at his apartment, found herself among
a group of his MIT contemporaries who were running huge companies and making millions. 'You should know,' said one of these
high-fliers, 'that Michael was the brightest of us all.'

Kaiser himself admitted to no attachments. He had a dog, which
he left with a friend in New York. His greatest joy in life, he said, was
to make things work.

The parallels with Webster were startling: both were single men
and single-minded with no life to speak of outside the theatre. Like
Webster, he never appeared flustered. Covent Garden was about to
pass from the hurly-burly of four chief executives in less than two
years to the deep, deep calm of Michael Kaiser.

But there was more to Kaiser than a good bedside manner and a
willingness to tell people what they wanted to hear. He represented
a change of style that caught English colleagues unprepared. One of
Kaiser's first acts was to dispense with the three-person secretariat
that had served the chief executive since Isaacs' time. He required
one secretary, and when she was out to lunch Michael Kaiser
answered the phone himself. There were to be no barriers or
formalities at the top.

Anthony Dowell was the first to be struck – dumbstruck – by the
new chief's style. A few days before Kaiser's arrival, the Royal
Ballet's leading male dancer, Tetsuya 'Teddy' Kumakawa decided to
break away and form his own troupe, the K Ballet. 'I'm very disappointed,' said Dowell. Two weeks later five more dancers defected
to join him, leaving the company with just three principal full-time
men. Dowell was devastated. 'What are we going to do?' he sighed.
'This is a terrific opportunity,' said Kaiser. 'Go out and hire the five
best male dancers in the world.' There was a deathly hush. No one
had ever suggested anything so bold at the Royal Ballet since
Nureyev shook the company's foundations. What is more, Kaiser
was the first person to run the company with real ballet know-how.

Kaiser's approach to problems was not to cover up or deny but to admit the difficulty and promise, 'we'll fix it'. His transparency was rare in the arts, and in the tight-lipped ROH it amounted to a cultural revolution. At one stage, when I challenged the budgets, he invited me in to go over the books, itemizing profit and loss with no apparent concern for commercial confidentiality. His candour was not so much refreshing as disarming. Within weeks, the press had turned from sour to supportive. Suddenly, everyone was willing Michael Kaiser to succeed. The *Guardian* headlined him 'The Turnaround King of Opera',[10] and the catchphrase caught on. Soon after, the *New York Times* reported that 'Mr Turnaround' had become his nickname. Kaiser made no objection. 'It does help to come from the outside,' he said, 'because my experience of troubled organizations is that when you are in the midst of all the problems, everyone is focused on the past. Who caused the problem? How did we get into this mess? They point fingers at each other, the staff blames the board, the board blames the staff. And no one is saying, "where do we go from here?"'[11]

It was not all smooth sailing from here on in. The first choice for artistic director of the Royal Opera turned them down. Francesca Zambello, the American director of *Paul Bunyan*, said she could not take the job, because no one would tell her who was in charge – herself as artistic director, or Kaiser as ROH executive director. In a letter to Southgate, she said, 'at present the managerial structure, and my own commitments, make this an enticing possibility best contemplated in the future.' To a press inquiry she added, 'I don't think they really know what they want. The company needs to rethink its whole role.'[12]

There was better luck on the conductor front. While Gergiev, Gatti, Rattle and Riccardo Chailly had declared themselves unavailable, and a campaign for Mark Elder, the former ENO music director, ran out of steam, a little-known London-born Italian entered the frame.

Antonio Pappano was music director of the Monnaie Theatre in Brussels and a regular at Bayreuth. He had the reputation of being able to work with anyone – indeed, he was the only conductor who could propitiate the volatile lovebirds, Angela Gheorghiu and Roberto Alagna.

Pappano had been working with voices since he was ten years old, coming home from school to a Marylebone studio to play piano for the singers his father was coaching. A family tragedy, the death of a sibling, took the Pappanos to a fresh start in America, but for Tony, just short of forty, the chance to lead Covent Garden was a wheel turned full circle. 'I have been told that I am on the list,' he remarked in Brussels that winter. 'I have not been formally courted but I'm being told what's going on.'[13] A fortnight later he was formally appointed.

Pappano had experienced Covent Garden at its worst, in 1989. 'It was a nightmare,' he said. 'I had, in the first seven nights of *Bohème*, seven different tenors. Jerry Hadley cancelled the première and Dennis O'Neill dropped out twice. Then *William Tell* was pulled one night and they asked me for an extra *Bohème* – and in the pit I found a *William Tell* orchestra. I thought I had a lot to say about *Bohème*, but the situation just got me in knots and it didn't go as it should. I got blasted in the press. People warned me, don't read the reviews.'

In another opera house, someone would have thrown an arm round his shoulder and taken him out to get drunk. At Covent Garden he was treated like a leper. 'I don't remember anyone in the house who was on my side. You walk around, and people know you've been blasted.' He had never returned. What swayed him was Southgate's insistence – Pappano was an EMI recording artist – and an instant rapport with Kaiser. In accepting the job, he insisted that Kaiser extend his own contract to 2005, so that they would have at least three years together in harness.

His appointment solved a nagging structural dilemma. Eyre had decreed that the Royal Opera needed an artistic director at the helm. Pappano said: 'It has to be clear that the music director is the artistic head of the house. He should be there at least seven months of the year. In addition to planning and conducting operas, he should be playing chamber music with the orchestra musicians, doing recitals with young artists.'

This was just what the doctor ordered. Pappano would be the first music director since Solti to know the nuts and bolts of an opera house, the intricacies of programming and the rewards of foresight. He would also be the company's youngest ever music director. The future was starting to look brighter.

At a topping-out ceremony, Chris Smith promised that Covent Garden would become 'a model of good practice in education and access'. Southgate declared that the building 'belonged to the nation', paid for by ordinary people out of their Lottery bets. A gaggle of local residents heckled the proceedings. Eerily, a hydraulic yellow van drew up to clean the street-lamps. On its side was the legend: David Webster Limited.

In the summer of 1999, Kaiser declared Covent Garden's financial crisis to be over. 'We will not be going back for more money to the Arts Council saying we need an extra bit otherwise we can't finish the building – that won't happen,' he said. 'Nor will we say we need an extra bit, otherwise we can't have the season we planned. While we want as much as we can get, I am realistic about the difficulties that all governments have in exceeding inflation when it comes to arts grants.'[14]

This was music to Chris Smith's ears. Not only was Kaiser planning to run a full season on twenty million pounds subsidy, but he was planning to raise an endowment to underpin new work. When the house reopened, said Kaiser, 'we are going to be in the best financial shape we have known in our history'.

For two dedicated years, Vivien Duffield had been going around tapping people and companies for money. 'We've got Vivien coming Monday morning,' one would hear. 'She thinks she's going to get fifty. She'll be lucky to get ten.' Duffield was a shrewd judge of donor character. 'I used to write on a piece of paper what I thought I was going to get, and I was usually right,' she said.

'It was quite businesslike with the corporates. We gave them something that they wanted. It was based on the Glyndebourne scale. They had sort of priced themselves into leagues beforehand. But I'm much better at individuals.'

She had perfected a technique of making a request that could not be refused. 'The only reason I can do it is that people do it to me, and I'm quite impervious about it,' she laughed. 'I go to Israel three times a year, where the word chutzpah was invented.

'There's a Jewish form of fundraising which my Uncle David was expert at. He'd get up at a dinner for Nightingale House (an old age home) and say, "Come on Shmulley, look what your wife's got round her neck, and look at that new car outside – what's the number plate? A new Bentley. What's this you're giving me? £10,000? Come on now, you can make it twenty." And he'd tear up the pledge. At least I haven't resorted to that.'

Duffield was tantalizingly close to her hundred-million target and focusing on small donations. She started a seat-naming campaign, in which anyone could put a plaque on a seat from £500 upwards. A number of ballerinas clubbed together and named a seat in memory of a man who used to send them flowers every night. One woman gave £5,000 for a seat in the stalls on which the anonymous plaque read: 'the seat in which I met the love of my life'.

On a rather grander scale, a pair of Darcey Bussell fans named her dressing-room and a woman whose mother had been in the chorus put her name on their rehearsal room. At the top of the range, three donors had given over ten million – herself, Sainsbury and the Floral Trust. Thirteen more had given over one million. With time running out, the total was in the upper eighties and stalling. During the Eyre review she had lost a million-pound pledge and she was busy trying to woo it back.

The final windfall came by a circuitous route. Alberto Vilar was a Cuban-American who made his fortune tracking new-tech stocks in the dawn of mass computing. He had been among the earliest investors in Microsoft and now he was giving large sums away to the places that gave him most pleasure.

He gave twenty-five million dollars to the Metropolitan Opera and four million more to the Salzburg Festival. He liked to be known as the biggest donor wherever he gave and loved seeing his name in lights. His favourite director was Franco Zeffirelli. When the Italian arrayed his forces on the Met stage, Vilar liked to say that he could see where every dollar was spent; he had no time for minimal stagings.

As co-ordinator of his munificence, he employed Charles Kay, Solti's former secretary, but Vilar liked to make his own decisions and was touchy about how he was received. At a post-concert dinner in London, he sat next to the banker Jacob Rothschild and his wife, Serena, who was involved with the Covent Garden appeal. They put him in touch with Sir Colin Southgate, but Vilar did not like what he was told. Southgate said he could not be the lead donor, since that honour had been claimed by Duffield and Sainsbury. He was about to walk away when Michael Kaiser suggested that, for ten million pounds, they could rename the Floral Hall after him. Others would claim credit for the donation, but Vilar made no secret of the clinching factor. 'If it hadn't been for Michael Kaiser,' he told a business friend, 'I would never have given money to Covent Garden.' Kaiser had given the donor all he wanted without yielding an inch on principle or precedence. Vilar was keen on education. The Vilar Floral Hall would help spread opera to new enthusiasts.[15]

*

One morning in the middle of the year, Sir Anthony Dowell was feeling weighed down by company reshuffles and continuing press attacks when he looked out of the window at the building site across Floral Street. 'Come on,' he said to his secretary, Jeanetta, and to Anthony Russell-Roberts, 'let's have a look.' After a hard-hat tour, Dowell said to himself 'it's going to be something wonderful'. He decided at that moment to see the Royal Ballet into its quarters, and then leave as quickly as possible. 'I have been through the mill in the last few years,' he exhaled.[16]

The building was breathtaking. The ballet rehearsal and dressing-rooms were bathed in sunlight, a far cry from dingy Baron's Court. The fourth-floor staff canteen had one of the best views in London and people ascending the escalator opposite the main entrance could catch a glimpse of Nelson's column if they inclined their heads to the right. There was a sun terrace running around half the roof, giving views of Whitehall and the River Thames. For the first time, the Royal Opera House was looking outward, behaving like a part of the great city.

The entrance halls were airy and marbled. Gone were the red baize curtains and the flunkey at the door, the choking of dust and the claustrophobic sensation, 'abandon hope all ye who enter'.

Jeremy Dixon, the architect, confessed himself 'amazed that the board didn't lose heart and give up two or three times during this process'. He had designed a huge backstage, with room for six sets to be stored intact and thirty more broken up (the rest were stored in Wales).

Everything had been constructed according to instructions given almost thirty years earlier. The potential of new technology hardly entered the picture. Barcelona, which was rebuilding the Liceo after fire in less than two years, had included planning for virtual-reality stage sets and live-relay screens around the lobby. The Met had introduced seat-back surtitles, so much easier on the eye than a screen hung above the proscenium. None of these innovations were considered at Covent Garden or mentioned to the architect. As technology hurtled ahead into a new millennium, this was definedly a twentieth-century building for two nineteenth-century art forms – a museum, to all intents and purposes, rather than a magnet for the lively arts.

*

Early in November, New Labour banned most hereditary peers from the House of Lords. Among those disenfranchised was the twelfth Earl of Drogheda, Derry Moore, photographer son of the former Covent Garden chairman. He lamented the passing of tradition in a *Guardian* diary and found greater distress among the lords who remained than among those who departed into history.

The ballet moved into their new quarters that week, thrilling to unaccustomed luxury. The orchestra checked in soon after, finding showers, lockers and proper shelves for their instruments. Some rehearsal rooms were unheated, others freshly painted, giving grief to the singers. On the 22nd, Cherie Blair bowled up to open the Linbury Studio Theatre, donated by John Sainsbury and Anya Linden. Her pregnancy was hot news and press photographers were out in force. A multi-ethnic audience of kids from local schools had been herded in to see their first ballet. 'For too long,' said Mrs Blair, 'the message that went out from this house was that arts are for the privileged few. All that has changed now.' The children sat mutely through a routine of classical ballet, livening up when the music turned minimalist and the dancing modern in *'Still Life' at the Penguin Café*. As the kids went off to consume boxed lunches in the Floral Hall, I saw the diminutive American director, Peter Sellars, leaving the stage door looking worried. Trouble? We would soon hear about it.

The next morning it transpired that Covent Garden was cancelling one of its three opening operas, and by far the most exciting – György Ligeti's *Le grand macabre*, imported from Salzburg where it had been a huge hit. The reason given was software failures, affecting the movement of scene-shifting wagons. The truth was slightly more complex. One stagehand admitted that they were inadequately trained – three weeks in a classroom before having to stage a full rehearsal. Half the stage crew were new, and the machinery was complex. 'One night it was the wagons, the next the hydraulics. No one knew why,' he said.[17] Kaiser had shed his jacket and put his shoulder to the wheel, to no obvious purpose except raising morale.

Cancelling the Ligeti opera relieved last-minute rehearsal pressure, but infuriated the composer and the conductor, Esa-Pekka Salonen, who were among the last to be told. Without Salzburg topping, the opening programme looked weakly repetitive – a new *Falstaff* with Bryn Terfel and a repeat of Birtwistle's *Gawain*. The ballet was no livelier than the usual Christmas fare.

A squalid row had broken out between the opera and the ballet as to who should go first on opening night. Haitink, on seeing Dowell's ballet programme, said it was far too long. He offered to boycott the opening night unless cuts were made. Dowell had designed a synoptic portrait of the Royal Ballet's work from 1946 to the present. He slashed his programme to an hour and seventeen minutes, shedding contributions by John Cranko and Jerome Robbins. Haitink was still not pacified, grumbling that it was too much for his poor orchestra, who would be overtired by the time they reached Wagner in the second half.

Although the evening was meant to open with Darcey Bussell dancing a spell from *Sleeping Beauty* with which she had put the house to rest thirty months before, Dowell decided to yield precedence in order to save the show. 'Would you like to go first?' he offered Haitink, who gracelessly accepted. The legend of two arts in one company had never seemed more ridiculous.

Tension mounted as the opening approached. Tradition, decorum and board preference dictated that it should be a black-tie occasion. A message arrived from Downing Street: did it have to be black tie? The Prime Minister hated dressing up. When the form was confirmed, Downing Street spin-doctors went tale-bearing to the tabloids about the toffs at Covent Garden. Some people in power never tired of playing class war.

On 1 December, Tony and Cherie Blair arrived in black tie, long gown and matching fixed grins. The Queen, with Prince Philip two scowls behind, glided through the portals in an ankle-length cream and gold dress designed to match the refurbished interiors. Sir Colin Southgate seemed to be forcibly restraining himself from taking Her Majesty by the arm. Vivien Duffield bobbed and curtsied, Michael Kaiser gave a trim little bow. In a breach with tradition, the royal party forsook the Royal Box and sat with the political classes, among them two ex-premiers, Thatcher and Heath. Of all the élite guests, Queen Elizabeth the Queen Mother, now ninety-nine years old, was the only one who seemed to be enjoying herself, perhaps remembering the night almost fifty-four years earlier when she had challenged the lack of refreshments. Tonight, it was free champagne for all and, as in 1946, nothing at all to eat.

Past chief executives jostled chairmen past and present, assuring one another that there were no hard feelings. The great and the good turned out in force. Only the gifted were absent. Joan Sutherland and

Kiri te Kanawa had not been invited. 'We weren't asked,' said Dame Joan tersely. Art took second place on the invitation list to social and political rank.

Colin Southgate was the first on stage, acclaiming the new opera house as 'the most technically advanced theatre in the world'. Then the microphone failed. BBC screens were twice blacked out during the evening by loss of power. There were no stage sets and the house felt unready. Chris Smith called it 'a miracle' and confessed there were times he never believed it would come into being. That afternoon he had been called to the floor of the Commons to admit that the hundred and twenty million pound Lottery grant he had approved for an Olympic stadium in Wembley had been a mistake since the space could not in his estimation accommodate both track and team-sport events. At least half the money was irrecoverable. With one stroke of the pen he had blown three-quarters of the amount of Lottery money invested in Covent Garden. Yet there was no howl from the tabloids, because the money was wasted with good sporting intentions, and no grilling from Kaufman because there was not as much fun to be had in exposing sporting negligence as there was in mocking the arts.

When the music finally struck up, spirits sank. Haitink had decided to open with the *Oberon* overture that Weber wrote for Covent Garden in 1826. Next came Domingo and Deborah Polaski in the love duet from *Walküre*. An assorted septet delivered the finale of *Fidelio*. It was a woefully becalmed festivity, lumpen with German dumplings and not a twinkle of light or an echo of the company's national identity. Two of the female singers were American, the third came from Lapland. Had England run out of sopranos who could sing a Beethoven set piece?

The ballet, by contrast, glittered and soared. Bussell reopened all eyes with *Beauty*'s Rose Adagio in the 1946 choreography, kicking off a chronological survey compiled with wit and fine taste. Ashton was remembered in clips from *Symphonic Variations*, *Cinderella* and later glories. Nureyev's role in *Bayadère* was revived by Irek Mukhamedov. Guillem swooped and swooned in MacMillan's *Manon* and Bussell and Jonathan Cope ran away with *Prince of the Pagodas*. The minimalist scores and modern choreography for '*Still Life*' *at the Penguin Café* and *Fearful Symmetries* showed that there was still some life remaining in dance, which is more than could have been said for the opera. When the curtain fell, first priorities had been restored. The ballet had triumphed at Covent Garden, while the opera seemed confused, stolid and uncertain. The wheel had turned full circle.

CHAPTER 13

Lie Back and Think of England
(2000–2100 European time)

EVER SINCE THE Festival of Britain in 1951, Labour had looked upon itself as the party of parties. The bash it put on for the opening of the third Christian millennium was designed to wow the world, no expense spared. A chain of fireworks along the Thames, an orange cloud of parachutists descending on Tower Bridge, the 'biggest ever' street parade and, to cap it all, a countdown entertainment at the Millennium Dome in the presence of the Queen and everyone who counted in New Labour's vision of New Britain. Paul Daniel and the orchestra of English National Opera performed a spiritual new meditation by Sir John Tavener, who protested at the absence of God's name in the text he had been given to set. Willard White, the West Indian-born bass, sang 'Amazing Grace'.

At the stroke of midnight, Tony Blair and Her Majesty clinked champagne glasses. He then *lèse-majesté*'d his arm into hers for a rendition of 'Auld Lang Syne'. After that, it was party all the way with a riot of Brazilian dancing and an 'erotic aerial ballet' beneath the brave new cupola. There was some muttering at an absence of indigenous relevance, but the show was intended to reflect a nation that had emerged from primordial insularity to embrace all the world had to offer in randomly equal opportunity.

The Dome, designed by the New Labour peer and former Arts Council deputy chairman Richard Rogers, emblemified the dawning century, its pylons stretching hopefully into the sky. Blair called it 'the envy of the world'. It had cost £758 million to build, of which a generous £449 million had come from the Millennium Commission, using National Lottery funds. This was almost six times the amount invested in the new ROH, and the Dome was not expected to survive longer than twenty-five years. Is it a visionary leap, wondered the novelist J. G. Ballard, 'or a gigantic folly, the equivalent of the South Sea Bubble, a vast balloon inflated by the promises of PR men?'[1]

The answer came with the speed of e-commerce. By the end of its opening week, the Dome was in trouble, running well below visitor targets and drawing glum reactions for the length of its queues and the mediocrity of its exhibits. By the end of the month, the Dome's operators had to go back to Millennium Commission for a sixty-million-pound 'loan' to enable them to continue trading. The money would be repaid from profits, they promised, but early projections indicated an annual loss of as much as twenty-three million pounds. 'This is a misuse of donated funds,' said the Institute of Charity Fund Managers.[2] Every pound that was poured into the Dome was a pound taken away from good causes and the arts.

The subsidy per Dome visitor amounted to thirty pounds, on top of the twenty pound admission price. This compared with £27.50 seat subsidy at the Royal Opera House, and eight pounds at Sadler's Wells.[3] The Dome was draining the nation of funds for education and enlightenment. A week into its second month, the Dome's chief executive, Jennie Page, was replaced by a Frenchman, a marketing executive from Euro Disney. The putative second Festival of Britain had made a mockery of national pride, bypassing the creative gene and substituting a rush of Gallic fast-sell gimmickry.

It was not the only post-war shibboleth to crack. 'Labour admits NHS in crisis,'[4] blared a front-page splash that winter as the crucible of the Welfare State proved unable to cope with a mild flu epidemic. Patients in Kent were shuttled across to French hospitals and German television viewers were warned to leave Britain fast if they felt sick. Britain had the lowest survival rate for heart disease and cancer in western Europe.

A fifty-five-year-old woman in Middlesborough was told that she would have to pay ten thousand pounds if she wanted a routine course of aggressive chemotherapy for ovarian cancer, as her local health authority could not afford it. 'I just didn't believe it,' said Jackie O'Donnell, 'because in this country we were brought up to believe that we would get the best treatment available.'[5] In Leeds, seventy-three-year-old Mavis Skeet was sentenced to death when her operation for oesophageal cancer was postponed four times until it became inoperable.

Tony Blair was shocked at this 'dreadful' latter case and accepted 'the responsibility to put this situation right'.[6] But it would take more than money to repair the nation's health. The NHS was now the largest employer in Europe, a behemoth in which cost control was all but impossible except in the most generalized forms. But no politician dared break it up. Of all the post-war values, the NHS remained a sacred shrine. Like a five-headed deity, no one believed it brought good health, but it could not be touched – just in case.

At the heart of its problems was a shortage of funds that derived partly from past economic crises and partly from expensive new drugs and treatments coming on to the market. When Viagra was released, promising renewed potency and mental equilibrium to men with erectile dysfunction, Blair's Health Secretary Frank Dobson announced at first that the pills, costing eight pounds each, would not be available on the NHS. He later modified his position, urging doctors to prescribe Viagra only in 'exceptional circumstances', such as paralysis victims. This advice was ruled illegal by a High Court judge,[7] but few health authorities could, in any case, afford to dispense the drug.

Spending on health in Britain was running at £55.7 billion a year, or 6.8 per cent of gross domestic product. This compared with 9.6 per cent in France, 10.7 per cent in Germany and 14 per cent in the United States. New Labour in its election campaign had promised an extra billion pounds for the NHS. Frank Dobson, when he entered office, was told that this would amount to roughly one week's spending, and would make no appreciable difference.[8]

Blair now pledged to raise health spending within six years to European levels, but much of the money was bound to be whittled away in wage rises for the gargantuan payroll, without appreciable improvements in patient care. Blair ordered the appointment of a national supervisor of critical care – a cancer 'czar', a heart 'supremo', swelling the bureaucracy still further.

There were two alternatives: either raise taxes, or encourage a higher uptake of private health insurance, as prevailed in the United States and most of Europe. Neither option was electorally acceptable, and no mainstream politician was prepared to propose more than a tinkering at the edges with this ailing relic of national consensus. England, on the threshold of a new millennium, was literally the sick man of Europe, its leaders unable to venture a cure.

The opening of the Royal Opera House was not much happier than the Dome. After the gala came Verdi's *Falstaff*, which Haitink conducted heavily, as if it were Wagner. Bryn Terfel played the comic hero with an apt blend of pomposity and self-pity, but the rest of the cast was undistinguished and Paul Brown's set resembled the BBC's cultish pre-school programme, *Teletubbies*. Backstage, crews wrestled with untested machinery and stubborn software.

By mid-January, twelve opera performances had been cancelled, including a schools matinée of *Gawain*, which left teachers and pupils bewailing their waste of curricular preparation. A ballet triple bill was abandoned mid-way through the performance when the sets would not budge. In *Nutcracker*, the Christmas tree failed to materialize and in *Gawain* the audience were kept waiting forty minutes for a trap-door to open. Many left during the delays to catch the last train home. There was not much by way of apology or compensation.

Patrons complained of a strident public address system and a lack of customer care at the front of the house, where the attendants were new and half-trained. 'I have been coming here for fifty-three years, and nobody knows me any more,' wailed a retired gentleman's outfitter.

The Crush Bar had been demolished and the space turned over to corporate entertainment. The fashionable round bars in the Floral Hall were crowded and lacked conviviality. The Hall itself looked like a cross between an airport concourse and a shopping arcade. It was soon to be hired out for barmitzvahs and weddings.

There were voluminous complaints about ticketing. Kaiser had promised to bring down prices. In fact, many seats were more expensive than before. A former ROH singer, Joan Carlyle, paid £150 for a seat with partial sightlines. Sir Peter Hall complained that not many people could, like himself, afford a pair of £150 seats for a *Rosenkavalier*. Chris Smith had let it be known that he did not want to see the 'same old faces' in the stalls and expected further price cuts to attract 'a better social mix'. There were, at last, facilities for the disabled, but MPs complained that twenty-four seats were far too few.

By mid-January, Bectu were demanding that the house should be shut until backstage problems were resolved. The Musicians Union said, 'our patience is running out'. The *Sunday Times* reported that the orchestra was in revolt and that a million pounds had been lost in the opening month. Kaiser kept his cool. 'All along we have evaluated whether we can get shows on safely and efficiently,' he said. 'So long as we can do that, we stay open.' The losses incurred had been about one-third of press guesstimates. He was negotiating with Bectu to allow all-night working on wagon tests.

In most other countries, the curtain would have fallen there and then. France, when it opened the Bastille Opéra for the glorious bicentenary of the 1789 Revolution, shut it again for the rest of the year until officials were satisfied that it worked. But this was England, where the state kept its hands off the arts until they lost money or offended ministers. Covent Garden could not afford to shut down for fear it would not be allowed to reopen. The Prime Minister hated the place, the culture secretary was looking to score points and the rest of the arts regarded it still as the whore of Babylon, a place of immoral and wasteful excess. Kaiser had no alternative but to put a brave face on the setbacks and carry on sweet-talking until the software came right. He was unable to propose radical measures without upsetting a fragile status quo. Like the NHS, the ROH was trapped in the misery of its own myth.

By March, matters had settled down sufficiently for people to attend the opera house in reasonable expectation that a show would start and finish on time, and they might retrieve their coats afterwards with less than half an hour's wait. A smile was seen on Anthony Dowell's drawn face, though that might have been an indication of demob-happiness. As Dowell put together tribute evenings to Ashton and MacMillan and the first revival for forty years of Ninette de Valois' *Coppélia*, televised live, his successor was about to be announced.

There were no fewer than fifty applicants, ten of them serious contenders. Kevin McKenzie of American Ballet Theater was Kaiser's favourite, along with Ross MacGibbon, a former RB dancer and busy filmmaker. Derek Deane, head of English National Ballet, was in the reckoning, as was Nureyev's Paris deputy, Patricia Ruanne, who had the support of the Sainsburys. Lynn Seymour put in a late bid, partnered by the choreographer Mark Baldwin. Parties formed behind Irek Mukhamedov, approaching the end of his dancing career, and Sylvie Guillem, who had just revived *Marguerite and Armand* with the Parisian Nicolas Le Riche, the first pair to dance the roles since Fonteyn and Nureyev.

The victor was an Australian, unknown in Britain. Ross Stretton, head of Australian Ballet, had not seen the Royal Ballet dance for three years but had strong views on its problems. 'I think it needs somebody to take a look from the outside, somebody with no axe to grind,' he said.[9] The company had to be 'remotivated' and would benefit from working with the European choreographers Jiri Kylian and Maurice Béjart, and their disciples. Kaiser, who had admired Stretton as a dancer at ABT, was impressed by his energy. Deborah MacMillan, who remembered him as one of her husband's New York principals, said: 'Kenneth thought Ross was a beautifully trained dancer, a perfect partner and a good company man.'[10] Not everyone was convinced that this was what the company needed. Since the death of MacMillan, whose works were danced in a dozen companies the world over, the Royal Ballet had not made a single contribution to dance repertoire. What it needed, more than Mr Motivator, was creative force at its helm, a choreographer who would remind the world of the uniqueness of English ballet, if such uniqueness still existed – and, if not, what was the company's purpose?

Another Australian, Gailene Stock, took over that month as head of the Royal Ballet School. She bemoaned the lack of good British male dancers. 'I am wondering why it is harder to find the raw talent here than it was in Australia,' she told Ismene Brown. 'Maybe it's the sedentary lives they lead in front of the television and the computer.'[11] Had English ballet fallen so low that it could be mocked and run by ex-colonials who, when Madam ruled the roost, had barely a tutu between them from Sydney to Perth? Certainly, its fortunes seemed to be on the slide. The men Dowell had imported to replace his defectors were Cuban, Russian and Swedish. Viviana Durante, the company's complete all-rounder, followed Adam Cooper into freelance exile. Stars of English National Ballet posed in their underwear for *Loaded*, a lads' mag, which billed them on its cover as 'Bra-less'. There was not much left to shed, it seemed, before ballet in Britain hit rock-bottom. Andrea Quinn, music director of the Royal Ballet, resigned after clashes with the Covent Garden orchestra and joined New York City Ballet.

Yet, early that year, the men of Matthew Bourne's unsubsidized *Swan Lake* returned for a second run in the West End, demonstrating that there was a viable audience for classical dance and an appetite for fresh ideas that seemed to have deserted the public sector. Bourne was staging *My Fair Lady* for the Royal National Theatre, but could not find the time or inclination to work with the Royal Ballet. He was about to make a bold move. In March, his company,

Adventures in Motion Pictures, took a lease on the vacant Old Vic, where Lilian Baylis had founded the public-spirited tradition, the stage where Ninette de Valois created English ballet. Bourne was sensitive to the symbolism. 'Anybody who knows me,' he said, 'knows that I love the history of theatre and dance, and the Old Vic is where British music and dance were born.'[12] It was a homecoming of sorts, perhaps a new beginning.

Elsewhere in the arts, resentments rumbled and heaved. Sir Richard Eyre, in a public lecture,[13] implored the Government to appoint a 'theatre czar' to rescue the drama sector from intensive care. Three symphony orchestras teetered on the brink of insolvency, awaiting a rescue package from the Arts Council that came with strings attached. The Council had squandered whatever trust it once owned among the arts to deal kindly and fairly with clients. Gerry Robinson, its chairman, announced that he would not serve a second term. Chris Smith formed a ministerial unit called Quest whose task was to monitor the Arts Council and, potentially, to take over arts funding in the event of its abolition, which many deemed desirable.

The saddest of spectres was Sir Peter Hall, obliged at seventy to work abroad because his own country would not sustain his brimming ambitions. Hall had asked the Arts Council for a half-million pound guarantee against loss – not a subsidy, he insisted – to continue running a repertory company that he had founded at the Old Vic and taken to the West End. They refused. New Labour was no friend to old age. Hall threatened to form an alternative Arts Council, made up of real artists, who would expose the ACE as a pen-pushing sham.

He went to America to direct Shakespeare in Los Angeles, and again to stage a cycle of ten new plays set in ancient Greece. 'I wanted to do it here with the Royal Shakespeare Company,' he lamented. 'They would have done it, but they haven't got any money. In Denver, population 3.5 million they found me eight million dollars. Here, population fifty-five million, nothing. It drives me mad, this country. Chris Smith is nice enough but he has no clout. The arts are starved of cash. Blair doesn't care. He isn't remotely interested. And I voted for him . . .'[14]

His was a common wail – that Governments of both parties refused to sustain the arts with amounts so tiny, 'they wouldn't even show up in the national accounts'.[15] Jeremy Isaacs, back in his television habitat, never tired of telling people how much easier it was to run an international opera house in Europe, with twice as much subsidy as in Britain. On the Continent, however, opera and ballet were state-run operations. Peter Jonas, the intendant in Munich, had a senior Treasury official sitting in an adjacent room to tell him what he could, and could not, put on. There was great respect for tradition in Bavaria, but limited room for adventure. The vitality of English opera and dance was rooted in a mixed economy of state and private subsidy, and Jonas would sometimes look back wistfully at the hair-raising risks he had taken at ENO.

In Europe, too, governments were cutting back on art subsidies in an age of mounting social costs. The German capital, Berlin, with three opera houses and seven orchestras, was facing severe rationalization. Italy was looking to reduce its thirteen opera houses, and La Scala was being encouraged to go private if it could find sufficient corporate sponsorship. France had stopped building cultural monuments, amid a rash of recriminations. The opera house in Lyon, lavishly rebuilt in 1993, was closed down after inspectors declared the stage and its machinery too dangerous for use. Similar problems afflicted the Bastille, the Bibliothèque Nationale and the Paris musical Conservatoire.

In England, the funding emphasis shifted away from live performance to capital conservation. The biggest expansion in British arts over the last decade of the twentieth century was the Tate Gallery, which built offshoots in Liverpool and Cornwall and a massive annexe opposite St Paul's Cathedral, designed to represent 'modern' – more precisely, post-modern – British art. Museum culture was redefining itself in an age of computers and virtual reality, while performing culture was mired in unchanged conditions of fixed labour costs, fickle audiences, and an ever-shrinking base of educated audiences who would spend their last penny to see a show. 'There must be vibrant audiences longing to come, fighting to come, pushing their way into spaces to live an experience that they feel is life-enhancing,' said Peter Brook, the theatrical doyen-in-exile. 'That is what theatre is about,' he told an awards audience, 'and yet – the opposite is true. The impossible-to-define theatre of next year, and the next hundred years, and the next millennium, will never happen unless that audience-cash-success criterion ... is also questioned, and with equal confidence one acclaims the bold work that empties the theatre and asserts the right to fail.'[16]

That right had been progressively withdrawn from the Royal Opera House in particular, and English performing arts in general, over a quarter of a century. The need for success produced safety-first programming which, in turn, foisted a fusty image upon lyric theatre. Opera, after its Big Bang mini-boom in the late 1980s, reverted overwhelmingly to its middle-class, middle-aged core audiences and ceased to be 'cool'.

In a culture of instant e-mails, two-minute pop-songs and whittled down attention spans, a full evening at the opera was more than most twenty-somethings could contemplate, let alone afford. The cross-section of teachers, clerical workers, college students, other ranks and curiosity seekers who thronged the Royal Opera House in its formative period were now banned – both by price and by self-perception. This was not the sort of place where young people would feel comfortable or find like-minded contemporaries. Unless some educational and economic miracle were to make opera irresistible and accessible once again to audiences of all ages and backgrounds, its claim to represent the nation would continue to be ridiculed as a privileged sham.

So where had it all gone wrong? How had a country which once put funding for the Royal Opera House before its daily bread ration reverted in prosperity to John Bull's cultural indifference? Had nothing improved in the national character after half a century of state-supported art?

As far as the ROH was concerned, executives and artists, past and present, overwhelmingly blamed its decline and fall on persistent and progressive underfunding. The bare statistics support their case. Between 1970 and 1997, Arts Council grants to Covent Garden rose from £1.4 million to £20 million. Over that period inflation octupled. In 1997, the grant was worth therefore half as much in purchasing value as it had been in 1970.[17] That is a severe and unsustainable decline, unforgivable in the view of arts supporters.

Seen from the Treasury side, however, the grant can be shown to have remained relatively constant in terms of general Government spending. It represented in 1997 exactly the same proportion of state expenditure as it had in 1970. Any shortfall had been happily compensated by private donations and sponsorships. The state, in this light, had done its bit.

Other factors entered the equation. The fees for stars and senior

staff exploded in the last quarter of the twentieth century,[18] making
the running of an international opera house the exclusive preserve of
the world's wealthiest cities. These sums were themselves dwarfed
by the soaring rewards for success in sports and light entertainment.
If Domingo commanded £20,000 for singing a role at Covent
Garden or the Met, it was a fraction of the million dollars he could
have earned from singing in the park, or of the ten million dollars
that a baby-faced Spice Girl could collect from a single record track.
Managerial salaries were comparably disproportionate. Webster,
who depressed his own wage packet to maintain a tight salary
structure, earned in 1948 roughly the same as Matt Busby, manager
of the Cup-winning Manchester United,[19] who was paid £1,750, plus
bonus. Michael Kaiser, equally frugal, received £125,000 in the year
2000, one-eighth of the published salary of Alex Ferguson, manager
of European Cup-winning Manchester United, who took home a
cool million.

The rewards in art and entertainment had become disproportionate to the creativity and effort involved, and distortionate to
general economic trends. To accuse the arts of extravagance, as
politicians habitually did, was to ignore the heartless exploitation of
working-class fans by club owners, record companies and the stars
themselves. The reasons for Covent Garden's decline were partly
self-inflicted, but they did not include wild indulgence, or, *pace*
Kaufman and Smith, persistent wastage of public funds. Nor could
underfunding be cited as the precipitant and principal cause. Money,
for once, was not the root of all evil.

The underlying cause was loss of purpose and relevance. When
Ninette de Valois founded Sadler's Wells Ballet, its aim was to
cultivate an English form of dance for a popular audience. Over time
and triumph, the company became international in reputation and
ability. What it stood for got lost in transition.

Ask its outgoing artistic director Anthony Dowell what the Royal
Ballet represents today, and he struggles for a definition:

I know the value of this company, what had been achieved. When
asked about my vision, I said that a classical company should
remain a classical company because that creates the best dancers,
and that's what I tried to move on. And a certain quality in the
package. I think I have kept alive certain things in the company
that do not exist in others.

Monica Mason, his deputy, speaks in terms of heritage preservation:

> For me, this is the best company in the world, because we have the best repertoire, the best working situation and the most extraordinary heritage from de Valois to the end of Anthony Dowell's reign. Since the 1930s there has been one continuous line running through. Most companies haven't had a history like that. It represents the most wonderful opportunity for young dancers to discover their talents in classical ballet.

Lynn Seymour, ever a dissident voice, challenged some of those assumptions:

> The Royal Ballet isn't doing anything to distinguish it from any other company, and in fact is quite a lot below the standard of other companies we see these days . . . I think the nation needs to feel a sense of ownership about English ballet – the same sense of ownership about Ashton as it feels about Shakespeare.[20]

But how to get to the point where the nation resumes its rightful ownership of English ballet is something no one can envision. De Valois' clarity of purpose and the need she identified for having a national ballet have faded in her successors and cannot perhaps be redefined so long as the founder casts her living shadow over the troubled proceedings.

The point of having an opera company at Covent Garden was that it should awaken and cultivate undeveloped realms of English culture and language. But the Royal Opera stopped singing in English. Then it disbanded its company of English singers. What survives is an orchestra, not of the best; a chorus at subsistence level; and an administration. The company cannot afford to tour the UK. Its national purpose has become invisible.

A former chairman, Claus Moser, defines its uniqueness through the continuity of its last three music directors:

> Why the opera house has been reborn is because we had three outstanding music directors in Solti, Davis and Haitink – it's like Karajan and the Berlin Philharmonic: the standards never slipped.

That traditional argument is meaningful, though only to a

diminishing caste of aesthetes. It is not a basis on which an artistic enterprise can attract broad public support.

The splendid bass singer John Tomlinson, a favourite Wotan at Covent Garden and Bayreuth, attacked domestic criticism of Covent Garden as 'parochial':

> Covent Garden is one of the three or four Eiffel Towers of the opera world, with Vienna, the Met, La Scala as the others. The tradition of opera as real music theatre is second to none in Britain, if only people would realize it.[21]

But how could they be expected to realize it, when only a minority within an arts-loving minority could afford to experience it. The cost of reducing tickets at Covent Garden to the levels of the Bastille or the Metropolitan Opera would amount to ten or fifteen million pounds a year, more than the entire subsidy for ENO. The Met and the Bastille kept tickets affordable by building new houses with four thousand seats. Covent Garden kept them exclusive by rebuilding with just 2,141 seats. This cardinal misjudgement alone will prevent the ROH from ever again becoming a popular venue.

'How much importance we attach to making opera and ballet accessible to all depends on what society we believe ourselves to be,'[22] intoned Jeremy Isaacs. His perception was typically accurate, but the face of society had changed in his lifetime and no longer shared his ideals. A country which was prepared to spend less than half on its health than the United States was also a country that would eke one-third as much to the arts as the German state. A mean, puritanical, pig-ignorant streak dominated the media agenda, and it precluded, as Tony Blair rightly perceived, any renewal of artistic altruism on the part of central Government.

What the arts had lost, apart from a reasonable level of funding, were their roots in a society that was changing both aspirationally and demographically. The ability to sing, dance, play the piano, write a poem or paint a picture to the best of one's ability was no longer prized in an Internet world where entertainment was obtainable at the press of a button and refinement was a suspect quality, tainted with politically-incorrect 'élitism'. The arts were scarcely taught in school, except with marks or careers in mind, and those who missed these skills at an early age would never learn to seek and appreciate the summits of art. The audience of the future was being eroded in the nation's schoolrooms. The J. B. Priestley characters who sought to 'better themselves' by attending concerts and operas were now more likely to pleasure themselves at a football match or disco.

As the improving dimension of the performing arts declined, so did their roots in English society. The second half of the twentieth century was a period of mass immigration, the diasporas arriving so thick and fast that they did not need to shed indigenous cultures and immerse themselves, as earlier waves had done, in a dominant host culture. Instead, there flourished a Joseph's coat of mini-cultures in which the western heritage of song and dance was but one contender among many. Its centrality could not be taken for granted in a multi-cultural society whose younger members sought a borderless breadth of experiences. Covent Garden could not claim to stand for England, when England was busily redefining itself.

Around one quarter of the populace of central London boroughs, those within an hour's journey of Covent Garden, were estimated to belong to ethnic minorities for whom the Royal Opera House meant little or nothing in terms of tradition, pleasure and aspiration.

The company's roots in its own city were thinning. Critically, the roots in its immediate locality were destroyed when the market was uprooted, the porters no longer whistling at passing ballerinas or lending a hand backstage, and many of the inhabitants affronted by the opera house's assaults on their environment. It was this loss of relevance and roots, more than any personal or financial failure, that brought successive ROH boards to their knees and prevented them from seeing beyond the end of their aquiline noses.

And then there were the residues of unresolved structural faults, going back to the company's formation. Maynard Keynes, when he created the ROH, intended to run it as an executive chairman, with a general administrator attending to daily business. Keynes died before the house was fully operational and the relative powers of chairman, board members and chief executive were never clarified. Conflicts could usually be settled over a cup of tea, but when it came down to a clash of personalities there was no constitutional framework on which to fall back. Many of the 1990s crises could be ascribed less to individual error than to institutional weakness. By the end of the first season in the reopened opera house, those frailties were fatally exposed.

Sir Colin Southgate had never got on well with his deputy, Vivien

Duffield. He allowed her to be removed from the board as soon as the money she had collected and donated was safely banked. Dame Vivien, honoured in the June 2000 birthday list, could do nothing but go gracefully. However, the board's ingratitude was duly noted by many who had given, or were thinking of giving, private donations. No American opera house would have treated a benefactor so shabbily.

That summer, relations between the board and executive director reached breaking point. Southgate is said to have resented the credit given to Kaiser for restoring the company, while Kaiser resisted having his decisions questioned and second-guessed by the chairman. The final straw was the appointment to the board of Peter Hemmings, retired manager of Scottish Opera and Los Angeles Opera and a man whose professional skills ran parallel to Kaiser's. Hemmings was there, potentially, to shadow the boss. 'This is not a board I can work with,' Kaiser told an American colleague. In the first week of June he crossed the Atlantic to pitch for top jobs at the Kennedy Center in Washington and the Lincoln Center in New York. On 19 June, he announced his resignation from the Royal Opera House. 'For personal reasons,' said Kaiser, 'it is time for me to return to my home.'

He had not settled well in London, missing his Manhattan friends and his dog, which had sadly died. But the principal reason for announcing his departure after only 19 months was neither social nor personal, but primarily structural. The imbalanced relationship between the board and its executive director had rendered the company effectively unmanageable.

Fingers were pointed at the board and a cry went up for Southgate's head, but the loss of a fifth chief in three years signalled that it was not so much the chairman as the system that was at fault. The board was appointed by a government which now contributed less than one-third of the budget. It no longer represented charitable supporters, disenfranchised with Vivien Duffield's departure, and took no heed of consumer views. Alberto Vilar, who had endowed the Floral Hall with ten million pounds and was planning to give more, sounded the alarm on the day that Kaiser quit. 'Michael was someone I could relate to and respect,' he said. 'I will need to know that his successor is someone I can work with.'[23]

Although Kaiser had never been expected to stay for life, his swift exit provoked a plummeting of morale and a sense of foreboding among the incoming opera and ballet chiefs, Antonio Pappano and Ross Stretton. The ROH remained conspicuously on the sick-list and in need of urgent reconstruction.

So what is to be done? The need for redefinition is urgent, for without it Covent Garden cannot survive. Four reviews in two decades – Priestley, Warnock, Stevenson, Eyre – failed to produce decisive change as politicians of both main parties fudged and fiddled. Given the near-certainty that no opera house will ever be funded to sustainable levels in a twenty-first century England, there are only two solutions on offer: the radical and the prudent.

The radical route separates performing companies from buildings. The ROH, Coliseum and Sadler's Wells would be put under a unified public administration. The Royal Ballet, Royal Opera, ENO, ENB, Ballet Rambert – and regional companies if they so wished – would each have a fixed residency period in its preferred house and a chance to bid for extra periods against foreign and commercial promoters, such as the Kirov and Raymond Gubbay. The performing companies would be relieved of the overheads of building maintenance and freed to concentrate on making art. The Royal Ballet and Royal Opera would shed their historic enmity and go their separate ways, fruitfully and sometimes collaboratively.

The building administration would shed the daily intrusion of artistic foibles and begin to formulate a performing-arts policy for the capital city, a policy in which repertorial risk could be safely balanced against box-office bankrollers. Both the ROH and Coliseum would have a resident orchestra, booked competitively by the season, playing with all comers. This would free the performing companies to take productions to the regions and abroad, working with local orchestras instead of expensively touring their own.

The plan is more likely to appeal to believers in a controlled economy – Eyre was 'enticed'[24] by it – but it has the virtues of saving money and, above all, liberating artists from internecine strife and unnecessary baggage. Radical plans, however, require political courage – a quality that is seldom to be found in bottom-of-the-table Cabinet ministers – along with a great deal of goodwill which has been conspicuously wanting in the performing arts industry. Without a fairly high level of mutual respect and tolerance between the performing companies, the plan cannot work.

There is a simpler option. It is called privatization and it is supported by strategists on all sides of the political spectrum, for reasons both negative and positive. Melvyn Bragg, the Labour peer, has urged that the ROH should be privatized because 'it is an albatross around the neck of arts subsidy'.[25] Graham Serjeant, the *Times* business columnist, has called for arts subsidy to be abolished altogether because most arts companies can be funded privately and the sums involved are so minute that they distort political judgement. Arts subsidy, wrote Serjeant, 'fuels disproportionate controversy' and thereby damages the arts.[26]

Critically, Governments no longer give money to the arts out of the goodness of their hearts. It is eked out with a show of reluctance and a degree of malice for the tabloids to chew. Sooner or later it will be cut off altogether. The Royal Opera House would be better off without it, sooner rather than later.

To sustain a privately-funded Royal Opera House requires two preconditions – a high and regular flow of donations and a substantial endowment to cover against loss. The first condition has always been deemed inapplicable to British circumstances, since the Treasury, in exchange for funding the Arts Council, has refused to allow donations to the arts to be set against personal tax.

No longer. In his Budget of March 2000, the Labour Chancellor Gordon Brown, persuaded by charities and the ACE chairman Gerry Robinson, made two important concessions. He allowed donations through the Gift Aid scheme to qualify for full tax relief, and absolved gifts of shares from Capital Gains Tax. The regime was not quite as liberal as the American way of giving, where a thousand dollars given to the Met would cost the donor five hundred dollars after tax relief, but it opened the way to large-scale benefaction. The shares concession was designed to attract dozens of newly-rich Internet entrepreneurs to leave their mark on the arts. Tax experts viewed the measures as revolutionary and attractive.

Raising money for the arts was becoming relatively easy. Vivien Duffield collected a hundred million pounds in two and a half years. Claus Moser who, as chairman of the ROH struggled to raise a million, now raised a hundred million for the British Museum Development Trust. The country was awash with cash and the desire to do good. Funding a private Royal Opera House would require twenty-five million a year, which was not beyond the end of a rainbow.

Raising the endowment might prove trickier. There was twenty-five million to start with, left over from Vivien Duffield's appeal; another hundred million should suffice. If the Government could be persuaded to donate its next five years' grant in a single cheque, that would set the ROH free in a single bound and shut the book on half a century of underhand conniving and mutual irritation.

The new ROH would have its own building, £125 million in the bank and no pretension to represent anything but itself. Its chairman would not be appointed or approved by Downing Street. He or she would be the biggest donor, the vice-chairman the second biggest. That is how it works, mostly, at Carnegie Hall and the Kennedy Center. The rest of the board would be chosen for what they can give, in cash and expertise. The moment public money stops flowing in, Covent Garden would cease to be a public issue – any more than Glyndebourne or Goodwood is a public issue. It would also become cheaper and simpler to run without having constantly to consult the Arts Council and conform to its labyrinthine twists of policy. Giving up state subsidy, the ROH would have nothing to lose but its chains.

Michael Kaiser has given the matter considerable thought. 'We are heading towards a no-subsidy situation,' he admitted, 'but it can't be done cold-turkey. I think about it a lot. I believe passionately in taking the arts to the widest possible public – not as a public right, but as a public responsibility.'[27]

Whatever the final outcome, those who care for English culture must demand that Covent Garden be put on a stable footing and spared the tortures of uncertainty as it resumes the quest for excellence. It has lost its flagship status and embodies few values beyond its own survival. It is an opera house, no more, no less. Its future should have no bearing on the state of the nation.

Notes

Chapter 1
Come Into the Garden, Awed
1. L. P. Hartley, *The Go-Between*.
2. Earl of Harewood in Rosenthal, *Two Centuries*, xii.
3. Author's interview.
4. Lady Tooley, author's interview.
5. Interview with Alexander Chancellor, January 1998.
6. Brougham, 18–19.
7. Dr Andrew Renton, author's interview.
8. Derek Wyatt, at House of Commons select committee on culture, 21.i.98.
9. Bracewell, 5.

Chapter 2
Drinks at the Bar. 6.45
1. Ziegler, 324.
2. Memorandum of 13.viii.1945, cf. Bryant, 363.
3. Orwell, *The English People*. Collins, 1947. Written between September 1943 and May 1944 (cf. Orwell, Collected Essays).
4. Orwell, loc. cit.
5. Taylor, 600.
6. Announcement by Sir John Anderson, incorporated in Arts Council Charter, 9.viii.1946.
7. Reported in *The Times*, 13.vi.1945.
8. BBC Broadcast, printed in *The Listener*, 12.vii.1945.
9. Bryant, 363.
10. Oscar A. H. Schmitz, *Das Land ohne Musik: Englische Gesellschaftsprobleme*. Munich (Müller), 1914.

11. Carey, 140.
12. Guthrie, 97.
13. De Valois, 77.
14. Atkins, Newman, 29.
15. Procter-Gregg, 153.
16. Related by Richard Bebb.
17. Clark, *The Other Half*, 25.
18. Ellis, 338.
19. Thomas Jones, 'The origins of CEMA', CEMA Bulletin, May 1942.
20. Macmillan, 305.
21. Mary Glasgow, in Milo Keynes, Essays (1975), 261–2.
22. Clark, *The Other Half*, 28.
23. Ellis, 434.
24. Sinclair, 34–5.
25. Clark, loc.cit, 26.
26. Russell, 71.
27. Keynes (ed.), Lopokova, 13.
28. Article in the *Observer*, 1947, cited in Ellis, 500.
29. Milo Keynes, Essays (1975), 4.
30. Landstone, 67.
31. Glasgow, in W. M. Keynes, Essays, loc. cit.
32. General Theory, 235.
33. loc. cit., 29.
34. Harrod, 462.
35. Skidelsky, vol 2, 537.
36. *Daily Telegraph*, Arts & Books, v.1998.
37. William Rees-Mogg, article in *The Times*, 10.xi.1983.
38. Including a 1994 biography 'for young people', by Jeffrey Escoffier, in a series of Lives of Notable Gay Men and Lesbians.
39. Skidelsky, vol 2, 537–8.
40. Skidelsky, vol 1, 67.
41. Skidelsky, vol 1, 248.
42. Quoted by Annan, 56.
43. Bell, 145.
44. Milo Keynes, Essays, 142.
45. *The Economic Consequences of the Peace*.
46. Skidelsky, vol 1, 287–8.
47. Grant diary entry, in Spalding, 204.
48. Skidelsky, vol 1, 349.

49. Spalding, 75.
50. Spalding, 210.
51. Skidelsky, vol 2, 93.
52. Spalding, 334.
53. In Milo Keynes, Essays, 49.
54. Milo Keynes, Essays, 3.
55. Hill and Keynes, 333.
56. Kavanagh, 116.
57. Milo Keynes, Lopokova, 81.
58. Kavanagh, 115.
59. Frederick Ashton in Milo Keynes, Lopokova, 117.
60. De Valois, 98.
61. Kirstein, 241.
62. Walker, 317.
63. loc. cit.
64. Lopokova, 170.
65. Hennessy, 102.
66. W. M. Keynes, Essays, 264.
67. Landstone, 67.
68. Walker, 316.
69. Kavanagh, 256.
70. Blunt, 231.
71. Clark, 131.
72. Blunt, 233.
73. Keynes, Essays, 269.
74. Recollection of John Denison, q.v., author's interview.
75. Clark, 131.
76. Blunt, 237.
77. Reid, 234–6 and Jefferson 190–3.
78. Foreword to Stephen Williams, *Come to the Opera!*, Hutchinson, 1947.
79. CGA, letter from Washington dated 6.xi.1944.
80. De Valois, 154.
81. Kavanagh, 308.
82. Guthrie, 195.
83. Webster, in CGB1, 63.
84. CGB1, 63.
85. CGB1, 63.
86. *Irish Times*, 28.ii.1946.
87. J. M. Keynes, Lopokova, 121.

88. Harrod, 623.
89. Beaton, 231.
90. W. M. Keynes, Essays, 270.
91. Drogheda, 226.
92. CGA, letter dated 23.ii.1945.
93. CGA, letter of 6.xi.1944.
94. CGA, trustees tribute to Keynes, 7.v.1946.
95. Guthrie, 197.

Chapter 3
Enter the Leader (1946–47)

 1. Quoted in Sked and Cook, 28.
 2. Alan Jefferson, conversation with the author.
 3. Healey, 69.
 4. Burton, 149.
 5. Interview with Delia Barnaby.
 6. Barnaby.
 7. See Drogheda, 232.
 8. John Denison, author's interview.
 9. CGA, 14.ix.1945.
10. CGA, 1.iv.1946.
11. Montague Haltrecht, interview with the author.
12. Shead, 10.
13. De Valois, 112.
14. Sir Edward Downes's comment to the author, July 1998.
15. Savage, 95.
16. See Lebrecht, *When the Music Stops*, 112–13.
17. Rosen, 248–9.
18. CGA, and Rosen, 250.
19. CGA, letter of 25.ii.1946. The chronology in Donaldson is inaccurate and misleading.
20. Rosen, 251.
21. Rosen, 253.
22. 'Delighted with Keynes letter(,) the view which is Clark's and mine.' (CGA, 16.iii.1946).
23. CGA.
24. CGA, 29.i.1958.
25. *The Other Half*, 132.
26. *The Times*, 17.vi.1946.
27. Source withheld by request.

28. Schoenberg, 75–6.
29. Brook (D.), 143.
30. Constance Shacklock, author's interview.
31. Author's interview.
32. Savage, 114.
33. CGA, 7.xii.1946.
34. Author's interview.
35. CGA memo, 12.xi.1946.
36. CGA: DW to Keynes, 1.i.1946.
37. Foreman, 270.
38. Mandinian, 19.
39. CGA: Ashton to DW, 14.x.1946.
40. Shead, 148.
41. Shead, 148–9.
42. Shead, 118.
43. Thomas, 45.
44. Private communication, 2.ii.1947.
45. Franklin, 124-5; the incident is corroborated by Irene Thomas, p.48.
46. Witnessed by Alan Jefferson, 1.x.1950, and related to the author.
47. Interview with the author.
48. CG25, p.26.
49. CGA, n.d., March 1946.
50. Langdon, 26.
51. Author's interview.
52. Interview with the author.
53. Thomas, 47.
54. Thomas, 66.
55. Drogheda, 232.
56. DNB, article by John Tooley.
57. Haltrecht, 22.
58. Clark, 129.
59. Glasgow memoirs, quoted in Witts, 460.
60. Witts, loc. cit.
61. Clark, 133.
62. Wheeler-Bennett, 362.
63. Drogheda, 230.
64. Wheeler-Bennett, 316.
65. Tucker, 47.

66. Wheeler-Bennett, 368.
67. CGA various memos, notably 22.vii.1946.
68. Wheeler-Bennett, 366.
69. Drogheda, 227.
70. Wheeler-Bennett, 367.
71. Drogheda, 227.
72. Wheeler-Bennett, 367.
73. CGA, memo of 25.iv.1947.
74. Drogheda, 230.
75. John Denison, author's interview.

Chapter 4
Overture and Beginners (1947–51)

1. Orwell, Essays, 'Writers Against Leviathan', 466.
2. Hollis, 131.
3. Tony Benn, at NHS 50th anniversary service.
4. In *The Listener*, 29.v.1941.
5. Carpenter, 156.
6. Lucas, 92.
7. Note written in 1993 to accompany EMI's release of a 1947 recording of *Grimes* excerpts. EMI CMS 7 64727 2.
8. Eric Blom in the *Birmingham Post*.
9. Scott Goddard in the *News Chronicle*.
10. Edmund Wilson, *Europe Without Baedeker*, NY, 1947, pp. 186-91.
11. Letter to Basil Wright's mother, dated 18.vi.1945, reproduced by permission of © the Trustees of the Britten-Pears Foundation and may not be further reproduced without permission.
12. Chronologically: Stockholm, Basle, Zurich, Tanglewood (US première, cond. Leonard Bernstein), Antwerp (1946); Brno, Milan, Copenhagen, Budapest, Hamburg, Mannheim, Berlin, Graz, Brussels, Paris (1947); New York, Los Angeles, Philadelphia, Boston, Oldenburg, Stanford University, Cal., San Francisco (1948); Helsinki, Strasbourg, Colmar (1949).
13. Evans recollections in 1993, notes to EMI recording CMS 7 64727 2.
14. *Evening Standard*, 14.vii.1946.
15. *Time and Tide*, October 1946.
16. Hinrichsen's Musical Year Book, 1947–8.
17. Blunt, 257.

18. Ashton and Piper quotes in Kavanagh, 338.
19. Kennedy, Britten, 49.
20. Apart from *The Partisans* by Inglis Gundry, which had an airing in St Pancras Town Hall in May 1946, and never since.
21. CGA, DW to Britten, 15.xi.1946.
22. CGA, 24.vii.1946 and other files.
23. CGA, Britten to DW, 15.v.1948.
24. CGA, DW to Britten, 14.vi.1948 © the Trustees of the Britten-Pears Foundation.
25. Haltrecht, 68.
26. Carey, 182.
27. CGA, minute of meeting on 24.vii.1946.
28. Carey, 184.
29. Covent Garden press statement, October 1946
30. Donaldson, 71.
31. Carpenter, *Envy*, 60.
32. Carpenter, loc. cit.
33. McArthur, 223.
34. Biancolli, vi.
35. Kells.
36. Desmond Shawe-Taylor, quoted Rosenthal, 576.
37. Interview with Susannah Herbert, *Daily Telegraph*, 2.v.1998.
38. Brook, 47.
39. Franklin, 121.
40. Franklin, 123.
41. Brook, 51.
42. Haltrecht, 126.
43. 12.xi.1949.
44. Author's interview.
45. *Sunday Times*, 13.xi.1949.
46. Brook, 59.
47. Coward, 172.
48. CGA, DW to JA, 25.vii.1947.
49. CGA: Weekly expenses of joint opera and ballet seasons.
50. CGA: E. Hale to Mary Glasgow, 27.i.1948.
51. Press reports, 5.i.1949.
52. *The Times*.
53. *News Chronicle*, 7.i.1949; information supplied by Webster: CGA.
54. *Daily Telegraph*, 17.i.1949.

55. CGA.
56. *Sunday Times*, 10.vi.1951.
57. John Denison, author's interview.
58. CGA: DW to Rankl, 2.iii.1950.
59. CGA: Wilson to Webster, 23.ix.1947.
60. CGA.
61. CGA: Wilson to Kenneth Stevenson, 15.i.1951.
62. Recollection by Constance Shacklock.
63. CGA: DW to JA, 16.xii.1949.
64. Author's interview, March 1998.
65. *Musical America*, 1.xi.1949.
66. De Valois, 187.
67. Robinson, 313.
68. Fonteyn, 113.
69. De Valois, 187.
70. Robinson, 315.
71. Clarke, 244.
72. Robinson, 309.
73. Kavanagh, 372.
74. Author's interview.
75. Channel 4 TV, 'Secret Lives', 4.ii.1999.
76. CGA: Jane Clark to DW, 3.v.1948.
77. Channel 4 TV, 'Secret Lives', 4.ii.1999.
78. Edwin Denby, *Ballet* magazine, viii.1952.
79. Shearer, author's interview.
80. *Musical America*, 1.xi.1950.
81. Author's interview.
82. Author's interview; source withheld by request.
83. Shearer, Menuhin, Sibley: author's interviews.
84. Christine Beckley, in Newman, 38.
85. Peter Gellhorn, author's interview.
86. Kennedy, 219.
87. Recollection by Joan Ingpen, author's interview.
88. Author's interview.
89. Eliot, 19.
90. Christine Rankl, interview with the author.
91. CGA: 2.iii.1950.
92. CGA: 2.iii.1950.
93. CGA: 3.iii.1950.
94. Recalled by Christine Rankl.

95. Elizabeth Latham, author's interview.
96. Desmond Shawe-Taylor in the *New Statesman*, 16.xii.1950.
97. Steven Rose, author's interview.
98. Savage, 128.
99. Savage, 128.
100. CGA: Clark to DW, 16.xii.1950.
101. Author's interview.
102. CGA, 10.ii.1951.
103. CGA, 9.ii.1951.
104. Information from Christine Rankl.
105. CGA: 20.iv.1951.
106. CGA: DW to Anderson, 7.v.1951.
107. Gellhorn, author's interview.
108. Langdon, 37,
109. CGA: Kerr to Rankl, 6.vi.1952.
110. CGA: DW to Rankl, 22.vi.1953.
111. CGA: DW to Wilfred Stiff, 31.vii.1962.

Chapter 5
First Act, Forbidden Acts (1951–59)

1. FOB, 9.
2. Samuel Johnson, 7.iv.1775.
3. FOB, 8–9.
4. FOB, 69.
5. op. cit.
6. Donoughue and Jones, 493.
7. Banham and Hillier, 176–89.
8. Castle, 192.
9. Tiratsoo, 103.
10. See Roberts, 243–85.
11. Goldschmidt, 72.
12. Recalled by Christine Rankl.
13. Letter from Mary Glasgow to Berthold Goldschmidt, 23.v.1950.
14. Berthold Goldschmidt, author's interview.
15. CGA: JB to DW, 9.v.1951.
16. CGA: Webster to Anderson, 19.v.1951.
17. Kennedy, Barbirolli, 225.
18. Neville Cardus (ed.), *Kathleen Ferrier, a memoir*. Hamish Hamilton, 1954, p. 52.

19. Savage, 139.
20. Hope-Wallace, 91.
21. CGA: EJD to DW, 29.xi.1952.
22. loc. cit.
23. Savage, 138.
24. Carpenter, Britten, 298.
25. Public Record Office document, cited *Guardian*, 17.viii.1998.
26. Eric Crozier, 'Writers Remembered: E. M. Forster', *The Author*, Winter 1990, p. 123.
27. Hope-Wallace, 98.
28. Channel 4: J'Accuse – Benjamin Britten.
29. *Sunday Telegraph*, 22.ii.1998.
30. *Observer*, 22.ii.1998.
31. Carpenter, Britten, 300.
32. cf Coward, 181.
33. CGA, letter of 9.xii.1951.
34. CGA, undated DW memo.
35. See Carpenter, Britten, 312.
36. Harewood.
37. CGA: BB to DW, 20.xi.1952: © the Trustees of the Britten-Pears Foundation and may not further be reproduced without written permission.
38. See Conway, 119–20.
39. Donald Mitchell and Hans Keller (eds.), *Benjamin Britten; A Commentary on his Works from a Group of Specialists*. Rockliff, 1952.
40. CGA: BB to DW, 28.v.1953.
41. Beaton diary entry for 4.xi.1952; Beaton, 243.
42. Savage, 142.
43. Colville, 715–6.
44. Letter to a friend quoted by Donald Mitchell in booklet for EMI recording of *Gloriana*, 1993.
45. Harewood, 138.
46. Drogheda, 239.
47. Rosenthal, *Mad*, 109.
48. CGA, DW file n.d. (assuredly 1958 from internal references).
49. Opera Annual 1954–5 (ed. Harold Rosenthal), p. 31.
50. Author's interview.
51. Haltrecht, 157.
52. Gay, 109.

53. See Drogheda, 285.
54. CGA: C. West to DW, 11.v.1950.
55. Recalled by Alan Jefferson.
56. CGA: DW to Clifford, 18.viii.1951.
57. *Opera*, Jan. 1954, p. 8.
58. Author's interview.
59. Major, 22.
60. Interview with *Classical Singer*, vol X, no. xii, October 1999, p. 7.
61. Braddon, 46.
62. Recalled by Miss Ingpen.
63. CGA: DW to Callas, 12.vii.1952.
64. *Manchester Guardian*, 9.xi.1952.
65. Braddon, 51.
66. Stassinopoulos, 131.
67. CGA, n.d.
68. Schwarzkopf, 202.
69. Personal communication.
70. John Tolansky: 'The Royal Opera, 50 glorious years'. Classic FM, 1.i.1997
71. Drogheda, 266.
72. Langdon, 49.
73. CGA: DW to BBC, 25.vii.1958.
74. Drogheda, 265.
75. Conrad, 318.
76. *Observer*, 18.ix.1977, from 1970 interview with Kenneth Harris.
77. Conrad, 325.
78. Harewood, 231.
79. Braddon, 97.
80. John Tooley, in John Drummond, 'A Price Worth Paying', Radio 3, tx 3.iv.1999.
81. Author's interview.
82. CGA: Pooley (AC) to JA, 14.ii.1952.
83. CGA: JA to Pooley, 20.ii.1952.
84. Norman Tucker, in Opera Annual 1954–5, p. 33.
85. Clark, *The Other Half*, 134.
86. Clark, op. cit.
87. Source withheld on request.
88. Information from John Denison.

89. CGA: K. Clark to Waverley, 18.xi.1953.
90. CGA: Waverley to KC, 10.xii.1953.
91. GDA, 1.i.1955.
92. CGA: Drogheda to Tooley, 22.vi.1972, adding: 'I don't think he will get in anybody's way. . .' Lund died 18.xi.1974.
93. *Opera*, Jan. 1956, William Mann.
94. *Dance and Dancers*, Aug. 1955, Peter Williams on *The Lady and the Fool*.
95. Interview with the author.
96. CGA, HDR file, 30.x.1950; not five pounds as reported by Rosenthal in his memoirs, p. 88.
97. Comments by Alan Jefferson and Ken Davison.
98. CGA: SW to DW, 29.vii.1953.
99. CGA: DW to HDR, 31.x.1958.
100. CGA: HDR to DW, 15.xii.1959.
101. CGA, 12.vi.1960.
102. *The Times*, 28.viii.1951.
103. Savage, 152.
104. Related to the author by Schuyler Chapin, Heifetz's agent; corroborated in Susannah Walton, 148.
105. Bayan Northcott, *Sunday Telegraph*, 21.xi.1976, quoted Kennedy, 188.
106. Tippett, 218.
107. CGA: SW to DW, 8.iii.1954.
108. 'This Opera Baffles Us Too, Say Singers'; article by James Thomas in *News Chronicle*, 26.i.1955.
109. Ross-Russell, 69.
110. 'This Opera Baffles . . .' loc. cit.
111. Tippett, 216.
112. *Daily Express*, 28.i.1955.
113. Verbatim first-hand account of the conversation reported to the author by Arts Council observer, John Denison.
114. Author's interview.
115. Gay, 157.
116. Comments to the author by Elsie Morison, Iris Kells, Elizabeth Latham and others.
117. *The Times*, 18.vi.1955.
118. *People*, 24.vii.1955.
119. Higgins, 268.
120. Carpenter, 335.

121. *Sunday Express*, 25.x.1953.
122. *Daily Express*, 9.iv.1959.
123. As Webster confided to John Denison.
124. Source withheld.
125. Kavanagh, 358.
126. CGA: Jane Clark to DW, 5.i.1953.
127. Drogheda, 237.
128. Author's interview.
129. BB to DW, 4.i.1957 (after 1st night of *Prince of Pagodas*) © the Trustees of the Britten Pears Foundation.
130. Stewart, 215.
131. *Daily Telegraph*, 9.vii.1956.
132. Stewart, 214.
133. CGA.
134. *Dance and Dancers*, Aug. 55, p. 5.
135. Buckle, 276.
136. Macaulay, 61.
137. See David Vaughan, 'London Revisited', *Dance and Dancers*, October 1956, p. 13.
138. Franks, 76.
139. Interview with the author, April 1998.
140. *Dance and Dancers*, October 1956, p. 5.
141. *Daily Express*, 4.x.1956.
142. *Dancing Times*, Nov. 1956, p. 73.
143. *Undine, Tagesbuch eines Ballets*. Munich (Piper), 1959; transl. Mary Whittall for DG recording 453-467-2.
144. John Lanchbery, interview with *Dance and Dancers*, March 1962.
145. Lecture at the Royal Society of Arts, 29.v.1957; *Dance and Dancers*, July 1957.
146. Downes, author's interview.
147. Author's interview.
148. Harewood, 159.
149. Author's interview.
150. Rosenthal, 660.
151. Author's interview.
152. Reported to the author by Miss Leigh.
153. CGA: DW to RK, n.d.
154. Gielgud, 185–6.
155. GDA: IB to GD, 1.vi.1956.

156. GDA, Waverley file, 28.ix.1956.
157. CGA: EJD to DW, 7.vi.1957.
158. CGA: EG to DW, 14.vi.1957.
159. See Ales Brezina, 'The first version of *The Greek Passion* by Bohuslav Martinů', Bregenz Festival brochure, 1999.
160. CGA: 9.xii.1957, RK to Opera Subcommittee chairman.
161. *The Times*, 27.vi.1956.
162. Drogheda, 247.
163. GDA, 14.v.1957.
164. Author's interview, 1982.
165. Author's interview.
166. Interviewed by John Drummond, 'A Price Worth Paying', Radio 3 3.iv.1999.
167. CG 25, p52.
168. Author's interview.
169. Sorley Walker, 318.
170. Wheeler-Bennett, 403.

Chapter 6
Short Interval: Champagne, Canapés and Nature Calls (1959–60)

1. Newton, 93.
2. Author's interview.
3. Strong, 48.
4. Information from Bill Beresford.
5. Walker, 320.
6. Donaldson, *A Twentieth Century Life*, 167.
7. Goodman, 303.
8. Author's interview.
9. Fane, 222.
10. Colin Clark, 48.
11. Lees-Milne, *Fourteen Friends*, 221.
12. Source withheld.
13. John Denison, author's interview.
14. GDA, Waverley file, 8.xi.1956.
15. Donaldson, *Twentieth Century Life*, 165.
16. Newton, 93.
17. Conversation with the author.
18. GDA: Drogheda to DW, 31.x.1960.
19. Private information.
20. Paul Findlay, author's interview.

21. Source withheld.
22. GDA: undated memo in Drogheda's hand.
23. Drogheda, 234.
24. Hansard, 23.i.1959
25. *Opera*, April 1958.
26. Tucker, 127.
27. John Denison, 'Subsidies for Opera in Great Britain', in Opera Annual 8, p. 23.
28. Author's interview.
29. Evans, 103.
30. Langdon, 52.
31. Zeffirelli, 148.
32. Langdon, 52.
33. Author's interview.
34. Schwarzkopf, 197.
35. Langdon, 52.
36. *Guardian* and *Financial Times*, 18.ii.1959.
37. Joan Ingpen, author's interview.
38. GDA: GD to DW, 10.i.1960.
39. Braddon, 122.
40. Related to the author by Joan Ingpen.
41. Culshaw, 293–4.
42. Culshaw, 295.
43. Author's interview.
44. John Tolansky: 'The Royal Opera, 50 glorious years'. Classic FM, 1.i.1997.
45. Haltrecht, 246.
46. Tolansky, loc. cit.
47. *Musical America*, September 1964, p. 12.
48. Advertisement, *Daily Express*, xii.1963.
49. Interview with the author.
50. Fonteyn, 175.
51. Channel 4, 'Secret Lives', 4.ii.1999.
52. Roboz/Monahan, 79.
53. Author's interview.
54. Newman, 93.
55. Sheila Bloom, in Newman, 95.
56. GDA: de Valois to DW, 15.ix.1960.
57. Author's interview.
58. Notes to meeting of 23.ii.1960.

59. Drogheda, 280.
60. Related by Solti to the author, February 1990.
61. Interview, Feb. 1990.
62. cf. Goodman 300, Haltrecht 260; and personal information.

Chapter 7
Act Two: Enter the Jew (1961–70)

 1. Larkin, 'Annus Mirabilis'.
 2. *Guardian*, 2.x.1999.
 3. Interviewed on BBC Radio 4, 'Front Row', 28.x.1999.
 4. Forman, 129.
 5. Heyworth, 264.
 6. CGA: Legge to DW, 9.ii.1960.
 7. Heyworth, 288.
 8. Information received from Andrew McGee.
 9. Information from Lotte Klemperer, Andrew McGee and others.
10. Letter from Lotte Klemperer to Webster, 19.v.1961, quoted by permission of the Otto Klemperer Archive, Zurich.
11. Observed by Bill Beresford.
12. Sutherland, 132.
13. Evans, 194.
14. *Times Educational Supplement*, anon.
15. *Daily Telegraph*, 9.iv.1963.
16. Lotte Klemperer, comment to the author.
17. Lucas, 148.
18. FT, 24.vi.1961.
19. Fonteyn, 204–5.
20. Fonteyn, 206.
21. Beaton, 345.
22. Fonteyn, 208.
23. Fonteyn, 209.
24. Maude Gosling, 'Nureyev in the West'. *Ballet Review*, Spring 1994.
25. Fonteyn, 209.
26. Comments to the author.
27. CGA, Nureyev file.
28. Nureyev, 122.
29. Nicky Johnson, author's interview.
30. Fonteyn, *Magic of Dance*, 67.
31. Seymour, 307.

32. Fonteyn, *Magic of Dance*, 67.
33. Newman, 120.
34. Buckle, 277.
35. Kavanagh, 472.
36. Beaton, 380.
37. Fonteyn, 221.
38. Channel 4, 'Secret Lives', 4.ii.1999.
39. Solway, 300.
40. Author's interview.
41. Author's interview.
42. Public Records Office, FO 371 184933, dispatch by British Ambassador, Madrid.
43. Buckle, 276.
44. Newman, 149.
45. Roboz, 79.
46. Sorley Walker, 291.
47. GDA: De Valois to Drogheda, 16.ix.1960.
48. Recounted by Sibley to the author.
49. GDA: Mark Bonham-Carter to Drogheda, 10.x.1962.
50. Author's interview.
51. Author's interview, February 1990.
52. Comments to the author.
53. cf. Roberts, 218.
54. Colville 649, entry for 30.v.1952.
55. GDA, file memo, 26.vi.1959.
56. Hansard, 10.xii.1959.
57. To the author.
58. Author's interview.
59. GDA, memo of the meeting, kept by Drogheda.
60. GDA, 27.xi.1962.
61. loc. cit.
62. GDA: GD to DW, 28.xi.1962.
63. CGA, Solti file, 21.vi.1963.
64. CGA: DW to GS, 21.x.1963.
65. Information from Valerie Solti.
66. BK comment to the author.
67. Solti archives.
68. Interview with the author.
69. Bernard Keefe, to the author.
70. Recalled by Ingpen.

71. GDA: GD to DW, 10.xi.1963.
72. GDA: GD to DW, 18.xii.1963.
73. Author's interview.
74. Ziegler, 134.
75. Conway, 139.
76. *The Times*, 27.xii.1963.
77. *Sunday Times*, 29.xii.1963.
78. *High Fidelity*, November 1967.
79. Kozinn, 12.
80. Donaldson, *Twentieth Century Life*, 185–6.
81. Hollis, 254.
82. GDA: JL to GD, 16.vi.1965.
83. Goodman, 265.
84. Recalled by John Denison.
85. Selbourne, 192.
86. *Spectator*, 1.iii.1957.
87. Comments to the author.
88. See Brivati, 50.
89. *Sunday Mirror*, 12.vii.1964.
90. Author's interview.
91. Recounted by John Denison.
92. Brivati, 117.
93. Author's interview.
94. Hollis, 260.
95. Hollis, 364.
96. Witts, 471.
97. Sinclair, 162.
98. Author's interview.
99. Recalled by Lord Gibson.
100. Author's interview.
101. Selbourne, 198.
102. Selbourne, loc. cit.
103. Author's interview.
104. Author's interview.
105. Author's interview.
106. Newman, 128.
107. *Dance and Dancers*, May 1964.
108. FT, 3.iv.1964.
109. Bill Beresford, author's interview.
110. Seymour, 222–3.

111. Author's interview.
112. Seymour, 230.
113. Seymour, 247.
114. GDA ballet file, Edward Perper to Sol Hurok, 3.vii.1963 et alii.
115. Seymour, 251.
116. Information from Ken Davison.
117. Fernau Hall and James Kelsey, *Ballet Today*, March/April 1965, pp. 16–18.
118. Tooley, 150.
119. GDA: GD to DW, 20.iv.1966.
120. Author's interview.
121. Seymour, 264.
122. GDA: MBC to GD, 22.xi.1966.
123. CGA: DW to FA 9.iii.1967.
124. *Observer*, 18.ix.1977 (from 1970 interview with Kenneth Harris).
125. Zeffirelli, 188.
126. *Guardian*, 22.i.1964.
127. CGA: Diamand to DW, 22.i.1964.
128. ROH press statement, 16.ix.1977.
129. Interview with the author, Barletta, 1987.
130. CGA: Gorlinsky to DW, 10.ii.1967.
131. CGA: Solti to Collier, 4.iii.1968.
132. GDA: GD to GS, 1.vii.1965.
133. GDA: GS to DW, 2.vii.1965.
134. Savage, 121.
135. Valerie Solti, author's interview.
136. Interview in *The Times*, 9.ix.1988.
137. GDA: GD to GS, 18.vi.1964.
138. GDA: GS to GD, 22.vi.1964.
139. GDA: GD to GS, 29.vi.1964.
140. Ken Davison, author's interview.
141. GDA: IB to GD, 10.ii.1964.
142. GDA: IB to DW, 25.ii.1964.
143. Fay, 71.
144. Hall, 222.
145. Solti, 19.
146. Interview with the author, vii.1997.
147. Alan Taylor, in Tolansky (CFMROH, 1.i.19.97).

148. Recounted to the author by Beresford.
149. Author's interview.
150. GDA: GD to DW, 2.viii.1965.
151. GDA: GD to BP, 7.ii.1965.
152. GDA: GD to Board, 28.x.1965.
153. *Sun*, 13.vii.1967.
154. Gay, 110.
155. CGA, Solti file, 31.iii.1964.
156. GDA: GD to GS, i.vii.1966.
157. CGA, 6.vii.1966.
158. Newton, 96.
159. FT, 21.ix.1964.
160. GDA.
161. GDA: AP to GD, 26.ix.1964.
162. GDA: GD to AP, 24.vi.1965.
163. GDA: AP to GD, 24.iii.1965.
164. GDA: GD to AP, 8.vii.1968.
165. GDA: IB to GD, 13.i.1970.
166. Author's interview.
167. Author's interview.
168. Ken Davison.
169. Bill Beresford.
170. Information from Lady Lightman.
171. Paul Findlay, author's interview.
172. Tucker, 127.
173. GDA: GD to DW, 21.xii.1967.
174. Observations by Bill Beresford, Alan Jefferson and others.
175. Author's interview.
176. Author's interview.
177. Author's interview.
178. Author's interview.
179. CGA, 29.iv.1968.
180. GDA: MBC to GD, 11.x.1971.
181. Kavanagh, 502.
182. Author's interviews.
183. Kavanagh, 508.
184. Author's interview.
185. Drogheda, 325
186. Recounted by Joan Ingpen.
187. John Rockwell, 29.viii.1973.

188. Gay, 153.
189. Clare, 67.
190. Clare, 52.
191. Tucker, 82.
192. Drogheda, 326.
193. GDA: CD to GD, 22.ii.no year.
194. Drogheda, loc. cit.
195. Private annexe to board minutes, 28.i.1969.
196. Goodman to GD, 15.iv.1969.
197. GDA, n.d.
198. Goodman, 305.
199. GDA: Harewood to GD, 9.iv.1969.
200. Private information.
201. GDA, undated report by Lord Robbins.
202. GDA: GD to Harewood, 7.i.1970.
203. Goodman, 306.
204. GDA: GH to GD, 18.iv.1972; GD to GH, 19.iv.1972.
205. GDA: GD to Lord Gibson, 4.xii.1972.
206. Conversation with the author.
207. Genista McIntosh, in Gottlieb and Chambers, 121.
208. FAZ, 25.iv.1970.
209. GDA: Kirstein to GD, 2.iv.1970.
210. Evans, 243.
211. *Daily Telegraph*, 13.v.1971.
212. Recounted by Valerie Solti.
213. Source: *About the House*, Spring 1971.

Chapter 8
The Long Interval: Propping up the Crush Bar (1971–87)

1. Heath, 309.
2. Hennessy, 383.
3. Hennessy, 384.
4. GDA: GD to Armstrong, 6.vii.1970.
5. Source withheld.
6. *The Times*, 5.i.1988.
7. Paul Findlay, author's interview.
8. Sleep, 84.
9. Buckle, 280.
10. GDA: GD to KM, 28.vii.1971.
11. GDA: KM to GD, 29.vii.1971.

12. *Guardian*, 3.xii.1970.
13. Interview with Harold Rosenthal, *Opera*, xii.1970.
14. William Mann, *The Times*.
15. *Opera Monthly*, July 1988, interview with Sam H. Shirakawa.
16. FT, 16.vi.1971.
17. GDA: PH to GD, 4.vii.1971.
18. GDA: GD to PH, 7.vii.1971.
19. GDA: PH to GD, 12.vii.1971.
20. CGA, quoted in Fay, 206.
21. GDA: Rayne to GD, 30.vii.1971.
22. Hall, 261.
23. Fay, 206, and personal information.
24. Hall, 230.
25. Lewis, 99.
26. GDA: JT to GD and Colin Anderson, 6.vii.1971.
27. Author's interview.
28. GDA: JT to GD, 28.ii.1972.
29. Interview with the author.
30. Author's interview.
31. The RPI Index stood at 513.9 in 1970, and 950.0 in 1975.
32. Castle, 441.
33. Author's interview.
34. Author's interview.
35. Gay, 158.
36. Fingleton, 94.
37. See Jenkins and d'Antal, 196.
38. Author's interview.
39. Fingleton, 95.
40. Donald McIntyre, in Jenkins and D'Antal, 183.
41. Cahill, author's interview.
42. Langdon, 166.
43. Reported to Joan Ingpen.
44. loc. cit.
45. Author's interview.
46. Reported by Kiri to the author.
47. Author's interview.
48. Baker, 27.
49. Sinclair, 188.
50. Lord Gibson, author's interview.
51. Claus Moser, author's interview.

52. Author's interview.
53. Goodman, 306.
54. Author's interview.
55. GDA: GD to Claus Moser, 31.xii.1973.
56. GDA: Goodman to GD, 10.vii.1972.
57. George Whyte, author's interview.
58. Author's interview.
59. GWA.
60. GDA: GD to JT, 28.vi.1972.
61. GDA: Goodman to GD, 6.xii.1972.
62. Tooley, 278.
63. Drogheda, 323.
64. Gordon, 43.
65. Recounted to the author by Vivien Duffield.
66. Heath, 394.
67. Fingleton, 111.
68. GDA: GD to KM, 17.i.1973.
69. GDA: MacMillan to GD, 1972, n.d.
70. Author's interview.
71. Newman, 175.
72. Deborah MacMillan, author's interview.
73. *Evening Standard*, 13.vii.1973.
74. GDA: JP-H to GD, 19.iv.1973.
75. GDA, 15.iv.1973.
76. GDA: CD to GD, 26.viii.1973.
77. GDA: Robbins to GD, 16.v.1973.
78. GDA: Kaslik to GD, 22.ix.1973.
79. GDA: GD to Pavitt, 10.x.1973.
80. GDA: GD to CM, 9.vii.1974.
81. GDA: GD to JT, 16.v.1973.
82. Author's interview.
83. Author's interview.
84. Author's interview.
85. GDA: GD to JP-H, 20.vi.1973.
86. GDA: CM to GD, 8.xii.1973.
87. Strong, 183.
88. Author's interview.
89. James Lees-Milne, *A Mingled Measure*, 177.
90. Drogheda, 348.
91. Interview with Harold Rosenthal, 'Music Weekly', BBC Radio,

     4.vi.1974.
 92. Author's interview.
 93. Author's interviews.
 94. Mattheopoulos, 161.
 95. *Financial Times*, 19.ix.1976.
 96. loc. cit.
 97. GDA: Moser to GD, 18.x.1976.
 98. Interview with Tom Sutcliffe, *About the House*, Summer 1974, p. 59.
 99. *About the House*, Christmas 1974, p. 10.
100. Mattheopoulos, 160.
101. Author's interview.
102. CFM-50.
103. Tooley, 44.
104. CFM-50, loc. cit.
105. Author's interview.
106. Interview with Max Loppert, *Opera*, August 1984, pp. 836–42.
107. *Classical Music* magazine, 9.vii.1988.
108. *Opera*, viii.1986, p. 876.
109. Author's interview.
110. Author's interview.
111. Gay, 143.
112. Mattheopoulos, 442.
113. Tooley, author's interview.
114. Author's interview.
115. Kavanagh, 555.
116. CGA: Gorlinsky to JT, 26.v.1977.
117. Ken Davison, to author.
118. Author's interview.
119. Author's interview.
120. CGA, 29.iii.1977.
121. Deborah MacMillan, author's interview.
122. Monahan, 34.
123. Radio 3, De Valois centennial tribute, v.1998.
124. Anonymity requested.
125. Author's interview.
126. Donaldson, 175.
127. *Opera*, August 1979, pp. 738–9.
128. *Opera*, October 1979, pp. 937–40.

129. Strong, 234.
130. cf. Clark Diaries, 17–18.
131. Hennessy, 346.
132. cf. Ranelagh, 80.
133. Annan, 347.
134. Hennessy, 589
135. Author's interview.
136. Strong, 335.
137. Goodman, 307.
138. Priestley, 4–5.
139. Author's interview with Ken Davison, *Classical Music* magazine, n.d.
140. Pick, 153.
141. Priestley, 52.
142. Quoted in Fingleton, 159–60.
143. Fingleton, 180.
144. Jenkins, 247.
145. Jenkins, 270.
146. *Time Out*'s Martin Hoyle, in Jenkins, 270.
147. Author's interview.
148. Mattheopoulos, *Bravo*, 57.
149. Author's interview, see *Sunday Times*, 13.x.1985 and 9.iii.1986.
150. *Classical Music*, 14.v.1988, p. 1.
151. CGA: JT to RN 11.ii.1981.
152. Solway, 427.
153. *Sunday Times* magazine, 26.iv.1981, p. 23.
154. *The Times*, 2.v.1981.
155. Ken Davison, private correspondence.
156. Sleep, 95.
157. Dowell to the author.
158. Findlay, author's interview.
159. Jeremy Isaacs, author's interview.
160. All quotes: GWA.
161. *Sunday Times*, 18.i.1987, interview with Robert Hewison.
162. GWA: GW to Moser, 10.iii.1987.
163. *The Times*, 2.iii.1987.
164. *The Times*, 3.iii.1987.
165. Author's interview.
166. Author's interview, *Sunday Times*, 22.vi.1986

167. Tooley to the author.
168. *Opera*, August 1986, p. 875.
169. Author's interview, *Sunday Times*, 5.x.1986.
170. Source withheld.
171. Isaacs, *Storm Over 4*, 197.

Chapter 9
Act Three, On a Spree (1987–96)

1. CGCA website, 10.x.1999.
2. Douglas Mason, 'Let's scrap the art of the state', *Evening Standard*, 13.v.1987.
3. Kings I, xxi, 19.
4. Wyatt, 346.
5. Author's interview.
6. *Classical Music*, 23.ix.1995, p. 11.
7. 'How Long Before Ofop Steps In?', *London Review of Books*, 16.iii.2000, p.226.
8. Richard Bebb, to the author.
9. Tooley, 202.
10. Source withheld.
11. *The Times*, n.d.
12. *Guardian*, 13.xii.1988, p. 35
13. Source withheld.
14. In *The Listener*, 20.iv.1989.
15. Loc. cit.
16. Solway, 496–7.
17. Taylor, 194–5.
18. Taylor, ix.
19. *Sunday Times* magazine, loc. cit. both Bussell and Eagling.
20. *Sunday Times* magazine, 18.xi.1990.
21. Isaacs, author's interview.
22. *The Times*, 31.i.1990, interview with Richard Morrison.
23. *Daily Telegraph* magazine, xii.2000.
24. Source withheld.
25. Findlay, author's interview.
26. Private communication.
27. Isaacs, 136.
28. loc. cit.
29. Interview with Ismene Brown, *Daily Telegraph*, 3.viii.1998.
30. Reg Wilson, in Bedell Smith, 160.

31. Confided to the author.
32. Author's interview, *Daily Telegraph*, 28.x.1993.
33. Source withheld.
34. Source withheld.
35. See Norman Lebrecht, 'Blight at the Opera', *Daily Telegraph*, 27.ii.1995.
36. *Daily Telegraph*, 21.vii.1995.
37. *Sun*, 21.vii.1995.
38. Interview in *Opera*, iv.1997, p. 396
39. *Opera*, loc. cit.
40. Author's interview.
41. *Daily Telegraph*, 1.v.1995.
42. Author's interview.
43. Author's interview.
44. *BBC Music* magazine, xi.1996, p. 59.
45. Author's interviews, June 1995.
46. Author's interview, April 1995.
47. *The House:* Settling Scores.
48. Tolansky, CFM-50, 1.i.1997.
49. Isaacs, 242.
50. Source withheld.
51. Isaacs, 244.
52. *Daily Telegraph*, 8.xii.1997.
53. *Independent*, n.d.
54. Pulford to Mary Allen, 4.ii.1996, copy in private possession.
55. Isaacs, 300.
56. Sources withheld.
57. 'Trouble at the House', a programme by Keith Cooper.
58. Author's interview.
59. Gottlieb, Chambers, 124.
60. *Daily Mail*, 23.x.1999, p. 24: 'Adultery, Deceit and the Secret Passion that Rocked the Royal Opera House'.
61. *Guardian*, 5.xi.1999, interview with Sabine Durrant.
62. *Guardian*, 9.ix.1998.
63. loc. cit.
64. Comments to the author.
65. Interview with BBC Radio 4 'Front Row', ix.1999.
66. Source withheld.
67. 'Trouble at the House' by Keith Cooper.
68. *BBC Music* magazine, xi.1996, p. 44.

Chapter 10

Act Four: Where's the Door? (January to August 1997)

1. *BBC Music* magazine, xi.1996, p. 45.
2. Gottlieb, Chambers, 126.
3. Antoinette Sibley, author's interview.
4. *Daily Telegraph*, 14.i.1997, interview with Jan Moir.
5. Source withheld.
6. *Daily Telegraph*, 10.v.1997.
7. Minutes of ROH/AC monitoring committee, 30.i.1997.
8. *Daily Telegraph*, 12.iv.1997.
9. Eye-witness account.
10. MA to JM, 20.iii.1997, doc. in Walker-Arnott report.
11. Article by NL, 5.iv.1997.
12. *Daily Telegraph*, 12.iv.1997.
13. *Daily Telegraph*, 10.v.1997, interview with Rupert Christiansen.
14. *Sunday Telegraph*, 29.iii.1998.
15. Source withheld.
16. Original letter in author's possession, published 20.iv.1997.
17. Submission by Chadlington to CMSC, 4.xi.1997.
18. *Daily Telegraph*, 10.v.1997.
19. Evidence to CMSC, p. xxiv.
20. loc. cit.
21. Isaacs, 315.
22. *Daily Telegraph*, 15.v.1997.
23. *The Times*, 14.v.1997.
24. *Daily Telegraph*, 15.v.1997.
25. *The Times*, 15.v.1997.
26. GM to Kaufman, 8.ix.1997, copy seen by author.
27. Author's interview.
28. Conveyed by Mary Allen to the author.
29. Source withheld.
30. *Daily Telegraph*, 26.iv.1997.
31. Board minutes, 30.vi.1997.

Chapter 11

Coming up for Eyre (September 1997 to November 1998)

1. Q.v. chapter two, p. 31.
2. Minutes to board meeting of 29.ix.1997, p. 9.
3. Author's interviews.

4. Allen, 9.
5. Allen, 57.
6. Parkinson, BBC1, 27.ii.1998.
7. Confided to the author.
8. Interview with the author.
9. Board minutes, 30.x.1997.
10. *Spectator*, 6.xii.1997, p. 15.
11. *Daily Telegraph*, 4.xi.1997.
12. *Guardian*, 7.xi.1997.
13. Interview with Michael Billington, *Guardian*, 2.v.1998.
14. *Daily Telegraph*, 5.xi.1997.
15. Allen, 120.
16. ROH board minutes, 19.xi.1997.
17. ROH board minutes, 24.xi.1997.
18. i.e. the Arts Council.
19. *Daily Telegraph*, 4.xii.1997.
20. 'Trouble at the House'.
21. *The Times*, 8.xii.1997.
22. Author's interview.
23. *Spectator*, 6.xii.1997, pp. 15–16.
24. *Spectator*, 13.xii.1997, pp. 20–21.
25. *Sunday Telegraph*, n.d.
26. CMSC, xviii.
27. Open letter to the National Campaign for the Arts, n.d.
28. Recounted by Albery.
29. Author's interview.
30. William Kay, 'Looking for a Fight', *Independent*, 2.ii.2000.
31. *Guardian*, 16.i.1998.
32. *Guardian*, 17.i.1998.
33. *Opera*, ii.1998, p. 144.
34. *Evening Standard*, 26.iii.1998.
35. *The Times*, 2.iv.1998.
36. Allen, letter to *The Times*, 3.iv.1998.
37. Gottlieb, Chambers, 15.
38. *Evening Standard* awards Savoy Hotel, 19.iii.1997.
39. Eyre to Russell Willis Taylor and Pelham Allen, 7.iv.1998.
40. Richard Eyre, *Utopia and Other Places*.
41. Author's interview.
42. All comments: interviews with the author.
43. Simon Jenkins, in the same column (1.vii.1998), curiously

asserted that 'Smith had deputed one of his own officials to write the Eyre Report.'

44. *The Times*, 19.vi.1998.
45. Eyre, pp. 31, 118.
46. *The Times*, 3.vii.1998, p. 35.
47. *Daily Telegraph*, 1.vii.1998, p. 20.
48. *Sunday Times*, 5.vii.1998, p. 1.
49. Eyre, 6.
50. *Guardian*, 3.vii.1998.
51. ROH press release, 7.vii.1998.
52. Two, actually.
53. Source withheld.
54. Memo leaked to *Evening Standard*, quoted in *Opera*, vii.1998, p. 766.
55. *Guardian*, 10.x.1998.
56. *The Times*, 27.x.1998.

Chapter 12
And so to Bed (December 1998 to December 1999)

1. *Guardian* and *Daily Telegraph*, 23.x.1998, *Jewish Chronicle*, 9.x.1998.
2. *Opera*, xii.1998, pp. 1405–6.
3. *Opera*, xii.1998, p. 140.
4. *Daily Telegraph*, 10.x.1998.
5. *Classical Music*, 10.x.1998.
6. *The Times*, 1.x.1998.
7. *Daily Telegraph*, 15.x.1998.
8. *The Times*, 19.x.1998.
9. *Daily Telegraph*, 13.ix.1998.
10. *Guardian*, 4.i.1999.
11. *NY Times*, 15.ii.1999.
12. Author's interview.
13. Author's interview.
14. *Daily Telegraph*, 23.vi.1999.
15. Source withheld.
16. *The Times*, 2.vi.1999.
17. Source withheld.

Chapter 13
Lie Back and Think of England (2000–2100 European time)

1. *Sunday Telegraph*, 8.i.2000.
2. *Daily Telegraph*, 28.i.2000.
3. cf. Rowan Moore, 'True Cost of a Great Day Out', *Evening Standard*, 18.i.2000.
4. *Guardian*, 9.i.2000.
5. *NY Times*, 10.ii.2000.
6. Interview with David Frost, BBC-1, 16.i.2000.
7. cf. *Daily Telegraph*, 17.v.1999.
8. Source withheld.
9. Interview with Ismene Brown, *Daily Telegraph*, 17.iii.2000.
10. *The Times*, 16.iii.2000.
11. *Daily Telegraph*, 18.iii.2000.
12. *Evening Standard*, 23.iii.2000.
13. At LAMDA, 23.iii.2000.
14. *Sunday Telegraph*, 26.iii.2000, interview with Gyles Brandreth.
15. Hall, interview with *The Times*, 13.iii.2000.
16. Peter Brook Awards, Theatre Museum, 9.xi.1999.
17. cf. CMCS, Appendix 3.
18. cf. Lebrecht, *When the Music Stops*.
19. Michael Crick and David Smith, *Manchester United, the Betrayal of a Legend*. Pelham Books, 1989, p. 21.
20. Interview with Ismene Brown, *Daily Telegraph*, 7.iv.2000.
21. Interview with Fiona Maddocks, *Observer*, 22.ii.1998.
22. Isaacs, 334–5.
23. Author's interview.
24. Eyre, 4.
25. *Daily Telegraph*, x.1998.
26. *The Times*, 23.xii.1999.
27. Comments to the author, March 2000.

Bibliography

A. Archives, newspapers, periodicals, reports, databases:

CFM-50   Classic FM documentary for fiftieth anniversary of ROH
CGA   Archive of the Royal Opera House, Covent Garden
CGB   Covent Garden Books (a series issued intermittently, 1947–60)
CG25   Covent Garden, 25 years of opera and ballet (exhibition catalogue), Victoria and Albert Museum, 1971
CMSC   Culture Media and Sport Committee, First report, The Royal Opera House, vol. 1. London, 25 November, 1997
DNB   Dictionary of National Biography, Oxford University Press, 1995
EYRE   The Eyre Review: The future of lyric theatre in London. The Stationery Office, 30. vi. 1998.
FOB   Festival of Britain catalogue, 1951.
GDA   Lord Drogheda's correspondence files (private collection)
GSA   Georg Solti archive (private)
GWA   George Whyte archive (private)

DTel   Daily Telegraph
FT   Financial Times
Gdn   The Guardian
MusAm   Musical America
NYT   New York Times
Op   Opera magazine
Obs   Observer
STel   Sunday Telegraph
STim   Sunday Times

B. BOOKS (major works consulted)
(place of publication is London, unless stated)

Mary Allen, *A House Divided*. Simon & Schuster, 1998.

Noel Annan, *Our Age*. Weidenfeld & Nicolson, 1990.

Dennis Arundel, *The Story of Sadler's Wells, 1683–1964*. Hamish Hamilton, 1965.

Harold Atkins and Archie Newman, *Beecham Stories*. Robson, 1978.

Janet Baker, *Full Circle*. Julia MacRae, 1982.

Mary Banham and Bevis Hiller (eds), *A Tonic to the Nation; the Festival of Britain, 1951*. Thames and Hudson, 1976.

Paul Banks (ed.), *Britten's Gloriana; essays and sources*. Woodbridge, The Boydell Press, 1993.

Cecil Beaton (ed. Richard Buckle), *Selected Diaries*. Weidenfeld & Nicolson, 1979.

Sally Bedell Smith, *Diana; the life of a troubled princess*. Aurum, 1999.

Quentin Bell, *Virginia Woolf*. 2 vols. The Hogarth Press, 1972.

Patrick Belshaw, *A Kind of Private Magic*. Andre Deutsch, 1994.

Louis Biancolli, *The Flagstad Manuscript*. William Heinemann, 1953.

Wilfrid Blunt, *John Christie of Glyndebourne*. Theatre Art Books (NY), 1968.

Alan Blyth, *Colin Davis*. Ian Allan (Shepperton), 1972.

Michael Bracewell, *England is Mine; pop life in Albion from Wilde to Goldie*. HarperCollins, 1997.

Russell Braddon, *Joan Sutherland*. William Collins, 1962.

Peter Brinson and Clement Crisp, *A Guide to the Repertory, Ballet and Dance*. David and Charles (Newton Abbot), 1980.

Brian Brivati, *Lord Goodman*. Richard Cohen Books, 1999.

Donald Brook, *International Gallery of Conductors*. Rockliff, 1951.

Peter Brook, *Threads of Time; a memoir*. Methuen, 1998.

Henrietta Brougham, Christopher Fox, Ian Pace, *Uncommon Grounds; the music of Michael Finnissy*. Ashgate, 1998.

Chris Bryant, *Stafford Cripps; the first modern Chancellor*. Hodder & Stoughton, 1997.

Richard Buckle, *Diaghilev*. Weidenfeld & Nicolson, 1979.

Humphrey Burton, *Leonard Bernstein*. Faber & Faber, 1994.

Angus Calder, *The People's War*. Panther Books, 1971.

Humphrey Carpenter, *Benjamin Britten; a biography*. Faber & Faber, 1992.

Humphrey Carpenter, *The Envy of the World; fifty years of the BBC Third Programme and Radio 3*. Weidenfeld & Nicolson, 1996.

Barbara Castle, *Fighting All the Way*. Macmillan, 1993.

Anthony Clare, *In the Psychiatrist's Chair*. Heinemann, 1992.

Anthony Clare, *In the Psychiatrist's Chair II*. Heinemann, 1995.

Kenneth Clark, *Another Part of the Wood*, John Murray, 1974.

Kenneth Clark, *The Other Half*, John Murray, 1977.

Mary Clarke, *The Sadler's Wells Ballet; a history and appreciation*. A. & C. Black, 1955.

Helen Conway, *Sir John Pritchard; his life in music*. Andre Deutsch, 1993.

Nöel Coward, *Diaries* (ed. Payne and Morley). Weidenfeld & Nicolson, 1982.

John Culshaw, *Putting the Record Straight*. Secker & Warburg, 1981.

Hugh David, *On Queer Street*. HarperCollins, 1997.

Norman Davies, *Europe*. Oxford University Press, 1996.

Michael De-La-Noy, *Eddy; the life of Edward Sackville-West*. Arcadia Books (2nd edition), 1999.

Frances Donaldson, *The Royal Opera House in the Twentieth Century*. Weidenfeld & Nicolson, 1988.

Frances Donaldson, *A Twentieth Century Life*. Weidenfeld & Nicolson, 1992.

Ninette de Valois, *Come Dance with Me; a memoir, 1898–1956*. Hamish Hamilton, 1959.

Bernard Donoughue and G. W. Jones, *Herbert Morrison; portrait of a politician*. Weidenfeld & Nicolson, 1973.

T. S. Eliot, *Notes Towards a Definition of Culture*. Faber & Faber, 1948.

E. L. Ellis, *T. J., A Life of Dr Thomas Jones, CH*. University of Wales Press (Cardiff), 1992.

Geraint Evans (with Noel Goodwin), *A Knight at the Opera*. Michael Joseph, 1984.

Ifor Evans and Mary Glasgow, *The Arts in England*. The Falcon Press, 1949.

Richard Eyre, *Utopia and Other Places*. Bloomsbury, 1993.

Julian Fane, *Eleanor*. Constable, 1993.

Stephen Fay, *Power Play; the life and times of Peter Hall*. Hodder & Stoughton, 1995.

David Fingleton, *Kiri*. Collins, 1982.

Margot Fonteyn, *Autobiography*. Hamish Hamilton, (rev. edn) 1989

Margot Fonteyn, *The Magic of Dance*. BBC Publications, 1980.

Denis Forman, *Persona Granada*. Andre Deutsch, 1997.

James Fox, *White Mischief*. Penguin, 1987.

David Franklin, *Basso Cantante*. George Duckworth & Co, 1970.

Bram Gay, *Trumpet Involuntary; an orchestral life*. Thames Publishing, 1995.

John Gielgud (with John Miller and John Powell), *An Actor and his Time*. Sidgwick & Jackson, 1979.

Tito Gobbi, *My Life*. Futura Books, 1980.

Arnold Goodman, *Tell Them I'm On My Way*. Chapmans, 1993.

Arnold Goodman, *Not for the Record* (selected writings and speeches). Andre Deutsch, 1973.

Charles Gordon, *The Two Tycoons*. Hamish Hamilton, 1984.

Vera Gottlieb and Colin Chambers (ed.), *Theatre in a Cool Climate*. Amber Lane Press (Oxford), 1999.

Tyrone Guthrie, *A Life in the Theatre*. Hamish Hamilton, 1960.

Tyrone Guthrie (ed.), *Opera in English*. Bodley Head, 1945.

F. E. Halliday, *An Illustrated Cultural History of England*. Thames and Hudson, 1967.

Montague Haltrecht, *The Quiet Showman; Sir David Webster and the Royal Opera House*. Collins, 1975.

Joan Hammond, *A Voice, a Life*. Victor Gollancz, 1970.

R. F. Harrod, *The Life of John Maynard Keynes*. Macmillan, 1951.

Roy Hattersley, *Fifty Years On; a prejudiced history of Britain since the War*. Little, Brown, 1997.

Peter Hennessy, *Whitehall*. Secker & Warburg, 1989.

Robert Hewison, *Culture & Consensus; England, art and politics since 1940*. Methuen (revised edition), 1997.

Christopher Hibbert, *Wellington; a personal history*. HarperCollins, 1997.

Patrick Higgins, *Heterosexual Dictatorship*. Fourth Estate, 1996.

Polly Hill and Richard Keynes (eds), *Lydia & Maynard; the letters of Lydia Lopokova and John Maynard Keynes*. Andre Deutsch, 1989.

Patricia Hollis, *Jennie Lee; a life*. Oxford University Press, 1997.

Philip Hope-Wallace, *Words and Music*. William Collins, 1981.

Editors of *Opera News, The Golden Horseshoe; the life and times of the Metropolitan Opera House*. Viking (NY), 1965.

Robert Hutchinson, *The Politics of the Arts Council*. Sinclair Browne, 1982.

Jeremy Isaacs, *Never Mind the Moon*. Bantam Press, 1999.

Jeremy Isaacs, *Storm Over 4*. Weidenfeld & Nicolson, 1986.

Alan Jefferson, *Sir Thomas Beecham; a centenary tribute*. Macdonald & Jane's, 1979.

Alan Jefferson, *Elisabeth Schwarzkopf*. Victor Gollancz, 1996.

George Jellinek, *Callas; portrait of a prima donna*. Anthony Gibbs and Phillips, 1960.

Garry Jenkins & Stephen d'Antal, *Kiri; her unsung story*. HarperCollins, 1998.

John Joel, *I Paid the Piper*. Howard Baker, 1970.

Thomas Jones, CH, LD, *A Diary with Letters, 1931–1950*. Oxford University Press, 1954.

Ludovic Kennedy, *On My Way to the Club*. Collins, 1989.

Michael Kennedy, *Britten*. J. M. Dent & Sons, 1981.

Michael Kennedy, *Portrait of Walton*. Oxford University Press, 1989.

Jürgen Kesting, *Maria Callas*. transl. John Hunt. Quartet, 1992.

John Maynard Keynes, *The General Theory of Employment, Interest and Money*. Macmillan, 1936.

John Maynard Keynes (ed. Donald Moggridge), *Collected Writings, volume XXVIII; social, political and literary writings*. Macmillan (for the Royal Economic Society), 1982.

Milo Keynes (ed.), *Essays on John Maynard Keynes*. Cambridge University Press, 1975.

Milo Keynes (ed.) *Lydia Lopokova*. Weidenfeld & Nicolson, 1993.

Lincoln Kirstein, *Mosaic; memoirs*. FSG (NY), 1994.

Allan Kozinn, *The Beatles*. Phaidon Press, 1995.

Heinrich Kralik, *The Vienna Opera*. Vienna, 1955.

C. P. Landstone, *Off-Stage; a personal record of the first twelve years of state-sponsored drama in Great Britain*. Elek, 1953.

James Lees-Milne, *Ancestral Voices*. Chatto & Windus, 1975.

James Lees-Milne, *Fourteen Friends*. John Murray, 1996.

James Lees-Milne, *Through Wood and Dale*. John Murray, 1998.

Roger Lewis, *The Real Life of Lawrence Olivier*. Century, 1996.

John Lucas, *England and Englishness*. The Hogarth Press, 1990.

John Lucas, *Reggie; the life of Reginald Goodall*. Julia MacRae Books, 1993.

Edwin McArthur, *Flagstad; a personal memoir*. Alfred A. Knopf (NY), 1965.

Lord Macmillan, *A Man of Law's Tale*. Macmillan, 1953.

Norma Major, *Joan Sutherland; the authorised biography*. Macdonald, 1987.

Edward Mandinian (photographer), *Purcell's The Fairy Queen; as presented by the Sadler's Wells Ballet and The Covent Garden Opera*. John Lehmann, 1948.

Arthur Marwick, *British Society Since 1945*. Penguin (3rd edition), 1996.

Lawrence D. Mass, *Confessions of a Jewish Wagnerite*. Cassell, 1994.

Martin Mayer, *The Met*. Thames & Hudson, 1983.

Richard Mayne, *Postwar; the dawn of today's Europe*. Thames & Hudson, 1983.

Barry Miles, *Paul McCartney; many years from now*. Secker & Warburg, 1997.

Andrew Motion, *The Lamberts*. Chatto & Windus, 1986.

Barbara Newman, *Antoinette Sibley; reflections of a ballerina*. Hutchinson, 1986.

Sir Gordon Newton (ed. Malcolm Rutherford), *A Peer Without Equal*. Privately published, 1997.

Nigel Nicolson, (ed.), *The Letters of Virginia Woolf* (vol. III). Hogarth Press, 1977.

Rudolf Nureyev (edited by Alexander Bland), *The Autobiography of Rudolf Nureyev*. Hodder & Stoughton, 1962.

Charles Osborne, *Giving it Away*. Secker & Warburg, 1986.

George Orwell, *The English People*. Collins, 1947.

Sonia Orwell and Ian Angus (eds), *The Collected Essays, Journalism and Lectures of George Orwell* (vols I–IV). Penguin Books, 1970.

John Percival, *Theatre in my Blood; a biography of John Cranko*. The Herbert Press. 1983.

Donna Perlmutter, *Shadowplay; the life of Antony Tudor*. Limelight Editions (NY), 1995.

John Pick, *Managing the Arts? the British experience*. Rhinegold, 1986.

V. S. Pritchett, *London Perceived*. Chatto & Windus, 1962.

Humphrey Procter-Gregg, *Beecham Remembered*. Duckworth, 1976.

Pierre-Jean Rémy, *Maria Callas; a tribute*. Macdonald and Jane's, 1978.

Andrew Roberts, *Eminent Churchillians*. Weidenfeld & Nicolson, 1994.

Philip Roberts, *The Royal Court Theatre and the Modern Stage*. Cambridge University Press, 1999.

Harlow Robinson, *The Last Impresario; the life, times and legacy of Sol Hurok*. Viking (NY), 1994.

Zsuzsi Roboz (with text by James Monahan), *British Ballet Today*. Davis-Poynter, 1980.

Carol Rosen, *The Goossens; a musical century*. Andre Deutsch, 1993.

Noel Ross-Russell, *There Will I Sing; a biography of Richard Lewis, CBE*. Open Gate Press, 1996.

Peter Rowland, *Lloyd George*. Barrie & Jenkins, 1975.

Bertrand Russell, *The Autobiography of Bertrand Russell, 1872–1914*. George Allen & Unwin, 1967.

Richard Temple Savage, *A Voice from the Pit; reminiscences of an orchestral musician*. David & Charles (Newton Abbot), 1988.

Erwin Stein (ed.), Arnold Schoenberg, *Letters*. Faber & Faber, 1964.

Elisabeth Schwarzkopf, *On and Off the Record; a memoir of Walter Legge*. Faber & Faber, 1982.

Meryle Secrest, *Kenneth Clark*. Weidenfeld & Nicolson, 1984.

Richard Shead, *Constant Lambert*. Simon Publications, 1973.

Andrew Sinclair, *Arts and Cultures; the history of the 50 years of the Arts Council of Great Britain*. Sinclair-Stevenson, 1995.

Alan Sked and Chris Cook, *Post-War Britain; a political history*. Penguin (4th edition), 1993.

Robert Skidelsky, *John Maynard Keynes; hopes betrayed, 1883–1920*. Macmillan, 1983.

Robert Skidelsky, *John Maynard Keynes; the economist as saviour, 1920–1937*. Macmillan, 1992.

Terry Slasberg, *The pleasure was mine . . . 40 years as a concert agent*. Thames Publishing, 1993.

Wayne Sleep, *Precious Little Sleep*. Boxtree, 1996.

Diane Solway, *Nureyev*. Weidenfeld & Nicolson, 1998.

Frances Spalding, *Duncan Grant*. Chatto & Windus, 1997.

Margaret Stewart, *English Singer; the life of Steuart Wilson*. George Duckworth & Co., 1970.

Joan Sutherland, *A Prima Donna's Progress*. Weidenfeld & Nicolson, 1997.

A. J. P. Taylor, *English History, 1914–1945*. Oxford University Press, 1966.

Irene Thomas, *The Bandsman's Daughter*. Macmillan, 1979.

Edward Thorpe, *Kenneth MacMillan; the man and the ballets*. Hamish Hamilton, 1985.

Michael Tippett, *Those Twentieth Century Blues*. Hutchinson, 1991.

Nick Tiratsoo (ed.), *From Blitz to Blair*. Weidenfeld & Nicolson, 1997.

John Tooley, *In House; Covent Garden, 50 years of opera and ballet*. Faber & Faber, 1999.

J. C. Trewin, *Peter Brook; a biography*. Macdonald, 1971.

Penelope Turing, *Hans Hotter; man and artist*. John Calder, 1983.

Katherine Sorley Walker, *Ninette de Valois; idealist without illusions*. Dance Books, 1998.

Ian Wallace, *Promise me you'll sing MUD*. John Calder, 1975.

Geoffrey Wansell, *Terence Rattigan; a biography*. Fourth Estate, 1995.

John W. Wheeler-Bennett, *John Anderson, Viscount Waverley*. Macmillan, 1962.

Eric Walter White, *The Arts Council of Great Britain*. Davis Poynter, 1975.

Richard Witts, *Artist Unknown; an alternative history of the Arts Council*. Little, Brown, 1988.

Hugo Young, *One of Us*. Macmillan, 1989.

Franco Zeffirelli, *Zeffirelli*. Weidenfeld & Nicolson, 1986.

Philip Ziegler, *London at War*, 1939–1945. Sinclair-Stevenson, 1995.

Philip Ziegler, *Harold Wilson*. HarperCollins, 1993.

Index